Students Can Relate to *Communication in Everyday Life*

Whether we are talking or texting, persuading or posting, turn-taking or tweeting, relationships play an essential role in all of the ways we choose to communicate throughout the day. We continuously manage and enact our relationships in our daily communication. In *Communication in Everyday Life*, Steve Duck and David T. McMahan highlight the inseparable connection between relationships and communication in every chapter to add insight and coherence to the full range of foundational communication concepts, theories, and skills covered in the introductory course. The second edition includes fresh new examples, the latest research, and enhanced learning tools that will encourage students to think critically, to relate communication theory to their everyday experiences, and to improve their communication skills in the process.

Praise for *Communication in Everyday Life*

"I loved Duck and McMahan. So did my students. . . . They found it understandable and easy to use."

—Donna L. Halper, *Lesley University*

"I have had numerous comments on the readability and tone of the text—students say they actually enjoy reading it!"

—Martha Antolik, *Wright State University*

"[This book] was definitely engaging, and every sentence made me want to continue. . . . I love how [this book] relates to the reader."

—Student, *Washburn University*

"A true relational approach that has real-world applicability. . . . Students reading this text should easily see the practical application of the concepts to their own lives."

—Martin Hatton, *Mississippi University for Women*

"This text, better than others I have reviewed, is a more comprehensive review of the field and introduces students to the gamut of the discipline. This is a true introduction to communication in everyday life."

—Jerry E. Fliger, *Toccoa Falls College*

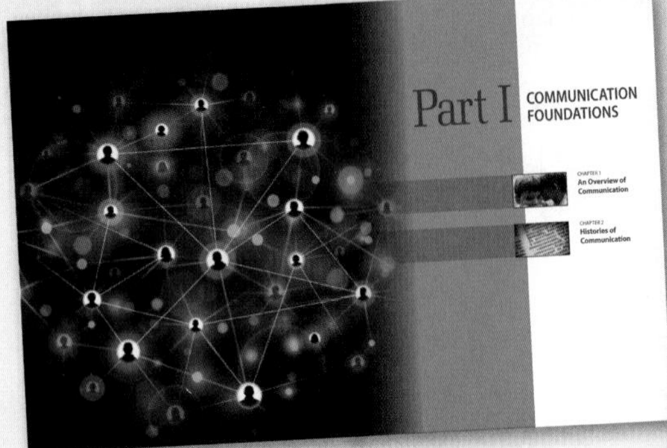

Revised Organization:

A new three-part structure—**Part One: Communication Foundations, Part Two: Communication Skills, Part Three: Communication Contexts**—provides an improved roadmap for students to chart their progress through the text. In response to feedback from users of the first edition, the authors have also reorganized their coverage of some topics to improve student understanding.

New Content:

Two new chapters—**Chapter 2: Histories of Communication** and **Chapter 15: Interviewing**—have been added to the second edition, expanding coverage of both theory and application. In addition, all chapters have been streamlined and thoroughly revised to include new examples, current research, and improved pedagogical features.

Updated Focus:

Chapter-opening **Focus Questions** now appear at the start of each chapter to encourage close reading on key concepts, theories, and skills. At the end of each chapter, **Focus Questions Revisited** help students review the chapter material.

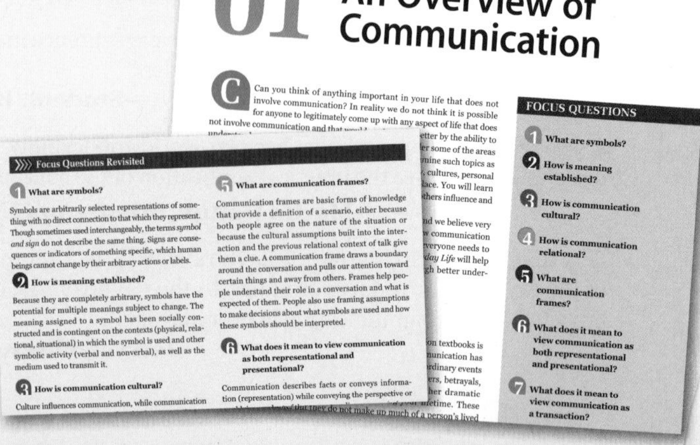

Enhanced Learning Tools:

Revised and updated pedagogical features in every chapter enrich the reading experience and encourage students to connect chapter material to their everyday lives.

- New **Analyzing Everyday Communication** boxes focus on critical analysis of real-life exchanges and relationships.
- New **By the Way** boxes use interesting and surprising pieces of information to highlight important topics throughout each chapter.
- New **Communication and You** boxes provide opportunities for self-reflection and self-assessment in each chapter.
- New **Disciplinary Debate** boxes ask students to use critical thinking skills to consider opposing views on key topics and theories.
- Updated **Ethical Issue** discussion questions have been moved from the end of the chapters to now appear in the margins alongside relevant chapter content.
- Updated **Make Your Case** boxes provide students with an opportunity to develop their own positions or to perform an exercise about the material.
- New **Skills You Can Use** boxes provide practical instruction on applying content to everyday life.
- New **Marginal Glossary Definitions** highlight important new terms right on the page, in addition to the full glossary at the back of the book.

By the way...

Saying "Hello" in Japanese

In Japanese, there are more than 200 ways for one person to address another according to protocols of respect and status differences recognized by the participants.

COMMUNICATION + YOU

Taking Things for Granted

You may not even be aware of how frames provide you with additional context and information in any communication interaction. After your next conversation with someone, take note of two or three key things that were said by this person.

QUESTIONS TO CONSIDER

1. What was taken for granted? What did you need to know in order to understand these things?
2. Do the same thing with someone with whom you share a different relationship. In what ways were the taken-for-granted assumptions the same, and in what ways were they different?

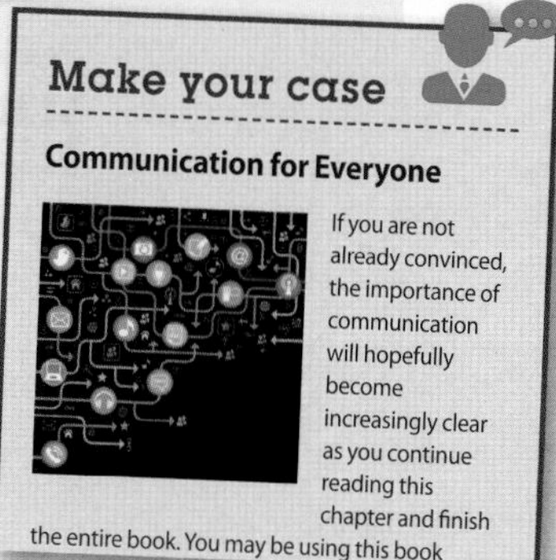

Make your case

Communication for Everyone

If you are not already convinced, the importance of communication will hopefully become increasingly clear as you continue reading this chapter and finish the entire book. You may be using this book

communication as interaction: an exchange of information between two (or more) individuals

communication as transaction: the construction of shared meanings or understandings between two (or more) individuals

ANALYZING EVERYDAY COMMUNICATION

Restaurant Research

We have begun to introduce new ways to analyze situations in your everyday life. The next time you go for a meal in a restaurant, take notes about the server–customer relationship.

QUESTIONS TO CONSIDER

1. How does the relationship get accomplished? For example, what is communicated/transacted by a server's uniform, style of speech (bubbly or bored), or manner (friendly or aloof)?
2. What impressions do you form about the server and his or her view of you?

DISCIPLINARY DEBATE

Skills or Theory?

The primary disagreement among early mass communication scholars and those already in journalism departments involved what should be their focus. Those already teaching journalism believed the focus should be more on skills and training. Mass communication scholars believed the focus should be on research and theory. Contemporary scholars taking an applied communication approach would probably be somewhere in the middle—seeking ways to use theory and research to improve communication in various settings.

QUESTIONS TO CONSIDER

1. Choosing from the two extremes, do you believe the discipline of communication should focus more on skills development or on theory and research?
2. Are the two extremes enough to justify separate disciplines?

ETHICAL ISSUE

Could being a disruptive member of a group be considered ethical?

Skills You Can Use: Adapting to Cultural Expectations

Communicating in a manner consistent with cultural expectations increases a person's ability to influence others. Consider how you might adapt or adhere to cultural expectations when planning to speak with another person, a group of people, or a large audience.

Key Concepts

communication as action 15
communication as interaction 15
communication as transaction 15
communication frame 12
constitutive approach to communication 16
frames 12
meaning 8
medium 10
presentation 13
representation 13
signs 7
social construction 8
symbols 7

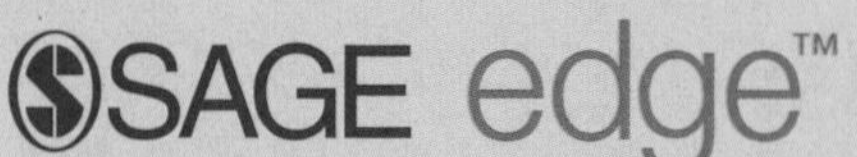

Give your students the SAGE edge at edge.sagepub.com/duckciel2e

SAGE edge offers a robust online environment featuring an impressive array of tools and resources for review, study, and further exploration, keeping both instructors and students on the cutting edge of teaching and learning. SAGE edge content is open access and available on demand. Learning and teaching has never been easier!

SAGE edge for students provides a personalized approach to help students accomplish their coursework goals in an easy-to-use learning environment.

- Mobile-friendly **eFlashcards** strengthen understanding of key terms and concepts.
- Mobile-friendly practice **quizzes** allow for independent assessment by students of their mastery of course material.
- A customized online **action plan** includes tips and feedback on progress through the course and materials, which allows students to individualize their learning experience.
- **Chapter summaries** with **learning objectives** reinforce the most important material.
- **Interactive exercises** and meaningful web links facilitate student use of internet resources, further exploration of topics, and responses to critical thinking questions.
- A **speech outline guide** helps students plan their speeches.
- **Speech topic ideas** give students a head start in developing their presentations.
- **Sample written speeches** show students examples of how to structure their speeches.
- EXCLUSIVE! Access to full-text **SAGE journal articles** that have been carefully selected to support and expand on the concepts presented in each chapter

SAGE edge for instructors supports teaching by making it easy to integrate quality content and create a rich learning environment for students.

- **Test banks** provide a diverse range of pre-written options as well as the opportunity to edit any question and/or insert personalized questions to effectively assess students' progress and understanding.
- **Sample course syllabi** for semester and quarter courses provide suggested models for structuring one's course.
- Editable, chapter-specific **PowerPoint slides** offer complete flexibility for creating a multimedia presentation for the course.
- **Multimedia content** includes original SAGE videos that appeal to students with different learning styles.
- **Lecture notes** summarize key concepts by chapter to ease preparation for lectures and class discussions.
- A **course cartridge** provides easy LMS integration.
- EXCLUSIVE! Access to full-text **SAGE journal articles** that have been carefully selected to support and expand on the concepts presented in each chapter to encourage students to think critically

---

For Additional Speech Resources

SpeechPlanner is an interactive, web-based tool that guides you through the process of planning and preparing your speech, one step at a time. Featuring practical tips, strategies, and useful examples designed to explain and illustrate every stage of the speech-making process, this valuable planner makes it simple and easy to create highly effective, successful speeches anywhere, any time. **SpeechPlanner** can be packaged for free with the print book.

Communication in Everyday Life

Second Edition

From Steve:
To Zach and Minnie, newly entered into the relational world

From David:
To Jennifer forever

Communication in Everyday Life

A Survey of Communication

Second Edition

Steve Duck

David T. McMahan

Los Angeles | London | New Delhi
Singapore | Washington DC

Los Angeles | London | New Delhi
Singapore | Washington DC

FOR INFORMATION:

SAGE Publications, Inc.
2455 Teller Road
Thousand Oaks, California 91320
E-mail: order@sagepub.com

SAGE Publications Ltd.
1 Oliver's Yard
55 City Road
London, EC1Y 1SP
United Kingdom

SAGE Publications India Pvt. Ltd.
B 1/I 1 Mohan Cooperative Industrial Area
Mathura Road, New Delhi 110 044
India

SAGE Publications Asia-Pacific Pte. Ltd.
3 Church Street
#10-04 Samsung Hub
Singapore 049483

Printed in the United States of America

A catalog record of this book is available from the Library of Congress.

ISBN 978-1-4522-5978-9

This book is printed on acid-free paper.

SFI label applies to text stock

14 15 16 17 18 10 9 8 7 6 5 4 3 2 1

Senior Acquisitions Editor: Matthew Byrnie
Associate Editor: Nancy Loh
Assistant Editor: Katie Guarino
Editorial Assistant: Gabrielle Piccininni
Production Editor: Amy Schroller
Copy Editor: Melinda Masson
Typesetter: C&M Digitals
Proofreader: Sarah J. Duffy
Indexer: Karen Wiley
Cover Designer: Gail Buschman
Marketing Manager: Liz Thornton

Contents

Preface xxi
A Personal Note to Readers xxvii
Acknowledgments xxix
About the Authors xxxi

PART I. COMMUNICATION FOUNDATIONS 1

1. An Overview of Communication 3
2. Histories of Communication 21

PART II. COMMUNICATION SKILLS 47

3. Identities, Perceptions, and Communication 49
4. Verbal Communication 69
5. Nonverbal Communication 89
6. Listening 111

PART III. COMMUNICATION CONTEXTS 131

7. Personal Relationships 133
8. Family Communication 155
9. Groups and Leaders 179
10. Communication in the Workplace 197
11. Health Communication 223
12. Culture and Communication 243
13. Technology and Media in Everyday Life 263
14. Public and Personal Influence 287
15. Interviewing 309

Glossary 342
Chapter References 351
Photo Credits 366
Index 367

Detailed Contents

Preface xxi
A Personal Note to Readers xxvii
Acknowledgments xxix
About the Authors xxxi

PART I. COMMUNICATION FOUNDATIONS 1

1. An Overview of Communication 3

Focus Questions 3
Everyday Communication and the Relational Perspective 3
What Is Communication? 4
Communication Is Symbolic 7
Communication Requires Meaning 8
Social Construction of Meaning 8
Meaning and Context 9
Verbal and Nonverbal Influence on Meaning 9
Meaning and the Medium 10
Communication Is Cultural 10
Communication Is Relational 11
Communication Involves Frames 12
Coordinating Interactions 12
Assigning Meanings 12
Perspectives 13
Communication Is Both Presentational and Representational 13
Communication Is a Transaction 14
Communication as Action 15
Communication as Interaction 15
Communication as Transaction 16
Focus Questions Revisited 17
Key Concepts 17
Questions to Ask Your Friends 18
Media Connections 18

2. Histories of Communication 21

Focus Questions 21
The Challenges of Writing History 23
The Development of a Discipline 24
The Development of Associations 25
The Emergence of Areas of Study 25
Rhetoric and Rhetorical Criticism 26
Interpersonal Communication 26
Mass Communication 27

Coming Together (Kind of) as Communication Studies 28
Troubles in Academic Paradise 28
Future of Communication and the Relational Perspective 29
Approaches to the Study of Communication 30
Social Scientific Approach 30
Assumptions 31
Methods 31
Experiments 31
Questionnaires/Surveys 31
Advantages 32
Disadvantages 32
Multiple Variables 32
Culturally Insensitive 32
Restrictive 32
Participant Accuracy 32
Convenient Samples 33
Interpretivist Approach 33
Assumptions 33
Methods 33
Data 34
Direct Observation and Participant Observation 34
Interviews 34
Textual Analysis 35
Advantages 35
Disadvantages 35
Limited Scope of Understanding 35
Researcher Accuracy and Perspective 35
Time-Consuming 35
Critical Approach 36
Assumptions 36
Methods 36
Advantages 36
Disadvantages 37
Areas of Study and the Relational Perspective 37
Communication Education and Instructional Communication 38
Communication Theory 38
Cultural Communication 38
Family Communication 39
Group Communication 40
Interpersonal Communication 40
Media 40
Health Communication 41
Organizational Communication 41
Persuasion 41
Political Communication 42
Public Relations 42
Rhetorical Criticism 42
Focus Questions Revisited 44
Key Concepts 44
Questions to Ask Your Friends 44
Media Connections 45

PART II. COMMUNICATION SKILLS 47

3. Identities, Perceptions, and Communication 49

Focus Questions 49
Do People Have a Core Self? 52
Different Moods 53
Different Situations 53
Different Relationships 53
Different Evaluations 53
Identities and Perceptions 54
Selecting 54
Organizing and Evaluating 55
Identities and Communication 55
Symbolic Identities and a Symbolic Self 56
Transacting Identities Symbolically 57
Symbolic Self 57
Self-Disclosure 58
Self-Description or Self-Disclosure 59
Dynamics of Self-Disclosure 59
The Value of Self-Disclosure 59
Passing on the Onion 60
Good, Bad, or Nothing 60
Dialectic Tensions 60
Identities and Boundaries 61
Narratives 62
Stories We Tell 62
Origin Stories 63
Shaping the Stories 63
Transacting Identity and Other People 63

Altercasting 64
Self as Others Treat You 64
Performative Self 64
Facework 65
Front and Back Regions 65
Focus Questions Revisited 66
Key Concepts 66
Questions to Ask Your Friends 66
Media Connections 67

4. Verbal Communication 69

Focus Questions 69
How Is Verbal Communication Symbolic? 69
Verbal Communication Involves Meaning 70
Denotative and Connotative Meanings 71
Words and Values 72
God Terms and Devil Terms 72
Verbal Communication Is Relational 73
Verbal Communication Transacts Relationships 73
Relationships Regulate Verbal Communication 73
Relationships and Shared Meanings 74
Conversational Hypertext 74
Verbal Communication Is Cultural 75
Verbal Communication Transacts Cultures 75
Cultures Regulate Verbal Communication 75
Cultural Ways of Talking 76
Verbal Communication and Frames 76
Recognizing Frames 77
Ways of Speaking 77
Accommodation: Adjusting Relational Frames 78
Verbal Communication Is Presentational 78
Telling Stories 78
Giving Accounts 79
Kenneth Burke's Pentad 79
Elements of the Pentad 80
Ratios of the Pentad 80
Functions of Verbal Communication 81
Influencing Others: Facework and Politeness 81
Facework 82
Face Wants 82
Maintaining Positive Face 82
Politeness Theory 82
Relationships and Everyday Talk 83
Instrumental Func tion 84
Indexical Function 84
Essential Function 84
Focus Questions Revisited 85
Key Concepts 85
Questions to Ask Your Friends 86
Media Connections 86

5. Nonverbal Communication 89

Focus Questions 89
What Is Nonverbal Communication? 90
Symbolic 90
Decoding and Encoding 90
Dynamic and Static 91
Guided by Rules 92
Cultural 92
Personal 92
Ambiguous 93
Less Controlled 94
Continuous 94
The Functions of Nonverbal Communication 94
Interconnects With Verbal Communication 94
Regulates Interactions 95
Identifies Others 96
Transmits Emotional Information 97
Attitude Toward the Other 97
Attitude Toward the Situation 97
Attitude Toward Yourself 97
Relational Meaning and Understanding 97
Types of Nonverbal Communication 98
Proxemics 98
Territoriality 98

Personal Space and Distance 99
Proxemics and Everyday Life 100
Kinesics 101
Posture 101
Gesture 101
Eye Contact and Gaze 102
Vocalics 103
Vocalics and Relationships 104
Vocalics and Regulation 104
Chronemics 105
Chronemics and Regulation of Interaction 105
Haptics 106
Focus Questions Revisited 107
Key Concepts 107
Questions to Ask Your Friends 108
Media Connections 108

6. Listening 111

Focus Questions 111
Why Is Listening Important? 112
Listening and Education 112
Listening and Career 113
Listening and Religion and Spirituality 113
Listening and Health Care 113
Listening and Relationships 113
Listening Objectives 113
Active Listening 114
Engaged and Relational Listening 115
Disengaged Listening 116
Engaged Listening for a Transactional World 116
Relational Listening 116
Recognizing and Overcoming Listening Obstacles 117
Critical Listening 120
Elements of Critical Listening 121
Evaluation of Plausibility 121
Evaluation of Source 121
Evaluation of Consistency 122
Evaluation of Evidence 122
Fallacious Arguments 122
Focus Questions Revisited 126
Key Concepts 127
Questions to Ask Your Friends 128
Media Connections 128

PART III. COMMUNICATION CONTEXTS 131

7. Personal Relationships 133

Focus Questions 133
What Are Personal Relationships? 134
Benefits of Personal Relationships 134
Relationships and What You Know 135
Filtering What You Know 135
Evaluating What You Know 135
Relationships and Support 135
Belonging and a Sense of Reliable Alliance 135
Emotional Integration and Stability 136
Opportunity to Talk About Oneself 136
Opportunity to Help Others 136
Provision of Physical Support 136
Reassurance of Worth and Value 137
Initiating Relationships: The Relationship Filtering Model 137
Talking to Strangers 137
Steps in the Relationship Filtering Model 138
Appearance 138
Behavior/Nonverbal Communication 139
Roles 140
Attitude/Personality 140
Transacting and Maintaining Personal Relationships 141
Composing Relationships Through Communication 141

Transforming Relationships 141
Relationship Talk: Direct 142
Relationship Talk: Indirect 142
Keeping Relationships Going Through Communication 143
Prospective Units 143
Introspective Units 143
Retrospective Units 143
Relational Dialectics 144
Contradiction 144
Change 145
Praxis 145
Totality 145
Internal and External Dialectics 145
Coming Apart 146
Symptoms and Sources of Decline 147
Deterioration in Communication 147
Destructive Conflict 147
Changes in Evaluative Standards 147
Major Transgressions 147
Inequity 148
Personal Reflection 148
Breakdown Process Model 148
Intrapsychic Process 148
Dyadic Process 150
Social Process 150
Grave Dressing Process 150
Resurrection Process 150
Focus Questions Revisited 151
Key Concepts 152
Questions to Ask Your Friends 152
Media Connections 152

8. Family Communication 155

Focus Questions 155
Families in Truth and Myth 156
Families as Social Ideals 156
Negative Aspects of Family 157
Families as . . . 158
Families as Frames 158
Family as Structures 158
Families as Communication Systems 160
Structure and Communication 160
Families as Systems 162
Characteristics of Systems 162
Viewing Families as Systems 162
Families in a System of Peer Culture 164
Children, Rules, and the Outside World 164
Families as Transacted Relationships 165
Transacting Family Life 166
Authority and Power 166
Norms and Rituals 167
Family Secrets 169
Family Storytelling 169
Information Flow: Kin Keeping and the Communication of News 170
Change and Development in Family Processes 171
Acute Change in Families 171
Long-Term Change in Families 172
Redeployment of Families and Their Communication 173
Families Communicate! 174
Focus Questions Revisited 174
Key Concepts 175
Questions to Ask Your Friends 175
Media Connections 176

9. Groups and Leaders 179

Focus Questions 179
What Is a Group? 179
Types of Groups 180
Characteristics of Groups 180
Cohesiveness 181
Avoiding Groupthink 182
Interdependence 182

Commitment 183
Dealing With Out-Groups 183
Group Norms 183
Member Roles 184
Formal Roles 184
Informal Roles 184
Task Roles 184
Social Roles 184
Disruptive Roles 185
Group Culture 185
Group Development and Decision Making 185
Group Decision Making Is About Relationships 187
Leadership 188
Leadership Styles 189
Task Leaders 189
Socioemotional Leaders 189
Leadership Power 190
Formal Power 190
Informal Power 190
More Types of Power 191
Leadership Vision 191
Leadership Ethics 192
Leadership Is Transacted 192
Focus Questions Revisited 193
Key Concepts 194
Questions to Ask Your Friends 195
Media Connections 195

10. Communication in the Workplace 197

Focus Questions 197
Learning About the Workplace 199
Socialization About Work 200
Metaphors of Organization 200
Early Learning About Work 201
Going to Work: The Workplace as a Special Frame 202
Going to Work: What Is Different, and What Is the Same? 203
Performance of Work Identities 204
Negotiating Relational and Work Goals 205
The Workplace as a Culture 206
Organizational Culture and Routines 206
Structuration Theory 207
Meaning Making 208
The Organization and Its Norms 209
Frames and Hierarchies: Formal Versus Informal Power 209
Industrial Time 210
Contact With the Public: Customer-Client Relationships 211
The Workplace as Relationships 212
Relationships as Workplace Challenges 213
Legitimate and Illegitimate Organizational Interference in Life 214
Spillover From Work Into Daily Life 215
Surveillance in an Organization 215
The Downside of Good Relationships at Work 216
Love, Sex, and Hate in the Workplace 217
Favors for Buddies 218
You're My Boss, but You Were My Friend 218
Employee-Abusive Communication 219
Focus Questions Revisited 220
Key Concepts 220
Questions to Ask Your Friends 220
Media Connections 221

11. Health Communication 223

Focus Questions 223
Patient and Provider Relationships 224
Patient-Provider Identities 224
How Patients and Providers Communicate 225
Improving Patient-Provider Communication 226
Benefits of Effective Patient-Provider Relationships 226

Satisfaction 226
Adherence to Treatments 226
Physical and Psychological Health 227
Malpractice Claims 228
Social Networks and Health 228
Social Networks and Health and Lifestyles 228
Eating and Exercising With Others 228
Smoking With Others 229
Drinking With Others 230
Social Networks and Support 230
Action-Facilitating Support 230
Nurturing Support 231
Secondary Goals of Social Support 231
Identity Goals of Social Support 231
Relational Goals of Social Support 232
Everyday Communication and the Foundation of Social Support 232
Communication Privacy Management 233
Media, Technology, and Health 234
Entertainment Media and Health 235
News Media and Health 235
Advertising Medications 236
Health Communication and the Internet 237
Searching for Information 237
Support 238
Connecting Patients and Providers 238
Focus Questions Revisited 239
Key Concepts 239
Questions to Ask Your Friends 240
Media Connections 240

12. Culture and Communication 243

Focus Questions 243
How Can Culture Be Identified and Studied? 245
Culture as Structure 245
Cross-Cultural Communication and Intercultural Communication 245
Limitations and Benefits 246
Culture as Transacted 246
Coded Systems of Meaning 247
Structure-Based Cultural Characteristics 248
Context 248
High-Context Cultures 248
Low-Context Cultures 249
Collectivism/Individualism 249
Collectivist Cultures 249
Individualist Cultures 250
Time 251
Monochronic Culture 251
Polychronic Culture 252
Future and Past Orientations 252
Conflict 252
Conflict-as-Opportunity Cultures 252
Conflict-as-Destructive Cultures 253
Managing Conflict 254
Transacting Culture 255
Culture Is Embedded Within Your Communication 256
Culture Goes Beyond Physical Location 256
Cultural Groups Are Created Through Communication 257
Co-Cultures 257
Speech Communities 257
Teamsterville and Nacirema 258
Cultural Membership Is Enacted Through Communication 258
Focus Questions Revisited 259
Key Concepts 260
Questions to Ask Your Friends 260
Media Connections 261

13. Technology and Media in Everyday Life 263

Focus Questions 263
Perceptions of Technology and Media 264
Cave Drawings and Other Concerns 264
Every Technology Is Relational 264
Impact of Technology 265
Technological Determinism 265
Social Construction of Technology 265

Social Shaping of Technology 266
The Relational Uses of Technology and Media 266
The Use of Technology and Media Is a Shared Relational Activity 266
Technology and Media Inform People About Relationships 267
Media Representations Inform About How Relationships Should Look 267
Media Representations Inform About How to Behave in Relationships 268
Technology and Media Function as Alternatives to Personal Relationships 268
Companionship and Relational Satisfaction From the Actual Use of Technology and Media 268
Companionship and Relational Satisfaction From Parasocial Relationships 269
Technology and Media Are Used in Everyday Talk 270
Technology and Media Provide a General Topic of Conversation 270
Talk About Technology and Media Impacts Their Value and Understanding 271
Talk About Technology and Media Impacts Their Dissemination and Influence 271
Talk About Technology and Media Promotes the Development of Media Literacy 271
Talk About Technology and Media Influences Identification and Relationship Development 272
Talk About Technology and Media Enables Identity Construction 272
Cell Phones: Constructing Identities and Relationships 273
Constructing Identities Using Cell Phones 274
The Meaning of Relational Technology 274
Relational Technology and Generations 274
Relational Technology and Social Networks 274
Technological Products and Service Providers 275
Ringtones 275
Performance of Relational Technology 275
Relating Through Cell Phones 276
Constant Connection and Availability 276
Boundaries and Closeness 276
Shared Experience 277
Social Coordination 277
Constructing Identities and Maintaining Relationships Online 277
Social Networking Sites and the Construction of Identities 278
Friends 278
Photographs 279
Media Preferences 279
Strategic 280
Public Disclosure 280
Online Communication and Relationships 281
Maintaining Relationships and Social Networks 281
Explaining the Benefits 282
Focus Questions Revisited 284
Key Concepts 284
Questions to Ask Your Friends 285
Media Connections 285

14. Public and Personal Influence 287

Focus Questions 287
Public Address and Relating to Audiences 288
Analyzing Audiences 288
Relationship With the Speaker 289
Relationship With the Issue and Position 289
Attitudes, Beliefs, and Values 290
Speeches to Convince and Speeches to Actuate 290
Speeches to Convince 291
Claims of Policy 291
Claims of Value 291
Claims of Fact and Claims of Conjecture 291
Audience Approaches to Speeches to Convince 292
Speeches to Actuate 292
Sequential Persuasion 292
Foot in the Door 293
Door in the Face 294
Pregiving 295
Emotional Appeals 295
Fear: Buy This Book and No One Gets Hurt! 297
Extended Parallel Process Model 297
Guilt: Have You Ever Seen Two Grown Professors Cry? 298
Lost Emotions 298
Compliance Gaining 299
Relational Influence Goals 299
Secondary Goals of Compliance Gaining 300

Compliance Gaining Strategies 300
Original Typology 301
Contextual Influences 301
Focus Questions Revisited 305
Key Concepts 306
Questions to Ask Your Friends 306
Media Connections 306

15. Interviewing 309

Focus Questions 309
Preparing for an Interview 310
Cover Letters and Résumés 310
Address Letter to Specific Person 310
Identify the Position 310
Summarize Qualifications and Promote Résumé 311
Reaffirm Interest and Request an Interview 311
Sign Off With Respect and Professionalism 311
Résumés 311
Name and Contact Information 312
Career Objective 312
Education and Training 312
Experiences 313
Skills 313
Activities 313
Interviews 313
Characteristics of an Interview 313
Types of Interviews 314
Employment Interviews 314
Performance Interviews 315
Exit Interviews 315
Persuasive Interviews 315
Information-Gaining Interviews 315
Problem-Solving Interviews 316
Helping Interviews 316
Pre-interview Responsibilities 316
Interviewer Responsibilities 317
Review Application Material 317
Prepare Questions and an Interview Outline 317
Gather Materials 317
Begin on Time 318
Interviewee Responsibilities 318
Gather Information 318
Prepare Questions 319
Practice 320
Professional Personal Appearance 320
Arrive on Time 320
Bring Materials 321
Turn Off the Cell Phone 322
Beginning an Employment Interview 322
Greeting and Establishing Appropriate Proxemics 322
Negotiating Relational Connection and Tone 323
Establishing Purpose and Agenda 323
Asking the Questions During an Employment Interview 324
Primary and Secondary Questions 324
Open and Closed Questions 325
Neutral and Leading Questions 325
Directive and Nondirective Questioning 326
Avoiding Illegal Questions 327
Answering the Questions During an Employment Interview 328
Adjusting the Interview Frame 328
Learning From Successful and Unsuccessful Interviewees 330
Answering Common Questions 331
Tell Me a Little About Yourself 331
What Are Your Greatest Strengths? 331
What Are Your Greatest Weaknesses? 331
What Do You Know About This Organization? 331
Why Do You Want to Work Here? 332
What Is Your Ideal Job? 332
Why Do You Want to Leave Your Current Job? 332
What Are Your Expectations in Terms of Salary? 332
Where Do You See Yourself in 5 Years? 333
Why Should We Hire You? 333
Dealing With Illegal Questions 333
Concluding an Employment Interview 334
Interviewer Responsibilities 334
Wrap-Up Signal 334
Summarize the Interview 334
Ask for Questions 334
Preview Future Actions and Schedule 334
Offer Thanks 334
Farewells 335
Interviewee Responsibilities 335

Ask Questions 335
Reinforce Qualifications and Enthusiasm 335
Inquire About Schedule (If Not Provided) 335
Offer Thanks 335
Farewells 336
Post-Interview Responsibilities 336
Interviewer Responsibilities 336
Assess the Job Candidate 336
Assess Personal Performance 337
Contact Interviewee 337
Interviewee Responsibilities 337
Assess the Interview 337
Send Follow-Up Letter 338
Avoid Irritating the Interviewer 338
Focus Questions Revisited 339
Key Concepts 340
Questions to Ask Your Friends 340
Media Connections 340

Glossary **342**
Chapter References **351**
Photo Credits **366**
Index **367**

Preface

Communication in Everyday Life has been written to provide students with a new kind of introduction to the central issues and topics of communication. Accordingly, it can serve as the course textbook for general education courses in communication, as the course textbook for survey courses taken by communication majors, and as a resource for anyone interested in the study of communication. Yet it demonstrates a fresh approach.

This book, therefore, includes discussions of material traditionally included in such textbooks. However, it also includes material conspicuously absent from other textbooks but increasingly relevant in the everyday lives of students, such as social media. Further, it allows all of these topics to cohere and coalesce by pointing out the *relational* basis of all communication as a major feature of students' everyday lives.

This book is written in a conversational tone with an acknowledgment that students arrive at college with various levels of academic preparedness and that students come from a number of different backgrounds with diverse life experiences.

Finally, this book recognizes the value of well-developed learning tools for students and the benefits of robust ancillary materials for both students and instructors.

In what follows, we will briefly introduce the focus on everyday communication and the relational perspective guiding this book. We will then examine pedagogical features, instructor support, and available ancillary materials.

Everyday Communication and a Relational Perspective

Topics in textbooks such as this one are frequently introduced only to be quickly left behind as students are introduced to ensuing topics. Issues of communication are discussed as if occurring in isolation, and a common thread or unifying theme is often absent. Like academic silos, each chapter houses a single topic, without any consideration about how topics may be interconnected and can be understood through a shared perspective.

The isolation of topics provides students with an artificial and unrealistic view of actual communication. It specifically obscures the interrelated nature of communication. For example, completely separating personal relationships and media conceals the fact that in real life such media as television and film are often consumed in the company of others, convey information about relationships, and serve as topics of everyday talk. Likewise, social media are explicitly used to conduct and maintain relationships, while health care and social support are based in relationship activity.

In addition to further separating topics, the lack of a common theme prevents students from recognizing how topics in communication fit and come together as part of a greater whole and how they might be studied in a coherent fashion. Not only is the everyday use of interpersonal communication a universal experience, but attempts to both teach and understand it are founded in teacher-student rapport and based around recognition of the universals of human experience.

Within this book, topics are frequently introduced and discussed in connection with other topics. Naturally, this approach runs the risk of focusing too much on these connections and not enough on each specific topic. However, it is accomplished in such a manner that students are reminded of other topics and provided with an awareness of the interconnected nature of communication.

When it comes to a unifying theme, *everyday communication* and a *relational perspective* will guide our exploration of communication.

Everyday Communication

The discipline of communication has traditionally focused on the "big" moments or seemingly extraordinary events of human interaction. These instances might include initial encounters, arguments, betrayals, or other dramatic occurrences. These events may be memorable, but they are not all that common.

In actuality, most of a person's life experiences and interactions with others are of the everyday, seemingly ordinary, and seemingly dull variety. This everyday communication might include brief conversations while getting ready for school or work, a quick text message between classes, or talking while watching video clips online (or sharing those clips as a means of expressing common interests and relationship). The content of these interactions might include schedules, the weather, what to eat, or any other seemingly mundane topic.

Everyday communication may not always be memorable, but it is very important. Beyond the frequency of this sort of interaction, it is through routine, seemingly mundane everyday communication that major portions of a person's life take shape. Everyday communication creates, maintains, challenges, and alters relationships and identities as well as culture, gender, sexuality, ethnicity, meaning, and even reality.

We will, of course, discuss major moments and events in human interaction when appropriate. However, we will always return to the significance of communication in everyday life and how references to everyday lived experiences will assist students in understanding the material.

Relational Perspective

The relational perspective is based on the belief that communication and relationships are interconnected. Relationships impact communication, and communication impacts relationships. Relationships flow into daily experiences, and all communication has a relationship assumed underneath it. At the same time, it is through communication that relationships are developed, maintained, and modified.

Relationships are an inherent part of any topic of communication. Relationships guide our use of verbal communication. Nonverbal communication conveys the type of relationship shared by two people. Interactions among those with whom a personal relationship is shared are often the basis of identity construction. Recognizing the type of relationship shared will assist people when engaged in the listening process. Families and groups can be understood not as structures but as the enactment of relational communication. Relationships influence health decisions and health-related activities. Culture and society are created and performed through relationships. People use media and technology relationally more than as individuals. Relationships often serve as the basis for influencing another person. And successful interviews involve the creation of relationships among interviewers and interviewees.

Given the variety of their educational backgrounds, demographic characteristics, and experiences, all students share the fact that their understanding of the world has been formed and influenced by relationships. The relational perspective makes the importance and operation of communication more understandable through direct connections to the experience of all students and therefore will facilitate classroom discussion while channeling and capitalizing on students' natural interests.

Pedagogical Features

We view the pedagogical features within textbooks as fundamental elements in the comprehension and incorporation of the material being presented. Rather than using them as meaningless filler or only to break up the text, we use them to provide students with a better understanding of the material and a better appreciation for its importance and application in everyday life. These pedagogical tools have been tested in our own and other classrooms and provide students with opportunities to enhance their learning.

Overview

To help guide the students, each chapter begins with a pedagogical overview: "These are the key items or issues you need to know about this topic. Now let's look at things in more detail." **Focus Questions** are also posed in the opening spread to further direct students through the chapter.

Chapter Boxes

The main body of the chapters includes the following pedagogical boxes: (1) Analyzing Everyday Communication, (2) By the Way, (3) Communication and You, (4) Disciplinary Debate, (5) Ethical Issue, (6) Make Your Case, and (7) Skills to Use. With the exception of Skills to Use, each of these boxes includes questions for students to further consider what is being discussed.

Analyzing Everyday Communication boxes encourage students to apply what they have learned in the analysis of everyday life situations. For instance, the culture chapter asks them to consider the television programs and fairy tales they enjoyed as children and the accompanying cultural themes.

By the Way boxes appear multiple times within each chapter and present students with additional information to ponder as they study the material. These boxes serve to enhance student interest in the material by providing unique or bonus information about what is being discussed. For example, the verbal communication chapter examines how media references are often used in everyday talk.

Communication and You boxes ask students to consider the material in relation to their lives and lived experiences. Specifically, this feature will sensitize students to issues and encourage them to become careful observers of the activities and events going on in their lives, compelling them to examine and apply the material. For instance, the health communication chapter has students consider a time when they struggled about whether or not to disclose private health information to another person.

Disciplinary Debate boxes encourage critical thinking by asking students to consider competing views within communication scholarship or positions that counter those presented in the text. For example, in the personal relationship chapter students are asked to consider whether relationships actually develop and end in stages as textbooks so often claim.

Ethical Issue boxes urge students to contemplate and develop a position regarding ethical quandaries that arise in communication. For instance, the media and technology chapter asks students to consider whether employers should use material on social networking sites, such as Facebook or Twitter, when making hiring decisions. These boxes appear three times within each chapter.

Make Your Case boxes provide students with opportunities to develop their own positions or to provide a personal example about the material. For example, in the listening chapter, students are asked to provide and respond to a time when they encountered problems with listening involving customer service.

Skills You Can Use boxes present students with guides to integrate the material into their lives. For instance, the group chapter discusses how recognizing the relational elements of a group can assist them when promoting a particular agenda or decision.

Photographs

Photographs included in each chapter also serve as pedagogical tools. Each photo caption is stated in the form of a question that corresponds with material being discussed. Students will be asked to examine the photograph and answer the accompanying question based on their understanding of the material. Rather than being open-ended, these questions have specific answers that appear on the the student study site: edge.sagepub.com/duckciel2e

End-of-Chapter Pedagogical Materials

Each chapter also ends with pedagogical materials that bring the overview and focus questions full circle. **Focus Questions Revisited** are implemented as a way of summarizing chapter material via pedagogical structure rather than as a simple (and usually ignored) chapter summary. Also, instead of including review questions, which often serve only to establish lower levels of comprehension, each chapter includes (a) Questions to Ask Your Friends and (b) Media Connections. These features enable students to further examine how the chapter material fits within their communicative lives as a whole. **Questions to Ask Your Friends** provide students with questions to ask their friends in order to further increase their awareness of the material and integrate it into their lives. In the culture chapter, for example, students are encouraged to ask their friends about what was challenging and what was rewarding about recent intercultural experiences. **Media Connections** lead students to draw from media in order to further explore the issues discussed in each chapter. For example, the relationships chapter instructs students to examine the Sunday newspaper section of marriages, engagements, and commitment ceremonies for similarities in attractiveness.

Conversational Tone

To further assist student learning, we have deliberately adopted an informal and conversational tone in our writing, and we even throw in a few jokes. We are not attempting to be hip or cool: Trust us; we are far from either, so much so that we are not even sure if the words *hip* and *cool* are used anymore. Instead, we use a conversational voice because we believe that it makes this book more engaging to read. Plus, we genuinely enjoy talking about this material. We want to share our enthusiasm in a way that we hope is infectious.

Instructor Support

Although a fundamental feature of the book is, of course, to update discussion of topics by integrating the latest research while providing a new relationally based perspective on the material normally included in traditional texts, this is a two-edged sword. A challenge associated with developing a new textbook—especially one offering an original approach and addressing more up-to-date issues of communication—is that many instructors already have their courses in good shape and do not need the extra burden of rewriting those courses to fit a completely new text. We have therefore sought to add material in a way that supplements and develops rather than replaces traditional material. By this means, we seek to support those teachers who have already developed useful courses and who want to add some spice from the newer research without having to completely revise their existing lectures and notes. Thus, although the present text updates much of the theory and research included in older-style texts, we have constructed this book to reflect the traditional basic text design. A host of ancillary materials are also available that would benefit both new and experienced instructors.

Ancillaries

Student Study Site

edge.sagepub.com/duckciel2e

SAGE edge offers a robust online environment featuring an impressive array of tools and resources for review, study, and further exploration, keeping both instructors and students on the cutting edge of teaching and learning. SAGE edge content is open access and available on demand. Learning and teaching has never been easier!

SAGE edge for students provides a personalized approach to help students accomplish their coursework goals in an easy-to-use learning environment.

- Mobile-friendly **eFlashcards** strengthen understanding of key terms and concepts
- Mobile-friendly practice **quizzes** allow for independent assessment by students of their mastery of course material
- A customized online **action plan** includes tips and feedback on progress through the course and materials, which allows students to individualize their learning experience
- **Chapter summaries** with **learning objectives** reinforce the most important material
- **Interactive exercises** and meaningful web links facilitate student use of internet resources, further exploration of topics, and responses to critical thinking questions
- A **speech outline guide** helps students plan their speeches
- **Speech topic ideas** give students a head-start in developing their presentations

- **Sample written speeches** show students examples of how to structure their speeches
- EXCLUSIVE! Access to full-text **SAGE journal articles** that have been carefully selected to support and expand on the concepts presented in each chapter

SAGE edge for instructors supports teaching by making it easy to integrate quality content and create a rich learning environment for students.

- **Test banks** provide a diverse range of pre-written options as well as the opportunity to edit any question and/or insert personalized questions to effectively assess students' progress and understanding
- **Sample course syllabi** for semester and quarter courses provide suggested models for structuring one's course
- Editable, chapter-specific **PowerPoint® slides** offer complete flexibility for creating a multimedia presentation for the course
- EXCLUSIVE! Access to full-text **SAGE journal articles** have been carefully selected to support and expand on the concepts presented in each chapter to encourage students to think critically
- **Multimedia content** includes original SAGE videos that appeal to students with different learning styles
- **Lecture notes** summarize key concepts by chapter to ease preparation for lectures and class discussions
- A **Course cartridge** provides easy LMS integration

A Personal Note to Readers

Communication in Everyday Life was developed with the belief that introductory communication courses play a central role in the discipline by attracting new majors, providing a foundation for upper-level courses, and supporting the entire academic community as important general education requirements and preparations for future life. The basic course is not just about training students in a discipline. It is about educating them more broadly for life beyond college and instilling within them an inquisitive curiosity that will serve them throughout their lives. It is one of the most important courses a student of any discipline will take.

Accordingly, we did not want to present students with a cookie-cutter book that looks and reads like every other textbook published in the past few decades. Many publishers encouraged us to do just that! Rather, if we were to develop a new textbook, it had to bring something fresh and meaningful to the study of communication.

We believe that our relational perspective and focus on everyday life provides students with a coherent structure to their study of communication and an opportunity to apply the material to their own personal and professional lives.

We believe that some traditional material such as verbal communication, nonverbal communication, and listening should be included in any introductory course. But other material such as social media and technology, culture, and family is conspicuously absent from other books in spite of being an integral part of students' lives.

We believe that a writing style can be achieved that is engaging and accessible to all readers at any level of academic preparedness. Students new to college should find the writing understandable while increasing their ability to study and comprehend the material. Students at advanced levels of preparedness should find the writing suitable for the collegiate level. No students should ever feel as if they are being presented with insultingly simple prose. Rather, the writing should be at appropriate and manageable levels and feel like it was written by humans.

We believe that books should not be written only for the "traditional student"—an assumed 18- to 22-year-old upper-middle-class student who does not work, whose parents are paying for college, and who plans on spending spring break on an exotic beach somewhere. We have nothing against such students, but we just recognize that many students are older, struggling financially, or are paying their own way through college. Many students work at least one job while going to school, and some of them have children of their own to care for as they study. Like ours when we were in school, their spring breaks will be spent working additional hours rather than lounging on the sand.

We believe that pedagogical tools within the text such as boxes and photos should be more than just meaningless filler and instead be focused on teaching and learning. Further, whenever possible, photographs should depict realistic-looking people in realistic situations rather than models or celebrities depicting unrealistic and theatrical communication.

Finally, we believe that ancillary materials such as self-quizzes, activities, and Internet resources should be developed to benefit students, new instructors, and experienced instructors alike. We also wanted to ensure that these ancillary materials were available to *all* students and not just those students purchasing a new copy of the book rather than a used copy of the book.

In order to substantiate, challenge, and build upon these beliefs, we engaged in extensive discussions with our fellow course instructors and directors as well as students throughout the United States and other countries. We wanted to know what they needed in a textbook, what worked and did not work with previous textbooks, and what innovations must be included. Primarily due to their input and encouragement during all facets of its development and production, the first edition of *Communication in Everyday Life* was met with an overwhelmingly positive response. These discussions continued once the first edition was published, and remained fundamental in the development and production of this edition.

This second edition has enabled us to advance the components that worked so well in the first edition and to include additional features and modifications to enhance its use in communication classrooms. In general, we have streamlined much of the text in order to increase its readability. Numerous tables and charts have also been included to help readers synthesize the material. Nearly all of the original photographs have been replaced, and many additional photographs have been included. Fresh and additional pedagogical boxes have been included in each chapter. In response to instructor and student comments, the coverage of some material has been rearranged, removed, increased, or added. The latest research and findings have been incorporated throughout each of the chapters, as have updated discussions and examples. We are thankful for the success of the first edition and are excited about the potential impact of the second edition.

We are passionate about the study of communication and are deeply committed to its instruction. It is our sincere hope that everyone who reads this book will experience improved understanding and enjoyment of communication. Thank you for providing us with the opportunity to share our enthusiasm for communication and the opportunity to demonstrate its importance and application in everyday life.

Steve and David

Steve Duck David T. McMahan

Acknowledgments

A book such as this one is a tremendous undertaking, and we are grateful to the many people who have contributed to the development of this volume. We are thankful to our students, both graduate and undergraduate, who knowingly or unknowingly provided observations, examples, and thoughtful discussion of the ideas presented here. We are also thankful to the instructors and students who have used the first edition of the book as well as our other books for allowing us into their classrooms. Many of them enabled us to live out the relational perspective through personal contact by phone and e-mail and through much-appreciated visits on campuses and at conferences. Their feedback and encouragement are greatly appreciated and have enhanced this volume in immeasurable ways.

Involvement in such books takes an enormous toll on relational life. We are extremely thankful to our respective families and friends. Their forbearance provides a supportive atmosphere for us to manage the long hours and extended absences required to bring such projects to completion. Beyond their acceptance of long absences and of seeing the back of our heads more often than the front of them as we sat at our computers, we are especially grateful for the suggestions and comments of Ben Lawson-Duck, Gabriel Lawson-Duck, and Jennifer McMahan as they withstood discussions about what we happened to be working on at a given moment.

Additionally, we would like to thank all of our parents, siblings, nieces and nephews, extended families, colleagues, acquaintances, strangers we have encountered, people we like, and people we despise, all of whom have provided us with ideas for a relational perspective of communication.

We also wish to extend our warm appreciation to Nancy Loh, Gabrielle Piccininni, Amy Schroller, and others at SAGE Publications who have assisted in bringing this book into existence. We remain thankful to copy editor extraordinaire Melinda Masson, who continues to be an absolute delight to work with and whose detailed eye and sensitivity to author voice position her without equal. Finally, we are grateful to our editor, Matthew Byrnie, for his helpful guidance, strong support, and confidence in this book's capability of being a meaningful tool for student learning and a positive influence in the discipline.

We are also indebted to the following people for their unstinting generosity in commenting on the textbook in spite of their incredibly busy schedules and for making many brilliant suggestions that we were all too happy to borrow or appropriate without acknowledgment other than here. They generously contributed to whatever this book in its turn contributes to the growth and development of the field. We could not have fully developed the relational perspective and conveyed the impact of everyday communication without their professionalism and thoughtfulness.

Susan Westcott Alessandri, *Suffolk University*

Martha Antolik, *Wright State University*

Colleen E. Arendt, *Fairfield University*

Megan N. Bell, *University of Minnesota at Crookston*

Marcia S. Berry, *Azusa Pacific University*

Sarah L. Cole, *Framingham State University*

Kevin Cummings, *Mercer University*

Katie Dawson, *University of Louisiana at Monroe*

Melissa K. Donley, *University of Northern Colorado*

Sarah Bonewits Feldner, *Marquette University*

Joy Goldsmith, *Young Harris College*

Jo Anna Grant, *California State University at San Bernardino*

Adam Gutschmidt, *Wright State University*

Donna L. Halper, *Lesley University*

Kathleen C. Haspel, *Fairleigh Dickinson University*

Kim Elizabeth Higgs, *University of North Dakota*

Julie Homchick, *Seattle University*

Dena Huisman, *University of Wisconsin at La Crosse*

William E. Hurt, *University of South Carolina at Beaufort*

Jacqueline A. Irwin, *California State University at Sacramento*

Vicki L. Karns, *Suffolk University*

Edith E. LeFebvre, *California State University at Sacramento*

Amy Lenoce, *Naugatuck Valley Community College*

Deborah Lewis, *Birmingham City University*

Melissa A. Maier, *Upper Iowa University*

Tino G. K. Meitz, *University of Tübingen*

Jonathan Millen, *Rider University*

Aimee E. Miller-Ott, *University of Hartford*

Jennifer Moreland, *The College of Wooster*

Heidi L. Muller, *University of Northern Colorado*

Alison N. Novak, *Drexel University*

Sivanes Phillipson, *Hong Kong Baptist University*

Ronda Picarelli, *California State University at Northridge*

Jeffrey H. Pierson, *Bridgewater College*

Joquina Reed, *Texas A&M International University*

Christine E. Rittenour, *West Virginia University*

Tracy R. Routsong, *Washburn University*

Terri L. Russ, *Saint Mary's College*

John H. Saunders, *Huntingdon College*

Susan Silcott, *Ohio University*

Arlene Swartzman, *University of Maryland University College*

Matthew R. Turner, *Radford University*

Patricia Turner, *Community College of Vermont*

Kyle Tusing, *University of Arizona*

Alice E. Veksler, *University of Connecticut*

Michelle T. Violanti, *University of Tennessee at Knoxville*

Bruce Wickelgren, *Suffolk University*

Julie Woodbury, *Hamline University*

About the Authors

Steve Duck taught at two universities in the United Kingdom before taking up the Daniel and Amy Starch Distinguished Research Chair in the College of Liberal Arts and Sciences at the University of Iowa, where he is a professor of communication studies also an adjunct professor of psychology. He is a Dean's Administrative Fellow and Chair of the Rhetoric Department. He has taught several interpersonal communication courses, mostly on relationships but also on nonverbal communication, communication in everyday life, construction of identity, communication theory, organizational leadership, and procedures and practices for leaders. Always, by training, an interdisciplinary thinker, Steve has focused on the development and decline of relationships from many different perspectives, although he has also done research on the dynamics of television production techniques and persuasive messages in health contexts. Steve has written or edited 60 books on relationships and other matters and was the founder and, for the first 15 years, the Editor of the Journal of Social and Personal Relationships. His book *Meaningful Relationships: Talking, Sense, and Relating* won the G. R. Miller Book Award from the Interpersonal Communication Division of the National Communication Association. Steve co-founded a series of international conferences on personal relationships. He won the University of Iowa's first Outstanding Faculty Mentor Award in 2001 and the National Communication Association's Robert J. Kibler Memorial Award in 2004 for "dedication to excellence, commitment to the profession, concern for others, vision of what could be, acceptance of diversity, and forthrightness." He was the 2010 recipient of the UI College of Liberal Arts and Sciences Helen Kechriotis Nelson Teaching Award for a lifetime of excellence in teaching and in the same year was elected one of the National Communication Association's Distinguished Scholars. He hopes to someday appear on a viral YouTube clip and be famous.

David T. McMahan has taught courses that span the discipline of communication, including numerous courses in interpersonal communication and personal relationships, media and technology, communication education, theory, and criticism. David's research interests also engage multiple areas of the discipline with much of his research devoted to bridging the study of relationships, technology, and media. This work encompasses discussions of media and technology in everyday communication, the incorporation of catchphrases and media references in everyday communication, and the relational aspects of the Internet and digital media. His diverse research experiences also include studies on symbolic displays of masculinity and violence in rural America, media-based political transformations of the world's nation-states, *The New York Times*' reporting of mass-murder suicide, and primetime animated series. In addition to authoring numerous books, his work has appeared in such journals as *Review of Communication, Communication Education,* and *Communication Quarterly,* as well as edited volumes. A tremendously-active member of the discipline, his endeavors include serving on a number of editorial review boards, serving as editor of the *Iowa Journal of Communication,* and serving as president of the Central States Communication Association (2015–2016). He has received multiple awards for his work in the classroom and has been the recipient of a number of public service and academic distinctions, including being named a Centennial Scholar by the Eastern Communication Association. He hopes to someday appear in an updated version of *The Andy Griffith Show.*

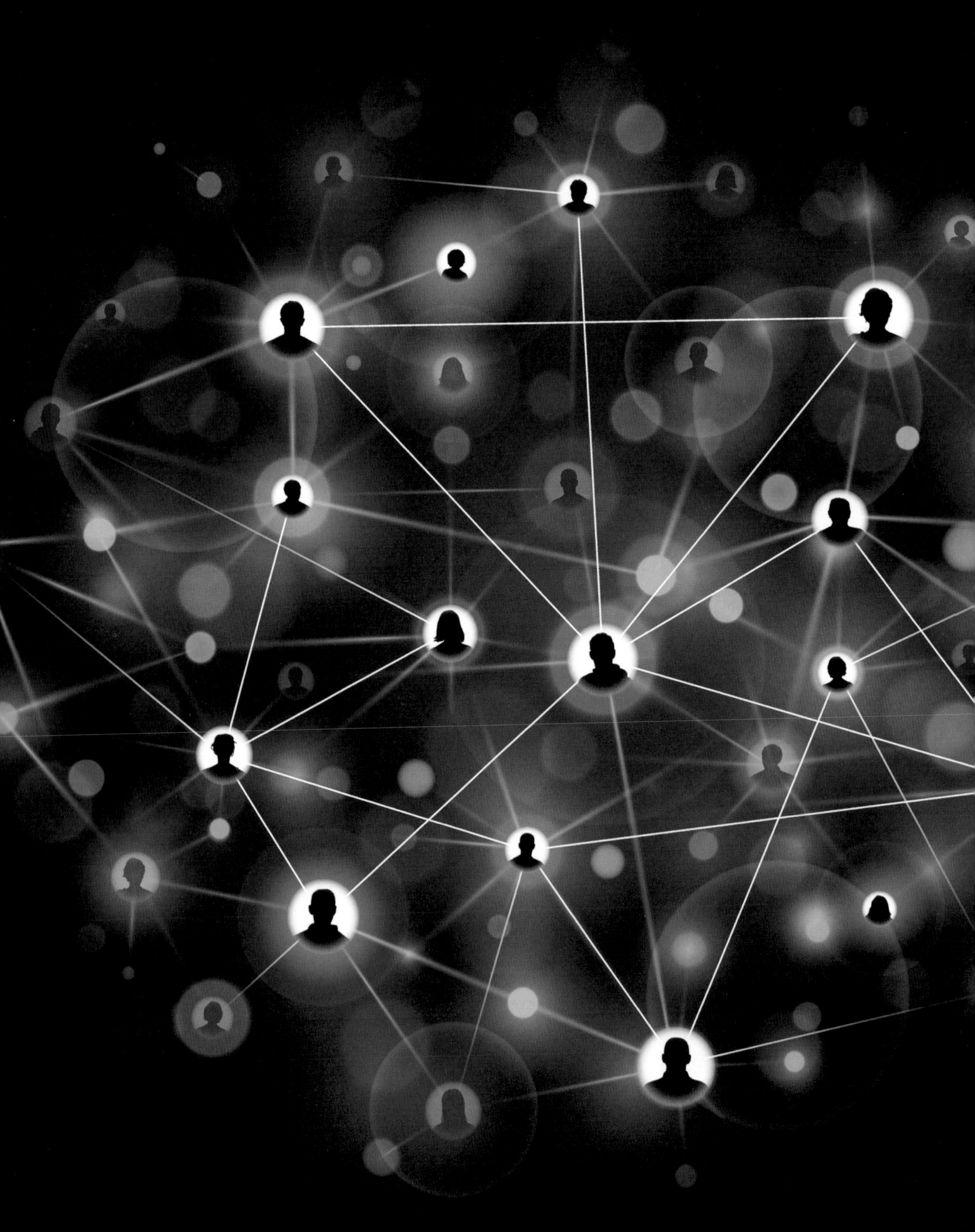

Part I COMMUNICATION FOUNDATIONS

CHAPTER 1
An Overview of Communication

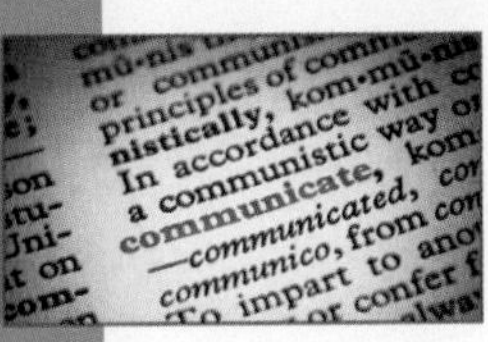

CHAPTER 2
Histories of Communication

Chapter Outline

Everyday Communication and the Relational Perspective

What Is Communication?

Communication Is Symbolic

Communication Requires Meaning

- Social Construction of Meaning
- Meaning and Context
- Verbal and Nonverbal Influence on Meaning
- Meaning and the Medium

Communication Is Cultural

Communication Is Relational

Communication Involves Frames

- Coordinating Interactions
- Assigning Meanings
- Perspectives

Communication Is Both Presentational and Representational

Communication Is a Transaction

- Communication as Action
- Communication as Interaction
- Communication as Transaction

Focus Questions Revisited

Key Concepts

Questions to Ask Your Friends

Media Connections

01 An Overview of Communication

Can you think of anything important in your life that does not involve communication? In reality we do not think it is possible for anyone to legitimately come up with any aspect of life that does not involve communication and that would not be made better by the ability to understand communication more thoroughly. Just consider some of the areas covered in this book. You will have the opportunity to examine such topics as friendships and romantic relationships, media, technology, cultures, personal and public influence, families, health care, and the workplace. You will learn about how your communication and the communication of others influence and actually develop these and many other areas of your life.

We are passionate about the study of communication, and we believe very strongly that you can benefit from knowing more about how communication works. We wrote this book partly because we believe that everyone needs to know more about communication. *Communication in Everyday Life* will help you better understand—and even improve—your life through better understanding communication.

FOCUS QUESTIONS

1. **What are symbols?**
2. **How is meaning established?**
3. **How is communication cultural?**
4. **How is communication relational?**
5. **What are communication frames?**
6. **What does it mean to view communication as both representational and presentational?**
7. **What does it mean to view communication as a transaction?**

Everyday Communication and the Relational Perspective

One thing making this book different from other communication textbooks is its focus on *everyday communication*. The discipline of communication has traditionally focused on the "big" moments or seemingly extraordinary events of human interaction. These instances include initial encounters, betrayals, disclosure of secret information, family upheavals, and other dramatic experiences you may occasionally encounter during your lifetime. These events may be memorable, but they do not make up much of a person's lived experiences. For instance, romantic relationships only rarely feature moments in which partners hold hands, gaze into one another's eyes, and share their deepest darkest secrets and declarations of unending love.

In actuality, most interactions of romantic partners are of the everyday, seemingly ordinary, or even seemingly dull variety. This everyday communication might include brief conversations as they get ready for work or school, a quick phone call or text between classes or during a break, talking in the car while in traffic, or chatting while watching television or videos online. The content of these conversations is seemingly mundane and may include topics such as schedules, weather, what to eat, what to watch on television, what bills need paying, or the source of a foul odor.

Is the connection between relationships and communication really that significant?

Everyday communication may not always be memorable, but it does *constitute* (i.e., compose) a person's life, and it happens to be incredibly important. It is through routine, seemingly mundane everyday communication that major portions of a person's life take shape. Everyday communication creates, maintains, challenges, and alters relationships and identities as well as culture, gender, sexuality, ethnicity, meaning, and even reality. Everyday communication should be studied not just because of its frequency in our lives but also because extraordinary things happen through everyday communication. When discussing all types of communication, we will continuously interconnect them with your everyday life and experiences.

Something else that sets this book apart from other communication textbooks is the relational perspective that we have developed through our books and research. The constant guide in understanding communication will be the relationships that you have with other people. The relational perspective is based on the belief that communication and relationships are interconnected. Any type of communication you ever participate in has a relationship assumed underneath it.

The relationship shared by people will influence what is communicated, how it is shared, and the meanings that develop. People generally talk with friends in a different way than with their parents. Coworkers generally talk with one another in a different way than with their supervisor. The meanings of communication also change depending on the relationships. For instance, saying "I love you" will take on different meaning if said to a romantic partner, a friend, a family member, a supervisor, or someone you just met. In turn, communication creates, reinforces, and modifies all relationships. Saying "I love you" can do many things. It can lead to the creation of a new relationship, strengthen a relationship, maintain a relationship, or result in the realization that people do not view a relationship in the same way. Ultimately, the link between relationships and communication is undeniable, and it can be used to study all communicative activity.

We sincerely believe that your life as a student, friend, romantic partner, colleague, and family member can be improved through the study of communication. Whatever your purpose in reading this book, and whatever your ultimate goal in life, we hope that it will enrich your life by sharpening your abilities to observe and understand communication activities going on around you.

By the way...

Citing Sources

You will notice that when we refer to someone else's work or ideas, we will list the surname of the author(s), a date, and a page number when quoting the author(s) directly. The date gives the year in which the original paper or book was published, and the page number is where the original quote can be located. This format is used in most social science textbooks and professional writing, with the full reference at the end of each chapter or at the end of the book. You may also be asked to use this format when you write your own papers or speeches.

QUESTIONS TO CONSIDER

1. Why do you suppose including references is so important?
2. Why would it be necessary for scholars to follow the same format when citing references?

What Is Communication?

In introductory chapters such as this one, you might expect the primary subject to be defined. In this case, you might be looking for an authoritative definition of *communication* that may very well show up on an examination you will take in the near future. Well, here is one you might like: *Communication* is the transactional use of symbols, influenced, guided, and understood in the context of relationships. Actually, that definition is not half bad, but it does not really do justice to what communication really entails. Your instructor may provide you with a better one.

There are a number of definitions of communication out there, and many of those definitions are very acceptable. Communication scholars Frank Dance and Carl Larson (1976) once compiled a list of 126 definitions of communication appearing in communication scholarship. Imagine the number of definitions that must have emerged in the four decades since then! Of course, education should go beyond memorizing a definition and rather should explore deeper issues or characteristics of an issue or a topic, so that is exactly what will be done in this chapter.

One fact that makes the study of communication unique, as opposed to, say, chemistry, is that you have been communicating your entire life. Previous experience with this topic can be very beneficial, since you will be able to draw from relationships and events in your own life when studying the material. You will even be able to apply the material—hopefully, improving your communication abilities and life in general along the way.

The drawback to previous experience is that people may not see the value in studying something that is such a common part of life. You may even be asking the "big deal" questions: What is so problematic about communication? Why bother to explain it? Don't people know what it is about and how it works? Communication is just about sending messages, right?

Make your case

Communication for Everyone

If you are not already convinced, the importance of communication will hopefully become increasingly clear as you continue reading this chapter and finish the entire book. You may be using this book for a required course in your major, a required general studies course, or an elective course. Make the case for a basic communication course being required for all graduates at your school. To get you started, people in the professional world consistently rank effective communication a vital trait for new hires and necessary for advancement.

QUESTIONS TO CONSIDER

1. What are some other reasons a communication course should be required?
2. Should students be required to take more than one communication course?

True: Most of the time, people communicate without thinking, and it is not usually awkward. However, if communicating is so easy, why do people have misunderstandings, conflicts, arguments, disputes, and disagreements? Why do people get embarrassed because they have said something thoughtless? Why, then, are allegations of sexual harassment sometimes denied vigorously, and how can there ever be doubt whether one person intentionally touched another person inappropriately? Why are some family members such a problem, and what is it about their communication that makes them difficult? Why is communication via e-mail or text message so easy to misunderstand? None of these problems would occur if people who asked the above "big deal" questions were right.

When first coming to the study of communication, many people assume that communication simply involves the sending of messages from person to person through the spoken word, text messages, or Facebook and Twitter updates. That basic view has some truth to it, but communication involves a lot more than merely transmitting information from Person A to Person B.

As you read this chapter, you will likely start to recognize that communication is more complex than it initially appears. Let's begin by examining a common situation, a restaurant server speaking to customers:

> "Hi! My name is Vera, and I'll be your server today. Our special is a bowl of soup for $3.95. If you have any questions about the menu, let me know."

Is communication simply the exchange of messages?

What you may already suppose about communication before studying it formally may be somewhat obvious in this example. Words are being used to convey information from one person to another person. Upon closer inspection, however, much more activity is taking place in this basic exchange.

The message is made up of words or symbols, which are used to allow one idea or representation to stand for something else. Taken-for-granted cultural assumptions are being made when these symbols are selected. "Menu" rather than "a list of all the food that we prepare, cook, and serve in this restaurant for you to choose for your meal" is said because it is assumed the customer will know the code word *menu* and its meaning in a restaurant as opposed to its meaning on a computer screen. If you are a member of a culture in which this sort of interaction is common, it all likely makes sense.

The server's message may also make sense because you know how to "perform/communicate restaurant." The comments are appropriate only in some places and at some times. If Vera was standing in the middle of a park screaming those words at everyone who passed by, you would likely think she was mentally unstable. They also make sense only at the beginning of the interaction, not during the meal or when the customer is leaving the restaurant.

Notice also how the message makes the interaction work in a particular way, setting up one person (server) in a particular kind of relationship with the other person (customer) while setting that relationship up as friendly and casual ("Hi," not "A thousand welcomes, great ones. Command me as you will, and I shall obey").

You have built-in expectations about the relationship between a server and a customer. You already know and take for granted that these relational differences exist in restaurants and that restaurants have "servers" who generally carry out instructions of "customers." Therefore, you expect the customer will be greeted, treated with some respect by the server, told what "the special" is, and asked to make choices. You know the customer will eventually pay for the food and that the server is there not only to bring food, water, the check, and change but also to help resolve any difficulties understanding the menu. Vera will answer any questions about the way the food is prepared or help if you need to find the restrooms. Both the customer and the server take this for granted; it is a cultural as well as relational element of communication.

This relatively brief encounter also demonstrates that communication is more than just the exchange of messages. It may appear as though a simple message involving the greeting, the speaker's name and job, her relationship to you, and the nature of the special on the menu is being sent to the customer. Beyond the transmission of a simple message, however, something will take place as a result of the message exchange. Further, worlds of meaning are being created, and personal perspectives are being displayed. Additional issues such as gender, status, power, and politeness are being negotiated. All of these things and much more are taking place within this simple exchange.

In the remainder of this chapter, we will introduce and begin our initial discussion of seven key characteristics of communication: (a) Communication is symbolic,

(b) communication requires meaning, (c) communication is cultural, (d) communication is relational, (e) communication involves frames, (f) communication is both presentational and representational, and (g) communication is a transaction. Examining these characteristics will provide a better understanding of what communication and its study really involves.

Communication Is Symbolic

All communication is characterized by the use of symbols. A **symbol** is an arbitrary representation of something else. This may be an object, an idea, a place, a person, or a relationship—to name only a few. As we discuss in the upcoming chapters, symbols are either verbal or nonverbal. Verbal communication involves language, while nonverbal communication involves all other symbols. Accordingly, a symbol can be a word, a movement, a sound, a picture, a logo, a gesture, a mark, or anything else that represents something other than itself.

To fully understand symbols, we can begin by discussing what they are not. Although the terms *symbol* and *sign* are sometimes used interchangeably, they do not represent the same thing. **Signs** are consequences or indicators of something specific, which human beings cannot change by their arbitrary actions or labels. For example, wet streets may be a sign that it has rained; smoke is a sign of fire. There is a direct causal connection between smoke and fire and between wet streets and rain.

Symbols, on the other hand, have no direct connection with that which they represent. They have been arbitrarily selected. For instance, the word *chair* has been arbitrarily chosen to represent the objects on which we sit, and other languages present the same item in different symbolic ways (i.e., *cathedra, sella, chaise, stoel,* and *zetel*). We call a chair a *chair* simply because the symbol made up of the letters *c, h, a, i,* and *r* has been chosen to represent that object. There is nothing inherent within that object that connects it to the symbol *chair*. There is nothing about the symbol *chair* that connects it to that object. Once again, a symbol is an arbitrary representation.

It is sometimes difficult to recognize that symbols are simply arbitrary representations. It sometimes might seem as though there is a natural connection rather than an arbitrary connection. A stop sign—or more appropriately stop *symbol*—is one example of how people tend to see symbols as naturally linked to what they represent. It may seem natural that a red octagon with the capital letters *S, T, O,* and *P* written in the middle would compel people to cease forward movement when driving an automobile. However, there is no direct connection between that symbol and that particular behavior. A giant cow placed on a pole could arbitrarily represent that same course of action just as naturally as the symbol people call a *stop sign* arbitrarily represents that action. There is no direct causal connection between a symbol and what it represents.

Because symbols are arbitrary representations of something else, they can be different in different cultures, and strangers need extra help. When Steve's mother first came to the United States from England, for example, she could find directions not to "toilets" but only to "restrooms," and she did not want a rest. Eventually, she had to

By the way...

Iconic Symbols

Symbols can be split into those that are iconic and those that are not. Both are representations of other things, but icons look like what they represent—for example, the airplane sign used to indicate the way to the airport. Other symbols do not have a pictorial connection to what they represent. For instance, the dollar sign does not look like a dollar bill.

QUESTIONS TO CONSIDER

1. Why do you suppose some objects become represented by iconic symbols, while others do not?
2. How close in appearance do you think a symbol must be to that which it represents in order for it to be considered iconic?

symbols: arbitrary representations of ideas, objects, people, relationships, cultures, genders, races, and so forth

sign: a consequence or an indicator of something specific, which cannot be changed by arbitrary actions or labels (e.g., "wet streets are a sign of rain")

As close to a cow placed on a large pole as we are going to get, this particular traffic sign is actually warning motorists of a cattle crossing rather than instructing them to stop. Are traffic signs really signs, or are they symbols?

ask someone. The euphemism *restroom* is not immediately obvious to cultural outsiders as a reference to toilet facilities. In other cultures—for example, in England—they may be referred to as "conveniences" or by a sign saying "WC" (meaning water closet). Even some indicators for restrooms within the U.S. culture are quite confusing, as they very clearly require a shared understanding of cultural reference points. For example, we have seen indicators for "Does and Bucks," "Roosters and Hens," "Pointers and Setters," and "Knights in Need and Damsels in Distress."

Making things even more difficult is the fact that the same symbol can mean a variety of different things even in the same culture. We talk more about meaning in the next section, but for now consider how the symbolic act of waving to someone can have multiple meanings (e.g., a greeting, a farewell gesture, or an attempt to gain attention). When David's cousin was 3 years old, he was asked to bring a yardstick to his dad who was planning on taking some measurements. His cousin promptly returned with a stick from the front yard.

The complexity of symbols is further evidence of the complexity of communication, but recognizing such complexities will enable you to begin developing a more advanced understanding and appreciation of communication.

By the way...

Setting a Record for Definitions

The word (symbol) *set* has the most definitions of any English word, with some unabridged dictionaries including over 400 meanings.

QUESTIONS TO CONSIDER

1. What are some other words that have many meanings? (To get you started, the second most "meaningful" word also has three letters and begins with the letter *r*.)
2. Can you come up with any words with a single definition? This question might be more difficult than you think.

Communication Requires Meaning

Communication requires that symbols convey **meaning**, what a symbol represents. Particular meanings, however, are not tied to only one symbol but can be conveyed in multiple ways using different symbols. For example, happiness can be conveyed by saying "I'm happy" or by smiling. Over the course of the relationship, you may have learned that frequency of talk is a meaningful indicator of a friend's emotional state. So that friend may indicate happiness just by talking more frequently than otherwise.

Social Construction of Meaning

Social construction involves the way in which symbols take on meaning in a social context or society as they are used over time. For instance, family members may use certain words or phrases that have particular shared meaning. The meanings of these words or phrases have developed through their use over time, and those unique meanings are recognized and understood by members of that family. The same thing occurs within larger cultural groups. Words and phrases used every day within

meaning: what a symbol represents

social construction: the way in which symbols take on meaning in a social context or society as they are used over time

the society to which you belong did not originate with previously established meanings. Rather, the taken-for-granted meanings attached to these symbols have developed through repeated and adapted use over time.

Meaning and Context

A single symbol or message can also have multiple meanings when used in different contexts. For example, the *physical context,* or the actual location in which a symbol is used, will impact its meaning. If you said, "There is a fire" while in a campground, it would mean something entirely different than if you said those exact same words while in a crowded movie theater.

The same symbols will also differ in meaning according to the *relational context,* or the relationship shared by the people interacting. Look again at the earlier example of saying "I love you." It means something vastly different said to you by your mother, your brother, your friend, your priest, your instructor, someone you have been dating for more than a year, or someone you have just met on a blind date.

The *situational context* will also impact the meaning of a symbol. Consider the phrase "I love you" said by the same person (e.g., your mother) on your birthday, after a fight with her, on her deathbed, at Thanksgiving, or at the end of a phone call. See Figure 1.1 for another example.

What type of communication context involves physical locations?

Verbal and Nonverbal Influence on Meaning

Accompanying verbal and nonverbal symbols will also impact meaning. For instance, the same words send different messages depending on how they are delivered. Using "I love you" as an example once again, consider those words said by a romantic partner in a short, sharp way; in a long, lingering way; with a frown; with a smile; or with a hesitant and questioning tone of voice. We discuss the interaction between verbal and nonverbal communication in greater detail later in the book. For now, however, just recognize how determining meaning is more complex than it may originally seem.

Figure 1.1 Meaning of Symbol Changing Over Time

In addition to physical, relational, and situational contexts, meanings generally assigned to symbols also change with the passing of time. Symbols such as the yellow ribbon around a tree, for instance, have held multiple meanings over time.

SOURCE: Griffin (2012).

DISCIPLINARY DEBATE

Power of the Medium

There is some disagreement among scholars in the discipline concerning the impact of a medium of technology. Some scholars believe that the primary medium used by members of a society determines social structure, cultural values, and even how people think. Other scholars believe that people determine how a medium is used and ultimately determine social structure and cultural values.

QUESTIONS TO CONSIDER

1. Do you believe technology has the power to shape society?
2. Do you believe that people have more control than technology?

Meaning and the Medium

The **medium**, or the means through which a message is conveyed, will also impact the meaning of a message. A medium might include sound waves or sight—especially when interacting face-to-face with someone. It can also include cell phones, text messages, e-mail, instant messaging, chat rooms, social networking sites, a note placed on someone's windshield, smoke signals, or many other methods of communication.

The topic is especially important in cases involving a medium. For instance, breaking up with a romantic partner can be accomplished using any of the means listed above, but some may be deemed more appropriate than others. Breaking up with someone face-to-face may be considered more appropriate than sending him or her a text message or changing your relational status on Facebook from "In a relationship" to "Single." Beyond the message of wanting to break up, additional messages, including how you view the romantic partner, the relationship itself, and yourself, are conveyed based on the medium used.

Skills You Can Use: Adapting to Cultural Expectations

Communicating in a manner consistent with cultural expectations increases a person's ability to influence others. Consider how you might adapt or adhere to cultural expectations when planning to speak with another person, a group of people, or a large audience.

Communication Is Cultural

ETHICAL ISSUE

Is communicating in a manner consistent with someone's cultural expectations but inconsistent with your normal communication style unethical?

Another characteristic of communication is that it is cultural. Different cultures make different assumptions and take different knowledge for granted. Each time you talk to someone, from your culture or another, you are taking knowledge for granted, doing what your culture expects, and treating people in ways the culture acknowledges. You are doing, performing, and enacting your culture through communication.

Ultimately, culture influences communication, while communication creates and reinforces these cultural influences. Consider what took place during your most recent face-to-face conversation with someone. Did you greet this person with a kiss or a handshake? Was there additional touch or no touch at all? How far were you standing from one another? Did you maintain eye contact? What were you wearing? Did you take turns talking, or did you talk at the same time? How did you refer to one another? What did you talk about? Did the physical setting impact what was discussed? How was the conversation brought to a close? What happened at the end? Your answers to these questions are based in part on cultural expectations.

medium: means through which a message is conveyed

When you follow these cultural expectations, you are also reinforcing them. Their position as the "proper" way to do things has been strengthened. Cultural expectations are also reinforced when someone violates them. Consider the most recent experience when you or someone else did something embarrassing. It was probably embarrassing because cultural expectations had been violated. Or, if there was no touch in your most recent face-to-face conversation, what would have happened if you had touched the other person? If touching would have been inappropriate, then the other person may have responded in a negative manner—enforcing cultural expectations.

By the way...

Saying "Hello" in Japanese

In Japanese, there are more than 200 ways for one person to address another according to protocols of respect and status differences recognized by the participants.

QUESTIONS TO CONSIDER

1. In what ways are respect and status conveyed when speaking English?
2. In what ways is disrespect conveyed when speaking English?

Communication Is Relational

As mentioned previously, communication and relationships are intertwined. Communication impacts relationships, and relationships impact communication. The ways in which communication and relationships are connected are fully explored throughout the book. For now, it is important to recognize that relationships are assumed each time you communicate with someone.

Watzlawick, Beavin, and Jackson (1967) originally put it a little differently, suggesting that whenever you communicate with someone, you relate to him or her at the same time. All communication contains both a content (message) level and a relational level, which means that, as well as conveying information, every message indicates how the sender of a message and the receiver of that message are socially and personally related.

Sometimes the relational connection between sender and receiver is obvious, such as when formal relational terms (e.g., *dad*) or terms unique to a relationship (e.g., *sweetie* or *stinky*) are included.

Quite often the relational connection between sender and receiver is less obvious. However, relational cues within communication enable you to determine, for instance, who is the boss and who is the employee. Yelling "Come into my office! Now!" indicates a status difference just through the *style* of the communication. Because the relationships between people often are not openly expressed but subtly indicated or taken for granted in most communication, the content and relational components of messages are not always easy to separate.

Exploring the relational characteristic of communication a bit further, it can be maintained that relationships create worlds of meaning for people through communication, and communication produces the same result for people through relationships. Group decision making, for example, is accomplished not just by the logic of arguments, agenda setting, and solution evaluations but also by group members' relationships with one another outside the group setting. Groups that meet to make decisions almost never come from nowhere, communicate, make a decision, and then go home. The members know one another, talk informally outside the group setting, and have personal likes and dislikes for one another that will affect their discussions about certain matters. Many decisions that appear to be made during an open discussion are actually sometimes tied up before the communication begins. Words have been whispered into ears, promises made, factions formed, and relationships displayed well in advance of any discussion.

ETHICAL ISSUE

Your communication with someone may appeal to certain relational obligations. For instance, friends may be expected to do certain things (give someone a ride) if they are truly friends. Is it ethical to appeal to such obligations, or is it simply part of being a friend? Are there any limits to what a person may ask someone else to do based on their relationship?

COMMUNICATION + YOU

Taking Things for Granted

You may not even be aware of how frames provide you with additional context and information in any communication interaction. After your next conversation with someone, take note of two or three key things that were said by this person.

QUESTIONS TO CONSIDER

1. What was taken for granted? What did you need to know in order to understand these things?
2. Do the same thing with someone with whom you share a different relationship. In what ways were the taken-for-granted assumptions the same, and in what ways were they different?

Consider examples from your life. Is everyone equal in your family? How are your interactions with friends different from your interactions with enemies? When watching television, does it make a difference whether you like the newscaster? Have you ever felt a connection to a character in a movie? On your last job interview, did the employer treat you like a potential valued colleague or an interchangeable worker? Are you more likely to contact some people through text messages and less likely to contact other people through text messages? We examine these questions and more throughout the remainder of the book.

Communication Involves Frames

Communication is very complex, but the use of frames helps people make sense of things. **Frames** are basic forms of knowledge that provide a definition of a scenario, either because both people agree on the nature of the situation or because the cultural assumptions built into the interaction and the previous relational context of talk give them a clue (Wood & Duck, 2006). Think of the frame on a picture and how it pulls your attention into some elements (the picture) and excludes all the rest (the wall, the gallery, the furniture). In similar fashion, a **communication frame** draws a boundary around the conversation and pulls our attention toward certain things and away from others.

ETHICAL ISSUE

Communicating by using words, terms, and knowledge shared by other people can include them in a conversation. At the same time, doing so can exclude individuals who lack that shared understanding. So two people might be talking in a way that excludes a third person who is present. Would you consider this scenario an unethical use of communication?

Coordinating Interactions

Frames help people understand their role in a conversation and what is expected of them. If you are being interviewed, for instance, your understanding of the interview frame lets you know that the interviewer will be asking questions and you will be expected to answer them. Likewise, your understanding of the restaurant frame helps you understand why one person is talking about "specials" and insisting that you make decisions based on a piece of laminated cardboard that lists costs of food. Your understanding of the classroom frame will inform you of what you should do as a student and how you should interact with your instructor and with your classmates. A shared understanding of these frames is what enables people to make sense of what is taking place to coordinate their symbolic activities.

frames: basic forms of knowledge that provide a definition of a scenario, either because both people agree on the nature of the situation or because the cultural assumptions built into the interaction and the previous relational context of talk give them a clue

communication frame: a boundary around a conversation that pulls one's attention toward certain things and away from others

Assigning Meanings

People also use framing assumptions to make decisions about what symbols are used and how these symbols should be interpreted. Your relationship with someone and your knowledge of that person, for instance, influence what can be taken for granted or left unsaid and what must be explained. Having both taught at the University of Iowa, when your authors talk with one another, we can include words or terms that presume knowledge of the university (such as *Hawkeyes* and *Pentacrest*).

These terms require a background of knowledge built into the interpretation of the words themselves, some of which depends specifically on knowing about the University of Iowa (e.g., that University of Iowa students are nicknamed *Hawkeyes* and that *Pentacrest* is the administration center). Each term would not need to be explained in our conversation because both of us know that the other one understands what those words, or symbols, mean.

Many conversations between close friends are "framed" by previous experiences and conversations—hence, the phrase *frame of reference*. In what ways can you work out that these women are friends and that they therefore share some history together that frames their interaction?

Perspectives

Communication frames are based in part on a person's perspectives of situations and relationships with others. These frames of perspective will greatly influence the coordinating of interactions and the assigning of meaning discussed above. They also explain why people do not always agree on what exactly is taking place.

Consider how instructors and students do not always frame situations and their relationships in the same way. For instance, when a student asks an instructor for an extension on an assignment, there are a number of factors influencing how both approach that interaction. A student may be considering personal demands at home, work, and other classes as valid reasons an extension should be granted. An instructor may be considering fairness to other students, maintaining accountability, and personal schedule constraints as reasons an extension should not be granted. A student may perceive the instructor as unwilling to provide an extension simply because he or she is mean or on a power trip. An instructor may perceive a student as simply being uncaring and lazy, which explains why the assignment could not be completed on time. A student may see him- or herself as a consumer paying for an education and expect instructors to satisfy his or her every whim. (Do not get us started on this one!) An instructor may perceive him- or herself in a superior role or view students more like clients—sometimes a person must tell clients things they do not want to hear. These are just as few examples of perspectives being used to frame an interaction. They certainly do not represent all perspectives, and some perspectives may be the total opposite of those presented here. Still, it gives you some idea about how a person's perspectives will influence communication frames being used during an interaction.

Communication Is Both Presentational and Representational

Another characteristic of communication is that it is both representational and presentational. Accordingly, although it normally describes facts or conveys information (**representation**), it also presents your particular version of the facts or events (**presentation**). Communication is never neutral. It always conveys the perspective or worldview of the person sending a message. Your communication with

representation: describes facts or conveys information (contrast with *presentation*)

presentation: one person's particular version of, or "take" on, the facts or events (contrast with *representation*)

Would sending a text message be considered an act, an interaction, or a transaction?

other people *presents* them with a way of looking at the world that is based on how you prefer them to see it.

At first glance, the notion of communication being both presentational and representational is difficult to grasp. Consider the following way of looking at this issue: When you speak to someone, you have a number of words—your entire vocabulary—that can be used to construct your message. You will choose some words to construct the message and not choose other words. You will arrange those words chosen in certain ways and not in other ways. Your selection of words and the arrangement of those words are meaningful acts. For instance, two different perspectives concerning people in the United States unlawfully are presented through using either the term *undocumented worker* or the term *illegal alien*. Your use of words and your construction of messages do not just represent ideas and information; these acts present your view of the world to others.

On some occasions, the presentation of these views is carefully developed. For example, imagine or recall a situation in which a friend has questioned something you have done, but you believed your actions were justified and wanted to explain this justification to your friend. In such cases you would likely select your words very carefully and thoughtfully, wanting your friend to view the situation from your perspective. Your message is conveying information (representational) while at the same time providing a glimpse into your perspective and how you want your friend to view the situation (presentational).

On other occasions, the selection of words may not be carefully planned but nevertheless presents your perspective to others. In fact, each time someone communicates, a worldview is being shared through the selection of terms, regardless of how much thought has gone into the construction of a message. Someone saying "I suppose I should probably go to work now" in a gloomy manner provides a glimpse into how that person views his or her job, presumably not favorably. Someone saying "I get to go to my communication class now" in an understandably excited manner provides a glimpse into how that person views the course, presumably very favorably.

The representational and presentational nature of communication is not limited to interactions between people but includes all types of communication. Consider the communication class example above. Our use of the descriptor *understandably excited* provides a glimpse into the worldview of your authors. When a liberal news channel reports political events, it picks up on different aspects of the news than a conservative news channel would. Both channels explain, analyze, and evaluate events differently. Each channel presents reality in the way it wants you to understand it. In this sense, you might want to think of representation as *facts* and presentation as *spin*.

Communication Is a Transaction

The transactional nature of communication is the final characteristic we will address in this chapter. When addressing communication as a transaction, though,

Figure 1.2 Communication as Action, Interaction, and Transaction

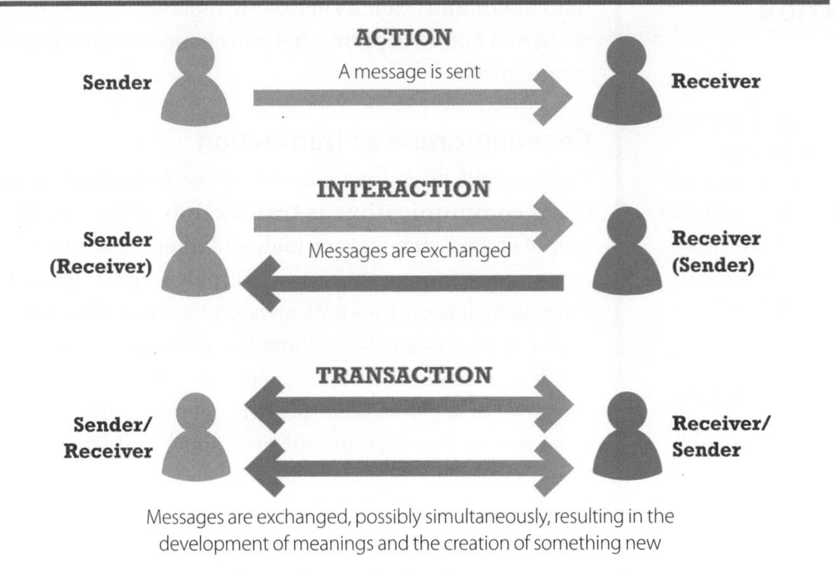

we first must address two other common ways of thinking about communication: communication as action and communication as interaction. As seen in Figure 1.2, each way of thinking about communication assumes something different about how communication works, with communication as transaction being the more sophisticated and more fruitful way of thinking about communication.

Communication as Action

Communication as action is simply the act of a sender sending a message to a receiver. Communication as *action* occurs when someone leaves a message on your voice mail, sends you an e-mail, or puts a message in a bottle in the ocean—that is, when someone transmits a message. So if Emalyn sends a text message to Corban, communication has occurred. It is pretty simple, really. However, it is not too interesting. If action was all there was to communication, we would be studying something else and not writing books about it. Communication as action could be developed slightly by questioning whether someone must *receive* a message for it to be communication. What if Corban does not check his text messages? Has communication truly occurred? That is about as far as we can take things, though. If communication was only an action, then there would really be no need to study it.

communication as action: the act of sending messages—whether or not they are received

communication as interaction: an exchange of information between two (or more) individuals

Communication as Interaction

Communication as interaction counts something as communication only if there is an exchange of information. In this much more typical perception of communication, someone sends a message, which is received by someone who in turn sends a message back to the original sender. Using the above example, communication takes place if Emalyn sends Corban a text, Corban receives the text from

ANALYZING EVERYDAY COMMUNICATION

Restaurant Research

We have begun to introduce new ways to analyze situations in your everyday life. The next time you go for a meal in a restaurant, take notes about the server–customer relationship.

QUESTIONS TO CONSIDER

1. How does the relationship get accomplished? For example, what is communicated/transacted by a server's uniform, style of speech (bubbly or bored), or manner (friendly or aloof)?
2. What impressions do you form about the server and his or her view of you?

Emalyn, and Corban then sends a reply to Emalyn. While this view of communication is slightly more advanced than communication as action, it remains limited in its scope and fails to capture what truly happens when people communicate.

Communication as Transaction

A more sophisticated and interesting way to see communication is **communication as transaction**, or the construction of shared meanings or understandings. For example, communication exists between Emalyn and Corban if, through their texts, they both arrive at the shared realization that they understand/know/love/need each other. In other words, communication in this sense is more than the mere exchange of symbols. The speakers get more out of it, and extra meanings are communicated above and beyond the content of the messages exchanged.

Communication is interesting and worthy of study not because it merely involves the exchange of messages but because something magical and extra happens in this process. Two people speak and trust is built (transacted); two people touch one another and love is realized (transacted); two people argue and power is exerted (transacted); a man holds the door open for a woman and either sexist stereotyping or politeness is transacted. In all cases, the communication message transacts or constitutes something above and beyond the symbols being exchanged.

If that was not enough reason to study communication, there is even more to consider. Communication does not just create meaning; it creates the stuff of life. This **constitutive approach to communication** maintains that communication creates or brings into existence something that has not been there before. From this point of view, communication does not just construct meanings. It is through communication that relationships are created, that cultures are created, that genders are created, that ethnicities are created, that sexualities are created, and even that realities are created. These are not only created through communication but also maintained, negotiated, challenged, and altered through communication.

For instance, relationships are not locations that we suddenly jump into—even though people refer to being *in* a relationship. Instead, relationships are quite literally talked into existence. It is through communication—especially words, but also nonverbal communication—that relationships are brought into being, and it is through communication that the maintenance, negotiation, challenges, and alterations of relationships occur.

So, returning to the question posed at the beginning of the chapter, there does not appear to be any part of life that does not involve communication. In fact, communication serves as the actual foundation for most of our life experiences. It is a fascinating area of study that provides a great deal of enjoyment and comes with continuous transformation and paths to explore. Those are some of the reasons we study communication. We are glad that you are joining us.

communication as transaction: the construction of shared meanings or understandings between two (or more) individuals

constitutive approach to communication: communication can create or bring into existence something that has not been there before, such as an agreement, a contract, or an identity

Focus Questions Revisited

What are symbols?

Symbols are arbitrarily selected representations of something with no direct connection to that which they represent. Though sometimes used interchangeably, the terms *symbol* and *sign* do not describe the same thing. Signs are consequences or indicators of something specific, which human beings cannot change by their arbitrary actions or labels.

How is meaning established?

Because they are completely arbitrary, symbols have the potential for multiple meanings subject to change. The meaning assigned to a symbol has been socially constructed and is contingent on the contexts (physical, relational, situational) in which the symbol is used and other symbolic activity (verbal and nonverbal), as well as the medium used to transmit it.

How is communication cultural?

Culture influences communication, while communication creates and reinforces these cultural influences. Each time someone communicates, he or she is taking knowledge for granted, doing what his or her culture expects, and treating people in ways the culture acknowledges. Culture is accomplished, performed, and enacted through communication.

How is communication relational?

All communication contains both a content (message) level and a relational level, which means that, as well as conveying information, every message indicates how the sender of a message and the receiver of that message are socially and personally related. Communication and relationships are intertwined. Communication impacts relationships, and relationships impact communication.

What are communication frames?

Communication frames are basic forms of knowledge that provide a definition of a scenario, either because both people agree on the nature of the situation or because the cultural assumptions built into the interaction and the previous relational context of talk give them a clue. A communication frame draws a boundary around the conversation and pulls our attention toward certain things and away from others. Frames help people understand their role in a conversation and what is expected of them. People also use framing assumptions to make decisions about what symbols are used and how these symbols should be interpreted.

What does it mean to view communication as both representational and presentational?

Communication describes facts or conveys information (representation) while conveying the perspective or worldview or slant of the person sending a message (presentation). Communication gives other people and audiences a way of looking at the world that is based on how the source of a message prefers them to see it.

What does it mean to view communication as a transaction?

Viewing communication as a transaction means understanding that communication is more than just the simple exchange of messages. Rather, communication involves the construction of shared meanings or understandings between two (or more) individuals. Moreover, communication constitutes, or creates, aspects of life such as relationships, culture, gender, and even reality.

Key Concepts

communication as action 15
communication as interaction 15
communication as transaction 16
communication frame 12
constitutive approach to communication 16
frames 12
meaning 8
medium 10
presentation 13
representation 13
signs 7
social construction 8
symbols 7

Questions to Ask Your Friends

1. Ask your friends to define communication. In what ways do their definitions align with the characteristics of communication discussed in this chapter? In what ways do their definitions counter these characteristics?
2. Ask your friends to consider the difference between signs and symbols. Do they find it difficult to view some symbols as being completely arbitrary?
3. Ask your friends whether a message must be received in order for communication to occur. What do their answers tell you about viewing communication as an action?

Media Connections

1. In what ways do song lyrics not merely entertain but also present particular ways of living, particular attitudes, and particular styles? Find examples that present relationships differently (e.g., from Maroon 5, Lady Gaga, Otis Redding, Toby Keith, Mel Tormé, The Beatles).
2. Watch a political discussion on a television news channel or online. How are opposing positions being presented? Is the distinction between representation and presentation obvious or hidden?
3. Watch the audio and visual coverage of a live event on television or online. Then read about the same event in a newspaper the next day. How does the medium impact your understanding of the event and the meanings you assign to the event?

Student Study Site

SAGE edge™

Sharpen your skills with SAGE edge at edge.sagepub.com/duckciel2e

SAGE edge for students provides a personalized approach to help you accomplish your coursework goals in an easy-to-use learning environment.

Chapter Outline

The Challenges of Writing History
The Development of a Discipline
The Development of Associations
The Emergence of Areas of Study
- Rhetoric and Rhetorical Criticism
- Interpersonal Communication
- Mass Communication

Coming Together (Kind of) as Communication Studies
- Troubles in Academic Paradise

Future of Communication and the Relational Perspective
Approaches to the Study of Communication
Social Scientific Approach
- Assumptions
- Methods
- Advantages
- Disadvantages

Interpretivist Approach
- Assumptions
- Methods
- Advantages
- Disadvantages

Critical Approach
- Assumptions
- Methods
- Advantages
- Disadvantages

Areas of Study and the Relational Perspective
- Communication Education and Instructional Communication
- Communication Theory
- Cultural Communication
- Family Communication
- Group Communication
- Interpersonal Communication
- Media
- Health Communication
- Organizational Communication
- Persuasion
- Political Communication
- Public Relations
- Rhetorical Criticism

Focus Questions Revisited
Key Concepts
Questions to Ask Your Friends
Media Connections

02 Histories of Communication

FOCUS QUESTIONS

1. How did the modern communication discipline develop?
2. What is the social scientific approach to communication?
3. What is the interpretivist approach to communication?
4. What is the critical approach to communication?
5. What are some of the major areas of study in the communication discipline?

The very fact that you are reading these words means you are now engaged in the study of communication. Congratulations! That shows a lot of character. We wish there were more people just like you.

Of course, studying communication is not an easy proposition, regardless of how rewarding it ultimately may be. If you take a chemistry course, other people will have a general idea of what you are studying. While there are naturally a few differences, the basic chemistry course and chemistry major look pretty much the same in colleges and universities throughout the land. The same thing goes for psychology, English, biology, and just about every area of study other than communication. Telling someone you are studying communication requires explaining what you are studying to others.

It is not just students who must explain what the study of communication involves. Instructors must do the same thing when telling people what they teach. To make matters even more challenging, instructors of communication do not always agree on what should be studied or how it should be studied.

Consider the number of names that departments specializing in the study of communication may be called. Some of them go by the following: *communication, communications, communication studies, communication arts, speech, speech communication, rhetorical studies, mass communication, media ecology,* and *media studies*. Then, there may be combinations of those names: *communication studies and media* or *speech and communication*. Then, there can be additional areas added to the name, such as *journalism, film, radio and television, theater,* and so on.

If you think that gets complicated, now consider the areas of study taking place in these departments. To give you some idea, Table 2.1 provides a list of interest groups within

COMMUNICATION + YOU

What's in a Name?

We will discuss the importance of naming things and the impact of doing so later in the book. For now, take a moment to consider what impact the name of an academic department has on how it is perceived by members of the department itself, by members of other departments, by students, by administration, and by people outside academia.

QUESTIONS TO CONSIDER

1. What is the name of the department devoted to the study of communication on your campus? How do you believe people perceive that department based on its name?
2. If there are multiple departments on campus devoted to the study of communication, how do people perceive them to be both similar and different?

the National Communication Association. There are other areas of study within the discipline of communication that are not listed. And there are many areas of study and approaches within each of those interest groups.

At this point, a person less dedicated than you might be tempted to say, "This is too hard. I'm just going to study something else." Before giving up and moving to an easier and much less fulfilling area of study, however, that person should consider why the discipline of communication is diverse and expansive.

Communication itself is expansive and diverse. It makes sense that the discipline devoted to its study is just as expansive and diverse. There is no area of your life that is not impacted in some way by communication.

Table 2.1 Interest Groups of the National Communication Association

African American Communication and Culture Division	Gay, Lesbian, Bisexual, Transgendered, and Queer Communication Studies Division
American Studies Division	Group Communication Division
Applied Communication Division	Health Communication Division
Argumentation and Forensics Division	Human Communication and Technology Division
Asian/Pacific American Caucus	Instructional Development Division
Asian/Pacific American Communication Studies Division	International and Intercultural Communication Division
Basic Course Division	Interpersonal Communication Division
Black Caucus	La Raza Caucus
Caucus on Lesbian, Gay, Bisexual, Transgender and Queer Concerns	Language and Social Interaction Division
Communication and Aging Division	Latino/Latina Communication Studies Division
Communication and the Future Division	Mass Communication Division
Communication and Law Division	Master's (College and University) Education Section
Communication Apprehension and Competence Division	Nonverbal Communication Division
Communication Assessment Division	Organizational Communication Division
Communication as Social Construction Division	Peace and Conflict Communication Division
Communication Centers Section	Performance Studies Division
Communication Ethics Division	Philosophy of Communication Division
Communication and Social Cognition Division	Political Communication Division
Community College Section	Public Address Division
Critical and Cultural Studies Division	Public Relations Division
Disabilities Issues Caucus	Rhetorical and Communication Theory Division
Elementary and Secondary Education Section	Spiritual Communication Division
Emeritus/Retired Members Section	Student Section
Environmental Communication Division	Theatre, Film, and New Multi-Media Division
Ethnography Division	Training and Development Division
Experiential Learning Division	Undergraduate College and University Section
Family Communication Division	Visual Communication Division
Feminist and Women's Studies Division	Women's Caucus
Freedom of Expression Division	

Communication itself is always changing and being transformed. This demands that the discipline devoted to its study also changes and transforms. When it comes to studying communication, this is a very positive characteristic. There is always something new to explore; there are always more questions to answer. We study communication, and so should you, in part, because it is an exciting and rewarding lifelong pursuit. There are sometimes disagreements concerning the ways in which communication should be studied. That is a positive characteristic as well. Competing voices in the discipline push everyone to work harder, examine his or her position more critically, and be exposed to other perspectives. Plus, different approaches generally result in new ideas that would not have been developed otherwise. Every perspective has brought something to the study of communication. Ultimately, the discipline is strengthened as a result of these competing and complementary views.

By the way...

Continued Disagreements

Disagreement is nothing new when it comes to the study of communication. It started with the ancient Greek schools of rhetoric and philosophy, which were often in conflict with one another. Rhetoricians wanted to persuade people by any means that was effective. Philosophers wanted to find only good, honest, truthful arguments. Dishonest means of persuasion were sometimes acceptable to rhetoricians but not to philosophers.

QUESTIONS TO CONSIDER

1. Would you rather be represented by a dishonest but effective attorney or an honest one?
2. What are some other areas of life in which this debate is still relevant?

The Challenges of Writing History

You may have noticed that the title of this chapter says *histories* of communication rather than *history* of communication. Having read the above paragraphs, you get the idea why writing a single history of the discipline is not legitimately possible. There are too many different perspectives and too many different origins.

The first necessary step in a history of the discipline, then, is to admit that it is one of many ways of reporting research developments and that many other ways of reporting the development of the discipline are possible. For instance, a person focusing on media would start at one point (perhaps the printing press), and a person studying interpersonal communication would start at another point (perhaps conversation studies at the turn of the last century). And do not forget that there are many competing views within those areas that might influence where to start and what to include.

Yet there are other issues regarding the writing and reading of history. We made the point in the first chapter that communication is both representational and presentational. Communication can describe *facts* and can offer a *spin* on those facts. So describing history is also presentational, with a particular spin put on things.

Each historian writes from a particular perspective and with particular major interests. One area of study in communication studies is devoted to **historiography,** which studies the persuasive effect of writing history in particular ways and the reasons why particular reports and analyses are offered by specific authors. The history of the United States of America written by a British historian in 1815 would be quite differently positioned from such a history written by an American historian, for example.

historiography: the study of the persuasive effect of writing history in particular ways and the reasons why particular reports and analyses are offered by specific authors

When looking at images such as this one, changes in focus will lead to changes in what is observed and how it is seen. How might this be similar to the development of histories?

It is also important to notice that the way history is written depends on many contemporary political and social forces that help to influence the report. For example, anyone who wrote a history of communication studies today without mentioning the important contributions made by women and people of color would simply be ignored. Nevertheless, even 25 years ago, such histories were offered as standard reading for students (e.g., Delia, 1987)—although authors were generally careful to point out that they were offering only one sort of history of the discipline. Similarly, the topics that are chosen for research and discussion depend on the historical circumstances in which the research is carried out. During World War II, there was much research about the effects of propaganda, leadership, and attitude change—topics that are particularly relevant in wartime. While those topics are still studied, there is much more emphasis today on studying topics of our time: cultural diversity, family secrets about sexual abuse or alcoholism, and the nature of family communication.

Finally, as we note in several chapters in the book, communication research and theory develop and change as scholars labor in their studies. One of the key goals of research is precisely to make developments and corrections to our understanding. Such changes lead to a reevaluation of what has happened and had been assumed to be true before. Occasionally, those studies that have previously been regarded as reliably *classic* are then seen in a new light that makes them less important. In their turn, the replacement *classics* also fade as new approaches and critiques become available. Therefore, the history that is written today will be different from the history that was written 50 years ago and from the history that will be written 50 years from now.

Rather than offering any hope of a definitive history of the discipline, we intend instead to offer at best some histor*ies* of communication studies or at least some ways of understanding how the discipline came to look the way it does . . . from our point of view!

The Development of a Discipline

When it comes to the origins of the communication discipline, people are likely to begin with Aristotle in the 4th century BCE. However, we can actually trace the roots of communication study to well before Aristotle. The first documented essay on communication was written around 3000 BCE, addressed to Kagemni, son of the Pharaoh Huni. The earliest existing book on effective communication is *Precepts,* written in Egypt by Ptahhotep around the year 2675 BCE (McCroskey, 1968).

We will start our discussion a bit later, admittedly skipping over a lot of material. We begin at the point when academic associations and academic departments dedicated to the study of communication began to develop. In the modern era, these are necessary components of an academic discipline and are thus a good place to begin.

The Development of Associations

The study of communication has taken place for thousands of years. As a formally established discipline, however, the study of communication is comparatively younger. While communication in its various forms had long been part of academic training, the first formally organized professional association devoted to its study, the Eastern Communication Association, was founded in 1910 (see Chesebro, 2010).

The first national association devoted to the study of communication, currently known as the National Communication Association, was established in 1914 as the National Association of Academic Teachers of Public Speaking. Always a contentious discipline, this association was founded by a rogue group of 17 members of the National Council of Teachers of English who did not believe enough attention was being given the study of oral address (Cohen, 1994).

Since the development of these first two academic associations, a number of associations within the United States and throughout the world have been developed. These associations are established based on region of the country (e.g., Central States Communication Association, Eastern Communication Association, Southern States Communication Association, and Western States Communication Association), state location (e.g., Iowa Communication Association), and interest (e.g., Kenneth Burke Society and International Association for Relationship Research). There is also an International Communication Association and a World Communication Association.

Aside from providing support for scholars and students of communication, these organizations provide the discipline with a *presence* in the larger academic community. The most important functions these associations provide are the publication of journals and the holding of conferences. Journals are where academic research is published. Table 2.2 provides a list of journals currently published by the National Communication Association and its four regional affiliates. Conferences, which are usually held annually, allow academics to come together to discuss issues related to the discipline and its instruction as well as to share and discuss research.

ETHICAL ISSUE

A link to the National Communication Association "Ethical Statements" can be found at www.natcom.org/publicstatements. Do you agree with the NCA Credo for Ethical Communication? Would you add, remove, or alter any of the statements?

Table 2.2 Communication Journals

National Communication Association
Communication and Critical/Cultural Studies
Communication Education
Communication Monographs
Communication Teacher
Critical Studies in Media Communication
Journal of Applied Communication Research
Journal of International and Intercultural Communication
Quarterly Journal of Speech
Review of Communication
Text and Performance Quarterly
Central States Communication Association
Communication Studies
Eastern Communication Association
Communication Quarterly
Communication Research Reports
Qualitative Research Reports in Communication
Southern States Communication Association
Southern Communication Journal
Western States Communication Association
Communication Reports
Western Journal of Communication

The Emergence of Areas of Study

As a formal academic discipline, then, communication got its start as a discipline devoted to the study of public speaking, debate, and performance. Public speaking tended to dominate in the early days of the discipline. A person did not study *communication*; rather, a person studied *public speaking* or *speech*. Public speaking's legacy is still evident in the discipline, especially within basic communication courses (Morreale, Hugenberg, & Worley, 2006).

Notwithstanding public speaking's position in the early days of the communication discipline, its importance in everyday life, or its position in many basic communication courses, it is no longer a major area of study within the discipline.

By the way...

The Position of Public Speaking

Public speaking as a common feature of many basic communication courses is actually not all that surprising. First, it is something that the communication discipline is still expected to teach by other disciplines in the academic community. Being able to construct a solid argument as done through public address is a necessary skill for students, and our discipline teaches it better than any other discipline. That is one of the reasons communication is a required course in most universities. Second, traditions do not go away that easily. There are still many instructors in the discipline who view public speaking as a vital area of the discipline. The term *speech* was included in the name of the national association until 1997.

QUESTIONS TO CONSIDER

1. Do you think public speaking should be included in basic communication courses?
2. Would not including public speaking have a positive or negative impact on the discipline of communication?

In what follows, we will discuss the three major areas that emerged during communication's first century as a formal discipline: (a) rhetoric and rhetorical criticism, (b) interpersonal communication, and (c) mass communication.

Rhetoric and Rhetorical Criticism

The study of rhetoric originated with the development and delivery of public address. Wealthy citizens sent their sons to learn from such wise people as Aristotle and Socrates. With the invention of writing, the study of rhetoric expanded into that realm as well. Accordingly, the development of formal sites of higher learning and academic departments as we now know them led to the placement of rhetoricians in departments of English.

Scholars more interested in the study of public address than the written word, however, eventually distanced themselves from the English discipline. These scholars argued what now seems obvious in hindsight—literature and public address and performance are not the same things.

Rhetorical criticism and theory developed student learning beyond the actual creation and delivery of a speech. In fact, it also enabled students to describe, interpret, and evaluate the spoken word.

The study of rhetoric underwent massive changes throughout the past century, as new techniques and perspectives were developed (Brock, Scott, & Chesebro, 1990; Olson, 2010; see Table 2.5 later in this chapter for a list of major approaches). However, rhetoric's value and position within universities were not readily called into question during its early emergence. This is likely due to its historical lineage and is in sharp contrast to what was experienced by the next areas of communication that we discuss.

Interpersonal Communication

During the same time that communication associations were being founded, there was an emerging interest in interactions between people. For instance, scholars studied such interpersonal concepts as characteristics of dyads and interaction rituals at the beginning of the previous century. By the late 1920s and early 1930s, articles about conversation were appearing in a journal of what would eventually be known as the National Communication Association.

The study of interpersonal interaction continued to grow and develop in subsequent decades, with scholars from multiple disciplines engaged in its study (Borisoff, Hoel, & McMahan, 2010). Scholars from newly developed speech departments, linguistics, psychology, sociology, and other disciplines were studying interpersonal communication but did not have their own academic home. Without an academic home shared by people with similar interests, it is difficult to collaborate on research, and there is limited influence in universities.

Departments devoted to the study of speech and rhetoric were also experiencing problems by the end of World War II. A *social scientific* (a term we will discuss in the next section) revolution had occurred during that period of time. Increasing numbers of scholars were engaged in scholarship involving experiments and statistical analysis. However, scholars in departments studying speech and rhetoric generally were engaged in other types of scholarship. As a result, departments needed to adjust if they were to remain relevant (Cohen, 1994).

So there was a group of scholars needing an academic home and a discipline needing to adapt to a new academic environment. Whether it was the number of speech researchers already studying conversation and interaction (McMahan, 2004), the oral tradition of speech departments (Wiemann, Hawkins, & Pingree, 1988), or a combination of factors, scholars studying interpersonal communication eventually found themselves in speech departments.

It should be noted, however, that this arrangement was far from peaceful. There were people in these departments being forced to study new subject matter and other people in these same departments needing to justify their research. Neither of these groups was really happy about the situation, and this tension continued for a number of years.

DISCIPLINARY **DEBATE**

Skills or Theory?

The primary disagreement among early mass communication scholars and those already in journalism departments involved what should be their focus. Those already teaching journalism believed the focus should be more on skills and training. Mass communication scholars believed the focus should be on research and theory. Contemporary scholars taking an applied communication approach would probably be somewhere in the middle—seeking ways to use theory and research to improve communication in various settings.

QUESTIONS TO CONSIDER

1. Choosing from the two extremes, do you believe the discipline of communication should focus more on skills development or on theory and research?
2. Are the two extremes enough to justify separate disciplines?

Mass Communication

A third major area of the discipline that played a key role in its development was mass communication. We have taken issue with the *mass* part of the term *mass communication* in other writings (Duck & McMahan, 2012). However, we will use the term here since that was what the area was generally labeled during the early development of the discipline.

As with interpersonal communication, scholars from multiple departments within universities engaged in the study of mass media such as newspapers, books, and eventually radio in the early decades of the previous century. And, as with interpersonal communication, an official academic home for scholars interested in this research did not exist.

Mass communication scholars found an initial home in journalism departments. Once again, as was the case with interpersonal communication, this arrangement was mutually beneficial to those studying mass communication and journalism. They were able to establish an academic home, while their research provided legitimacy for journalism education. Until that time, many universities did not consider journalism worthy of graduate study (Carey, 1979; Wilcox, 1959). However, just like interpersonal communication, mass communication scholars did not get along with those already in those departments.

Coming Together (Kind of) as Communication Studies

The way we just ended the sections on rhetoric, interpersonal communication, and mass communication makes it sound as if nothing has happened for the past few decades. That is far from the truth. In fact, a great deal has happened since the initial founding of the discipline. For the sake of time and space, we will provide you with a condensed version.

As mentioned above, public speaking is still an area of study in many basic communication courses. However, it has a limited presence in the discipline in terms of advanced courses.

Rhetoric continues to be a notable area in the discipline. However, its study is no longer limited to public address. Instead, rhetoric is more likely to study all contexts of communication, including media content, technology, and even architecture.

The study of interpersonal communication continued to grow in popularity at the undergraduate and graduate levels. A departure from earlier research in this area, the study of interpersonal communication tends to focus on close personal relationships rather than simply two people talking with one another. It is now a dominant presence in the discipline of communication.

Mass communication and journalism are still connected to some extent in some universities. However, the study of media is most likely to occur in another department and is generally considered an area of communication studies. A primary reason for this separation is the introduction of other media. Radio was already in homes by the 1940s, and television was introduced in the 1950s. There were simply areas of mass communication to study other than newspapers. Also giving rise to its move away from journalism, scholars in departments of communication became increasingly interested in the study of media and welcomed scholars and students with comparable interests. As with interpersonal communication, the study of media is now a major area in the discipline of communication.

Of course, as mentioned earlier, there are a number of areas studied within the discipline of communication beyond rhetoric, interpersonal communication, and media. Some of the more common areas of study will be discussed later in the chapter.

It is important that students of communication be aware of some of the challenges still facing the discipline and work together to address and overcome these challenges. What are these challenges?

Troubles in Academic Paradise

As communication enters its second century as a formal academic discipline, things are looking pretty good. In many colleges and universities, departments related to communication studies are listed among those with the largest numbers of majors. Further, the knowledge and skills taught in the discipline are among the most sought after by employers. It is a respected and powerful area of study.

With all of these great things, we do not want to dampen your spirits. However, there are some problems in the discipline that are connected to its development. First, as mentioned above and as with other disciplines, women, people of color, and members of many other groups have been historically excluded from playing significant roles in the development of the discipline. Unfortunately, this was true even a few decades ago. We would like to believe that the discipline has been more active than other disciplines when it comes to correcting this injustice. However, more needs to be done, and the discipline will only improve with the addition of more unique voices.

A second problem connected to the development of the discipline explains why there exist so many different names for departments studying communication but also results in troubling consequences (see Borisoff et al., 2010; McMahan, 2004, for extended discussion). The discipline was essentially divided from the outset, with rhetoric, interpersonal communication, and media frequently being studied in different departments. As a result, there are sometimes multiple departments studying communication on a single campus, which places communication scholars in direct competition for university resources and prevents them from developing a unified front. This separation impacts students more indirectly than faculty, but everyone is ultimately affected.

The initial division, especially among interpersonal and media scholars, has also hindered the scholarly development of the discipline. Frequently, scholars in one area know little about research conducted in other areas. This separation of interests would not be harmful if not for the interconnected nature of communication. Interpersonal communication and media are intertwined everywhere but in the discipline devoted to their study. Scholars in both areas would benefit by incorporating one another's research.

As with the inclusion of multiple voices, we are hopeful that more communication scholars will begin seeing the value of merging the interconnected areas of the discipline. It will lead the strengthening of the discipline and increase its value for students even more.

Future of Communication and the Relational Perspective

History writing frequently tends to assume that everything stops at the present. It also tends to assume that the present is the way that things *should* be, the result of a "logical unfolding" of developments that are described within.

Assuming that the development of the discipline has not yet finished, then, we must assume it is still continuing. If the discipline of communication studies has not evolved to a final state of perfection as a result of previous historical and intellectual forces, then where is it to go next?

If you do not know our answer to this question by the time you finish reading this book, then our time spent writing this textbook has not been worthwhile. We are unable to see any area of communication studies to which a relational perspective could not be taken. The chapters represented in this book are on traditional topics studied by undergraduates in communication majors and basic courses nationwide. We have been able to give all of these topics a relational twist and to show that underneath all of these traditional topics is a presumption about the nature of personal relationships and their influence in everyday life.

The future of the discipline can benefit from applying our relational perspective even more broadly. We hope that our overview in this chapter and the other chapters in this book convince enough people to take our particular view of the topic and to push forward for those social changes that are necessary to make the future foreseen in this book become a reality.

Table 2.3 Approaches to the Study of Communication

APPROACH	SOCIAL SCIENTIFIC	INTERPRETIVIST	CRITICAL
Assumptions of the World	Objective, causal, and predictable world	Subjective, arbitrary, and uncertain world	Subjective world in which there is an imbalance of power
Truth	A single Truth exists	Multiple truths exist since there exist multiple perspectives and no fixed reality	Multiple truths exist, but those of some groups have greater influence than those of others
Communication	Predictable and controllable	Creative and indeterminate	Struggle for power
Goals	Description, correlation, and prediction	Description and understanding	Uncover power imbalances and possibly eliminate
Primary Methods	Experiments Questionnaires/surveys	Observation Interviews Textual analysis	Interviews Textual analysis
Advantages	Explains observable patterns of communication; researcher objectivity; studies are relatively easy to conduct	Draws attention to impossibility of truly objective research; provides deep understanding of communication; examines natural communication	Directs researchers toward the recognition and study of societal inequalities
Disadvantages	Numerous methodological problems	Limited scope; possible inaccuracy; subjectivity of researcher; time-consuming	Challenges associated with accepting the view of researcher as all-powerful and appropriate

Approaches to the Study of Communication

As we have just discussed, the very nature of communication is expansive, and numerous challenges have been experienced in the development of the discipline. It is nevertheless possible to identify certain styles of research and scholarship in communication studies. While there are many approaches to the study of communication, we will focus on the three that have had the most influence: (1) social scientific, (2) interpretivist, and (3) critical. Table 2.3 provides an overview of these approaches.

Although the summary that follows is necessarily brief, it will give you some sense of the different styles of investigation and study that you may come across while reading books on communication or pursuing your own research. As you consider these approaches, we encourage you to be mindful of a couple of things. First, while these approaches are presented separately and at times may seem to be in opposition, many communication scholars do not view them as mutually exclusive. Scholars can and frequently do engage in more than one approach. In fact, your authors have engaged in all three approaches at one time or another when conducting research. Second, in some instances, research may encompass more than one approach. Common examples of this dual approach are studies using both interpretivist and critical approaches. With these things in mind, we can now begin our exploration.

social scientific approach: views the world as objective, causal, and predictable; researchers using this approach primarily seek to describe communication activity and to discover connections between phenomena or causal patterns

Social Scientific Approach

The **social scientific approach** to communication studies views the world as objective, causal, and predictable. It can involve laboratory experiments, precise measurements of behavior, and an emphasis on statistical numerical analysis of what is studied. Researchers using this approach to study communication seek to describe communication activity and to discover connections between phenomena or causal patterns.

Using this approach, researchers might seek to *describe* patterns of communication among close friends. They might also seek to determine whether there is a *connection* between favorable comments by professors and student performance. They might attempt to determine whether supportive communication *causes* children to behave in a more positive manner.

By the way...

The Name Game

Social science tends to have standardized definitions for terms and usually (but not always) to use those definitions in similar ways. This means, for example, that two different social scientists will portray or represent or measure "silence" in the same way—such as a period of five seconds or more when no one is speaking.

QUESTIONS TO CONSIDER

1. What problems might occur when social scientists do not define terms in similar ways?
2. Is it possible to define terms in exactly the same way?

Assumptions

The social scientific approach assumes that Truth (with a capital *T*) exists. Truth is independent of the researcher and will be discovered by different researchers using the same methods. If this Truth exists, certain assumptions must be made.

First, reality is objective and exists externally to human beings. What this means is that a person's world is made of real things that will be experienced and reacted to in generally the same way by everyone.

Second, because a true reality exists, human communication is predictable, and causal connections can be uncovered. Once these connections are uncovered, we can learn what behaviors are connected, and we can learn what will likely occur in certain circumstances.

Methods

The social scientific approach primarily uses *experiments* or *questionnaires/surveys* to study communication.

Experiments

Experiments generally involve the manipulation of a person's experience to determine how he or she will respond. This sort of manipulation could be as simple as having some people experience one thing and having other people experience something different. Participants in an experiment conducted by Williams (2013), for instance, played video games using either a traditional handheld controller or motion-based controls to determine whether the type of control influences hostility, identification with the game avatar, or sense of immersion within the game.

Questionnaires/Surveys

Questionnaires or surveys are used to gather information from people. While experiments usually provide data observed by researchers, questionnaires or surveys provide data reported to the researcher by participants (Metts, Sprecher, & Cupach, 1991).

One type of questionnaire or survey asks people to recall a particular situation or interaction. Studying the ways in which college students talk to instructors about disappointing grades, for example, Wright (2012) asked participants to recall a recent disappointing grade and answer questions about the conversation with their instructor about that grade.

Another type of questionnaire or survey provides people with a scenario and asks them to respond based on that situation. For instance, Donovan-Kicken, McGlynn, and Damron (2012) studied the ways in which people in stressful circumstances avoided questions from friends by providing students with hypothetical situations to consider.

Advantages

The social scientific approach to communication has some advantages. First, studies are relatively easy to mount and can involve large numbers of participants, especially when it comes to questionnaires.

Second, there is often strong agreement between different types of social scientists about the way in which assessments can be made of behavior. The statistical analysis of data generally conducted with social scientific research takes the investigator out of the equation and does not allow subjective interference in the interpretation of results.

Perhaps the main advantage of the social scientific approach is its ability to explain patterns of observations theoretically and to derive new predictions from previous work. We are better able to understand communication and recognize patterns accordingly.

Disadvantages

While advantages to the social scientific approach do exist, there are a number of disadvantages or problems to this approach. First, the primary assumption of this approach has been challenged. Human behavior tends to be creative and unpredictable rather than fixed and predictable. It can also be argued that people create their own unique realities rather than simply react to an established shared reality.

Multiple Variables

The remaining problems with the social scientific approach deal with the methodology that tends to be used with this approach. First, a number of variables affect communication and cannot all be identified. For instance, a researcher can have someone play a violent video game and then measure that person's behavior. However, there are multiple influences on that person's behavior beyond playing that video game. Even though researchers are careful to take many factors into account, it is impossible to take everything into account.

Culturally Insensitive

Research methods are often culturally insensitive. Experiments and questionnaires are frequently created in ways that do not take into account differences in race, religion, gender, sexuality, education, national origin, age, socioeconomic status, and so on. In many cases, dominant social views are privileged over others.

Restrictive

Similarly, when constructing questionnaires, the researcher may impose too much restriction on subjects. The construction of a questionnaire presents the sorts of questions that the investigator wishes to ask, but these may be the wrong questions.

Participant Accuracy

Participants may not always be honest about the answers provided to researchers. Frequently, people who respond tell a researcher what they think he or she wants to hear or what they think makes them look good ("social desirability effect"). Through direct observation, for example, the Middletown Media Studies project found that people use twice as much media as they report using on surveys and questionnaires (Papper, Holmes, & Popovich, 2004).

Why are college students the participants in the majority of research?

Convenient Samples

Convenient samples of participants are often used when conducting social scientific research. Researchers frequently use participants who are nearby and readily accessible to take part in an experiment or to complete a questionnaire. Since researchers tend to be professors, those nearby and convenient participants tend to be students. Accordingly, communication scholars and others who study human behavior know a great deal about the communication and behavior of college students. However, the communication and behavior of college students is not representative of that of other groups.

Interpretivist Approach

The **interpretivist approach** to the study of communication seeks to understand and describe communication experience. It frequently involves observation of communication in natural settings as opposed to a laboratory. It also uses interviewing and textual analysis to study communication.

Assumptions

The interpretivist approach rejects the idea that a single reality exists and causal connections can be discovered. Communication is seen as creative, uncertain, and unpredictable. Therefore, interpretivist scholars do not believe that Truth (with the capital *T*) can be discovered or that it even exists.

In further contrast to social scientific approaches, interpretive approaches reject the idea that research can ever be value free. Researchers are seen as personally interpreting whatever is being studied based upon their knowledge and perspectives. From this point of view, neutrality cannot exist, so no researcher can ever be truly objective.

Methods

The interpretivist approach to communication frequently uses *grounded theory* to analyze collected data (Glaser & Strauss, 1967). Grounded theory, as its name suggests, works from the ground up and focuses on observations grounded in data and developed systematically. The researcher first gathers data on a particular topic. These data are then examined over and over with the expectation that knowledge and understanding will emerge.

interpretivist approach: views communication as creative, uncertain, and unpredictable, and thus rejects the idea that a single reality exists or can be discovered; researchers using this approach primarily seek to understand and describe communication experience

ETHICAL ISSUE

Prior to conducting any research involving humans, scholars must have their study approved by a review board to ensure that the study is ethically sound and will not harm the participants. This approval must be gained even when conducting direct observation. Unlike participants taking part in an experiment, completing a survey, or being interviewed, people being observed in natural settings frequently do not know they are being studied. Do you consider it ethical to study people who do not know they are being studied?

This method of analysis might be confusing without understanding the data being analyzed and knowing how the data were collected. So we need to clarify those two issues. In what follows, we discuss the data being analyzed and the common methods used in data collection using the interpretivist perspective.

Data

When people come across the term *data*, there may be a tendency to associate it with numbers. As opposed to social scientific research, however, the data used in interpretivist research tend not to be quantitative or number-based.

Rather, the data used in interpretivist research are actually symbolic activity. These data might include, for example, nonverbal behaviors when interviewing or words spoken when interacting with an enemy. Numerous instances of interviewing or enemy interaction would be gathered and recorded in some manner. The nonverbal behaviors and words used in each situation would then be analyzed.

Direct Observation and Participant Observation

Now that we have discussed the data that are being analyzed, we can examine various ways in which the data are gathered. Direct observation and participant observation, sometimes referred to as ethnographic research, involve observing communication and gathering information (data) about its use in natural settings.

When conducting direct observation, researchers observe communicative activity by a particular group but do not engage in these interactions themselves. Among other ethnographic methodology, Chang (2012) used direct observation to examine Chinese criminal courtroom communication.

Participant observation requires researchers to interact with the group but do nothing that would alter what would have otherwise taken place. David (McMahan, 2011) used this method by working at a rural tavern in order to study the physical altercations that take place within them.

What advantage might gathering data through interviews have over gathering data through a questionnaire?

Interviews

Interviews are also frequently used when conducting interpretive research. Data collected through interviews result from asking participants questions and engaging in general conversation with them about a particular issue of communication. In a way, interviews can be a lot like questionnaires completed by participants. However, interviews allow researchers to ask follow-up questions and probe deeper into the information being provided by participants. Norwood (2013a, 2013b), for example, interviewed parents of transgendered people and was able to gauge their general reactions to their children's change but also to follow up with specific questions that paid attention to particular answers.

Textual Analysis

Textual analysis involves the analysis of recorded communication, which could be visual, auditory, or both. Textual analysis conducted as part of interpretivist research frequently takes the form of conversation or discourse analysis. Essentially, verbal communication taking place during an interaction is specifically analyzed, often by using a written transcript of the interaction. Holt (2012), for example, used conversation analysis to examine the ways laughter is used to neutralize complaints.

Advantages

Like the social scientific approach to the study of communication, the interpretivist approach has both advantages and disadvantages. One advantage of this approach is that it provides a deep understanding of communication that cannot be gained through other perspectives. Another advantage of the interpretive approach is that communication is more likely to be studied in a natural context. A laboratory experiment, for instance, makes it easier for researchers to control what happens, but it can never fully replicate what happens naturally. What happens in a laboratory does not happen naturally, and vice versa.

Finally, the interpretivist approach draws to our attention the inability of scholars to be truly objective. All observers have their own biases and interpretative styles. Even a social scientist is trained to observe and evaluate data in particular ways.

Disadvantages

There are also a number of disadvantages to the interpretivist approach and the methodology used in its study.

Limited Scope of Understanding

First, interpretivist work seems to commit to individual levels of analysis without the possibility of making any broader understandings of human communication. In other words, we learn a great deal about the communication of very specific people through interpretivist research. This knowledge increases our understanding of communication in a general sense and has value. However, it is not transferable to the study of other specific people. And it does not allow for a wide-ranging understanding of communication.

Researcher Accuracy and Perspective

Another issue with this approach involves believing the researcher. If people view things differently, who is to say that the researcher's observations and conclusions are accurate? It is possible that another researcher might discover something entirely different. Further, researchers using interpretivist methods may impose their own values and understandings when studying the communication of others. Especially when conducting direct and participant observation, researchers are often outsiders, or not an actual member of the community they are studying. Accordingly, they are never able to fully understand the communication taking place from the perspective of the group being studied.

Time-Consuming

Compared to methods primarily used in social scientific research, the methods used when taking an interpretivist approach are very time-consuming. It takes a great deal of time and energy to conduct these studies, especially when it comes to collecting the data.

Make your case

Pick Your Approach

Both the social scientific approach and the interpretivist approach come with advantages and disadvantages. Scholars may use one approach when conducting a research project and then use the other when conducting a different research project.

QUESTIONS TO CONSIDER

1. With those things being said, which approach do you think is the better one, and why?
2. Should scholars be required to choose and use only one approach in all their research? Why or why not?

Critical Approach

The **critical approach** to communication seeks to identify the hidden but formidable symbolic structures and practices that create or uphold disadvantage, inequity, or oppression of some groups in favor of others. Scholars taking this approach study who has power within a societal group, who does not have power, how power is maintained, and how existing power differences are challenged.

Assumptions

The critical approach to the study of communication assumes that there is a built-in structure in society that gives advantage to one set of people rather than another. Accordingly, certain members of society have a greater ability to impose their values and establish the nature of taken-for-granted aspects of society than do other people.

This oppression and advantage is transacted or exercised through communication as well as through other means. Some groups of people have greater opportunities to express and convey their thoughts feelings and experiences, while other groups of people are repressed and have limited opportunities to be heard or recognized.

Another concern of some critical scholars is that only certain types of experiences are valued and expressed in a given society precisely because of the power dynamics that are contained in that society.

Methods

The methods used in the critical approach are very similar to those used in interpretive approaches. Examining issues of power and gender, for example, Harris, Palazzolo, and Savage (2012) used interviews to study the ways in which sexism is reinforced when people talk about intimate partner violence.

Another method used by those taking a critical approach involves the analysis of texts. As with interpretivist research, these texts might be transcripts of interactions. They might also be those of such media products as television, music, and movies. For instance, through a textual analysis of the television programs *Brothers & Sisters* and *Six Feet Under*, Dhaenens (2012) demonstrated how heteronormativity, a cultural bias toward opposite-sex romantic relationships, has resisted representations of gay male domesticity.

Advantages

The critical approach has been very important in redirecting the thinking of communication scholars toward the awareness of inequities in society at large. Critical theorists have encouraged us not only to identify inequalities but also to make it our goal to eradicate them. To the extent that the theorists are able to be successful in this venture, people in the future will participate equally in relationships and invest and benefit equitably from their communication in everyday life.

critical approach: seeks to identify the hidden but formidable symbolic structures and practices that create or uphold disadvantage, inequity, or oppression of some groups in favor of others

Disadvantages

Of course, the critical approach is not without its challenges. One of the problems faced by the critical approach is the criticism that it is giving itself power and the right to identify the nature of inequity and how it might be challenged. Are those who engage in critical scholarship—including your two authors—really so important that they can best determine what sorts of inequity matter more than others and determine the possibility of their elimination? What gives us the right to make the call?

Along those lines, it can never be clear whether an assessment of power is accurate. As with those taking an interpretivist approach, critical scholars are very often not a part of a group being studied. Accordingly, their understanding will never be as complete or as accurate as actual members of a group. For example, a strict military discipline of the Roman army was not regarded as unreasonable or oppressive but was voluntarily accepted by the people as part of the system. Contemporary groups may very well view differences in power as acceptable, or a difference in power may exist only from the perception of an outside reviewer. The challenge of critical scholars, again, is dealing with the questions of how we know we are correct and what gives us the right to make such judgments.

ETHICAL ISSUE

Is it ethical for a communication scholar to claim a particular group is wrong because perceived inequality may exist in its communication styles or social structure? A reasonable person would easily point out that unequal treatment based on gender, race, religion, or sexuality is wrong. However, how far should scholars, and society for that matter, take issues of power?

Skills You Can Use: Power and Privilege

You do not have to conduct research to be aware of issues of power and privilege in everyday life. Such issues can be discovered in conversations with friends, family, and coworkers; advertisements; news reports; and television programs, among other areas. You will be able to sharpen your skills as a communicator by making yourself aware of how differences in power and privilege are evident in all communication.

Areas of Study and the Relational Perspective

In this remaining section of the chapter, we introduce various areas of study in the discipline of communication. We also discuss how these areas can be studied from a relational perspective. As with previous sections of the chapter, we must address its limitations.

First, space prevents us from going into great detail about these areas. However, some of these areas have entire chapters devoted to them later in the book. Even then, we encourage you to explore independently and more thoroughly the areas you find particularly interesting. As mentioned previously, there is always something additional to examine and more questions to answer when it comes to the study of communication.

Second, not every area of communication will be included. Those that are included have a major presence in the discipline, but that does not mean that those not included are less valuable. Plus, new areas are always being created. Again, we encourage you to explore the entire discipline of communication. You will benefit from it a great deal.

Communication Education and Instructional Communication

The discipline of communication is unique in that a major area of study is devoted to improving its instruction. Communication education involves the teaching of communication itself. Instructional communication involves the study of teaching as communication. Both areas are dedicated to improving instruction.

According to Richmond and Frymier (2010), major programs of research in these areas include nonverbal immediacy, teacher power, teacher credibility, affinity seeking, humor, clarity, social-communication style and orientation, teacher misbehaviors, argumentativeness, and verbal aggression, among many other areas related to instruction and learning. Communication apprehension, an area of study developed by McCroskey (1970, 2010) and subsequently by multiple scholars, has received perhaps the most attention in this area.

Relationships develop in the classroom and within all academic contexts among students and instructors, among students and advisers, among students themselves, and among instructors themselves. Understanding the relationships of instruction is necessary to understanding learning and best instructional practices.

Communication Theory

Communication theory actually touches on quite a few areas of the discipline, with different theories dedicated to different contexts of communication. A theory is used to understand and explain something. However, like most things, it is not as simple as that. Scholars disagree about what a theory should look like and about what a theory should be used to accomplish. Remember, though, disagreements within the discipline can be a good thing.

The development of theory within the discipline has enhanced the legitimacy and strength of the discipline in the academic community. Some theories used in the discipline of communication have fallen out of favor, and new theories are being introduced. Table 2.4 provides a few that you may come across within this book and as you explore the discipline.

Relationships are fundamental to every single theory of communication. All-encompassing statements such as this one are often problematic and set up for challenge. However, we honestly cannot name a single theory that does not directly or indirectly involve relationships. Incorporating a relational perspective can be used to better understand and enhance existing theories while serving as the basis for theoretical development.

Cultural Communication

The discipline of communication has strong interest in cultural influences. Jackson (2010) notes the existence of four areas of cultural communication study. *Intracultural communication* examines communication within a single culture. *Intercultural communication* examines communication when members of different cultural groups interact. *Cross-cultural communication* compares the communication of different groups. *Critical cultural communication* examines issues of power within cultural contexts and seeks to contest hegemony and promote social justice. As we discuss in Chapter 12, abstract notions such as culture can be understood and recognized through relationships. Further, it is through relationships that culture is actually developed, enacted, maintained, and altered.

Table 2.4 Theories of Communication

Agenda Setting
The issues people view as important and how they think about those issues are based on the agenda of the news media.

Cognitive Dissonance
People prefer their actions to be consistent with their attitudes, beliefs, and values, because inconsistency creates negative feelings.

Communication Accommodation
People adjust their communication styles to indicate a connection with those with whom they wish to gain approval or develop a relationship.

Communication Privacy Management
People create and manage privacy boundaries in their relationships.

Coordinated Management of Meaning
Social meanings and realities are co-constructed when people communicate.

Cultivation
Heavy television viewing causes people to believe that the world is more dangerous than it actually is.

Cultural Studies
Media organizations and subsequent media content maintain the dominant ideologies of the powerful and elite in society.

Elaboration Likelihood Model
Persuasion occurs through central routes (scrutiny of message) and peripheral routes (mental shortcuts based on cues other than message itself).

Face Negotiation
People from collectivist cultures and from individualist cultures differ in the importance placed on the concept of "face" and differ in the ways in which they deal with conflict.

Media Equation
People use the same social rules and expectations when interacting with technology as they do when interacting with other people.

Muted Group
Since language tends to be man-made or -dominated, it supports the exclusion and depreciation of women.

Relational Dialectics
The continuous interplay among contradictory needs comprises relationships.

Social Exchange Theory
Relationship status and interactions are based on people's perceptions of costs and rewards of being in a given relationship.

Social Information Processing
People who meet online can develop close relationships just as they do face-to-face; in fact, online relationships may be hyperpersonal or even more intimate, given the nature of online communication.

Social Judgment
Explains how people may respond to a range of positions surrounding a particular topic or issue.

Social Penetration
Intimacy or closeness in a relationship occurs through gradually disclosing increasingly personal information.

Speech Codes
Communication and culture are inherently connected, and unique cultures develop unique codes of communication with distinct psychology, sociology, and rhetoric.

Standpoint
Different positions on a social hierarchy provide different perspectives, and the views of less powerful groups in a society are likely to be more accurate than the views of more powerful groups in society.

Symbolic Interactionism
People respond to things, situations, and others based on how they assign meaning to these things; symbol using is seen as a basis for the development of society and membership in society.

Uncertainty Reduction
When two people meet, their primary goal is to reduce uncertainty about one another and their relationship.

Family Communication

The study of family communication is often placed under the broad umbrella term of *interpersonal communication*. Many relationships are studied under that term, including romantic relationships, friendships in their various forms, and even social relationships. However, given its particular societal importance and the number of scholars studying this area, family communication has emerged as a specific area of study in its own right (see Turner & West, 2015).

Relationships are naturally the primary area of study within family communication. The many topics of investigation within this area include family structure, specific relationships within family units, and issues such as conflict, divorce, traditions, storytelling, violence, and celebration.

Group Communication

As with family communication, the study of group communication is pretty much what you would expect it to be. According to Gouran (2010), small-group research emerged as a major area of discipline beginning in the 1970s. Gouran has also isolated key perspectives within this area that include the following: (a) functional theory of communication in decision-making groups, (b) the decision development perspective, (c) symbolic convergence theory, (d) structuration theory, (e) bona fide groups theory, and (f) socioegocentric theory. Group communication has been strengthened in recent years through the study of leadership communication.

In Chapter 9, we examine how group communication can be better understood by taking a relational perspective. People within groups rarely have zero history with one another. Rather, they enter into group situations with preexisting relationships that influence their interactions and decision making. Group members with little shared history or few preexisting relationships often anticipate future connection or, at minimum, generate relational alliances and adversaries within the group.

Interpersonal Communication

Interpersonal communication has become a general term for the study of relationships. In past decades, scholars studying interpersonal communication primarily viewed it as something that happens when two separate individuals come together. Communication was seen as little more than the way inner thoughts were shared and how two people asserted their individuality and achieved their personal goals.

Scholars increasingly study the ways in which relationships, identities, and meanings are created through interactions themselves. Of course, relationships then serve as the foundation for all other communication and human activities. Much more interesting than it used to be, if you ask us!

Media

The study of "mass communication" has moved well beyond newspapers. *Media* and *media studies* are now the more appropriate and recognized terms for this area of exploration. There are three primary areas of media study, each incorporating an array of approaches and methods.

One area of study examines the impact of technology, or a particular medium, on the construction of knowledge, perceptions, and social systems. For instance, scholars may study the ways in which the Internet has changed what counts as knowledge and how people perceive information.

A second area of study entails media content. A broad area of study, scholars exploring this area might examine particular television genres or how video game content supports the dominant views of a society.

ANALYZING
EVERYDAY COMMUNICATION

Converging Relationships and Media

The use of media is often done with others. For instance, people may play video games with friends and watch television with family members. The next time you find yourself in such a situation, consider what might be taking place.

QUESTIONS TO CONSIDER

1. How is using media together impacting your relationship?
2. How does using media with others impact your actual use of those media and how they are understood?

The final primary area of study examines people's reactions to technology and media content. In the past, scholars viewed technology and media content as powerful agents capable of manipulating users and audiences. More recently, communication scholars have recognized that people actively interpret media content in a variety of ways and use media content and technology for a number of different reasons.

As we discuss in Chapter 13, the formation and maintenance of relationships occur in part through their use of technology. Further, people's use and understanding of technology and media content are based largely on relationships.

Health Communication

Lederman (2010) has traced the origins of the study of health communication to the 1980s. Early research in this area focused on interactions between patients and doctors and public campaigns concerning health issues. Since that period of time, health communication has been one of the fastest-growing areas of the discipline. It has also grown beyond doctor-patient communication to provider-patient communication in recognition of patient interactions that take place among many types of health care providers.

Communication involving any treatment or health-related issues is now studied under the banner of health communication. Accordingly, this communication can occur within social networks of friends, family, and acquaintances as well as among health care providers. Further, the study of health campaigns and information sharing is increasingly focused on Internet use when seeking medical information.

As we discuss in Chapter 11, relationships among providers and patients as well as among providers provide great insight into communication taking place and health care in general. Further, health information is frequently gained through social networks, and health information gained online or through media is accessed through the context of relationships.

Organizational Communication

The study of organizational communication involves communication taking place within an organization or a workplace. The sharing of information within an organization was an original focus of this area of study. Increasingly, those studying organizational communication are concerned with the processing of information and the creation of meanings within organizations and workplaces.

As we discuss in Chapter 10, the workplace and organizations in general are best viewed as relational enterprises through which meanings are developed and shared understandings are created or challenged. Organizations are essentially created by relationships, and that is how their operation and productivity are carried out.

Persuasion

The study of persuasion can easily be traced back to ancient Greece and the Roman Empire. It can also be argued that the study of persuasion led to the initial interest in interpersonal interaction among those teaching in speech departments. Influenced by many studies of persuasion and attitude change in psychology (e.g., Hovland, Janis, & Kelley, 1953), many researchers who were interested in persuasion and had received rhetorical training began to turn away from the traditional focus of rhetorical analyses (speeches) and toward other forms of communication.

The study of persuasion essentially examines the ways in which people's thinking and behavior can be modified (changed, strengthened, weakened, and so on). Given those broad parameters, persuasion naturally can involve many contexts and areas of communication, such as interpersonal communication, media, and others discussed within this section of the chapter. And depending on whom you ask and the context, persuasion can be called *coercion, compliance, brainwashing, influence, manipulation, indoctrination,* or *propaganda* (Gass & Seiter, 2011). It could also be argued that symbol using is inherently persuasive.

Regardless of the context and purpose of persuasive study, relationships play a fundamental role in nearly every regard. We discuss the impact of relationships on public and personal influence in Chapter 14.

Political Communication

As with persuasion, the study of political communication can be traced back to the days of ancient Greece and the Roman Republic. According to Trent and Friedenberg (2010), however, it emerged as a formal area of the discipline in the 1970s and fully developed in the early 1980s. There are a number of topics of study within this area of the discipline. Scholars in this area study, for instance, campaign strategy, voter behavior, campaign advertisement, news media coverage, candidate speeches, and candidate debates. While the majority of research is focused on political campaigns, scholars may also examine communication once a politician is elected. Further, the use of the Internet as a political tool has invigorated this area of the discipline.

Relationships play a key role in political communication. Candidates generally want to develop positive relationships with voters, who will then be more likely to cast a vote on their behalf. Relationships are formed within campaign staffs and among campaign volunteers. An extraordinarily important consideration in political communication research must be the impact that talk about candidates and political issues among friends, family, and acquaintances has on voters' perceptions and actions.

Public Relations

The study of public relations entails understanding the ways in which organizations (and increasingly high-profile people) communicate and should communicate with the general public. Specifically, the study of public relations is concerned with determining how organizations can influence how the public views them and their activities.

In a very obvious sense, especially given the second word in the name of this area, the study of public relations is about developing relationships between organizations and the public. Further, as with political communication, an important area of concern within this area of study must be the ways in which organizations are discussed among people who share relationships.

Rhetorical Criticism

If rhetorical criticism can be recognized as the analysis of symbolic activity, then it can easily be argued to serve as the basis of all communication study. Certainly, a convincing argument can be made for that perspective. If we examine rhetorical criticism specifically, however, we can witness its tremendous development as an area of study within the discipline of communication.

Rhetorical criticism, as mentioned earlier in this chapter, has developed well beyond the study of public address. It is just as likely, if not more likely, to entail the analysis of digital communication, cartoons, memorials, billboards, and the human body as it is the analysis of a speech (see Olson, Finnegan, & Hope, 2008).

As rhetorical criticism has developed, so has the number of approaches dedicated to its study. As we did with the earlier table dedicated to communication theories, Table 2.5 lists a few of the rhetorical approaches you may encounter within this book and throughout your study of communication.

As with theories of communication, approaches to rhetorical criticism directly or indirectly involve relationships. They can all be applied in some manner to the study of personal relationships. Further, incorporating a relational perspective, by simply exploring how relationships are involved with these approaches, can result in their further development and understanding. Any analysis or study of symbolic activity could be strengthened through the recognition of relationships.

Table 2.5 Approaches to Rhetorical Criticism

Approach	Description
Neo-Aristotelian	Essentially applies such Aristotelian concepts as ethos, pathos, logos, invention, arrangement, style, and delivery to the analysis of the public address of speakers.
Historical	Views a causal connection between historical events of a given era and public address taking place.
Eclectic	An early break from traditional criticism, this approach rejects the notion that there is a specific starting point for the rhetorical analysis—such as a speaker—and leaves it to the critic to decide which elements of symbolic activity are most worthy of examination.
Epistemic	Examines the methods through which knowledge systems such as language are used to create a certain perspective or view of the world.
Dramatistic	Incorporates symbolic concepts and methods developed primarily through the writings of Kenneth Burke, such as the pentad, identification, and form.
Fantasy Theme	Examines how socially shared rhetorical visions are developed and become deterministic, or how symbolic realities become shared among people or a society as a whole.
Narrative	Examines the ways in which stories are used to both convey information and influence people.
Sociolinguistic	Views language, specifically the ways in which a society regulates and uses it, as fundamental to perceptions, attitudes, beliefs, values, and institutions.
Generic	Classifies symbolic activity into categories based on shared characteristics.
Social Movements	Another break from speaker-centered criticism, this approach examines collective or group activities and discourse meant to challenge societal norms and power structures.
Feminist	Multifaceted approach that (a) uncovers patriarchal underpinnings of symbolic activity, (b) examines the rhetoric of previously neglected women of history, and/or (c) incorporates women's issues and perspectives into existing and emerging rhetorical theory and criticism.
Content Analysis	Systematically identifies observable and/or underlying characteristics of messages (especially media products) to determine possible meanings and effects.
Media Analysis	Examines how modes of communication or technologies influence meanings, perceptions, knowledge, and social systems.
Postmodernist	Often in a quest to promote democracy, this approach views symbolic activity as (a) unique to each situation, (b) understood and experienced differently by every individual, and (c) based on power structures that influence not only symbolic activity itself but also its analysis by critics.
Queer Theory	Multifaceted approach that (a) views sexuality as fluid, socially constructed, and an essential influence on symbolic activity and (b) uncovers heteronormative underpinnings of symbolic activity.

Focus Questions Revisited

How did the modern communication discipline develop?

The modern discipline of communication developed as increasing numbers of scholars became interested in the study of communication, accompanied by the creation of academic associations and of academic departments devoted to the study of communication.

What is the social scientific approach to communication?

The social scientific approach believes in the existence of a single reality that causes people to communicate in predictable ways, thereby enabling communication to be studied empirically.

What is the interpretivist approach to communication?

The interpretivist approach does not believe that a single reality exists but rather believes that multiple realities are created symbolically, thereby requiring communication to be studied in a subjective manner.

What is the critical approach to communication?

Critical approaches focus on how power is constructed, challenged, and maintained through communication, thereby seeking to identify the hidden but powerful structures and practices that create or uphold disadvantage, inequity, or oppression of one subgroup of society by any other.

What are some of the major areas of study in the communication discipline?

Some areas within the discipline of communication include (1) communication education and instructional communication, (2) communication theory, (3) cultural communication, (4) family communication, (5) group communication, (6) health communication, (7) interpersonal communication, (8) media, (9) organizational communication, (10) persuasion, (11) political communication, (12) public relations, and (13) rhetorical criticism.

Key Concepts

critical approach 36
historiography 23
interpretivist approach 33
social scientific approach 30

Questions to Ask Your Friends

1. Ask your friends how they would define communication studies. How do their definitions compare with the histories offered in this chapter?
2. Ask your friends if they believe a single reality, external to human beings, exists or if they believe human beings create their own realities. Would their response make them more of a social scientist or more of an interpretivist?
3. Ask your friends if they would stretch the truth on a first date assuming it would guarantee the date went well and that they would never be found out. Do they believe it more important to tell the absolute truth even if it means the date will not go well? Many people are on their "best behavior" during a first date and may not communicate as they normally do. Do your friends believe this qualifies as being untruthful?

Media Connections

1. Watch or listen to a news broadcast. What elements of rhetoric can be studied? What elements of media can be studied? What elements of interpersonal communication can be studied? How might a relational perspective of communication be used to bridge these areas of study?
2. Watch or listen to a political speech. What elements of rhetoric can be studied? What elements of media can be studied? What elements of interpersonal communication can be studied? How might a relational perspective of communication be used to bridge these areas of study?
3. Watch a television sitcom. How are male and female characters portrayed? In what ways are traditional gender roles being upheld? Watch carefully! Even when it appears as if traditional gender roles are being challenged, these traditional roles are often being reinforced.

Student Study Site

Sharpen your skills with SAGE edge at edge.sagepub.com/duckciel2e

SAGE edge for students provides a personalized approach to help you accomplish your coursework goals in an easy-to-use learning environment.

Part II COMMUNICATION SKILLS

CHAPTER 3
Identities, Perceptions, and Communication

CHAPTER 4
Verbal Communication

CHAPTER 5
Nonverbal Communication

CHAPTER 6
Listening

Chapter Outline

Do People Have a Core Self?
- Different Moods
- Different Situations
- Different Relationships
- Different Evaluations

Identities and Perceptions
- Selecting
- Organizing and Evaluating

Identities and Communication
- Symbolic Identities and a Symbolic Self
- Self-Disclosure
- Dynamics of Self-Disclosure
- Narratives

Transacting Identity and Other People
- Altercasting
- Performative Self

Focus Questions Revisited

Key Concepts

Questions to Ask Your Friends

Media Connections

03 Identities, Perceptions, and Communication

Did you know that you develop multiple identities throughout the day? Before making an appointment for psychological evaluation, recognize that we are not talking about a medical disorder. Everyone constructs multiple identities as part of their everyday relational lives. Consider the many relational roles a person establishes in everyday life. A person may at once be a friend, sibling, parent, and child. That same person may be a student, coworker, supervisor, or customer. Within these various roles, when interacting with different people, and when interacting in different contexts, a person may be passive, strict, caring, detached, feminine, or masculine. That same person may end the day cheering for a sports team in a group of die-hard fans or taking part in an online discussion about a favorite web series. Each of these aspects of daily experience requires the development of a different identity.

Just as the primary subject of a textbook is usually defined in an introductory chapter, a reader can generally expect to find a definition of the main topic or topics of a given chapter in the opening pages of that chapter. However, as we saw when attempting to define *communication* in Chapter 1, defining terms is not always a simple task. Throughout this chapter, we will develop what is meant by *identities*. For now, an **identity** can be simply defined as who a person is. There is more to it than just that, of course. And, determining *who a person is* is not that straightforward or even possible. For now, though, that simple definition can set us on our exploration of this area.

Before jumping fully into the chapter and to clarify what might be meant about determining who a person is not being straightforward or possible, we need to discuss a few key ideas. First, *people do not possess a core self.* The notion that people construct multiple identities may be somewhat unique. From the introductory paragraph, this idea might make sense to you. However, there exists a general idea that people are who they are. Each person is often thought to possess a core self or an established personality developed from previous experiences and other factors. This core self may drive decisions and becomes known to others in part through actions but more specifically through revealing information about one's self to others.

Theorists have described this idea as the "Onion Model" (Altman & Taylor, 1973) because it suggests an inner core covered up with layer after layer of information and characteristics right out toward the surface skin. If you cut an onion in half, you will see the way the analogy works. This suggests to some theorists that they can describe getting to know someone as working their way toward the core, cutting through the outer layers one after the other in order to reach the central "truth."

FOCUS QUESTIONS

1. Does it make sense that someone has a true core self?
2. How do perceptions influence identities?
3. What does it mean to say that identities are symbolic constructions?
4. What is the difference between self-description and self-disclosure?
5. What is the role of narratives in the construction of identities?
6. How do other people influence identity construction?

identity: a person's uniqueness, represented by descriptions, a self-concept, inner thoughts, and performances, that is symbolized in interactions with other people and presented for their assessment and moral evaluation

How do daily interactions with other people form or sustain your identity? What is being communicated here about gender, identity, and culture?

In actuality, people do not possess a central, unchanging self influencing actions and waiting to be revealed through disclosure. (Since this is a common assumption, however, we will discuss this idea within the chapter.) People may have developed and possess core values and beliefs. They may also have a particular biological makeup and physical characteristics that influence the way they communicate with others and—probably more so—the way others communicate with them. However, people construct multiple, sometimes contradictory, identities through communication with others.

Second, *identities, communication, and relationships are interconnected,* which explains the placement of this chapter near the beginning of the book, even before we discuss verbal and nonverbal symbols. A *person* is using verbal and nonverbal symbols, so it is necessary to establish who that person might be. Even more importantly from our approach, a *relator* is using verbal and nonverbal communication. So, an individual is using symbols but doing so within the context of relationships.

At the same time, as we will discuss further within this chapter and still others to come, it is the use of symbols through which these identities and relationships are being transacted, or created. Your identities influence your communication, while communication influences your identities. This notion may be somewhat difficult to comprehend, and we discuss this matter in more detail later in the chapter. For now, basically think of yourself as clay (clay has certain characteristic qualities and properties) and communication as the potter (the clay can be molded and shaped).

Moreover, while identities connect communication to meaning, they also connect people relationally. For instance, we become friends with people whose identities and personalities we like. Not only that, it is through these relationships that our social understanding of identities is tested and established.

Third, *society provides you with ways to describe and evaluate identities and personalities.* Categories like *gluttonous, sexy, short, slim, paranoid, kind, masculine,* and *feminine* are all available to you. Society tells you how to be "masculine" and "feminine." It indicates such things as "guys can't say that to guys" (Burleson,

DISCIPLINARY **DEBATE**

What Is an Identity?

Many different areas of study are concerned with the issue of "identity." However, despite the importance of this concept, there is very little agreement about the way in which identity should be understood. Some scholars regard it as perfectly obvious that there is a "central core" of identity that an individual "has" and that is essentially unchanging. Other scholars take the position that an individual's identity is constructed in the course of interaction with other people. They believe that a person's behavior and "personality" are influenced by the situations and social circumstances in which the individual is placed. A third position is that the notion of personality—and identity—is itself a construction of our society that is meaningless in other cultures and therefore not a central truth about human beings.

QUESTIONS TO CONSIDER

1. Where do you come down in this debate?
2. Are these positions mutually exclusive, or is there some truth to all of them?

Holmstrom, & Gilstrap, 2005), restricting the way men can give one another emotional support. Society also places more value on some identities than others. In many instances, a "coward" would be a less valuable identity than would a "hero." Adding another consideration into the mix and something we will discuss later in this chapter, cultural groups and societies do not always agree on what an identity looks like or how it is valued.

How many people in this photo are performing a social role and its accompanying identity requirements? Be sure to justify your answer.

Finally, *people perform their identities with others*. This idea means that rather than *having* an identity, people are *doing* an identity. Further, just as there does not exist a core self, this idea may initially appear somewhat odd. However, consider the following question. If you happen to see an adult and a child together and determine the adult is the child's parent, how did you conclude that to be the case? The answer is likely that the person was *acting* like a parent, doing certain things and communicating the way a parent would communicate.

When people perform identities associated with social roles, they are not being fake and are not necessarily being dishonest—although one would hope the pilot getting ready to fly a plane is actually a pilot or the doctor getting ready to perform surgery is actually qualified! Rather, they are acting in ways that both society and they perceive to be associated with identity.

Performing identities associated with particular roles may be easy to understand and accept. Other types of identity performance tend to be a bit more challenging to grasp, at least initially, but will be discussed further within this chapter. Take the example of masculinity and femininity from above. People perform being masculine, and they perform being feminine. These performances are based on what a society or cultural group establishes as masculine and feminine. And a given person sometimes performs in a masculine manner and sometimes performs in a feminine manner, depending on the situation and the people with whom an interaction is taking place.

Having discussed some of the key ideas to be explored within this chapter pertaining to identities, there is one more thing to consider before we get started. You may have very perceptively noticed that the word *perception* is included in the chapter title.

The transaction of identities is guided in part through perceptions of oneself, other people, and situations. **Perception** involves how a person views the world, organizes what is seen, and evaluates information, all of which will influence symbolic activity. It is therefore important to include such material in discussions of identity.

perception: process of actively selecting, organizing, and evaluating information, activities, situations, people, and essentially all the things that make up your world

The ideas presented above set the discipline of communication and this textbook apart. Identities, relationships, cultural membership, and the like are not located within people or embedded within their minds. They are instead created symbolically through communication with others. Now that these general ideas have been established, we can begin exploring them in more detail.

Do People Have a Core Self?

After reading the introduction to this chapter, you know what our answer to this question is going to be: No, they do not. However, we will justify that response a bit more within this section. As a result, you will be introduced to a traditional yet flawed approach to the study of identities. And knowing why this approach is not necessarily accurate will provide you with a more accurate understanding of identities.

Mentioned in the opening of this chapter, the Onion Model sees identity as analogous to an onion where deeper and deeper layers of more intimate information about a person are found beneath previous layers (see Figure 3.1). A cross-section of the onion reveals these layers as well as the central core at the very heart of the onion. According to this model, the central core is very rarely reached by others. For instance, a person may get to know someone else broadly but in a shallow way—a broad *V* cut a couple of layers deep into the onion. Or a person may get to know someone's identity in a narrower but deeper cut—a narrow *V* cutting through several layers. Because it seems pretty simple and because people may feel that who they are is fairly stable and is deeply embedded within them, this model has persisted as a "commonsense" model of identity, despite the lack of research support for it (Altman, Vinsel, & Brown, 1981).

Partly on grounds of a lack of supporting research, despite the frequency with which it is reported in communication texts, and partly on logical grounds, we reject this model, and here is why. We will start with Bob.

Bob is a really nice guy. He is loyal, trusting, open, honest, comforting, caring, active in organizing charitable events (especially for kids who are mentally challenged), a fabulous cook (he specializes in the cuisines of other cultures), and devoted to his aging parents. He is active in the local parent-teacher association and does long Saturdays coaching and refereeing the blossoming mixed-sex soccer group that he started.

At work, Bob is the most hated officer in the Border Protection branch of Homeland Security. There is no one who is such a completely ruthless, nasty, dogged,

Figure 3.1 The Onion Model

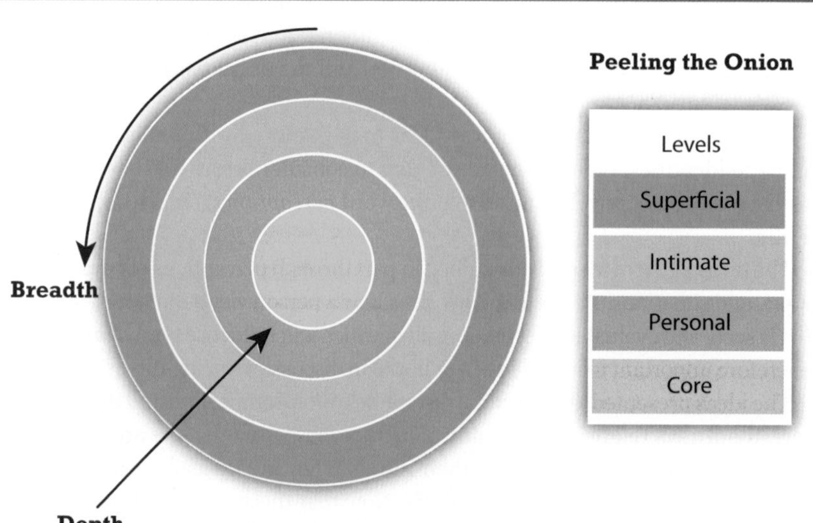

suspicious, awkward cuss. He is a complete pain to others, and there is no one better at interrogation. He nails people who make illegal applications for a green card and has the highest record in the whole border area for catching cheats. He regularly has grown, otherwise secure adults breaking down in tears in his office. If you get interviewed for immigration by Bob and are not 100% straight up, then he will get you.

Who is the real Bob? Does he have an evil twin? No, he just constructs multiple identities throughout his everyday life, just like everyone else does. Multiple experiences in everyday life call into question having a core self or identity. We will examine some examples in the remainder of this section.

ETHICAL ISSUE

Of course, we are maintaining that people construct multiple identities and act or communicate in different ways with different people, in different situations, and so on. There is no true core self or person to be discovered, and people will not act the same way in all situations. Having said that, though, people who behave differently around different people are sometimes accused of being "fake." Are these people being unethical? Also, is it unethical to accuse someone of being fake?

Different Moods

You may feel outgoing and confident some days and communicate with others accordingly. Other days, you may feel more reserved and insecure, and this is reflected in your communication with others. Well, people can have mood swings as a result of periodic hormonal imbalances, gluten intolerance, or just having had a series of really unfortunate events happen to them on a bad hair day. Many changes in mood are temporary, relatively unimportant, and reversible. Get the hormones back into balance, avoid certain foods, and let the sun shine in, and then most people will be back to their same old self. However, these fluctuations are a problem for anyone who sees identity as fixed or layered like an onion.

Different Situations

A person may be unfriendly and distant when at school but funny and sociable when at work. This person may be more confident and comfortable at work than at school. Or this person may have yet to make friends at school with whom he or she can interact in a sociable manner. It is also possible that this person views his or her time at school as serious business, and he or she wants to remain focused. Whatever the case might be, the point is the same. People transact multiple identities given different situations and different areas of their lives. A person does not have a fixed identity, and a layered onion is not an accurate way to think about the transaction of identities in everyday life.

Different Relationships

People also transact multiple identities given the many different relationships shared with others. You may act one way around your friends and an entirely different way around your relatives. Different relational identities are constructed based on the relationships being transacted. Once again, if people had an unchanging core self, there would be no change in communication and behavior around different people. However, this change takes place, occasionally in dramatic ways.

Different Evaluations

Sometimes people evaluate the same person in vastly different ways. For instance, you may know someone whom you view as kind, yet one of your friends sees the person as nasty. Or two professors may argue about whether a particular student is intelligent or

By the way...

Pillar of the Community or Serial Killer?

Dr. Harold "Fred" Shipman was a family practitioner in England, working in two practices in the 1980s and 1990s and even appearing on TV in a discussion about the way to treat mentally ill patients. He was seen by many as a pillar of the community. He was also England's most prolific mass murderer and in January 2000 was convicted of murdering 15 patients. Subsequent inquiries revealed that he was directly responsible for the murders of at least 215 people, and that figure is now regarded as a serious underestimate.

QUESTIONS TO CONSIDER

1. How do we ever know who someone "really" is?
2. Can we ever know who someone "really" is?

Make your case

College for Traditional and Nontraditional Students

Consider nontraditional students and identities. Nontraditional students have the same concerns as all students, such as getting their work done on time and receiving good grades. However, they view themselves differently. Nontraditional students frequently return to school after working for several years. Perhaps they have decided that their line of work is not challenging enough, or they recognize that their full potential is not being realized, or perhaps they have lost their job in a rough economy. Many of these students have already been successful outside of the classroom, yet they are very apprehensive about *entering* one. Such students are used to being obeyed—to being someone to whom people turn for advice, a leader, a mentor, and an example.

Now consider traditional students. These students most likely experienced success in high school. Many entering students graduated high school with honors, participated in many activities, received a number of awards and distinctions, were well known in their school, and were admired by others. Now, these students may view themselves as adrift in a sea of people who were more successful in their own high schools and are now classmates in college competing for grades.

QUESTIONS TO CONSIDER

1. Which is the *real* person: the successful professional and authoritative leader or the obviously older student in a classroom where previous experience counts for very little?
2. Which is the *real* person: the standout high school student who excelled at everything or the awkward first-year student seeking some sort of recognition?

Return to these questions once you have read the entire chapter and see if your responses have changed.

someone who stands no chance of improving. If every person had just one identity at the core of his or her personality and everyone perceived it identically, then these competing evaluations would make no sense. Yet such varying evaluations of people happen quite frequently.

Sometimes even a single person will evaluate another person in vastly different ways. If people really had a stable core inside a set of layers that we could peel away to reach "the truth," then we would never be able to change our mind about someone. If someone were a good and loyal friend, he would never turn into an enemy unless he had a personality transplant. Yet you have most likely had the experience of seeing someone in a different light over time.

Identities and Perceptions

Consider further the notion introduced above that one person's evaluation of another person changes over time. Could identity be a matter of *perception* rather than *fact?* Something transacted between two communicators, rather than something set in a stone onion? When a stranger does something rude, your first thought may be to blame personality ("This is an evil person, perhaps with psychopathic tendencies"). Or you might put it down to an identity that was constructed during childhood when the person had some bad experiences. (Lawyers often explain their clients' bad behavior in such terms.) On the other hand, that "rude stranger" probably sees his or her identity in personality terms, too, but more favorable ones—as a decent person who is being irritated by an annoying stranger (you!)—and may walk away thinking, "What a jerk!" Notice that these are representations, attributions, or claims, based on perception and not facts. They are based on the way one person perceives and understands the evidence.

Within this section, we will examine how perceptions influence the development of identities and meanings. These perceptions are based on relational and cultural understandings. And they involve the process of actively selecting, organizing, and evaluating information, activities, situations, and people, and essentially naming and giving significance to all the things that make up your world.

Selecting

Receiving stimuli does not necessarily mean you will recognize their presence or direct your attention to them. Imagine going up to a friend whose concentration is focused on reading *Communication in Everyday Life*. You greet her by saying hello or by saying her name, but she does not seem to recognize you are speaking. This person continues to focus solely on the book. You speak again, a little louder this time, and still receive no response. You may tap her on the shoulder to get her attention or hit her gently over the head with your new copy of *Communication in Everyday Life*. You are not being ignored; this person simply does not attend to the sound of your voice. In short, she is attending to the world *selectively*.

Everyone selects and focuses more on some things than others. If something stands out for whatever reason, you are more likely to focus your attention on that. If you scan a room of people wearing similar clothing, you will likely focus on the one person whose clothing is dissimilar to that of the others. On the other hand, **selective exposure** means you are more likely to expose yourself to that which supports your values and attitudes. You will be more likely to pick up on activities that support your views of the world, and you will pay less attention to those that do not. If you view yourself as a competent person, you will be more likely to pick up on compliments and less likely to focus on criticism. The opposite, of course, would happen if you viewed yourself as an incompetent person.

Organizing and Evaluating

Your observations of the world are selectively chosen and then organized in ways that allow you to retrieve them when necessary. New information is connected to previous information that is already organized and stored as your own characteristic way of looking at the world (through your identity goggles). **Schemata** are mental structures that are used to organize information in part by clustering associated material. For example, information about relationships can be stored and connected in "relationship" schemata and drawn upon when needed. Since this information is stored in a relatively accessible manner, it can be used to make sense of what you are experiencing and to anticipate what might happen in a given situation. For instance, you may think to yourself, "This is a friendship. I know what to do in it."

Your organizational goggles are constantly being updated based on new experiences and evaluations of their meaning to you. This system seems efficient. However, it is not without its disadvantages. George Kelly (1955) maintained that a person's processes are "channelized" by the ways in which events are anticipated. As a result, certain ways of acting become more deeply ingrained in your thinking. Imagine running the end of a stick in a straight line over and over in the same spot on the ground. Eventually, an indentation begins to develop and becomes deeper as you continue to run the end of that stick in the same place. You create a rut, and the same thing can happen with ways of behaving and viewing the world. The more you behave in a certain way and the more often you view the world in the same way, the deeper and more ingrained it becomes in your thinking. After a while, it becomes difficult to imagine behaving in another way or viewing the world in a different way. It is, however, based on your perceptions and experience of the world, so identity influences what you see, hear, or believe about the world. These are **personal constructs**, individualized ways of construing or understanding the world and its contents. These are your identity goggles that prescribe the way you tend to see things and selectively categorize and attend to them. As such, your habitual ways of seeing and perceiving are a component of identity that affects your presentation of that identity to other people.

selective exposure: the idea that you are more likely to expose yourself to that which supports your values and attitudes, that you will be more likely to pick up on activities that support your views of the world, and that you will pay less attention to those that do not

schemata: mental structures that are used to organize information in part by clustering or linking associated material

personal constructs: bipolar dimensions used to measure and evaluate things

Identities and Communication

We began this chapter by broadly questioning the idea that people have a true inner self. In the next section, we started to take this idea apart by showing that people understand identities based in part on their perceptions of others and by using socially constructed labels. We now will spend the remainder of the chapter discussing how identities are symbolically created and performed. These symbolic creations and performances are transacted though interactions with others. They are

COMMUNICATION + YOU

Identifying Yourself

How would you describe yourself? Would you give your national, ethnic, gender, sexual, age, social class, or religious identity, or anything else?

Now check the categories that you can use to personalize your profile on Facebook or another social networking site. People are asked to identify themselves by association with particular categories such as favorite videos and music, hobbies, and sexual orientation.

QUESTIONS TO CONSIDER

1. Are these the categories you would use to describe yourself to a child, an employer, or a new neighbor?
2. Would you consider your social networking site profile to be an accurate representation of how you view yourself and how others view you?

also based on and understood through relationships with others and cultural memberships.

Before talking about the particular symbolic activities, though, let's briefly examine how identities involve cultural membership and relationships. First, and obviously, some identities are based on group membership such as being an Asian American, a graduate of a particular university, or a part of a labor union. And some identities are based on personal relationships such as being a parent, child, and friend.

These group and relational identities take us further away from the notion of an inner core self, since they rely on other people. They also show that a person can simultaneously construct many identities, and a person has a choice in the identity emphasized at a given moment. Sometimes, for example, a person will emphasize his or her identity as a parent. Other times, that person will emphasize his or her identity as a child.

Second, it is through relationships that much identity work takes place. Our relationships with others provide us with opportunities to develop who we are and how we want to be perceived by others. It is through relationships that we develop trust so that we may disclose personal information about ourselves. And we come to understand ourselves through our interactions with others. A person cannot have a concept of self without reflection on identities via the views of other people with whom he or she has relationships. Further, it is through relationships that our understanding of cultural norms and values develops, something we will talk about more in Chapter 12.

Finally, cultural membership informs people about the value of identities and the proper ways of constructing those identities. And your identities are based in part on the beliefs and prevailing norms of the society in which you live. When you communicate with other people in your culture, you get information about what works and what does not, what is acceptable and what is not, and how much you count in that society—what your identities are worth. For example, the dominant culture in the United States typically values ambition, good looks, hard work, demonstration of material success, and a strong code of individuality. People stress those values in their talk (the American Dream, winners) or else feel inadequate because they don't stack up against these values (losers).

Symbolic Identities and a Symbolic Self

With those ideas in mind, we will begin by considering how identities are created and performed symbolically and how, without symbols, we could not even perceive ourselves as unique individuals.

Transacting Identities Symbolically

Identities can be understood as being transacted symbolically through communication with others. Who we understand ourselves to be and how we want others to perceive us at a given moment is established through our use of symbols. Essentially, our multiple identities are created and performed though verbal and nonverbal communication.

Sorts of identities might include personal identities (kind, mean, hardworking, lazy, fan of musicals), relational identities (parent, child, friend, enemy), social identities (customer, employee, supervisor), and those identities involving biological sex, race, sexual orientation, and national or regional origin, which are relatively stable and unchanging. Tracy (2002) refers to the latter type of identities as *master identities*. It is with this type of identity that some people argue that people do possess a core, unchanging self, but that is not necessarily the case as will be explained below.

Transacting personal identities includes communicating and behaving in ways culturally understood to represent those characteristics. For example, a kind person might talk in ways and do things that people would consider kind. Or a fan of musicals might spend the day humming the soundtrack of *Rent* when not talking about his or her favorite Broadway performers. Transacting relational and social identities includes communicating and behaving in ways culturally associated with those roles. For instance, a parent will communicate as a parent is expected to communicate and will do parent-type stuff, whatever that happens to be.

Then, we get to master identities. It is here, again, where people might claim that a core self exists. After all, they might argue, a person is born a male or female, born a particular race, born homosexual or heterosexual, and born in a particular place. While all true, cultural understanding and norms influence the symbolic activities associated with these categories. Further, a person may choose to not conform to those symbolic activities or may choose to emphasize or disregard these identities when communicating with others. So, while master identities are those a person may be born with, they are ultimately socially and symbolically created and performed.

By the way...

Sexual and Gender Identities

Sexual and gender identities are not necessarily as straightforward as being able to say "I am a homosexual" or "I am a female."

QUESTIONS TO CONSIDER

1. How might transsexual individuals, transgendered individuals, and those individuals who do not view themselves as belonging to any established sex or gender category call traditional notions of identity into question?
2. Are any identity categories still relevant, or are they essentially meaningless?

Symbolic Self

If not for symbols, there would be no need to talk about people being unique or enacting particular identities.

Your identity is shaped by culture and the people you interact with, and this affects the way you communicate and receive communications. This is because you can reflect that your "self" is an object of other people's perceptions and that they can do critical thinking or listening about you as well. In short, your identity is a **symbolic self**, a self that exists for other people and goes beyond what it means to you; it arises from social interaction with other people. As a result, you fit identity

symbolic self: the self that is transacted in interaction with other people; that arises out of social interaction, not vice versa; and hence that does not just "belong to you"

What is meant by a symbolic self, and why do we have to account to other people for who we are?

descriptions into the form of narratives that you and your society know about and accept. Hence, any identity that you offer to other people is based on the fact that you all share meanings about what is important in defining a person's identity. This matters in communication because the identity that you adopt will alter your ethos—your ability to be taken seriously and to be persuasive.

Another way of thinking about identity, then, is in terms of how broad social forces affect or even transact an individual's view of self. This set of ideas is referred to as **symbolic interactionism**. In particular, George Herbert Mead (1934) suggested that people get their sense of self from other people and from being aware that others observe, judge, and evaluate their behavior. How many times have you done or not done something because of how you would look to your friends if you did it? Has your family ever said, "What will the neighbors think?"

Mead (1934) called this phenomenon the human ability to adopt an **attitude of reflection**. You think about how you look in other people's eyes or reflect on the fact that other people can see you as a social object from their point of view. Guided by these reflections, you do not always do what you want to do; instead you do what you think people will accept. You may end up doing something you don't want to do because you cannot think how to say no to another person in a reasonable way. You cannot just stamp your foot and shout "I *won't!*"

Your identity, then, is not yours alone but is partly adopted from society and so affects your credibility. Indeed, Mead (1934) also saw self as a transacted result of communicating with other people: You learn how to be an individual by recognizing the way that people treat you. You come to see your identity through the eyes of other people, for whom you are a meaningful object. People recognize you and treat you differently from everyone else.

Self-Disclosure

Now that we have talked in general about how identities are symbolically constructed and understood, we can talk about specific ways in which this takes place. One way that people establish identities is by telling people about themselves. If you ask people to tell you who they are, they will tell you their name and start revealing information about themselves, usually with stories that place their self in various contexts, but they will tend to use socially prescribed terminology about identity. We will begin by telling you a bit about Steve Duck.

symbolic interactionism: how broad social forces affect or even transact an individual person's view of who he or she is

attitude of reflection (symbolic interactionism): thinking about how you look in other people's eyes, or reflecting on the fact that other people can see you as a social object from their point of view

Steve Duck is a proper name—a first requirement socially for identifying oneself—and it indicates to someone in your culture that the person is male and has to put up with many very unoriginal jokes about his name. Although he has lived in the United States of America for more than 30 years, he is a Brit, or English as he prefers to think of it. His family comes from Whitby in North Yorkshire, England, where the first recorded Duck (John Duck) lived in 1288. John Duck and Steve Duck share the same skeptical attitude toward authority figures. John is in the historical record because he sued the Abbot of Whitby over ownership of a piece of land. John was descended from the Vikings who sacked and then colonized Whitby in about 800 AD (*Duck* is a Viking nickname-based surname for a hunchback. Have you ever ducked out of the way of anything? If so, you have crouched like a hunchback.)

Steve Duck is also relatively short for a man, is bald but bearded, likes watching people but is quite shy, and can read Latin. Steve likes the music of Ralph Vaughan Williams, enjoys doing cryptic crosswords, knows about half the words that Shakespeare knew, and has occasionally lied. He resents his mother's controlling behavior, was an Oxford college rowing coxswain (cox'n), loves reading Roman history, and is gluten intolerant. He thinks he is a good driver and is proud of his dad, who was a Quaker pacifist (that antiauthority thing again) who won three medals for bravery in World War II for driving an unarmed ambulance into the front line of a war zone in order to rescue two seriously wounded (armed) comrades. Steve has had two marriages and four children, carries a Swiss Army knife (and as many other gadgets as will fit onto one leather belt), and always wears two watches. He is wondering whether to get the new Swiss Army knife that has a data storage capacity, a laser pointer, and a fingerprint password.

Self-Description or Self-Disclosure

Notice that some of this information about Steve's identity involves characteristics people might use to describe him without knowing him personally (e.g., male, bearded, short, bald, two watches). This **self-description** usually involves information about self that is obvious to others through appearance and behavior. If you wear your college T-shirt, talk with a French accent, or are tall, these characteristics are available even to strangers. In many cases, characteristics of self-description position a person within categories (e.g., national, racial, or ethnic groups). It is not really an individual identity but is more about group membership.

Some points in Steve's description of himself count as **self-disclosure**, the revelation of information that people could not know unless a person makes it known to them. In the above example, these are the points that describe particular feelings and emotions that other people would not know unless Steve specifically disclosed them. The *resents, is proud of, enjoys, thinks,* and *is wondering* parts give you a view of his identity that you could not directly obtain any other way, though you might work it out from what Steve says or does. Self-disclosure often involves the revelation of private, sensitive, and confidential information. Values, fears, secrets, assessments, evaluations, and preferences all count as such confidences that you share with only a few people.

ANALYZING EVERYDAY COMMUNICATION

Disclosure

Analyze three recent interactions with people you would consider, respectively, a friend, an acquaintance, and a stranger.

QUESTIONS TO CONSIDER

1. What disclosure, if any, took place during these interactions?
2. What does this tell you about disclosure and relationships?

self-description: description that involves information about self that is obvious to others through appearance and behavior

self-disclosure: the revelation of personal information that others could not know unless the person *made* it known

Dynamics of Self-Disclosure

Self-disclosure is an important aspect of identity construction and has a long history in the discipline of communication. Accordingly, we will spend a bit more time examining this issue. As we will discuss, self-disclosure has traditionally been viewed as favorable and fairly straightforward. Like most things, though, it is more complicated than one might originally think.

The Value of Self-Disclosure

Self-disclosure was traditionally seen as beneficial to identity construction and personal relationships. Jourard (1964, 1971) originally wrote about self-disclosure as making your identity "transparent" to others. People who are transparent in this way are acting in the most psychologically healthy manner. Early research also connected self-disclosure with growth in intimacy. Classic reports (e.g., Derlega, Metts, Petronio, & Margulis, 1993) found that the more people become intimate, the more they disclose to each other information that is both broad and deep. Also, the more you get to know someone's inner knowledge structures, the closer you feel to him or her.

Closeness generally develops only if the information is revealed in a way that indicates it is privileged information that other people do not know. For example, if a person lets you (and only you) know the secret that he or she has a serious invisible illness (such as diabetes, lupus, or prostate cancer), an unusually strong fear of spiders, or a significantly distressed marriage, you feel valued and trusted, because that person let you into his or her inner life.

Passing on the Onion

The above all makes sense to a certain extent, but it seems as if we are slicing into that onion again. The truth is that, as Dindia (2000) points out, the revelation of identity is rarely a simple progression and is certainly not just the declaration of facts leading to instant intimacy. Self-disclosure is a dynamic process tied to other social processes and how you disclose yourself over time. It continues through the life of relationships and is not a single one-time choice about whether to disclose or not. Part of your identity is the skill with which you reveal or conceal information about yourself and your feelings, as any good poker player knows.

The above also would lead a person to assume that self-disclosure is always beneficial, self-disclosure is always desired and welcomed, and no topic is off-limits, since the more a person discloses, the better things are going to be. However, none of these assumptions would be true.

Good, Bad, or Nothing

When someone self-discloses information, three possibilities may occur. First, it is possible that you will feel honored that someone trusts you with his or her secrets. And that person may be successfully creating a desired identity.

Another possibility is that you do not like what people are telling you or they disclose too much information. Petronio and Durham (2008), for example, found that too much disclosure is sometimes far from a good thing. In this case, both the relationship and the identity work may suffer.

The third possibility is that you simply do not care about what you are being told. Disclosure itself does not make a difference to a relationship; the relationship makes a difference to the value of disclosure. If you feel the relationship is enhanced by self-disclosure, it is. If you do not, then the relationship does not grow in intimacy.

Dialectic Tensions

Even when the relationship is one in which disclosure might be welcomed, it is not *always* welcomed. There are times when people want to provide personal information and want to receive personal information from others. And there are times when people do not want to provide or receive personal information. Baxter (2011) identifies a push-pull **dialectic tension** of relationships. These tensions occur whenever you are of two minds about something or feel a

dialectic tension: occurs whenever one is in two minds about something because one feels a simultaneous pull in two directions

simultaneous pull in two directions, and we will talk more about relational dialectics in Chapter 7.

Some communication scholars (e.g., Baxter, 2011; Baxter & Braithwaite, 2008) suggest that there simply is no singular core of identity but a dialogue between different "voices" in your head. For example, in relationships, you want to feel connected to someone else, but you do not want to give up all of your independence. You can see how you—and your identity—can grow by being in a relationship, but you can also see that this comes at a simultaneous cost to your identity, independence, and autonomy. Such a view significantly affects the way in which you visualize communication, not as a message sent by one inner core to another, but as something jointly created by two people.

The autonomy–connectedness dialectic is only one dialectic tension. Another is openness–closedness, where people feel social pressure to be open yet also want to retain control over private information. This tension leads to people sometimes giving out and sometimes holding back information about themselves and takes us fully back to self-disclosure. In any relationship, a person can feel willing to reveal information sometimes but crowded and guarded at other times. A personal relationship is not a simple experience any more than identity is. Each affects the other over time. Also, you may tell different versions of your identity to different audiences on different occasions.

How do you explain the fact that a person can experience different sides of self and hold different views simultaneously?

So, once again, recent research undermines the idea of a core self that is stable when *producing* communication and is steadily revealed during the growth of intimacy. The idea of the transaction of the self in communication is much more credible.

Identities and Boundaries

Rather than all information being available for disclosure, people negotiate boundaries of privacy with others (Petronio & Durham, 2008). These boundaries are determined in part by the relationship. One difference between friendship and mere acquaintance, for instance, is that you have stronger boundaries around your identity for acquaintances than you do for friends. Also, as Hess (2000) notes, you may simply not like some people. You do not want these people to know "personal stuff" and may actively limit what they find out. Even when it comes to close relationships, Caughlin and Afifi (2004) have shown that intimate partners prefer to completely avoid certain topics that may provoke a partner.

Petronio and Durham (2008) deal with the inconsistencies in the revelation of information by pointing to the importance of boundary management of the topics within different relational settings. People experience a tension between a desire for privacy and a demand for openness differently in different relationships. Couples make up their own rules for controlling the boundaries of privacy. So, for example, two people may define, between themselves, the nature of topics that they will mention in front of other people and what they will keep to themselves. A married couple may decide what topics to discuss in front of the children, for instance, and these

ETHICAL ISSUE

If you have a guilty secret and are getting into a deep romantic relationship with someone, should you tell him or her early on or later? Or should you not tell him or her at all?

topics may change as the children grow older. In other words, people show, employ, and work within different parts of their identity with different audiences at different times.

One of Petronio and Durham's (2008) key points is that the suitability of something for disclosure is itself affected by relational context and by agreement between the partners. There are no absolutes.

These researchers also draw attention to the ways in which a couple can decide how much to disclose. Amount, type, or subject of self-disclosure can be a topic for discussion (often called *metacommunication* or communication about communication). In contrast to Jourard's (1964, 1971) idea that there are absolute rules about self-disclosure of identity, Petronio (2002) demonstrated that it is a matter of personal preference, worked out explicitly between the partners in a relationship through communication.

The upshot of this discussion of self-disclosure questions identity as a straightforward, layered possession of your own inner being. Your self-disclosure and your identity are jointly owned by you and a partner. There is more to identity than just *having* or *revealing* one, then. The norms of appropriateness for reciprocity, the rules about amount of revealed information (especially negative information), show that there is a relational context for communication about identity.

Skills You Can Use: Transacting Identities Online

People develop impressions of others through social networking profiles. Consider what your profile says about you, and ask yourself whether your profile conveys the identity or identities that you desire. If not, think about what might be changed to help construct the desired identities. If your profile is working, think about how it can be further enhanced and if it will be the one you use five years from now. Look back over what you have read in this chapter that would help you to make decisions about these particular questions.

Narratives

Self-disclosure may be accomplished through story form, but we will discuss narratives as a separate way that people construct identities. People often use stories to tell others something about themselves and help shape a sense of who they are for others. In fact, people tell stories about themselves and other people all the time and pay special care to what they say, particularly for occasions like job interviews, sales pitches, and strategic communication of all sorts. You may have noticed that you adapt stories of your identity to a social context. You are influenced by both society/culture and the specific persons to whom you do the telling.

Stories We Tell

A report about your identity characterizes you by means of a memory or history in its narrative or a typical or an amusing instance that involves character (your identity), plot, motives, scenes, and other actors. Even when you reveal an inner self, this story organizes your identity in ways other people understand in terms of the rules that govern accounts, narratives, and other social reports. As Kellas (2008) has pointed out, narratives can be an *ontology* (how I came to be who I am), an *epistemology* (how I think about the world), an *individual construction,* or a *relational process,* such as when romantic partners tell the story about how they first met.

How is your sense of identity represented by connections to the past?

Origin Stories

Reports about an identity have a narrative structure that builds off a sense of origin and a sense of continuity. The self comes from somewhere and has roots—"I'm Hispanic," "I'm a true Southerner," "I'm a genuine Irish McMahan."

Identity comes in part from narratives of origin. These can be personal, cultural, or species ("What was my great-grandfather like?" "Where did I come from?" "Where did our culture come from?" "How did humans get started?"). A sense of origin leads, for most people, straight back to their family, the first little society that they ever experienced (Huisman, 2008). The family experience is the first influence on a person's sense of origin and identity. It gives the person a sense of connection to a larger network of others. Indeed, in African American cultures, "the family" can be seen as a whole *community* that goes beyond the direct blood ties that define family in other cultures. Your earliest memories give you a sense of origin as represented by your experiences in a family-like context.

Shaping the Stories

Stories about you must fit with what your societal audience believes to be coherent and acceptable. It is not just that you *have* a self but that you shape the *telling* of your identity in a way that your audience (culture, friends) will accept. When Bob from earlier in the chapter, a nontraditional student, a Purdue fan, or a fraternity/sorority member talks about achievement or activities, the story is probably told differently to friends, former coworkers, Indiana University fans, or the dean of students.

Transacting Identity and Other People

The shaping of stories to suit a particular audience highlights the importance of other people in the transaction of identities. In fact, we could get philosophical and consider, similar to whether a tree falling in the woods without anyone around makes any sound, whether someone attempting to construct an identity without anyone around is really constructing an identity. For example, is the Broadway musical fan mentioned previously creating an identity when humming along to show tunes alone in the car? Or does the development of identities require someone else being there?

There is actually no need to get too philosophical at this point. A more important consideration is identity construction that takes place because of other people, either because of their actions and communication or simply through interactions with them. In what follows, we will examine altercasting, treatment from other, and the performative self.

ETHICAL ISSUE

Consider situations in which imposing an identity onto someone might be considered unethical. Is it unethical to tell people that they are strong when attempting to get their assistance with lifting a heavy object? Is that situation unethical if you really do not believe they are strong? Is encouraging your classmates by telling them that they are smart and will do well on an upcoming exam unethical, if you really do not believe either to be true but are saying it to help?

Altercasting

We will begin with **altercasting**, which involves the work that someone's communication does to impose, support, or reject identities of others (Tracy, 2002). Altercasting refers to how language can give people an identity and then force them to live up to the description, whether positive or negative (Marwell & Schmitt, 1967). For example, you are altercasting when you say, "As a good friend, you will want to help me here" or "Only a fool would . . ." These label the listener as a certain kind of person (or not), by positioning the person to respond appropriately (as a friend or not as a fool). Even such small elements of communication transact your identity and the identities of those people around you.

Altercasting may also refer to the rejection of someone's identity. Just because someone attempts to create an identity does not mean that it will be accepted. It could just as easily be rejected by other people. You may know someone who attempts to come off as tough or dominant, but other people may reject this identity. Rather than trembling in this person's presence, people may make fun of this person or do things to intimidate this person.

On the other hand, altercasting may also refer to communication that accepts and supports the identity of someone. Perhaps people do accept that person's tough and dominant identity. In this case, their communication may support this tough and dominant identity by giving that person more space or not making eye contact with that person.

In all of these situations, the communication of other people is influencing the transaction of someone's identity. The construction of identity does not take place in isolation; rather, it depends in part on other people.

Self as Others Treat You

How people perceive themselves and their attempts to construct identities are influenced by the ways in which they are treated by others. Both directly and indirectly, your interactions and communication with other people shape your views of yourself.

Relationships connect through communication to the formation of your identity. If other people treat you with respect, you come to see yourself as respected, and self-respect becomes part of your identity. If your parents treated you like a child even after you had grown up, they may have drawn out from you some sense that you were still a child, which may have caused you to feel resentment. If you are intelligent and people treat you as interesting, you may come to see yourself as having a different value to other people than does someone who is not treated as intelligent. You get so used to the idea that it gets inside your "identity" and becomes part of who you are, but it originated from other people, not from you.

If you are tall, tough, and muscular (not short, bald, and carrying a Swiss Army knife), perhaps people habitually treat you with respect and caution. Over time, you get used to the idea, and identity is enacted and transacted in communication as a person who expects respect and a little caution from other people (Duck, 2011). Eventually, you will not have to act in a generally intimidating way in order to make people respectful. Your manner of communicating comes to reflect expected reactions to you. Although your identity begins in the way you are treated by other people, it eventually becomes transacted in communication.

altercasting: how language can impose a certain identity on people, and how language can support or reject the identity of another person

performative self: a self that is a creative performance based on the social demands and norms of a given situation

Performative Self

Another way that people influence identity construction is just by being there. They provide you with an audience for which to perform. Identity is not just *having* a symbolic sense of self but *doing* it in the presence of other people and doing it well in their eyes. Everyone *does* his or her identity for an audience, like an actor in a play. **Performative self** means that selves are creative performances based on the social demands and norms of a given situation. As we will now discuss, you try to present the right face to people you are with and do your identity differently in front and back regions.

Facework

Facework is part of what happens in everyday communication, and people have a sense of their own dignity. This gets transacted in everyday communication by polite protection of the person's "face."

This idea is about the performance of one's identity in public, the presentation of the self to people in a way that is intended to make the self look good. Erving Goffman (1959) indicated the way in which momentary social forces affect identity portrayal. Goffman was interested in how identity is performed in everyday life so that people manage their image to make everyone "look good" (Cupach & Metts, 1994). The concept of "looking good" of course means "looking good *to other people*." It is therefore essentially a relational concept.

It takes you one step closer to looking at the interpersonal interaction that occurs on the ground every day. Rather than looking at society in an abstract way, Goffman (1959) focused on what you actually *do* in interactions. In part, your portrayal of yourself is shaped by the social needs at the time, the social situation, the social frame, and the circumstances surrounding your performance.

By the way...

Physical Attractiveness

Physically attractive people often act confidently because they are aware of the fact that other people find them attractive. On the other hand, unattractive people have learned that they cannot rely on their looks to make a good impression. They need other ways of impressing other people (e.g., by developing a great sense of humor; Berscheid & Reis, 1998). In a phrase, you come to see yourself as others see you.

QUESTIONS TO CONSIDER

1. To what extent do you find that this research confirms your own experiences in life?
2. Do you think this applies to other such characteristics as intelligence and talent?

Front and Back Regions

Goffman (1959) differentiated a **front region** and **back region** to social performance: The front region/front stage is *not a place* but *an occasion* where your professional, proper self is performed. For example, a server is all smiles and civility in the front stage of the restaurant when talking to customers. This behavior might be different from how he or she performs in the back region/backstage (say, the restaurant kitchen) when talking with the cooks or other servers and making jokes about the customers or about being disrespectful to them. But again, the back region is not just a place: If all servers are standing around in the restaurant before the customers come in and they are just chatting informally among themselves, the instant the first customer comes through the door, their demeanor will change to "professional," and they will switch to a front-region performance.

That means the performance of your identity is sprung into action not by your own free wishes but by social cues that this is the time to perform your "self" in that way. An identity is a performance. It shows how a person makes sense of the world not just alone but within a context provided by others.

Any identity connects to other identities. You can be friendly when you are with your friends, but you are expected to be professional when on the job and to do student identity when in class. So is this what allows Bob from earlier in the chapter to be "two people," one at work and one in the social community?

Individuals inevitably draw on knowledge shared in any community, so any person draws on information that is both personal and communal. If you change from thinking of identity as about "self as character" and instead see it as "self as performer," you also must consider the importance of changes in performance to suit different audiences and situations.

front region: a frame where a social interaction is regarded as under public scrutiny, so people have to be on their best behavior or acting out their professional roles or intended "face" (contrast with *back* region)

back region: a frame where a social interaction is regarded as not under public scrutiny, so people do not have to present their public face (contrast with *front region*)

Focus Questions Revisited

Does it make sense that someone has a true core self?

Like an urban myth, this way of looking at identity, which has no basis in research and has been abandoned by the theorists who proposed it, still feels like it *ought* to be right and is repeated unscientifically in many communication textbooks. Perhaps it is something we would like to believe, but as shown during the chapter it is basically a worthless idea, even when placed up against common sense.

How do perceptions influence identities?

The transaction of identities is guided in part through perceptions of audiences and situations. Factors such as how a person views the world, organizes what is seen, and evaluates information will influence symbolic activity and, accordingly, the construction of identities.

What does it mean to say that identities are symbolic constructions?

Identities can be understood as being transacted symbolically through communication with others. Who we understand ourselves to be and how we want others to perceive us at a given moment is established through our use of symbols. Essentially, our multiple identities are created and performed though verbal and nonverbal communication.

What is the difference between self-description and self-disclosure?

Self-description usually involves information about self that is obvious to others through appearance and behavior. Self-disclosure involves the revelation of information that people could not know unless a person makes it known to them.

What is the role of narratives in the construction of identities?

People often use stories to tell others something about themselves and help shape a sense of who they are for others. People adapt stories of their identity to a social context. They are influenced by both society/culture and the specific persons to whom they do the telling.

How do other people influence identity construction?

Identity construction takes place because of other people, either because of their actions and communication or simply through interactions with them. Such influence involves altercasting, treatment from other, and the performative self.

Key Concepts

altercasting 64
attitude of reflection 58
back region 65
dialectic tension 60
front region 65
identity 49
perception 51
performative self 64
personal constructs 55
schemata 55
selective exposure 55
self-description 59
self-disclosure 59
symbolic interactionism 58
symbolic self 57

Questions to Ask Your Friends

1. Discuss with your friends or classmates the most embarrassing moment that you feel comfortable talking about, and try to find out what about the experience threatened your identity. What identity were you projecting at the time, and what went wrong with the performance?

2. Have your friends look at how advertisers sell the image of particular cars in terms of what they will make the owner look like to other people; the advertisers recognize that identity is tied up in material possessions. Discuss with your friends the following topics: How is your identity affected by your preferences in music, the Web, fashion magazines, resources, or wealth?

3. Get a group of friends together and ask them each to write down what sort of vegetable, fish, dessert, book, piece of furniture, style of music, meal, car, game, or building best represents their identity. Read the responses out loud and have everyone guess which person is described.

Media Connections

1. Watch the movie *Sideways* (Payne, 2004) and fast-forward to the veranda scene during which Miles talks to Maya about his preference for wine and it becomes apparent that he is using wine as a metaphor about himself. He projects his identity through his knowledge about the subtleties of wines. Basically he uses it to describe himself, and his hope is that Maya will learn to understand him.

   Maya: You know, can I ask you a personal question, Miles?
   Miles: Sure.
   Maya: Why are you so into Pinot?
   Miles: [laughs softly]
   Maya: I mean, it's like a thing with you.
   Miles: [continues laughing softly] Uh, I don't know, I don't know. Um, it's a hard grape to grow, as you know. Right? It's, uh, it's thin-skinned, temperamental, ripens early. It's, you know, it's not a survivor like Cabernet, which can just grow anywhere and, uh, thrive even when it's neglected. No, Pinot needs constant care and attention. You know? And in fact it can only grow in these really specific, little, tucked away corners of the world. And, and only the most patient and nurturing of growers can do it, really. Only somebody who really takes the time to understand Pinot's potential can then coax it into its fullest expression. Then, I mean, oh its flavors, they're just the most haunting and brilliant and thrilling and subtle and . . . ancient on the planet.

2. Collect examples that demonstrate how media representations of ideal selves (especially demands on women to be a particular kind of shape, but try to be more imaginative than just these images) are constantly thrown in our path.

3. How do television talk shows encourage us to be open, honest, and real? Do these programs teach us anything about the "right" ways to be ourselves?

Student Study Site

SAGE edge™

Sharpen your skills with SAGE edge at edge.sagepub.com/duckciel2e

SAGE edge for students provides a personalized approach to help you accomplish your coursework goals in an easy-to-use learning environment.

Chapter Outline

How Is Verbal Communication Symbolic?

Verbal Communication Involves Meaning
- Denotative and Connotative Meanings
- Words and Values

Verbal Communication Is Relational
- Verbal Communication Transacts Relationships
- Relationships Regulate Verbal Communication
- Relationships and Shared Meanings

Verbal Communication Is Cultural
- Verbal Communication Transacts Cultures
- Cultures Regulate Verbal Communication
- Cultural Ways of Talking

Verbal Communication and Frames
- Recognizing Frames
- Ways of Speaking
- Accommodation: Adjusting Relational Frames

Verbal Communication Is Presentational
- Telling Stories
- Kenneth Burke's Pentad

Functions of Verbal Communication
- Influencing Others: Facework and Politeness

Relationships and Everyday Talk
- Instrumental Function
- Indexical Function
- Essential Function

Focus Questions Revisited

Key Concepts

Questions to Ask Your Friends

Media Connections

04 Verbal Communication

A man walked into a bar. A second man walked into a bar. A third one didn't . . . because he ducked. You know the word *bar,* and you most likely know that in some cultures jokes and stories often start with the phrase "A man walked into a bar." Such cultural knowledge frames expectations about the story being told. A *frame,* you recall from Chapter 1, is a context that influences the interpretation of communication. However, the word *bar* has different meanings. If you were faintly amused by the opening sentences here, it is partly because the word is used in the first sentence differently than you expected on the basis of the frame of the story. The punch line works only because you are misled—twice—into thinking of a different kind of "bar." Familiarity with the story's cultural form frames your expectations in a way that pulls the last sentence right out from under you. Language has a grammatical structure, but when used conversationally, it uses cultural and relational assumptions.

Verbal communication involves the *use* of language. Notice that the word *use* is emphasized in this definition. When discussing verbal communication, communication scholars do not simply look at language but rather explore the ways in which it is used when interacting with others. *Language* is just a collection of symbols that can be arranged in a particular order according to a particular grammar. Remember, though, that symbols themselves have no meaning. Words, like all symbols, are given meaning when they are put into use. Within this chapter, we explore the ways in which language is put into use.

This chapter is structured somewhat differently than others within this book. In exploring verbal communication, we will essentially be following the characteristics of communication discussed in Chapter 1. Accordingly, we will talk about how verbal communication is symbolic, involves meaning, is relational, is cultural, involves frames, is presentational, and is transactive. Doing so will reinforce those characteristics for when they are not explicitly addressed but still involved when discussing other types of communication. The application of those characteristics when discussing verbal communication will also provide a clear understanding of verbal communication in everyday life.

FOCUS QUESTIONS

1. How is verbal communication symbolic?
2. How does verbal communication involve meaning?
3. How is verbal communication relational?
4. How is verbal communication cultural?
5. What frames your understanding of verbal communication?
6. What is the presentational nature of verbal communication?
7. What are the functions of verbal communication?

How Is Verbal Communication Symbolic?

The answer to the opening question is pretty obvious if you have already read the introductory paragraphs of this chapter. If you have not read them, why are you starting here? Go read them, and we will wait. . . . All right, the answer is: Verbal communication involves the use of language, which is made up of symbols.

verbal communication: the use of language

Why might this pairing of street signs be amusing to a citizen in the United States, and what is taken for granted by those who understand the joke?

Symbols are arbitrary representations of something else, which means there is no direct connection between a symbol and what it represents. When it comes to the word *chair,* used as an earlier example of symbols, there is no natural connection between an object on which you sit and the five letters *r, h, c, a,* and *i* arranged in the order *c, h, a, i, r*. That symbol is just used to represent that object.

As a result of the arbitrary nature of symbols, the meanings applied to words are somewhat ambiguous. There is often some degree of agreement on the meanings that should be applied to words, but there is never complete agreement on the meaning associated with any word, even the most basic and common words. Consider the brother and sister who asked their parents if they could keep in the family's tiny apartment the stray dog they had found. Agreeing without actually seeing the dog, the parents expected to find a small dog only to find an extremely large Great Dane. The meaning the parents applied to the symbol *dog* did not fully correspond with the meaning the children intended when using that symbol.

We will talk more about meaning in the next section, but for now notice the use of *applied* in the last paragraph. It is not that words *have* meanings but that meanings *are applied to* words. Symbols have no inherent meaning. They are given meaning along with value and power when they are used during interactions among people. This fact does not mean that studying language is meaningless—many of our linguist friends would certainly take issue with that notion. However, as much as your authors enjoy learning new words and studying the development of languages, we find the actual use of words more interesting. It is through the actual use of language that meanings develop. Moreover, it is through the use of language, along with other symbolic activity, that relationships, identities, cultures, and realities are transacted. Now that is really fascinating!

By the way...

Taa

Of the thousands of languages worldwide, the most complicated may be Taa, which is primarily spoken in Botswana. It has 112 distinct sounds, more than any other language. (For comparison, English has around 45 sounds, depending on the dialect.) Making Taa particularly complicated, the majority of the words start with one of 83 sorts of clicks.

QUESTIONS TO CONSIDER

1. If you speak more than one language, what does that tell you about the arbitrary nature of symbols?
2. If you only speak one language, do you think this makes the arbitrary nature of symbols more difficult to grasp?

Verbal Communication Involves Meaning

So, we know that verbal communication is symbolic and that meanings are established through its use. And, later in this chapter, we explore how people go about assigning meanings using a communication frame. Before tackling that issue, though, we need to examine what *meaning* actually means. Words are given the following two types of meaning:

denotative and connotative. Taking things one step further, words are also given value based on the meanings applied.

What factors might be influencing the conversation of these two people?

Denotative and Connotative Meanings

Words, as with all symbols, can be given multiple meanings depending on how they are used and the circumstances surrounding their use (Ogden & Richards, 1946). **Polysemy** is the term used to recognize that there can be multiple meanings given to the same word. If all symbols can have several different meanings, then each time you speak or hear a word, you must determine which meaning applies.

Denotative meaning is the general meaning of a word. It is the meaning or meanings appearing next to each word in the dictionary. (*Dictionary* and *denotative* both obviously start with the same letter, if you need help remembering the term on an examination.) If you point at a cat and say, "Cat," everyone will know that the sound denotes the object that is furry and whiskered and currently sleeping on your keyboard as you read this book.

Denoting the same object or idea by the same words is an obviously fundamental requirement for communicating. Conversation works only when people can assume that they share the world by using the same words to denote items. Remember, there is never complete agreement by individuals on the meanings of any word, but there is often at least some overlap of meanings. The polysemic nature of words can make determining intended meaning a challenging task, though.

DISCIPLINARY **DEBATE**

Language and Perception

Developed from the writings of Edward Sapir and Benjamin Whorf (Sapir, 1949; Whorf, 1956), the **Sapir-Whorf hypothesis** proposes that "you think what you can say." In other words, the names that make verbal distinctions also help you make conceptual distinctions rather than the other way around. Essentially, the language you speak impacts how you view the world. Other scholars oppose this notion of linguistic relativism and might ask the first question as follows.

QUESTIONS TO CONSIDER

1. English speakers have a word for the front of the hand (*palm*), but no single word for the back. According to the Sapir-Whorf hypothesis, does this mean that English speakers should not be able to tell the difference?
2. To what extent do you believe language shapes how people view the world?

Connotative meaning refers to the overtones and implications associated with a word or an object. For example, cats are seen as independent, cuddly, hunters, companions, irritations, allergens, stalkers, stealthy, and incredibly lucky both in landing on their feet all the time and in having nine lives. If you talk about a friend as a "pussycat," you are most likely referring to the connotative meaning and implying that he is soft and cuddly and perhaps stealthy, companionable, and lucky. You are unlikely to be referring to the denotative meaning and warning people that he or she is actually, secretly a cat and has fur and sleeps on keyboards.

Since connoting involves the implications of a word, some words carry baggage that can elicit an emotional response. Consider, for instance, the different emotions stirred up by the words *patriot* and *traitor*. The first connotes many good feelings of loyalty, duty, and faithfulness. The second connotes bad qualities like deceit, two-facedness, untrustworthiness, and disloyalty. These connotations are

polysemy: the fact that multiple meanings can be associated with a given word or symbol rather than just one unambiguous meaning

denotative meaning: the identification of something by pointing it out ("that is a cat")

Sapir-Whorf hypothesis: the idea that it is the names of objects and ideas that make verbal distinctions and help you make conceptual distinctions rather than the other way around

connotative meaning: the overtones, implications, or additional meanings associated with a word or an object

By the way...

Hello, Officer Fife

Media references are often used in conversations because of associated connotative meanings (McMahan, 2004). For instance, a police officer might be called "Barney Fife" or "Chief Wiggum," characters from *The Andy Griffith Show* and *The Simpsons*, respectfully, to highlight cowardice or ineffectiveness.

QUESTIONS TO CONSIDER

1. Think about some of the conversations you have recently had during which media references were used. Why do you suppose they are effective when used in conversations?
2. Do you use media references more with some people than with other people?

extra layers of meaning atop the denotation of a person as one kind of citizen or the other.

Words carry strong and varying connotations in particular cultures (Jiqun, 2012) and within particular relationships. As a result, your ability to understand someone improves as you know more about the associations he or she makes to certain words, either culturally or personally.

Words and Values

As a result of their denotative and connotative meanings, words are generally given particular values in a society. Like meanings the values associated with words have developed over time and are reinforced and socially constructed. Consider the characteristics of values encoded through words in Table 4.1.

God Terms and Devil Terms

Recognizing that words and all symbols are given value within societies, communication philosopher Kenneth Burke (1966) made a distinction between God terms and Devil terms. **God terms** are powerful terms that are viewed positively in a society. **Devil terms** are equally powerful terms that are viewed negatively in a society. In the United States, such a term as *freedom* may be considered a God term, while such a term as *al-Qaeda* may be considered a Devil term. (See Table 4.2 for some other examples.) However, God and Devil terms are not absolutes for everyone in the same society. Depending on your political point of view, for example, such words as *Bush* or *Clinton* or *Obama* may be one or the other. Furthermore, societal views of God or Devil terms may change with the passing of time. Within the United States, for example, *democracy* has been viewed as both (Engels, 2011).

Table 4.1 Values Encoded Through Words

Values encoded through words can be positive or negative.
Communication studies would naturally be positive, while *terrorism* would likely be negative.

Values encoded through words can be shared by individuals.
If you tell your instructor, "I deserved a B on this paper, but you gave me a C+," both you and the instructor recognize that a B is "better than" a C+ in the framework of meaning related to grades.

Values encoded through words can differ among people.
People may react differently to the words *Republican, Democrat, conservative, liberal, capitalism,* and *socialism.*

Values encoded through words can change over time.
The word *nice* generally has a positive association now. However, it was originally used when referring to someone as ignorant, having been derived from the Latin word for ignorant, *nescius.*

God terms: powerfully evocative terms that are viewed positively in a society (contrast with *Devil terms*)

Devil terms: powerfully evocative terms viewed negatively in a society (contrast with *God terms*)

Table 4.2 God and Devil Terms

God terms in the United States	Liberty, Justice, Equality, American Dream
Devil terms in the United States	Communism, Torture, Prejudice, King George III

God and Devil terms also exist in personal relationships. For instance, one partner may know what topics should not be mentioned around the other partner—his or her Devil terms. On the other hand, certain terms might be so unquestionably revered by a partner that their use can always bring about a positive reaction. Consider how a society's God and Devil terms are also reinforced through relationships. Sometimes a partner may act on behalf of society by saying, "Oh! You shouldn't say such things!" In such a statement, he or she is reinforcing, and reminding the other person of, the norms of society and its God and Devil terms.

Make your case

God Term or Devil Term?

People can assign different values to any particular word. What is a God term to one person may be a Devil term to another.

QUESTIONS TO CONSIDER

1. Which of the words below would you consider God terms, and why?
2. Which would you consider Devil terms, and why?

Abortion	Facebook
Banker	Natural
C (course grade)	Politician
Cigarettes	Raw Food
Exercise	Twitter

Verbal Communication Is Relational

Verbal communication is also relational. Accordingly, verbal communication influences relationships, and relationships influence verbal communication. Whenever you communicate verbally, a particular relationship is presumed with another person, the members of a group, or an audience. Another way of thinking about this is that when you are verbally communicating, you are also relating.

Verbal Communication Transacts Relationships

As we will maintain later in the chapter and again on the chapter dedicated to personal relationships, it is through verbal communication and other symbolic activity that relationships are developed and maintained. They are symbolic creations, literally talked into existence. That statement may be difficult to wrap your head around at this point, but it will become clearer after we cover that idea later on.

Relationships Regulate Verbal Communication

Relationships influence the meanings that are given to words and the words that are actually used. As mentioned in Chapter 1, the words "I love you" have different meanings attached depending on the relationship in which they are spoken. Saying those words to a romantic partner would mean something different than saying those words to a friend. Moreover, relationships influence what words are uttered in the first place. Regardless of great customer service, you would not expect a checkout person at a grocery store to say that to you as a customer.

Here as well, we see relationships being created through verbal communication. The very fact that you would or would not say something reinforces the existence of a particular relationship! With friends, for example, we draw on words differently than we do in work relationships, family relationships, and school relationships. Specific relationships are also reinforced through the meanings and intentions we assign to the words of others. Kirkpatrick, Duck, and Foley (2006) noted that enemies do not trust each other to mean what they say, each suspecting the other's words to be a lie or a misdirection.

COMMUNICATION + YOU

Talking With Your Friends

You and your friends probably have several examples of shorthand words and phrases for reminding one another of events, feelings, or people who populate your relational history. You may also have special nicknames for people known only to you and your partner or close friends.

QUESTIONS TO CONSIDER

1. What are some examples of these words, phrases, and names, and what do they tell you about your relationships?
2. Have you ever been the "out-of-towner" in a group of friends, where you did not understand shorthand words or phrases and needed them to be explained to you?

Relationships and Shared Meanings

We can take the relational nature of verbal communication a bit deeper, by looking at the creation and recognition of shared meanings. The more personal your relationship is with someone, the better you can understand his or her intentions and meanings. Part of becoming closer to other people is learning how they tick—an informal way of saying that you understand their worlds of meaning. When you know people better, you also know better than strangers what they mean when they make certain comments.

Relationships are transacted in part through shared meanings and patterns of communication. In other words, the understandings shared by you and a friend represent not only common understanding but also your relationship. No one else shares the exact understandings, common history, experiences, knowledge of the same people, or assumptions that you take for granted in that relationship. When you talk to people, you use words that refer to your shared history and common understandings that represent your relationship. Relationships presume common, shared knowledge.

Think for a minute about what happens when a friend from out of town comes to visit, and you go out with your in-town friends. You probably notice that the conversation is a bit more awkward. You are required to do more explaining. For example, instead of saying, "Landan, how was the hot date?" and waiting for an answer, you must throw in a conversational bracket that helps your friend from out of town understand the question. You may say, "Landan, how was the hot date?" and follow it with an aside comment to the out-of-towner ("Landan has this hot new love interest he has a *real* crush on, and they finally went out last night").

Conversational Hypertext

Talk among people who share a personal relationship is characterized by a great deal of conversational hypertext (Duck, 2002). The term **conversational hypertext** refers to coded messages within conversation that an informed listener will effortlessly understand.

conversational hypertext: coded messages within conversation that an informed listener will effortlessly understand

You know what hypertext is from your use of the Internet, and how you talk to people works the same way. In conversation, people often use a word that suggests more about a topic and would therefore show up on a computer screen in blue, pointing you to a hyperlink. For example, you might say, "I was reading Duck and McMahan, and I learned that there are many more extra messages that friends pick up in talk than I had realized before." This sentence makes perfect sense to somebody who knows what a "Duck and McMahan" is, but others may not understand. On a computer, they would use their mouse to find out more by clicking on Duck and McMahan and being taken to edge.sagepub.com/duckciel2e. In a conversation, they would "click" on the hypertext by asking a direct question: "What's a Duck and McMahan?"

In relationships, shared meanings and overlaps of perceptions make communication special and closer. You and your friends talk in coded, hypertextual language all the time and probably do not even recognize when you are doing it, because it seems so natural in your personal relationship. Only when you encounter someone who does not understand the code, such as the out-of-town friend in the example above, do you probably recognize the hypertext and realize that it needs to be unpacked, expanded, or addressed directly for the out-of-towner.

By the way...

Speaking and Social Class

Somewhat connected to our discussion here, Basil Bernstein (1971) made a distinction between restricted codes and elaborated codes. **Restricted code** leaves a great deal unsaid, with the assumption being that other people will understand because of shared connections and accompanying shared knowledge. **Elaborated code** leaves very little unsaid, with the assumption being that people would not be able to understand otherwise. Examining class differences and education, Bernstein maintained working-class children struggled because they communicated in a restricted code, while middle-class children succeeded because they were able to communicate using both codes.

QUESTIONS TO CONSIDER

1. Do you believe class distinctions of this sort exist today?
2. If so, are they still transacted in part through restricted and elaborated codes?

Verbal Communication Is Cultural

Verbal communication is also cultural, much in the way that it is relational. Accordingly, verbal communication influences culture, and culture influences verbal communication. Whenever you communicate verbally, cultural assumptions are presumed involving appropriateness and meanings within a given society or group.

When discussing culture, we are not just talking about such nation-states as the United States and China. Also included in discussions of culture are any groups of people who share distinct meanings and styles of speaking. Embedded within these distinct meanings and styles of communication are the values and beliefs of those cultural groups.

Multiple cultural groups exist within larger nation-states, and as a result you likely belong to many of them. They might include cultural groups involving your life on campus, at work, and within your community.

Verbal Communication Transacts Cultures

It is through verbal communication and other symbolic activity in which cultures are developed and maintained. Like relationships, cultures are symbolic creations. Cultural groups are distinct and brought into being because of the way in which their members communicate. We talk more about this idea in Chapter 12, but in the meantime, consider the fundamental role that relationships play in this process. It is through our relationships that we come to understand cultural ways of communicating. You have learned culturally appropriate ways of talking through interactions with family, friends, neighbors, classmates, coworkers, and even the person at a fast-food drive-through.

restricted code: a way of speaking that emphasizes authority and adopts certain community/cultural orientations as indisputable facts (contrast with *elaborated code*)

elaborated code: speech that emphasizes the reasoning behind a command; uses speech and language more as a way for people to differentiate the uniqueness of their own personalities and ideas and to express their own individuality, purposes, attitudes, and beliefs than as a way to reinforce collectivity or commonality of outlook (contrast with *restricted code*)

Cultures Regulate Verbal Communication

Cultures influence the meanings that are given to words and the words that are actually used. Some cultural groups curse more than others, for instance. You are so good at communicating culturally and are so skilled at moving seamlessly in and out of various groups that you may not even recognize that you are doing it. Aware or not, you communicate in unique ways when among members of different cultural groups because of the meaning systems and norms of those groups.

ETHICAL ISSUE

Note how sexist, racist, and heteronormative language is both relational and cultural and always places one group of people in an inferior position relative to another group of people. Is it ever ethical to use this kind of language?

For instance, you would likely talk in distinct ways when interacting within on-campus culture and work culture. Here, like relationships, cultures are being created through verbal communication, since the fact that you would or would not say something reinforces those cultures.

Cultural Ways of Talking

To understand the nuances involved in talking culturally, we can examine categories of cultural talk. These styles of cultural talk are usually applied to nation-states, and we take issue with such broad characterizations in Chapter 12, but they will illustrate our point here. These styles of talk have unique meaning systems, values, and styles. Table 4.3 provides definitions and examples of talk attempting to get someone to finish a project at work.

Table 4.3 Cultural Styles of Talk

Feminine and Masculine

Feminine talk is nurturing, harmonious, and compromising (Arrindell et al., 2013).

I hope you can finish this project soon and am certain you will do a good job. Let me know if you need any additional assistance.

Masculine talk is tough, aggressive, and competitive (Arrindell et al., 2013).

If you cannot complete this project now, I will replace you with someone who can.

High-Context and Low-Context

High-context talk relies heavily on the context in which it takes place. Words are used sparingly with a great deal left unsaid. Relationships among people are extremely important (Samovar, Porter, & McDaniel, 2010). In the following example, the cultural implications of friendship (which would probably entail prompt work) are used to get the person to complete the project.

It is good to have a friend working on this project.

Low-context talk is straightforward, and the message itself says everything. Relationships are separated from the message as much as possible (Samovar et al. 2010).

This project needs to be completed soon, because it is behind schedule and completing it after the deadline will be harmful for you, me, and everyone in this company.

Collectivist and Individualist

Collectivist talk stresses group benefit and harmony rather than personal needs and advancement (Du & King, 2013; Gudykunst, 2000; Morsbach, 2004).

Completing this project soon will benefit the team a great deal.

Individualist talk stresses individual needs and achievement (Du & King, 2013; Gudykunst, 2000; Morsbach, 2004).

Completing this project soon would look good on your yearly evaluation.

feminine talk: that which is characterized as nurturing, harmonious, and compromising (contrast with *masculine talk*)

masculine talk : that which is characterized as tough, aggressive, and competitive (contrast with *feminine talk*)

high-context talk: that which is characterized as relying on the context in which it takes place, with words used sparingly and the relationship shared by interactants being extremely important (contrast with *low-context talk*)

low-context talk: that which is characterized as straightforward, with the message speaking for itself and relationship separated from the message as much as possible (contrast with *high-context talk*)

collectivist talk: that which is characterized as stressing group benefit and harmony rather than personal needs and advancement (contrast with *individualist* talk)

individualist talk: that which is characterized as stressing individual needs and achievement (contrast with *collectivist talk*)

Verbal Communication and Frames

Frames assist people in making sense of communication by drawing attention to how they should be communicating, how they might expect others to communicate, and how they should assign meanings to symbols being used. Conversational frames are used to make sense of and assign meaning to verbal communication.

You are better able to communicate with another person when both of you recognize that frames are shared. Sometimes these frames are assumed. At other times, frames are signaled by means of various relational, cultural, and personal cues. For example, saying "Let's not be so formal" is a direct way of saying that you are in the "friendly frame." Saying "Take a seat and make yourself comfortable" is more indirect but has the same effect.

The woman on the left is telling her friends how the chaos around her house prevents her from ever having any time to herself. The friend in the center is providing assurances that her concerns are warranted and that she is a valuable person. The friend on the right is getting ready to tell her to stop complaining and get over herself. Which cultural styles of talk are these friends demonstrating?

Of course, difficulties may arise if people are using different frames of understanding. Different frames may be used unknowingly. Different frames could be used purposefully, especially if people do not perceive the situation or their relationships in the same way.

Recognizing Frames

A number of types of conversational frames may be applied when interacting with others. As just discussed in the preceding sections, relationships and cultures influence how verbal communication is used and what it means. Accordingly, your understanding of relationships and cultures enables you to use them as frames when assigning meaning to verbal communication. The physical location can also be used when assigning meaning, such as when you engage in "restaurant talk" rather than "classroom talk" by asking your instructor a question about course content rather than requesting that your instructor bring you a tasty beverage.

Ways of Speaking

In everyday communication, the form of language selected to express thoughts and emotions carries important relational messages. The form of language used also enables people to properly frame an interaction. When talking with friends, your language is probably informal and simple. When talking with your instructor or with a boss, your language is probably formal and bit more complex.

Forms of language can generally be categorized as either *high code* or *low code* (Giles, Taylor, & Bourhis, 1973). **High code** is a formal, grammatical, and very correct way of talking. **Low code** is an informal and often ungrammatical way of talking. Consider the difference between saying "My state of famishment is of such a proportion that I would gladly consume the complete corporeality of a member of the species *Equus caballus przewalskii*" and "I'm so hungry I could eat a horse." The first statement is written in high code, and the second is written in low code.

When interacting with someone in a close relationship and when feeling relaxed, people are more likely to use low code. High code is more likely to be used when speaking to someone with whom a person is unfamiliar or someone with greater power or higher social rank. It is also more likely to be used when a person is uncomfortable or views the interaction as formal. Knowing these differences in codes will enable you to understand the frames that you or others may be using when communicating and how the participants and the situation are being perceived.

high code: a formal, grammatical, and very correct—often "official"—way of talking

low code: an informal and often ungrammatical way of talking

By the way...

Git 'er done!

Linguists like Ferdinand de Saussure (Komatsu, 1993) draw a distinction between *langue* (pronounced "longg") and *parole* (pronounced "pa-rull"). **Langue** is the formal grammatical structure of language that you read about in books on grammar. **Parole** is how people actually use language, with informal and ungrammatical phrases that carry meaning all the same. "Git 'er done!" is an example of parole but would earn you bad grades in an English grammar course (langue).

QUESTIONS TO CONSIDER

1. Why do you suppose people write one way and speak to people a different way?
2. Why do English courses not teach both ways?

langue: the formal grammatical structure of language (contrast with *parole*)

parole: how people actually use language: where they often speak using informal and ungrammatical language structure that carries meaning to us all the same (contrast with *langue*)

accommodation: when people change their accent, their rate of speech, and even the words they use to indicate a relational connection with the person to whom they are talking

convergence: a person moves toward the style of talk used by the other speaker (contrast with *divergence*)

divergence: a person moves away from another's style of speech to make a relational point, such as establishing dislike or superiority (contrast with *convergence*)

Accommodation: Adjusting Relational Frames

Frames can be adjusted during an interaction. People choose particular ways of interacting and can change them just the same, adjusting the interaction to fit another person or as a result of changes in feelings or in the relationship that occurs during the course of the interaction.

Giles and his colleagues (Giles, Linz, Bonilla, & Gomez, 2012; Giles, Taylor, & Bourhis, 1973) have shown that people will change the words they use as well as nonverbal communication (discussed in the next chapter) to indicate a relational connection with the person to whom they are talking. They called this process **accommodation** and identified two types: convergence and divergence.

In **convergence**, a person moves toward the style of talk used by the other speaker. For example, an adult converges when he or she uses baby talk to communicate with a child, or a brownnosing employee converges when he or she uses the boss's company lingo style of talk.

In **divergence**, a person moves away from another's style of speech to make a relational point, such as establishing dislike or superiority. A good example is how computer geeks and car mechanics insist on using a lot of technical language with customers, instead of giving simple explanations that the nonexpert could understand. This form of divergence keeps the customer in a lower relational place.

Verbal Communication Is Presentational

Verbal communication, as with all symbolic activity, can be both representational and presentational. It is representational in that it can be used to name things and convey information. Accordingly, the word *cat* is used to represent that animal to others. You do not have to draw a picture, bring a live cat, or act out its behaviors on your hands and knees. If you think about it, even though it is generally taken for granted, the representational nature of verbal communication and the development of symbol using by humans is incredible.

Perhaps less obvious but equally powerful is the presentational nature of verbal communication. The use of verbal communication also provides information about the perspective and worldview of the person sending a message. Your selection of words when describing a scene, persuading someone, discussing another person, or simply talking about the weather is meaningful and conveys your worldview to others. All verbal communication is presentational, but when people tell stories and provide accounts, its presentational nature is particularly recognizable.

Telling Stories

Much of everyday life is spent telling stories about yourself and other people. Suggesting that storytelling is one of the most important human tendencies, Fisher (1985) coined the term *Homo narrans* (Latin for "the person as a storyteller or narrator").

A **narrative** is any organized story, report, or prepared talk that has a plot, an argument, or a theme, or can be interpreted as having one. The term *narrative* covers what is involved when you say *what* people are doing and *why* they are doing it. This applies whether talk includes funny events, tragic events, significant emotional experiences, relational stories (meeting new people, falling in love, arguing, making up, and breaking up), or describing one's day.

Narratives are particularly presentational, because speakers do not just relate facts but also arrange the story in a way that provides their perspective. Quite often, stories are told in a way that makes the speaker appear favorable.

People tell stories every day, whether about the crazy commute that made them late to work or a funny interaction with a bank teller. How do you know that one of the people in this photo is telling a story, and what role does storytelling seem to play in their relationship?

Giving Accounts

Although narratives appear on the surface just to report (represent) events, they frequently account for (present) the behaviors. **Accounts** are forms of communication that offer *justifications* ("I was so mad"), *excuses* ("I was really tired"), *exonerations* ("It wasn't my fault"), *explanations* ("And that's how we fell in love"), *accusations* ("But he started it"), and *apologies* ("I'm an idiot"). Accounts "go beyond the facts."

Giving an account involves telling a story that justifies, blames someone for, or calls for someone to account for what happened (Scott & Lyman, 1968). The facts reported in accounts are actually quite presentational. Indeed, the description of something contains spin that explains the facts being reported. For example, your friend may say, "I just failed a math test. It was way too hard." Both statements appear to be facts. One is actually an explanation for why your friend failed (the test was too hard). It is also a presentational account—a personal view about the reason for the failure (the test was too hard).

Listen with fresh ears to everyday conversation, and you will start to hear accounts much more often. Think about their structure and what it tells you about the relationship shared by the person providing the account and the person receiving the account. For example, you do not bother to justify yourself to people whose opinions you do not care about. Also, you would not justify yourself to an enemy in the same way you would to a friend. You expect the friend to know more about your background and to cut you some slack. Relationships impact whether accounts are given and how they are structured.

ETHICAL ISSUE

Should the stories you tell always be true? Why or why not?

Kenneth Burke's Pentad

The presentational nature of verbal communication is a fundamental component of everyday communication and personal relationships. Therefore, it stands to reason that being able to analyze the presentational aspects of communication and narratives you encounter would be beneficial.

Kenneth Burke's **pentad** is composed of five elements that explain the motivation of symbolic action. Essentially, Burke was interested in determining the reasons why people used the words that they did. Burke correctly recognized that the use of words results in meanings beyond their denotative meanings or connotative meanings. The very act of using words is meaningful. The key to fully understanding communication is understanding the motives of the people communicating. The selection of words provides clues to understanding motives and provides insight into the perceptions of symbols used.

narrative: any organized story, report, or talk that has a plot, an argument, or a theme and in which speakers both relate facts and arrange the story in a way that provides an account, an explanation, or a conclusion

accounts: forms of communication that go beyond the facts and offer justifications, excuses, exonerations, explanations, or accusations

pentad: five components of narratives that explain the motivation of symbolic action

By the way...

Would You Believe Six Fingers?

After originally developing the pentad, Kenneth Burke (1969) would sometimes include a sixth element: *attitude.* Describing this term, he noted that building something with a hammer would involve an instrument, or *agency.* Building something with diligence would involve an *attitude.* So, the pentad may actually be a hexad.

QUESTIONS TO CONSIDER

1. What are some examples of narratives and accounts focused on attitude?
2. Although not stated, what might have been the attitude accompanying agency in the example from Table 4.4?

Elements of the Pentad

There are five elements of the pentad, a name conveniently and not coincidentally derived from the Greek word for "five." In Table 4.4, you will find the names of these elements and what they involve. You will also see how the following event might be categorized: *Following an argument and as soon as she got home, Jessie sent Casey a text message stating she wanted to end their relationship.*

As you consider the terms of the pentad, notice that they are all elements that make up a good story or narrative. It is a good bet that within any story, each one of these elements will be included. However, not all of them will be given the same amount of attention or provided the same emphasis.

The element or elements emphasized in a story provide information about the speaker's motivation and how he or she wants others to understand the situation. Stories are not simply narrations of events but personalized ways of telling. When a person highlights certain elements of the pentad and not others, he or she is presenting his or her view of the world.

We can use your academically challenged friend from a previous example to illustrate what we mean. Suppose your friend says the following after doing poorly on an examination: "That room was so cold, it was difficult to concentrate on the test." In this example, the *scene* is being emphasized as the important element of the story. Your friend is not taking responsibility as an *agent,* instead blaming the location of the act.

Table 4.4 Elements of the Pentad

Act	What happened	Jessie ended her relationship with Casey
Scene	Situation or location of the act	Immediately following an argument; Jessie's home
Agent	Who performed the act	Jessie
Agency	How the act was accomplished	Through sending a text message
Purpose	Why the act took place	To end a relationship

Ratios of the Pentad

The elements of the pentad can be used and understood individually. However, they are also interconnected. Burke (1969) likened them to five fingers on a hand, separate and yet interrelated and used together.

Narratives and accounts may use more than one element of the pentad when framing outcomes or situations as inevitable. When doing so, the outcome or situation seems almost natural, unavoidable, and unquestionable. Table 4.5 provides some ratios for you to consider. Keep in mind that there exist many more. We encourage you to construct your own using the elements of the pentad to better understand them and recognize them in your everyday life.

Table 4.5 Accounting Using Ratios

Agent:Act	*Uses a person's character to explain actions* • He's the kind of guy who does that. • Friends don't let friends drive drunk.
Scene:Act	*Uses a situation or circumstances to justify action* • Desperate times call for desperate measures. • This is war, and harsh methods are needed to obtain the truth from prisoners.
Scene:Agent	*Uses a situation to explain the kinds of characters who are found there* • Politics makes strange bedfellows. • Miami, Florida, is a sunny place for shady people.

Functions of Verbal Communication

The use of verbal communication and all symbolic activity is transactive. Things are accomplished beyond the exchange of symbols. On its most basic level, verbal communication enables people to symbolically represent objects, ideas, places, and so on. As mentioned above, using the word *cat* makes things a lot easier than getting down on all fours and acting like a cat. It is also less embarrassing than if you had to go so far as to start licking your leg, coughing up a hairball, and shedding. Video of that behavior would have a nonstop ticket to YouTube!

Verbal communication does more than just represent, though. It presents the worldviews of others, as just discussed. It is used to influence other people. It also creates meanings, realities, relationships, identities, and cultures. We mentioned in Chapter 1 that the stuff of life is created, transformed, and maintained though verbal communication and other symbolic activity.

These ideas are explored in more detail within later chapters. For now, we want to explore two important functions of verbal communication. First, we will examine the use of verbal communication when influencing others. We will then examine its relational functions.

Influencing Others: Facework and Politeness

As people interact with one another in everyday life, they generally want to be viewed as favorable to others. They want to be accepted and to be viewed with respect. There are also many times throughout the day that they will need to impact the behaviors of others. This impact can be as minor as asking someone to pass the ketchup to as major as asking a huge favor. Influencing how we are viewed by others and influencing the behaviors of others involve facework and politeness.

Skills You Can Use: Telling Stories and Providing Accounts

Kenneth Burke's (1969) pentad can help you analyze the stories and accounts of others. However, it can also be used as you develop your own. Consider when it might be more appropriate to emphasize scene, agent, act, agency, and purpose when sharing particular stories and accounts with others.

By the way...

Nonverbal Facework

Although *face* is used as a metaphor, it is worth noticing how often people who are embarrassed or who feel foolish cover their faces with their hands. It is an almost automatic reaction to shame or to the recognition that they have done something foolish.

QUESTIONS TO CONSIDER

1. We talk about nonverbal communication in the next chapter, but how do you think nonverbal communication is used with facework?
2. Which do you think is more important in facework, verbal communication or nonverbal communication?

Facework

Cupach and Metts (Cupach & Metts, 1994; Metts, 2000) use the term **facework** when referring to the management of people's face, meaning dignity, respect, and acceptance. In most cases, people want to be viewed in a positive manner by others, and those others may include anyone with whom an encounter is shared. Accordingly, people desire positive face regardless of whether interacting with a close friend or with classmates, colleagues, instructors, employees at a store, or even strangers on the street. For instance, people tend to get angry when ignored by store employees while shopping. The anger likely comes not just from having one's time wasted but also from not feeling respected. At the same time, store employees may not feel respected when being yelled at by a customer.

Face Wants

People have positive face wants and negative face wants. **Positive face wants** refer to the need to be seen and accepted as a worthwhile and reasonable person. Positive face wants are dealt with and satisfied quite frequently through verbal communication. For instance, you often hear people pay compliments like "You are doing a great job" or "How very nice of you."

Negative face wants refer to the desire not to be imposed upon or treated as inferior. The management of this last type of face want is perhaps the most familiar. For example, you may hear people say things like "I don't mean to trouble you, but would you . . ." or "Sorry to be a nuisance, but . . ." Our personal favorite from students, "I have a *quick* question," implies that it will not be a lot of trouble or a big imposition to answer it.

ETHICAL ISSUE

Should you always be polite and save people's face when they do something embarrassing?

Face concerns are evident in everyday communication among those sharing a relationship (see Charee, Romo, & Dailey, 2013). Use of either type of face allows you to manage your relationships by paying attention to the ways people need to be seen in the social world. The behaviors are therefore a subtle kind of relational management done in talk.

Maintaining Positive Face

Sociologist Erving Goffman (1971) promoted the notion that *face* is something managed by people in social interactions. People cooperate to maintain positive face for one another and to avoid negative face for one another.

An example of helping others to maintain a positive face and avoid a negative face may occur when they make a mistake or do something embarrassing. In such cases, people trivialize an embarrassing mistake by saying "Oh, don't worry about it" or "I do that all the time." In effect, they are saying that they do not see the other person's behavior truly as an indication of who he or she really is. They are trying to let him or her off the hook as a person and are distinguishing his or her momentary actions from his or her self as a socially appropriate being.

facework: the management of people's dignity or self-respect, known as "face"

positive face wants: the need to be seen and accepted as a worthwhile and reasonable person (contrast with *negative face wants*)

negative face wants: the desire not to be imposed upon or treated as inferior (contrast with *positive face wants*)

Politeness Theory

As mentioned above, people must impact the behaviors of others throughout daily life. When this is done, there is a chance that positive face can be diminished and negative face can be imposed. Linguists Penelope Brown and Steven Levinson (1978) developed a theory of politeness to describe the ways that people deal with these possibilities.

While there is a chance that face will be threatened, not all face-threatening acts are equal. When determining the size of the face threat, the following three things must be considered: (a) the relationship shared by the interactants, (b) the power difference of the interactants, and (c) the size of the imposition. Some relationships are more likely than others to make impositions appropriate. For instance, asking a friend to help you move is more acceptable than asking an acquaintance. Differences in power may make impositions more appropriate. For instance, a boss asking an employee to move a box would be more acceptable than a coworker of the same standing asking another coworker to do the same thing. The sizes of impositions also differ. Asking someone to open a window is less of an imposition than asking someone to give you a ride to the airport.

Determining the size of the face-threatening act assists people when determining the best way to impact someone else's behavior. Table 4.6 offers various politeness strategies for you to consider.

ANALYZING EVERYDAY COMMUNICATION

Look at What I Can Do

Think about a situation where you overheard two people talking and you could tell—you just *knew*—that they were not close but that one of them was trying to impress the other and get into a relationship with him or her.

QUESTIONS TO CONSIDER

1. What did you notice that made you sure you were right about the person doing the "impressing"?
2. How did you know whether or not the other person was impressed?

Relationships and Everyday Talk

Another important function of verbal communication is its use in the development and maintenance of relationships. Duck and Pond (1989), apart from being our favorite combination of author names, came up with some ideas about the way relationships connect with talk in everyday life. They pointed out that talk can serve the following three functions for relationships: (a) instrumental, (b) indexical, and (c) essential.

Table 4.6 Politeness Strategies

Bald on Record	*Act directly without concern for face needs. Likely used when an imposition is small or appropriate given relationship of interactants.* • I need you to help me move next weekend. • I need you to give me a ride to the airport.
Positive Politeness	*Focus on positive face of the person, often through flattery or offering something in return.* • You are so strong. Could you help me move next weekend? • If you would give me a ride to the airport, I would fill your car up with gas.
Negative Politeness	*Acknowledge possibility of negative face, offering regrets or being pessimistic.* • It is a lot to ask, but would you mind helping me move next weekend? • I don't suppose you would be able to give me a ride to the airport?
Off Record	*Hint or present the request in a vague manner.* • I sure could use some help moving next weekend. • I don't know how I am going to get to the airport.
Avoidance	*Sometimes the face-threatening act is so large, it is avoided entirely.* • Lift with your knees. • Start walking.

Talk in friendships or relationships can de described in terms of three functions: instrumental, indexical, and essential. Which function of talk would you use to describe the two men in this photo?

Instrumental Function

The **instrumental function of talk** occurs when what is said results in the accomplishment of a goal in the relationship. The instrumental function of talk in relationships is illustrated whenever you ask someone out for a date, to a party, to meet you for coffee, to be your friend, or to be just a little bit more sensitive and caring. What you say reveals a goal that you have in mind for the relationship, and talk is the means or instrument by which you reveal it. Anything you say that serves the purpose of bringing something new to or changing anything about the relationship is an instrumental function of talk in relationships.

Indexical Function

The **indexical function of talk** demonstrates or indicates the nature of the relationship between speakers. You index your relationship in *what* you say to someone and the *way* that you say it (nonverbal). If you say in a sharp tone "Come into my office; I want to see you!" you are not only being discourteous, but you are indicating that you are superior to the other person and have the relational right to order him or her around. If you say in a pleasant tone "Would you happen to have a free moment? I would appreciate it if we could meet in my office," you are indicating respect for the other person and indicating relational equality. The content and relational elements of the talk occur together. In your talk with other people, you constantly weave in clues about your relationships. The fact that you would say some things to some people and avoid saying those things to other people exhibits different relationships.

Essential Function

The **essential function of talk** happens when talk makes a relationship real or brings it into being. The essential function of talk often occurs through the use of coupling references or making assumptions that the relationship exists. People very easily underestimate the extent to which talk and its nonverbal wrapping *are* a relationship.

Verbal communication creates and embodies relationships both directly and indirectly. Direct talk would be such statements as "You're my friend" and "I love you." Indirect talk, which recognizes the relationship's existence but does not mention it explicitly, would include such questions or statements as "What shall we do this weekend?" and "Let's do something really special tonight." The essential function of talk operates in less obvious ways as well. Examples of these less obvious forms of talk include frequent references to *we* and *us* along with the use of nicknames.

Of course, when two people are in a relationship, they do not spend every moment with each other. You experience absences, breaks, and separations in your relationships. These may be relatively short (one person goes shopping), longer (a child goes to school for the day), or extended (two lovers get jobs in different parts of the country).

Because these breaks occur, there are ways to indicate that, although the interaction may be over, the relationship itself continues. For example, you might say "See you next week," "Talk to you later," or "In the next chapter we will be discussing nonverbal communication."

instrumental function of talk: when what is said brings about a goal that you have in mind for the relationship, and talk is the means or instrument by which it is accomplished (e.g., asking someone on a date or to come with you to a party)

indexical function of talk: demonstrates or indicates the nature of the relationship between speakers

essential function of talk: a function of talk that makes the relationship real and talks it into being, often by using coupling references or making assumptions that the relationship exists

Focus Questions Revisited

How is verbal communication symbolic?

Verbal communication is the use of language. Words are symbolic representations.

How does verbal communication involve meaning?

Words have denotative meaning and connotative meaning. Denotative meaning is the general meaning of a word. Connotative meaning refers to the overtones and implications associated with a word or an object. Words are also given particular value in a society.

How is verbal communication relational?

Verbal communication influences relationships, and relationships influence verbal communication. Whenever you communicate verbally, a particular relationship is presumed with another person, the members of a group, or an audience. Another way of thinking about this is that when you are verbally communicating, you are also relating.

How is verbal communication cultural?

Verbal communication is cultural, much in the way that it is relational. Verbal communication influences culture, and culture influences verbal communication. Whenever you communicate verbally, cultural assumptions are presumed involving appropriateness and meanings within a given society or group.

What frames your understanding of verbal communication?

Frames used to understand communication can involve relationships, cultures, settings, and other factors influencing communication. These frames can be recognized and established through the form of language. They can also be adjusted during the course of a conversation.

What is the presentational nature of verbal communication?

The selection of words when speaking is meaningful and provides information about the perspective and worldview of the person sending a message. All verbal communication is presentational, but when people tell stories and provide accounts, its presentational nature is particularly recognizable.

What are the functions of verbal communication?

Verbal communication is used to represent other things. In doing so, verbal communication also provides information about the worldview of others. It is used to influence other people. It also creates meanings, realities, relationships, identities, and cultures.

Key Concepts

accommodation 78
accounts 79
act 80
agency 80
agent 80
avoidance 83
bald on record 83
collectivist talk 76
connotative meaning 71
convergence 78
conversational hypertext 74
denotative meaning 71
Devil terms 72
divergence 78
elaborated code 75
essential function of talk 84
facework 82
feminine talk 76
God terms 72
high code 77
high-context talk 76
indexical function of talk 84
individualist talk 76
instrumental function of talk 84
langue 78
low code 77
low-context talk 76
masculine talk 76
narrative 79
negative face wants 82

negative politeness 83
off record 83
parole 78
pentad 79
polysemy 71
positive face wants 82
positive politeness 83
purpose 80
restricted code 75
Sapir-Whorf hypothesis 71
scene 80
verbal communication 69

Questions to Ask Your Friends

1. Try conducting a conversation with one of your friends where you use only high code. Afterward, ask your friend how long it took to notice something wrong or inappropriate in the situation.
2. Ask your friends if they ever find it hard to know when you are kidding and what makes it hard.
3. Have your friends report an occasion when they caught someone in a bold-faced lie and how they knew. How did they handle it, based on what you know about facework?

Media Connections

1. Find news stories that are structured in ways that illustrate the pentad.
2. Language used on social networking sites and when making comments online tends to be more argumentative than that which is used elsewhere. Collect examples of argumentative language use online and consider why such language use is more prevalent online.
3. What techniques do news anchors use on television in order to relate with their audience and seem friendly, likeable, and credible?

Student Study Site

SAGE edge™

Sharpen your skills with SAGE edge at edge.sagepub.com/duckciel2e

SAGE edge for students provides a personalized approach to help you accomplish your coursework goals in an easy-to-use learning environment.

Chapter Outline

What Is Nonverbal Communication?

- Symbolic
- Decoding and Encoding
- Dynamic and Static
- Guided by Rules
- Cultural
- Personal
- Ambiguous
- Less Controlled
- Continuous

The Functions of Nonverbal Communication

- Interconnects With Verbal Communication
- Regulates Interactions
- Identifies Others
- Transmits Emotional Information
- Relational Meaning and Understanding

Types of Nonverbal Communication

- Proxemics
- Territoriality
- Kinesics
- Eye Contact and Gaze
- Vocalics
- Chronemics
- Haptics

Focus Questions Revisited

Key Concepts

Questions to Ask Your Friends

Media Connections

05 Nonverbal Communication

Imagine that you are deaf. There are no sounds. You cannot hear speech, though luckily you can read lips, gestures, body posture, eye movements, and facial expressions. How do you think the ability to see these accompaniments of speech will help you to understand what is spoken aloud for those who can hear?

Now imagine that you can hear. Ask yourself the same question. How does the ability to "read" other aspects of human behavior add to or help you interpret what is being said? How far do you believe that you rely on the nonverbal behavior of a speaker to interpret the meanings of the speech, and which is more important: what is said or what is done nonverbally?

Nonverbal communication is any symbolic activity that communicates a message other than words. This definition covers a very wide range of topics: facial expression, hand movements, dress, tattoos, jewelry, physical attractiveness, timing of what happens, distance, tone of voice, eye movements, the positioning of furniture to create atmosphere, touch, and smell—and that is not an exhaustive list.

Nonverbal communication is used differently by different cultures. In deaf culture it is a substitute for speech and has its own complex signs and codes. In Mediterranean cultures, especially Italian, it is used as a perpetual accompaniment of speech with much arm and hand movement as well as facial expressions changing for emphasis and clarity. However, it is a mistake to resign it to only special cultural examples. Nonverbal communication is always present during face-to-face interactions and carries messages over and above the words you speak. For example, a smile makes your words seem friendly, but a sneer makes the same words seem sarcastic. Nonverbal communication may go along with verbal communication, but not always. You might say "I'm *not* angry" but look as if you are really angry. Or you might say "I love you" and only have to exchange a glance with your partner for him or her to see that you really mean it. Accordingly, nonverbal communication *frames* talk and assists in determining its meaning.

Nonverbal communication can also frame other people's assessments and judgments of you and your identity, your status and power, and your sincerity in what you say. It can further indicate how you feel about other people. The way you move, look, and sound conveys relational messages to others. All nonverbal communication conveys something about your sense of relaxation and comfort with the person with whom you are speaking. Nonverbal communication also indicates your *evaluation or assessment* of that person. In short, nonverbal communication is an essential *relational* element of all interaction, and you cannot have interactions without nonverbal communication; nor can you have interactions without

FOCUS QUESTIONS

1. What is nonverbal communication?
2. How does nonverbal communication interconnect with verbal communication?
3. How does nonverbal communication regulate interactions?
4. How does nonverbal communication identify people?
5. How does nonverbal communication transmit emotional information?
6. What are the most common types of nonverbal communication?

nonverbal communication: any symbolic activity other than the use of language

What features of nonverbal communication can you use to form an impression of this person?

the *relational messages* that nonverbal communication sends.

Since nonverbal communication has been tied up with your communication all of your life, it might be difficult to fully appreciate its importance. However, consider difficulties that may arise when nonverbal cues are absent, such as when texting or sending an e-mail. Even if that example does not convince you, the value in understanding nonverbal communication will soon become apparent as you read this chapter. Increasing your understanding of nonverbal communication may also increase your effectiveness in interpreting the messages of others and in conveying your own messages.

What Is Nonverbal communication?

While a definition of nonverbal communication was provided above, a more complete examination is needed in order to better understand and appreciate it. As we engage in a deeper exploration of nonverbal communication, we will address the characteristics it shares with verbal communication. For instance, both verbal and nonverbal communication are symbolic and share many of the same characteristics, such as being personal, ambiguous, guided by rules, and linked to culture. We also discuss characteristics unique to nonverbal communication, such as its continuous nature and that it is often beyond our full control. This comparison will help you understand the workings of nonverbal communication and should also add to your understanding of verbal communication, with which it often occurs (Knapp & Hall, 2002; Remland, 2004).

By the way...

Remember Silence!

Silence is a nonverbal behavior and can convey many meanings, from "dumb insolence" to tacit agreement. The law assumes that whoever is silent or raises no objection agrees (*Qui tacet consentit*). Silence is also polite: When someone in authority is speaking, you should not interrupt. However, as every schoolchild knows, it can also indicate ignorance of the answer to a question!

QUESTIONS TO CONSIDER

1. Have you ever used silence as a way to communicate nonverbally? Why did you choose to do so?
2. When has someone else's silence made you uncomfortable? Why do you think you felt that way?

Symbolic

Nonverbal communication involves the use of symbols. Accordingly, everything we discuss about symbols in Chapter 1 applies to nonverbal communication. In this regard, nonverbal communication and verbal communication are alike, with both being symbolic. The key difference between them is that verbal communication involves the use of language and nonverbal communication involves all other symbolic activity.

Decoding and Encoding

Nonverbal communication requires decoding and encoding. **Decoding** is the act of assigning meaning to nonverbal symbols. When decoding a nonverbal message, you draw meaning from something you observe. For example, if somebody blushes unexpectedly, you might decode that

decoding: drawing meaning from something you observe

Table 5.1 Characteristics of Effective Decoding

Effective decoders *attend* to whether others pay attention to nonverbal communication and seem to understand it. A skilled decoder will determine whether the person with whom he or she is interacting seems to pick up on nonverbal cues being provided.

Effective decoders *bond* with others and watch for signals others send about comfort in the situation. A skilled decoder will notice when a speaker is anxious and will smile more often or reward the speaker with head nods and encouraging nonverbal communication to put him or her at ease.

Effective decoders *coordinate* with others and respond to cues so the interaction runs smoothly with no awkward silences.

Effective decoders *detect* the undercurrents of a speaker's talk by attending carefully to eye movements and gestures that "leak" what the speaker truly feels.

as meaning he or she is embarrassed. Effective decoding increases the chances of accurately assigning meaning to the messages of others. It will also enable you to determine a person's emotions. Successful medical and sales professionals tend to be good decoders (Puccinelli, Andrzejewski, Markos, Noga, & Motyka, 2013; Sheeler, 2013). Table 5.1 provides characteristics of effective decoding.

Encoding is the act of using nonverbal symbols to convey meaning. When encoding a nonverbal message, you put your feelings or other information into behavior. For instance, if you are feeling happy, you tend to *look* truly happy. Effective encoding increases the chances that others will accurately assign meaning to your messages. It will also enable you to put your feelings "out there" and help other people "get" what is going on inside you when so desired. Skillful actors, teachers, and politicians tend to be good encoders (Koppensteiner & Grammer, 2010). Table 5.2 provides characteristics of effective encoding.

encoding: putting feelings into behavior through nonverbal communication

dynamic: elements of nonverbal communication that are changeable during interaction (e.g., facial expression, posture, gesturing; contrast with *static*)

static: elements of nonverbal communication that are fixed during interaction (e.g., shape of the room where an interaction takes place, color of eyes, clothes worn during an interview; contrast with *dynamic*)

Dynamic and Static

Nonverbal communication can be both dynamic and static (Roberts et al., 2009). **Dynamic** nonverbal communication is that which is changeable during an interaction. We will discuss specific types of nonverbal communication more completely later in the chapter, but for now examples include eye contact, facial expression, voice, and gestures. As you talk with someone, for example, your eye contact will vary, your facial expressions will change, elements of your voice will change, and various gestures will be incorporated.

Static nonverbal communication is that which does not change during an interaction. Examples of static nonverbal communication are clothing, hairstyle, body art,

Table 5.2 Characteristics of Effective Encoding

Effective encoders *affirm* others through encoding approval and liking while talking. Examples of this behavior include smiling and maintaining eye contact.

Effective encoders *blend* their nonverbal communication with their verbal communication to allow for consistency between what is spoken and what is conveyed nonverbally.

Effective encoders are *direct* by striving to make their nonverbal communication clear and as unambiguous as possible.

Effective encoders exhibit *emotional clarity* so that the emotions of their words are matched by their nonverbal expression of emotion.

and piercings, as well as general surroundings such as the arrangement of furniture or the color of the walls. Although some of these things may change during the course of an interaction, most often they do not change.

Guided by Rules

Nonverbal communication is guided by rules. Rules guide the choice of nonverbal symbols that should be used in specific situations and with certain people. The appropriateness of greeting someone with a kiss depends on whether he or she is your romantic partner, an attendant behind the counter at a gas station, or someone from a culture where a kiss on the cheek is an accepted greeting even between persons of the same sex (Russia or Italy, for example). Rules also guide evaluation of nonverbal behavior. A brisk handshake is evaluated differently than a hearty handshake; a slight smile is evaluated differently than a broad smile (Dolcos, Sung, Argo, Flor-Henry, & Dolcos, 2012).

As opposed to those guiding verbal communication, the rules guiding nonverbal communication are learned indirectly and primarily through your interactions with others (Remland, 2004). This course may be the first time you have ever formally studied nonverbal communication, but you have been studying verbal language in school for years. In your English classes, for example, you learned the difference between nouns, verbs, adjectives, and adverbs and about proper sentence structure. In grade school, you learned vocabulary skills and the meanings of certain words. With nonverbal communication, you have learned nearly everything, from the meaning of particular nonverbal symbols to the structure of their use, informally throughout your lifetime as you have interacted with other people.

How can body art be both cultural and personal?

Cultural

Nonverbal communication is linked to cultural appropriateness (Matsumoto & Hwang, 2012). Cultures vary on the meanings and appropriateness of nonverbal behaviors. In the United States, eye contact is often viewed as a display of courtesy, honesty, and respect. In other countries, making eye contact, especially with a superior, is considered improper and highly disrespectful. Further, many gestures are acceptable in some cultures but impolite or offensive in others. There also exists a host of cultural differences involving space, touch, time, and other nonverbal behaviors.

There exist no universally understood nonverbal behaviors. Some nonverbal behaviors and symbols are perhaps universally recognized (the smile, for example), but they do not necessarily have universal meaning in the same contexts (Remland, 2004). Further, there may be similarities among nonverbal behaviors, but there are subtle differences among different cultural groups (Elfenbein, 2013).

Personal

Nonverbal communication can be very personal (Guerrero & Floyd, 2006). Similar to verbal communication, you develop your own personal meanings and use of nonverbal symbols. A person's use of some nonverbal symbols may even become idiosyncratic over time. Some people may not like to hug or be hugged, for example. One person may view the peace sign as cliché and may look at celebrities flashing the peace sign at cameras with disdain. Another person may view this sign as still having great meaning and value and may regard its use with admiration. Others still may wear their hair in a distinctive style or wear unique clothing.

How might Winston Churchill's lifting of two fingers to represent "victory" be considered ambiguous?

Ambiguous

Nonverbal communication is highly ambiguous, even more than the meaning of verbal communication. Indeed, the meaning of nonverbal communication is often unclear without additional information from context or communication frames. The ambiguous nature of communication can actually be valuable, though. When flirting, for instance, the associated nonverbal behaviors can mean many different things. Eye contact, a quick or sustained glance, a smile, or even a wink can be used either to flirt with someone or just to be friendly. Here, ambiguity is useful because it releases the pressure to receive the desired response. If the other person is interested, the response transacts your ambiguous message as flirtatious. If the other person is not interested, the response transacts your ambiguous behavior as "just being friendly" (Goodboy & Brann, 2010).

Although nonverbal communication is ambiguous, that does not mean that it is impossible to determine its meaning. You can more accurately interpret the meaning of nonverbal communication by recognizing that it occurs as part of a system and is related to other parts of an interaction. Table 5.3 examines four clues to consider when assigning meaning.

Table 5.3 Assigning Meaning to Nonverbal Communication

Verbal Communication	Nonverbal communication is understood in part to the *verbal communication* used with it. It can affect how words are understood, and words can affect how nonverbal communication is understood. Someone caressing your thigh and saying "I love you" is doing something different than someone touching your thigh and saying "Is this where it hurts?"
Other Nonverbal Communication	Any nonverbal communication has a relationship to *other nonverbal communication* that happens simultaneously. If someone is staring at you with a scowl and clenched fists, you can assume that the stare is intended as a threat; if the stare is accompanied by a smile and a soft expression, it is intended as friendly. Likewise, a smile accompanied by agitated gestures, sweating, or blushing probably means the person is nervous, but someone smiling and looking relaxed with an open posture is probably feeling friendly and confident.
Physical / Situational Context	The interpretation of nonverbal communication depends on the *physical context and situational context* of the interaction. If someone stares at you in class, it feels different from a stare across a crowded singles bar. A scream at a sports match probably means your team just scored, but a scream in your home could indicate the discovery of a rodent.
Relationship	How nonverbal communication is interpreted is also affected by your *relationship* to another person. If the person caressing your thigh is a nurse, you're probably right to assume that the touch is part of a treatment or medical exam, so stay there and get well. If the person is a stranger in a park, it's time to leave—quickly.

DISCIPLINARY DEBATE

Controlled Nonverbal Communication

We maintain that nonverbal communication is less controlled than verbal communication. However, some people (such as con artists and actors) can train themselves to appear certain ways and even control their heart rates and other physical features.

QUESTIONS TO CONSIDER

1. Does this mean that nonverbal communication is actually easy to control with enough practice?
2. Can some nonverbal communication be controlled while other nonverbal communication is uncontrollable?

Less Controlled

Nonverbal communication is less subject to control than is verbal communication. You might be able to keep from calling someone you dislike a jerk, but nonverbally you may be expressing your displeasure unknowingly through dirty looks or changes in posture and distance.

Nonverbal behaviors often occur without your full awareness and reveal how you really feel (Pretsch, Flunger, Heckmann, & Schmitt, 2013). This nonverbal betrayal of someone's internal feelings is known as **leakage**. Because your spontaneous nonverbal communication is more difficult to control than your verbal communication, people are more likely to believe your nonverbal over your verbal messages—especially when the two are contradictory. People rely more on what you do than on what you say.

Continuous

Nonverbal communication is continuous and ongoing. If nothing else, you will always be communicating nonverbally through your physical appearance. More to the point, when interacting face-to-face, you begin communicating nonverbally before you start talking and will continue communicating after you stop. You can stop communicating verbally, but you cannot stop communicating nonverbally.

ETHICAL ISSUE

Now that you are learning more about nonverbal communication, would it be ethical to use this knowledge to your advantage when interacting with people who do not possess this knowledge?

The Functions of Nonverbal communication

Nonverbal communication has many functions in everyday life, some of which reinforce verbal behavior, some of which regulate interactions, and some of which serve to identify people. It also registers people's emotional states or displays their attitudes about themselves, the other person in the interaction, or their comfort level. Nonverbal communication further establishes relational meaning and understanding.

Interconnects With Verbal Communication

One function of nonverbal communication involves its interconnection with verbal communication. Your interpretation of verbal meaning is often framed by accompanying nonverbal elements, such as tone of voice, facial expression, and gestures.

Your nonverbal communication might *repeat* your verbal communication, sending a corresponding nonverbal message. For example, when you say hello to someone from across the room, you might wave at the same time.

Alternatively, nonverbal messages can *substitute,* or be used in place of, verbal messages. For example, you might just wave to acknowledge someone and not say anything.

Nonverbal communication is often used to *emphasize* or highlight the verbal message. If you have ever gone fishing and described "the one that got away" to your friends, you have no doubt used nonverbal communication to emphasize just how big

leakage: unintentional betrayal of internal feelings through nonverbal communication that fish really was by holding your arms out wide to indicate its gargantuan length. A verbal message can also be emphasized through your tone of voice. When you tell someone a secret, for example, you may use a hushed voice to emphasize its private nature.

How can nonverbal communication regulate interactions by beginning or ending a conversation?

When nonverbal communication is used to *moderate* verbal communication, it plays down a verbal message. For instance, a doubtful tone of voice and the slight scrunching of your face and shoulders could indicate uncertainty. If your supervisor did this while saying "I may be able to give you a raise this year," you would probably not expect a raise. By moderating the verbal message nonverbally, your boss is letting you know there is uncertainty in that statement.

Your nonverbal communication can also *contradict* your verbal communication—sometimes intentionally, such as when you are being sarcastic ("Oh, nice job!" said angrily when someone spills coffee on you). Contradiction may occur unintentionally as well: for instance, when someone charges into a room, slams the door, sits down on the couch in a huff, and says "Oh, nothing" when you ask what is wrong. Contradiction is not always obvious, but you are generally skilled at detecting it—especially when you share a close, personal relationship with the speaker. Faced with contradiction, you will likely believe the person's nonverbal over verbal communication. Why? (Hint: Spontaneous nonverbal communication is less subject to your control than is verbal communication.)

Regulates Interactions

Nonverbal communication also helps regulate interactions. Nonverbal communication aids in starting or ending interactions. Used to determine whether you should actually engage in interactions with another person, nonverbal communication helps you know when to send and when to receive verbal messages.

Regulators are nonverbal actions that indicate to others how you want them to behave or what you want them to do. One familiar regulator occurs at the end of most college classes: Students begin closing their books and gathering their belongings to signal to the instructor that it is time to end class. Other regulators include shivering when you want someone to close the window or turn up the heat, a look of frustration or confusion when you need help with a problem, and a closed-off posture (arms folded, legs crossed) when you want to be left alone.

Nonverbal communication can indicate whether you will actually engage in conversation. If one of your friends walks past you at a rapid pace with an intense look on his or her face, it shows that he or she is in a hurry or not in the mood to talk. In this case, you might avoid interacting with your friend at this time. If someone looks frustrated or confused, however, you may decide to interact with him or her because the nonverbal behavior signals a need for help.

Nonverbal communication also serves to *punctuate* how you talk to other people; it starts and ends interactions and keeps them flowing. Specifically, nonverbal communication creates a framework within which interaction happens in proper sequence. Most of the time it is perfectly effortless and unconscious, but you must

regulators: nonverbal actions that indicate to others how you want them to behave or what you want them to do

Make your case

Static or Changing Nonverbal Communication

Note the date (1973) of Kendon and Ferber's greeting ritual research. When discussing touch later in this chapter, we reference works by Heslin and Jourard, which were conducted at around the same time (1974 and 1971, respectively). In a later chapter, we encourage you to be cautious when using references that are dated. However, some material may stand the test of time. There are two cases for you to make here.

QUESTIONS TO CONSIDER

1. Has Kendon and Ferber's greeting ritual research stood the test of time, or have changes in greetings occurred since it was conducted?
2. Will the meanings of some nonverbal behaviors never change, or is all communication and meaning open to change?

act to get in and out of conversations. For example, you may have to "catch the server's eye" when wanting to order in a restaurant.

Elaborate nonverbal rules are followed to begin and to break off interactions. Consider what happens when you see someone walking toward you in the distance and wish to engage in conversation. Kendon and Ferber (1973) identified five basic stages in such a greeting ritual, as shown in Table 5.4.

Nonverbal communication also signals the end to an interaction. You may, for example, stop talking, start to edge away, or show other signs of departure, such as looking away from the other person more often or checking your watch. You might also step a little farther back or turn to the side. When the interaction is coming to an end, speakers join in rituals of ending, such as stepping back, offering a handshake, or stating directly that it's time to go.

Identifies Others

Nonverbal communication also functions to identify specific individuals. Just as dogs know each other individually by smell, humans recognize one another specifically from facial appearance. You also use physical cues like muscles, beards, skin color, breasts, and the color of a person's hair to identify him or her as a particular sex, age, race, or athletic ability.

Clothing is an identifying signal for someone's sex (men rarely wear dresses), personality (whether a person wears loud colors, sedate business attire, or punk clothing), favorite sports team, and job (police, military, security). Clothing can also identify changes in people, such as whether they have a special role today (prom outfits, wedding wear, gardening clothes).

People can also distinguish others' scents: What perfume or cologne do they wear? Do they smoke? Are they drinkers? People often do not comment on these kinds of clues, but if your physician smells of alcohol, you may well identify him or her as professionally incompetent to deal with your health concerns.

Table 5.4 Kendon and Ferber's (1973) Five Basic Stages of a Greeting Ritual

Stage	Description
1. Sighting and Recognition	Occurs when you and another person first see each other
2. Distant Salutation	Used to say hello with a wave, a flash of recognition, a smile, or a nod of acknowledgment
3. Lowering Your Head and Averting Your Gaze (to Avoid Staring)	As you approach the other person you break off your visual connection until you get close enough to talk and be heard
4. Close Salutation	Most likely involves some type of physical contact: a handshake, a kiss, or a hug, which brings you too close for a comfortable conversation
5. Backing Off	Taking a step back or turning to the side to create a slightly larger space, the actual size of which is dictated by the type of relationship you share with the other person

Transmits Emotional Information

An additional function of nonverbal communication is to convey emotional information (Sanford, 2012). When you are angry, you scowl; when you are in love, you look gooey; when you feel happy, you smile. Nonverbal communication actually allows you to convey three different kinds of emotional information as follows.

Nonverbal Communication and Anxiety

Think about a situation where you felt uncomfortable in the presence of another person. Inside, you may have been filled with anxiety. Consider how the other person could have known that you were anxious; for example, you may have been sweating, blushing, agitated, speaking too fast, or jumpy.

QUESTIONS TO CONSIDER

1. What did you do to try to conceal your nerves?
2. Have you ever seen other people trying to appear calm, but you weren't fooled? What behaviors gave away their anxiety?

Attitude Toward the Other

Nonverbal communication conveys your *attitude toward the other person*. If your facial expression conveys anxiety, viewers assume you are frightened. If your face looks relaxed and warm, viewers assume you are comfortable. If you care about what your instructor has to say, you fall silent when a lecture begins; talking in class (instructors' biggest complaint about students) makes it difficult for people to hear but also shows lack of respect.

Attitude Toward the Situation

Nonverbal communication conveys your *attitude toward the situation:* Rapidly moving about while talking conveys a message of anxiety. Police officers often see fidgeting and an inability to maintain eye contact as indicators of a person's guilt.

Attitude Toward Yourself

Nonverbal communication conveys information about your *attitude toward yourself.* If a person is arrogant, confident, or low in self-esteem, it is expressed through nonverbal behaviors. Arrogance shows up in nonverbal actions, such as facial expression, tone of voice, eye contact, and body posture. If someone stands up to his or her full height and faces you directly, you might assume that he or she is confident. Conversely, if he or she slouches and stares at the ground, you might assume that he or she is shy, lacks confidence, and is insecure.

Relational Meaning and Understanding

Nonverbal communication is a silent *relational* regulator. Your relationships with others inform your everyday communication, and your everyday communication develops relationships. Regulation of interactions serves to regulate engagement, politeness, coordination of action, and sense of pleasure in the interaction—all of which are ultimately relational in effect. The appearance of others enables you to distinguish and make judgments about them. Appearance also forms the basis of relational attraction. In fact, you often are attracted to people with facial and bodily features very similar to your own.

Although people do not always have as much space as they would like, what term is used to represent the need for people to establish space as their own?

Types of Nonverbal Communication

So far we have discussed nonverbal communication as if it is a single thing. Actually nonverbal communication has many different elements used collectively in the construction and interpretation of meaning, the development of identity, and the enactment of relationships. In what follows, we discuss types of nonverbal communication individually to provide a more detailed explanation, but keep in mind that nonverbal communication works as a whole system comprising all these elements.

Proxemics

Proxemics is the study of space and distance in communication. The occupation of space and the distance you maintain from others conveys messages about control, acceptance, and relationships. We will begin our discussion with space, which is used in different ways and conveys different meanings. For instance, some space is established to serve certain purposes such as living rooms, bedrooms, kitchens, offices, and bus shelters. Wherever you happen to be right now, you are occupying space. You may have exclusive control over this space, such as where you live. Or you may simply be occupying space established as your own for the time being such as a table in a public location like a library or coffee shop.

Skills You Can Use: Arranging Your Space

Your arrangement of the space in your interaction can make another person feel more comfortable or less comfortable and make that person feel more in control or less in control. Consider ways in which the arrangement of space that you control can be adjusted according to the types of relationships you wish to achieve when people enter your space.

Territoriality

The need to establish space as your own is somewhat of a human need. **Territoriality** is the establishment and maintenance of space that people claim for their personal use. Knapp and Hall (2002) point out three types of territory that you may establish: primary, secondary, and public. *Primary territory* is space that you own or have principal control over. This space is central to your life and includes such spaces as your house, room, apartment, office, or car. How you maintain and control this space communicates a great deal to those around you. Decorating your home in a particular fashion not only provides you with a sense of comfort but also informs others about the type of person you may be or the types of interests you may have. Even in dorm rooms, though they are generally less than spacious, roommates find ways to assert ownership of "their" areas (Erlandson, 2012).

You establish *secondary territory* as your own through repeated use, even if it is space that is not central to your life or exclusive to you. A good example of secondary territory is the room where your class is held. Chances are pretty good that you and your fellow students sit in the exact same seats that you sat in on the first day of class.

proxemics: the study of space and distance in communication

territoriality: the establishment and maintenance of space that people claim for their personal use

Even though this space does not belong to you, others associate it with you because of repeated use. Accordingly, if you came to class one day and someone was sitting in "your" seat, you might get upset or uncomfortable if you were forced to sit elsewhere.

Public territory is space open to everyone but available for your sole temporary occupancy once established as such. These spaces might include park benches, seats in a movie theater, and tables at a library. Secondary and public territory can involve the same type of physical space, such as a table at a restaurant, so consider the following example. If you go to the same restaurant every day for lunch and always sit at the same table, eventually it will become your secondary territory. Although it is open to everyone, once you claim that space for your temporary use, you assume exclusive control over it for the time being and would not expect anyone to violate that.

There are cultural variations in the use of public territory. In the United States, for example, if you and your date went to a restaurant and were seated at a table for four, the two additional seats would remain empty regardless of whether other people were waiting to be seated. In many European countries, however, it would not be surprising if another couple you do not know were eventually seated at your table.

Markers, used to establish and announce your territory, are surprisingly effective. People mark space by putting their "stuff" on it. Markers are common when using public territory that is open and unrestricted. For example, when you lay a jacket over the back of a chair, you have claimed that chair. Should someone want to move the chair, he or she would probably ask your permission rather than simply removing the jacket and taking the chair. Markers are often used to indicate privacy and control, and you feel uncomfortable if someone else enters the space without permission. People meet this "invasion" with varying degrees of disapproval, but blood pressure frequently goes up (Guerrero & Floyd, 2006).

By the way...

Religious Practices

Note that in many religions (e.g., Judaism and Islam) women and men are allocated different spaces within religious buildings and may not interact during religious ceremonies. In weddings, for example, the male and female participants may be separated by a physical barrier or a symbolic one such as a sheet, indicating what is the "proper" place in that religion for the fully active male participants and the restricted participation of the women.

QUESTIONS TO CONSIDER

1. Have you ever encountered this type of territoriality? If so, how did you respond to it?
2. If you have never encountered this type of territoriality, how do you think you would have responded if you had?

Personal Space and Distance

You carry around with you an idea of how much actual space you should have during an interaction. This idea will be affected by your status, your sex, and your liking for the person with whom you are talking. It also will be affected by the situations in which you find yourself. **Personal space** refers to that space legitimately claimed or occupied by a person for the time being.

All of us have a **body buffer zone**, a kind of imaginary aura that we regard as part of ourselves. People differ in the size of their body buffer zone. If you step into the body buffer zone that someone feels is his or her "space," even if it is beyond what you would normally expect, you may be in for trouble. Your friends and family can enter your body buffer zone more freely than other people. You react to space and its use depending on the kind of situation in which you find yourself.

An early pioneer of personal space research, E. T. Hall (1966) distinguished among intimate distance (contact to 18 inches), personal distance (18–48 inches), social distance (48–144 inches), and public distance (12–25 feet). Although valuable,

personal space: space legitimately claimed or occupied by a person for the time being; the area around a person that is regarded as part of the person and in which only informal and close relationships are conducted

body buffer zone: a kind of imaginary aura around you that you regard as part of yourself and your personal space

Figure 5.1 Hall's (1966) Four Types of Personal Space

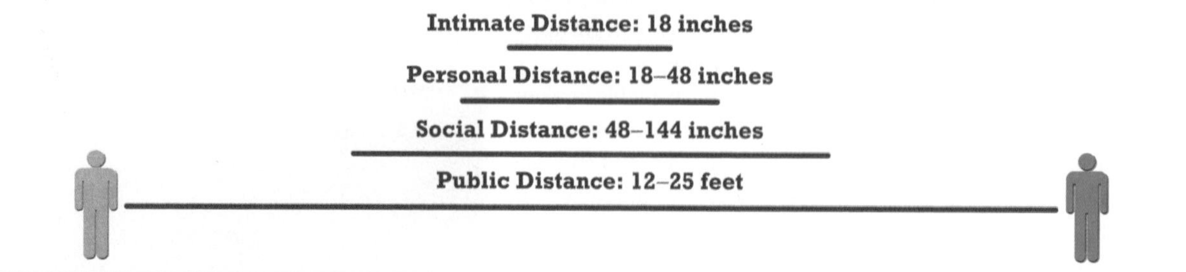

this early research does not explain cultural differences. For instance, it has become accepted that people from Latino and Arab cultures require less space for each type of encounter than do Northern Europeans and North Americans. Nevertheless, these types of personal space are frequently referenced when discussing space and distance and are illustrated in Figure 5.1.

Proxemics and Everyday Life

The meaning of space or distance is framed by your relationships with others. What it means for someone to stand mere inches away from you will differ depending on whether he or she is a friend, an adversary, or a complete stranger. Close friends are literally closer to you—people generally stand closer to people they like. Similarly, a friend moving the backpack you placed on a table in order to sit near you would mean something entirely different than a complete stranger doing the same thing.

Your use of space and distance enacts these relationships. Subordinate individuals tend to give more space to individuals in leadership positions. An employee, for example, would stand at a greater distance when talking with an employer than with a coworker, indicating the superior–subordinate nature of that relationship and enabling both interactants to perform their respective roles.

Physical space is often laid out to indicate and perform leadership or power roles. A formal chair of a meeting sits at one end of the table, usually in a special seat, and everyone else lines up along the length of the table at right angles to the chair. In contrast, a more secure or less formal leader might sit anywhere at the table. From seemingly minor physical facts about the distribution and use of space, then, you can determine relational information about the people in a setting—who is in charge and who is not—as well as the leader's preferred style of interaction, formal or informal.

Space and distance also allow relational negotiation to take place. For instance, a friend who desires a more intimate relationship with you may begin standing a bit closer to gauge your reaction. Similarly, a subordinate decreasing the amount of space granted to a superior may be indicating a desire for a more equal relationship. Either attempt could be accepted or rejected depending on the other person's view of the relationship. Such relational negotiation frequently takes place in families once adolescent sons or daughters start to claim bedrooms as their own space that is now private from invasive parents.

Space and distance also guide interactions with others. If your friend has books, papers, and other material spread out over a large space, it could indicate that he or she prefers to be alone. In this case, you might ask your friend before you move these items to the side, or you might avoid going over altogether. Your instructor working in his or her office with the door wide open could be indicating that he or she is available to see students. Still, you would probably attempt to knock or at least announce yourself before entering the office, because you are essentially invading the instructor's primary space. The reaction of your friend sitting at a table or your instructor working in the office—looking up and smiling or expressing annoyance—will probably dictate what you do next, which brings us to the next element of nonverbal communication.

Notice the difference between these two photos. The first photo is a scene from a Western city in which people are noticeably uncomfortable with their lack of personal space. The second photo captures Japanese train pushers, whose job is to cram as many people onto the subway car as possible. Little consideration is given to personal space in this Eastern city. What imaginary aura that people regard as part of themselves is obviously more restricted in the latter photo?

Kinesics

Kinesics refers to the movement that takes place during the course of an interaction. While interacting, you may move around quite a bit, shift position, walk around as you talk, cross and uncross your legs, lean forward on a table, or sit back in a chair. Kinesics can be broken down into postures and gestures. In every case, whether separately or in combination, these cues convey messages about your relationship to others, about the subject you are discussing (discomfort or relative ease), or about the situation as a whole.

Posture

The position of your body during an interaction may be relaxed and welcoming or tense and off-putting. For example, someone draping him- or herself over a chair will look very relaxed, and someone sitting up straight or standing to attention will not.

In an open posture, the front of the body is observable, and in a closed posture, the front of the body is essentially shut off, usually because the arms are folded across the chest or the person is hunched over. Both types of posture convey the three attitudes noted before: (1) attitude about self (confidence, anxiety, shyness, a feeling of authority), (2) attitude about others (liking, respect, attention), and (3) attitude about the situation (comfort, ease). An open posture conveys positive messages, and a closed posture conveys negative messages. When someone feels "down," he or she tends to look "down," slumping over, slouching, and generally being depressed (*depressed* means "pressed down"). These postures send messages about a person's relaxation, attention, confidence, comfort, and willingness to communicate.

Gesture

Gesture can be defined as a movement of the body or any of its parts in a way that conveys an idea or intention or displays a feeling or an assessment of the situation (Peace, Porter, & Almon, 2012). Suppose you were in a foreign country, one of your friends suffered heatstroke, and no one knew the word for *dehydrated* in that country's language. You would likely indicate your need for water by making a "drinking" gesture.

kinesics: the study of movements that take place during the course of an interaction

ANALYZING EVERYDAY COMMUNICATION

Mirroring Nonverbal Behavior

People often find that they unconsciously adopt a similar posture to another person in an interaction (for example, they fold their arms when the other person does). Go to a public space on campus and observe individuals who are talking to or interacting with others.

QUESTIONS TO CONSIDER

1. Did people's nonverbal behavior mirror that of others they were with?
2. Did you notice any differences in the verbal communication between individuals who mirrored the behavior of people they were with and those who did not?

When people think of gestures, hand or arm movements most often come to mind, but facial expressions also count as gestures for our purposes. Quite frequently, your face and the rest of your body work together to express meaning. For instance, when a person is expressing an emotion, the face will provide information about the exact emotion being expressed, and the body will provide information about its extent. You could, for example, be angry and scowling while your body is fairly loose and fluid, indicating low-intensity anger. However, you could be scowling, holding your body tight and rigid, and almost shaking, which would indicate great anger and tell others to use their knowledge of proxemics to give you plenty of space!

Gestures can be split broadly into two sorts: those that represent feelings or ideas not necessarily being expressed in words (emblems) and those that visualize or emphasize something said in words (illustrators). **Emblems** are not related to speech in the sense that they do not help illustrate what is being said, although they may clarify what a person means. Consider conductors directing bands and orchestras, police officers directing traffic, and coaches signaling plays. Emblems can nevertheless be translated into verbal expressions; for example, you recognize that bouncing the palm of your hand off your forehead means "How stupid of me! Why didn't I think of it before?"

Illustrators are directly related to speech as it is being spoken and are used to visualize or emphasize its content. For example, turning your palm down and then rotating it as you describe how to unscrew a bottle cap is an illustrator, and scrunching up your face while saying "This tastes disgusting" is an illustrator using facial expression. Like other nonverbal communication, gestures can also regulate interaction. While making a speech, you might raise a finger to draw attention to the fact that you wish to make a key point.

Eye Contact and Gaze

Eye contact refers to the extent to which someone looks directly into the eyes of another person. In the United States, someone who "looks you in the eye" while talking is generally seen as reliable and honest. On the other hand, someone with shifty eyes is treated as suspicious and untrustworthy. **Gaze**—distinguished from eye contact, where both interactants look at each other—describes one person looking at another and, most of the time, is seen as rewarding. Most people generally like to be looked at when they are talking to someone else. In fact, if you gaze at a speaker and smile or nod approvingly, you will probably find that the speaker pays more attention to you, looks toward you more often, and engages in eye contact with you. (However, this is a culturally relative point, and in Eastern cultures eye contact is disrespectful and an inferior in the hierarchy should look away from a superior. In this case, gaze aversion is a sign of respect.)

Although most eye contact is positive, it can also convey negative messages. A wide-eyed stare can convey disbelief or a threat. Years ago, Ellsworth, Carlsmith, and Henson (1972) stood at the intersections of roads and stared at some drivers and not others. Those who were stared at tended to drive away more speedily, suggesting

emblems: gestures that represent feelings or ideas not necessarily being expressed verbally

illustrators: gestures that visualize or emphasize verbal communication

eye contact: extent to which someone looks directly into the eyes of another person

gaze: involves one person looking at another person

that a stare is a threatening stimulus for flight. Gaze can therefore be threatening and negative as much as it can be enticing and positive.

Some people (shy people, for example), afraid that others will evaluate them negatively, tend to decrease eye contact (Bradshaw, 2006), which cuts out negative inputs from other people. For shy people, this is a distinct advantage, but it also reduces the amount of information they can gather about a listener's reaction to what they say. Many outsiders assume that decreased eye contact is evidence of other social flaws, such as deception, so a shy person who avoids eye contact through fear of feedback may eventually create an impression of being shifty and unreliable. Burgoon, Coker, and Coker (1986) found that gaze aversion produces consistently negative evaluations of interviewees. Typically, unconfident behavior (as in shy people) involves not only low eye contact but also nervous speech, poor posture, tendency for long silences in conversation, and lack of initiative in discussion.

Eye contact is also used to regulate interactions. Some characteristic patterns of eye movements go along with talk in conversations to regulate its flow. The speaker tends to look at the listener at the start and end of sentences (or paragraphs, if the speaker is telling a longer tale) but may look away during the middle parts. A listener who wishes to speak will tend to look hard at the present speaker, and a person asking a question will look right at the person to whom it is directed, maintaining his or her gaze while awaiting a reply. Listeners look at speakers more consistently than speakers look at listeners. When giving a speech to a group or large audience, it is important that you not only look at your audience (rather than at your notes) most of the time but also distribute your gaze around the room, looking both left and right.

Interaction is further regulated through use of eye contact to manage turn taking (described below), a kind of eye-based "over and out." In cultures where simultaneous speech is taken as a sign of impoliteness, rather than of active and desirable involvement in the interaction, eye contact is used to end or yield a turn (a speaker looks longer toward the audience at the end of sentences), as well as to request a turn (a listener establishes longer eye contact with a speaker in order to signal willingness to enter the conversation). You leave a conversation by breaking off eye contact (typically 45 seconds before departure) and then, when the talking stops, turning toward an exit.

Vocalics

Vocalics, sometimes called paralanguage, refers to vocal characteristics that provide information about *how verbal communication should be interpreted* and about *how you are feeling* and even about *yourself*. When being sarcastic, your tone of voice will let others know if they should evaluate your words as serious or as part of a joke. The tone of your voice might be strained when you are angry or high-pitched when you are anxious. You can recognize some people you know simply by the sound of their voice. You can even tell things about people you do not know based on the sound of their voices. The voice can provide information about a person's place of origin, age, and sex. The sound of someone's voice also impacts perceptions of his or her credibility and attractiveness.

vocalics (paralanguage): vocal characteristics that provide information about how verbal communication should be interpreted and how the speaker is feeling

Pitch involves the highness or lowness of a person's voice. If you want to get technical, it involves the frequency of sound waves that are produced when you speak. Higher pitches produce more sound waves than lower pitches. Some people speak naturally at a very high pitch, while other people speak in a lower tone. People often use changes in the pitch of their voice to emphasize the parts of a sentence that they think are the most important.

pitch: highness or lowness of a person's voice

Rate is how fast or slow you speak, generally determined by how many words you speak per minute. People average around 150 words per minute when speaking, but differences certainly exist among individuals. When a teacher wants you to pay special attention to what is being said, he or she will sometimes slow down so you realize the importance of the point. Someone who speaks too fast is likely to be treated as nervous or possibly shy. In everyday life, where people are relaxed among friends, their speech rate tends to be lively and fluent rather than stilted or halting. In stressful circumstances, however, their speech rate may be hesitant or uneven.

Volume is the loudness or softness of a person's voice. Like variations in pitch and rate, some people naturally speak louder or softer than others. When speaking, changes in volume can provide emphasis to your words by indicating importance or poignancy. Increases and decreases in volume can also convey emotional feeling.

Silence, or the meaningful lack of any sound, is a surprising part of vocalics. You may have heard the seemingly contradictory phrases "Silence is golden" and "Silence is deadly." Depending on cultural, contextual, and relational factors, both of these phrases can be true. Most people in the United States—especially on a date or in an interview—meet silence or a prolonged break in conversation with discomfort. In other cultures, prolonged silence is not only tolerable but also may be expected. Silence can indicate embarrassment, anxiety, or lack of preparation as well as shyness, confusion, or disrespect. It can also be used to show anger or frustration, such as when you give someone the "silent treatment." Silence can also be an indication of relational comfort, that people do not feel pressured to keep the conversation going.

ETHICAL ISSUE

If a member of another culture is breaking a rule of nonverbal communication in your culture, should you tell him or her? Why or why not?

Vocalics and Relationships

This brings us to the use of vocalics and relationships. Giles (2008) shows that people can indicate their membership in a particular group by the way they use vocalic nonverbal behavior. For instance, if you are from the South, you might use a heavier accent in your conversation with others from your state or region, but you might tone down your accent when talking to people from the Northeast. Where people wish to maintain a distance from the person they are talking to, they will diverge, or hang on to differences in accent. When they want to become closer to the other person, they will tend to converge, or match their way of talking to the other person's. You may notice yourself copying the speech styles of people you like. Farley, Hughes, and LaFayette (2013) found that not only do people's voices change when talking with a romantic partner, but other people can also distinguish whether someone is talking with a romantic partner or a friend based solely on the sound of the person's voice.

Vocalics and Regulation

In addition to sending relational messages, people use vocalics to regulate their interactions. **Backchannel communication** involves vocalizations by a listener that give feedback to the speaker to show interest, attention, and a willingness to keep listening. For instance, *Uh-huh* may be used to encourage someone else to keep talking. Backchannel communication also involves vocalizations that a speaker wishes to keep speaking. *Um* might be used to indicate that a speaker does not want to yield the floor because he or she still has something to say but has not yet decided what.

The most common use of vocalics in regulating your interaction is with **turn taking**, which is when you hand over speaking to another person. This handover happens much less obviously than does a radio form of communication, where a trucker, for example, says "over" or "comeback" to indicate that he or she has finished speaking

rate (of speech): how fast or slowly a person speaks, generally determined by how many words are spoken per minute

volume: loudness or softness of a person's voice

silence: meaningful lack of sound

backchannel communication: vocalizations by a listener that give feedback to the speaker to show interest, attention, and/or a willingness to keep listening

turn taking: when one speaker hands over speaking to another person and wants another person to respond. In your normal interactions, you do not need to say "over" because, in addition to eye movements discussed above, you can tell from changes in pitch, rate, and volume that he or she wants you to begin speaking. For example, when someone asks a question, raising the pitch of his or her voice afterward serves to prompt you that the questioner now expects an answer. You also know when people are coming to the end of what they want to say because they will generally slow down somewhat and drop the pitch of their voice. That is how students know when a lecture is coming to an end and that they should start closing their books!

Chronemics

Chronemics encompasses use and evaluation of time in your interactions, including the location of events in time (see Kalman, Scissors, Gill, & Gergle, 2013). For example, the significance of a romantic encounter can often be determined by when it occurs. You might see a lunch date as less meaningful than a late-night candlelit dinner. Whether you are meeting for lunch or dinner, however, your meal will have a time structure and pattern. You probably have the salad before the ice cream.

Chronemics also involves the duration of events. Boring lectures seem to last forever. You may also have had the experience that people often end their college romances after about 18 months or during the spring semester, when one partner might be graduating or going away for the summer. You are quite likely to comment if you run into someone whom you have not seen for "a-a-a-ges." Also, you would probably feel the need to apologize if you left an e-mail unanswered for too long, did not answer a text message, or were late for an appointment.

Cultural differences in attitudes toward time also exist; some cultures especially value timely completion of tasks over attention to relationships, respect, or status, while others place the priorities exactly in reverse, feeling that it is discourteous to get down to the task before taking plenty of time to create a good relational atmosphere first.

By the way...

Touch and Diplomacy

In some cultures men and women are not allowed to touch, and more specifically heads of state or religious leaders are not allowed to touch women. This leads to some diplomatic issues when, for example, a visiting female dignitary is not allowed to touch, or in this case shake hands, with a religious leader. Such cases have to be carefully managed since a refusal to shake hands is usually regarded as an insult in the United States. For this reason, U.S. media never showed the moment of greeting between former Secretary of State Hillary Clinton and leading Arab heads of state.

QUESTIONS TO CONSIDER

1. Do you consider cultural norms to be more important than diplomatic norms?
2. When two cultures disagree about appropriate communication, how do you think the issue should be resolved? In other words, which cultural norms should be given priority?

Chronemics and Regulation of Interaction

Chronemics can affect the structure of interactions. You have an expectation about the number of milliseconds that are supposed to elapse between one person finishing speaking and the other joining in. When this timing gets disrupted, interaction becomes uncomfortable for everybody—one reason why people who stammer or who are shy create difficulty for others in interaction by not picking up the conversational baton when they are expected to (Bradshaw, 2006). You also recognize that when someone is really paying attention to you and is interested in what you are saying, he or she will tend to be engaged and maintain "synchrony." He or she will not allow too much time to elapse between utterances and try to synchronize his or her interaction and behavior with yours. In addition, you can indicate interest in somebody else by answering his or her questions promptly, a chronemic activity. You also convey information about your knowledge and expertise by keeping your

chronemics: the study of use and evaluation of time in interactions

What nonverbal communication seems to indicate that these two people like each other?

talk flowing freely and by not allowing yourself too many hesitations. Both fluency and the absence of hesitation count as chronemic elements of nonverbal communication since they are about the timing of speech.

Haptics

Haptics is the study of the specific nonverbal behaviors involving touch. These days there is also "haptic technology," and the ability to touch, enlarge, and swipe your smartphone screen is one of the newer developments. When people get into your personal space, they will likely make actual physical contact with your most personal possession, your body. Touch is used not only as a greeting to start an interaction (a handshake or a kiss) but also in ceremonies, whether baptism, the confirming laying on of hands, holding a partner's hands while making wedding vows, or as a means of congratulation from a simple handshake to a pat on the back to those piles of players who form on top of someone who made a game-winning score or play in sports.

Psychologist Sidney Jourard (1971) observed and recorded how many times couples in cafés casually touched each other in an hour. The highest rates were in Puerto Rico (180 times per hour) and Paris (110 times per hour). Guess how many times per hour couples touched each other in the mainland United States? Twice! (In London, it was zero. They never touched.) Jourard also found that French parents and children touched each other three times more frequently than did American parents and children.

Heslin (1974) noted that touch, of which there are many different types, has many different functions, as shown in Table 5.5. These forms of touch show positive feelings, but each could also produce negative feelings: Someone you feel close to shakes your hand instead of hugging you, or someone you are not close to tries to hug you. Touch can also indicate influence. Have you ever seen a politician who places one arm on the back of a visiting foreign dignitary to indicate a place to which the person should move? The two actions together serve to indicate politely to the other person where the next stage of a discussion or proceedings will take place. Touch can also serve as a physiological stimulus, for example, in sexual touch or from a reassuring back rub.

haptics: the study of the specific nonverbal behaviors involving touch

Table 5.5 Heslin's (1974) Functions of Touch

Functional/professional	Touch is permitted by the context—for example, during a medical exam, someone you hardly know may touch parts of your body that even your best friend has never seen.
Social/polite	Touch is formal—for example, a handshake.
Friendship/warmth	Touch is an expression of regard.
Love/intimacy	Touch is special, permitted only with those with whom you are close.

As with all other nonverbal communication, touch can play a role in interaction management. For example, you can touch someone on the arm to interrupt the flow of conversation. Also you both begin and end encounters with handshakes on many occasions, indicating that the beginning and ending of the interaction have essentially relational consequences because you imply, through touch, continuance of the relationship beyond the specific interaction.

From the previous discussion of nonverbal behavior you can see that it is an essential part of communication in everyday life and one that is by no means unimportant. Indeed, when nonverbal communication has, according to some research, 4.3 times more influence than the words that are spoken, it would be foolish to overlook its wide-ranging use to convey power, status, feelings, and clarity to the meaning of words.

Focus Questions Revisited

What is nonverbal communication?

Nonverbal communication is everything that communicates a message but does not include words. Nonverbal communication is (a) symbolic, (b) encoded and decoded, (c) both dynamic and static, (d) guided by rules, (e) cultural, (f) ambiguous, (g) less controlled than verbal communication, and (h) continuous.

How does nonverbal communication interconnect with verbal communication?

Nonverbal communication can repeat, substitute, emphasize, moderate, and contradict verbal communication.

How does nonverbal communication regulate interactions?

Nonverbal communication regulates interaction by initiating interactions, enabling turn taking, and defining when interactions have reached their end. It does this through eye movements, vocalics, and gestures, among other things.

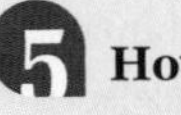

How does nonverbal communication identify people?

Physical appearance, voice, clothing, and even smell can be used to identify people.

How does nonverbal communication transmit emotional information?

Nonverbal communication actually allows you to convey three different kinds of emotional information: attitudes toward the other person, attitudes toward the situation, and attitudes toward yourself.

6 What are the most common types of nonverbal communication?

Common types of nonverbal communication include the following: (a) proxemics, (b) territoriality, (c) kinesics, (d) eye contact and gaze, (e) vocalics, (f) chronemics, and (g) haptics.

Key Concepts

backchannel communication 104
body buffer zone 99
chronemics 105
decoding 90
dynamic 91
emblems 102
encoding 91
eye contact 102
gaze 102
haptics 106
illustrators 102
kinesics 101

leakage 94
nonverbal communication 89
personal space 99
pitch 103
proxemics 98
rate 104
regulators 95
silence 104
static 91
territoriality 98
turn taking 104
vocalics 103
volume 104

Questions to Ask Your Friends

1. Ask your friends how good they believe themselves to be at determining when other people are not telling the truth.
2. Ask your friends whether they can tell when you are embarrassed or uncomfortable even though you might not tell them. What nonverbal behaviors inform them of your embarrassment or discomfort?
3. Ask your friends whether they think they could get away with telling you a lie.

Media Connections

1. Look for television news stories involving police putting people into cars. What percentage of police touch the person's head? In what other circumstances, if any, do people open the car door for someone else and then touch the head of the person getting in? What do you think is being conveyed?
2. How many news stories can you find where a fight got started because someone felt another person was "looking at him in a funny way" or infringing upon his personal space?
3. How do television shows use the placement of furniture to add something to the story?

Student Study Site

SAGE edge™

Sharpen your skills with SAGE edge at edge.sagepub.com/duckciel2e

SAGE edge for students provides a personalized approach to help you accomplish your coursework goals in an easy-to-use learning environment.

Chapter Outline

Why Is Listening Important?

- Listening and Education
- Listening and Career
- Listening and Religion and Spirituality
- Listening and Health Care
- Listening and Relationships
- Listening Objectives

Active Listening

Engaged and Relational Listening

- Disengaged Listening
- Engaged Listening for a Transactional World
- Relational Listening

Recognizing and Overcoming Listening Obstacles

Critical Listening

- Elements of Critical Listening
- Fallacious Arguments

Focus Questions Revisited

Key Concepts

Questions to Ask Your Friends

Media Connections

06 Listening

What if we told you that we could provide you with the secret to academic success, career advancement, and improved relationships? The truth is that we can tell you one secret to these things, and it is something many people rarely consider: listening.

Effective listening entails more than merely going through the motions of hearing what someone says. Effective listening means being active in hearing what is said. This means paying careful attention to what your partner says. It also requires assessment of the evidence and arguments your partner presents, looking out for fallacies in arguments, and being engaged, critical, and relationally aware of underlying themes and rhetorical visions in what the speaker says. In short, an active listener is one who recognizes and overcomes the many obstacles to listening encountered in everyday communication and makes a good relational connection with the speaker. As you will find out, listening is a very demanding and exhausting activity!

In this chapter, we discuss the objectives for listening, such as relational development, gaining and comprehending information, critical evaluation, enjoyment, and therapeutic goals. We also address active listening and discuss how *listening* and *hearing* are not the same thing. Discussions of listening frequently do not go beyond the active listening process, but we discuss ways to maximize your listening skills and emphasize the importance of being "other oriented"—focused not on your own reactions but on what the other person is trying to say.

People listen more effectively on some occasions than on others; however, you may not be fully aware of the many *obstacles* to listening. We address these obstacles and discuss how you might overcome them. You may very well be a listening champion once you finish studying this chapter! Even if you do not receive an award for listening, your listening skills will significantly improve, assisting you in school, your career, and your relationships.

The final part of this chapter is dedicated to critical listening. Being critical does not necessarily mean finding fault or disagreeing with messages, but it does involve determining their accuracy, legitimacy, and value. This process may lead just as often to a positive evaluation of a message as to a negative evaluation of a message. We discuss the prevalence of critical evaluation in everyday life and examine the four elements of critical evaluation. We also explore the use of fallacious arguments based on faulty reasoning or insufficient evidence. Fallacious

FOCUS QUESTIONS

1. Why is listening important enough to have an entire chapter devoted to it?
2. What are the objectives of listening?
3. What does it mean to listen actively?
4. What are engaged and relational listening?
5. What obstacles must people overcome to listen well?
6. What is critical listening, and why is it so important?
7. What are fallacious arguments?
8. Can you identify a "hasty generalization," a "bandwagon appeal," and an "equivocation" in commercials?

arguments, actually quite evident in everyday communication, appear in many of the commercials you come across each day. After reading this chapter, you will be better equipped to recognize—and not be fooled by—these.

Why Is Listening Important?

Listening is the communication activity in which people engage most frequently. In fact, studies conducted over the past 90 years have consistently ranked listening as the most frequent communication activity (Barker, Edwards, Gaines, Gladney, & Holley, 1980; Janusik & Wolvin, 2009; Rankin, 1928; Weinrauch & Swanda, 1975). All the same, very few studies have been devoted to it recently, and most sources cited to support claims about listening are quite old. One of the most recent studies examining the amount of time spent listening found that people dedicate nearly 12 hours daily to listening-related activities, such as talking with friends, attending class, participating in a business meeting, or listening to music on an iPod (Janusik & Wolvin, 2009). In other words, you probably spend half of each day *listening!*

As frequently as people engage in listening, its significance in daily life is not always valued. People may tend to take this essential communication activity for granted. Perhaps the most pervasive activity of everyday life (Halone & Pechioni, 2001), listening is nevertheless crucial to everyday interactions in a number of important contexts.

Listening and Education

Listening—often the primary channel of instruction at all levels of education—is a fundamental element in instruction and key to academic success. Listening is also a critical component in the relationships that develop between students and their instructors and between students and their academic advisors. Both instructor–student and advisor–advisee relationships demand effective listening by everyone involved. Yet active listening remains the least taught and most taken for granted type of communication skill (see Beall, Gill-Rosier, Tate, & Matten, 2008).

Skills You Can Use: **Listening**

We will remind you to do so when examining obstacles to effective listening, but as you read this chapter, consider the ways in which your listening in the classroom can be enhanced. Also, consider how interactions with your instructors, your classmates, your advisors, and others with whom you share an academic-based relationship can be improved through engaged and relational listening. As you read on, imagine specific situations where you could apply what you are learning. For example, think about how you could make better contributions in class, if you have really understood what your teacher/classmates are trying to say, and whether your learning has increased by paying closer attention to what other people say. Active listening really will become a skill you can develop to your benefit.

Listening and Career

Effective listening skills are also crucial to career success and advancement. Employers frequently rank listening as one of the most sought-after skills. Furthermore, most success and achievement from both organizational and personal career standpoints can be connected in large measure to effective listening (see Flynn, Valikoski, & Grau, 2008). This is true not only in jobs like social work or pastoral duties or being a really good investigative journalist or interviewer but in listening carefully to what others say in business meetings or strategy sessions and paying close attention to customer concerns. Surveying the importance of listening in all professions and its significance in developing occupational areas, one listening scholar concluded that "job success and development of all employees, regardless of title, position, or task will continue to be directly related to the employees' attitudes toward, skills in, and knowledge about listening" (Steil, 1997, p. 214).

Enabling someone to talk about a problem or concern is known as what type of listening?

Listening and Religion and Spirituality

Although in this context it has received less attention from researchers, listening is also an important component in religion and spirituality. Surveying this context, it was noted that listening in this area includes *intra*personal listening when engaged in meditation and prayer. *Inter*personal listening occurs in such instances as listening to sermons or music and studying sacred and holy texts (Schnapp, 2008).

Listening and Health Care

Listening is also a fundamental element of health care. The extent to which both patients and providers listen effectively has a tremendous impact on whether correct diagnoses are established and on whether patients accurately follow provider instructions. Listening is also vital to successful communication among health care workers.

Listening and Relationships

Listening also plays a fundamental role in relationship development and maintenance. When both partners engage in effective listening, they tend to have more successful, longer lasting, and more positive relationships. A sure recipe for failure is when either partner fails to engage in effective listening and makes up his or her own (probably incorrect) reasons for the other's attitudes and behaviors. Effective listening is an essential component of every action that takes place within relationships at all stages of development.

Listening Objectives

While people may have a primary objective for listening, a single communicative exchange can have multiple goals. Table 6.1 presents these listening goals in isolation, but keep in mind that all listening situations may entail more than one objective.

Table 6.1 Listening Objectives

Relational Development and Enhancement	People may engage in listening for the development and enhancement of relationships. Through listening, you can gain a greater understanding of yourself, your partner, and the relationship—even when these are not being discussed directly.
Gaining and Comprehending Information	People also listen in order to gain and comprehend information. As a student, you are likely well aware of this listening objective as you listen to lectures during class or to a classmate during a class discussion.
Critical Listening	The goals of critical listening include evaluating the accuracy of a message as well as its value in a given situation. For example, you may listen critically to a salesperson discussing a product. Critical listening may lead to negative or positive evaluations of the message.
Enjoyment and Appreciation	People also listen for enjoyment or appreciation: listening to a friend tell a story about a recent trip, listening to music on an iPod, or listening to crickets chirp and birds sing while walking through a wooded area. The objective of these listening experiences is to gain pleasure.
Therapeutic Listening	Therapeutic listening enables someone to talk through a problem or concern. Examples of therapeutic listening include listening to a coworker complain about a customer or client and listening to a neighbor talk about financial difficulties. In these situations, the person might simply be needing to express certain anxieties or frustrations, might be seeking approval or justification for feelings, or might be seeking advice and counsel about appropriate actions.

Active Listening

Many people use the terms *hearing* and *listening* interchangeably, but they are not the same. **Hearing** is the passive physiological act of receiving sound that takes place when sound waves hit your eardrums. If someone starts beating on a desk, the resulting sound waves will travel through the air and hit your eardrum, the act of which is an example of hearing. As the act is passive, you can hear without really having to think about it.

Listening is the active process of receiving, attending to, interpreting, and responding to symbolic activity. As opposed to hearing, listening is active because it requires a great deal of work and energy to accomplish. It is also referred to as a process rather than an act, since multiple steps or stages are involved. If someone beats on a desk in a rhythm that another person recognizes and correctly interprets as Morse code, then listening has occurred. (See below discussion of *interpreting*.)

The first step in the listening process is the act of **receiving** sensory stimuli as sound waves that travel from the source of the sound to your eardrums. As you continue reading, keep in mind that the entire listening process is not just about hearing or about aural stimuli. Multiple sensory channels, including taste, touch, smell, and sight, can be used to make sense of a message you have received.

Attending to stimuli occurs when you perceive and focus on stimuli. Despite constant flooding with competing stimuli, you pick up only on some. The stimuli that receive your attention are those most necessary to accomplish the task at hand. In a conversation with your boss about an important issue, for example, you will probably attempt to concentrate on what he or she is saying rather than on competing stimuli, such as other conversations taking place nearby or music playing in the background.

The third step in the listening process, **interpreting**, is when you assign meaning to sounds. You use multiple sensory channels and accompanying stimuli when

hearing: the passive physiological act of receiving sound that takes place when sound waves hit a person's eardrums

listening: the active process of receiving, attending to, interpreting, and responding to symbolic activity

receiving: the initial step in the listening process where hearing and listening connect

attending: the second step in the listening process when stimuli are perceived and focused on

interpreting: the third step in the listening process when meaning is assigned to sounds and symbolic activity

listening, especially sight and visual stimuli. Returning to the earlier example of a person beating on a desk, if you see his or her hand hitting the desk each time that sound is received, this cue will assist you in making sense of what you hear—whether it is Morse code or not. Likewise, noticing a smile or a scowl when a person is speaking to you will help determine whether he or she intended a caustic remark as a joke or as a serious retort.

Responding is your reaction to the communication of another person. Responses, or feedback, to messages occur throughout the entire communication. Even though you give a verbal response to a comment, you may express yourself nonverbally. Responding to a message while it is being received, even a snarky smile or an approving nod, can show another person your reaction to what is said. In addition to letting someone know you are listening, any kind of active or unintended response enables the sender to know how you feel about the message.

After receiving a message, you may respond with verbal feedback in which you explain your interpretation of the message. **Reflecting**, sometimes referred to as *paraphrasing*, involves summarizing what another person has said in your own words to convey your understanding of the message ("I understand you to mean that our team has until the end of the week to finish the project"). Sometimes these reflections or paraphrases are accompanied by requests for clarification or approval ("Do you mean it will be impossible to receive my order by the first of the month?"). Reflecting primarily assists in ensuring accurate understanding of the message, but it serves the secondary function of exhibiting attentiveness to the message and concern about its accurate interpretation.

By the way...

Giving Others Feedback

Traditional positive feedback or response to a message includes leaning forward, smiling, and nodding your head in agreement, while negative feedback or response includes leaning away from the source, frowning, and shaking your head in disagreement. Feedback can also include looks of shock, excitement, boredom, and confusion.

QUESTIONS TO CONSIDER

1. Do you think it helps your interactions if you control some of these reactions, or is it better to be perfectly natural?
2. What if you are a therapist, social worker, or pastor? Should you ever let yourself look shocked at what clients or parishioners say to you, or will that send the signal that you are critical rather than "there for them"?

Engaged and Relational Listening

The process of active listening described above has traditionally been viewed as the ideal method of listening. This description is OK for the most part. Nevertheless, participating in the communication process involves more than listening carefully to what is said, even if you listen intently and can repeat it. *A tape recorder can accomplish both of these things.*

Essential for truly effective listening is being engaged and relationally aware. Engaged and relational listening involves attending carefully to what the speaker means or perhaps has left unsaid. When doing so, a listener can repeat not only the essence of what has been said, by giving a clear and evidently accurate report of what was said, but will report also the matters that were relevant but left unsaid. "Duck and McMahan is not only an inexpensive book compared with the competition but is up to date and engaging." (Translation: "My professor, Steve Duck, had us write 'anonymous' comments on this book before he gave us grades. He wrote this book with David McMahan, and the way he tells it, other books are short on vision and lack decent evidence. I wanted a good grade, so I went heavy on the praise.")

Engaged listening means making a relational connection with the source of a message. Not just listening actively, engaged listening involves caring, trusting, wanting to know more, and feeling excited, enlightened, attached, and concerned.

responding: final step in the listening process that entails reacting to the message of another person

reflecting (paraphrasing): summarizing what another person has said to convey understanding of the message

engaged listening: making a personal relational connection with the source of a message that results from the source and the receiver actively working together to create shared meaning and understanding

Customer service representatives often appear to be listening actively, but they do not really understand the point of view of the customer. If they attempted to make a personal connection with the customer and actively worked to create shared understanding, what type of listening would they be doing?

Disengaged Listening

Perhaps the best way to explain what we mean by engaged listening is by first demonstrating what it is *not*. Examples of disengaged listening include standard attempts to be friendly and positive in boilerplate responses to technical support questions and apologies from the bank/airline/hotel after receiving a complaint. Most of these responses start off by saying how important you are while the rest of the message in both form and content conveys a contrasting meaning. "Your call is *very* important to us. Please stay on the line until the next available agent is free. And by the way, how do you like old violin music played right into your earpiece? We have all of Vivaldi's [1678–1741] classical *Four Seasons,* and that is likely how long you will wait."

Engaged Listening for a Transactional World

Engaged listening enables you to grasp a deeper understanding of the message that goes beyond what can be achieved through mere active listening. Take reflecting, the routine approach to active listening described earlier. While you may be able to paraphrase or repeat what you hear, this ability does not guarantee you will actually understand the overtones of what is said. For example, active listeners may be able to understand and "reflect" that when someone says, "As a father, I am against the military occupation of Freedonia," he is stating opposition to the situation in a foreign country. Active yet disengaged listeners, however, may miss the deeper significance of the first three words. Apparently irrelevant to the rest of the sentiment expressed, they were probably uttered because the role of "father" is central to *the speaker's view of self* and to *the speaker's view of his relationship with others* and therefore constitute a major part of what he wants to tell the world. Engaged listeners would be able to pick up on this additional meaning (perhaps he is concerned that his child may be drafted to fight in Freedonia).

ETHICAL ISSUE

Although therapeutic listening conveys concerns for others, when would you consider it appropriate to suggest that a friend seek professional assistance instead of continuing to expect you to listen and advise upon his or her problems?

Relational Listening

Relational listening involves recognizing, understanding, and addressing the interconnection of relationships and communication. Vital to understanding how your personal and social relationships are intrinsically connected with communication, listening relationally will also enhance your understanding of your personal relationships and the meaning of communication taking place. When engaging in relational listening, you must address two features of communication and relationships: how communication impacts the relationship and how the relationship impacts communication.

All communication between people in a relationship will impact that relationship somehow. Some exchanges may have a greater impact than others, but all communication will exert influence on the relationship. Relational listening entails recognizing this salient feature of communication, considering how a given message impacts the relationship, and addressing this impact in an appropriate manner. The relationship people share will also influence what is (or is not) communicated, how it is

relational listening: recognizing, understanding, and addressing the interconnection of relationships and communication during the listening process

Table 6.2 Questions to Consider When Receiving a Message

1. What impact does this message have on my understanding of this relationship?
2. What impact may this message have on the other person's understanding of this relationship?
3. Does this message correspond with my understanding of this relationship?
4. Is something absent from this message that would correspond with my understanding of this relationship?
5. Is this message being communicated in a manner that corresponds with my understanding of this relationship?
6. What does this message mean based on my understanding of this relationship?
7. What does this message tell me about the other person's understanding of this relationship?

Make your case

Dealing With Customer Service Agents

The job of a customer service representative is typically to respond to questions and requests from customers, which requires a good deal of listening in order to provide customers with the information they need. Recall an experience with a customer service representative in which you felt that you were not listened to.

QUESTIONS TO CONSIDER

1. What about the customer service representative's responses made you feel this way?
2. If you were training customer service providers, how would you prepare them to be good listeners? Could you become a listening consultant?

communicated, and its meaning. Relational listening when receiving a message would thus entail addressing the questions listed in Table 6.2.

How you answer these questions will determine the actions that result from the message you receive. First, these questions will guide your actual response to the message, given your relational understanding of its meaning and its impact on your relationship. Second, your answers to these questions will change your perception and understanding of the relationship. Sometimes these changes in perception and understanding will be quite profound, while other times your perception and understanding will be only slightly modified. All communication will change your relationship, once again underscoring the importance of listening.

Recognizing and Overcoming Listening Obstacles

Effective listening is fundamental in the development of shared meaning and understanding. It accounts for the positive attributes derived from interactions with others. But let's not get too rosy: Listening sometimes goes bad and results in negative outcomes and problems in relationships. What are these obstacles and problems?

Environmental distractions result from the physical location where listening takes place and competing sources (Wood, 2009). If you have tried listening to a friend when loud music is playing at a restaurant or bar, for example, or if people are whispering in class or texting while you are attempting to focus on your instructor, you already know how environmental factors can hinder effective listening. However, a host of environmental distractions can obstruct listening, and these distractions go beyond competing sounds that make it difficult to hear and pay attention. The

environmental distraction: obstacle to listening that results from the physical location where listening takes place and competing sources

ANALYZING EVERYDAY COMMUNICATION

Listening Obstacles in the Classroom

Listening has a profound impact on classroom performance. As you explore obstacles to effective listening, consider how you can enhance your listening abilities in the classroom by recognizing and overcoming these obstacles.

QUESTIONS TO CONSIDER

1. Which of these obstacles do you find most common in the classroom? What can you do to manage them?
2. What sorts of distractions have you discovered that prevent good understanding of what is said in class?

temperature of a room can distract you from fully listening if it happens to be uncomfortably warm or cool. Activity and movements of people not involved in a conversation can also distract you from focusing on a message being received.

Medium distractions result from limitations or problems inherent in certain media and technology, such as mobile phones or Internet connections. You have probably needed to include the phrases "Are you still there?" and "Can you hear me now?" in a conversation with someone when at least one of you was using a cell phone. You also likely have continued talking long after a call has been disconnected only to realize the disconnection when your phone starts ringing in your ear. Such distractions make it very difficult not only to pick up on the words being spoken but also to fully concentrate on the message. Similar to problems encountered with cell phones, problems involving poor connections and delays also occur when using instant and text messaging, making it very difficult to concentrate on the messages being exchanged.

Source distractions result from auditory and visual characteristics of the message source. Vocal characteristics—for example, an unfamiliar or uncharacteristic tone and quality of voice, extended pauses, and such repeated nonfluencies as *um, uh,* or *you know*—can distract you from listening to someone's message. A person's physical appearance, proxemics, haptics, and artifacts may also serve as distractions. For instance, someone may be standing too close to you or touching you more than you find appropriate or comfortable.

Factual diversion is a frequent problem that students experience when taking notes while listening to a lecture in class. It occurs when so much emphasis is placed on attending to every detail of a message that the main point becomes lost. Students become so intent on documenting every single detail that they lose the main point of the discussion. Imagine you are in a history course studying the American Revolution. The instructor is discussing Paul Revere's "midnight ride," which just so happens to be her area of expertise. As a result, throughout the discussion she offers multiple details about this infamous ride, including the type of buttons on Revere's jacket, the color and name of his horse, the temperature, and even what he ate for breakfast that morning. You begin to furiously write them all down in your notes. In fact, you note every single detail but one—the purpose of his ride! You know the color and name of his horse but not what he was doing on top of it. When you focus too much on every detail of a message, you very likely will miss the main idea.

Semantic diversion takes place when people are distracted by words or phrases used in a message through negative response or unfamiliarity. People tend to respond positively or negatively to words they encounter. The intensity of this response will vary, with some words eliciting a strong or weak response in one direction or the other (Osgood, Suci, & Tannenbaum, 1957). Semantic diversion occurs when your response to a certain word used during a message causes you to focus unnecessary attention on that word or prevents you from listening to the rest of the message. For example, you may hear a word that elicits a strong negative response, such as a racial or sexual slur, and focus on your feelings about that word rather than fully attending to the rest of the message.

medium distraction: obstacle to listening that results from limitations or problems inherent in certain media and technology, such as mobile phones or Internet connections

source distraction: obstacle to listening that results from auditory and visual characteristics of the message source

factual diversion: obstacle to listening that occurs when so much emphasis is placed on attending to every detail of a message that the main point becomes lost

semantic diversion: obstacle to listening that occurs when people are distracted by words or phrases used in a message through negative response or unfamiliarity

Semantic diversion also involves letting unfamiliar words or phrases cause us to stop listening to or shift our attention away from the message. People often encounter unrecognizable words in a message; for instance, during a lecture your instructors may occasionally use a word with which you are unfamiliar.

COMMUNICATION + YOU

Becoming a Good Listener

Some people are very good listeners, while others might be poor listeners. Being aware of what obstacles stand in the way of listening, and observing good listeners, can help to strengthen your listening skills. Hopefully (after finishing this chapter), you can call yourself a good listener!

QUESTIONS TO CONSIDER

1. Which of your friends, family members, classmates, or coworkers would you consider *good* listeners? What behaviors do these people enact when interacting with others? In what ways could their listening still improve?
2. Which of your friends, family members, classmates, or coworkers would you consider *poor* listeners? What behaviors do these people enact when interacting with others? In what ways could their listening improve?

Content (representational) listening occurs when people focus on the content level of meaning, or literal meaning, rather than the social or relational level of meaning. Content listening occurs when you focus solely on the surface level of meaning and fail to recognize or engage in determining deeper levels of meaning. A classmate may remark, "This project I have been working on is more difficult than I expected." If you listen only at the content level, you may see this statement as a mere observation. However, it may very well have a deeper meaning. Listening at a deeper level may uncover that this classmate needs your assistance, is seeking words of motivation, or is determining if your relationship is one that would provide such support.

Selective listening occurs when people focus on the points of a message that correspond with their views and interests and pay less attention to those that do not. Essentially, people pick up on the parts of a message that correspond with their views or that they find most interesting and disregard the rest. Imagine meeting a friend for lunch when you are particularly hungry. Upon meeting your friend, he begins telling you about his morning. You drift in and out of the conversation until he asks what restaurant you prefer. At that moment, you become very interested in the conversation and focus on what is being discussed.

Egocentric listening occurs when people focus more on their message and self-presentation than on the message of the other person involved in an interaction. This type of listening is frequently observed during disagreements or arguments when people concentrate so much on what they are going to say next that they fail to listen to others. Perhaps you are in the middle of a heated discussion with a rival coworker and have just come up with a brilliant sarcastic remark. You cannot wait until your coworker's lips stop moving so that you may use this line. The problem is that you have stopped listening to your coworker. You are so absorbed in developing and presenting your own message that you have failed to listen to his or hers.

Wandering thoughts occur when you daydream or think about things other than the message being presented. This lack of attention happens to everyone from time to time. No matter how intent you are on focusing on a message, your mind wanders, and you start thinking about other things. Consider listening to a lecture in class when your mind starts to wander. You think about a high school classmate, the great parking space you found last week, where you will eat after class, or a YouTube video that you have seen at least 20 times.

Wandering thoughts are caused not necessarily by lack of interest in the topic but rather by the connection between the rate of speech and the ability to process

content (representational) listening: obstacle to listening when people focus on the content level of meaning, or literal meaning, rather than the social or relational level of meaning

selective listening: obstacle to listening when people focus on the points of a message that correspond with their views and interests and pay less attention to those that do not

egocentric listening: obstacle to listening when people focus more on their message and self-presentation than on the message of the other person involved in an interaction

wandering thoughts: obstacle to listening involving daydreams or thoughts about things other than the message being presented

Why are wandering thoughts so common?

information, which can directly impact listening comprehension (Preiss & Gayle, 2006). People speak on average between 100 and 150 words per minute, but listeners process information at a rate of between 400 and 500 words per minute. An effective way to overcome this obstacle is to take advantage of the extra time by mentally summarizing what the speaker is saying. This strategy will enable you to remain focused, as well as increase your understanding of the message.

Experiential superiority takes place when people fail to fully listen to someone else because they believe that they possess more or superior knowledge and experience than the other person (Pearson & Nelson, 2000). If you have worked at the same job for a number of years, you might choose not to listen to a recently hired employee's suggestion about your work. You might feel that because you have more experience in the position, you do not need to listen because you will not hear anything new. Unfortunately, the new hire's suggestion might be good, but you will never know because you did not listen.

Message complexity becomes an obstacle to listening when a person finds a message so complex or confusing that he or she stops listening (Wood, 2009). At times, you may listen to a person discussing a topic that you feel is beyond your grasp. You may try to listen intently to comprehend what is being discussed, but you just find it too confusing and difficult to understand. In this situation, you feel tempted to stop listening because you believe you cannot glean anything valuable from paying further attention. You might, however, actually gain some understanding from continuing to listen, and the discussion might actually start making sense. Unfortunately, you will lose this understanding if you continue to ignore the remainder of the message.

Past experience with the source becomes an obstacle to listening when previous encounters with the message source lead people to ignore the message. You may know people who habitually lie or who seem to be wrong about nearly everything they say, and your past experience with these individuals may compel you to not listen to them. Although they may have something worthwhile to say, you will never know because you decided not to listen. Of course, just because you should listen to that person does not mean that you should believe what he or she tells you. We talk more about the need to critically examine messages in the next section.

experiential superiority: obstacle to listening when people fail to fully listen to someone else because they believe that they possess more or superior knowledge and experience than the other person

message complexity: obstacle to listening when a person finds a message so complex or confusing that he or she stops listening

past experience with the source: obstacle to listening when previous encounters with a person lead people to dismiss or fail to critically examine a message because the person has generally been right (or wrong) in the past

critical listening: the process of analyzing and evaluating the accuracy, legitimacy, and value of messages

Critical Listening

Critical listening does not mean being negative about what you hear; it means judging/assessing what you hear, and this assessment may end up being positive. Critical listening involves analyzing the accuracy, legitimacy, and value of messages and evidence produced to support claims. Critical listening can just as easily result in a positive as a negative valuation of a message. Much like movie critic Roger Ebert (1942–2013), who rated movies with either a "thumbs down" or a "thumbs up," you may evaluate messages positively or negatively. In addition, a message will likely have both positive and negative qualities, in which case you decide whether the positive attributes outweigh the negative or vice versa. Few messages can be evaluated as entirely negative or entirely positive, with the actual evaluation ranking somewhere in between. Rather than "thumbs up" and "thumbs down," perhaps "thumbs slightly askew upward" and "thumbs slightly askew downward" are more appropriate. So critical judgments are not black-and-white but involve many shades of gray.

Are there some types of relationships or areas of life that do not require critical evaluation?

Critical evaluation encompasses every aspect of daily life and all symbolic activity. People are constantly being called to make critical evaluations and judgments as they encounter others' messages and general life experiences. Your critical choices can range from major life-altering decisions, such as deciding to attend college, to seemingly less important but still significant decisions, such as which television program to watch or where to meet a friend for lunch. The need for critical listening pervades your daily life.

Elements of Critical Listening

Now that we have introduced critical listening, we can examine the four elements that compose it.

Evaluation of Plausibility

Some messages seem legitimate and valid whenever you first listen to them. When encountering other messages, however, you immediately get the feeling that something is just not right. Even if you cannot immediately pinpoint the problem with these messages, you feel as if something is amiss. When you experience these feelings, you are evaluating the **plausibility** of the message, or the extent to which it seems legitimate (Gouran, Wiethoff, & Doelger, 1994). You might not believe that diaper-wearing winged monkeys were spotted flying over campus because this event is implausible. The plausibility of other messages might not be as obvious, but something might still strike you as problematic. For example, an automobile dealership guaranteeing "free maintenance for life on all new cars sold this month" may strike you as plausible but problematic. You may feel that the message does not provide sufficient information or is not entirely genuine. When you are unsure of a message's legitimacy, it is best to follow your instincts. The evaluation of plausibility is your first line of defense as a critical listener, and often your first impression of a message is accurate.

Evaluation of Source

When critically examining a message, you must evaluate its source. As mentioned when discussing listening obstacles, you may know people who never provide you with good advice or who always seem to be wrong about everything. While you should still listen to these people in case they offer a worthwhile message, your past experiences with them may dictate the degree of belief and value that you place on their messages. The **status of the source** will also impact the extent to which you

plausibility: the extent to which a message seems legitimate

status of the source: obstacle to listening when a person's rank, reputation, or social position leads people to dismiss or fail to critically examine a message

critically engage a message. People tend to be more critical of messages from individuals of equal status than of those from higher-status individuals. For instance, you may not critically evaluate a message from your instructor because you assume he or she will be correct (Pearson & Nelson, 2000).

ETHICAL ISSUE

Consider a situation in which you were engaged in therapeutic listening and a friend told you in confidence that he or she was doing something harmful or dangerous, and really meant it (not just saying "Grrr! I could have killed her for making that comment!" but actually appearing to mean it). Would it be appropriate to tell someone else if you believed it would prevent your friend from being harmed or harming others? If you believe it would be proper to tell someone else, in what circumstances would this behavior be appropriate?

Evaluation of Consistency

Consistency concerns whether the message is free of internal contradiction and in harmony with information you already know is true (Gouran et al., 1994). Earlier in this chapter, we mention the importance of listening. If we contend later in the chapter that listening is not very important in your everyday life, this contradiction should strike you as problematic. One of these two statements is obviously wrong or misrepresented, and this contradiction might lead you to question the information being provided as well as the rest of the things we have told you in the book.

Consistency also entails whether the information provided agrees with information you already know as true. If someone is describing the best route to travel through the South and mentions that "once you enter Mississippi, just keep driving south until you reach Tennessee," you might question the message given your previous knowledge that Tennessee is actually located north of Mississippi. The information being offered is not consistent with previous information you know to be true.

Evaluation of Evidence

As a critical listener, you must also evaluate the evidence by considering the following criteria: verifiability, quantity, and quality. **Verifiability** indicates that the material being provided can be confirmed by other sources or means (Gouran et al., 1994). If someone tells you during the day that the sky is blue, you can verify this by going outside and looking for yourself. If someone tells you Alexander Hamilton was shot in a duel with Aaron Burr, you can verify this by confirming the information in a book about these historic figures. Some material may be more difficult to verify, in which case you must evaluate other aspects of the message.

When it comes to the *quantity* of evidence, there is no magic number to indicate a well-supported argument or claim. Such judgment is based on other evaluations of a message as well as the quality of evidence that is included, but the more arguments, data, and people that are consistent with it, the better.

Evaluations of *quality* include determining such issues as a lack of bias, sufficient expertise, and recency. Information from most sources slant in one direction or another when it comes to issues, but some sources may be very obvious about their point of view, such as material from pro-life groups and pro-choice groups. You should also determine the expertise of the sources being used. A newspaper reporter may be an expert in journalism, but that does not make him or her an expert source about fitness or military strategy, if writing such articles. Finally, you must determine whether information provided is recent or outdated. Given your knowledge of the issue, is information that is five years old outdated (as it would be in discussion of computers) or sufficiently current (key points in discussion of ancient Babylon really are not changing much at this moment)?

consistency: a message is free of internal contradiction and is in harmony with information known to be true

verifiability: an indication that the material being provided can be confirmed by other sources or means

fallacious argument: an argument that appears legitimate but is actually based on faulty reasoning or insufficient evidence

Fallacious Arguments

Engaging in critical listening requires the recognition of **fallacious arguments**, or those that appear legitimate but are actually based on faulty reasoning or insufficient evidence.

Argument against the source occurs when the source of a message, rather than the message itself, is attacked. This fallacy is traditionally known as *argument against the person* or *ad hominem (to the human being) argument,* but we prefer to call it *argument against the source* to recognize the growing trend in attacking not only people but also media sources. Political analysts are often guilty of this fallacy. For instance, you might hear a political analyst say, "The senator's latest proposal is not acceptable because he is nothing but a pathological liar." Rather than critically evaluating the actual proposal, the analyst attacks the source of the proposal. Challenging the source of a message instead of the message itself may indicate the message as sound; otherwise, the flaws of the message would be challenged. Sometimes actual media sources or systems are challenged. For instance, when discussing a television news segment you just watched with a friend, he might say, "That cannot be right because television news is biased against the current administration," challenging not the information within the segment but the media source of the information.

DISCIPLINARY **DEBATE**

Questioning the Source

Arguing against the source rather than the message is considered a fallacious argument. However, are there times when it would be appropriate to question the source of the message? Scholars do not want to encourage us to believe everything said by a person who has always told the truth in the past, because this may well be the exceptional case. Nor is it wise to dismiss everything a known liar says. Remember Aesop's fable of the "boy who cried wolf" who was not believed when his report was true? One of the key things that the military, the fire brigade, and the police have to be trained to do is to treat every report as "true" because the consequences of getting it wrong are so severe. So every bomb threat in an airport is treated seriously.

QUESTIONS TO CONSIDER

1. Have you ever been in a situation where you questioned the source of a message? If so, was that a good decision?
2. Have you ever been in a situation where you should have questioned the source but did not? If so, why did you not question the source?

Appeal to authority happens when a person's authority or credibility in one area is used to support another. Sports heroes and actors, for example, have been used to sell everything from magazine subscriptions to underwear. However, just because a person has particular knowledge or talent in one area does not mean he or she is knowledgeable or talented in all areas. Ask most college administrators to change the oil in an automobile and see what happens!

Appeal to people (bandwagon appeal) claims that something is good or beneficial because everyone else agrees with this evaluation. Consider the many products that boast their own popularity in advertisements: "Squeaky Clean is the nation's top-selling brand of dish soap" or "See *British and Redneck Professors Go to Vegas,* the movie that audiences have made the number-one comedy for two weeks in a row." No mention is made of dexterity in removing grease from pans or of wonderful acting. These products' *popularity* is offered instead, and you are asked to join the crowd. As a critical listener, you should recognize when the "appeal to people" fallacy is being used as the reason to purchase something, and you should question why other evidence was not provided.

Appeal to relationships occurs when relationships are used to justify certain behaviors and to convince others of their appropriateness. Communication scholar Erin Sahlstein (2000) has noted that people often refer to the relationship they share with another person in an interaction when attempting to convince him or her to behave a certain way. When

argument against the source (fallacious argument): when the source of a message, rather than the message itself, is attacked (also called ad hominem argument)

appeal to authority (fallacious argument): when a person's authority or credibility in one area is used to support another area

appeal to people (fallacious argument): claims that something is good or beneficial because everyone else agrees with this evaluation (also called *bandwagon appeal*)

appeal to relationships (fallacious argument): when relationships are used to justify certain behaviors and to convince others of their appropriateness

By the way...

Following the Crowd

Sometimes it is not the messages of others that make people susceptible to the appeal to people fallacy but rather their own thought processes. People may convince themselves of the value of an object or a behavior because they see lots of other people using or doing it. Making a decision based on what you perceive others to be doing is referred to as social proof (Cialdini, 1993). One interesting thing you can try is getting some friends to stand in a particular place and look up to a tall building.

QUESTIONS TO CONSIDER

1. How many other people convinced themselves that if your group was looking up, then there must have been something to see, so they looked up as well?
2. Do you think some people are more likely to follow the crowd than other people are likely to do so?

someone says, "Could you be a real good friend and give me a ride to the library?" the inclusion of the relational term *friend* underscores the existence of the relationship and reminds the other person of behaviors and duties associated with that sort of relationship. You might expect a "friend" to provide transportation when requested, but not an "acquaintance." The use of relational terms also justifies requests being made. A "friend" *could make* and *be asked to make* this sort of request without great loss of face by either interactant. Appealing to a relationship may be somewhat legitimate but also fallacious. Asking a friend for a ride to the library is one thing; asking a friend to drive the getaway car while you rob a convenience store is another. Certain obligations are associated with each type of relationship, but each responsibility also has limitations. Critical listeners determine when the use of relational terms is legitimate and when it is unreasonable.

Latin for "after this; therefore, because of this," ***post hoc ergo propter hoc*** argues that something is caused by whatever happens before it. According to this logic, the following statement is true: A man kissed a woman, and two weeks later she was pregnant; therefore, the kiss was responsible for her pregnancy. You likely see the inherent problem with this statement. Admittedly, the above example may seem a bit obvious. However, the use of this sort of reasoning is actually quite common and frequently evident in advertising.

Cum hoc ergo propter hoc argues that if one thing happens at the same time as another, it was caused by the thing with which it coincides. Once again, we are dealing with a Latin phrase. *Cum hoc ergo propter hoc* translates into "With this; therefore, because of this." As with its *post hoc* companion, this fallacy argues that one event causes another due to their association in time. While *post hoc* argues that something occurring *before* something else is the cause, *cum hoc* argues that something occurring *at the same time* as something else is the cause. Someone might remark, "I wore a new pair of socks on the day of my communication midterm and earned an A on the test. Wearing new socks must have been the reason I scored so high. From now on, I'm going to wear a new pair of socks each time I take a test." If this were all it took to score well on an examination, life would be pretty sweet! Wearing new socks at the same time you ace an examination, however, will not guarantee you a high score on your next exam. If you really want to improve your exam scores, try visiting **edge.sagepub.com/duckciel2e.**

Although quite common and often very convincing, these fallacies are difficult to prove when challenged. Upon recognizing them, as a critical listener, you may question and expect the speaker to prove two things: First, does a direct link actually exist between what is deemed the cause and what is deemed its effect? Second, if a link between the cause and its effect exists, did any additional variables work to produce the effect?

ETHICAL ISSUE

When would you consider an appeal to relationships appropriate, even when it is in fact a fallacy? When would you consider it entirely inappropriate?

***post hoc ergo propter hoc* (fallacious argument):** argues that something is caused by whatever happens before it; Latin for "after this; therefore, because of this"

Hasty generalization arises when a conclusion is based on a single occurrence or insufficient data or sample size. Asked about where to purchase a new car, someone might remark, "My coworker bought a car at that dealership east of town, and it broke down a week later. If you buy a car at that dealership, it will probably be a lemon." Just because the dealership sold a faulty car once does not mean it will sell another defective car. Sometimes, the hasty generalization is based on a small sample size. In other words, the people involved or questioned are not significantly representative of a given population. When defending a new policy on campus, someone might say, "I asked people in my algebra class, and they all agreed that a campus-wide attendance policy is a good idea. So I guess the policy is a good one that the students like." Simply because a few people agreed with this policy in one class does not mean it is good or that the majority of students agree with the policy.

Red herring describes the use of another issue to divert attention away from the real issue. This fallacy is especially common when someone wishes to avoid a particular topic. When talking about the cost of higher education, you might hear "I find it difficult to fathom that you insist on addressing higher-education funding when the spotted pygmy squirrel is on the verge of extinction" or "Sure, the cost of higher education is staggering, but so is the cost of health care, which has become a major burden on millions of people." During an argument between romantic partners, you might hear the following use of a red herring: "Why are we talking about me going out with my friends when we should be talking about your inability to commit to this relationship?" This example contains a strategic attempt to divert attention away from the issue of going out with friends by dragging commitment to the relationship across the conversational trail.

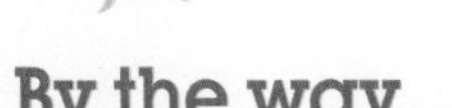

By the way...

An Interesting Piece of Trivia

The name "red herring" comes from the phrase "draw a red herring across the trail," derived from the practice of 17th-century dog trainers. They would drag a smoked ("red") herring across the trail of a fox to determine how well dogs could remain focused on the original scent (Urdang, Hunsinger, & LaRouche, 1991).

QUESTIONS TO CONSIDER

1. Has anyone ever tried to use a red herring in a conversation with you? If so, did it work, and why or why not?
2. Have you ever tried to use a red herring? If so, did it work, and why or why not?

False alternatives occur when only two options are provided, one of which is generally presented as the poor choice or one that should be avoided (Pearson & Nelson, 2000). One flaw in this reasoning is that there are usually more options than the two provided. Traveling by plane, for example, comes with the likelihood of delays caused by mechanical problems and the always kind and supportive airline personnel who have been known to use false alternatives by explaining, "You can either endure a delay while we find a plane that is functional, or you can leave as scheduled and travel in a plane that is not working correctly." Waiting for a functional plane seems much better than facing possible mechanical problems after takeoff. However, this overlooks the other equally probable option: having a functional plane available to begin with by ensuring proper maintenance is accomplished well before the flight is scheduled to depart. As a note of caution, pointing out this option to airline personnel at the gate will decrease your chances of receiving an upgrade on that particular flight!

In addition, quite possibly the option deemed less favorable is not as negative as it is portrayed, and the preferred option is not as beneficial. Likewise, an auto mechanic may explain, "You can either replace the serpentine belt in your car now or face being stranded should it end up breaking at one of these cracks." It is possible that the serpentine belt does not need immediate repair, as well as that you would not be stranded somewhere should it actually break. Such claims and options often

***cum hoc ergo propter hoc* (fallacious argument):** argues that if one thing happens at the same time as another, it was caused by the thing with which it coincides; Latin for "with this; therefore, because of this"

hasty generalization (fallacious argument): when a conclusion is based on a single occurrence or insufficient data or sample size

red herring (fallacious argument): the use of another issue to divert attention away from the real issue

false alternatives (fallacious argument): occurs when only two options are provided, one of which is generally presented as the poor choice or one that should be avoided

By the way...

Commercials

Watch television and analyze the commercials being aired. Pay attention to the claims that are made not only in words but in images (note that most people in advertisements are relatively young and attractive, but you relate certain kinds of products—life insurance, for example—to certain kinds of actors, who are usually white haired but never bald; they all have a full head of white hair and tend to wear sweaters). Some particular racial groups may be used to advertise certain kinds of products instead of others.

QUESTIONS TO CONSIDER

1. What fallacious arguments are evident in these commercials? Are some forms of fallacious arguments more prevalent than others?
2. Can a picture or a video or an image be "fallacious," or is it an example of associating products with images in a way that encourages people to make fallacious inferences? ("If you buy this car," for example, "you will have a fast and attractive life surrounded by lots of rich and attractive people.")

go unchallenged unless a person recognizes this fallacy and critically examines the statements being made.

Composition fallacy argues that the parts are the same as the whole (Pearson & Nelson, 2000, p. 118). According to this fallacy, any student at your school could be picked at random to represent all students at your school. Common sense tells you that one person cannot accurately represent an entire group of people, but this fallacy nevertheless remains quite common. Consider how often entire populations are represented in newspaper articles by one person or perhaps a few people. An article might say, "Students on campus are in favor of the tuition increase to pay for the new sports complex. When asked about the increase in tuition, sophomore Steven Taylor noted, 'If it takes an increase in tuition to replace the old sports complex, that's what needs to be done.'" This report essentially says that if one student (part) is in favor of the tuition increase, all students (whole) are in favor of it as well.

Division fallacy argues the whole is the same as its parts (Pearson & Nelson, 2000, p. 118). For instance, when being set up on a date by a friend, you might argue, "Everyone you have ever set me up with has been a loser, so this person is going to be a loser too." This statement essentially reasons that if previous dates have been losers (whole), this date (part) will also be one.

Equivocation relies on the ambiguousness of language to make an argument. The equivocation tactic is frequently used in commercials. You might hear an announcer proclaim, "Squeaky Clean dish soap is *better!*" This sounds good, but you cannot be certain what Squeaky Clean is actually better than. Is it better than using no dish soap at all or washing dishes by dropping rocks into the sink? Is it better than other brands of dish soap? The use of equivocation leaves such questions unanswered, often the point of this fallacy. When ambiguous words and phrases, such as *improved, bargain, good value, delicious,* or *soothing,* are used, listeners must fill in the context on their own, which often results in a product or an idea being received in a much more positive manner than warranted. The makers of Squeaky Clean dish soap could say, "We never said *it was better than all other brands;* we just said it was *better.*" While this tactic is tricky, this statement would be absolutely true. The good news is now that you are able to recognize the use of equivocation, you will be well equipped to find the best dish soap—whatever *best* means!

But you are better for having read this chapter. That we guarantee.

composition fallacy (fallacious argument): argues that the parts are the same as the whole

division fallacy (fallacious argument): argues the whole is the same as its parts

equivocation (fallacious argument): relies on the ambiguousness of language to make an argument

»»» Focus Questions Revisited

Why is listening important enough to have an entire chapter devoted to it?

Listening is not only the communication activity in which you engage most frequently but also fundamental to success in education, careers, and relationships. Often the most common activity in classrooms, listening has been directly linked to academic achievement, is one of the most sought-after skills by employers, and is critical to success and advancement in the workplace. Effective listening in relationships leads to greater satisfaction and is essential for successful relational development.

2 What are the objectives of listening?

There are five objectives of listening:

1. Relational development and enhancement
2. Gaining and comprehending information
3. Critical listening
4. Enjoyment and appreciation
5. Therapeutic listening

Even though these objectives were discussed in isolation, remember that a single communicative exchange can involve multiple listening goals.

3 What does it mean to listen actively?

Active listening is a process of receiving, attending to, interpreting, and responding to symbolic activity. Receiving auditory stimuli is the first step in the listening process. Attending occurs when you perceive and focus on stimuli. Interpreting involves assigning meaning to sounds and symbolic activity. Responding, the final step in the active listening process, entails reacting to this symbolic activity.

4 What are engaged and relational listening?

Engaged listening and relational listening are advanced types of listening that demand more of the listener than active listening. The engaged listening process entails making a personal relational connection with the source of a message that results from the source and the receiver actively working together to create shared meaning and understanding. Relational listening involves recognizing, understanding, and addressing the interconnection of relationships and communication.

5 What obstacles must people overcome to listen well?

You may encounter a number of obstacles to listening. There are various kinds of distraction to good listening, such as environmental noises, an uncomfortable situation, a disconcerting partner, "something on your mind" that makes it hard to focus, and difficulty hearing what the person says (whether because of an accent or the fact that the person mumbles or a problem with your own hearing). Recognizing, dealing with, and overcoming these obstacles is crucial to effective listening.

6 What is critical listening, and why is it so important?

Critical listening is the process of analyzing and evaluating the accuracy, legitimacy, and value of messages. Involving the evaluation of a message's plausibility, source, argument, and evidence, critical listening has a profound impact on personal relationships, learning, and the evaluation of persuasive messages.

7 What are fallacious arguments?

Fallacious arguments are those that appear legitimate but are actually based on faulty reasoning or insufficient evidence, and we list several examples to help you understand what is legitimate and what is not. Practice hard listening out for these fallacies. The ability to recognize fallacious arguments will enable you to become a more critical listener, a keener reader of course materials in any discipline, and a better writer when it comes to your own papers for classes.

8 Can you identify a "hasty generalization," a "bandwagon appeal," and an "equivocation" in commercials?

Well, if not, then look back over the relevant sections of the chapter!

Key Concepts

appeal to authority 123
appeal to people (bandwagon appeal) 123
appeal to relationships 123
argument against the source 123
attending 114
composition fallacy 126
consistency 122
content (representational) listening 119
critical listening 120
cum hoc ergo propter hoc 124
division fallacy 126
egocentric listening 119
engaged listening 115
environmental distractions 117

equivocation 126
experiential superiority 120
factual diversion 118
fallacious arguments 122
false alternatives 125
hasty generalization 125
hearing 114
interpreting 114
listening 114
medium distractions 118
message complexity 120
past experience with the source 120
plausibility 121
post hoc ergo propter hoc 124
receiving 114
red herring 125
reflecting (paraphrasing) 115
relational listening 116
responding 115
selective listening 119
semantic diversion 118
source distractions 118
status of the source 121
verifiability 122
wandering thoughts 119

Questions to Ask Your Friends

1. Ask a friend to recall a time when he or she misunderstood someone else. Have your friend describe the situation and determine if problems with listening had anything to do with the misunderstanding. If so, how could the misunderstanding have been prevented through effective listening behaviors, and how could you now "coach" your friend to avoid the same mistake next time?

2. Now that you have read the chapter and learned some better ways to listen, ask your friends if they consider you a good listener or not. What suggestions do they have for improving your listening, and how far can you now translate that advice into the technical terms you have learned in this chapter?

3. Ask a friend to describe a time when he or she made a purchase based on the recommendation of a salesperson that he or she later regretted. Was a lack of critical listening partially responsible, or was the salesperson using tricks of persuasion that your friend overlooked? What suggestions could you offer your friend when making future purchases? If all else fails, David's wife is an excellent shopper and can offer more tips.

Media Connections

1. Find videos of two people talking. These videos could include actual interactions or fictionalized interactions such as a television program or movie. Select one video in which one or both of the interactants are listening effectively, and select another video in which one or both of the interactants are listening ineffectively (presidential debates are often good examples of the latter). What led you to characterize them as effective and ineffective, respectively?

2. Watch a political talk show, such as *Fox News Sunday*, *Meet the Press*, or *The O'Reilly Factor*. What obstacles to listening are evident during interviews and panel discussions on these programs? How do you think it helps or distracts the viewer to have interviewers interrupt the proceedings so often?

3. Concurrent media exposure occurs when two or more media systems are used simultaneously. For example, you may be using the Internet while listening to the radio or reading a newspaper at the same time you are watching a movie on television. What impact might concurrent media exposure have on listening to media?

Student Study Site

SAGE edge™

Sharpen your skills with SAGE edge at edge.sagepub.com/duckciel2e

SAGE edge for students provides a personalized approach to help you accomplish your coursework goals in an easy-to-use learning environment.

招廣告
新
華
營專
MING KEE
L KINDS OF EMBROIDERIES
2739 3806
get wicked
The Arc
Brasserie
End
終止

Part III COMMUNICATION CONTEXTS

CHAPTER 7
Personal Relationships

CHAPTER 8
Family Communication

CHAPTER 9
Groups and Leaders

CHAPTER 10
Communication in the Workplace

CHAPTER 11
Health Communication

CHAPTER 12
Culture and Communication

CHAPTER 13
Technology and Media in Everyday Life

CHAPTER 14
Public and Personal Influence

CHAPTER 15
Interviewing

Chapter Outline

What Are Personal Relationships?

Benefits of Personal Relationships

Relationships and What You Know

Filtering What You Know

Evaluating What You Know

Relationships and Support

Initiating Relationships: The Relationship Filtering Model

Talking to Strangers

Steps in the Relationship Filtering Model

Transacting and Maintaining Personal Relationships

Composing Relationships Through Communication

Keeping Relationships Going Through Communication

Relational Dialectics

Coming Apart

Symptoms and Sources of Decline

Breakdown Process Model

Focus Questions Revisited

Key Concepts

Questions to Ask Your Friends

Media Connections

07 Personal Relationships

FOCUS QUESTIONS

1. What are personal relationships?
2. What are benefits of relationships?
3. How are relationships initiated?
4. How are relationships transacted and maintained?
5. How do relationships come apart?

As you read and study this chapter, we want you to reconsider the way many people think about relationships. Specifically, they are not just about emotion. Rather, relationships are about knowledge, ways of understanding the world, and connecting people symbolically (Duck, 2011). Relationships are a fundamental part of what you know about the world, how to act, what to think, what to value, and what to believe.

Placing relationships at the heart of your knowledge and reality systems may very well be something you have not considered before, but all our previous chapters have been connecting relationships to other aspects of communication. Now we want to speak directly to the question of the ways in which relationships have directly affected what you know and how you know it. Think about the following questions and answers.

When you were younger, who taught you the proper way to behave through example or through punishment if you misbehaved? Most likely it was a parent or guardian. It may have also been another relative, a friend of the family, or a neighbor.

When you grew older, how did you learn which behaviors were considered admirable and resulted in social status and which behaviors were to be avoided? The above answers may also apply here, but you may want to add your friends.

From the very beginning of this book, we have discussed how communication transacts or creates meanings, realities, knowledge systems, cultures, and identities. Well, guess where that communication takes place. You've got it . . . *relationships!* You have developed what you know, how you view the world, and who you are through interactions with family, friends, romantic partners, neighbors, classmates, colleagues, enemies, acquaintances, and the list continues. The development of your knowledge, worldview, and self never ends, by the way. They are continuously being transformed, reinforced, and otherwise altered through relationships.

Within this chapter, we will examine the value of relationships as ways of knowing the world. We will also explore the development of personal relationships and their place within your everyday life. To begin, though, we need to figure out exactly what personal relationships are and what makes them so personal.

As you read this chapter, there will not be a great deal of discussion about media and technology. This chapter is intended to be focused on the very basics of personal relationships. Once this foundation is provided, however, it is important to recognize the mutual influences of personal relationships,

Make your case

Social or Personal Relationships?

It is possible for social relationships to be transformed into more personal ones, as when you repeatedly visit the same store and the servers get to know you and may even greet you by name when you come in. However, if all of those employees retired, you might still go to the same store and just start off social relationships with the new employees. More difficult to explain is the way in which personal relationships develop from two strangers meeting for the first time to their becoming good friends.

QUESTIONS TO CONSIDER

1. At what point does a social relationship become a personal relationship? For instance, at what point might acquaintances be recognized as friends?
2. How can you tell? Hint: Consider the communication taking place.

media, and technology. Chapter 13 brings these areas together, but as you read this chapter, consider how technology and media influence the ideas being presented.

What Are Personal Relationships?

A range of different relationship types can be recognized. These types of relationships are represented by different styles of communication. For instance, some relationships may be characterized by formal communication (business acquaintances) or by informal communication (friends). These types of relationships are also understood and appreciated differently within a culture. For instance, *friend* is a relational category that might be evaluated positively, while *enemy* is a relational category that might be evaluated negatively. Ultimately, relationships can be placed into two broad categories: social relationships and personal relationships.

Social relationships are those in which the participants are interchangeable and communicate using socially understood norms and roles. These involve people with whom a close relationship is not necessarily shared. Your relationships with store clerks, bus drivers, and restaurant servers are generally social ones. When interacting with a store clerk, you are both playing specific social roles and communicating in a fairly standard manner. If one of you were replaced by someone else, the communication taking place would not be very different.

Personal relationships are those in which the participants are irreplaceable and communicate in close, unique ways. Unlike social relationships, personal relationships involve people who cannot be replaced by someone else. Your relationships with friends, family, and romantic partners are generally personal ones. When interacting with a particular friend, you are using patterns of interaction and meaning systems exclusive to that particular relationship. Even if there are some similarities with the patterns of interaction and meaning systems used with other friends, they are still unique and different.

As you consider these categories of relationships, note that social relationships and personal relationships are not permanent or mutually exclusive. Social relationships can become more personal. If you often frequent a restaurant, for example, a more personal relationship could develop with a regular server. A personal relationship could develop from what would generally be recognized as a social relationship.

social relationships: relationships in which the specific people in a given role can be changed and the relationship would still occur (e.g., customer–client relationships are the same irrespective of who is the customer and who is the client on a particular occasion; compare with *personal relationships*)

personal relationships: relationships that only specified and irreplaceable individuals (such as your mother, father, brother, sister, or very best friend) can have with you (compare with *social relationships*)

Benefits of Personal Relationships

Positioning relationships as vital to your world, as we do throughout this book, it stands to reason that there are benefits to engaging in them. Within this section, we are going to discuss two particular areas of value that personal relationships provide: ways of knowing and support.

Relationships and What You Know

Everyday communication reinforces both your relationships and what you know. All forms of communication show how you rely on your connections with other people to filter your knowledge and help you critically evaluate events, people, and situations. Because communication involves information, the people you know and with whom you spend your time affect your knowledge. They influence the messages you send or attend to, the information you believe, the type of critical thinking you do, and how you evaluate the outcomes. So, not just a *result* of communication, relationships are also significant in the opposite process, the formation and transaction of knowledge.

Filtering What You Know

Relationships exert influence on the distribution of information. You tell secrets to your friends that you would not tell to strangers, and news travels through networks of folks who know one another (Bergmann, 1993; Duck, 2007). Certain information, not just pertaining to personal relationships but pertaining to the world in general, is shared among members of social networks.

Evaluating What You Know

Communicating with others also offers opportunities for people to test their knowledge of the world. If you happen to speak erroneously, for example, people around you might offer corrections. Likewise, those around you may offer different views of the world that challenge your understandings. On the other hand, interactions with others may support your beliefs and views of the world.

In general, the latter is much more likely to occur—the reason being that people typically prefer to hang out with those who share similar attitudes and beliefs (Byrne, 1997; Kerckhoff, 1974; Sunnafrank, 1983; Sunnafrank & Ramirez, 2004). Not surprisingly, you tend to respect the judgments of your friends and enjoy talking with them because they often reinforce what you believe (Weiss, 1998). Of course, there will occasionally be disagreements, but for the most part, you and your friends talk in ways that support mutually shared views of the world (Duck, 2011).

Relationships and Support

Relationships also provide you with various forms of support. Robert Weiss (1974) identified six specific areas where relationships provide us with something special, needed, or valued. These are **provisions of relationships**, the deep and important psychological and supportive benefits that relationships provide. Everyday communication provides these provisions seamlessly and often without being obvious.

Belonging and a Sense of Reliable Alliance

A major benefit that people gain from relationships is belonging and a sense of reliable alliance. Feeling connected with others provides a sense of stability and provides feelings of comfort. In fact, such assurances may be one reason why users are

ETHICAL ISSUE

Given all the benefits of personal relationships, it would seem that having many of them would be advantageous. A person can have many friends. Is it ethical to have more than one romantic partner?

By the way...

Friends as Influencers

The marketing world knows about the power of the connection among relationships, information flow, critical thinking, and knowledge. Marketers use word-of-mouth campaigns that exploit the fact that we respect our friends' opinions about the right purchases to make and what is "cool." In the latest marketing fad, "buzz agents" are paid to tell their friends about particular products, thereby creating "buzz" and influencing people to buy them (Carl, 2006). Think about items you have purchased; it will likely dawn on you that your clothing style as well as the cell phones and computers that you buy may be influenced by your group membership as well as specific friends you have.

QUESTIONS TO CONSIDER

1. How have friends influenced past purchases you have made?
2. How have you influenced past purchases of your friends?

provisions of relationships: the deep and important psychological and supportive benefits that relationships provide

COMMUNICATION + YOU

How Needy Are You?

Now that you know about Weiss's (1974) provisions of relationships, pay close attention to your everyday communication and try to identify instances where one of the provisions is invoked. Think about what sorts of relationship tend to encourage which sorts of provision—or do all relationships encourage all of the provisions? Ask yourself whether your observations show that friends are more likely to ask for physical support than other people, and consider whether social relationships employ different provisions from personal relationships.

QUESTIONS TO CONSIDER

1. Who is more likely to request emotional integration? Is there a sex difference?
2. Could we begin to categorize relationships according to the provisions that they most often rely upon, or are we looking for all/any of these provisions whenever we talk to people anyway?

drawn to social networking sites (Quinn & Oldmeadow, 2013). Relationships also enable people to feel that someone is there for them if they are ever in need of assistance. Sometimes there may be a desire for people to state this support explicitly. Most of the time, however, people just learn from daily interaction that someone looks after their interests and cares for them (Leatham & Duck, 1990).

Emotional Integration and Stability

Personal relationships also provide people with opportunities to express and evaluate emotions. As is also discussed in Chapter 14, people experience emotions physically (e.g., increased heart rate) but rely on societal and relational definitions to understand what they are experiencing (e.g., anger, love, fear). A person's understandings of and reactions to emotions have developed in large part through the ways they are experienced and discussed by people within his or her social network. Within some families, for instance, the expression of such negative emotions as fear or sadness is done openly, while such negative emotions are generally hidden within other families. In fact, much of a person's understanding of emotion comes from interactions within the family (see Sanchez-Nunez, Fernandez-Berrocal, & Latorre, 2013).

Opportunity to Talk About Oneself

A key provision of personal relationships is the ability to talk about one's self. This activity is not only enjoyable but also provides opportunities to derive other relational provisions, such as those mentioned above and others mentioned below. People like to put themselves into their talk, offer their opinions and views, be important in stories they tell, and otherwise be part of a narrative of their own lives that makes them appear valuable and good. Indeed, one of the main things that makes a relationship more rewarding to people is a sense of being known and accepted (Duck, 2011).

Opportunity to Help Others

People also like the feeling of being there for others, and relationships provide opportunities to do just that. A request for advice, for instance, is flattering and implicitly recognizes one's value and significance, yet another provision discussed below. Accordingly, assisting people with whom a relationship is shared can offer the provider of that support with equal if not surpassed personal benefits (Straus, Johnson, Marquez, & Feldman, 2013).

Provision of Physical Support

Relationships provide physical assistance when needed. Physical support includes needing help from others to move a heavy piano, fix your computer, or look after

How does your end-of-day communication with other people transact your relationships? How are the relationships between people here conveyed and transacted in talk?

your pet rat while you are on vacation. These are favors that friends do for one another as part of the role of friendship. Of course, different relationships are generally associated with different forms of physical support, and different types of support are offered with changes in age (Kahn, McGill, & Bianchi, 2011).

Reassurance of Worth and Value

People may find a subtle reassurance of their worth when someone gives up time for them by providing physical support. You would certainly find it confirming if someone said, for example, "Good job" or "Drop that jerk—you deserve better anyway." More important, relationships show people how others see the world, how they represent/present it, what they value in it, what matters to them, and how one's own way of thinking fits in with theirs. In such talk and action, they reassure one's worth and value as a human being (Duck, 2011).

Initiating Relationships: The Relationship Filtering Model

Thus far in the chapter, we have talked about what personal relationships are and the benefits of those relationships. In what follows we will discuss how relationships are initiated, how relationships are created and maintained during everyday life, and how they end or are transformed.

We will begin by examining how two people move from being strangers to developing a close personal relationship. You have encountered and met a lot of people throughout your lifetime and continue to do so. Of those many people, only a few have become someone with whom a close personal relationship is shared. Why, then, do some people become more than just strangers? Turns out, it begins with talk.

Talking to Strangers

If you were taught not to talk to strangers at age 5, it was probably sound advice. However, that warning probably applied to the creepy guy standing on the corner and not the child next to you on the playground. It is still a good idea to avoid the creepy guy on the corner, but if people did not talk to strangers, personal relationships would never develop.

Think about meeting and getting to know strangers. When you meet strangers, all you have to go on initially is how they look and sound. In everyday life when basic personal information is missing, you seek this information by asking questions. Interactions among strangers focus on information gathering and providing information. Topics tend to be noncontroversial, such as your general background and perhaps some basic personal views and interests. This information mostly appears inconsequential. After all, who really cares which high school someone attended, where a person works, or whether he or she has any children?

How do relationships grow or change, and how does this show up in talk?

Well, these seemingly trivial bits of information actually provide background information that can be useful to new acquaintances. If the other persons go on to make evaluative remarks about their school, they could be giving helpful insights into their general attitudes, ways of thinking, and values. These pieces of information are important in building pictures of themselves for others to perceive and evaluate. These pictures will help you determine whether to get to know them better or whether a personal relationship with them might be desirable. Keep in mind that it is not a one-way decision. They are engaged in the same process—the same *filtering* process.

Steps in the Relationship Filtering Model

The more you get to know people, the better your map of their worlds of meaning and whether you want to continue pursuing a personal relationship. For instance, when classes begin, most of your classmates are, at best, little-known acquaintances. Yet you share some experiences and knowledge that would create some common topics to talk about if you happened to get stuck in an elevator or ended up walking across campus with one another after class ended. You would have some common topics of knowledge and at least some idea of each other's positions on issues.

Steve's (Duck, 1998, 1999) **Relationship Filtering Model** suggests that people pay attention to different cues in sequence as they get to know one another. Basically, you use whatever evidence is available in order to form an impression of another person's underlying thought structure and worldview. Your original model of the person will receive micro-adjustments as you take in new evidence and realize that such modifications need to be made as you meet the person on successive occasions and in different contexts.

The sequence in which you pay attention to characteristics of other people is basically the sequence in which you encounter them: (1) physical appearance, (2) behavior/nonverbal communication, (3) roles, and (4) attitudes/personality.

At each point in the sequence, some people are filtered out as people you do not want as partners. Only those people who pass all filters become friends or romantic partners. The model follows the intuitive process through which you get to know people layer by layer. It assumes your basic goal is to understand others on the basis of whatever cues are available at the time. At each deeper level, you get a better understanding of how they tick, and you let them deeper into your world. See Figure 7.1 for an illustrated depiction of the model in action.

Appearance

When you first meet people, you may make assumptions about them just on the basis of their appearance. You can observe their age, race, sex, dress, number of tattoos and body piercings, height, and physical attractiveness.

Relationship Filtering Model: demonstrates how sequences of cues are used to determine which people are selected to develop close relationships

Although these cues do not necessarily provide accurate information, people make inferences from such cues to the inner world of meaning. The Relationship Filtering Model assumes that you filter out people who do not appear to support

Figure 7.1 The Relationship Filtering Model

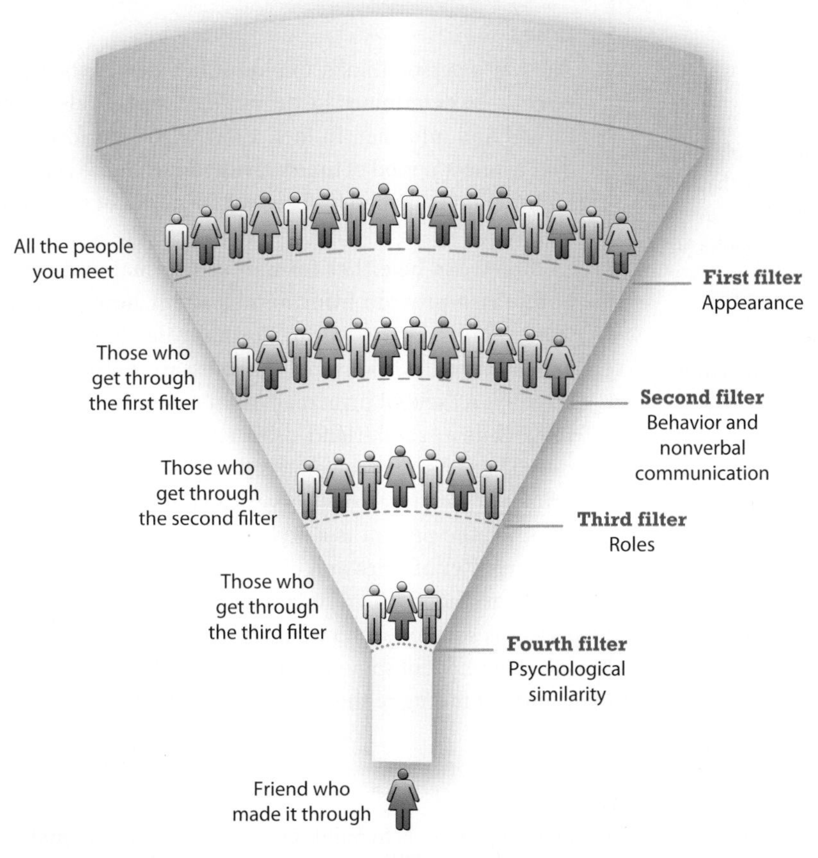

your ways of seeing the world and would therefore not be a prospect for a personal relationship. Thus, if you perceive yourself as more of a conformist, someone with an extremely unusual hairstyle may not be someone with whom you would seek a personal relationship. On the other hand, someone with a conventional hairstyle may be someone with whom a personal relationship is possible.

Behavior/Nonverbal Communication

Those who make it through the appearance filter must then pass through the behavior/nonverbal filter, which gives new clues to the way a person thinks. The way that people act is a fairly accurate way of determining some aspects of how they think. For instance, as we saw in Chapter 4, the way people stand or hold themselves can indicate arrogance, depression, confidence, anxiety, or fear. Thus their inner world of meanings, beliefs, and values about themselves is exhibited through their behaviors and actions. Deductions based on nonverbal behavior can sometimes be very accurate. On other occasions, the way in which someone behaves may lead to wrong assessments until more information is collected.

As you evaluate the actions of others, you determine in part whether they view the world in the same manner as you. Also, you determine whether this is someone with whom you enjoy spending time and communicating with further. Maybe you are into people who push little old ladies into traffic. If so, you may have found a potential

By the way...

Do People Match Up on Physical Attractiveness?

The "matching hypothesis" maintains that people tend to be attracted to those whom they perceive to have roughly the same level of attractiveness as they have. In fact, people are often attracted to those who look a great deal like themselves!

QUESTIONS TO CONSIDER

1. Do you think these ideas have any merit based on your own experiences or observations?
2. Do you think the matching hypothesis can be applied to both romantic relationships and friendships?

relational partner. If not, that person will probably not make it past this filter.

Roles

The way a person thinks and his or her view of the world can also be determined by the performance of roles, both formal and informal. In fact, viewing role performance over a longer period of time provides much more accurate information than merely observing instances of nonverbal behavior.

Roles can be either formal or informal and can in both cases provide information about how a person thinks and sees the world. Formal roles have specific expectations, while informal roles are defined more broadly. A "school principal" is an example of a formal role, while a "good friend" is an example of an informal role. The ways a person enacts the formal role of "school principal" might give observers a chance to determine whether the person is a strict, rule-bound tyrant or a generous and supportive interpreter of rules and discipline. The ways a person enacts the informal role of being a "good friend" might give observers a chance to determine whether the person is someone who would be there when needed. In all cases, observing the role enactment of someone enables people to strengthen, modify, and correct their understanding of the ways in which that person views the world.

Attitude/Personality

The ultimate goal of the filtering process is to build the best model you can make of someone's belief structures and personality. The more you understand someone and the more he or she appears to support your world of meaning, the more you like it. Hence the final filter is based on exact information about someone's personality as derived from self-disclosure (see Chapter 3).

In all of your filtering interactions, you are really trying to find out what people are like at the level of their deeper worlds of meaning, so you aim all the questions you ask and all the communication strategies you adopt toward finding these deeper selves. The more fully you understand somebody, the more you understand how he or she thinks.

However, relationship development cannot be equated to simply revealing and gathering information. Rather, relationship development is dependent on the interpretation of this information (Duck, 2007). In other words, the relationship grows not from the information that you learn about the other person but from how you "go beyond" it by making inferences about a person's worlds of meaning. For instance, learning that someone grew up on a farm provides limited information about the person's worldview. It is necessary to learn and determine how the person views that experience and how growing up on a farm may have impacted his or her ways of thinking.

As mentioned throughout this section, the more a person's view of the world and meaning systems seem to correspond with your own, the more likely you will want to form a relationship with him or her. If a person moves through these filters, then the development of a close personal relationship is possible. In what follows, we will turn our attention to the ways in which relationships are created and maintained.

Transacting and Maintaining Personal Relationships

Before getting into our discussion of the ways in which relationships are created and maintained, we need to note how these processes have frequently been presented in past research. Previously, relationships have been assumed to develop based on the amount of communication taking place. They were also assumed to develop in orderly stages common to all relationships.

Thinking about relationships in this way makes something very complicated seem uncomplicated and manageable. However, the beliefs represented in this research are inventions of researchers and not the way relationships actually develop. Relationships do not develop in a nice, neat, straightforward manner. And while certain culturally recognized markers of development may be shared with other relationships, all relationships have developed in unique ways.

With that in mind, we will first discuss the ways in which relationships are composed and maintained through communication. We will then examine the theory of relational dialectics.

Composing Relationships Through Communication

Relationships are partly essentialized and indexed through communication. If you have not yet read or need a refresher on Chapter 4, this means that relationships are brought into existence (transacted) through communication and that types of relationships are categorized accordingly through communication.

The *essential function of talk* happens when talk makes the relationship real or talks it into being. The use of coupling references and assumptions about the relationship's existence made when communicating are example of this sort of talk.

The *indexical function of talk* demonstrates or indicates the nature of the relationship between speakers. What you say and how you say it reveals intimacy (closeness) levels, power differences, and other characteristics of relationships.

Transforming Relationships

If relationships are composed through communication, it stands to reason that they are transformed through communication. When the type of relationship shared moves from one to another (acquaintances to friends, dates to romantic partners, lovers to enemies, or spouses to divorcées), you are moving across the boundaries between different types of relationships in your culture. Accordingly you say and do different things together.

Relationship development and transformation can be seen as a change in communication based on the information individuals know (or have assumed) about each other's ways of thinking about

By the way...

Culture and the Development of Relationships

Development of relationships is really a cultural ideal. It is assumed that relationships will develop from initially meeting the ultimate romance in a warm, fuzzy, and uncomplicated way. In the stark cold daylight of real life, the development of a relationship is far more complex. One person might not want it to move ahead too fast and may resist his or her partner's attempts to make it grow. Some people might be wary of letting others into their lives and will try hard to keep them at a distance—the intrusive neighbor, the undesirable coworker, or the unwanted romantic who won't take no for an answer. Hess (2000) indicated that people have an extensive range of communicative strategies for keeping disliked people at a distance, from simply ignoring them to treating them as objects to direct and open hostility and antagonism.

QUESTIONS TO CONSIDER

1. Have you ever used any of these strategies?
2. What do you suppose some of the other strategies may be?

the world (Duck, 2011). Any change in a relationship involves change in content of talk and the style of communication.

The transformation of a relationship is generally the result of at least one partner, if not both, driving it toward more intimacy or less intimacy. More intimacy may be achieved by introducing intimate topics and changing to more relaxed styles of talk. Less intimacy may be achieved by avoiding the discussion of intimate topics and engaging in talk that is sharper and less welcoming.

Relationship Talk: Direct

Relationship transformation can also occur through communication about the relationship. This communication may be direct or indirect. People engage in direct relational communication in special ways, on special occasions, and with very special care. Any direct talk about a relationship forces the partners to focus on its explicit definition.

People often have difficulty raising and discussing certain topics in a relationship (Petronio, 2013). Hearing "Let's talk about our relationship" has caused many an otherwise brave individual to contemplate running away and hiding under a blanket! This response has been historically common among men (Acitelli, 1988), and cultural differences also emerge in how talk about a relationship is perceived (Theiss & Nagy, 2013).

Ultimately, you cannot talk about the relationship without ending up somehow defining it and its meaning to the two partners involved. For at least one of them, the result may be unwanted. One may hope that the relationship is defined as stronger and has a better future than the other person is willing to accept. The best outcome is that the two people agree to see the relationship in a particular way that they both accept.

Relationship Talk: Indirect

Fortunately for us cowards, most communication about a relationship—and the communication that most often results in transforming relationships—is indirect. Asking someone "Will you have sex with me?" is a direct and very high-risk strategy whereas many indirect strategies are more effective without being threatening (e.g., a warm kiss, a bunch of flowers, a deep sigh, a longing look, or even a smart or sexy outfit).

For this reason, flirtation is one of the key ways people push the envelope in relationships through indirect communication. Flirtation is a safe way to propose relationship growth. First, it generally serves as an indirect form of relationship question. Second, it can be taken as a simple statement of fact, a friendly joke, or something more sexually or relationally loaded. If the person you flirt with

Skills You Can Use: Determining the Status of a Relationship

We have discussed a number of ways in which relationship status is conveyed through communication. By listening very carefully to the way that people speak to one another, you can tell how their relationship is going. As we go on below to describe the changes in communication that accompany decline in relationships, you may be able to helpfully step in to assist a friend whose relationship is in trouble before being asked for help.

is interested in a relationship, the response will accept the relationally loaded reading of the message. If the person is not interested, the message can be treated as fun or fact and nothing more.

The man in this photo just said, "We'll see you this weekend." Which type of relational continuity constructional unit is being displayed here?

Keeping Relationships Going Through Communication

Communication not only composes and transforms relationships but also maintains relationships when people are apart. Such communication may be especially important in long-distance relationships (Sahlstein, 2004, 2006) but are common in all personal relationships. Sigman (1991) called this sort of communication **relational continuity constructional units (RCCUs)**. In less complex and more memorable terms these are simple conversational symbols that indicate a relationship continues to exist even when the partners are physically distant. These symbols can be divided into *prospective, introspective,* and *retrospective* types.

Prospective Units

Prospective units provide recognition that an interaction is about to end but the relationship continues. In essence, prospective units refer to a coming absence, and they create a conversational leapfrog that gets you over it. Prospective units include saying "Let's set the agenda for next time" or "See you later."

Any form of communication that suggests the likelihood of the partner's return is considered a prospective unit. For example, if one partner leaves a toothbrush in the other's apartment, the toothbrush indicates the missing partner will likely return. It offers recognition that the absence is temporary but the relationship remains intact. Sigman (1991) referred to such nonverbal evidence as "spoors," like the track marks made by deer in snow, that indicate the partner's previous physical presence (and expected return).

Introspective Units

By contrast, *introspective units* are direct indications of a relationship's existence during the physical absence of one partner. The difference between introspective units and prospective units is that prospective units note that the absence is *about to happen* whereas introspective units acknowledge it *already has*. Examples include wedding rings worn when away from the spouse, as well as text messages and photos of friends, romantic partners, and family on your cell phone.

Retrospective Units

Retrospective units directly recognize the end of an absence and the reestablishment of the relationship through actual interaction. The most familiar nonverbal example is a hug or handshake or kiss upon greeting. The most common forms of conversation that fit this category are catch-up conversations and talk about the day (Vangelisti & Banski, 1993; Wood, 2006).

relational continuity constructional units (RCCUs): small-talk ways of demonstrating that the relationship persists during absence of face-to-face contact

By reporting on their experiences during the day, partners emphasize their psychological togetherness, as well as a shared interest in one another's lives and the events that happened in those lives during their physical separation. Hence, in these

ANALYZING EVERYDAY COMMUNICATION

How You Use RCCUs

Consider the ways in which you greet people and end interactions with them. What sorts of indications are made in these comments that imply the continuation of a relationship during absences or its continuation through an absence that has just ended? Now take a look at yourself and then around your living space and make a list of how many items there are essentially introspective RCCUs.

QUESTIONS TO CONSIDER

1. How many photos of friends and family do you have?
2. Are you wearing jewelry, rings, or other indications of your relationships to other people? How about your T-shirts and indicators from your dress style that you belong to particular groups?

communicative moments, or "end-of-the-day talks," with your partner or friends, you are relating to each other as well as simply reporting what happened. The talk reestablishes the relationship.

Relational Dialectics

You may have noticed in your relationships that you have needs that seem to oppose one another. Sometimes you want to be around your friends; sometimes you want to be away from your friends. Sometimes you want to talk with your family; sometimes you do not want to talk with your family. Sometimes you want your romantic relationship to be monotonous and stable; sometimes you want your romantic relationship to be unpredictable. Well, we have good news for you. These competing needs do not mean that you are crazy or that your relationships are messed up. In fact, they are indications that you and your relationships are normal.

Relational dialectics is the study of contradictions in relationships, how they are played and how they are managed. Developed by Baxter and Montgomery (1996; Baxter, 2004), the study of dialectics adheres to four guiding assumptions: contradiction, change, praxis, and totality. In what follows, we will examine these guiding assumptions. We will then introduce the three internal dialectics and three external dialectics that comprise your relationships.

Contradiction

From a dialectic perspective, contradiction is a necessary component of relationships. A **contradiction** involves the interplay between two things that are connected at the same time they are in opposition. That may be difficult to grasp, so consider the following: In order to know what it is like to be with someone, you need to know what it is like to be without someone. In this regard, those two conditions are opposed yet connected.

ETHICAL ISSUE

Is it ethical to lie to someone in order to satisfy a contradictory need, if it is done to help the relationship?

There are competing needs within relationships that make up these contradictions. We addressed some of these competing needs in the introduction to this section. These needs are equally necessary in any relationship and must all be satisfied in one way or another.

People in relationships strive to strike a balance between these needs. However, they inevitably are drawn to one need or the other. When one need is satisfied, the competing need must be addressed, and people are drawn to satisfy that one.

To understand being drawn toward an opposing need, consider what happens when traveling with someone. In relationships, there is a need to spend time with your partner and also a need to spend time away from your partner. Say you have been traveling with someone for hours or even days. You have spent a great deal of time with this person, perhaps without any break at all. Chances are good that when this happens, you cannot wait to get away from that person and be by yourself. It is not that you do not like that person—even though it might feel that way. Rather, you have fully satisfied one need and are being drawn toward the other because it has not been satisfied at all.

relational dialectics: the study of contradictions in relationships, how they are played out and how they are managed

contradiction (relational dialectics): interplay between two things that are connected at the same time they are in opposition

Change

So, in order to satisfy these competing and equally necessary needs, you are constantly being pulled toward some needs and away from others. Accordingly, there is constant **change** in your relationship. In order to make sense of relationships, it is sometimes tempting to think of them as stable. In reality, there is nothing stable about relationships. They are always changing.

Even if we were not talking about dealing with contradictions, we would still be talking about change as a fundamental component of personal relationships. You change every second of every day, and the same holds true for the other person in your relationship. It stands to reason that the relationship is changing as well. As Steve has said previously, relationships are *unfinished business*. There is always something going on, and that something is changing the relationship.

Praxis

The notion of **praxis** reminds us that "people are at once actors and objects of our own actions" (Baxter & Montgomery, 1996, p. 13). You make a lot of choices in relationships. Those choices do not just impact the relationship or your partner. Rather, those choices impact you as well. Accordingly, the actions you perform as an actor will have consequences that will impact you.

When it comes to contradictions in your relationships, how you manage them will have an impact on you, your partner, and the relationship. Everything that you do and everything that you say in relationships will have an impact of some sort. The impact can be large, small, good, bad, anticipated, unanticipated, immediate, delayed, recognized, or unrecognized. Be assured, though, all actions in a relationship have consequences.

Totality

Finally, **totality** emphasizes the complex nature of personal relationships. From a dialectic perspective, contradictions cannot be studied apart from other contradictions, without considering where they are taking place, or without recognizing that relationships involve more than one person. Contradictions must be understood as being interconnected with other contradictions. Contradictions must also be understood in the cultural, physical, and situational contexts in which they occur and in which they are managed. Contradictions must be understood as being experienced by everyone in a relationship, but that does not mean that they experience them at the same time or need them to the same degree.

Internal and External Dialectics

Having discussed the four guiding assumptions of dialectic research, we can now examine specific dialectic tensions, which make up personal relationships. While numerous contradictions can be studied, we will look at those most commonly studied in both their internal and external forms.

Internal dialectics are those occurring within a relationship itself. These would involve contradictions within a romantic relationship, a friendship, a family, a group at work, and so on. **External dialectics** are those involving a relational unit and other relational units or people within a social network. These include contradictions involving a romantic couple and other romantic couples or involving a romantic couple and their family members. The internal and external dialectics are defined and illustrated in Tables 7.1 and 7.2, respectively.

change (relational dialectics): movement in relationships that occurs in part through dealing with relational contradictions; in relationships, change is the constant element; relationships are perpetually in motion, unfinished business, and constantly evolving

praxis (relational dialectics): the notion that activities of the partners in a relationship are a vital component of the relationship itself; people are both actors and the objects of action in relationships

totality (relational dialectics): the notion that relational contradictions do not occur in isolation from one another and that the whole complexity of relationships must be taken into account as each element or part of the relationship influences other parts

internal dialectics: those occurring within a relationship itself

external dialectics: those involving a relational unit and other relational units or people within their social networks

Table 7.1 Internal Dialectics

Connectedness-Separateness (Connection-Autonomy)	*The need to be with a relational partner and the need to be away from a relational partner.* • Friends may choose to spend time engaging in shared activities and spend other time engaging in individual activities. *Also, the need to be seen as connected with a relational partner and the need to be seen as an individual.* • A younger sibling may enjoy being known as a successful older sibling's brother or sister. However, younger siblings may also want to be seen as their own person and known for their own achievements.
Certainty-Uncertainty (Novelty-Predictability)	*The need for predictability and routine in a relationship and the need for novelty and change in a relationship.* • Romantic partners may regularly have pizza delivered on Friday evenings but occasionally have a date night out.
Openness-Closedness	*The need to talk with a relational partner and the need to not talk with a relational partner.* • Roommates may talk with one another while watching television and not talk while reading or studying. *Also, the need to disclose some information to a relational partner and to not disclose other information to a relational partner.* • A child may be willing to share information to parents about school but not about what happens when out with friends.

Table 7.2 External Dialectics

Inclusion-Seclusion	*The need for people in a relationship to be around others in a social network and the need for people in a relationship to be by themselves.* • Parents may enjoy spending time with their children, but they must also spend time alone together.
Conventionality-Uniqueness	*The need for people to feel as if their relationship is like the relationships of others and the need to feel as if their relationship is special.* • A wedding or commitment ceremony may include traditional elements and at the same time include distinctive elements.
Revelation-Concealment	*The need to let others know of the existence of a relationship and the need to prevent others from knowing of the existence of a relationship.* • Someone having an affair may be tempted to let some people know about it and also ensure that other people do not know about it. *Also, the need to disclose some information about the relationship to outsiders and the need to hide other information about the relationship from outsiders.* • A family may work together to conceal the addiction of a parent to non–family members.

Coming Apart

While some relationships are maintained and continue, other relationships do not always work out and may come apart. In what follows, we will examine symptoms and sources of relational decline and deterioration. We will then explore the process of relational breakup.

Symptoms and Sources of Decline

Wood (2000, pp. 222–238) has offered six symptoms and sources of decline in personal relationships: (1) deterioration in communication, (2) destructive conflict, (3) changes in evaluative standards, (4) major transgressions, (5) inequity, and (6) personal reflection.

These factors in relational decline and deterioration, of course, do not exist independent of one another. Each one may be promoted by the others. For instance, feelings of inequity may lead to deterioration in communication and vice versa.

As relationships come apart, people, especially couples, find it harder to interact and tend to become more hostile and unsympathetic in their behaviors toward each other. What are the signs that these partners are in distress about their relationship?

Deterioration in Communication

Deterioration in communication strikes at the heart of personal relationships. Deterioration can take the form of a reduction in the usual amount of communication, a reduction in the quality of communication, and a negative tone of communication. Communicating becomes problematic and labored rather than smooth and seemingly uncomplicated. Relational dialectics reminds us that not communicating is sometimes just as necessary as communicating in relationships. However, deterioration in communication involves a decrease in the amount and type of communication that generally occurs in a given relationship.

Destructive Conflict

When relationships are coming apart, conflict may become prominent and overshadow more positive elements of the relationship. Here, it is especially evident how negativity created through destructive styles of conflict can be both a symptom and a source of decline. It is also especially evident how each of these six factors is interconnected with the others. Destructive conflict and deterioration in communication seem to go hand in hand.

Changes in Evaluative Standards

Sometimes relationships no longer seem as good and as satisfying as they once did. This change in assessment can be due to changes in the relationships itself, such as a deterioration of communication. It can also be the result of changes in the standards used to evaluate a relationship. Our personal needs at a given period of time will also influence what we desire from a relationship and what we are looking for in a relational partner. Relationships are also evaluated by comparing them to alternatives and determining whether we are getting as much or more out of them as the effort we are putting in (Thibaut & Kelley, 1959).

Major Transgressions

Consider a major transgression as anything that will get you on *The Jerry Springer Show*. These transgressions could be what many people consider deal breakers in a relationship, such as cheating or similar offense or betrayal. There are a few things to consider with major transgressions. First, not everyone agrees on what a major transgression is. Second, a major transgression does not necessarily mean the end of a relationship. Finally, it is not the action itself that causes relationships to end. Rather, as Wood (2000) reminds us, "the meaning partners assign to events and the

By the way...

Do Relationships Really End?

We talk about relationships coming to an end. In many cases, however, a relational connection between two people continues. Former friends may become enemies. Romantic couples may become friends. In these cases, relationships end in their current form, but another type of relationship may emerge.

QUESTIONS TO CONSIDER

1. How might communication between enemies who used to be friends differ from communication between enemies who never were friends?
2. How might communication between friends who used to be romantic partners differ from communication between friends who never were romantic partners?

ways they manage the events shape how the problems will affect a relationship and the possibility of repair" (p. 232).

Inequity

People sometimes determine that they are putting more into a relationship than they are receiving. This does not mean that it will automatically lead to problems or that the relationship will come to an end. However, people generally want to feel as if they are being treated equally and fairly. They do not want to feel as if they are doing all the work in a relationship while the other person is doing little or nothing at all. It is impossible to legitimately quantify the effort put into a relationship and the benefits received from a relationship. At the same time, perceptions of equality will often guide people's understanding and evaluation of their relationships.

Personal Reflection

People spend a great deal of time away from their relational partners, providing many opportunities to think about and evaluate their relationship. Personal reflection can be positive or negative. It can, therefore, lead to positive evaluation and growth of a relationship. During periods of decline, however, things seem a bit more negative than they may have seemed otherwise. Good things do not seem so good. Bad things seem worse. The overall negative atmosphere of relationships in decline increases the negative evaluations and meanings assigned.

Breakdown Process Model

So what happens when relationships come to an end? Well, all relationships are different and end in unique ways. However, there are some similar processes that people tend to experience when their relationship breaks down. Steve (Duck, 1982; Rollie & Duck, 2006) has proposed a basic model to explain the workings of relational breakdown. This model focuses on the uncertainties surrounding the end of relationships, which involve the partners and others in the network. It also focuses on the types of communication taking place during various points of the breakdown.

In what follows, we will examine the five processes that tend to occur following dissatisfaction with the relationship. Dissatisfaction is not a slippery slope that leads to a relationship's end. If that does occur, though, the following five processes generally take place: (a) intrapsychic, (b) dyadic, (c) social, (d) grave dressing, and (e) resurrection. Figure 7.2 shows the Breakdown Process Model.

intrapsychic process: part of the process of breakdown of a relationship where an individual reflects on the strengths and weaknesses of a relationship and begins to consider the possibility of ending it

Intrapsychic Process

In the **intrapsychic process**, a person reflects on the strengths and weaknesses of a relationship. He or she considers whether or not the relationship should be ended. There are advantages and disadvantages to both continuing a relationship

Figure 7.2 The Breakdown Process Model

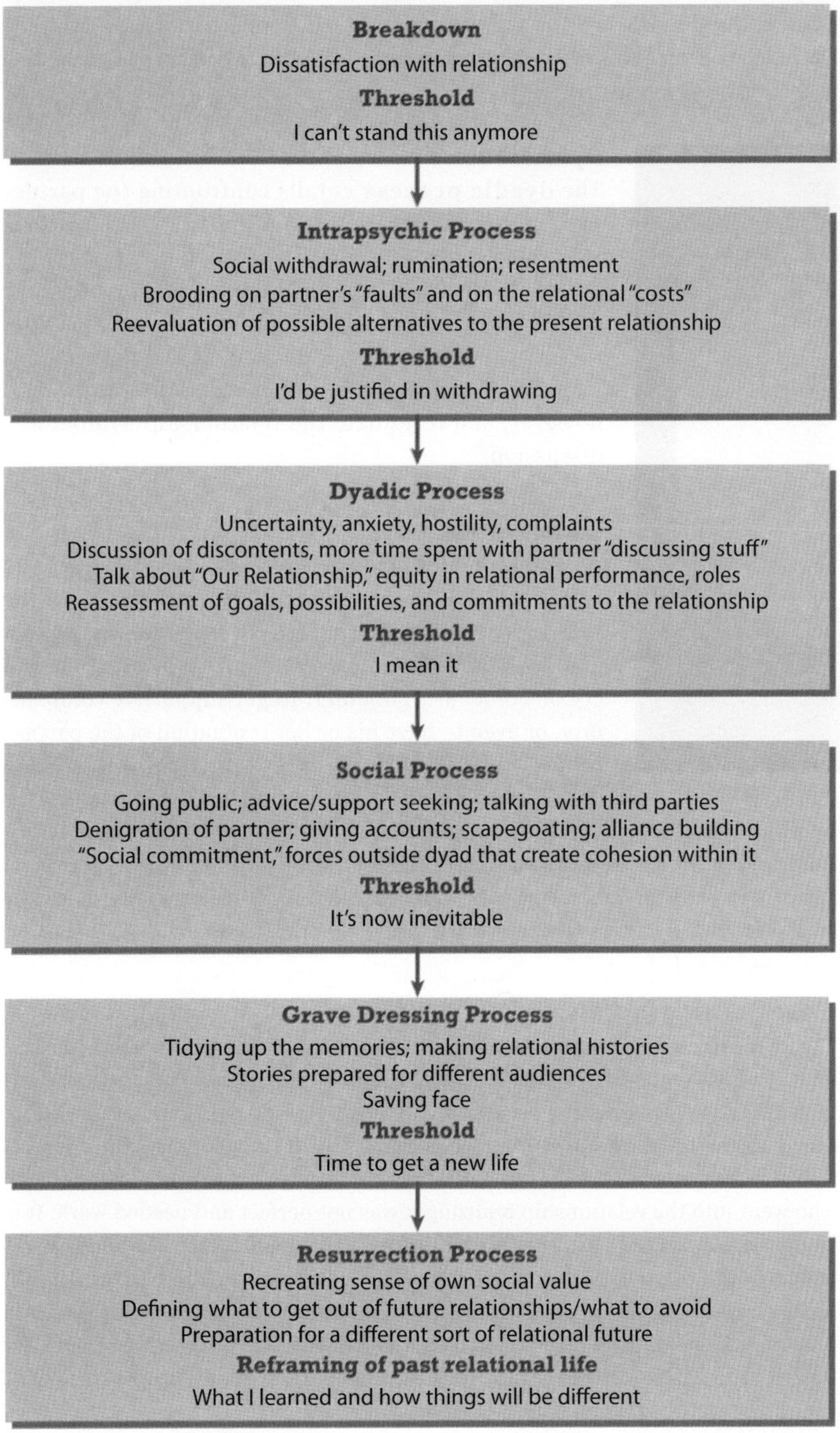

Breakdown
Dissatisfaction with relationship
Threshold
I can't stand this anymore

↓

Intrapsychic Process
Social withdrawal; rumination; resentment
Brooding on partner's "faults" and on the relational "costs"
Reevaluation of possible alternatives to the present relationship
Threshold
I'd be justified in withdrawing

↓

Dyadic Process
Uncertainty, anxiety, hostility, complaints
Discussion of discontents, more time spent with partner "discussing stuff"
Talk about "Our Relationship," equity in relational performance, roles
Reassessment of goals, possibilities, and commitments to the relationship
Threshold
I mean it

↓

Social Process
Going public; advice/support seeking; talking with third parties
Denigration of partner; giving accounts; scapegoating; alliance building
"Social commitment," forces outside dyad that create cohesion within it
Threshold
It's now inevitable

↓

Grave Dressing Process
Tidying up the memories; making relational histories
Stories prepared for different audiences
Saving face
Threshold
Time to get a new life

↓

Resurrection Process
Recreating sense of own social value
Defining what to get out of future relationships/what to avoid
Preparation for a different sort of relational future
Reframing of past relational life
What I learned and how things will be different

ETHICAL ISSUE

Do you think that someone who is ending a relationship has an ethical duty to explain to the other person why he or she is doing so?

and ending a relationship. When a person is dissatisfied with his or her relationship, however, the advantages of leaving are highlighted over the disadvantages of staying. Likewise, the disadvantages of staying are highlighted over the advantages of staying. During the intrapsychic process, a person tends to withdraw, reflect alone, and pull back from his or her partner.

Do relationships develop and break down in a linear fashion?

Dyadic Process

The **dyadic process** entails confronting the partner and openly discussing a problem with the relationship. This confrontation may be unpleasant or lead to greater understanding and forgiveness. Partners may decide to actively work on improving the relationship, take a break from the relationship, or end the relationship. Some people choose not to engage in this process, however, and terminate the relationship without any discussion.

Social Process

The **social process** involves telling other people in one's social network about the relationship problem. In the social process, the person actively seeks greater contact and communication with third parties to get advice, to cry on someone's shoulder, to get supportive commentary, or even to have his or her evaluation of the partner confirmed. Through the social process, a person is seeking either help to keep the relationship together or support for his or her version of why it has come apart. In this latter case, he or she is essentially laying the groundwork for ending the relationship. Members of a social network (friends, family, neighbors, and acquaintances) are generally shared by both relational partners. Therefore, it is important to have them on your side.

Grave Dressing Process

The **grave dressing process** involves creating the story of why a relationship died and erecting a metaphorical tombstone that summarizes its main points from birth to death. The grave dressing process involves storytelling, and you have probably heard a lot of breakup stories yourself. The most usual form of breakup story follows a narrative structure that portrays the speaker as a dedicated but alert relator who went into the relationship realizing it was not perfect and needed work. It is also possible that both partners were mature enough to realize their relationship was not going to work out, so they made the tough but realistic decision to break it off. Inherent within the grave dressing process and often included in breakup stories is praise for the relationship. Such statements as "I have learned something from all of this" or "There were some good times" are often made. Essentially, people are providing a eulogy for the relationship.

Resurrection Process

The **resurrection process** deals with the ways people prepare themselves for new relationships after ending an old one. The end of a particular relationship is not the

dyadic process: part of the process of breakdown of relationships that involves a confrontation with a partner and the open discussion of a problem with a relationship

social process: telling other people in one's social network about dissatisfaction and about possible disengagement or dissolution of a relationship

grave dressing process: part of the breakdown of relationships that consists of creating the story of why a relationship died and erecting a metaphorical tombstone that summarizes its main events and features from its birth to its death

resurrection process: part of the breakdown of relationships that deals with how people prepare themselves for new relationships after ending an old one

end of all relational life. Once any single particular relationship has finished, one of people's major tasks is to begin seeking a replacement. That is why the term *rebound* is so prominent and understood in society. Beyond actually getting back on the relational horse, the resurrection process involves preparing oneself to reemerge as a relational being. Keeping the metaphors rolling, the final nail has been placed in the coffin of the past relationship, and it is time to move forward. This process is both public and private. Publically, in part through grave dressing, a person is positioned in a positive manner and as someone capable of being in a relationship. Privately, a person comes to terms with past mistakes and difficulties, while determining what he or she wants to get out of future relationships and how past mistakes and difficulties will be avoided in the future.

DISCIPLINARY **DEBATE**

Are There Stages in Relationships?

The Battle of Cannae pitted Carthaginian forces against Roman forces in 216 BCE. It went down in history as the worst defeat for Rome and as one of the most devastating battles to ever take place. This battle received particular attention from the ancient Roman historian Livy. In describing Livy's work, however, O'Connell (2011) points out "because he was an amateur writing for amateurs, his battle descriptions focus on clarity and take place in distinct stages. Given the chaos of actual combat, this helps make the mayhem more coherent, but it definitely warps reality" (p. 9). Although we are attempting to avoid comparing relationships with wars, communication scholars have long argued about whether relationships develop or breakdown in clear, distinct stages.

QUESTIONS TO CONSIDER

1. What do you think? Is relationship research in support of stages picking up on a real fact about human relational life, or is it simply picking up on the way people like to think about and describe their relational life, whether or not it is what they actually do?
2. Does describing the development of personal relationships as occurring in distinct stages obscure what actually happens?

Focus Questions Revisited

What are personal relationships?

Personal relationships are those in which the participants are irreplaceable and communicate in close, distinct ways. Unlike social relationships, personal relationships involve people who cannot be replaced by someone else.

What are benefits of relationships?

Relationships are significant for the formation and transaction of knowledge—the creation of the world of meaning you inhabit. Relationships also provide you with various forms of support. Robert Weiss (1974) identified six specific areas where relationships provide us with something special, needed, or valued.

How are relationships initiated?

The more you get to know people, the better your map of their worlds of meaning and whether you want to continue pursuing a personal relationship. The Relationship Filtering Model suggests that people pay attention to different cues in sequence as they get to know one another. The sequence in which you pay attention to characteristics of other people is basically the sequence in which you encounter them: (1) physical appearance, (2) behavior/nonverbal communication, (3) roles, and (4) attitudes/personality.

How are relationships transacted and maintained?

Relationships are brought into existence (transacted) through communication, and relationships are categorized through communication. Relationship development and transformation can be seen as a change in communication based on the information individuals know about each other's ways of thinking about the world. Any change in a relationship involves change in content of talk and the style of communication. Relationships are kept going through communication.

How do relationships come apart?

The breakdown of relationships is marked by changes in both the topic of conversation and the audience to which the person communicates. In the early parts of a breakup when an individual is simply contemplating ending a relationship, he or she tends to withdraw from social contact and become very brooding. The second phase of a breakup is characterized by confrontation with a relational partner and less time spent with other friends. A third phase develops where the person decides to tell friends and associates about the breakup and to enlist their support. In the fourth phase, the person develops and tells a story to the world at large, explaining how the breakup occurred and making himself or herself "look good." The final (resurrection) phase is characterized by communication aimed at developing new relationships and letting go of the past.

»»» Key Concepts

certainty-uncertainty dialectic 146
change (relational dialectics) 145
connectedness-separateness dialectic 146
contradiction (relational dialectics) 144
conventionality-uniqueness dialectic 146
dyadic process 150
external dialectics 145
grave dressing process 150
inclusion-seclusion dialectic 146
internal dialectics 145
intrapsychic process 148
openness-closedness dialectic 146
personal relationships 134
praxis (relational dialectics) 145
provisions of relationships 135
relational continuity constructional units (RCCUs) 143
relational dialectics 144
Relationship Filtering Model 138
resurrection process 150
revelation-concealment dialectic 146
social process 150
social relationships 134
totality (relational dialectics) 145

»»» Questions to Ask Your Friends

1. Write the story of your most recent breakup. Does it follow a neat progression? Have a friend read it and ask you questions about particular details. Does this questioning make you want to revise your narrative in any way?
2. What turning points are there in relationship growth or decline that you and your friends believe you can identify through talk?
3. The next time your friends ask, "How was your day?" ask what they think they are accomplishing. Enter into a broad and fulfilling discussion on retrospective RCCUs and how even small talk serves to maintain relationships during absence.

»»» Media Connections

1. Look at several Sunday newspaper sections on marriages and engagements. Check for similarities in attractiveness level between the people involved. Next take these pictures and cut them down the middle. How easy is it to reconnect the right people?
2. Take any movie where a romance develops between two main characters. Does it either develop or dissolve according to the proposal made in this chapter, and if not, how?
3. What models of "true romance" are presented in different kinds of movies?

»»» Student Study Site

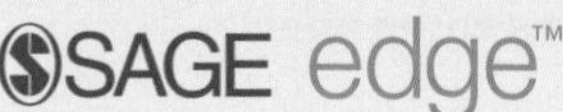

Sharpen your skills with SAGE edge at edge.sagepub.com/duckciel2e

SAGE edge for students provides a personalized approach to help you accomplish your coursework goals in an easy-to-use learning environment.

Chapter Outline

Families in Truth and Myth

- Families as Social Ideals
- Negative Aspects of Family

Families as . . .

- Families as Frames
- Families as Structures
- Families as Communication Systems
- Families as Systems
- Families as Transacted Relationships

Change and Development in Family Processes

- Acute Change in Families
- Long-Term Change in Families
- Redeployment of Families and Their Communication

Families Communicate!

Focus Questions Revisited

Key Concepts

Questions to Ask Your Friends

Media Connections

08 Family Communication

FOCUS QUESTIONS

1. What is a "family," and how can communication in everyday life contribute to an understanding of what counts and what does not?
2. What sorts of diverse forms of "family" are recognized in different societies/cultures?
3. What are the possible ways in which a "family" may be defined, and which one is best for a communication scholar?
4. What types of everyday communication in a family *transact* the nature of family life?

Societies treat the family as so important an institution that they give it special tax breaks, emphasize it in religion, and idealize it in media and even fairy tales. On this view, divorce is a bad thing (Devil term; see Chapter 4), and family is a good thing (God term; see, again, Chapter 4). *Family communication* has recently become a hot topic, partly because the family is a primary source for early socialization. Your parents or guardians are the first of Society's Secret Agents to shape the ways in which you think about almost everything, from your own self to your views about the world in general. Family communication instills and frames cultural values from the beginning and is a key starting point for your sense of self and identity (Chapter 3). However, for good or ill, you mostly can't choose your family members, and they are yours forever.

But what exactly *is* a "family"? Think about two puzzling recent news stories before you get going. First, one news story raises some interesting questions. It claimed that a happily married couple, both given up for adoption at birth, later discovered to their horror that they were in fact twins, and their marriage, even though it was a happy one with children, was forcibly terminated by the law. OK, it turned out not to be true, but what if it had been? The couple had not known that they were genetically related, and the marriage was a successful one up to that point. Why could they not be a "family"?

A second story is definitely true (BBC News, 2006). In this case a Japanese woman in her 50s gave birth to her own grandchild, having acted as a surrogate mother for her daughter whose womb had been removed as a result of cancer. The daughter had donated her own eggs, the eggs had been fertilized in vitro using the daughter's husband's sperm, and the fertilized egg had then been transplanted into the grandmother to carry through term to birth. Just after the birth, the daughter and her husband formally and legally adopted the child, and the grandmother/birth mother formally and legally renounced any rights to the child as her own. Physically the "grandmother" was the mother; genetically she was the grandmother. What do you see as her role in the *family?*

As the chapter progresses, we will teach you to focus less on family structure and more on the communication that makes the structure work. A deeper and more revolutionary question left for the end of the chapter is whether you should classify people as "family" according to some social structural categories that are used by lawyers and demographers or according to the communication styles that members use to *transact* family life

By the way...

The Family and Society

According to Mr. Justice Coleridge, "We are experiencing a period of family meltdown . . . as catastrophic as the meltdown of the ice caps," and its effects pose "as big a threat to the future of our society as terrorism, street crime or drugs. . . . *[A]lmost all of society's social ills can be traced directly to the collapse of the family life*" (BBC News, 2008, ¶ 8, 10, italics added).

Actually, similar statements about the downward trend of society and its root cause being the collapse of the family have been made throughout history by people in the times of Abraham Lincoln, the Plymouth Pilgrims, and even the Roman poet Horace. Perhaps the "good old days" were never really that good.

QUESTIONS TO CONSIDER

1. What reasons are there to agree with Justice Coleridge's statement that we are currently experiencing a period of family meltdown?
2. What reasons are there to disagree with Justice Coleridge's statement that we are currently experiencing a period of family meltdown?

and share worlds of meaning. As Kathleen Galvin (2007) noted, "The greater the ambiguity of family form, the more elaborate the communicative processes needed to establish and maintain identity" (p. 1). We will teach you in this chapter that a "family" essentially depends on a set of interconnected *communicative* relationships.

FAMILIES IN TRUTH AND MYTH

Because the family is seen as the root of socialization and a small form of "society" itself, it is given special attention in modern life. However you think of a "family," there is a strong tendency to (a) separate it from other forms of relational interaction and (b) idealize the concept.

Families as Social Ideals

Politicians, religious officials, and tax collectors all like the idea of the family. Most religions have something explicit and direct to say about the importance of the family in the belief system (e.g., there is some version of "Honor thy father and thy mother," or respect is due particularly to your parents and elders).

The media and politicians also bombard you with images of *good* families, and there are debates about the way a family may be constituted. There is a strong heteronormative pressure; there is a suspicion of countries or religions that permit polygamous relationships. Bigamy is illegal, and adultery—which threatens the family bonds—is disapproved; partners without children are not seen as a "family" (Steuber & Solomon, 2012); there is a discussion in society of whether biological parents separated from a child at birth are the "true family" as compared to the child's lifelong foster caregivers or adoptive parents.

These views are essentially positive, conservative, and static: They see a "family" as a stable structure, usually with a definite power hierarchy. A traditional view denotes a husband and wife plus 2.4 kids and a quartet of silver-haired grandparents somewhere in the background. This traditional group is represented in advertising as happy, supportive, quite comfortably wealthy, and harmoniously understanding. The family is usually depicted eating a meal or driving around in a newly purchased automobile—while the older generation is usually represented as advice givers. You are also subtly influenced in other ways: for example, to get family calling plans for your phones, a cultural fact that emphasizes the people you *should* be calling.

Families are therefore supposed to be good for us. Le Poire, Hallett, and Erlandson (2000) identified two key defining functions as *nurturing* and *control:* A family nurtures, supports, and sustains its members, not only emotionally and educationally but also financially. The family also exerts control over behavior (often thought of as parental control over children but actually much more than that, since it teaches children about the nature of society and the world—**socialization**). There is a large set of social **rules** or norms for "family" that monitors the way in which family life should be carried out. Many of these are similar to the issues discussed in Chapter 3, where individual identity is responsive to larger social pressures. Labeling particular people as a

socialization: the process by which a child comes to understand the way the surrounding culture "does things"—that is, holds certain values to be self-evident and celebrates particular events or festivals

rules: norms for "family" that monitor the way in which family life should be carried out

"family" is a powerful way to establish *expectations* about how they should feel about one another and communicate affection, loyalty, or membership.

Negative Aspects of Family

All the same, the fact is that families often present very negative experiences for people at least some of the time (Coleman & May-Chahal, 2003; May-Chahal et al., 2012). Many teenagers come to dislike their parents (for either a short or a long period) as part of the process of establishing an independent identity. Early experiences with parents can lead to decreased self-esteem or to insecurities in later life relationships. Distant and aloof parents tend to produce children whose later personal relationships are characterized by distance, aloofness, persecuted vigilance, and insecurity (Rowe & Carnelley, 2005; Rowe et al., 2012).

Although rates are declining, the family has long been known as the most violent social institution outside of the military (Straus, Gelles, & Steinmetz, 1980), and by no means are all families functional or even fun (May-Chahal & Antrobus, 2012). People are more likely to be assaulted, abused, or even murdered by a family member than by a random stranger (see Figure 8.1). Most people's personal acquaintance with violence is represented by, and restricted to, their interactions with family members (Coleman & May-Chahal, 2003). In part this is simply a consequence of the fact that, being close and intense, families tend to communicate all the extremes of emotion. Their everyday communication may convey at one time or another both love and hate, both peaceful coexistence and outright open conflict. They also provide plenty of opportunities for a very rich range of emotional experiences to be shown toward one another.

So if the "family" is not always the realization of a social ideal and is not always positive, what is it, and how can an understanding of communication in everyday life help us understand it?

Figure 8.1 Murder by Intimate Partner, 1976–2004

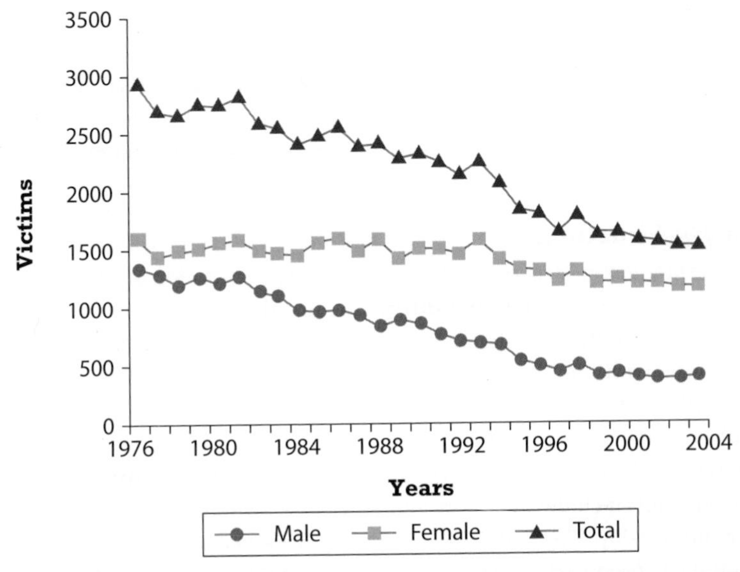

SOURCE: http://www.silentwitness.net/sub/violences.htm.

Make your case

Families as Controllers of Access to Media

Children have access to more types of media than ever before, through personal e-mail accounts, Facebook, and cell phones. Parents, on the other hand, have increasingly less control over their kids' access to media, and whom their kids talk to or interact with. In addition, online communities, texting, and digital devices that adolescents use to keep in constant contact with peers may detract from the parent-child relationship.

QUESTIONS TO CONSIDER

1. How should parents respond to their children being members of an online community? Should children have to be "friends" with their parents on Facebook?
2. Do you think that the relationships between parents and adolescent children who are in constant contact with their peers via these various media channels suffer as a result?

FAMILIES AS . . .

Segrin and Flora (2005) identified three ways of defining "family": structural, functional, and transactional. *Structural definitions* term a "family" as people who are related by blood, law, or adoption; *functional definitions* focus on the behaviors that make a family work well, such as mutual support, socialization, and financial assistance; *transactional definitions* are based on the communication that takes place within a group in a way that builds a sense of family identity. This last definition is of course the most appealing definition for communication scholars.

Families as Frames

For many purposes, families are seen primarily as social or demographic *structures* that contain and connect particular individuals (for example, two parents and a child, mother and partner, father and son, daughter and aunt, stepparent and stepchild). This way of seeing "family" is structural or genetic: who is in it, who is biologically or legally related to whom, who is older, who is a parent, who is offspring. You could map that structure by indicating dates of adoptions, deaths, births, and marriages as a way to show who was in the family at a particular time. This represents the family as an interconnected group of individuals. This is the information, after all, that most people use when they construct a family tree—for example, names, dates, relationships, and events that specify inclusion or exclusion from the group.

Le Poire (2006) noted that this particular structure of a family can be defined according to (a) *biological ties* (genetics, bloodlines, or biological connectedness), (b) *legal definitions* based on a person's suitability to be a parent or a person's right to have custody of the children after a divorce, or (c) *sociological definitions*. This third set is based not only on the two foregoing kinds of category but also on those groups that self-define themselves as families with an expectation of future functioning as a "family." Many African Americans, for example, define "family" to include **kin networks** (cousins, second cousins, children of cousins, uncles, aunts, and even long-term friends). These considerations omit one factor that we will consider later—namely, communication as a means of defining family life (Galvin & Bylund, 2009).

kin networks: the extended relational network of cousins, second cousins, children of cousins, uncles, aunts, and even long-term friends who are considered family, too

nuclear family: the parents plus their genetically related children

extended family: a family that has at its center a nuclear family but also includes grandparents, aunts, cousins, and all other living forms of blood relatives

family of origin: the family where you are the child of two parents, and in the majority of cases you will have spent some of your life with one or both of them

family of descent: the whole historical family tree from which you are descended, both living and dead

Family as Structures

If you see families as structures, then your first representation of a family is likely, in this society, to be a **nuclear family** (i.e., just the parents plus their children) (Le Poire, 2006). Importantly, however, every nuclear family also is a small family subgroup within a larger family conceptual group. Two parents and the kids are nested within a wider group of the grandparents, cousins, broader families of both parents, and many more strange add-ons of aunts, uncles, in-laws, and many relatives they may never even meet—the **extended family**. In Japan, an extended family includes ancestors long since dead, whom the living have a duty to honor and worship. The living accept a strong responsibility to procreate in order to continue to produce future honor and worship for this group and for themselves after their own death (Golliher, 2006). You can also consider **family of origin** (the parents you were born to), **family of descent** (the clan or historical family tree that you branch from), **family of generativity** (the one you may start for yourself), or **family of choice**. This latter may be one created through adoption, for example, or may simply be the group of people you decide is your "true" family even though there is no genetic connection. When parents adopt nongenetic offspring, divorce, or remarry other partners, then so-called **blended families** are the result (Afifi & Hamrick, 2006). This means that one parent's children may spend at least some of their time in a family where children of another adult are present as "brothers or sisters." The creation of one blended family can sometimes mean that the children of divorced parents experience daily life in two "families." This is described as a **binuclear family**—that is, two families based on the nuclear form (for example, the children's father, their stepmother, and her children, if any, as well as the children's mother and their stepfather and his children, if any).

How many different types of family can you identify in this illustration? Are there any that are omitted, and would you have included all the ones that are illustrated here?

The one defining feature of such traditional views of a "family" is a transgenerational concept that involves the existence of at least one member of one generation who is the responsibility of at least one member of another generation (Duck, 2007). This structural arrangement can take many shapes. The traditional heterosexual nuclear family of one male and one female and their offspring has now been supplemented by many other diverse possibilities, such as families we choose (Weston, 1997) or even one adult and a dog. An incomplete list of possibilities is two same-sex parents; communal rearing groups; fostering; adoption; grandparents, aunts, or uncles raising their direct or indirect descendants; and single-parent families.

Single-parent families can arise from several circumstances. For example, singleness may be a choice, a preference, or an unwanted outcome (e.g., as a result of an undesired divorce or unexpected death). A person may not wish to be encumbered with a permanent partner even after having a child or children. You can therefore distinguish those single-parent families where there has never been more than one parent from those single-parent families where there was previously more than one parent. In the latter case, one of them chose to leave for whatever reason or has been involuntarily removed from a direct parental role by divorce, death, or other circumstances such as serious chronic illness or imprisonment. Many military families operate effectively this way even though both partners are still alive but one is away on active service. In addition, any couple may choose to have no children of their own, but the traditional definition of family means you will not count them as a family unless the couple is looking after their own parents instead (Sahlstein, Maguire, & Timmerman, 2009).

Now consider other increasingly prevalent forms of family, whether resulting from different original pairings of parents or from reconnection of different parents into a blended family. As Regnerus (2012) indicates, forms of family that have two same-sex parents are increasingly frequent. Obviously everything that can happen to heterosexual parents can happen there too, including socialization, love, caring, support, separation, blending, abuse, self-sacrifice, and family stress. Two same-sex parents may adopt unrelated children, may parent the existing genetic offspring of one or both of them, or may newly generate children from one partner and a willing or paid surrogate or donor and then bring those children up themselves.

family of generativity: the family where you are one of the parents of at least one child

family of choice: a family created through adoption, or simply the group of people you decide is your "true" family even though there is no genetic connection

blended family: when parents adopt nongenetic offspring, divorce, or remarry other partners, then so-called blended families are the result

binuclear family: two families based on the nuclear form (e.g., the children's father, their stepmother, and her children, if any, as well as the children's mother and their stepfather and his children, if any)

single-parent family: family where there are children but only one parent caregiver; singleness may be a choice, a preference, or an unwanted outcome (e.g., as a result of an undesired divorce or unexpected death)

Families as Communication Systems

The difficulties for communication scholars of using such structural definitions are now obvious. A family tree would not tell you anything about the *personal and communicative relationships* between the people in the family structure. What if you are incredibly close to one parent but feel distant from the other one and so do not talk with that parent as much as with the other? What if your family structure was disrupted (by death or divorce, for example), and you feel really bad about the fact that you never get to see your kids? What if one of your parents or siblings abused you physically, sexually, or verbally, and you are now almost terrified of intimacy with anyone else? What if your family was so happy that you enter every relationship feeling very self-secure, with total confidence and self-respect, and you find it easy to trust everyone else you meet (or what if they treated you so badly you can never trust anyone)?

How would any of that show up in a simple structural representation like a family tree? Clearly, it would not, but it might show up in the *patterns of communication*. Some of these feelings and experiences are more than likely to affect family communication, self-concept, identity, relationships with other people, and life goals in ways not registered on the simple diagram of family structure.

ETHICAL ISSUE

Is it unethical for some family structures to be privileged or favored in society while other family structures are viewed negatively?

Structure and Communication

There actually is a method—the genogram—for representing some of these details, and it can be found at www.genopro.com/genogram. In a genogram the basic family tree structure is embellished with various emotional and historical information that helps both the person and (say) a therapist make more sense of the communication and different perspectives in the family than the structure does alone. You may want to try creating a genogram, either as a class exercise or purely for your own pleasure or enlightenment. Basically, instead of just looking at the names and their relationship to one another, you start to ask questions about the emotional connections and attitudes. First draw a picture of the family structure, but then add to it an emotional map that shows communication patterns, preferences, and antagonisms. For example, "X was Y's sister, but no one in the rest of the family except Y would talk to her because X had once insulted their mother very nastily" or "B's father would always treat him disrespectfully after he came out." Not all fathers like all of their daughters equally well, not all siblings like one another equally strongly, and the mere existence of membership in a family is not a guide to the strength of feelings between the members. Figure 8.2 is a genogram for Harry Potter that clearly illustrates both biological *and* relational ties. Hence we emphasize how the family is transacted through communication.

Several scholars have identified the ways in which family communication can be broken into different categories. These represent the structure in terms of the style

DISCIPLINARY DEBATE

Is Biology Thicker Than Communication?

Concepts like "blood is thicker than water," "separated at birth," and "brothers reunited after 60 years" suggest strongly that people see genetic relationships as more significant than other ways of viewing "family." Two biological brothers who have been separated for 60 years are not likely to know much about one another or their respective lives, and they have no shared memories, family photos, or family experiences. At the same time, politicians and others often treat the biological family as the bedrock of society.

QUESTIONS TO CONSIDER

1. Is this essentially saying that genetics matters more than experience, or that family communication or shared experience is not one of its defining features?
2. Do you believe that a person should stay in a family with an abusive and violent parent? Or can the bonds of blood and genetics be broken if a parent mistreats other family members?

Figure 8.2 Genogram Example for Harry Potter (written by J. K. Rowling, www.jkrowling.com)

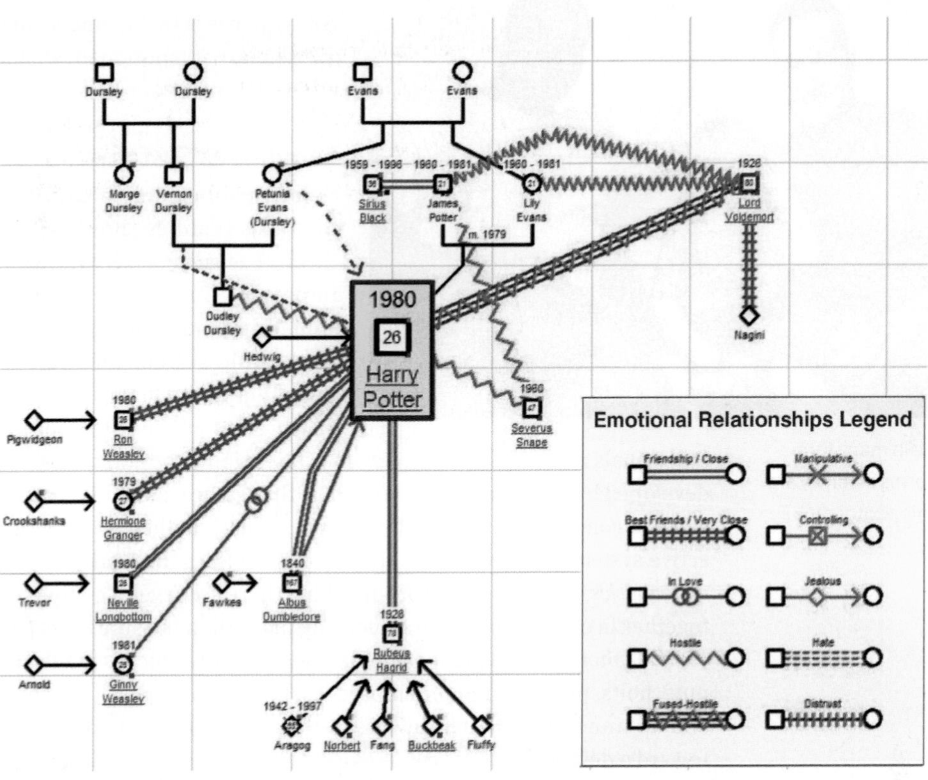

SOURCE: http://www.genopro.com/genogram/

NOTE: Names and descriptions have been collected from the Harry Potter books written by J.K. Rowling and from Wikipedia (www.wikipedia.org).

of communication that is adopted there. Koerner and Fitzpatrick (2002), for example, describe family communication along two dimensions: *conformity orientation* and *conversation orientation*. Conformity orientation describes "the degree to which family communication stresses a climate of homogeneity of attitudes, values, and beliefs," whereas conversation orientation describes "the degree to which families create a climate in which all family members are encouraged to participate in unrestrained interaction about a wide array of topics" (Koerner & Fitzpatrick, 2002, pp. 85–86).

These two dimensions create a four-category typology of family communication that can be used to typologize families by comparing their positions on each dimension, whether high or low on each: (a) *Protective* families are high in conformity orientation and low in conversation orientation. Family members place a value on conformity to family norms and do not permit or expect discussion of alternatives. (b) *Pluralistic* families are the opposite on both dimensions: high in conversation orientation but low in conformity orientation. Such families encourage conversation about rules and enjoy discussion, innovation, and diversity of lifestyle, so it is not offensive to break family rules if it raises a worthy issue for discussion. (c) *Consensual* families are high in both conformity and conversation orientation. In these families, parents expect children to obey rules but provide opportunities to discuss and question these rules, as long as there is ultimately agreement about how the rules should be followed in the future. (d) *Laissez-faire* families are low in both conformity and conversation orientation. These families have lax rules and do not talk about them much. One consequence is that members of such families are somewhat emotionally distant from each other (Koerner, 2006).

Families come in many forms. What three forms of family are depicted in this photograph?

Families as Systems

Some scholars use a different approach that sees families (however defined structurally) as *systems.* **Systems theory** is an important way to understand families—as something made up of parts but operating as a whole system that can achieve functions that individuals alone cannot and that also creates an environment in which those individuals must exist (Griffin, 2012). The original notion of systems theory was developed by Von Bertalanffy (1950). Although he was a biologist, he foresaw the value of conceiving of many things as systems, whether machines, human interactive systems, or ecosystems. In some disciplines the study of systems is called *cybernetics,* and in the case of a machine there are several components that work together in order to produce something more than the sum of its parts (*nonsummative wholeness*). A great example is a motorcar, which is made up of individual nuts, bolts, pipes, computer chips, cogs, levers, and wheels, which altogether can end up transacting something greater than the sum of its parts, namely motion toward a destination.

Characteristics of Systems

Cybernetic systems are *goal-oriented* and *self-regulating;* that is, they keep a check on their own activity and adjust themselves in response to input from the environment. The classic example of this is the thermostat, which reads the temperature and turns on a heating or cooling device whenever the temperature gets out of range. As soon as the temperature is restored to the desired level, the thermostat serves to turn off the heating or cooling device but continues to read the environment in order to discover when it should reactivate the appropriate device. Such systems show *hierarchy* among component parts and environment, in that one component tends to be in charge of others (e.g., the engine drives the wheels). Yet the parts are also *mutually interdependent,* and the performance of one influences the success of the total system (*common fate*). If one part of the motorcar ceases to function (e.g., if a wheel falls off), then the system (motor car) will no longer be able to achieve its objectives (going to a destination) until the part is repaired.

systems theory: deals with (among other phenomena) family and social events as systems made up of parts but operating as a whole system that can achieve functions that individuals alone cannot and that also creates an environment in which those individuals must exist; the behavior of one part (person) affects the atmosphere and behavior of other parts (persons) of the family

Viewing Families as Systems

Using the same sorts of key terms (*nonsummative wholeness, goal orientation, self-regulation, hierarchy, interdependence,* and *common fate*), several family scholars began to apply systems theory to families (Bateson, 1972; Watzlawick, Beavin, & Jackson, 1967). Such researchers (Bosticco & Thompson, 2005) pointed out that families are like systems in many ways, particularly in terms of their *mutual interdependence, hierarchy, common fate,* and *self-regulation.* Most families have a power hierarchy, and all members share a common fate and depend on one another for their outcomes and performance to some extent. For example, if one member of the family becomes ill, then the performance of the other members at various tasks—like going to work—may be influenced (in this instance a parent may have to take a day off work in order to look after a sick child).

What impact does reading storybooks have on the socialization of children?

This kind of *interdependence* can work in different ways too, and a classic example is where one parent is an abuser or an alcoholic and the other members of the family are forced to adapt their behavior to this (Wright & Wright, 1995). The whole system of the family is affected by the one individual having an alcohol dependency or being abusive. The children may learn to be very cautious around a drunken parent who could become violent. Not only is their behavior influenced by the behavior of another part of the "system" in the present, but it may cause them to become hypervigilant in all future relationships.

Skills You Can Use: **Communication and Substance Dependency**

If you have any experience with alcoholism or the effects of alcohol or drug dependence on the operation of a family system, then use your familiarity with communication concepts and your skills at finding evidence to take a look at Le Poire et al. (2000), one of the few approaches to these common and serious issues that uses communication as the basis for assessment.

As systems theory would predict, it sometimes turns out to be difficult to cure an individual alcoholic in a family, because over time the family members come to find creative ways to deal with the alcoholism, and they get locked into using them. A classic example is the case where a family prefers the drunk parent to be incapably drunk, because that way he or she is not as dangerous to other people as when in a state of more capable alertness. It has also been reported that some spouses prefer their partners when drunk because they are funny. Somewhat surprisingly, then, it is rather hard to cure alcoholism if you do not treat the family as a system but merely treat the individual as an alcoholic with an individual problem. Indeed, family systems therapists often will not work alone with children in therapy. If they take the child out of the system and try to help the child as an individual but then put the child back into exactly the same unchanged system, the child will not have the power to change it, and the symptoms will recur.

However, in abusive families the abusing person will never be invited to attend joint sessions. This is one of the protections for potential victims that the therapeutic system endorses. Aside from the obvious risks to the victim's safety from attending a meeting of this kind, such a "systems" approach implies dual ownership of the abusive behavior, which may not be true, and could potentially increase the victim's misperception that the abuse is his or her own fault. It is therefore important to recognize that a systems analysis is a theoretical approach to the problem that can identify practical issues that need to be treated without a systems analysis on

By the way...

Peer Pressure and Peer Support

One of the major influences on children's development of smoking habits and attitudes toward drugs is the sort of influence that happens not only in the family but also in the adolescent peer group. Why might this be? Well, one reason is that adolescents are particularly sensitive to issues of rejection, inclusion, and popularity, so the nature of adolescent communication about drugs, smoking, and alcohol might be expected to have a lot to do with "being one of the in-crowd." Many adolescents reported that they were pressured by their peers into taking up smoking or drugs, and some influential communication programs have been developed to help them resist such pressures (Colby et al., 2013).

QUESTIONS TO CONSIDER

1. How do you think communication programs would help adolescents to resist peer pressure?
2. Aside from smoking, drinking, and other dangerous behaviors, can peer pressure ever be a positive thing?

top. The fact that a victim is systematically abused does not require the conclusion that the victim is in any way "responsible" for the abuse. One observation that surprises many outsiders, however, is the fact that many victims *feel* responsible even when they obviously are not. In the case of Amanda Berry, who recently escaped from 10 years of imprisonment in Cleveland, for example, it is quite possible that despite the obvious evidence to the contrary, she might feel that she somehow contributed to her fate. Therapists recognize this syndrome and are prepared to deal with it.

Families in a System of Peer Culture

In addition to internal dynamics that work as systems, families exist within other connections of people and can be characterized as "systems" from that point of view—wheels within wheels. Any family system can also be seen as placed in networks of other structures, systems, and social connections that affect its experience. A network is a complex set of groups to which any individual belongs. For example, two parents may have different sets of friends and may work in different places where they know different sets of people as well as knowing people in common. Their children play with children from other families, go to school and meet peers, and as adolescents will certainly communicate with a **peer culture** that may influence their behavior.

In short, the family does not live in isolation but has connections with other groups, and these networks can influence the way in which family life is experienced. Galvin (2007) notes that redeployed families (our term) face a problem of presenting their identity as a family group to the outside world that sees them as not "normal." This faces the family with the issue of "discourse dependency"—that is, a way in which they frame and represent themselves to one another and to the outside world through their communication. For example, Suter (2006) analyzed the way in which children may be faced with explaining to their friends why they have two mommies, so their family structure is not simply a personal matter between them and their two parents.

The effects of peer culture can also wash back into the family, as when children bring their friends home or adolescents adopt the styles and habits of their peer group in contrast to those usually used within the family. This often generates a familiar and predictable form of adolescent rebellion against the previously experienced family norms and practices (Pickhart, 2013).

Children, Rules, and the Outside World

Children have multiple models in a complex, interconnected, networked world. Parents are not the only influence to which children are accountable: First of all, the school system calls them to account, but increasingly through the teenage years, adolescents' peer groups become more influential in their decisions. As the children develop, their social world begins to extend beyond the parenting and family group to a wider world of schoolteachers, friends, and peers, all of whom can influence the

peer culture: the set of attitudes and beliefs that create influence from children or adults of the same age/generation as the target person

way in which the children learn and behave. As children get old enough to become active outside their home family environment, so too they discover that there are different ways to perform a family life. Your family and your friends' families do many things, like celebrating birthdays and holidays and even everyday living, in different ways, as you will know if you have ever been to a sleepover at a friend's house.

However, the peer group does not simply communicate influence but is also most often the group that is consulted when an adolescent has questions about sexuality, in particular in seeking information about sexual experiences. Teenagers tend to ground their information about morals from their parents or family groups, but their communication about actual sexual practices is much more likely to be derived from the adolescent network (Lloyd & Anthony, 2003).

As children grow older, the family's influence on them changes. Schools exert an influence on family activities and the timetabling and priorities given to family experience. This means that childhood evening time spent together is now exchanged for separate time as the child does homework or school-related activities, and various kinds of "spillover" enter family life. This spillover is not only from school and the child's wider network. Parents' work organizations may require them to do assignments that cut into family time, or adolescents may want their peers to stay out late when their parents want them home. Parents may want to control adolescent access to computer time whereas adolescents expect to be able to contact their networks through technology whenever they want. Of course, this changes the nature of communication within the family. So with the family, it is important to consider more than its structure and to consider the interaction of its parts and how these all work communally to transact the full experience of family life.

More subtly, each of these groups has a thought world/world of meaning attached to it, and these may be in conflict in various ways. For example, your friends and your family may have different attitudes toward achievement in school or toward sexual relationships outside of a marriage. Although family and parents start out being the most powerful influences on children, as the children grow up, their exposure to other sources of information and to other people provides them with new and often competing ideas and values.

Families as Transacted Relationships

We noted that family communication seems to be both a hot topic and an interesting one with lots of clear connections to your own personal life. It is hardly surprising that family communication is a growing area, because the family context is one that exemplifies many of the issues we have previously discussed.

First, a family offers most of the provisions of relationship that friendship and romance supply. In Chapter 7, we note that relationships provide such resources as *reliable alliance, emotional integration,* and *support,* and the same is true of the family. A family also tends to have its own styles, rituals, and practices—for example, its own norms and rituals that represent a shared world of meaning. **Norms** are the habitual rules for conducting any family activity, and **rituals** are particularly formalized ways for handling, say, the routines of mealtimes or birthday gift giving. There are many other issues of family dynamics, for communication with stepchildren or siblings and family rituals that represent classic instances of basic forms of communication. Also management of boundary dialectics influences what a given family believes is "private" information. As another example, patterns of support, argument, and conflict in families may be different from one another even if the underlying forms are similar to those in dyads.

norms: the habitual rules for conducting any family activity

rituals: particularly formalized ways for handling, say, the routines of mealtimes or birthday gift giving in a family

COMMUNICATION + YOU

Your Family and Its Communication

Every family has its own traditions or rituals, usually passed down from generation to generation. Look at any of your family's rituals and analyze the ways in which it communicates something centrally important to the identity of the family.

QUESTIONS TO CONSIDER

1. How does the ritual "perform" family life, and what central features of that family does it tend to emphasize?
2. Reconsider the earlier "Make Your Case" box about family constraints on media use. How does media use in your family stack up against the questions that were asked in that box?

The four different styles of family communication noted earlier (protective, pluralistic, consensual, laissez-faire) suggest different responses by parents to a child's increased access to peer networks, which these days are increasingly conducted through such relational media as cell phones, Facebook, Twitter, and Internet social sites. Whereas permissive parents are unlikely to show much interest in their child's access to such media, protective parents are much more likely to take control and to restrict their child's use of social media. This in turn is likely to influence the child's access to peers who make frequent use of those media and therefore transacts a different form of social life for the child.

By the way...

Respect for Parents

In the 16th century, English offspring were expected to stop what they were doing and to stand in silence, as a mark of respect, when their father came into the room whether or not they were grown adults themselves (Stone, 1979).

QUESTIONS TO CONSIDER

1. When you were a young child, how did your communication with your parents or guardians indicate respect for them, or how did it not?
2. Did this communication change as you grew older? If so, in what ways did it change?

Transacting Family Life

The move to considering behaviors, rituals, and norms means that you are looking at families no longer as groups (i.e., *institutions* or *structures*) so much as performances or sites of communication. This is an important shift of emphasis. You might recognize that family communication provides a link to discussion in Chapter 3 on the influences of interaction with significant individuals on your identity.

Authority and Power

First, families are more than categories: They have norms and power structures within them that are transacted in communication. There is, especially when children are young, a firm authority structure in a family that means that decisions are not effectively made between equal beings. There is, at least at first sight, an **authority structure** in a family, one more firmly enforced in some families, religions, and cultures than others. Some stress the role of one parent as head of the family; others stress equality of all the mature members. However, there is an unstated structure also. If your parents decide that the toddling young members of the family will go with them to the Ozarks for the weekend, then they do: The toddlers don't get to vote; they're just taken to the place, willingly or not.

authority structure: in some families the authority structure stresses the role of one parent as head of the family; others stress equality of all the mature members

As the younger family members mature, then the family communication may become increasingly inclusive and consultative about some activities, though most middle-class parents seem to press their children involuntarily to accept opportunities that involve piano lessons, dancing, or sports. In the teen years, the "children" become more independent and make a lot of their own choices, so the notion of family decision making gets quite differently executed. It is important, then, not to transfix the "family" as only one sort of entity. Its styles of communication are constantly changing as the family members grow older. It grows, changes, and develops in form and style, as its component members all age and mature or decline with the passage of time. Therefore you miss something important if you do not look within the category ("family") and explore the way changes are transacted in communication.

Consider how the above definition of family authority is too simplistic and too inclined to overlook the way in which authority is not a simple rigid hierarchy but a communication practice. Can't a child exert power over a parent by throwing a tantrum or being obstinate? Who has the power then? Isn't every screaming child basically letting the neighbors know how wicked and incompetent the parents really are? That's a kind of communicative power, and it certainly affects family experience. So power can be *formally* structured in a family, but it can also operate *informally* or bidirectionally. The **bidirectionality hypothesis** (Pettit & Lollis, 1997) recognizes that power can work in two directions. That is, at some points and times it works one way when parents control or influence their young kids, but power also goes the other way and sometimes kids can control or influence parents.

Norms and Rituals

Families have their own specific norms and rituals. The norms may be based on family beliefs about the proper way of indicating respect for elders, for example. They may also relate to equality of members where everyone must be heard as equal and having the same value, especially as the children are old enough to make real contributions to discussions and decisions. Also families have rituals. Take a moment to think about the ways in which your family *does* routine events and celebrations. How do you "do dinner" or "do vacations" or "do birthday parties"? Are these rituals organized in the same way that they are done in your friends' families? Probably not. There are no standard ways for families to conduct their lives, though there will be some sort of broad agreement in a given culture about how a set of family activities should occur, the events families recognize and celebrate, and the ways in which they carry out their rituals of life.

Carol Bruess and Anna Hoefs (2006) describe an amusing family ritual concerning gift giving, where one person always ends up with a wooden cat puzzle that was once given to a member of the family. It was a surprisingly odd gift, so it ended up becoming a family joke. Instead of throwing away an unwanted gift, the family turned it into a ritual where the last person to be given the cat puzzle one year always gives it as "the gift" to another member next year. The ritual of discovering who got stuck with it this year is part of the family enjoyment of gift giving at Christmas that adds to the fun and makes the family reconnect with its history or hypertext as discussed earlier (this refers to the sorts of terms in a conversation that are packed with taken-for-granted meaning and yet can be unpacked with a direct question, rather as hypertext in a Wikipedia article can be read as part of the sentence [taken for granted] or clicked to unpack the further information). Families also own private knowledge as family members relationally connected by this shared joke. The ritual serves to remind the family of a playful way in which it transacts and enjoys something within its structure as a set of members. The ritual reestablishes the "we-ness" of the family group. In short, the ritual re-creates and reestablishes the relational reconnection of the family. Once again, then, if you see a family as only a structure, then you miss the symbolic importance of such communicative rituals in transacting relationships.

bidirectionality hypothesis: the idea that power can work in two directions; that is, at some points and times it works one way when parents control or influence their young kids, but power also goes the other way and sometimes kids can control or influence parents, for example, by throwing temper tantrums

Take the blended family again as a specific case. It has to create its own new rituals and norms, just like any other family, but these are most likely somewhat different from the practices of each of the separate preblended arrangements. Baxter, Braithwaite, Bryant, and Wagner (2004) studied the quiet tensions and difficulties created within blended families and how they show up in the communication of the family, especially as it handles boundaries of privacy and disclosure with a new member (the new stepparent, for example). Baxter et al. explored the communications between a stepchild and a stepparent and the difficulty in handling the question of closeness and distance (which the authors describe as the *dialectic of integration*). Galvin (2007) also notes that integration often involves negotiations and significant implications for the family, especially in the different levels of commitment acceptance and connection implied by whether a child refers to his or her stepfather as "my mother's husband," "Brad," "my stepfather," "my other Dad," or even just plain "Dad."

ETHICAL ISSUE

Would "forcing" a ritual on a "new" family member be unethical, if the person really does not want to join in? Would it be unethical for a "new" family member to refuse joining in on a ritual, if joining in would make other people happy?

The communication between the stepparent and stepchild also showed a problem based on the stepchild's (un)willingness to grant the stepparent any kind of legitimacy in a parent role. Finally, as a special case of the openness-closedness dialectic that we have noted before, the stepchild-stepparent relationship is particularly sensitive to the issue of candor and discretion. Both participants are very much aware of the eggshells upon which they would be walking if they were to talk about any personal or private material, at least until they have established a reliable level of relationship where complete trust exists. The experience of a blended family, then, is determined very largely by the communication patterns that take place within it.

In both cases, people find it very difficult to adjust communicatively to the structural changes although many make the transition very successfully. A remixed family, like a remixed music track, has some of the features of the original but may have significant differences that make it original in its own way. The communication processes change, and the family transacts itself differently. The key issues are not just to do with the structure of the newly created unit. Sometimes there are power issues and ways of living life in the new structure that are different from what was done in the old ones, but these are also connected to routine and organizational issues. Both children and adults feel a sense of loss of the old relationship as well as recognizing the challenges of the new one. In the case of adoptees, there are also issues of "loss" felt as they reach adulthood and wish to know more about their biological origin (Powell & Afifi, 2005).

We could again treat these merely as structural issues and look at the size of the group or the power changes in a structure that modify its form. Indeed there are occasions where this is truly relevant, as when two families blend and so have to live in the same accommodation that used to house only one of them, with children sharing bedrooms that used to be their own personal space, for example. More interesting for our purposes, however, is the issue of communication along with the other changes.

All of these studies suggest that it is extremely difficult for people who move between one form of family and another to negotiate what the privacy boundaries are and what information counts as secret, or personal. The sense of specialism about the information is transmitted in family communication that creates these difficulties and has nothing to do with the structure/membership of the family itself.

Sandra Petronio (2002) noted that all family members, not just members of blended families, must negotiate quite frequently about *privacy* and its violation.

This is particularly important during the years when children become adolescents who might now expect parents to respect their rooms as private areas, for example. Furthermore, there are questions as to whether parents should open children's e-mail, eavesdrop if they are offered the chance, or go through an adolescent's personal possessions looking for such things as drugs (Petronio & Durham, 2008). Occasionally parents use direct invasion tactics like this or sometimes provide unsolicited advice, which may also be a violation of privacy.

That people are in the same family does not mean they necessarily agree about the preferences and decisions that should be made. There are often issues of communication **boundary management** and **privacy management** to be dealt with. These are, in everyday communication, most often related to personal information that specific persons or members may have and that others do not know. For example, one parent may allow a child a special secret treat on the condition that the other parent is not told—we know a family where there are "DTMs [Don't Tell Moms]" where the other members carry out an activity, such as eating candy, knowing that the mother might have preferred it not to happen. Other examples come from the ways in which siblings may work together to defeat parental control, backing one another up in ways that resist parental authority, such as "covering" for one another during absences or when challenged by the parent (Nicholson, 2006).

ANALYZING EVERYDAY COMMUNICATION

Communication and Authority in the Family

Authority structures can vary widely from family to family. Consider how your own family is structured.

QUESTIONS TO CONSIDER

1. What is the authority structure in your family, whether formal or informal, and are these two forms the same?
2. How has that changed as you have aged? What have been the influences upon your family and its changing?

Family Secrets

In addition, there may be family secrets that the members agree to conceal from other people outside the family group, such as alcoholism in one parent, a teenager's fight with a drug problem or anorexia, the fact that an uncle is confined in a mental institution, or that one person committed a serious misdemeanor that has not yet been detected. The keeping of such secrets can be either toxic or bonding. Several researchers (e.g., Cohen, 2013) have reported many studies of this form of communication in families and the ways in which families transact the concealment of such secrets. Such communication not only protects the family reputation in the outside world but also serves to bind the members together through the playing out of their shared secret. Such secrets are private knowledge holding them together and are part of the important dynamic of family secrets (as is the DTM—it bonds together the father and the children by creating a relational boundary that encloses and connects them).

Family Storytelling

A final important communicative aspect of families is the process of **family storytelling**, which acts as an important mechanism for the creation of a sense of **family identity**. A family identity is an important aspect of an individual's connection to the world and image of self, and as Huisman (2008) showed, it revolves around intergenerational storytelling, where the elders talk about dead relatives or relate stories about particular family characters who defined the essence of being "a Karatza" or "a Dreber." Jody Koenig Kellas and April Trees (2006) have shown the

boundary management: focuses on the way marital couples manage talking about private matters with each other and how they coordinate communication boundaries in balancing a need for disclosure with the need for privacy

privacy management: see boundary management

family storytelling: families have stories about remarkable figures or events in their history that help define the nature of that particular family; telling such stories is a way of bonding and uniting the family as well as identifying some of its key characteristics

family identity: a family identity is a sense of the special or unique features of the family; often revolves around intergenerational storytelling, where the elders talk about dead relatives or relate stories about particular family characters who defined the essence of being a member of their family

What could this child learn from the stories told about his father's experiences in the military?

importance of **family narratives** in this process, not only in indicating a family's sense of itself in general but also in indicating how it deals with difficult experiences. In the process of telling stories about their significant events, families create a shared sense of meaning about the family experience, whether it is something positive like a birth or an adoption or something negative such as a death or divorce. The point is that when a family starts to develop a common story about such events as these, the members blend their own individual and personal experiences together into a shared story that marks and creates—and hence transacts—the family history. In particular, in extended families in the United States, the elders often describe the way in which immigration and inclusion into the American culture were negotiated in their early days as settlers (Huisman, 2008).

Information Flow: Kin Keeping and the Communication of News

Long-distance relationships (LDRs) apply to families as well, once the children have left the nest. When children move away from home, many issues arise, and the empty-nest parents are left conducting the relationship with their offspring at a distance. Erin Sahlstein (2006, 2010) has noted that this brings out one particular function of certain members of the family who serve to do "**kin keeping**"; that is, they act as a reservoir for information about members of the family, and they pass it to the others. For example, one person could end up being told everything that happens in the lives of everyone else in the family and then act as a central hub-and-spoke system for passing the information along to everyone else. Sahlstein uses the example of her mother, who keeps her up to date about what has been happening to her brother and other members of the family whom Erin does not contact so often. Her mother always knows what is going on with everyone. In this way, she still keeps the family together, and this is what is meant by the "kin-keeping function."

However, there is another aspect of information flow that does not make you stop and think—because it seems so normal and natural that it is simply taken for granted. Give some thought to the way in which you would spread the news that you have found a new romantic partner and are thinking of moving in or that you are about to become engaged or married or are expecting a child. Whom would you tell first about such news (or, in the case of an unexpected and unwanted pregnancy, from whom might you wish to keep the news)? Most of you have an understanding that if you are close to your parents, they should be told before other people find out. Family members might have a right to expect to be told privately before they find out on Facebook.

In other words, such communication is not just about messages but is about the relational priorities that are indicated by the way in which information is spread around. Information flows through the family system in a way that reflects the closeness of the relationships that people have with one another and operates in a way that sustains the hierarchy or the strength of the particular relationships (Duck, 2011). In short, the transmission of information is done in a way that supports (or at least represents the strength and nature of the bonds in) the family system. Information flow does not just happen randomly: It serves a transactive function in the maintenance of family and personal relationships.

family narratives: in the process of storytelling families create a shared sense of meaning about the family experience, whether it is something positive like a birth or an adoption or something negative such as a death or divorce

long-distance relationships (LDRs): relationships characterized by the distance between partners that prevents them from meeting face-to-face frequently (e.g., commuter marriages or relationships where one person lives on the East Coast and one on the West Coast)

kin keeping: the act of serving as a reservoir for information about members of the family, which is passed along to the other members of the network

Change and Development in Family Processes

Whatever form a family takes, its structure—and hence the influence of structure on the family processes and communication patterns—will change with the passage of time. Some of these changes are seen as normal growth—new children are born; children go to school; children become more independent, turn into adolescents, leave home, and start families of their own; the parents age and need to be looked after and eventually die.

By the way...

Who Runs the Family?

Consider the following dialogue from the classic movie *My Big Fat Greek Wedding* (Zwick, 2002):

Toula Portokalos: Ma, Dad is so stubborn. What he says goes. "Ah, the man is the head of the house!"

Maria Portokalos: Let me tell you something, Toula. The man is the head, but the woman is the neck. And she can turn the head any way she wants.

QUESTIONS TO CONSIDER

1. Can you think of examples from your own family that tell whether or not this portrait is accurate?
2. Do you think this portrait is accurate in some cultures and not in others?

Acute Change in Families

Other changes are seen as fractures in the surface of normality: divorce, separation, chronic illness of one adult, death of a relatively young parent in an otherwise still intact family. Other forms of fracture in the family are also transacted in discourse. Buzzanell and Turner (2003) found that traditional (husband breadwinner) family roles tend to be underscored within discourse used to describe job loss, financial strain, and necessity of dual incomes. The wife supports the family, but their communication maintains the husband as financial leader and primary decision maker.

Both big and gradual changes are transacted in dynamic patterns of communication. These too are not only changing all the time but occasionally respond to dramatic events such as family members' need to console one another during unexpected grief. For example, although some couples don't have kids, the original pair-bond couple is responsible for the formation of a nuclear family, and the addition of children will change the dynamics of the communication in a number of ways as a result of the transition to parenthood or the decision to adopt. The addition of a (first) child brings significant difficulties/differences in the communication patterns and relational behaviors that follow. Indeed, the transition to parenthood is a very significant stressor for couples: Satisfaction with the marital relationship tends to decrease sharply soon after this point (Kayser & Rao, 2006).

ETHICAL ISSUE

Family narratives involving past generations are not always accurate, due to the passing of time or blatant revision. So, an ancestor may not have been the war hero he or she is made out to be. And the many years grandma spent in prison are described as her extended vacation. Is it unethical for families to revise their histories, if doing so makes them feel better about themselves?

Although you could see the addition of children as a simple structural change, it is the communicative consequences that are the most interesting here. When there are children present, the focus of attention and the nature of tasks about which the couple communicates will necessarily change too (Socha & Yingling, 2010). No couples spend their dating or romantic time together talking about diapers and sleep patterns, but the couple with a new baby does that far more often than they might want. When there are no children to consider, the couple can act much more spontaneously than when they must consider the children as well. The need to arrange babysitters so that they can have some "alone time" is not something that romantic couples ever have to take into account when they are youthful and hormonally active. After commitment to a long-term partnership and the addition of children, however, romantic talk tends to get pushed aside in favor of discussion of practical child-rearing tasks, and this in part accounts for the decreasing couple satisfaction that is associated with the addition of children (Rholes, Simpson, & Friedman, 2006). The couple gains new topics for conversation (feeding schedules, the dangers of electric sockets, and the most desirable sorts of fluffy toys). Their communication also loses some of the old styles (especially romantic and relaxed topics and the chance to have spontaneous

What might the children be learning from seeing their parents fight like this?

and uninterrupted talk). In both cases the dynamics of communication transact the changes in family structure.

Although this is a quite striking example, less extreme changes to everyday communication happen all the time in any family "structure" as the participants grow up or get old or become ill or are faced with the decisions of life that arise in any family. Communication topics change from issues of schooling, job choice, instruction, and discipline to appropriateness of rules for "child" behaviors as the child grows older. Parents will talk between themselves and with the child about play possibilities (is the child old enough for a sleepover yet?). Also talk will turn to permissions or disputes about dating, and there are many communicative changes when the children become teenagers and establish their independence or eventually leave home.

Long-Term Change in Families

Consider the changes that are continuous, long-term, and two-sided in family life. In addition to the sudden and drastic changes when children are added, relationships within a family change relentlessly with age across the life course (Socha, 2012). There are alterations to the dependency structures that exist as parents and children age. Your parents may be fit and well right now, but give it another 40 years and you may be looking after your parents in the same sorts of ways they looked after you when you were merely a dependent and inept bundle. The helpless babies who were looked after by parents eventually find, as adults, that the roles are reversed, and they end up caring for their relatively helpless elderly parents in return (Blieszner, 2006).

How will communication change, do you think, when your parents cannot move about on their own, cannot hear what the doctor says, or cannot remember medical instructions given by health professionals? The *structure* of the family will be the same as before (the same people are in it, the same ones are parents, the same ones are children). However, you can expect the *communication dynamics* to change as the elder members become more, not less, dependent on the younger ones and the younger ones become more, not less, responsible for caring for the older members. For example, Petronio, Sargent, Andea, Reganis, and Cichocki (2004) noted that elderly patients often ask to be accompanied by family member "advocates" during visits to a physician. This raises numerous privacy dilemmas, as the advocates necessarily violate knowledge and privacy boundaries while protecting the health of their parent. This situation can also unwittingly lead to the dialogue with the physician being directed more in their direction than in the direction of the patient, who is typically treated as superfluous to the dialogue. All the same, the elderly parent relies heavily on his or her family member to make decisions on his or her behalf. This is just one example of the ways in which the same basic family structure communicatively transacts alterations over time to fundamental family matters, to power, to dependency patterns, and to family life itself.

In short, a family is always dynamic and changing; something is usually going on in it. When you look at it as a structure or as a group of members, the nuclear family is the same right through until someone is added to it or someone is taken away. Viewed more dynamically as a communication system, family communication is obviously always changing within that basic framework, even when the membership stays the same.

Redeployment of Families and Their Communication

What problems might "weekend parents" experience in handling their kids?

Any form of family redeployment is tough to handle for everyone concerned, whether occasioned by addition of children, divorce, or empty nesting. The divorced or separated partners experience many difficulties and strains about their own personal experiences as they enter negotiations about ownership of property and maintenance payments. They may struggle to make joint decisions about the children's future when they may have experienced loss of trust in the relational partners with whom they are required to discuss it all. These kinds of communications are particularly difficult. Separated parents often also experience subsequently poor relationships with their own children, partly as a result of difficulty in maintaining contact and sometimes because their ex-partner undermines them in the minds of the children.

Although you may normally think of the difficulties that happen between the adults or the consequences for the children when a divorce occurs, consider the special case of divorced parents who are separated from their children. Stephanie Rollie (2006) wrote about the particular case of NRPs—nonresidential parents (those divorced parents who live away from their kids and see them only on weekends). She was interested in their strategies for maintaining relationships with their children. She pointed out a particular difficulty that they have in negotiating the absence-presence-absence cycle that is an essential part—indeed, the defining characteristic—of their relationship with the child. It is obviously stressful for both the NRP and the child to keep being reminded that they must once again be separated. It is important for the parent, as the older person with more insight and control over such behaviors, to be able to remind the child of the continuing existence of the parent-child relationship during the periods of separation. It turns out that the parents use the same sorts of relational continuity constructional units (RCCUs) discussed in Chapter 7—the small-talk means of recognizing and recording the fact that the relationship is still continuing even when the partners are *not* face-to-face and may be apart from one another.

Most NRPs are able to do this by giving the children photographs or toys that remind them about the absent parent (these would be **introspective units**). Sometimes the residential parent with custody has such a bad experience with the divorce that he or she will not let these items be taken into the house, so the child is deprived of the various ways to be reminded about the absent parent. NRPs make a lot of use of **prospective units** about future meetings, even laying out ideas for future behavior in order to show their continued interest in the child ("Be good" or "Don't forget to do your homework" are examples here).

These examples are lively instances where talk is used to continue family relationships that are otherwise difficult to maintain, but they exemplify the same principles that are used in all forms of relationships. When people say, "See ya later" or "What time shall we meet tomorrow?" this everyday method of sustaining relationships conceals a simple mechanism for continuing relationships in their present form, even in the family, reconfigured family, or disassembled family, even if this particular interaction is ended.

introspective units: one of three types of relational continuity constructional units that keep the memory of the relationship alive during the physical separation of the members involved; introspective units are reminders of the relationships during an absence, examples being photographs of a couple, wedding bands, or fluffy toys that one partner gave to another

prospective units: one of three types of relational continuity constructional units that keep the memory of the relationship alive during the physical separation of the members involved; prospective units are recognitions that a separation is about to occur

Families Communicate!

You will not be surprised that our general idea is the same as the one we spelled out before. Relationships even in the family are always under the influence of other relationships and respond to the direct personal inputs of other people and the activities of other SSAs (Society's Secret Agents) to support social norms and conventions. The nested groups of networks, neighbors, and extended family within which a nuclear family exists are not simply a convenient academic idea. They represent and carry out the living interactions of society as its Secret Agents—the people who live in it—act to reinforce their habits, actions, and opinions for one another.

When you are thinking about "family communication," you must recognize that within any given family there occur different networks of connection. You might think of "family communication" in simple terms. For example, the family may have secrets, like an alcoholic parent, that everyone in the family treats as private information together, and such secrets can be bonding or toxic. However, the different pairs of people in the family may talk to one another in different ways that are by no means common to everyone. We'd expect the adults to talk to one another in ways different from the communication that occurs between a younger brother and sister, but each child may talk to each of the parents differently, feeling preferred by one rather than the other, for example. That is, communication within the family will always depend on the specific relationships of the particular people involved at the time. For example, you and your brother, you and your father, and your mother and your sister may talk to each other differently, and this cannot be characterized as "family communication" as a whole.

Families communicate between parents and child(ren) and among siblings but also are influenced by and responsive to the forces outside the family itself. You are particularly shaped by society's views about what "family" looks like. For example, you may argue whether "gay marriage" creates a family, whether lesbians may adopt children, or about the role that "natural parents" may have in rearing a child if those natural parents are teenagers themselves. Note then that the family, whatever form you envision, is not only a system of its own but a system within a system of other influences and networks.

Although our first thoughts were about the structure of a family, you end up where this book always ends up: The family is another instance where relationships between people are done communicatively and dynamically. In important ways they show bidirectionality of influence and mutual interdependence. These are instances of the essential and inescapable effects of relational forces on all types of communication wherever you look.

Focus Questions Revisited

What is a "family," and how can communication in everyday life contribute to an understanding of what counts and what does not?

Although a family tree can indicate who is whose parent/cousin/grandparent, it does not indicate anything about the dynamics of communication that occur within the family, nor does it indicate who hates whom or who prefers whom. Yet families have specific ways of communicating, and often the closeness of the personal relationships between people are not simply reflected by the structural or genetic connections that the individuals have to one another. By placing greater emphasis on the communication patterns that occur within the family, we were able to demonstrate that families transact their relationships with one another in important ways that are not predictable simply from structure alone. Galvin (2007), in particular, has pointed out the ways in which families are discourse dependent.

What sorts of diverse forms of "family" are recognized in different societies/cultures?

Different sorts of families (as structures) are nuclear families, extended families, kin networks, families of origin, families of descent, families of generativity, families of choice, blended families, stepfamilies, single-parent families, and same-sex families.

What are the possible ways in which a "family" may be defined, and which one is best for a communication scholar?

From the point of view of communication studies, the analysis of the messages that people send one another in a family structure is merely a starting point that represents communication as just action (the messages send information but do not actually change or transform anything). More sophisticated views pay attention to bidirectional aspects of family communication and treat the communication as interaction, where the response of one person to another is relevant to the "meaning" of the communication. However, we have taught you that families actually transact themselves through communication, and this indicates that the interaction of people itself transacts a feeling of connectedness among them. In short, the ways in which a family communicates are themselves ways of being/creating/making a family what it is.

What types of everyday communication in a family *transact* the nature of family life?

Everyday communication in families can be about something or nothing. There are many little ways in which families conduct their norms and customary patterns of behavior. There are also such things as family secrets, the importance of managing boundaries around the privacy of the individuals involved, dialectics, family storytelling, and information flow. These all are also relevant to the understanding of a family as is the kind of style of communication that each individual shows in the presence of the others. The structure—the family tree alone—does not tell you whether the mother was secretive, dominating, or fun to be with; nor does it show the brutality or selfishness of a father—it shows merely that he was the father. Yet the communication that transacts family life is exactly of this emotional and relational sort. To understand the life of a family, you need to know how its members interact, what identity has been transacted, and who they are in each other's eyes before you know what it is like to be in that family.

Key Concepts

authority structure 166
bidirectionality hypothesis 167
binuclear family 159
blended family 159
boundary management 169
extended family 158
family identity 169
family narratives 170
family of choice 159
family of descent 158
family of origin 158
family of generativity 159
family storytelling 169
introspective units 173
kin keeping 170
kin networks 158
long-distance relationships (LDRs) 170
norms 165
nuclear family 158
peer culture 164
privacy management 169
prospective units 173
rituals 165
rules 156
single-parent family 159
socialization 156
systems theory 162

Questions to Ask Your Friends

1. Does family conflict matter more than conflict at work? Why or why not?
2. How do your friends' family members do Thanksgiving or other holiday rituals, and how does that compare with the way your family does it?

3. How do your different friends do their family life in ways that (a) correspond with or (b) are different from how others do it? For example, what do friends with same-sex parents call their moms and dads?

Media Connections

1. In what ways are unity and harmony in the family depicted in the media? Do you find that the family is shown as essentially stable and comforting even if there are hiccups (even in comedy shows)?
2. Can you find TV shows that debunk the idea that families are happy, functional units? See the film *Loverboy* or watch *Family Guy* or *The Simpsons*.
3. How has the representation of the family changed in the media over the last several decades? Compare the film *Pleasantville* and the old TV show *Leave It to Beaver* with *Family Guy* or *The Simpsons*. What's different? Consider the different families in *Game of Thrones*. How does the Lannister family compare with the Starks in the way the father treats the children?

Student Study Site

Sharpen your skills with SAGE edge at edge.sagepub.com/duckciel2e

SAGE edge for students provides a personalized approach to help you accomplish your coursework goals in an easy-to-use learning environment.

Chapter Outline

What Is a Group?

- Types of Groups

Characteristics of Groups

- Cohesiveness
- Interdependence
- Commitment
- Group Norms
- Member Roles
- Group Culture

Group Development and Decision Making

Group Decision Making Is About Relationships

Leadership

- Leadership Styles
- Leadership Power
- Leadership Vision
- Leadership Ethics
- Leadership Is Transacted

Focus Questions Revisited

Key Concepts

Questions to Ask Your Friends

Media Connections

09 Groups and Leaders

Groups impact our lives in a number of ways, and we do not even have to be a member of a group for this to happen. For instance, committees in Congress influence the enactments of laws governing our lives. Job interview panels can result in a dream job. There are many types of small groups that might be part of your everyday experience: study groups, board meetings, sorority/fraternity committees, friends deciding what kind of pizza to order on Friday night, chat rooms, or focus groups.

Groups are composed of people who share relationships, often relationships existing outside of that group setting. These relationships influence the communication taking place within a group, leadership within a group, and decisions that are made by a group. For example, a group may include some members who are close friends, and this friendship brings with it shared understandings unknown to other group members and possibly guaranteed support should one friend bring forth a proposal. On the other hand, members of that group might be rivals or enemies, which might lead to a lack of trust within the group setting and obstructions when making decisions. The study of groups simply cannot be legitimately separated from the study of relationships, we say, though it has been in most previous books!

Communication scholars ask a number of questions about groups, but we focus on those dealing with group development and decision making and on leadership. Before this, however, we examine what groups actually are.

What Is a Group?

Is a group just one more person than a dyad and one person short of a crowd? Or is it less a matter of numbers and more one of how groups communicate or transact their *groupness?* Well, a group requires at least three people. And a group cannot be so large that people are unable to fully contribute or unable to perceive themselves as anything more than a collection of individuals without a shared purpose. In a way, then, the number of people does matter.

However, it would be unwise to think of a group simply in terms of numbers. A person could not just put, say, five people together in the same room and call them a group. Groups interact not because of their composition (numbers or types of people) but because of the kinds of communication occurring between specific people involved.

FOCUS QUESTIONS

1. What is a group?
2. What are the characteristics of a group?
3. How do groups form and make decisions?
4. What are the styles of group leadership?
5. What are the types of leadership power?
6. What is meant by leadership vision and leadership ethics?
7. How is leadership transacted?

What exactly is a group, and what makes it different from an assembly, a collective, or a team? How many of each of these can you see in this picture?

Thus, a group is more than just a collection of a few people. Rather, groups are transacted, or created, through communication and relationships. However, we still have not discussed what makes a group special and unique from other things transacted through communication and relationships.

To begin answering the question posed in the header of this section, think of any group to which you belong. You have hit one important feature of groups—your sense of membership. A group comes into being once people recognize and identify themselves and others as *members* of the same group. Beyond the recognition of membership, a simple assembly or collection of people is not really a group unless it has a *common purpose*. That is, people are collected together to achieve a particular goal.

Types of Groups

Groups are commonly classified according to their purposes and features. The five primary types of groups and their characteristics are summarized in Table 9.1. As you review this table, keep in mind that types of groups are ultimately differentiated through their communication and the ways in which members treat one another relationally. In some cases, such as with formal groups, members will treat one another formally and follow standardized and regulated ways of speaking. In other cases, such as with networking groups, the ways in which people treat each other and communicate are much less formal. In all cases, communication and relationships are transacting these groups.

Characteristics of Groups

So, groups involve people who recognize shared membership and who have a common purpose for being together. Thus, a bunch of folks waiting for a bus is not a group. They meet the number criterion and have a common purpose, but they do not communicate and do not share a sense of membership. Groups are ultimately transacted through communication and relationships, which serve not only to create groups but also to set apart different types of groups.

Having discussed these basic features of groups, we can now examine key characteristics of groups. In what follows, we will examine how groups involve

COMMUNICATION + **YOU**

Communicating Belonging and a Shared Purpose

Analyze the interactions of a group to which you belong and determine what types of communication create a sense of belonging and shared purpose. A class discussion group, for example, shares a sense of membership, which may be why you keep texting the member who never shows up to meetings; and you also share a sense of purpose: You are all in this to get an A, and the AWOL person is going to bring down your grade!

QUESTIONS TO CONSIDER

1. What are some other groups you belong to?
2. Do you feel closer to people you are in a group with, compared to those you are not in a group with?

Table 9.1 Types of Groups

TYPE OF GROUP	PRIMARY/FUNDAMENTAL PURPOSES	FEATURES	EXAMPLES
Formal	Task oriented, general management oversight, outcome focused, often legislative or formally structured to run an organization	Membership restricted/delegated Attendance expected Clear structure Power vested in the chair/leader Agenda followed Possible formal rules for turn taking, voting, and other activities	Congress, congressional committees, debate clubs, shareholder meetings, annual general meetings of organized bodies, executive committees of unions, student government organizations, legislative assemblies
Advisory	Task specific, usually evidentiary or evaluative, with the intention of producing an outcome that is a focused "best solution" to a specific problem or arrangement of an event	Membership specific/restricted Possible structure Possible chair Possible agenda Discussion usually open and informal Critical and evaluative argument of different proposals encouraged	Sorority and fraternity social affairs committees, homecoming committees, juries, accident investigation boards, review boards for awards and prizes
Creative	Evaluation of concepts or creation of new products or approaches to complex problems	Membership usually invited Lack of structure Primary purpose is generation of as many ideas as possible to evaluate at a later time Members discouraged from critical comment on the ideas generated	Brainstorming; consciousness raising; creativity groups; focus groups; test-bed groups for developing specifications and criteria for complex projects, such as the beta versions of new software; advertising logo development teams
Support	Advising, comforting, sharing knowledge, spreading information, and raising consciousness about specific issues	Membership loosely defined Members come and go as needed Participation generally voluntary	Alcoholics Anonymous, breast cancer survivors, grief support groups, study groups, PFLAG (Parents, Families and Friends of Lesbians and Gays)
Networking	Obtaining, building, or sustaining relationships, usually online	Membership not defined Members join and leave as desired	Chat rooms, social networking groups, Twitter, Facebook

(a) cohesiveness, (b) interdependence, (c) commitment, (d) norms, (e) roles, and (f) cultures.

Cohesiveness

A characteristic of groups is cohesiveness among group members. **Cohesiveness** describes people working together and feeling connected. Beyond existing relationships outside the group setting, relationships among group members can be established through common motives and goals (Northouse, 2012). Cohesiveness

cohesiveness: working together and feeling connected

By the way...

Rules for Conducting Formal Meetings

Formal groups frequently conduct business using guidelines established by *Robert's Rules of Order.* This book was originally written by Brigadier General Henry Martyn Robert and published in 1876. He distinguishes the ranks of motions, the orders and sequences in which they are to be considered, and stresses particularly the role of order in the discussion of business. What general would do otherwise?

QUESTIONS TO CONSIDER

1. Have you ever been part of a group, as a student or otherwise, with specific rules on how the group was run? If so, did all the group members "follow the rules"?
2. In what ways might specific rules both help and hinder a group?

in groups is performed communicatively and essentially comes down to a communicational concept where people coordinate their talk and action as a result of their relationships with one another.

Group effectiveness or success largely depends on members working together cohesively (Evans & Dion, 2012; Gully, Devine, & Whitney, 2012). You may have seen a motivational poster of a team of rowers all pulling their oars together. They are synchronized and cohesive. If they pulled their oars whenever they felt like it rather than all at the same time, their oars would clash and the boat would go nowhere (take it from Steve, an Oxford rowing coxswain who shouted out the rate and speed with which the rowers should row).

Group effectiveness or success also depends on members feeling connected and cohesive. Again, this can come from existing relationships outside the group and can come from coordination of communication and actions. However, it also comes from maintaining morale, civility, and good relationships between group members. In this sense, cohesiveness is a primary output of groups' social emotional exchanges in talk and thus is a transactional and relational consequence of communication.

Avoiding Groupthink

Although cohesiveness has been found to assist group effectiveness, a negative consequence of cohesiveness has been identified. An attempt to be cohesive at the expense of anything else can sometimes get in the way of a group's effective functioning. If everyone wants to keep everyone else happy rather than make tough decisions, this leads to a special kind of *conformity*. Sometimes, people would rather preserve good relationships than make good decisions.

Irving Janis (1972) famously referred to this negative kind of consensus-seeking cohesiveness as **groupthink**. In groupthink, members place a higher priority on keeping the process running smoothly and agreeably than they do on voicing opinions that contradict the majority opinion (or the opinion of the leader). The group prefers the well-being of its members, morale, and teamwork at the expense of proper critical evaluation of ideas. Groupthink can result in faulty decision making because a group prefers to be a *happy* ship rather than a ship going in the right direction. So although usually a good thing, cohesiveness can lead to negative consequences.

groupthink: a negative kind of consensus seeking through which members place a higher priority on keeping the process running smoothly and agreeably than they do on voicing opinions that contradict the majority opinion (or the opinion of the leader)

interdependence: the reliance of each member of a team or group on the other members, making their outcomes dependent on the collaboration and interrelated performance of all members (e.g., a football team dividing up the jobs of throwing, catching, and blocking)

Interdependence

Another characteristic of groups is the division of labor in a way that leads to **interdependence**. That is, everyone relies on everyone else to do a specific part of the overall job well. A group cannot function properly if its members do not work interdependently. Interdependence, however, is not simply an abstract concept that something is based on the ways in which people interact. Rather, it works as a transacted outcome of the communication between group members. In sports teams, for instance, the coaches have the job of communicating and coordinating the team members' performances in a way that pulls everything together. At the same time, especially in cultures in which individual achievement is appreciated, it is sometimes important that the contributions of individual members to the group are recognized (Purvanova, 2013).

Commitment

Group members usually show commitment to each other and to their group's goals when a group is working well (Harden Fritz & Omdahl, 2006). One transactive feature that makes a group a "group" is that individual members share a commitment to the overall group goals. They want to be team players, and this shows up in their talk and behavior (Meeussen, Delvaux, & Phalet, 2013). The members may also show commitment to one another, watching each other's backs and looking out for one another. This helps the whole group move forward toward its goals. The group shows commitment to individual members through caring for their welfare, as well as aiming to achieve the goals of the group.

Dealing With Out-Groups

Keep in mind, though, that not all members of a group are necessarily committed to group goals or to other members. Group members do not always trust each other, share common goals, and want what is best for everyone. Factions within the group, based on existing relationships or those created within group activity, may not agree with the direction of a group, or they may just want to make life difficult for other group members. Surely you have met these types!

Out-groups are cells of disgruntled members who feel undervalued, mistreated, disrespected, not included, or overlooked. These members can be either disruptive or constructive. A good leader, something we will talk about later in the chapter, can turn around their sense of exclusion by using them to challenge and question group assumptions, by listening carefully to their concerns, and by making the majority members of the group discuss more options, reflect more carefully on their opinions, answer challenges, and rethink their arguments. This tends to make groups consider their decisions and assumptions more carefully and ultimately to see the out-group cell as a useful part of the larger group rather than a simple nuisance. It also helps prevent groupthink.

By the way...

Division of Labor

In football, not everyone can be a quarterback; people in the offense have different jobs than those in the defense. The work is divided because the team as a whole shares a purpose: namely, winning the game. The ultimate success of the whole team will depend on whether every member does an assigned job. If everyone tried to do the same task (all tried to throw the ball, all tried to block the other team, all tried to catch passes), it would be ineffective because the other jobs would not get done.

QUESTIONS TO CONSIDER

1. Using any of the groups you previously listed as an example, think about a time when multiple members caused a disruption by attempting to do the same thing. How did your group address this situation?
2. In what ways could the group have addressed the situation more effectively?

Group Norms

Groups usually expect particular behavior from members. **Group norms** are informal and formal rules and procedures guiding group behaviors. For example, there may be formally established rules for speaking or turn taking. Some norms are informally understood as proper behavior in a particular group, such as whether joking is allowed or whether criticism of other members is acceptable. Group norms are established in face-to-face group settings and are also evident in computer-mediated and virtual group interactions (Moser & Axtell, 2013).

The norms that are established generally reflect the values of the group, especially those concerning communication and relationships. For instance, if group members value creative and open thinking and communication, lower-ranking members may speak first so that they will not mold their responses in support of senior members and will not fear reprisals by senior members if they should disagree.

out-groups: cells of disgruntled members who feel undervalued, mistreated, disrespected, not included, or overlooked; these members can be either disruptive or constructive

group norms: rules and procedures that occur in a group but not necessarily outside it and that are enforced by the use of power or rules for behavior

Sidelining a player for an offense during a soccer game is a good example of a particular group behavior. What is that?

ETHICAL ISSUE

What conditions would make it wrong, and what conditions would make it right, to blow the whistle on your group for wrongdoings irrespective of the consequences to you personally?

Sometimes a group member just does not want to follow group norms (Frings, Hurst, Cleveland, Blascovich, & Abrams, 2012). Most groups have their own **group sanctions**, or punishments for violating norms. For example, an unruly member—one who persistently violates the norms—may be thrown out of a meeting and so is silenced, losing participation in, and influence on, the group. Everyone else in the group may "shun" a dissenter both outside and inside the meetings. Shunning or excluding people from participation in the group, or not even acknowledging their presence, is a very powerful social, relational, and communicative punishment (Nezlek, Wesselmann, Wheeler, & Williams, 2012).

Member Roles

Group members also take on particular **group roles**, involving certain positions or functions within a group. You know about roles from movies: A role is when someone acts out a part that fits in with parts other people play in a performance. It is important to note, then, that the performance of a role is not a single activity. Rather, it requires the participation and influence of other people who join in the performance. Group roles are generally placed within five categories: (1) formal roles, (2) informal roles, (3) task roles, (4) social roles, and (5) disruptive roles.

Formal Roles

In formal groups, there are **formal roles**, specific functions to which members are assigned and that they are expected to perform within that group. These roles frequently have such titles as chair, vice chair, and secretary. Sometimes, these roles are about the hierarchy of the group, and they let you know something about the formal powers that are delegated to each individual.

Informal Roles

Both formal and less formal groups may see the enactment of **informal roles**, those to which someone is not officially assigned but that serve a function with a group. For example, a group member may be a joker, someone who cracks jokes and keeps up everyone's spirits during meetings. Another group member may be a taskmaster, someone who keeps the group on task during meetings. In these cases, the group members have not been officially assigned to these roles but are recognized as performing these roles through repeated patterns of interaction.

Task Roles

Task roles are those functioning to ensure a group achieves its goals and is productive. These roles may be either formal or informal. A chair, for instance, is formally responsible for ensuring that a group achieves its goals. Other group members informally take on task roles. For instance, group members may provide information; seek information; clarify information, ideas, and activities; evaluate information, ideas, and activities; and serve other task-related functions.

Social Roles

Social roles are those functioning to encourage group members and to develop and maintain positive communication and relationships among group members. These roles are generally informal and might include encouraging quiet group members to speak, praising the contributions of group members, relieving tension, managing conflict among group members, and praising group efforts as a whole.

group sanctions: punishments for violating norms

group roles: positions or functions within a group (see *disruptive roles, formal roles, informal roles, social roles, task roles*)

formal roles: specific functions to which group members are assigned and that they are expected to perform within the group

informal roles: those to which someone is not officially assigned but that serve a function with a group

task roles: those functioning to ensure a group achieves its goals and is productive

social roles: those functioning to encourage group members and to develop and maintain positive communication and relationships among group members

Disruptive Roles

Of course, group members do not always function in a productive manner. **Disruptive roles** are those functioning in opposition to group productivity and cohesion. These are certainly informal in nature and might include blocking progress by reintroducing and opposing previous decisions, withdrawing from the group or avoiding discussions, calling attention to oneself, and getting the group off-topic by discussing unrelated matters.

ETHICAL ISSUE

Could being a disruptive member of a group be considered ethical?

Group Culture

The above characteristics of groups work together in the creation of a **group culture**, shared patterns of interactions both reflecting and guiding beliefs, values, and attitudes of the group. Group culture is evident in such symbolic activity as how members talk to one another, the clothes they wear while working as a group, or the special terms and language or jokes they use. For example, members of some groups talk in a very formal and polite manner, while members of other groups talk in ways that are extremely informal. Further, members of a group may use terms unique to that group, such as language unique to specific professions. These communicative acts transact the culture of a group.

Communicating culturally within a group accomplishes some very important things. First, it reinforces what the group believes and values. For instance, Mumby (2006) illustrates this influence of group culture when he writes about his experiences as a college student working in a manual labor job. The other workers mocked the fact that, with all his "college boy" intelligence, he could not drive some of the machinery as well as they could. The very use of the term *college boy* to describe him represents, in talk, the group culture that "book learning" is less important than practical skills.

disruptive roles: those functioning in opposition to group productivity and cohesion

group culture: the set of expectations and practices that a group develops to make itself distinctive from other groups and to give its members a sense of exclusive membership (e.g., dress code, specialized language, particular rituals)

Communicating culturally within a group also enables the group to accomplish its goals. If members of a group had to reestablish expected ways of communicating and behaving each time they came together, there would not be much time available for actual work. Knowing what to expect and how to act saves time and allows group members to get down to business whenever they meet. Beyond specific styles of communication, utilizing specialized language also promotes the accomplishment of group goals through ensuring shared understanding among group members. Ultimately, group members are able to work together, developing group cohesion.

Finally, communicating culturally within a group enables group members to establish membership in a group. A sense of membership and belonging by members is one of the key criteria of a group. Communicating like other members of a group and sharing a similar meaning system with members of a group lead to acceptance by other group members and feelings of connection. Again, we see the development of group cohesion through group culture. When group members communicate culturally, they are transacting not only group culture but also group membership.

ANALYZING EVERYDAY COMMUNICATION

Differentiating Groups

One person may simultaneously be a member of very different groups, with different values and cultures. Analyze the norms, roles, and cultures of two groups to which you belong.

QUESTIONS TO CONSIDER

1. How are these norms, roles, and cultures transacted through communication and relationships?
2. What does this tell you about differences in the respective values of these groups?

Group Development and Decision Making

In addition to characteristics of groups, scholars studying group communication frequently focus on group

DISCIPLINARY DEBATE

Studying Groups

Much communication scholarship on small groups is based on research experiments where members have never met before and will never meet again. Collections of people, very often students, gather in a group in order to make a decision about something. Dignified by the name zero-history groups, these groups are much more importantly zero-future groups. They tell us almost nothing about the operations of real-life groups that have a real-life relational connection to one another. Except in artificial laboratories where researchers almost never attend to relational factors, all ongoing groups are typified by relationships that have a bearing on their interactions, their culture, their cohesiveness, and their decisions. Beliefs about groups are based on specific kinds of research, and if that research is flawed, so are the resultant conclusions.

There has been some recognition of the need to study bona fide groups (Frey, 2003; Putnam & Stohl, 1990). These studies use real groups in real settings. At the same time, artificial groups continue to be used and were the basis for many traditional notions about groups.

QUESTIONS TO CONSIDER

1. Do you think groups might behave differently when the people involved know they are being observed in an experiment? Why or why not?
2. Why do you think some scholars continue to use zero-history groups?

development and decision making. Before examining this area, however, it is necessary to acknowledge limitations in research dedicated to its study addressed in the "Disciplinary Debate" box. Because the relational aspect of groups has been largely ignored in research, we are necessarily confined to traditional literature that offers nonrelational accounts of the ways in which groups develop. These accounts are frequently based on artificial groups in laboratories or based simply on reviewing existing literature of the topic (see Smith, 2001).

Students sometimes wonder why information is included in textbooks and classroom discussion that is then discredited or evaluated negatively. We, just like your instructors, want to make sure you are familiar with ideas and research that have played an important role in the development of this area. Further, understanding the limitations or problems inherent within the material will enable you to develop critical thinking skills and better understand, in this case, important characteristics of actual group development and decision making.

With those thoughts in mind, we can now examine traditional notions of group development. Table 9.2 presents a five-stage model proposed by psychologist Bruce Tuckman (1965). Notice that apart from a reference to guidance by a leader, this description of group formation is relationship-free and topic/goal focused. Such generalizations would also lead a person to believe that all groups function and communicate in much the same manner.

Table 9.2 Tuckman's Five Stages of Group Development

1. **Forming:** The group comes into existence and seeks direction from a leader about the nature of its tasks and procedures.
2. **Storming:** The group determines leadership and roles of its members.
3. **Norming:** The group establishes its procedures to move more formally toward a solution.
4. **Performing:** Having established how it will perform its task, the group now does so.
5. **Adjourning:** The group reflects on its achievements, underlines its performative accomplishments, and closes itself down.

A similar stage model proposed by communication scholar Aubrey Fisher (1970) is presented in Table 9.3. In Fisher's model, there is acknowledgment that people get to know one another during the creation of the group. However, the importance of this relational fact for subsequent decision making is absent. Also absent from this model is the fact that a group could preexist a particular meeting.

There are other models of group development and decision making, but the two presented here are indicative of these models for the most part (see Smith, 2001). In these models, development and

Table 9.3 Fisher's Model of Group Progression

1. **Orientation**: Group members get to know one another and come to grips with the problems they have convened to deal with.
2. **Conflict**: The group argues about possible ways of approaching the problem and begins to seek solutions.
3. **Emergence**: This occurs when some daylight of consensus begins to dawn. The group sees the emergence of possible agreement.
4. **Reinforcement**: The group explicitly consolidates consensus to complete the task, or the leader may do it for the group by thanking everyone.

decision making is a linear process. Communication is frequently taken for granted or thought to be similar in all group experiences. Relationships tend to be absent altogether.

Group Decision Making Is About Relationships

The components and characteristics of groups (membership, common purpose, cohesiveness, interdependence, norms, roles, and cultures) are all in their own way relationship concepts. For whatever reason, however, relationships are generally absent when considering group decision making. Nevertheless, group decisions are influenced by outside relationships and interactions.

Groups are made up of *people*. Members have relationships with one another *outside* as well as *inside* their meetings. After the formal discussion, when the group splits up, the members go on with the rest of their lives, which can mean chatting to other group members in places outside the group. Real-life groups exist continuously both as *groups* (e.g., "The work team meets every Friday," "The study group is Wednesday night," "The book club meets every Thursday") and as *relators* whose lives may be connected outside the group (e.g., two members of the same work team may be friends, study group members may also be neighbors, book club members could be in the same family).

What (usually undesirable) characteristic of groups is depicted in this photograph?

Formal group decision making can be seen theoretically as if it were a rational type of interaction, where groups sit around and work through decisions smartly and thoughtfully. This just seems to be wrong, and if you have ever sat in on a group making a decision, you will know that. Relationships influence what happens within the group.

Three Scotsmen in 1877 judge a prize canary, their equivalent of a beauty pageant. Which of Fisher's stages do they portray?

Separating decision making into the activities of groups in meetings overlooks just how much persuasion of group members actually occurs in other settings for other reasons. Sometimes, people vote for a proposal not because it is compelling but because they like the person who proposed it or dislike the person who opposed it, for instance.

Not really about arguments and abstractions, group interaction and decision making are about emotions, feelings, and relationships—not so much a battle of *ideas* as a battle between *people who have ideas* and persisting relationships with one another.

Leadership

Groups usually have a leader. A person's first thought about *leadership* is that it involves a formal position in which a specific person has power over the others in the group. Examples of such positions might include a boss in the workplace, a team leader in a task group, a chair of a committee, or an elder of a religious community. Such people are required to communicate authoritatively, to run the agenda, and to move the group forward in particular ways that others should follow.

However, there are a few problems with the notions that leadership involves a formal position and that leadership activities include the same or similar activities. First, as we discussed earlier in the chapter, there are many different types of groups, and these groups do not share the same level of formality. Accordingly, there may not be a designated leader of a group. Rather, a leader or leaders may emerge within a group.

Second, leadership is not the same across all possible domains. Even if we were to focus on a formally recognized leader, a Pope is not a four-star general is not a grocery store manager is not a classroom discussion leader. The styles and requirements for successful leadership in these roles differ. If styles and requirements of leadership were developed to fit all possible areas, they would be so general that they would not have any consequence or value as indicators of success in leadership.

Finally, even within a single organization, as people are rising through the system, they pass through leadership roles of different sorts and scopes. Hence, in order to become one kind of leader you must first have been successful at a lower rank.

Skills You Can Use: Distinguishing the Relational Politics of Group Discussion

Recognizing the relational elements of groups will greatly assist you when promoting a particular agenda or decision. Groups are not structured as bodies, numbers, and depersonalized decision makers. Within a general structure sit real human beings who have relationships with one another. Consider what relationships exist in groups to which you belong and how you can use this knowledge during future group interactions.

For example, in the military, a person goes through captain, colonel, brigadier general, and two-star general before becoming a four-star general. What is true of one level of leadership may have no application to other levels of leadership. A general may need to inspire troops in battle with a vision for the future, whereas a captain merely needs to keep them on target and assure them that they will all do well as a team and survive to fight another day.

In what follows, we will examine four key components in the study of leadership: (a) leadership styles, (b) leadership power, (c) leadership vision, and (d) leadership ethics. We will then specifically discuss how leadership is transacted through communication and relationships.

Which communicative and relational skills make a leader a good leader?

Leadership Styles

The classic discussion of leadership, since Bales (1950), has divided leaders into those who are focused on the task and those who focus on the socioemotional well-being of the members of the group. **Task leaders** focus on the performance of tasks to ensure the achievement of group goals. **Socioemotional leaders** focus on group member satisfaction and well-being.

Task Leaders

- stress the activity of the group,
- keep members on topic,
- follow the agenda,
- make sure decisions get made,
- are responsible for defining the group's intended accomplishment,
- are charged with directing what happens to fulfill the set tasks of the group,
- make sure the group reaches a conclusion at the end of its allotted meeting time,
- summarize what got done in a meeting, and
- set the agenda for the next meeting.

Socioemotional Leaders

- pay attention to how everyone feels in the group,
- ensure that members feel comfortable with the decision-making process,
- allow everyone to get a turn in the discussion,
- make members happy with the outcome,
- keep the personal relationships between group members on an even keel, and
- manage people's "face" and handle their feelings.

ETHICAL ISSUE

Some say that leaders must use authority to mobilize people to face tough decisions when the followers are struggling with change and personal growth. Others stress that leaders should take care of and nurture their followers. What do you think?

When considering task leadership and socioemotional leadership, there are some key points to recognize. First, there are times when a group requires more task leadership and times when a group requires more socioemotional leadership. Effective leadership requires understanding when each type of leadership is required. Second, different types of groups will require different types of leadership. Task-oriented leadership may be more expected in formal groups than in informal groups, for instance. Next, gender and cultural differences and stereotypes may influence expectations and success of each type of leadership (Carli & Eagly, 2011; Chhokar, Brodbeck, & House, 2012). Further, a person may be good at one type of leadership but poor at the other type. Of course, a person may be good at both elements of the group process, and the ability to understand and use member emotion will assist

task leaders: those focusing on the performance of tasks to ensure the achievement of group goals (compare with *socioemotional leaders*)

socioemotional leaders: those focusing on making group members feel comfortable, satisfied, valued, and understood (compare with *task leaders*)

both types of leadership (Emery, 2012). Finally, task leadership and socioemotional leadership may come from different people in a group.

Leadership Power

Leadership generally involves power within a group, and this power can be broadly categorized as formal and informal. In both cases, this power is transacted through communication and, especially in terms of the latter, is best understood through recognizing the influence of relationships. Within this section, we will examine both types of power and then look at more specific types of power.

Formal Power

A leader is said to have **formal power** when power has been formally given or recognized by a system or group. For example, the chair of a group may be recognized as possessing formal power within the group. Just because a person possesses formal power does not mean that this person will be effective, though. Another member of the group may be more respected and have more influence than the chair.

Informal Power

In that case, the other member of the group may be said to have **informal power**. This type of leadership power has not been formally granted but rather has been developed through the group's interactions. This power is often based on liking, relationships, and communication competence. There may be a formally designated group leader, but group members generally go along with the wishes and direction of someone else in the group. In other cases, a group may not have a designated leader, but someone rises up and is able to exert influence on the other members.

We will spend a bit more time discussing informal power, because it is not always as straightforward as one person being more powerful than a chair or someone rising up from among equals. In fact, there may be an informal power base working beneath the scenes or in conjunction with a more formal power arrangement.

Take, for example, Hepburn and Crepin's (1984) study of the relationships between prisoners and guards in a state penitentiary. The formal structure of power seems obvious: The guards are in control, and the prisoners are not. But think again. The system cannot work if only formal power is taken into account. Informal power must also be taken into account within this system.

First, the prisoners outnumber the guards. At any time, if they acted together, they could overpower a single guard, whether or not the guard is carrying weaponry.

Second, the guards' superiors take note of how they handle prisoners. Particular guards get a reputation for being good with prisoners, while other guards are seen as incompetent. The good ones receive bigger pay raises than the others. Once again the prisoners can influence the outcomes for the guards in unexpected ways.

If the prisoners choose to communicate cooperatively with a particular guard, the superiors will see that guard as doing the job well. If the prisoners decide to make a particular guard's life difficult by disobeying orders or showing disrespect in their talk, he or she will be frequently pulled into conflicts. The superiors will eventually see this as evidence of inability to get the job done well.

So the guards need to play along, communicating with prisoners in a constructive and amiable way that helps them develop decent working relationships so they can do their job at all. So who *really* has the power?

formal power: that which is formally allocated by a system or group to particular people (compare with *informal power*)

informal power: operates through relationships and individual reputations without formal status (e.g., someone may not actually be the boss but might exert more influence on other workers by being highly respected; compare with *formal power*)

An informal system of power also exists among the prisoners: Some prisoners are top dogs while others are not. The guards must pay attention to this informal hierarchy and not treat them all equally. Otherwise, the prisoners will stir up trouble for the guards. Again, power is transacted into being by how two parties relate and communicate.

Power in groups, then, is not always as clear as it seems from group structure. As you can tell, power is always a transactional concept and is always related to relationship dynamics. It depends on acceptance by followers as well as on its execution by a leader.

More Types of Power

French and Raven (1960) went further and distinguished five specific types of power. These are presented in Table 9.4, and we will return to them in Chapter 14.

Table 9.4 French and Raven's Five Types of Power

TYPE OF POWER	FEATURES	EXAMPLES
Legitimate	Created by a person's office rank or official status	Designated chair of a group
Expert	Created through special knowledge of a particular topic	Group member with special knowledge of topic or issue being considered
Referent	Created by the allegiance of one group of people to another person or group	Group member who is respected by other members and whom other members may wish to emulate
Reward	Created by the power to give benefits to other people, or to manage or withhold them	Group member who promises support on an upcoming vote in return for earlier favor
Coercive	Created by the power to punish (as distinct from withholding of rewards, this means actual application of punishment)	Chair of group sanctioning or not allowing a member to participate

Notice, then, that the exercise of power is more complicated than it may appear at first. It is derived from many sources. Also note that a single person can often have more than one of these types of power. For instance, the chair can have both legitimate and coercive power. A group member may have expert power through specialized knowledge of a topic and also have referent power as a respective member of the group.

Leadership Vision

It is often claimed in major textbooks about leadership that it is essential for a leader to have a "vision" (Kantabutra & Rungruang, 2013; Northouse, 2012). This has become so much of a mantra in business and leadership courses that very few people take the time to evaluate what it means. The first mistake is one that we already noted, to assume that "leadership" is a unified entity and that it manifests itself in the same way in a grocery store manager, a classroom discussion leader, a Pope, and a four-star general. Clearly, these different types of leaders do not all need "visions," or at least not ones of the same type. No four-star general is going to make an Easter plea for world peace as the Pope does every year! The focus and scope of the visions they should have are also different, with higher-ranking people being expected to

Make your case

Are Leaders Born or Made?

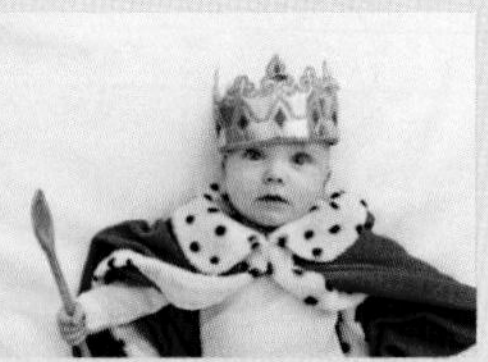

Some areas of study such as business management focus on traits and personalities of leaders. Scholars in communication focus more on leadership styles and on the ways in which leaders form and lead groups in the successful completion of tasks so that group members feel that their contributions are recognized and appreciated. It may very well be that a leader has a strong personality or is a person who can focus on task accomplishment and socioemotional qualities of interactions. Despite this, the nature of leaders' communication is what contributes to these concentrations, and the nature of their personality is itself conveyed through communication as discussed in Chapter 3.

QUESTIONS TO CONSIDER

1. Do you believe that leaders are born or made?
2. Can people be trained to be better leaders by having their communication skills trained to a higher level using some of the techniques indicated in this book?

steer the boat and people lower down the chain just needing to keep their production or sales targets in sight.

Any broad statement about the fact that "a leader needs a vision" (Northouse, 2012) is clearly going to be wrong. However, it is very often motivating for the members of a group to believe that their leader has some idea of where the group will be headed and what they will be doing. People in groups commonly want to be led, and they want to believe that the leader is taking them somewhere useful. They may have their own ideas as to whether the leader is taking them in any useful direction, but that is a matter for discussion and group agreement. A good leader will be able to create consensus in a group through the mechanisms that we have already discussed.

Leadership Ethics

Another claim made in books and research on leadership is that ethical leadership is a prerequisite for success (Jordan, Brown, Treviño, & Finkelstein, 2013; Northouse, 2012). Many students write course assignments about this with great conviction, but cannot define the nature of ethics. Is it ethical to praise people when they do not deserve it, even if the phrase will motivate them to do better? Is it ethical to hold back information from people because it will improve their performance? Is it ethical to give everyone the same reward when some people work harder than others?

Although each of these questions leads to its own complexities, anyone who writes about ethics in leadership needs to take a good look at the last 20 years and see how many cases he or she can come up with where politicians, business leaders, and others in positions of trust have clearly violated their ethical responsibilities and are not paying the slightest bit of attention to what the books on leadership tell them they should be doing. It is even clearer that however many books on ethics and leadership leaders have read and however many seminars on ethics they have attended that have stressed the point that ethics matter, they nevertheless are behaving in ways that are pure examples of avarice, greed, and irresponsibility.

Maybe it says that ethics matter in the leadership textbooks and classes, but clearly many political, business, and social leaders do not find ethics too constraining a burden. The main problem with the ethics question in leadership is that it is context-bound and often dependent on a whole range of complexities that interlock. Decisions are rarely independent of one another, and particular actions cannot always be assessed without reference to other activity. This is particularly true of people's feelings of obligation to relationships and to the value of doing favors for people they wish to impress or who have done them favors. Relationships strike once more!

Leadership Is Transacted

The preceding discussions within this chapter really mean that leadership is not a trait and that there are complicated social influences from other people in a group. These influence how a leader behaves—and relationships between group members are part of that. This really means that leadership is a *relational process,* not a trait.

Leadership is a communicative relationship between one person and others such that when one gives a direction and another gladly carries it out, leadership has been successfully *transacted* in the interchange. Leadership is embedded not *in a person* but in *communication and relationships between people.*

It is true that a leader, manager, director, or department head has real control over resources that other team members need. But French and Raven (1960) teach us that these apparent powers can be undermined by the existence and use of other kinds of relational power. Sometimes, particular members of decision-making groups come up with consistently better ideas than the designated leader, and eventually people start to see those members as the true influencers. Or sometimes followers just refuse to obey.

You may have noticed the use of the term *team* when referring to groups—especially those taking place in the workplace. This term, although overused and almost cliché, has a rhetorical spin that presents interdependence, cooperation, effective division of labor, common goals, coordination, and mutual respect, so now leadership books tend to emphasize teamwork. This is not so different in effect as the topic of "cohesiveness" that we covered earlier, but it is a relational communicative term. Relational aspects of an effective team are at least as important as the group's task outcomes. Hence, messages in teams place emphasis on making people feel valued as well as getting the job done (Clampitt, 2005).

Any nasty despot can force slaves to build pyramids, but very few leaders can make their underlings feel important afterward. Julius Caesar's leadership qualities included making a point of knowing the names of as many of his men as humanly possible—he had a staggering memory—and addressing each one personally as often as he could. By paying attention to their feelings as people, he built his legions into formidable teams that would do for him what they would do for no one else (Dando-Collins, 2004). The same characteristic was true of Scipio Africanus who eventually defeated Hannibal and also of General Bernard Montgomery in World War II who beat Rommel (O'Connell, 2011).

Effective teams and their leaders are always interdependent. They all attend to personal relationships and carry out the friendly and respectful communication necessary for truly "personal" relationships. Personal communication transacts a collaborative climate, strong personal commitment, high regard for other team members, and a unified commitment to excellence.

Focus Questions Revisited

1 What is a group?

A group is more than just a collection of a few people. Groups are transacted through communication and relationships. A group comes into being once people recognize and identify themselves and others as members of the same group. Beyond the recognition of membership, a simple assembly or collection of people is not really a group unless it has a common purpose. Types of groups include (a) formal, (b) advisory, (c) creative, (d) support, and (e) networking.

 What are the characteristics of a group?

Key characteristics of groups include (a) cohesiveness, (b) interdependence, (c) commitment, (d) norms, (e) roles, and (f) cultures.

 How do groups form and make decisions?

Although research on group communication has too frequently used groups with zero history among members, there are a number of models of group development and decision making. These models usually view group development and decision making as a linear process. Communication is frequently taken for granted or thought to be similar in all group experiences. Relationships tend to be absent altogether. Recognizing the impact of relationships and interactions outside of group interactions will enhance this area of study.

 What are the styles of group leadership?

Leadership style is categorized into focusing on the task and focusing on the socioemotional well-being of the members of the group. Task leaders focus on the performance of tasks to ensure the achievement of group goals. Socioemotional leaders focus on group member satisfaction and well-being.

5 What are the types of leadership power?

Leadership power can be broadly categorized as formal and informal. Formal power is that which has been formally given or recognized by a system or group. Informal power is that which has not been formally granted but rather has been developed through the group's interactions. More specific types of power include (a) legitimate, (b) expert, (c) referent, (d) reward, and (e) coercive.

 What is meant by leadership vision and leadership ethics?

Books on leadership frequently note the need for leadership vision. However, there are too many "visions" in existence for that to have much meaning beyond talking points in business seminars. Yet it is very often motivating for the members of a group to believe that their leader has some idea of where the group will be headed and what they will be doing. People in groups commonly want to be led, and they want to believe that the leader is taking them somewhere useful. Another claim made in books on leadership is that ethical leadership is a prerequisite for success (Northouse, 2012). At the same time, many political, business, and social leaders do not find ethics too constraining a burden. The main problem with the ethics question in leadership is that it is context-bound and often dependent on a whole range of complexities that interlock, especially those involving relationships.

 How is leadership transacted?

Leadership is a communicative relationship between one person and others such that when one gives a direction and another gladly carries it out, leadership has been successfully transacted in the interchange. Leadership is embedded not in a person but in communication and relationships between people.

Key Concepts

adjourning (Tuckman's group development) 186
advisory group 181
coercive power 191
cohesiveness 181
conflict (Fisher's group progression) 187
creative group 181
disruptive roles 185
emergence (Fisher's group progression) 187
expert power 191
formal group 181
formal power 190
formal roles 184
forming (Tuckman's group development) 186
group culture 185
group norms 183
group roles 184
group sanctions 184
groupthink 182
informal power 190
informal roles 184
interdependence 182
legitimate power 191
networking group 181
norming (Tuckman's group development) 186
orientation (Fisher's group progression) 187
out-groups 183
performing (Tuckman's group development) 186
referent power 191

reinforcement (Fisher's group progression) 187
reward power 191
social roles 184
socioemotional leaders 189
storming (Tuckman's group development) 186
support group 181
task leaders 189
task roles 184

Questions to Ask Your Friends

1. How does your group of friends decide what to do on Friday night? Ask your friends this question to determine their perspective. Which processes discussed in this chapter can you see at work there?
2. Who do your friends think is a good leader, and what makes a person so?
3. What group norms and rituals can you identify in the small groups and organizations to which you belong? Ask your friends in these groups this question and then compare answers.

Media Connections

1. The following four movies offer good instances of groups in action and cover some of the concepts discussed in this chapter: *Office Space, Apollo 13, 12 Angry Men* (the original Henry Fonda black-and-white version), and *The A-Team*. Each movie demonstrates something different about groups. The opening sequence of *Office Space,* for example, gives you a good idea of a group culture, and some of the characters represent different leadership styles (analyze Lumbergh's—ugh!—power and leadership style). *12 Angry Men* demonstrates how a task leader can bring emotionally led individuals back on track by using promotive communication but also handle the socioemotional concerns of different members. *Apollo 13* demonstrates aspects of leadership and group norms. Finally, *The A-Team* demonstrates a number of such group characteristics as group roles, interdependence, and cohesion.
2. The next time you are in a group, pay attention to any discussions about media. For instance, someone might bring up a television program viewed the previous evening or a newly discovered website. In what ways could such discussions be considered disruptive communication? In what ways could such discussions actually enhance group relationships?
3. Watch any reality show with groups. How do groups form, what are their dynamics and transactions, and what are their weaknesses?

Student Study Site

SAGE edge™

Sharpen your skills with SAGE edge at edge.sagepub.com/duckciel2e

SAGE edge for students provides a personalized approach to help you accomplish your coursework goals in an easy-to-use learning environment.

Chapter Outline

Learning About the Workplace
- Socialization About Work

Going to Work: The Workplace as a Special Frame
- Going to Work: What Is Different, and What Is the Same?
- Performance of Work Identities
- Negotiating Relational and Work Goals

The Workplace as a Culture
- Organizational Culture and Routines
- The Organization and Its Norms
- Frames and Hierarchies: Formal Versus Informal Power
- Industrial Time
- Contact With the Public: Customer-Client Relationships

The Workplace as Relationships
- Relationships as Workplace Challenges
- Legitimate and Illegitimate
- Organizational Interference in Life
- The Downside of Good Relationships at Work

Focus Questions Revisited

Key Concepts

Questions to Ask Your Friends

Media Connections

10 Communication in the Workplace

When we ask students to tell us what their workplace is like, they say things like "My restaurant is very upscale, and I really like the people and the customers I work with"; "I work in a fitness center, and the manager is a control freak"; or "I used to work at a corporate head office, and the people really got on my nerves, which is why I decided to come back to college." They also tell us stories about the way a colleague had advised them not to pay too much attention to one particular company rule because nobody ever really enforced it but that they should always be sure to show up early when one particular shift manager was on duty because she was very strict about timekeeping. They also get plenty of advice from more experienced employees about how to get bigger tips or what to do if a customer complains. In short, they answer specific questions about experience in terms of other people and relationships.

When we ask the broader and more abstract question "What comes to mind when you think about work or the workplace in general?" they envision something different from their own personal experiences and instead talk of leaders and followers/employees, managers and peons, law offices with strict lines of report, corporate businesses where sales departments and marketing departments are often in conflict, nonprofit organizations with specific rules and cultures, and other arrangements of management. They tend to think, in short, in terms of *structure*.

In the case of corporate organizations, they talk about the corporate head office, managerial hierarchies, vice presidents and middle management, chain of command—the sort of structure that is often represented in organizational flowcharts. These are hierarchically organized charts that show who reports to whom. Although most students do not experience their workplace quite that way, they do recognize it as a general way of thinking about the workplace as an organization. Yet in their own experience, they notice how work is a place that makes meaning between people, where a particular culture exists, and where "the way things get done around here" is passed on to new employees not only by instructions from the boss but by individuals telling one another stories about how they dealt with a difficult situation that might arise in the new employee's interactions with customers. So again, thoughts about "structure" are really translated into communication, and we can apply our usual analysis.

Accordingly, we will start by looking at organizations in this familiar structural way and move on to show a better and more recent approach for understanding organizations. You have already learned from the family chapter (Chapter 8) to make this move: to see structure (official formal structures) as

FOCUS QUESTIONS

1. Where do people learn about the workplace?
2. Going to work: What do you need to know?
3. How are organizations constituted as a "culture" of interaction and relationships between members?
4. Is the workplace best explained by a relationship approach?

transacted (brought into being) in interpersonal communication. In this same way, "the workplace" and "organizations" are transacted in communication through relationships (who knew?). The goal of this chapter is to teach you how to move from the traditional structural views of organizations toward an approach based on communications that make a workplace what it is. Interestingly, this same move is happening in management and business schools where leadership is now seen as a relational skill rather than as the use of structural power to get people to do your will (Northouse, 2012). Democracy and civil mutual respect are also regarded as essential to good workplace ethics nowadays (Northouse, 2012), and these turn out to be communicative and transactional as well.

A moment's thought will make it clear that relationships do not exist in an organization between faceless structural units called "Sales" and "Marketing" but rather exist between *individual* members of those groups. They know one another and have long-term relationships with one another. In fact *workplace* is a misleading term in some respects as it directs your attention away from (long- or short-term) personal relationships and toward places and impersonal structures between abstract organizational units. Members of a sales "team" know one another. People in an organization deal with other individuals from different organizations in order to do business *transacted* through communication in relationships between them.

Surprise! The "workplace" is (and organizations generally are) best viewed as a relational enterprise that involves meaning making, rhetorical visions, and everyday communication. This fact is often disguised by abstract terms like *conflict management* (which, of course, happens between individuals) or *leadership* (of individuals by other individuals) or *decision making* (by individuals interacting face-to-face or through technology). Corporate organizations project an identity by having employees wear identifying uniforms, or they conduct business with customers face-to-face, giving away pens with company logos and often much more substantial company gifts. They often have special jargon for communication in the workplace, while they project themselves to the public by the same means we have already discussed in the identity chapter (Chapter 3). These terms, however, also connect to culture and speech codes. Organizations and workplaces are, in effect, small cultures after all. (Note from your culturally diverse authors: The British English word here for "coworkers" is *workmates,* making them sound friendly and connected rather than simply people who show up at the same place and work together like cogs in a system. One culture assumes that they will bond together; the other assumes that they will have to be made to.)

Organizations handle their public image through communication (public relations) and try to establish loyalty to their brand by calling their workers not "employees" but "associates." They also present their "valued customers" as loyal allies of their organization (so they don't go and buy someone else's product instead!). Organizations try to be seen as individual entities, and always want to be your friend (for example, "Like a good neighbor, State Farm is there." Weiss's [1974] *reliable alliance* that was discussed in Chapter 7, anyone?). They have public relations offices not only to project a good image to the public but also to prepare corporate rhetorical strategies for dealing with catastrophes and are judged by the way they handle them in public (whether with an apology or with a defensive response; Ice, 1991).

Finally, hierarchy is a defining characteristic of organizations, and any organization has top people and bottom people, those who command and those who obey, those who make decisions and those who carry them out. If you view an organization as a structure, you will not find it surprising that this leads to a significant managerial bias in research. It is geared toward the power structure and established order, where "workers" have no real power. Where organizations seek ways to maximize output and profit, they may not care if the result does nothing to make the company more enjoyable for the workers. Organizations, which often sponsor such research, believe that the power lies in management and leadership, so they are most interested in improving those aspects of organizational operations.

Any sort of formal power structure, however, sometimes can be undermined and undercut by the informal relationships between participants. A poor boss may in fact inspire no confidence or respect among subordinates, who undermine authority by disobedience, resistance, or private jokes about the jerk who is supposed to be "Our Dear Leader."

This chapter, then, incorporates our general attempt to reconceptualize all traditional phenomena in interpersonal communication as driven by, and carried out through, interpersonal relationships. Traditional topics (like the nature of work, leadership, the culture of the workplace, and relationships between people in organizations) can be reconceptualized as based on our relational perspective.

What is this picture telling us about the nature of work and the glossy expectations of professional success? How is it sending messages of what professionals look like and what they do?

Learning About the Workplace

One very influential approach to leadership and organizations proposes that they are sites of *meaning making* (Weick, 1995). This general idea fits very well with what we are saying in this book. People develop understanding, rhetorical visions, and predispositions or expectations about how to behave and perform in specific frames. Other people help them do it. If this were not a general principle of communication in everyday life, then it would not apply to the workplace, but it does. We get our ideas about work from Society's Secret Agents right out of the crib and are conditioned by TV, movies, and other experiences to accept what "work" is like and how "professionals" look, act, and operate.

How do we come to understand the meaning of work and to perform our roles within it? There are many ways in which people tend to think of the workplace. Some are developed in childhood and reinforced in later life; some are derived from practical experience with the norms and organizational culture of a company; and some are refined by the relational interactions that occur among the specific people who work there. If we invited you to join the Suck/Cess Team at Duck & McMahan's Drain Cleaning Company ("We can even unclog memories"), you would already have expectations about how to dress, how to behave in a professional manner, and how to think about rising to the top (it's not the sort of company where you want to stay at the bottom very long).

By the way...

Metaphorical Depictions of the Workplace

Early cinema (Charlie Chaplin in *Modern Times* [1936] or the silent movie *Metropolis* [1927]) represented the metaphor of organizations as machines. These films suggested that the machine has the effect of turning workers into robots, a fear that was very real in society in those days as mechanization of jobs on the assembly line began to occur more frequently (and nowadays those jobs very often are indeed done by robots or computers). In a more recent example, if you have seen *Office Space,* you may recall the receptionist who spends the first 5 minutes of the movie routinely and sequentially (and in a chirpy mechanical voice) repeating robotically, "Corporate Accounts Payable . . . Nina speaking . . . Just a moment." And so on, 8 a.m. to 5 p.m., day after day. Other depictions of the workplace, from *The Office* to *House* to *Mad Men,* represent it as something tedious and irrelevant, bound by rules, which can be broken by a crazy genius, or essentially a place grounded in a lack of ethics, where the achievement of a goal is justified by any means of achieving it.

QUESTIONS TO CONSIDER

1. How have these depictions of the workplace influenced your life?
2. What do you expect the workplace will be like in the future?

Socialization About Work

It is important to see how communication contributes to your understanding of organizations and also to see how your socialization teaches you to treat the workplace as a special kind of *frame*. Much of your thinking about organizations is created by the language (especially the metaphors) that you use to describe it (Chapter 4) and also by your learning before you ever enter the workplace (especially in the family and at school). After all, there is something like 15 years of childhood and socialization that can form the basis for your expectations about what "work" is all about before you ever get there. Often one of the highlights about school is the visits from the police and fire services whose personnel come and demonstrate all their "cool gear," and from such experiences children get an impression about the significance of this kind of work in society.

Metaphors of Organization

One strong influence on thinking in general is the use of metaphors, and there are many different metaphors for organizations, such as organizations as machines; organizations as cultures; and organizations as instruments of domination.

Gareth Morgan (2006) specifically points out how metaphors structure ways of seeing and thinking that guide the ways in which managers and members of organizations view them. A *machine metaphor* represents organizations as standardized by repetition, specialization, or predictability.

Modern management techniques that were previously guided by this metaphor have sought to escape from it. They seek to make the workplace more welcoming. Workers' voices should be listened to so that they do not simply feel like cogs in a machine or anonymous numbers on a list. Their value to the company or the organization is something that must be recognized and valued by management (Sias, 2009). That is why there are now endless (and often detested) "bonding weekends" and "team-building exercises." However many times you play trust games with some colleagues, you can never forget that time they betrayed you into holding the bag for some major snafu. And, of course, a lot of the trust games are simply silly.

Other metaphors focus on *organizations as cultures* based on shared meaning, and the notion of "sharing" presupposes relationships between people. However, the concept of *organizational culture* is one that readily springs to mind, and the atmosphere in particular organizations can be very different; "atmosphere" is very apparent to people who work in different organizations and may even come across to the customers themselves. Most organizations try to create an atmosphere of friendliness and the valuing of customers by the use of such phrases as "Your call is very important to us," but you know, as mentioned in Chapter 6, on many "help lines" you will sit there listening for 20 minutes to the music of Vivaldi's *Four Seasons* and that if you hear that bloody "Springtime" violin piece anymore you will go nuts. Some companies even go so far as to say, for example, "Univision™ doesn't just have viewers. We have relationships. Relationships with millions of people who say they simply cannot live life without us" (Univision, 2008). But why would anybody *want* a deep personal relationship with his or her defense attorney?

For most people, organizations are not seen as friends but are more likely to be seen metaphorically as *instruments of domination* that not only shape the workers' behavior but even control or manipulate their thoughts and ideologies. This metaphor is extremely common because most people feel that work is not only undesirable but actually oppressive. Most people would rather be out fishing or shopping or bicycling than moving containers of trash from place A to place B or sitting in boring meetings or driving delivery trucks. It is very clear that in order to become a member of any workplace you are faced with the *connectedness-separateness dialectic* (see Chapter 7). You give up lots of your freedom in order to devote most of your time to working for your employer, when you would rather be doing something else. However, in the early part of your life you learned that work is unavoidable (unless you happen to be an extremely wealthy horse-owning nontaxpayer), but you also learned subtly that society values those who "aim for success" (except for Donald Trump, of course).

Early Learning About Work

Vocational anticipatory socialization is the preparation for becoming a worker and begins in a child's early life through family interaction and exposure to the media. You first learned about the nature of work and the workplace through socialization in your families. Cockburn-Wootten and Zorn (2006) note that many families tell stories about the nature of work experiences, some of them funny, some of them poignant, but all conveying to young children something about the nature of work. As a child, you heard adults talking about the work that they do, and you were able to gain some sense of whether they see it as important or simply something that they reluctantly do in order to feed the family. A child's attitude toward the workplace can be affected by such ordinary comments, whether they are about the nature of particular professions or the nature of the colleagues with whom the adult individual lives life during the long daily period of absence from the family. For children who have not yet experienced the workplace, these kinds of stories, comments, and conversational pieces are formative.

Family stories about work, of course, are often structured to express and emphasize certain values such as the payoffs of hard work or the ways to break the rules and get away with it (Cockburn-Wootten & Zorn, 2006). Each conveys something to the child about the mysteries of the workplace. Such stories may emphasize the swirling together of the leisurely "true" individual self and the necessarily but reluctantly "working self." The workplace may be described by a parent as a source of stress or as a source of income (or both) but as something for which the growing child must prepare and for which a so-called Protestant work ethic is often induced—the drive to achieve success through hard work (Allen, 2006).

vocational anticipatory socialization: the preparation for becoming a worker; takes place from early moments of childhood onward, including through exposure to the media and depiction of the workplace in comedy and other shows

Other stories stress the dangerous nature of, say, a firefighter's job and extend that fact to the identity that encompasses the individual and admirable heroes who perform the work. The ultimate media message of *World's Wildest Police Videos* is that the police always catch criminals, who are frequently described as "punks" and often presented as inept and hopeless losers. In its own way, this program conveys messages about the value of police work to society and the ultimate folly of breaking

By the way...

What Did Your Parents Tell You About Work?

When Steve's father brought his boss home to dinner when Steve was 7 and his younger brother was 5, it was presented as a very significant event where they had to dress up smartly and be on their absolute best behavior. Although they did not realize what was at stake about the importance of behaving well in the presence of a boss, as a matter of fact they soon realized—even at their young ages—why their father hated his work so much.

QUESTIONS TO CONSIDER

1. In what ways do you think that your approaches to understanding the workplace were influenced by the ways in which your parents or guardians reported their work experiences?
2. If you have children (if not, imagine you do), what might their impressions of the workplace be, based on your reports?

the law. As well as being engaging and informative about police work, it serves as yet another example of Society's Secret Agents at work, infiltrating and reinforcing society's values into our ordinary life and reinforcing the idea that police are incorruptible heroes who make life safer for the rest of us, which is fine as long as we don't watch news stories about criminals getting away with it and police being prosecuted for corruption.

Through such socialization, people develop shared cultural understandings of work and its place in society and personal life. There is often, for example, a straightforward identity connection between job and person through the God term (Chapter 4) of one's profession (doctor, nurse—to say nothing of professor!) or the status and social structure associated with other kinds of workers such as dentists, janitors, lawyers, or meatpackers. Identity becomes embedded in these terms and shows us that people derive much of their sense of identity from their job. Also much of their social identity is established by their workplace and the function they perform there (see Chapter 3). So also does a sense of the role of the "boss" as related to that of the "workers" become instilled in the child's mind. Bosses tell you what to do, and you are supposed to do it. Your goals as an individual may be placed alongside those of the organization itself, and your success or failure may be judged according to your success in "climbing the ladder." You are taught that it is better to be a boss than a peon. You should aim to progress through promotion, or else you will be seen to have failed. And if only you can become an astronaut . . . or a communication graduate . . . or a *Deadliest Catch* fisher . . .

Such vocational anticipatory socialization instills dominant beliefs like TGIF (thank goodness it's Friday) or "a case of the Mondays" that reinforce the idea that for many people work is simply a necessary evil between weekends. In this way people learn that there is a difference between "work" and "relationships" and certainly a tension between "work" and "family" (Totten, 2006). Work happens when you are constrained by the organization; "relationships" happen in the evening or on weekends when you are relaxing. On the other hand, you are presented with many glossy images of the positive side of work—and particularly of success at work (think *Mad Men*). In both cases, shared societal rhetorical visions about work are consistent with our general "take" on the world in this book.

Going to Work: The Workplace as a Special Frame

There are important differences between the workplace and normal everyday life experiences with friends and associates—at least on the surface—and it is these differences upon which much research has focused (Sias, 2009). Indeed, a workplace is special in many important respects, mostly framed through learning, language, and life. Furthermore, these are developed in large part through the communicative efforts of managers or leaders within an organization (Fairhurst & Sarr, 1996). In the terms used in Chapter 4 (to describe *presentation* versus *representation*), this means that a leader or a manager or an organization or a workplace itself presents (rather than represents) certain options of meaning and interpretation as preferable over others. This is an important principle in understanding the way in which workplace practices frame perspectives concerning talk and relationships. Of course, although the workplace has special practices and codes, it is also important to recognize that these overlie the usual practices and codes of everyday life.

We extend to the workplace what you have learned about relational narratives and sense making in other chapters. In doing so, we first explore the direct continuation of aspects of interpersonal communication into the new frame of the workplace. Second, we apply some of our analysis of transaction of communication to the workplace itself. We begin by looking at what people import into the workplace, and then we examine the workplace as a place in itself and look at the talk there, asking what workplace talk does to transact the organization. This is another way of asking how people "perform" the workplace. We then apply the transactional nature of communication to the workplace itself, examining how workplace talk sustains and transacts organizations.

When you are at work, you are in a different *frame* where you perform identities connected to work. Everyday life patterns and practices are extended into the new context and frame the workplace. However, these can be constrained or even altered by the workplace frame.

Going to Work: What Is Different, and What Is the Same?

Continuation of identity imports your normal practices of everyday talk into the workplace. Since everyday talk is usually recreational or relational, the *instrumental purpose* of the workplace affects the nature of talk at work and so can reshape the way in which talk operates to transact your identity (Mokros, 2006). For example, the workplace constrains the kinds of identity you can perform (Chapter 3) and requires that you adopt a professional working identity. A striking example is in the armed forces when the first part of boot camp training is to break down an individual's sense of personal identity and to replace it with a highly trained, disciplined, unquestioningly obedient uniformity as one of a team of people who carry out automatically whatever orders may be given (almost as if they were in college!).

In less extreme cases, you share the rhetorical vision that you will be expected to dress in a particular way (a suit, a uniform, overalls, a logo shirt). Also organizations usually require you to dress differently than you dress at leisure. The nonverbal communication (Chapter 5) that takes place through these styles of dress carries messages of connection to the organization and requires you to perform roles not done elsewhere. Dress may also indicate your position in the organization, whether you wear a certain kind of military insignia on your sleeve or whether you have a peaked cap and epaulets (pilot) or an apron (flight attendant). The organizational relationship between one person and another is conveyed by nonverbal cues. Management is referred to as white-collar workers while laborers are described as blue-collar workers. The symbolic distinctions of workplace dress are thus built into language and ways of understanding hierarchy in relationships (Chapter 7).

You will also be expected to adopt a new "working identity" and adapt to that culture. This may involve learning new *speech codes*, jargon, and idioms that are appropriate to a particular workplace (remember the server in Chapter 1) and adapting your speech to represent your **professional face**. In many professional settings, you will be required to learn the jargon that is appropriate to the job and will be expected to adopt high code (Chapter 4) when interacting with customers, clients, or other people involved in the

continuation of identity: parts of your identity carry over from your normal practices of everyday talk into the workplace, but some parts of your identity are transformed by the workplace

professional face: the behaviors, courtesy, and comportment that are appropriate for people to present to others in a workplace

By the way...

Attitudes Toward Customers in the Workplace

In the movie *Waiting...*, the boss is presented as an idiotic and ineffective jerk whom the workers despise along with the diners. The cooks and servers play tricks on diners by spoiling the food of people who complain. They also play an obscene game in the kitchen in order to distract themselves from the boredom of the job. Two memorable (bottom) lines from the movie are "Never [mess] with the people that serve you food!" and "What happens in the kitchen ends up on the plate." If you have worked in a restaurant or food establishment, you probably have comparable stories to tell, but you probably still go out for special meals, despite what you know about the secret life of the kitchen.

QUESTIONS TO CONSIDER

1. If you have ever worked in a customer service job, how did your work experiences change the way you behave as a customer?
2. If you have never worked in a customer service job, how might you imagine the experience to be?

same organization. You may be able to express your own personality in particular ways that fit with this professional face; servers, for example, can often project their personal style into the role of server in a way that maximizes their tips. However, in a wholesale produce market, the interpersonal performance of relational preferences (liking, disliking) can affect whether a given merchant gets a good or bad deal on the produce that he or she wishes to purchase (Mokros, 2006).

Performance of Work Identities

On top of whatever you take into the workplace, the organization attempts to overlay special formats of identity constructed for the workplace. They reflect the conduct of workers' relationships not only with one another but with customers and clients. Although Chapter 3 focused on the personal identities that we perform, the workplace requires conflicting sets of performances. The workplace has some influence on the way talk molds identity at work, partly through power dynamics that are built into the workplace, making some people officially powerful and some less powerful. For example, the server in Chapter 1 has less power than the diners in that she is expected to carry out their instructions. Relationally, however, she has informal power and can at any time decide to delay the serving of their order or place other people ahead of them in her list of service. We pointed out also that she has to adopt a stylized form of greeting required by her role and that she is identified as a server by the clothing that her organization requires her to wear in order to indicate that she is someone on duty to perform roles for the customer (asking questions related to food, taking orders, delivering food). Her working identity requires her to be polite but not overly chatty and to focus rapidly on the task of taking diners' orders and, ultimately, their money.

Is this sergeant "only doing his job"? What is happening to the recruit and his sense of identity?

In the workplace, interactions are also subject to language performances that facilitate the completion of the organization's tasks. Talk tends to be formal and structured and to focus on the professional deportment of the person involved. Police officers say "10–4," or "Copy that," not "Yep" or "Got it." Airline pilots address the control tower in special codes that are meaningless outside the organizational frame in which they work. When an alarmed pilot shouted "No gear, no gear!" to the control tower after observing another plane coming in to land with its landing wheels still up, for example, it prevented a catastrophe (National Transportation Safety Board, 1993).

Outside of that special context his shout would have meant nothing. In short, there often is jargon and special language to be learned for the workplace (see Table 10.1). Special language gives you special positioning and expert involvement in the workplace. It identifies you as a special person within an organizational frame and also as an expert who knows special terms that outsiders do not.

Table 10.1 Examples of Workplace Jargon and Special Language

PROFESSION	JARGON	TRANSLATION
Police Officer	1. "Copy that"	1. "Yes," "Got it."
	2. "MO"	2. "Modus operandi"—a criminal's typical pattern of behaviors when conducting a crime.
Airline Pilot	1. "No gear!"	1. "A plane's landing gear has not deployed properly."
	2. "Roger"	2. "I understand."
University Teacher	1. "GPA"	1. "Grade point average"—a measure of a student's level of achievement overall.
	2. "Midterm"	2. A method of assessing student progress.
Therapist	1. "Borderline"	1. A client with a particular personality disorder.
	2. "Intake"	2. A special form for admitting a new client to the practice.

From your performances in the workplace you also learn that it is inappropriate to play around in ways that are entirely appropriate in friendships. When one is in the front region of performance in the workplace, it is inappropriate to behave sloppily or unprofessionally. On the other hand, in the back region, where there is more of a relaxed atmosphere, playfulness may be encouraged as a way of building a sense of community and team membership (Mokros, 2006). You learn to distinguish very clearly between the front and back regions here also.

Negotiating Relational and Work Goals

One clear difference between work and everyday life is that **instrumental goals** are predominant at work ("Get the job done") whereas **relational goals** are predominant outside work ("Have a social life"). Instrumental goals can involve direct delegation of duties. They can also involve a direct assessment of performance in ways that are not expected in everyday conversation with friends. Typical *relational goals* involve intimacy and support. By contrast, goals at work are more focused on *tasks and achievement* of organizational objectives. The instrumental purposes required at work will affect the nature of talk and reshape the way in which talk operates. You must focus on issues of task management.

Another clear difference at work is that the talk tends to construct distance and **formality/hierarchy** in certain parts of the organization (e.g., between management and workers). Thus, work represents a strain or restraint on relationships as an individual is forced to adopt a professional face rather than a personal identity (Chapter 3). For example, it is essential in a working environment that the tasks of the workplace are performed adequately and efficiently. This may involve the clear explanation of a particular task to subordinates and the delegation of specific activities to those who must carry them out. By contrast, in your friendships, the delegation of tasks and the spelling out of particular activities that must be performed are relatively small parts of your conversational life ("Hey, Joy, don't forget to order the pepperoni toppings!").

Although there are instrumental goals in our everyday relationships such as asking someone out on a date, the *essential function of talk* (Chapter 7) is much more

instrumental goals: are predominant at work and are directed at completion of duties; can also involve a direct assessment of performance

relational goals: typically involve intimacy and support and usually serve recreational or supportive purposes

formality/hierarchy: creates distance between workers and management and can represent a strain or restraint on relationships as an individual is forced to adopt a professional face rather than a personal identity when dealing with people at work

to the front and center of your conversations outside of the workplace. The conflict between essential goals in relationships and predominantly instrumental ones in the workplace may be difficult for people to manage. This may strain their performance of their usual identity, as there is a conflict between the role of worker and the role of friend.

Outside of the workplace, people may have the purpose of developing their relationships and may make use of self-disclosure in a way that develops intimacy (Chapters 3 and 7). However, at work, the development of long-term intimacy is not one of the purposes of conversation. A salesperson working in a large department store simply needs to present and project a friendly face rather than a face that leads to the development of intimacy with customers. Relationships at work don't develop in intimacy, and at work they are often specifically prohibited from doing so (even *consensual* sex can lead to dismissal).

The Workplace as a Culture

At work, little bits of knowledge are invaluable, such as knowing the photocopier etiquette. But such things are not always part of the formal training, which is usually concerned with "bigger issues" like the president's welcome message to a college.

Socialization into the workplace is done most often through special, if occasionally very brief, training that involves at least being shown the ropes by another employee. Although the organization expects that this will involve watching corporate videos, attending management team training sessions, going to retreats, and doing bonding exercises, individuals may form relationships with others in the organization that undercut these things. Such socialization also involves the instillation of the organizational culture into its newest members.

Organizational culture is a popular notion, but it is a difficult one to pin down. It is important to recognize the fundamental truth that *people* are part of, not detached from, systems that influence them. People carry around their history in any organization or group—as a structure; as agreed memory; as meaning; as narrative; as persuasive practices. Their relationships to one another in the workplace, then, are key to understanding it.

Organizational Culture and Routines

Bastien, McPhee, and Bolton (1995) reported a longitudinal case study of an administrative unit of a large nonfederal government organization following the election of a new chief executive officer (CEO). They were interested in the ways that attempts to change the climate become the dominant characteristic of the emerging situation as a new CEO begins to impose a character on the organization. For example, if a new CEO wants people to treat one another differently, it is not as easy as just making a decree about it. People have long-standing relationships with each other that the new ordinance may undermine.

In most cases, of course, such changes are minor or illusory. Much that has gone on before continues to go on the way it always has—partly because the workplace consists of existing relationships between people who have had long-term histories of interactions with each other in particular roles. These patterns of interaction emphasize that people are neither purely free co-constructors of social reality nor simple pawns moved around by abstract social structural forces. In fact, their existing interpersonal relationships with each other produce and reproduce social systems and their structures—through social interaction and long-term relations, much as Society's Secret Agents reinforce our views about what is acceptable behavior in public.

Structuration Theory

Giddens's (1991) **structuration theory** points to the regularities of human relationships that act as rules and resources drawn on to enable or constrain social interaction. Examples are norms or habitual expectations of how to communicate and relate to one another. You can certainly reinterpret structures as relational expectations that transact the "workplace," organizations, leadership, and performance—a complex way of saying what we just said! The relationships and expectations become a context for future interaction. Giddens smartly changes the notion of *structure* in organizations from static or objective hierarchies into something *structured by the transactions* themselves and the communication between people in everyday life relationships within the organization.

In essence, the distinction between structure (rules, policies, and resources) and systems (patterns of relations) amounts to a *duality of structure*—two different ways of creating the same eventual outcome. Also vital to this theory are *organizational production and reproduction* over time (including specific organizational practices such as communicative behavior and material reality). It is no surprise that organizations produce and reproduce themselves over time through conversations between the individuals within the organization. For example, people refer to previous experiences or decisions that have been made; people remember the way things used to be done; and as each new person enters and older people leave, passed down from one workplace generation to the other is a system of beliefs and practices about how the organization works.

In the workplace, then, there are certain things that get *done* in the relational talk more noticeably than in other places. These create the kinds of repetition of structure that Giddens (1991) emphasizes. They all take their force from the way they are repeatedly enacted in talk and relationships, however, and not from the formal structures that exist as abstract forms. For example, if your instructor tells you to answer a question and you do so, then you have transacted the power of your instructor over you. There is no *abstract structure* that forces you to answer. Instead you do so because you understand the norms and customs of the organization and you transact them in your behavior, based on knowledge of proper relationships with the instructor.

This means that organizational climate is not a property of organizations but an interpersonally and relationally *transacted* product of communication based on the relationships between people. By constantly referring to a particular theme (customer satisfaction, for example), workers in the workplace make it a theme of the organization's culture. It therefore experiences **sedimentation**, or is laid down into the organization by the workers' talk and everyday relational practices: The repetitive structuration of talk/repetitive patterns of communication and relationships gradually drops to the bottom like sediment in a river and so affects the future course that the river takes, as it were.

In other words, the "structures" that matter in an organization are not physical buildings or the formal hierarchical organization "reports to" charts but derive from the sedimented ways in which the people have repeatedly reinforced their relational and conversational interactions. It is these repetitive conversational

structuration theory: points to the regularities of human relationships that act as rules and resources drawn on to enable or constrain social interaction

sedimentation: the process by which repeated everyday practices create a "structure" for performance in the future, as a river deposits sediment that alters or maintains its course over time

ANALYZING
EVERYDAY COMMUNICATION

Workplace Communication

In any organization to which you belong, listen for the number of times somebody says "That's the way we do things around here" or makes an equivalent claim.

QUESTIONS TO CONSIDER

1. In what way do such statements establish and continue the norms of an organization and invalidate anybody raising questions or new ways of doing things?
2. How do you hear people counteracting such claims, and what is the outcome?

patterns and topics that create any sedimented structures that an organization has in its practices of work. This suggestion is referred to as a **structurational approach** and serves to create those structures that we see as organizations. It is very much like saying that a village is not simply the buildings but the people and the interactions that they have with one another: It is more of a community than a set of houses.

Structurational approaches therefore offer basically a social constructivist and critical approach looking at how people enact and enable or contain future interactions through their talk. Surprise! "Structure" is all about communication and *relationships!*

Workplace culture, workplace groups, and workplace communities consist of thinking, relating, reflective people who monitor their own behavior and tend to repeat it rather than reinvent a new style each day (who has time?). It is easier to take the path of least resistance—the way we have always done things around here, the way you and I interacted yesterday, or the way our relationship was before today (take another look at relational continuity constructional units, described in Chapter 7). Thus a daily routine of relational interaction in the workplace ultimately becomes the basis for future interaction.

The format into which new recruits are introduced and the patterns of existing relationships into which they must fit become key—perhaps individuals may get minor things to change a little bit, but ultimately the organization continues through its existing patterns of talk and relationships among the individuals who live their lives within it. Thus the appearance of "structure" in an organization really depends entirely on the relationships and familiar patterns of communication that repeat themselves in everyday life, even in the workplace. You can give incoming first-year students a tour of the buildings, but that doesn't teach them how things work inside of them or which are the best instructors. These latter aspects of the college come from other people, not from a map.

Meaning Making

We mentioned earlier Weick's (1995) notion that meaning making lies behind the activities of organizations and people at work. He interprets such "organizing" of expectations as a result of the human search for meaning. Humans attempt to make sense of a stream of events by using recipes, guides, norms, or selective attention to events as a means of reducing equivocality or uncertainty. Weick does not emphasize the preexisting relationships between people and their rhetorical visions as we do, however.

Most often the way in which people do this organizing of experience is through interpersonal communication about what is going on or through framing the situation in particular ways that allow good contexts for expectations to be discussed (Fairhurst & Sarr, 1996). Fairhurst (2007) extends this notion to the idea that norms and other meaning systems are transacted in the discourse between people in an organization—again, though not stated directly by Fairhurst, this is a relational point. In other words, it is talk between people who have existing relationships with one

structurational approach: to look at how people enact and enable or contain future interactions through their talk

another that creates and reinforces frames and norms rather than vice versa. To this we would add that the continuity of relationships between people over time tends to reinforce both talk and norms. Since discourse presumes that at least a basic relationship exists between the speakers—otherwise it could not occur—it is relationships that lie at the base of all organizational "structures."

The workplace can be placed in a frame of *moral ordering* and a social ordering or an *interaction order* (Duck, 2011). The workplace is understood within a particular sequence and structure for behavior that is particular to the place where it is done (scene:act ratio) so that judgments can be made about people's performance. The performance of a work identity is evaluated relative to the norms of the workplace and also relative to relational needs where the two conflict.

The Organization and Its Norms

Your school probably has a document called something like "The Code of Student Life," and this describes behaviors that the school expects you to carry out and those it expects you to avoid. For example, it will talk about civility in the classroom and the punishment that you can expect for plagiarizing or copying other people's work. Just as in groups (Chapter 9), organizations develop *norms* that establish and clarify the expectations that will apply while you are a member of the organization. Norms are parts of structures as traditionally perceived, and so are rules and resources. A norm is an unstated rule that is understood to be represented in a pattern of behavior, whereas rules and resources are more formally stated. These appear to represent formal power or at least resources to which someone can refer in order to exert power. "It says here in paragraph 9 subsection 2a that you must not [do what you did], so you're fired." The real question is how this works relationally and the extent to which such organizational norms are actually about relationships.

Frames and Hierarchies: Formal Versus Informal Power

One evident norm or rule in an organization is expectation of hierarchy—indeed hierarchy is a defining characteristic of organizations. Organizations offer guidelines but also constrain the activities of individual workers by insisting that messages work through the chain of command, for example. Employees often compensate for weaknesses in the chain of command by forming informal communication networks and resistance ("Let's work more slowly for Duck & McMahan's Drain Cleaning Company until they fire the terrible supervisor. That'll clog 'em up!"). However, as we have noted, these actually come down to relational activities.

So before you get carried away with the mistaken notion that we are talking about structures in a traditional sense, let's take another look at how norms and rules actually work in an organization through relationships and talk. We already wrote in Chapter 9 about the differences between formal and informal power. In any organization there are people designated as the powerful and the powerless, but even norms and documents can be challenged or amended when they create relational tensions. In fact, positions can be reversed when the powerless activate the key buttons in the whole enterprise: acceptance and deference. If the powerless refuse their deference to those who are placed in authority over them, then those people have no authority over them. Slaves can revolt like Spartacus (and threaten the society as a whole) or workers can strike, and the basic operation of the business itself is placed at risk.

Workers may refuse to obey or may choose to resist management and its instructions (Mumby, 2006). Resistance may be done in talk or behavior that shows a worker's lack of respect for the management. For example, Mumby reports one of the workers in his organization made a point of reading the newspaper when he was supposed to be working and of talking negatively about the management and its inability to stop him from doing so.

Other forms of resistance to management may be captured in talk that shows reluctance to do the work or actual withdrawal of effort that involves individuals taking longer to do the job than they know they actually need. Those who read newspapers when they should be working or who talk disrespectfully about management are projecting personal identities as resistant and uninvolved relative to the norms that are expected in the workplace. In their own way, through their everyday communication practices, they are doing their own tiny but personal "identity thing" to resist an organizational culture.

Stereotyping can also be used to resist membership or inclusion of particular individuals in the organization, and it can be reflected in talk. Mumby (2006) reports on a job he took as a student in an organization that involved large amounts of manual labor. His inclusion in the organization was initially resisted by the permanent employees who resented college students being allowed to take temporary positions in a job where they were experts and permanently employed. As part of their working banter, they performed "working-class masculinity." This involves demonstration of physical strength but also knowledge about technical machinery, which would be lacking in someone with a college education who had only "book learning" at his or her disposal, not practical skills (Mumby, 2006).

They continually referred to his inability to operate machinery that they easily and effectively used day to day. Indeed, they were particularly overjoyed when he drove a large tractor into a ditch and had to be pulled out by others who were more used to operating the machine. From that point on, as mentioned in Chapter 9, they referred to him as "college boy," a tactic for excluding him from membership with the other manual laborers in the group, who did not go to college. Ultimately, however, they began to accept him because he passed or avoided other tricks and traps that they set for him, so he earned their ultimate respect and was eventually included in their relationships (Mumby, 2006).

Industrial Time

One feature of the workplace, which is characteristic of that set of circumstances and different from others, is that people there, as in any other culture, have a specific approach to time—in this case "industrial time." Before clocks were accurate, the predominance of agricultural work led to a vague approach to time based on the seasons, crop cycles, and the availability of daylight. There was very little need for punctuality as we understand it today (see Chapter 12 on polychronic and monochronic cultures). Once clocks had been introduced and industry had turned to a more repetitive performance of specific kinds of work using machines, it became important for employers to count the number of minutes when a worker was actually doing work for which he or she was paid by the minute or the hour.

This introduced the notion of **industrial time**, which is the time a person is actually counted as being at work and therefore is paid for doing such work. In the same way that individuals are able to show resistance to other work ethics, they resist the management's control over their time at work and become clock-watchers, downing tools at exactly 5:00 P.M. when their shift ends. This is a form of resistance that is obviously based on relationships of solidarity/connection with other workers as opposed to

industrial time: the attention to punctuality and dedication to a task that is connected with the nature of industry (clocking in, clocking out, lunch breaks, etc.)

management. And we have both noticed a curious tendency for undergraduates to snap their folders shut and start packing the bags two minutes before the end of a lecture! Why is that? They often miss the most interesting bits of a concluding summary.

The workers also talk about time and the amount of time that it should take to do a job. Workers often set about covering for one another during absences or periods of lateness—for example, "clocking in" to work for someone who has not arrived on time and will otherwise be penalized by the managers if they find out. These kinds of interpersonal favors for one another make the workplace operate through a relational base that brings workers together in a sense of community that resists management that otherwise would have perfect control over workers' personal time.

Contact With the Public: Customer-Client Relationships

First, it is necessary to distinguish between customer *relations* (customer service) and customer relation*ships,* which are defined by the boundary between the workplace and its external environment. In the first case, the customer is part of the work environment for the time when the customer is receiving service. In the second case, an attempt is made to establish a relationship that outlasts the temporary connection between customer and server. In the 1980s it was realized that it is far more expensive for an organization to acquire new customers than it is to retain old ones. At that point, Berry (1983) coined the term *relationship marketing* and emphasized the value to organizations of building constructive and long-term relationships with their clients.

A number of techniques have been used to retain customer loyalty even to the extent of an organization claiming to be friends with its customers as noted above in the case of Univision™. However, the differences between friendship in the real world and the kinds of friendship an organization attempts to establish with its customers are many and important. For example, self-disclosure is an important element of friendship development in the real world as we saw in Chapters 3 and 7. However, no organization is going to disclose its business plans to its customers even though it might want to obtain as much of your personal information as it can extract from you without seeming intrusive. So you can bet your bottom dollar that the self-disclosure between a large organization and yourself will never be equalized or reciprocal: In fact, your bottom dollar is what the organization wants.

Equally important are such elements as trust and commitment in everyday relationships. It can take a very long time for two individuals to build up a sense of mutual trust, and it is difficult for organizations to shortcut this process. However, the concept of relationship marketing is an interesting confirmation of the breadth that can be developed from the perspective we are taking in this book (Carl, 2006). Organizations

COMMUNICATION + YOU

How You Relate to Product Branding

Susan Fournier (1998) demonstrated that many people define themselves in terms of brands to which they feel particularly loyal and even see themselves in terms of such products as shampoo or motorcycles (Harley rider) as defining characteristics of their identity. Fournier and Alvarez (2012) showed the validity of the relationship premise of the level of consumers' lived experiences with their brands. Consumers simply see themselves in terms of the products that they consume and often feel loyal to the brands that "make them who they are." More than this, though, they experience an actual relationship with the brand and feel it is comforting.

QUESTIONS TO CONSIDER

1. Are there any brands that you are loyal to? Why are you loyal to them?
2. How do you feel when you use or consume those brands?

What seems to be going on in this photograph, and what would you say is the problem with what is happening?

attempt to reproduce friendships in their customers even though this rarely works in the same way as relationships between individuals in real life (Chapter 7).

The Workplace as Relationships

People have traditionally confused "organization" with physical and hierarchical structure rather than considering it as something, like families and groups, that is *transacted* in discourse. Yet relationships are the true driving force of any organization. Relationships and relating are built into any existing organizations that have long-term histories, memories of working together in the past, and/or recollections of how things were done last time a similar problem arose. Indeed the cyclical rhythms of the workplace exist only in memories and talk about memories. All of these factors are overlooked in traditional ways of seeing organizations as physical or bureaucratic structures, which are as natural as ways to think of organizations as they are traditional.

As Sias (2009, p. 1) notes, "The daily activities in a typical organization . . . occur in the context of interpersonal relationships" (see Table 10.2). The relationships at work are usually *involuntary,* and people do not usually choose their coworkers: They are just there when you are hired. If you're lucky, you'll find them friendly and welcoming, and you may even become friends—or more—with them.

The converse of that, however, is often a problem in organizations: You cannot always get away from your coworkers even if you don't like them. However, the same point is true in both cases: Problems and successes in the workplace both have a relational basis. This is usually celebrated in organizational communication literature as a relatively novel approach these days and also as obvious. "Good working relationships" like "good communication" generally are accepted as the cure for all organizational ills

Table 10.2 Some Daily Activities of Organizations That Occur in the Context of Interpersonal Relationships

1. directing	12. interviewing
2. collaborating	13. reporting
3. information gathering	14. gossiping
4. information sharing	15. debating
5. rewarding	16. supporting
6. punishing	17. selling
7. conflict	18. buying
8. resolution of conflict	19. ordering
9. controlling	20. managing
10. feedback	21. leading
11. persuasion	22. following

SOURCE: Sias, (2009, p. 1).

and as the basis for all organizational successes. Managers are encouraged to become friendly with their workers, up to a point that does not border on sexual harassment and certainly to nurture and mentor them rather than just order them about. The problem is that it is all too easy to regard such terms as *leader, manager, worker,* and others that operate in organizations in the workplace as generalized abstractions rather than as *real face-to-face interactions between real people.*

We have said that relationship processes are the basis for the workplace, but we have not talked about friendship and romance in the workplace—or even strong hatred. What happens when relationships at work get personal? The workplace contains many different kinds of relationships, some of which are good and some of which are bad. Some people get along well; some do not. Some relationships get very close, and that can create suspicions or "political issues" for the other workers in the same place. Likewise, if you are friends with someone who then gets promoted, what happens to the relationship?

Relationships as Workplace Challenges

Parts of an organization do not always act in concert and occasionally attempt to undermine one another. Sales teams sometimes promise the impossible in order to make a sale, and the technicians who have to make the product as specified simply cannot live up to the promise. A product may look good to the designers, but the bean counters in accounting are not able to find the dollars to make it happen.

Of course, every introductory textbook with a chapter on organizational communication deals with these issues and with the conflict that is based on differences in the internal communication between managers and workers in the workplace. These issues should not be ignored, but we are more interested in the problems of communication that arise from the relationships between people there rather than the managerially biased issues of how an "organization" (seen as a structure) communicates down its "structural" chains of command and lines of management. There are other books where you can read about that if it interests you. Here we give it all a very quick summary before moving on to what we think really matters: relationships between the people in the workplace.

The standard problems within organizations are assumed to result from managers' failure to "communicate" properly with their workers. For example, it tends to be an assumption by the manager that "if I know it, then everyone must know it." This leads to a series of difficulties for the workers who simply do not know what the manager or leader knows and yet require it in order to operate effectively. It is therefore important for managers to make their staff openly aware of what they know and everything relevant to the workers' performance. The problem is that people say such things without defining what "communication" means. You now know that communication as action can be entirely ineffective, like posting company policies on a notice board and hoping people read them. Communication must be at least interactive, where the two sides interact and do active and critical listening (Chapter 6). Best, however, is if it is communication as transaction, such that the interaction builds trust, confidence, a sense of membership and belonging, and mutual interest.

Make your case

Should an Organization Interfere With Relationships in the Workplace?

Romantic relationships often develop in the workplace. Adults who have full-time jobs spend a majority of their waking hours at work, so this is not a too surprising.

QUESTIONS TO CONSIDER

1. Do you think that people in an organization should not be allowed to have consensual romantic relationships with one another, or is it an unfair restriction on their freedom if an organization bans such relationships?
2. What sorts of circumstances might alter your judgment? Make an argument that supports your opinion and indicate how you would make decisions about the appropriateness of such a relationship.

By the way...

Spillover From Work to Home and Vice Versa

Now that you have read most of this chapter, you may recognize some of the complexities about modern life and communication. As the world of work becomes more reliant on such facilities as computer usage, the Internet, purchases online, and Google searches, so there has developed an expectation that managerial staff will check their e-mail at all times of the week, day and night. (Please note that smart instructors never do this, so do not e-mail instructors at ridiculous hours and expect an immediate response.) This makes it hard for people to differentiate the two spheres of activity, and they now no longer act as if the workplace and the rest of life are distinct and separate areas of life. Students take their laptops with them when they are out sunbathing, and often use social time concurrently with media usage (or, even more unthinkable, they may check Facebook during lectures!).

QUESTIONS TO CONSIDER

1. Does a distinction between leisure time and work time any longer make sense, or do the two forms of life basically intersect in the modern world?
2. Is the notion of "spillover" from work to home just a simplistic idea now that work and the rest of life are so closely interwoven anyway?

Another common belief is that everybody hates bureaucracy and that leaders should not burden themselves or their workers with bureaucratic written policies and procedures. However, such a refusal to clarify policies and procedures can lead to confusion. When something is written down, at least everyone can refer to the same document in order to resolve confusion. This is compounded when managers fail to understand the importance of communication or else assume that it just happens. It is very important that managers ensure that communication has actually taken place with those people who need to know the information and that the policies are enforced.

As you learned in Chapter 6, active listening is an extremely important part of communication in everyday life, and it is a significant contributor to good working relationships. Many managers believe that it is their job to tell employees what to do and that employees have no place in directing the enterprise. However, many employees have important things to say, and a good manager will be willing to listen in the ways that we indicated in Chapters 6 and 9. Managers need to listen to their workers, and personnel need to listen to one another before it is too late and the communication problems result in a catastrophe. Personal communication between managers and employees or among employees can use an existing relational base between the people in order to pick from a collection of data the information that is important.

Proper—that is, interactive and transactive—communication in an organization is made more effective when group members question one another and ask pertinent questions in order to avoid groupthink (see Chapter 9). It is important for good managers and effective workers to respect and value what they hear other people saying and to clarify that they have correctly interpreted it. Each person in an organization needs to take responsibility for speaking up when he or she doesn't understand a communication and for making suggestions about ways to improve communication in the organization.

Legitimate and Illegitimate Organizational Interference in Life

In everyday relationships you recognize limits on the questions that you can ask people without breaking relational rules. In the workplace, however, these rules may be different. The workplace occupies a legitimate place in people's lives but sometimes spills over into the parts of life that used to be private, nonwork areas, at least while people are at work. The frequent use of the Internet, cell phones, and various technologies that blur the difference between work space and home space, for example, means that we are often unable to draw sharp distinctions between whether someone is at work or at home.

This can lead to some negative consequences for the home life, whereas the developments of technology can lead to some interesting relational consequences for the workplace itself. Workers are often expected to be available by e-mail 24/7, and they accept calls on their cell phones even during weekends. In essence, these come down to the question of your rights to keep the workplace out of your home and your rights over your privacy at work. What, then, are your relational rights in connection with other people in the workplace, and what legitimate limits are there that you can expect to be honored? You might even discuss them in class. We expect that your instructor has some unexpressed thoughts about student e-mails.

Spillover From Work Into Daily Life

Like a family or a friendship, no organization exists alone in the social world; instead one has multiple points of contact with other organizations and people and their lives. One obvious problem is that people may bring home their work problems and be preoccupied during family time. A corresponding problem that goes the other way is that a personal problem at home can have a negative impact on someone's performance at work (Goodman & Crouter, 2009). If my partner or child is sick, then I will be anxious to check frequently that things are not getting worse, or I may not be able to concentrate on the project. These are known as "spillover effects," and although apparently they occur in unrelated spheres of life, they demonstrate that the different relational worlds in which a person moves cannot be so easily separated.

Totten (2006) noted that there is also a difficulty in negotiating familial and professional roles. Role negotiation occurs when a person has two competing roles to enact at once, such as representing oneself as both a responsible employee and a caring parent if a child is sick at home. There are many occasions when an individual is faced with a choice between doing the work of the workplace and doing the work of parenting. The spillover of one kind of caring may spoil one's attention to the other. A sick kid can mean you have to cancel clients, take a day off work, or eat into your holiday or sick time, let alone seeing the key project you were working on fall slowly past its deadline. Although one has a clear duty to attend to the needs of one's family and particularly young children, it is also clear that an organization has certain rights to expect an employee to perform roles that are required as part of the job he or she is paid to do.

Surveillance in an Organization

Organizations have a legitimate right to expect not to be the victim of theft by their employees and vice versa. By the same token, they may have a right that you do not use your personal computer in the office for playing Internet war games during office hours or watching *Game of Thrones*, a point of view shared by some fellow workers who otherwise feel cheated by their coworkers (Zweig & Webster, 2002). Misuse of employer resources, whether physical resources or time that is being paid for, is a serious problem. The issue comes down to a relational one because the employer's response amounts to an invasion of personal privacy and a breach of relational trust. Zweig (2005) explored surveillance and electronic performance monitoring and noted that these cross the basic psychological spaces and boundaries between the employer and the employee—and hence create a different type of relationship between them.

ETHICAL ISSUE

Is it unethical for an employer to expect an employee to work at home? Does it make a difference if the employee is paid hourly and not "on the clock" or if the person is salaried and expected to achieve a particular output?

Most workers accept that it is legitimate for an organization to keep an eye on what its workers do and to carry out other practices related to ensuring the efficient completion of work. For example, it is reasonable for employers to expect that someone who is contracted to work for a certain number of hours per day at a particular place should actually do so, and that he or she should not call his or her family and have extended chats instead of working (perhaps except in the case of

DISCIPLINARY **DEBATE**

Information Is Power, but How Much Power Should Organizations Have Over Your Private Life?

Why would you resent secret company surveillance? If your boss is looking over your shoulder and catches you writing personal e-mails during company time, you would probably accept it as your fault. On the other hand, if the organization routinely monitors your e-mail—which it probably does, as a matter of fact—you might feel that your privacy is being invaded. Why might this be so? Reflect on nonverbal communication in Chapter 5 and consider whether there are any parallels in the situations of nonverbal violation and electronic violation.

QUESTIONS TO CONSIDER

1. Would it be OK for a company to check through all employees' purses and pockets before they left at the end of the day in case they were stealing paper clips?
2. Is it OK for a company to report customers' personal buying preferences to another company with different marketing strategies?

family emergencies). Definitely he or she should not bring in a camp bed and take a deep sleep during work time. All of these things would be seen as unreasonable by coworkers.

Zweig (2005) showed that some forms of "intrusion" are regarded as acceptable, even if not desirable, within the parameters of the employer-employee relationship. Some supervision is seen as a violation of personal liberty—for example, the opening of employees' mail or unreasonable searching of bags and clothing. On the other hand, it is regarded as an acceptable part of the duties of the job that one may be timed and observed or told what to do or moved from one task to another at the will of the manager. Would you accept the same rules if your friends proposed them?

Just as in other relationships, people regard themselves as having charge of certain kinds of private information in the workplace—that is, information over which they have ownership and control (Petronio, 2002). There is a certain boundary within which people will tolerate intrusions by an employer as long as this is done with one's express or implicit permission. When permission has not been given, a psychological and relational barrier gets crossed, and this changes the nature of the relationship between employer and worker. Reconsider Chapter 3 and what was acceptable as self-disclosure and what was not. Does this apply equally to relationships at work? What questions about your private life is it legitimate for your boss or coworkers to ask?

Although such issues are realistic in organizations that take a traditional and managerially focused approach to the workplace, the issues that concern the majority of workers in the workplace are based on interpersonal matters: communication in everyday life and relationships.

The Downside of Good Relationships at Work

So far we have focused on the importance of relationships, essentially distinguishing members from nonmembers (by jargon or clothing, for example), the differences in number of participants and interactions in any given organization and knowledge of membership that individuals in an organization have, and the different sorts of membership that are possible in an organization. Now we turn to the interpersonal issues in the workplace, and we of course emphasize communication and relationships.

We noted earlier in the chapter that there is a distinction between relational goals and the instrumental work goals of the workplace. This raises a number of questions for you to think about concerning cases where work spills over into relational life or where relational life spills over into work. In the previous section, we looked at work spilling over into private life, and in this section we will look at the opposite: What happens when friendship or romance spills over into the workplace?

Relationships at work: In what ways might personal relationships at work have a negative effect on productivity?

Love, Sex, and Hate in the Workplace

You may have noticed that we have written so far as if the workplace contains only particular types of interactants and they are basically limited to customers and salespersons, leaders and followers, or members of sales and marketing. We have emphasized the individual nature of relationships that occur when salespeople and marketing people hold meetings with one another, but it is obvious that the workplace can contain a number of different levels of relationship from friendship to outright hostility or sexual harassment. How does the depiction of relationships between the sexes in *Mad Men* (purporting to be about the 1960s) diverge from what is acceptable today?

In extremely broad terms, the types of relationships in the workplace can be strict, formal, hierarchical, collegial, or a mix of the four. In the cult movie *Office Space* the creepy manager, Lumbergh, attempts in an ingratiating way to be overly friendly and informal while still exercising power and authority. The mismatch between the two is part of the problem that makes the workplace so unpleasant for his subordinates, and he is judged as insincere because of this discrepancy.

In *Mad Men,* both Don Draper and Roger Sterling are sexual predators and feel no constraints when it comes to taking advantage of their female secretaries or other employees. The problem that we identified at the beginning of the chapter is that there is a natural inborn conflict between the demands of the workplace and the demands of relationships. The workplace represents an interaction order—that is, it is based on rules. Every workplace has its own norms and behaviors that emphasize the team and the cooperative performance of teamwork in order to fulfill instrumental goals most enjoyably for those involved. On the other hand, friendship is not supposed to be instrumental. What happens, then, when people who work together become friends, and is it good for them or for the organization or not?

Obviously if the relationship veers over the line into sexual harassment, then it is bad for everyone and not acceptable. We say more about this later, but this is an extreme and despicable form of behavior that is further off the charts than anything that concerns us at the moment. Let's first deal with less extreme problems.

Kram and Isabella (1985) identified three different types of friendly or collegial relationships between people in an organization. All three types—*information peer relationships, collegial peer relationships,* and *special peer relationships*—are described in detail in Table 10.3.

There is particular suspicion when two members in the same place become romantically involved (Dillard & Miller, 1988), and a fear may exist that information

ETHICAL ISSUE

It is ethical for a boss to initiate a romantic relationship with an employee? Is it ethical for an employee to initiate a romantic relationship with a boss?

Table 10.3 The Three Types of Friendly or Collegial Relationships Between People in an Organization

Information Peer Relationships	• Low on personal self-disclosure, but information about the task is freely and openly discussed • Civil and cordial but not close
Collegial Peer Relationships	• Individuals at work regard one another as friends and act in all respects in ways indistinguishable from friends outside the workplace; that is, they self-disclose and joke around and arrange to meet outside the workplace for social events
Special Peer Relationships	• Characterized by very high openness, self-disclosure, and intimacy • Virtually indistinguishable from best-friend relationships outside of the workplace

SOURCE: Kram & Isabella (1985).

shared with one person will be automatically transmitted to the second. Therefore in the workplace caution can develop if a budding romance is suspected. Workers not only expect the productivity of the lovers to go down as they spend more time adoring one another but also tend to be careful in their dealings with members of a romantic couple or others who are known to be close friends (Sias, 2009).

Favors for Buddies

One of the ways in which organizations and workplaces operate is through the interpersonal relationships among the people in those places and organizations. As a sales manager, you may be prepared to cut a special deal for someone in another organization because you know him or her personally. Therefore your organization benefits from a sale it otherwise might not make. The other organization benefits from the relationship that you have with its buyer and therefore gets something it wants at a cheaper rate than it could get from the competition. In the supply side of an organization (the sources from which it buys the parts to make the product that it then sells to other customers), these sorts of favorable relationships are vital ways for the organization to cut its costs (C. Heal, personal communication, May 23, 2008).

Although it appears on the surface that commercial transactions are carried out between one organization and another, in fact they are done through the personal relationship between one member (or several members) of one organization and those of another over the phone, in group meetings, on e-mail, or by other interpersonal means. It is vital for organizations to maintain good personal relationships among the individuals who do this sort of business on their behalf. Once again, then, "organizational work" is done at the relational level.

You're My Boss, but You Were My Friend

Many people in the workplace develop friendly relationships with one another when they are at the same level because it makes their work easier. However, it can create problems when one of them is promoted over the other (Zorn, 1995), assuming that friends at work are freely chosen and real. However, the expectations of friendship require the revelation of self and perhaps secrets. This may pose no threat to anyone while the two individuals remain at the same level in the hierarchy of the organization. However, if one of them is promoted to a rank higher than the other, then the information acquired during the friendship may become a source of conflict, particularly if the information leads to a negative assessment of a person's capacity to fulfill the job properly (Zorn, 1995).

In addition, the knowledge that a person is friends with the boss on a personal level can have an adverse effect on the other members of the same team. They naturally enough expect that the friends will look after one another and may even act as a team in the political arena of the organization. Workers tend to become suspicious that the boss will show favoritism toward friends, and this suspicion, of course, has an undesirable effect on morale.

ETHICAL ISSUE

Is it unethical for a boss to be friends with an employee?

Employee-Abusive Communication

Sometimes workers are not nice to one another, and it is only recently that communication researchers have begun to understand the frequency of hostile workplaces and bullying. It is a question not just of personal criticism or attacks on appearance but of "emotional tyranny . . . of the weak by the powerful" (Waldron, 2000, p. 67). Backstabbing gossip and derogatory talk about other employees are also examples of employee-abusive communication. In fact, many forms of contemptuous or discounting messages are available in the workplace just as they are in other places. The workplace has often been the home to hostile interviews, but in the everyday running of an organization, the kinds of talk that go on and count as abusive run from offensive jokes to shunning and ostracism to the ignoring of an individual's requests or withholding important information that the person needs in order to complete the job properly (Lutgen-Sandvik & McDermott, 2008).

Sexual harassment is an obvious example of employee abusive communication when it is defined as "any unwelcome sexual advance or conduct on the job that creates an intimidating, hostile, or offensive working environment. Any conduct of a sexual nature that makes an employee uncomfortable has the potential to be sexual harassment" (England, 2012, p. 3). Although we have frequently pointed to the evident sexism and sexual harassment that were prominent in the 1960s as depicted by the TV show *Mad Men,* it would be entirely too complacent to suggest that the culture of modern organizations has changed in such a way that sexual harassment has been eliminated. Rather it is the case that more organizations are aware of the legal liabilities that follow from improper policing of this aspect of their culture and have become much more sensitive to the realization that victims often are telling the truth and not, as used to be assumed, simply making things up. Most colleges have a policy about sexual harassment that makes it clear it should not be part of their culture, and if you find that this is not a promise that is honored in your institution, then you should immediately report it to someone who can institute organizational/cultural change.

sexual harassment: "any unwelcome sexual advance or conduct on the job that creates an intimidating, hostile, or offensive working environment; any conduct of a sexual nature that makes an employee uncomfortable" (England, 2012, p. 3)

Skills You Can Use: Does a Communication Scholar Understand the Workplace Better Than Anyone Else?

The research literature in interpersonal communication concerning the workplace is most often biased toward hierarchies, structures, and a managerial point of view, as stated earlier. The question that we want you to consider is the extent to which the literature on "organizations" actually applies to real life as you know it from any workplace you have ever experienced.

Focus Questions Revisited

Where do people learn about the workplace?

People's ideas about the nature of work and the workplace are obtained early in childhood through family stories and discussions with others at school or through the media, which present certain professions and jobs as more or less valuable than others and stress the importance of work as part of identity or the value of "success."

Going to work: What do you need to know?

An organization can be viewed as a simple structure as in an organizational chart or as a sedimented set of practices that are transacted through repetitive communication, memory, narrative, and routine daily discourse. A better way of looking at the workplace, however, is as a set of interpersonal relationships between specific individuals.

How are organizations constituted as a "culture" of interaction and relationships between members?

Although we often talk about organizations transacting business with other organizations, in fact these transactions occur at the face-to-face interpersonal level between individuals or groups of individuals who know one another, and this is a relational activity. It is important to focus away from looking mostly at the managers in the situation and to look at the everyday discourses between other employees who transact their relationships within the organization.

Is the workplace best explained by a relationship approach?

Since the workplace is another frame for real interactions and although it has hierarchical structures, there is no reason to suppose that relationship types there are different from those anywhere else, especially as these may be transacted in communication.

Key Concepts

continuation of identity 203
formality/hierarchy 205
industrial time 210
instrumental goals 205
professional face 203
relational goals 205
sedimentation 207
sexual harassment 219
structurational approach 208
structuration theory 207
vocational anticipatory socialization 201

Questions to Ask Your Friends

1. Ask your friends if they get offended by other students in a large lecture class listening to an iPod through the whole lecture. Does it disrupt their learning in the lecture or not? Are colleges right to assume that it does?
2. Ask your friends how they would react to the discovery that you recommended a particular product to them but you had been paid by a large organization in order to make the recommendation. Would they assume that you were acting in their best interests and really believed in the product (Carl, 2006)?
3. What is the most interesting example that you and your friends can produce about the way in which front and back regions operate in the workplace?

Media Connections

1. Several movies and TV shows depict organizations and behavior in the workplace that could help illustrate ideas presented in this chapter—for example, *Office Space, The Office,* or *Waiting . . .*
2. Occasionally, organizations fall over their own rules or objectives and make serious errors because of disobeying their own rules or following them too closely. Watch *Titanic* for examples of organizational hierarchy tripping itself up.
3. What organizational cultures exist, and what is the difference between them as represented by *Mad Men* versus almost anything else, or between the Drug Enforcement Administration and drug cartel cultures in *Breaking Bad?*

Student Study Site

Sharpen your skills with SAGE edge at edge.sagepub.com/duckciel2e

SAGE edge for students provides a personalized approach to help you accomplish your coursework goals in an easy-to-use learning environment.

Chapter Outline

Patient and Provider Relationships
- Patient-Provider Identities
- How Patients and Providers Communicate
- Improving Patient-Provider Communication
- Benefits of Effective Patient-Provider Relationships

Social Networks and Health
- Social Networks and Health and Lifestyles
- Social Networks and Support
- Secondary Goals of Social Support
- Everyday Communication and the Foundation of Social Support
- Communication Privacy Management

Media, Technology, and Health
- Entertainment Media and Health
- News Media and Health
- Advertising Medications
- Health Communication and the Internet

Focus Questions Revisited

Key Concepts

Questions to Ask Your Friends

Media Connections

11 Health Communication

Health communication is not something that is confined to visits to a doctor's office or a hospital but instead occurs in communication and everyday life. It comprises lifestyle choices people make, how they talk with their friends and families about illness and health, the kinds of social support that they give and receive, decisions to reveal or conceal private information about pain or fear, media images and appeals splashed over billboards or the sides of buses and on TV, and Internet activity. Life expectancy and disease survival rates are even highly correlated with the number of friends that you have and how much you talk to people every day (Duck, 2007). In short, health communication is very much built into both everyday communication and relationships.

Emphasizing the role of communication in health may seem somewhat curious at first. Many people may consider that health issues are confined to the physical or biological and not connected to the symbolic or relational. Health and illness are indeed very much physical, but how we think about them and respond to them is very much symbolic and relational.

This shift in thinking may be a bit confusing, so let us consider the example of cancer. From a physical or biological standpoint, this disease involves the abnormal activity or breakdown of cells within a body. However, what it *means* to have cancer or what it *means* for a friend, romantic partner, or family member to have cancer is symbolic, and cancer has relational effects. For example, it may restrict movement, reduce energy, decrease sociability, increase tiredness, and make people feel uncomfortable "being seen like this." How societies or cultures *respond* to cancer is symbolic and relational. How people *deal* with the disease is symbolic and relational.

Health communication is a broad area within the discipline of communication. So, this chapter serves as a broad introduction to this area by examining three key topics of health communication: (1) patient-provider relationships, (2) social networks, and (3) media and technology.

Although health communication is not confined to medical settings, patient-provider relationships and their corresponding interactions have a tremendous effect on everyday experience and health decisions. Unfortunately, communication between patients and providers is often problematic and counterproductive, with many patients feeling treated dismissively by doctors who think they are gods. On the other hand, many doctors feel frustrated that patients cannot remember simple instructions on how to take their pills. We examine typical patient-provider interactions and discuss suggestions for developing more effective patient-provider relationships.

FOCUS QUESTIONS

1. How do patients and providers generally communicate?
2. How can patient and provider communication be improved?
3. How do social networks influence lifestyle choices through everyday communication?
4. How do social networks provide support?
5. In what ways do media and technology impact issues of health?

How might the development of each patient-provider relational identity facilitate this patient's disclosure about his concerns to his therapist? What are the risks of each approach?

We then explore the impact of social networks on health, examining the influence of friends, families, and others on lifestyle choices or willingness to accept health advice and the influence of everyday communication on social support. Since health issues are often considered very personal and private, we also discuss how people decide whether to share this information with others.

Finally, we examine how media and technology influence health communication and what people make of government health campaigns. We explore how entertainment and news/health media impact people's lifestyle choices, their understanding of health and illness, and their expectations of treatment. Then, we discuss the use of the Internet when searching for health-related information and when seeking social support and ask you to think about the way in which the availability of health webpages on the Internet may have made a physician's job easier or more difficult.

Patient and Provider Relationships

Patients and providers (medical doctors, nurses, dentists, dental hygienists, optometrists, physical therapists, psychologists, and so on) meet in a variety of circumstances. Patient need for expert help runs the whole gamut from "Stop me dying when I don't even know where I am and have no control over anything at all" (Secklin, 2001) to "I've got this embarrassing itch, and all I want is for you to fill out a form prescribing the best cream for it, because the over-the-counter stuff that I can get for myself doesn't work."

Expectations of the proper or ideal relationship between patients and providers, the actual development of their relationship, the construction of relational identities, and the nature of their interactions will be guided by these situations and cultural expectations surrounding health.

Patient-Provider Identities

As with all relationships and identities, those created during patient and provider interactions are co-constructed. As such, both parties are responsible for the relationships and identities created during the interaction. However, interactants may not always agree with or approve of the relationships and relational identities being created.

Altercasting, as we discussed in Chapter 3, involves the ways in which a person's communication influences the identity of another person. Altercasting can work in two ways. First, a person's communication can force a particular identity on another person. A patient saying to a provider, "Well, you are the expert, so what do you suggest I do?" positions the provider a certain way and compels him or her to live up to that label.

Second, as a person attempts to create a particular identity, the communication of another may either affirm or negate that identity. If a patient suggests a particular

Table 11.1 Patient-Provider Identities

Machines and Mechanics	Providers are viewed as competent experts analytically diagnosing a physical problem and then fixing it. Patients are passive and allow the expert mechanic to give them a proper tune-up with little or no input or objection.
Children and Parents	Patients and providers display more emotional and personal involvement compared with the mechanistic view. However, the provider clearly portrays a dominant role of expert while the patient assumes a submissive and dependent role. This approach is generally the most common.
Consumers	Patients are increasingly viewing themselves as paying providers for specific information and expecting them to carry out their wishes. This view transacts the patient role as an increasingly dominant one.
Partners	Patients and providers work together to solve a problem and are viewed as equals, each bringing special knowledge to the interaction. The provider possesses unique medical knowledge, and the patient possesses unique knowledge about his or her physical and emotional state. Although this view is increasingly supported by medical professionals and patient groups, it is sometimes difficult to achieve due to preconceived notions of the patient and provider relationship along with unwillingness or inability on the part of both patients and providers.

treatment option to a provider, who in turn replies, "I am the expert, so you had better let me decide what is best for you," then the provider is combating the identity being created by the patient.

Based on cultural and individual expectations, Athena du Pre (2005, pp. 222–227) has noted the following identities created in patient and provider interactions: (a) machines and mechanics, (b) children and parents, (c) consumers, and (d) partners. These are presented in Table 11.1.

How Patients and Providers Communicate

Patient and provider interactions most often transact relationships that place the patient in a passive role and place the provider in a dominant role, as outlined in the machine-mechanic relationship and the child-parent relationship, both of which require a large degree of trust of the physician by the patient. Driven by traditional and cultural norms, such interaction styles can interfere with the communication and wellness processes in certain circumstances.

Providers tend to dominate interactions with patients through questions and directives. Through directives, or commands, the dominant position of providers is further substantiated. Of course, a provider telling a patient to breathe deeply, cough, open wide, or sing a chorus of "Moon River" may have legitimate medical backing. At the same time, it clearly places the provider in a dominant position and may consequently hinder a patient's ability to question the provider and to participate in decision making regarding his or her treatment, with such participation clearly being best when the patient is informed, is knowledgeable, and understands the situation to the fullest.

Providers also focus most often on establishing a patient's physical problems rather than psychosocial problems (social and relational issues accompanying or even causing illness). This approach likens patients to machines and gives no account to relevant emotional and relational needs. When patients attempt to incorporate

machines and mechanics (patient-provider relationship): providers are viewed as competent experts analytically diagnosing a physical problem and then fixing it; patients are passive and allow the expert mechanic to give them a proper tune-up with little or no input or objection

children and parents (patient-provider relationship): the provider clearly portrays a dominant role of expert while the patient assumes a submissive and dependent role; this view of provider and patient relationships is the most

consumers (patient-provider relationship): patients viewing themselves as paying providers for specific information and expecting them to carry out their wishes

partners (patient-provider relationship): patients and providers work together to solve a problem and are viewed as equals, each bringing special knowledge to the interaction

such issues into the interaction, providers tend to interrupt them and refocus on physical symptoms. Consequently, providers may miss opportunities to discover the actual cause of a patient's problem or miss relevant treatment opportunities.

Further complicating matters is an unwillingness of some patients to fully disclose their medical concerns to providers. Especially when dealing with personal or embarrassing issues, patients tend to avoid disclosing information that would be pertinent to providers. In fact, patients undergoing a medical examination sometimes delay disclosing the real reason for their visit until a provider is getting ready to leave the room. These "doorknob disclosures" generally result in another medical evaluation or interview being conducted, resulting in further delay for the next patient (du Pre, 2005).

Improving Patient-Provider Communication

A number of health communication scholars have noted the importance of a patient-provider relationship based on partnership or mutuality, in which the interactants share control of the interaction and equally negotiate an understanding of patient needs and treatments (e.g., du Pre, 2005; Roter & Hall, 2006; Wright, Sparks, & O'Hair, 2012). Such a relationship can only be established through extensive transformations of existing patient-provider communication patterns.

Roter and Hall (2006, pp. 6–20) have outlined seven communication principles that would vastly improve existing interactions among patients and providers. In Table 11.2, we examine the primary ideas behind these seven communication principles, whose recognition and subsequent incorporation could assist in the development of effective patient-provider relationships.

By the way...

Front-Office Staff

A point rarely researched and recognized by practitioners is that the relationships and communication established by front-office staff can greatly influence overall patient satisfaction. The health care providers can be very good in themselves, but the patient may already feel badly treated or disrespected by a dismissive or overhasty office staff before the physician even shows up.

QUESTIONS TO CONSIDER

1. How do you suppose front-office staff might impact the benefits of effective patient-provider relationships being discussed here?
2. Why do you think scholars have not focused on this area?

Benefits of Effective Patient-Provider Relationships

We can now examine the positive outcomes resulting from effective patient-provider relationships. These benefits include satisfaction with the encounter, greater likelihood of adherence to treatments, improved physical and psychological health, and even a decrease in malpractice lawsuits.

Satisfaction

Effective patient-provider relationships can enhance feelings of patient satisfaction, which is increasingly recognized as an important goal in addition to the traditional goal of patient recovery or survival (Wright et al., 2012). In fact, studies indicate that patient satisfaction is significantly connected with communication among patients and providers (Martin, Roter, Beach, Carson, & Cooper, 2013). Patient satisfaction is a consequence of communication taking place at various points throughout care (Venetis, Robinson, & Kearney, 2013) and may involve face-to-face, digital, and other types of interaction (Ye, Rust, Fry-Johnson, & Strothers, 2010).

Adherence to Treatments

Effective patient-provider relationships also increase the likelihood that patients will adhere to treatments and lifestyle

Table 11.2 Patient-Provider Communication Principles

Patient-provider communication should acknowledge . . .	
Patient Stories	Stories reveal what people perceive as the most important details or elements of a situation. They hold crucial information pertaining not only to physical symptoms but also to the psychological and relational issues connected with a specific patient's illness.
Patient Expertise	Patients should be considered experts about their unique situation, regardless of how common the illness or medical concern. As such, their expertise and contributions should be valued as greatly as those of providers.
Provider Expertise	Beyond utilizing specialized medical knowledge to confirm illness and to set forth treatment options, providers should use their knowledge to educate patients. Sharing their expertise with patients in a manner that is clear and understandable can enhance patient-provider relationships and improve the health and healing process.
Physical and Psychosocial Connections	There exists a powerful connection between health and everyday life. Both patients and providers do not always recognize the importance of everyday life experiences and instead focus their attention on biological causes. A holistic understanding of patient experiences can improve diagnoses and treatment options.
Emotions	The expression, recognition, and subsequent transacted meaning of emotion impact patient-provider relationships just as they do other relationships. Patients and providers should recognize the profound influence of emotion and their mutual emotional investments.
Reciprocity	As with any relationship, patients will act in accordance with provider interaction styles (positive or negative) and vice versa. Both patients and providers must recognize the influence of reciprocity on their relationship, treating each other with respect and recognizing the concerns and needs of each other.
Roles and Expectations	Patients and providers should recognize the influence of traditional roles and expectations while attempting to establish a more constructive relationship and more effective communication styles. They must clearly express their expectations of the relationship, the interaction, and each other.

recommendations established by providers (Wright et al., 2012). Adherence to treatment may result from improved understanding on the part of patients and from improved confidence in both providers and their own abilities to remember and follow treatment guidelines (Dorflinger, Kerns, & Auerbach, 2013; Martin et al., 2013; Schoenthaler, Allegrante, Chaplin, & Gbenga Ogedegbe, 2012).

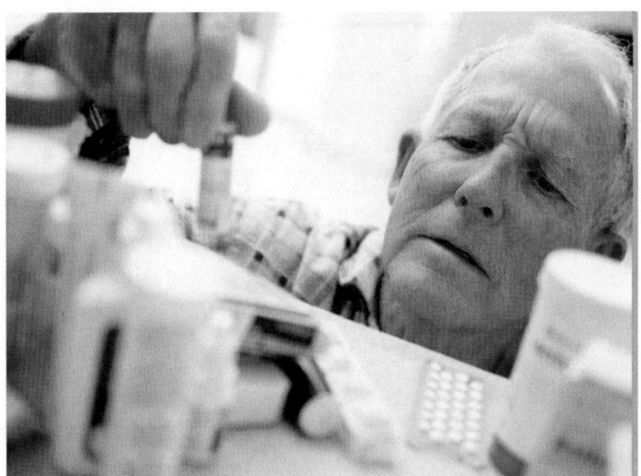

Elderly patients or those undergoing complex treatments sometimes have difficulty remembering the regimen of pills and medications they should take. How could a physician facilitate a patient's adherence to the prescribed treatment?

Physical and Psychological Health

Effective patient-provider relationships also enhance the physical and psychological health of patients (Wright et al., 2012). It is fairly easy to understand how effective patient-provider communication can enhance patient physical and psychological health, since it increases adherence to treatments. If the physician is right, then this will increase the likelihood that patients will overcome a particular ailment

Make your case

Proper Patient-Provider Relationships

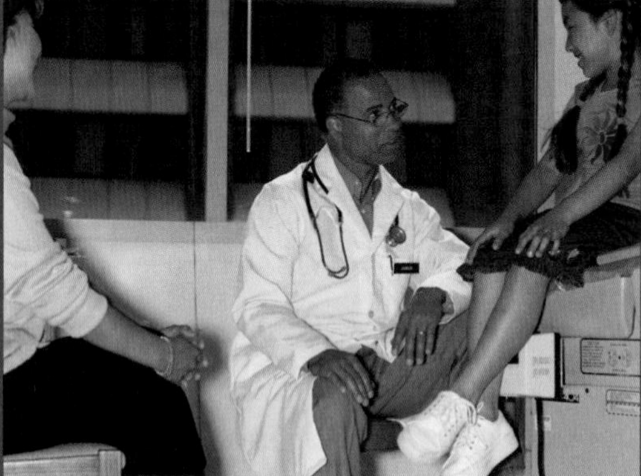

We have championed the need for a reciprocal relationship between patients and providers. Think about whether there might be any drawbacks to this type of patient-provider relationship.

QUESTIONS TO CONSIDER

1. Do you believe a different type of relationship would be more advantageous, such as providers having a dominant role or patients having a dominant role?
2. If so, what would be the advantages of such a relationship, and what would be the disadvantages?

and feel pretty darn good about it as a result. Beyond adherence, however, effective communication increases the chances that providers will ask the right questions during evaluations and that patients will be willing to be forthcoming, freely supplying providers with information that they do not otherwise know and that could speed their arrival at a proper diagnosis. Effective patient-provider communication will also decrease patient anxiety and stress related to the interaction and overall medical concerns, because the patient feels accepted, understood, and safe (Bankoff, McCullough, & Pantalone, 2013).

Malpractice Claims

And now, one for the medical providers out there: Effective patient-provider relationships may decrease malpractice lawsuits (Wright et al., 2012). Medical providers do not often get sued when a patient's health improves. However, overall communication patterns of providers influence the likelihood that a malpractice claim will or will not be filed. Patient-provider communication is especially important when problems are encountered during treatment (Duclos et al., 2005).

Social Networks and Health

Having discussed the impact of relationships with providers, we will now examine how relationships with friends, family, acquaintances, and other members of social networks have an impact on health. Social networks influence many of the lifestyle choices people make, from eating and exercising to smoking, drinking, and taking drugs. Social networks also provide various forms of support. In what follows, we will examine the influence of social networks on health and lifestyle. We will then look at the support provided by social networks, secondary goals of social support, and how everyday communication serves as a foundation for social support. Finally, we will explore the communication privacy management theory to better understand how people manage private health information.

Social Networks and Health and Lifestyles

Social networks influence the decisions people make regarding health-related issues and overall lifestyles, both good and bad. The nature of health, its importance, the evaluation of health advice, and the meanings of health and lifestyle choices are all transacted in interactions with others.

Eating and Exercising With Others

Beyond genetic predispositions, your family members have an incredible influence on your food consumption and your exercise habits through both their actions and the ways in which they talk about these things (Berge, Arikian, Doherty, & Neumark-Sztainer, 2012). For instance, food is often ritually connected with holidays and celebrations in families, and it is possible that you associate food with joy and happiness.

Some families may incorporate healthy diets and exercise in their everyday lives and talk, which reinforces these behaviors among family members.

Along with family, friends have a profound influence on diet and exercise decisions (Fitzgerald, Fitzgerald, & Aherne, 2012; Flatt, Agimi, & Albert, 2012; Salvy, De La Haye, Bowker, & Hermans, 2012). Research indicates that people with overweight friends tend to be overweight themselves, although the direction of causality is hard to establish: Do overweight people choose overweight friends, or do people who choose overweight friends become larger themselves afterward?

While it may be an epidemic, obesity cannot be caught like a cold, but it can be influenced by your friends' rhetorical visions about fitness, food, and size. Behaviors and talk about food and exercise influence people's attitudes and the decisions that are made about diet, exercise, and ordering the supersized meal. Your friends' eating habits and exercise routines may influence or set the standards for your own. Part of the reason people are influenced in this manner is through comparing themselves with others. Beyond this reason, however, are the meanings attached to food and to exercise that have been transacted through interactions.

ANALYZING EVERYDAY COMMUNICATION

What Are You Going to Order?

Restaurant employees indicate that if one person at a table orders dessert, the likelihood that others will greatly increases. The next time you are at a restaurant, pay attention to the ways in which orders of those dining together compare.

QUESTIONS TO CONSIDER

1. Do people ask what a dining companion plans to order because of curiosity, or do you suppose people ask this question to determine how their own order might be perceived?
2. Have you ever changed your mind about what you wanted to order after hearing someone else's order (e.g., changing your order from a burger to a salad after your dining companion ordered a salad)?

Smoking With Others

Attitudes toward smoking and smoking-related behaviors are strongly connected to social networks (Lakon & Valente, 2012). Like other health and lifestyle behaviors, smoking is frequently a shared relational activity. For instance, smoking might be a way to forge and maintain relational connections with colleagues and classmates through bonding activities like sharing cigarettes or lights or the fact that smokers must meet outside in certain areas. Of course, a person passing a construction crew placing tar on the road and thinking "I would sure like to inhale some of that along with some tasty nicotine and other carcinogens" must have an addiction. However, relationships with others through the social bonding provided by commonly shared smoking habits have consistently been listed as one of the perceived benefits of smoking (Nguyen, Von Kohorn, Schulman-Green, & Colson, 2012).

In addition to smoking as a shared relational activity, people's talk about their smoking serves to minimize the perceived risks. This talk consequently influences the likelihood that a person will continue the behavior. In case you have not heard, SMOKING WILL KILL YOU! Most people have heard the warnings, but many otherwise intelligent people continue this behavior. DeSantis (2002) has examined the ways in which talk among a group of smokers collectively crafts and reinforces *pro*smoking arguments that refute established findings, decrease the impact of antismoking messages, and minimize cognitive dissonance and anxieties connected with the activity. When this occurs, the smokers manage to reinforce each other's rhetorical vision that the dangers of smoking have been misrepresented by evil statisticians or lying governments.

Social networks also influence attempts to cease smoking. This influence can be negative. For instance, smokers often report negative relational consequences when attempting to stop smoking such as a decrease in the number of (smoking) friends (Pingree et al., 2004). On the other hand, this influence can be positive. Friends and family may just as frequently provide support, encouragement, and guidance when a person is attempting to quit smoking. Such social networking sites as Quitnet.com even provide support for smokers trying to cease this behavior (Myneni, Iyengar, Cobb, & Cohen, 2013).

Drinking With Others

Alcohol consumption is another lifestyle behavior associated with relationships. In fact, drinking alone has been listed as a potential sign of alcoholism! As is the case with food, alcohol often plays a prominent role in holidays and special occasions. And, as is the case with diet and exercise, both family and friends impact the use of alcohol.

The role of alcohol and talk about drinking alcohol in families is a significant indicator of a person's attitudes toward drinking and his or her consumption of alcohol (Jayne, Valentine, & Gould, 2012). A person's use of alcohol is strongly influenced by parents' consumption of alcohol and talk about alcohol within families.

Friends also influence the use and consumption of alcohol. Drinking among college students continues to be a problem on many campuses, resulting in physical, academic, relational, and legal problems for many students. Pressures to drink in general are often based on relational obligation, and those who try to avoid the consumption of alcohol often experience relational distress as a result (Yang, Davey-Rothwell, & Latkin, 2012). For new students, drinking at parties is frequently viewed as a way to establish social capital in a new environment (Buettner & Debies-Carl, 2012). Ironically, through talk about alcohol and updates on social networking sites, there is a tendency to believe that drinking is more common than it actually may be among one's social network (Fournier, Hall, Ricke, & Storey, 2013). These beliefs may result in perceiving that alcohol consumption is necessary in order to fit in when it may very well not be necessary.

Social Networks and Support

Now that we have examined the impact of social networks on health decisions and behaviors, we can examine the ways in which members of social networks provide support. This support can be an important element when managing illness and any number of health and wellness issues (Uchino, 2009).

The two primary types of social support are (1) action-facilitating support and (2) nurturing support (du Pre, 2005). **Action-facilitating support** involves providing information or performing tasks for others. **Nurturing support** involves helping people feel better about themselves and the issues they are experiencing. Although separated as two categories, action-facilitating support and nurturing support are often connected in their application as you will see as we go along.

action-facilitating support: providing information or performing tasks for others

nurturing support: helping people feel better about themselves and the issues they are experiencing

Action-Facilitating Support

Action-facilitating support includes informational support and instrumental support. **Informational support** involves providing someone with information in order to increase his or her knowledge and understanding of health issues. For instance, someone dealing with hypertension may be provided with information found online by a friend. As we will discuss later in this chapter, half of searches for health information on the Internet are related to someone else's health or medical situation (Fox & Duggan, 2013).

informational support: type of action-facilitating support providing someone with information in order to increase his or her knowledge and understanding of health issues

Providing someone with information not only increases his or her understanding of the situation and ability to make informed decisions but also increases his or her feelings of competence and value, issues related to nurturing support. Accordingly, when you provide someone with a piece of information, you are doing more than just that. You are reinforcing the existence of the relationship, you are reinforcing his or her importance, and you are validating his or her ability to make his or her own decisions. As with most actions, additional symbolic meaning is inherent in the provision of information as relational support.

These same meanings are evident with **instrumental support**, which involves performing tasks for someone. For instance, you might perform tasks around the home when a friend is too sick to do them for him- or herself, or you might give someone a ride to the doctor. Doing such things, once again, goes beyond the mere completion of tasks and additionally entails personal and relational reinforcement.

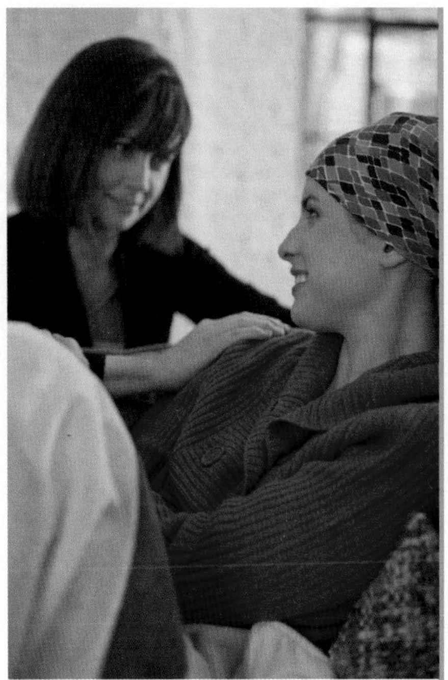

In what ways can social support help improve a patient's health?

Nurturing Support

Nurturing support includes emotional support and esteem support. **Emotional support** enables people to express their feelings and to have those feelings validated by others. Providing people with the opportunity to express their emotions can prove very beneficial in the coping and healing process. Emotional support also involves making people feel valued by letting them know that they are needed and that others care for them. Health problems may lead people to view themselves as a burden to others. This form of support also entails reinforcing relational connections by letting those experiencing health problems know that others will stick around even when things get rough.

Esteem support involves making someone feel competent and valued. Health problems are often accompanied by a perceived lack of control, which is often increased by well-meaning assistance and advice from others. Consequently, people may begin to feel as though they are incapable of normal activities or of making their own decisions. This form of support promotes feelings of competence and ability by allowing and encouraging people to act on their own and to take part in decision making related to their care.

Secondary Goals of Social Support

While the goals of social support just discussed frequently receive the most attention, there exist secondary goals of both those seeking and those providing social support. These secondary goals are just as significant as the primary goals, and in fact, it could be argued that fully understanding the primary goals would be impossible without them. These secondary goals involve identities and relationships.

Identity Goals of Social Support

Identity goals inherent in social support are connected with face wants, discussed in Chapter 4. People desire to be seen as worthwhile and as decent overall (positive face wants) and do not wish to be imposed upon or treated in a negative manner (negative face wants). The possibility of negative face arises with every request for or offer of social support. Asking for a ride to the hospital, for example, may place a person in an inferior position and may also be seen as imposition of a burden on the person being asked. Accordingly, people must manage their interactions in a way that ensures the prevention

instrumental support: type of action-facilitating support performing tasks for someone

emotional support: type of nurturing support enabling people to express their feelings and to have those feelings validated by others

esteem support: type of nurturing support making someone feel competent and valued

of negative face or in a manner that minimizes negative face. ("Pardon me. I hate to bother you, but I seem to have stapled my eyelid to my knee. Could I trouble you for a ride to the hospital? I would drive myself, but if I did, I'd likely pass out and crash.")

Providing or receiving social support can be consistent or inconsistent with transacted identities. Consequently, people may struggle with the desire to create particular identities that may be hindered through support actions. Of particular concern for those providing social support is a desire to be viewed as competent and reliable. A lack of autonomy or independence is a key concern for those seeking or receiving social support.

Relational Goals of Social Support

Closely associated with identity goals, relational goals also guide social support. Of primary concern are the expectations surrounding relationships. Although the communication transacting relationships is a more important indicator of potential social support than the actual type of relationship, certain relationships are expected to fulfill social support functions (Carl & Duck, 2004). A friend would usually be expected to provide support in times of need whereas an acquaintance might not be, for instance. When a relationship provides the support expected, this reinforces the relationship and may very well make both relational partners feel better about themselves and the relationship. On the other hand, when a relationship does not provide the support expected, a person might experience disappointment and rejection along with feeling even worse about the situation than before.

Everyday Communication and the Foundation of Social Support

The foundation of social support is established in everyday communication with others. It is here in everyday communication where people establish their beliefs about the likelihood of receiving support from members of their networks along with expectations surrounding how support will be potentially acquired and fulfilled when needed. Everyday communication in general serves to underscore the existence and continuance of a relationship, thereby establishing the possibility that someone could serve as a resource for support if the occasion arises.

Of course, it is important to recognize that it is not the existence of a relationship itself that guarantees the probability of support but rather it is the communication that transacts that relationship. A person may be considered a friend, but this does not ensure that he or she would be able and willing to provide you with the right kind of support you might seek when dealing with health issues or that the support provided would be accurate and appropriate. That person might be great to go shopping with on the weekend or to discuss sports with but would not be someone you would seek out in times of emotional or health need. On the other hand, another person you consider a friend may be someone you would seek out in times of need, someone you are confident would be willing and able to provide you with competent support.

What this ultimately means is that beyond the instrumental and relational objectives fulfilled through everyday communication, there are inherent supportive functions of everyday communication as well. Further, every time you speak with someone you are establishing a basis for support in the future.

As discussed in Table 11.3, there are six supportive functions of everyday communication: (1) information, (2) perpetuation, (3) detection, (4) ventilation, (5) distraction, and (6) regulation (Barnes & Duck, 1994).

Table 11.3 Supportive Functions of Everyday Communication

Information	Everyday communication with members of a social network enables people to determine who might be a reliable source of support when needed. It also provides insight into the nature of social support. Observing how such support actions as advice giving, resource granting, and others are constructed and evaluated allows people to develop proper frames to better understand and enact social support.
Perpetuation	Perpetuation is concerned not with *determining* potential sources of support but rather with *maintaining* sources of support. Everyday communication serves to sustain relationships and enable their continuance. It helps ensure that sources of support are readily available when necessary.
Detection	Everyday communication provides a baseline from which people may perceive the communication of others. There exist certain patterns of interaction that people come to expect from those in their social networks (such as being talkative or subdued). Purposefully or not, changes in these patterns could be a signal that someone is in need of support.
Ventilation	Everyday communication allows for the ventilation of stress and worries, allowing people to feel better and preventing stress and worry from becoming a major problem. Talking about problems with others can be a productive way of managing concerns and anxieties.
Distraction	Sometimes the best way to deal with a problem is by not dealing with it—at least for a while. Since everyday communication is often viewed as mundane, routine, trivial, and light, it is often a welcome alternative to discussions of major health issues and problems.
Regulation	Everyday communication serves as a regulation mechanism in two ways. First, since everyday communication is often viewed as trivial or mundane, social support can be sought and provided with seemingly less consequence when compared with social support sought and provided during moments of deep discussion. Second, everyday communication can serve as a precursor to deeper discussions. Broaching the topic during the course of everyday communication allows people to evaluate another person's response and determine whether or not a more in-depth discussion or increased disclosure of the issue would be warranted and worthwhile.

Communication Privacy Management

When it comes to social support for a health issue, who is provided with such information and the extent to which that information is disclosed become important factors. Within your social network, there are some people with whom you will disclose such information and some people with whom you will not. For example, college students may be more likely to reveal risky behaviors to friends and siblings than to parents (Aldeis & Afifi, 2013). Further, some information will be shared while other information will remain hidden. For instance, a person may not fully reveal past sexual encounters when discussing such matters with a new romantic partner (Nichols, 2012).

Petronio's (2002, 2013) **communication privacy management theory** explains how people create and manage privacy boundaries in their relationships, and her approach can enable you to better understand how health information may or may not be revealed. Since it deals with private information, *self-disclosure* rests at the heart of this theory. Self-disclosure deals with the revelation of private, sensitive, and confidential information (see Chapter 3).

Private information comes with perceived *ownership*. A person's private information is considered something that is owned and, consequently, something that one can control. This control entails determining who is given access to information and the right to keep some information private. Ownership can be personal or collective.

ETHICAL ISSUE

Cultures and people differ on the extent to which medical information should remain private. Do you consider your health information to be private? Who should have access to that information? Who should be denied access to that information? If your condition is genetic, should your family be told?

communication privacy management theory: explains how people create and manage privacy boundaries in their relationships

COMMUNICATION + **YOU**

Revealing Private Information

Deciding whether or not to reveal private information about yourself to someone can be a difficult choice. Consider a time when you struggled with determining whether to reveal or conceal private information.

QUESTIONS TO CONSIDER

1. What impact did your decision have on your relationship with the person to whom you revealed or from whom you concealed the information?
2. What impact did your decision have on you personally? Would you make the same decision if given a second chance?

Personally, a mother may decide when to reveal her HIV status to her children (Tenzek, Herrman, May, Feiner, & Allen, 2013). Collectively, a family may choose to keep a teenager's alcoholism hidden from those outside the family (Petronio, 2010).

Of course, what one person considers private information may not be considered private information by another person. Some people, for instance, are more likely to talk about "hooking up" and sexual promiscuity than other people (Holman & Sillars, 2012). These people have erected different *privacy boundaries,* or borders between what is considered private and what is not.

Once erected, these privacy boundaries will vary in their degree of *permeability.* Relationships often determine the actual permeability of these boundaries. As mentioned above, depending on the degree of closeness and relational type, some people will be allowed access to information while other people will be denied access.

Access to private information demands *coordination* by those involved. People must cooperate to keep boundaries intact and to ensure that information revealed is not misused by the recipient. Whether or not explicitly stated, certain topics may be avoided in a relationship. For instance, a friend may know that a person does not like talking about his or her excessive drinking and avoids that topic. Coordination also entails ensuring that when private information is shared, it is not used against the person or spread to others who were not intended to receive the information.

Boundary turbulence occurs when people struggle to coordinate privacy rules and boundaries. For instance, people dealing with infertility must determine what to reveal or conceal when the issue arises in conversation (Bute, 2013). Such decisions may lead to strengthening boundaries, loosening boundaries, and developing ways to manage the topic depending on relational connections and situations.

Media, Technology, and Health

Media and technology are fundamental components of everyday life and greatly influence health communication. Health issues make up a great deal of media and technology content, including television programs, newspaper and magazine articles, advertisements, and Internet sites. This content influences people's lifestyles, awareness of health issues, and understanding of health issues, as well as how people talk about health both with their social network and with their health provider.

In what follows, we examine the impact of media and technology on health communication. First, we examine the impact of entertainment and news programming on health communication, including awareness and expectations. We then examine commercials and print advertisements for prescription drugs. Finally, we explore the use of the Internet and its impact on health communication.

Entertainment Media and Health

Health care has long been a staple of entertainment programming. Since the introduction of television, for instance, a vast number of television dramas and comedies have focused on medical professions. Health-related issues on these and other programs, along with depictions of health-related issues through other media sources, may influence audience awareness and understanding of these issues. Indeed, much of the information people possess about health and wellness has come from media. Even when health information is gained through talking with other people, the original source of the information may likely have come from media.

Unfortunately, media depictions of health-related issues are frequently inaccurate, which may lead to inaccurate perceptions of health care. For instance, certain types of illness are much more prevalent in entertainment media than others, and these illnesses are much more prevalent among fictional patients than they are among actual patients (Primack et al., 2012; Rasmussen & Ewoldsen, 2013). Illnesses portrayed on television, for example, are often more critical and dramatic (poisoning) than chronic and enduring (heart disease), even though the latter is much more common (Hetsroni, 2009). Additional representations including demographic characteristics of both patients and medical providers portrayed in media do not correspond with those of actual patients and medical providers (Hether & Murphy, 2010; Hetsroni, 2009; Jain & Slater, 2013) along with roles of certain medical personnel (Turow, 2012) and with patient-provider interactions (Gross, Stern, Silverman, & Stern, 2012).

Entertainment media may also lead to inaccurate understandings and expectations of medical treatment. For example, some media portrayals of medical treatment are simply wrong (Moeller, Moeller, Rahey, & Sadler, 2011). On the other hand, some media portrayals of medical treatment are correct and, in the case of CPR (cardiopulmonary resuscitation), may actually be correctly used by audience members when needed (Eisenman, Rutetski, Zohar, & Stolero, 2012). At the same time, audience members may not be provided with accurate expectations. In the case of CPR specifically, an earlier study found survival rates of fictional characters receiving CPR to be much higher than among real patients (Diem, Lantos, & Tulsky, 1996). More recent studies have found survival rates on current programs to be more accurate. Still, these studies caution that medium-term and long-term outcomes are often unseen and may provide audience members with unrealistic expectations after all (Harris & Willoughby, 2009).

Ending this section on a somewhat positive note, media portrayals of health care have sometimes been criticized for potentially giving audiences false hope through depictions of medical miracles. In the early days of television, especially, medical providers were portrayed as perfect, and patients always seemed to survive. Now, while inaccurate depictions of health care continue in media, a patient may be better off in a real hospital rather than a fictional hospital. The mortality rate of fictional hospital patients has been shown to be nine times higher than the mortality rate of real hospital patients (Hetsroni, 2009).

ETHICAL ISSUE

Is it ethical for entertainment media to provide inaccurate views of medical conditions in order to make a program more dramatic and suspenseful even though viewers may develop inaccurate understandings?

News Media and Health

Television news programs, newspapers and magazines, and general health programming are also sources of information and misinformation about health. Like

DISCIPLINARY DEBATE

Media and Lifestyle Choices

Some people would like to blame media for causing people to develop unhealthy body images, drink, smoke, and engage in sexual promiscuity. Other people argue that doing so simplifies these problems and avoids personal responsibility. There are, of course, many contributing factors to people's lifestyle choices, most notably social networks as discussed earlier. Ultimately, media do influence people's perceptions and understanding of the world, and it is important to recognize the potential influence on lifestyles.

QUESTIONS TO CONSIDER

1. What degree of influence do you think media have on lifestyle decisions?
2. Do you think media influence some people more than other people?

entertainment programming, news and health programming can lead to increased awareness and understanding of health-related issues, which can be very beneficial, but this information may also be inaccurate and misleading.

Certain health and illness issues are more frequently addressed in news media than others. For example, some cancers (male reproductive, lymphatic, and thyroid) have been found to be underreported by news media, while other cancers are overreported (breast, blood/leukemia, pancreatic, and bone/muscle) based on incidence rates (Jensen, Moriarty, Hurley, & Stryker, 2010).

When health and illness issues are included in news media, many inaccuracies and contradictions are often reported (MacKenzie, Chapman, Barratt, & Holding, 2007). Furthermore, health and illness issues are often presented in ways that may be misleading. Kinsella (1989) argued that news media tended to avoid coverage of AIDS early on due to viewing it primarily as a disease affecting gay males. When coverage of the epidemic eventually increased, little attention was given to transmission of the disease, which mischaracterized the actual risks for the entire population.

News media frequently provide audiences with social and moral meanings of health-related issues. As with any development of meanings, those encouraged by news media are biased toward certain perspectives. For instance, an analysis of a decade's worth of news reporting about weight issues and obesity discovered that thinness is associated with moral virtue and obesity is associated with poor individual choices. Such reporting, it can be argued, reinforces cultural stereotypes by overlooking both biological causes of obesity and socioeconomic associations (Saguy & Gruys, 2010).

Advertising Medications

Got a hangnail? Have we got the drug for you! Duck and McMahan Hangnail Fixer-Upper is all you need to rid yourself of fingernail frustration. Warning: May cause dizziness, irregular heartbeat, shortness of breath, weight gain, weight loss, nausea, uncontrollable itching, putrid odors emanating from the body, increased and uncontrollable bowel movements, loss of teeth, impaired vision, paranoia, and death. Put an end to your hangnail worries with Duck and McMahan Hangnail Fixer-Upper.

Before you look for this product at your local pharmacy, we can reassure you that it does not really exist. However, the wording of this advertisement may sound familiar to you given the dramatic increase in direct-to-consumer advertising of medications. In case you are wondering why drug manufacturers would list all of the horrible side effects of their medication, the reason is FDA (Food and Drug Administration) compliance. When the benefits and virtues of a drug are included in an advertisement, the side effects must be included as well. When only the name of a drug is mentioned and you are simply encouraged to ask your doctor about it, the side effects do not have to be included.

By the way...

Daffy's Elixir Salutis

Appearing in 1708, an advertisement for Daffy's Elixir Salutis was the first advertisement for a patent medicine in an American newspaper (Young, 1992). Today, advertisements for medication are commonplace in magazines and on television.

1. How closely do you pay attention to advertisements for medication?
2. Do you think these advertisements have an effect on how you view these medications?

Direct-to-consumer advertising impacts health communication in both positive and negative ways (Frosch, Grande, Tarn, & Kravitz, 2010). First, it increases patient awareness of illnesses treated by the medications. This increased awareness could be beneficial if a patient recognizes legitimate symptoms from the commercial or advertisement and seeks medical treatment, but it could very well lead to unnecessary treatments and overmedication. Much of the direct-to-consumer advertising includes symptoms that everyone has occasionally.

Second, it increases patient awareness of an available treatment option. Once again, this increased awareness could be beneficial but has potentially negative outcomes. Drug treatments focus on physical elements of illness and tend to overlook psychosocial and other factors contributing to the illness as well as nonmedicinal treatments. Further, such advertising increases the prescription of certain medications even though other medications may be just as if not more effective.

Third, direct-to-consumer advertising increases the likelihood that patients will take a more active role in discussions with providers. An increased awareness may encourage patients to feel more equivalent to providers. However, information gleaned from a brief commercial or print advertisement is usually quite limited, and the potential problems caused by the drug are generally not fully realized. Accordingly, providers must spend time reeducating patients, limiting time available to discuss other issues and concerns about a patient's illness and treatment options.

Health Communication and the Internet

The Internet has had a tremendous impact on health communication in recent years. In what follows, we will examine the use of the Internet for health information, coping and support, and patient-provider connections.

Searching for Information

Research conducted by the Pew Research Center's Internet and American Life Project indicates that 72% of Internet users have searched for health information online within the past year. Underscoring the relational components of health, of those people seeking online health information, half searched for information on behalf of someone else (Fox & Duggan, 2013). Table 11.4 presents the types of health information Internet users search for online in order of frequency.

Table 11.4 Searching for Health Information on the Internet

Specific disease or medical condition
Specific medical treatment or procedure
Weight control
Health insurance, Medicare, or Medicaid
Food safety or recalls
Drug safety or recalls
Advertised drug
Medical test results
Caring for an aging relative or friend
Pregnancy and childbirth
Reducing health care costs

SOURCE: Fox & Duggan (2013).

In what ways do people use the Internet in connection with health issues?

Support

The Internet is also being used as a support mechanism. Many support groups are now available online and are beneficial for their convenience and relatively easy access along with providing an outlet for people who are physically unable to attend formal support group meetings or people who choose not to attend face-to-face meetings for personal reasons. Online support groups have been found to benefit users through multiple forms of social support (Beaudoin & Tao, 2007; Lindsay, Smith, Bellaby, & Baker, 2009; Loane & D'Alessandro, 2013; Mo & Coulson, 2008).

Support also comes in the form of information from others. Thirty percent have consulted online medical reviews of health care services and treatments. Twenty-six percent of Internet users indicate reading about someone else's health or medical issues on news groups, websites, or blogs. Sixteen percent have searched for people online who might share the same health concerns (Fox & Duggan, 2013). The number of Internet users seeking online support will likely increase as familiarity with and access to the Internet continue to increase.

Connecting Patients and Providers

In a way, we are ending the chapter in a similar way in which we began the chapter: examining patients and providers. The Internet is increasingly used as a means of connecting patients and providers. Although the numbers are still small, some providers are connecting with their patients through social networking sites (Mathews, 2013). Providers are able to supply patients with general medical information and encourage healthy lifestyle choices between visits. Patients are provided with another means of contacting providers when needed. Social networking site connections may encourage the partner identity examined earlier, enabling both the patient and providers to play active roles in health care and treatment. Although there may be advantages to these social networking site connections, there also exist concerns about privacy and relational boundaries.

The Internet is also being used for patient evaluation and treatment by providers (Mathews, 2012). Rather than interacting in a doctor's physical office, for instance, patients and providers interact virtually or through webcams. Virtual and online interactions provide such benefits as decreased costs, increased accessibility, and increased convenience. However, there are concerns about the risk of misdiagnosis and potential deception. Such online treatment is a relatively new phenomenon, but as with other uses of the Internet, it is likely to become more common with the passing of time.

ETHICAL ISSUE

Is it ethical for providers and patients to be Facebook friends or to be connected through other social networking sites?

Skills You Can Use: Critically Evaluating Information

Unfortunately, people do not always engage in the critical evaluation of material discovered online (Hargittai, Fullerton, Menchen-Trevino, & Thomas, 2010). One study found that only 15% of Internet users seeking health information online always checked for the source and date of the information (Fox, 2006). You can improve your searches and find better information by always determining the credibility of the source and the recency of the health information you find online.

Focus Questions Revisited

How do patients and providers generally communicate?

Often based on traditional expectations and relational prototypes, patient-provider communication generally transacts relationships that place the patients in a passive role and place the provider in a dominant role. Ultimately, patients and providers may transact the following identities: (a) machines and mechanics, (b) children and parents, (c) consumers, and (d) partners.

How can patient and provider communication be improved?

Acknowledging factors such as patient stories, patient expertise, provider expertise, physical and psychosocial connections, emotions, reciprocity, and roles and expectations can improve patient-provider relationships. Effective patient-provider relationships can result in increased patient satisfaction, greater adherence to treatments, improved physical and psychological health, and a decrease in malpractice lawsuits.

How do social networks influence lifestyle choices through everyday communication?

The nature of health, its importance, the evaluation of health advice, and lifestyle choices are all transacted in communication with others. For instance, obesity can be influenced by your friends' rhetorical visions about fitness, food, and weight. Further, certain lifestyle behaviors such as smoking and drinking are shared relational activities.

How do social networks provide support?

The two primary types of support provided by social networks are (1) action-facilitating support and (2) nurturing support. Action-facilitating support involves providing information or performing tasks for others. Nurturing support involves helping people feel better about themselves and the issues they are experiencing. There also exist secondary goals involving identities and relationships.

In what ways do media and technology influence issues of health?

Health issues make up a great deal of media and technology content. This content influences people's lifestyles, awareness of health issues, understanding of health issues, and how people talk about health both with their social network and with their health provider. Entertainment media, for instance, can increase awareness of medical issues and procedures but may lead to inaccurate perceptions and expectations of health and medical procedures. Further, news media tend to focus on certain health and illness issues while neglecting others. Additionally, direct-to-consumer advertising increases patient awareness of illnesses treated by the medication, increases patient awareness of available treatment options, and increases the likelihood that patients will take a more active role in discussions with providers. Finally, the Internet serves as a source of information about a variety of health issues and as a means of managing health-related concerns. It is increasingly used to connect patients and providers.

Key Concepts

action-facilitating support 230
children and parents (patient-provider relationship) 225
communication privacy management theory 233
consumers (patient-provider relationship) 225
emotional support 231
esteem support 231
informational support 230
instrumental support 231
machines and mechanics (patient-provider relationship) 225
nurturing support 230
partners (patient-provider relationship) 225

Questions to Ask Your Friends

1. Have a friend describe his or her most recent visit to a doctor's office. What key elements are included in the story? What do these key elements tell you about how your friend perceived the visit?
2. Ask your friends to describe the ideal relationship between patients and providers. What do their responses tell you about how people view patient-provider relationships and what people want these relationships to be like?
3. Have a friend tell you about a time that he or she received support from someone in his or her social network that was very beneficial. Why would your friend characterize the support as beneficial?

Media Connections

1. Watch a fictionalized medical comedy or drama on television. How might the portrayal of health and illness influence people's expectations of medical treatment?
2. Read a newspaper article about health issues or medical concerns. What support, if any, does the author provide? Do you find the information provided in the article to be credible?
3. Search online for information about a health question you may have or can come up with (say, leprosy). What information is available to you? Do you find the information helpful? If so, how might the information be incorporated into your life? If not, how might the information be improved?

Student Study Site

SAGE edge™

Sharpen your skills with SAGE edge at edge.sagepub.com/duckciel2e

SAGE edge for students provides a personalized approach to help you accomplish your coursework goals in an easy-to-use learning environment.

Chapter Outline

How Can Culture Be Identified and Studied?

- Culture as Structure
- Culture as Transacted
- Coded Systems of Meaning

Structure-Based Cultural Characteristics

- Context
- Collectivism/Individualism
- Time
- Conflict

Transacting Culture

- Culture Is Embedded Within Your Communication
- Culture Goes Beyond Physical Location
- Cultural Groups Are Created Through Communication

Focus Questions Revisited

Key Concepts

Questions to Ask Your Friends

Media Connections

12 Culture and Communication

To begin our exploration of culture, we want to address three issues. First, when most people think of culture, they tend to think of it as something involving *other* people—wearing unusual clothes, eating strange foods, participating in odd customs, living in unique structures (bamboo huts, Roman temples, Chinese pagodas), and doing strange things with coconuts and tulips.

However, what is considered abnormal by one culture is normal to another. In fact, *you* perform cultural practices and communicate in ways that those from another culture might regard as odd, even though these practices and ways of communicating may seem to you to be natural and right. For instance, if you follow a traditional U.S. approach to time, what do you make of the fact that many cultures would view arriving at a very specific time quite strange, utterly obsessive, absurd, and valueless? After all, you should stop to smell the roses—or the tulips. In short, it seems just as normal and natural and right to the Japanese, the Italians, the Serbo Croatians, and the Tutsi to act the way they do as it does to you to do what you do.

Believing that your culture is the benchmark for all others is called **ethnocentric bias**: Your own cultural way of acting is right and normal, and all other ways of acting are variations of the only really good way to act (yours!). If this manner of thinking seems familiar, you are not alone, and it does not necessarily make you a bad person. However, appreciating and recognizing the value of other cultures will assist you personally and professionally, especially given an ever-expanding multicultural world. Doing so will also increase your appreciation for and understanding of your own culturally limited behaviors. Adolf Hitler, the Ku Klux Klan, the New Black Panthers, and the Muslim Brotherhood are obvious examples of ethnocentric bias but are so extreme that they might close your mind to the possibility that ethnocentric bias is less obvious in many cases and simply closes one's mind to reception of other views from different cultures.

Now we are not saying that if you have ethnocentric bias you are a new Hitler or Eva Braun, but we are pointing out the danger of taking ethnocentric bias to an extreme. We all have some degree of such bias in our worlds of meaning. If we are able to recognize it, then we can perhaps cut it away and become more open-minded. Few Americans question politicians who claim that the United States is "the best country in the world" or that "the U.S. education system is the best in the world," but they could not—and neither could the politicians—tell you how the education system works in Denmark or Mongolia, so the comparison claim is misleading without specific evidence.

FOCUS QUESTIONS

1. What does it mean to view culture as structured?
2. What does it mean to view culture as transacted?
3. How is communication organized to reflect cultural beliefs about context, collectivism/individualism, time, and conflict?
4. What does it mean to say culture is coded into communication?
5. What does it mean to say that cultural groups are created through communication?
6. How do people enact cultural membership through communication?

ethnocentric bias: believing that the way one's own culture does things is the right and normal way to do them

The view that one's own cultural styles of communication are the normal ways of communicating and that other ways of communicating are variations of normal communication is known as what type of bias?

Second, many people think of culture as something that is possessed or something to which a person belongs. Actually, you do not just have or belong to a culture; you *transact* and *perform* culture. This notion is similar to that discussed in Chapter 3 when examining identities. Identities and cultures are transacted (or constructed) symbolically and performed when interacting (or relating) with other people, and so are families—so why not "culture"? Culture is created symbolically, not through positioning in a physical location.

Of course, relationships remain fundamental to the actual creation and maintenance of culture. Using the relational perspective to examine identities in Chapter 3, we noted that the only way you ever meet *society* is through other people. Similarly, your exposure to *culture,* whether your own or another, is not exposure to an abstraction. You meet culture when you encounter people performing that culture; you perform your own culture when you communicate with other people. Society's (and Culture's) Secret Agents are the very friends you meet; other people on the streets; human beings you observe, read about, or see online or on television; and everyone who communicates with you.

Third, culture is not only geographical, although that is the way we most often think of it. Within the United States or the United Kingdom or Japan or even the Seven Kingdoms, there are many different styles and cultures. As the chapter proceeds, we indicate that such classifications as "gender" can be cultures, and so can "bikers"; the lesbian, gay, bisexual, and transgender (LGBT) community; "Beliebers"; political groups; and religious congregations. Each of these sets has a code of meaning, a bank of key terms, rituals, beliefs, and practices or styles that constitute a "culture" that is not bound by nationality alone. We discuss later that even *working class* is a label referencing culture embodied in styles of speech and codes of practice. So your passport does not define your cultural identity—your communication does.

In what follows, therefore, we examine the two primary approaches to identifying and studying culture: structured and transacted. From a structural approach, we discuss cultural differences concerning context, individualism/collectivism, time, and conflict. Examining culture as a transaction, we further explore the connection between culture and communication using a relational perspective. Specifically, we examine how culture is embedded in communication and how cultural membership is enacted or denied through communication.

As you study the material in this chapter, it is important to be as detached as possible and to treat your own culture as objectively as you treat others—as far as that can be achieved. Cultural influences run so deep within your routine talk and relational performance that you do not recognize them at first, but this chapter shows you how. Also note the importance these days that is placed on diversity. It is not just other people who benefit from diversity, but all of us get our minds opened by exposure to other cultures: Think study abroad.

ETHICAL ISSUE

Do you consider ethnocentric bias to be unethical?

How Can Culture Be Identified and Studied?

We begin our exploration by examining how culture has been identified and studied. As mentioned above, the two primary ways in which culture has been examined are as a *structure* and as a *transaction*. The most common approach to studying culture has been to view it as a "national" structure. Increasingly, however, the limitations of this perspective have become more obvious. Nevertheless, this approach has provided a wealth of information about culture and should not be shoved aside without full consideration.

COMMUNICATION + YOU

Culture and Minorities

As Nakayama, Martin, and Flores (2002) point out, White adults and especially "White children do not need to attend to the norms and values of minority groups unless they have direct exposure in their neighborhoods and schools. Minority children, however, are exposed to and compare themselves to [the dominant] white cultural norms through television, books, and other media" (p. 103). Whereas White people can act without knowledge or sensitivity to other cultures' customs in a White society, minority groups are rapidly disciplined for failing to observe White cultural norms. Consider these findings with particular reference to the ways in which the "dominant" or "preferred" cultural identifiers are usually taken for granted and invisible. This means you need to think about the ways in which the powerful people in society are *not* called upon to "explain themselves." Note that it is, for example, LGBT members of our society who are called upon to "justify" their behavior, not heterosexuals; that it is women whose promiscuous sexual behavior is subject to negative comments, not men's (compare use of the word *slut* with use of the word *player*); and so on.

QUESTIONS TO CONSIDER

1. Do you agree with what is stated above?
2. If you are a minority, did you compare yourself to White cultural norms when you were growing up? If you are White, were you aware of cultural norms of minority groups?

Culture as Structure

Viewing *culture* from a structural standpoint has a long history in the communication discipline. This way of seeing culture focuses on large-scale differences in values, beliefs, goals, and preferred ways of acting among nations, regions, ethnicities, and religions. We could therefore differentiate Australian, Indian, Japanese, Dutch, and Canadian cultures. Clear and simple distinctions could be made between Eastern and Western cultures and the communication styles displayed among people of these areas.

Cross-Cultural Communication and Intercultural Communication

A great deal of valuable research has been conducted from a structural standpoint, examining communication within and among nations or physical regions. This research is usually referred to as cross-cultural communication or intercultural communication.

Cross-cultural communication compares the communication styles and patterns of people from very different cultural/social structures, such as nation-states. For example, Seki, Matsumoto, and Imahori (2002) looked at the differences in intimacy expression in the United States and Japan. They found that the Japanese tended to think of intimacy with same-sex friends in relation to such expressive concepts as "consideration/love" and "expressiveness" *more* than did the Americans. The Japanese placed *more* stress than the Americans on *directly* verbalizing their feelings when considering intimacy with mother, father, and same-sex best friend. On the other hand, Americans placed more value than

cross-cultural communication: compares the communication styles and patterns of people from very different cultural/social structures, such as nation-states

ANALYZING EVERYDAY COMMUNICATION

Reinforcement of Cultural Norms

Consider the television programs and fairy tales you enjoyed as a child and their accompanying cultural themes. For example, many children's programs in the United States stress the importance of a person's individuality and his or her ability to achieve everything he or she desires through hard work, patience, and determination (*Cinderella, The Little Engine That Could*). This belief accompanies the U.S. beliefs in rugged individualism, achievement, and the "American Dream." Other national stories were studied many years ago by McClelland (1961) in an attempt to discover the underpinnings of achievement in different societies. He found that several children's stories popular in a particular culture supported the idea of the Protestant work ethic and subtly introduced children to the idea of the importance of achievement in that society.

QUESTIONS TO CONSIDER

1. What was your favorite program as a child?
2. What themes were reinforced in those programs?

the Japanese on *indirectly* verbalizing their feelings for others. Examining the influence of social networks on romantic relationships, Jin and Oh (2010) discovered that Americans tend to involve their friends and family in romantic relationships more often than Koreans. Social networks among Americans also provide more support for romantic relationships.

Intercultural communication deals with how people from these cultural/social structures speak to one another and what difficulties or differences they encounter, over and above the different languages they speak (Gudykunst & Kim, 1984). Chiang (2009), for instance, examined office-hour interactions involving international teaching assistants and American college students. Potential linguistic and cultural issues were isolated, and strategies for improving communication among these groups were offered.

intercultural communication: examines how people from different cultural/social structures speak to one another and what difficulties or conflicts they encounter, over and above the different languages they speak

Limitations and Benefits

This view of culture has provided a better understanding of different groups and has improved interactions among people, but it is not without its limitations. For example, when you start looking at cultures as identifiable national or regional groups, you rapidly notice some important points: First, *multiple* "cultures" exist in one national or regional group. The United States contains straight and gay cultures, old and young cultures, redneck and Minnesotan cultures, and Republican and Democrat cultures. Second, multiple *social communities* coexist in a single culture and talk amongst themselves as part of their conduct of *membership* (for example, bikers, car mechanics, vegetarians, and ballet dancers all exist within "American culture").

Nevertheless, from a communication point of view, we can study how all members of a nation partake of the customs or beliefs of the nation and its communication patterns and styles. Although broad, such distinctions seep down to the individual way of thinking, and are built into meaning systems used in everyday communication. Accordingly, while a social community of construction workers (or any other group) may communicate in unique ways, members' styles of communication are still impacted by the larger social structure in which they are embedded (for example U.S. construction workers communicate in ways different from how U.K. construction workers communicate and expect cups of tea—"tea breaks"—much less often).

Culture as Transacted

As we have maintained throughout this book, it is through communication (or symbolically) that most of social life is transacted. Culture is no exception. You belong to sets of people who share meanings and styles of speaking, systems of beliefs, and customs. In other words, you live your life in the context of communicating sets of individuals who transact universes of thought and behavior, which are supported through unique cultural styles of communication.

Cultural beliefs and values are established and reinforced through everyday communication. You are constantly reminded of them by your contacts with other people (Society's/Culture's Secret Agents). Your conformity to culture is constantly and invisibly reinforced in the daily talk that happens informally in the interactions with such agents and even strangers. The nature of culture and your connection to society is conducted through the specific relationships you have with others whom you meet frequently or with whom you interact daily. This stretches down to gendered culture, and as noted in Chapter 3, there can be norms such as "guys can't say that to other guys" (Burleson, Holmstrom, & Gilstrap, 2005).

The Harajuku area of Tokyo is a popular destination for teenagers, many of whom dress in such cultural styles as Gothic Lolita, visual kei, and decora. Are artifacts such as clothing the primary distinctions between cultural groups?

Cultural groups are recognized as such when some consistency and distinctiveness is observed in their behavior or communication. For example, the *shared relational* use by Goths, punks, and emos of symbols like hairstyles, body piercing, cutting, and self-harm along with a relevant music genre and vocabulary transacts their identity and collectively forms the Goth, punk, or emo culture. Similarly, rednecks and redneck culture have been identified and caricatured through particular stories and jokes (for example, by Jeff Foxworthy, Larry the Cable Guy, and David McMahan).

Coded Systems of Meaning

What makes this approach to studying culture different from a structural approach is that culture is seen as a **coded system of meaning**. Culture is not just a structured bureaucratic machine but a set of beliefs, a heritage, and a way of being that is *transacted* in communication. From this point of view, then, you can think of culture as a meaning system, and any group with a system of shared meaning is a culture. Farmers, athletes, gamers, members of business organizations, comic book fans, health professionals, truckers, fast-food employees, and musicians could all be considered members of a unique culture. The list of unique cultural groups is virtually unending.

Although conventional "structural" views of culture can still provide a great deal of valuable information, they tend to overlook numerous, distinct meaning systems within larger structure-based labels such as *nation-state*. You cannot legitimately maintain that everyone in the United States communicates the same way, that everyone in Lithuania communicates the same way, that everyone in India communicates the same way, or that everyone in any other nation-state or region communicates the same way. There are many different cultures within the United States (and other nation-states) communicating in very unique ways.

If we examine how culture is symbolically transacted, then we can explore how styles of communication serve to include people in or exclude people from cultural communities and groups. We can focus on how people "speak themselves into culture" and how membership in a particular culture is done through communication.

coded system of meaning: a set of beliefs, a heritage, and a way of being that is transacted in communication

By the way...

Watch a Culture in Action

Go to a public space where members of a unique cultural group are gathered and observe the ways they communicate. (Naturally, avoid dangerous places and situations. We do not want you injured and cannot send the Unsullied to rescue you.) There are many groups from which you may choose, but based on some of those mentioned here, you might observe farmers at a cattle auction barn, comic book fans at a comic book store, or truckers at a truck stop. (If you do not want to leave your comfortable couch, then write notes about the differences between Dothraki culture and the culture of Qarth.)

QUESTIONS TO CONSIDER

1. What is unique about their communication?
2. What does their communication tell you about their cultural beliefs and values?

Structure-Based Cultural Characteristics

Although we have indicated that it is far too simplistic to equate culture *exclusively* with nation-states or regions, some very broad differences between such groups have been observed and should be taken into account. All members of a nation or citizens of a country are impacted in some way by the most general communication styles, as you soon discover if you go on study abroad.

Children learn to view the world in culturally appropriate ways as they learn to communicate and interact with others. For example, small children may be rushed from the store by embarrassed parents who have just been asked loudly, "Why is that man so ugly?" and they will certainly be taught a culture's nonverbal rules: "Look at me when I'm talking to you" and "Don't interrupt when someone is talking." "Remember to say thank you" is another way children are taught culture's rules about respect and politeness. During your childhood and introduction to culture (socialization), you learned how to behave, interact, and live with other people at the same time as you learned to communicate, because culture is wrapped up in language. These styles of behavior readily became more and more automatic—and hence were automatically included in your later communication—as you grew up. If this did not happen, you could not communicate with other people in your society. Thus, learning to communicate includes learning the habits of your particular culture or society.

It makes sense to look at the rich list of differences uncovered among cultures—even if these sometimes amount to stereotypes that you hold about other nations when representing how people there *typically* act. In what follows, we examine the following cross-cultural characteristics: (a) context, (b) collectivism/individualism, (c) time, and (d) conflict. As these communication styles and meanings are discussed, keep in mind how they are learned and reinforced through interactions with friends, families, and others with whom relationships are shared.

Context

Context involves the emphasis placed on the environment, the situation, or relationships when communicating. Some cultures tend to leave much unsaid, with the assumption that others will understand what is meant based on such influences as circumstances and the relationships among those communicating. Other cultures tend to be more explicit and straightforward when communicating, rather than relying on contextual factors. Cultures are accordingly categorized as being either high-context or low-context.

high-context culture: a culture that places a great deal of emphasis on the total environment (context) where speech and interaction take place, especially on the relationships between the speakers rather than just on what they say (contrast with *low-context culture*)

High-Context Cultures

Some societies, known as **high-context cultures** (Samovar, Porter, & McDaniel, 2010), place a great deal of emphasis on the total environment or context where speech and interaction take place. In a high-context society, spoken words are much less important than the rest of the context—for example, the relationships between the people communicating. It is much more important for people to indicate respect for one another in various verbal and nonverbal ways than it is for them to pay close attention to the exact words spoken.

In such countries as China and Iraq, for example, a person's status in society is extremely important, and people tend to rely on shared history and their relationship to the speaker/audience. In Iraq and some African countries, additional importance may be attached to a person's religious or tribal group to assign meanings to conversation. Such cultures greatly emphasize relationships among family members, friends, and associates. Therefore, it is regarded as ethical to favor one's relatives or as fair to give contracts to friends rather than to the highest bidder. Everything is connected to this background context of relationships and other personal contexts of status, influence, and personal knowledge.

Low-Context Cultures

By contrast, when communicating in a **low-context culture**, the message itself is everything. It is much more important to have a well-structured argument or a well-delivered presentation than it is to be a member of the royal family or a cousin of the person listening (Samovar et al., 2010).

In a low-context society, therefore, people try to separate their relationships from the messages and to focus on the details and the logic. Detailed information must be given to provide the relevant context, and only the information presented that way counts as relevant to the message. In low-context societies, people usually recuse (remove) themselves from decision-making roles if a friend or family member is involved. Nepotism, or favoritism shown to a family member or friend, is evaluated negatively in low-context cultures.

By the way...

Learning About Your Culture

Cultural beliefs and values are first learned in childhood and then reinforced by relationships throughout your entire life. In this way, you do your culture by using the filters you learned in your early years without even realizing it, rather like wearing glasses. The lenses, for example, affect what you see to make perception more effective. Most of the time, people are not aware of wearing glasses because of their lenses' "transparency," but nevertheless, they affect what the wearer sees and how she or he sees it. So too with culture: Though it shapes and to some extent distorts perceptions and focus, people are largely unaware of culture and how it affects them.

QUESTIONS TO CONSIDER

1. How might your own culture be seen through the eyes of someone from a different culture?
2. What are some things about your own culture that seem strange, if you really think about it?

Collectivism/Individualism

An entire chapter of this book is dedicated to identity (Chapter 3), but the very notion of a personal identity is more of a Western than an Eastern idea. Some cultures stress collectivism/togetherness, and some stress individualism/individuality.

One interesting example of a culture that stresses the importance of not being outstanding is originally a fictional culture created by the Scandinavian author Aksel Sandemose through his imagination of a village called Jante. The law of Jante (Table 12.1) expresses the importance of not rising above the group as an individual, a sort of anti–tall-poppy law, with 10 rules that over time have come to be real in many parts of Scandinavia, which has adopted them as a cultural norm.

Collectivist Cultures

As traditionally noted (Gudykunst, 2000; Morsbach, 2004), Eastern societies, such as Japan, tend to be **collectivist**—that is, to stress group benefit and the overriding value of working. Collectivist cultures place importance on the whole group, stressing common concerns and the value of acting not merely for oneself but for the common good. Accordingly, in a collectivist culture, your value is based on your place in a system—portraying you as just a single bee in a beehive—more than your special and unique qualities as an individual.

low-context culture: assumes that the message itself means everything, and it is much more important to have a well-structured argument or a well-delivered presentation than it is to be a member of the royal family or a cousin of the person listening (contrast with *high-context culture*)

collectivist: subscribing to a belief system that stresses group benefit and the overriding value of working harmoniously rather than individual personal advancement (contrast with *individualist*)

By the way...

Conflict of "Culture" Within an Organization

There often exist contextual-based differences between the marketing or sales force in a business and the technicians or engineers who actually make the product. We would consider these differences to be *cultural* differences as we are defining the concept. For marketing team members and salespeople, it is very important to have good relationships with their customers and with a network of other sales personnel, a culture of high context and centering on other people and relationships with them (from the work chapter [Chapter 10] or your personal experience, you may have some ideas about why this matters). For the technicians who actually make and service products, it is more important that accurate information be conveyed to customers than that the customers be made to feel good interpersonally. This is a low-context culture where the emphasis is not on relationships but on "facts" and "truth." These cultural differences of emphasis sometimes lead to conflict between the same organization's marketing and technical personnel.

QUESTIONS TO CONSIDER

1. Have you ever experienced a conflict of culture as described above? If so, how was it managed?
2. In what ways can conflicts of culture be both beneficial and negative?

Table 12.1 Definition of the Law of Jante

There are 10 rules in the law as defined by Sandemose, all expressing variations on a single theme: *You are not to think you're anyone special or that you're better than us.*

The 10 rules state:

1. *You're not to think you are anything special.*
2. *You're not to think you are as good as us.*
3. *You're not to think you are smarter than us.*
4. *You're not to convince yourself that you are better than us.*
5. *You're not to think you know more than us.*
6. *You're not to think you are more important than us.*
7. *You're not to think you are good at anything.*
8. *You're not to laugh at us.*
9. *You're not to think anyone cares about you.*
10. *You're not to think you can teach us anything.*

In the book, the Janters who break this unwritten "law" are treated with suspicion or actual hostility, as their behavior breaks the town's wish to preserve harmony, social stability, and uniformity. In short, the individual must uphold the collective uniformity. Important from our perspective is the fact that the "law" was transacted in speech: "The Law of Jante was not merely a set of laws, *it was the very core of the speech of the people, all they ever said could be traced straight back to the Law of Jante*" (Sandemose, 1936, p. 28, italics added).

These characteristics are developed and reinforced through personal relationships and interactions with others. Within a collectivist society, an individual who acts to achieve personal rather than collective goals would be viewed as simply selfish and disrespectful. He or she would be brought back into line and made to adopt the values of community and collectivity. Such reprimands, especially made by someone with whom a close relationship is shared, would bolster the prevailing view of that society.

Individualist Cultures

Western societies, such as the United States, are generally characterized as **individualist**, or focusing on the individual personal dreams, goals and achievements, and right to make choices (Gudykunst, 2000; Morsbach, 2004). Individual desires and freedoms are emphasized, and your value is measured according to your personal accomplishments.

individualist: one who subscribes to a belief system that focuses on the individual person and his or her personal dreams, goals and achievements, and right to make choices (contrast with *collectivist*)

As with collectivist cultures, these characteristics are reinforced through relationships. Contrary to collectivist cultures, within individualistic cultures, personal achievement is lauded and reinforced through conversations with others. For instance, supervisors may talk with employees about the development of personal goals and post "employee of the month" placards to single out individual achievements. Next time you see such a placard, think of it as an example of American cultural ideals being transacted before your very eyes!

DISCIPLINARY **DEBATE**

Is Culture an Overall Ethnic or National Concept?

Some research presents a sharp distinction between individualist and collectivist cultures. Other scholars are becoming skeptical about such hard-and-fast distinctions, noting that although some large-scale differences exist, there is lot more subtlety and distinctiveness within a culture that is identified only by nationality or ethnicity. Not all Japanese people behave in identical ways or have exactly the same priorities, although a tendency toward collectivism is much stronger there than in some other national cultures. Two different popular authors have tried to identify what is special about being English, and they reached different conclusions. Jeremy Paxman (1999) wrote that the English were "polite, unexcitable, reserved, and had hot-water bottles instead of a sex-life," whereas Kate Fox (2005) emphasized the underlying importance to the English of humor and not taking anything too seriously.

QUESTIONS TO CONSIDER

1. Can you think of examples in U.S. culture where the individual is required to subordinate personal goals to the collective good?
2. If you can, does this undercut the whole idea of the great distinction between collectivism and individualism?

Time

Cultures are also categorized and differentiated according to their views of time. Consider how time is perceived in the United States: *Time is money*. Time is valuable, and so it is important to not waste it. Therefore, showing up on time helps create a positive impression. Many employees are required to punch in on a time clock or log into a computer system when arriving and leaving work, so precise time at work can be measured. If a person consistently arrives late for work, he or she will likely lose the job. Of course there is a range of views about this in any culture, and some progressive companies like Google and Apple explicitly replace this (obsessive?) attitude about time with something else (relaxed attitudes to time in the workplace, although they do not totally abandon the idea the time at work is a key notion). However, the fact that they explicitly abandoned a culturally normative way of treating time is a statement about the usual importance of time and the culture, such that they emphatically replace it as evidence of their special way of doing work.

Because cultures differ in how they view time, the importance of brisk punctuality, as opposed to that of leisurely relationship building, is also given different weight. This broad difference of emphasis on time is labeled as a distinction between monochronic and polychronic cultures.

Monochronic Culture

If you think of time as a straight line from beginning to end, you are thinking in terms of *monochronic time,* where people do one thing at a time or carry out connected tasks only because it helps them work toward particular goals with tasks in sequence and communication fitting into a particular order.

Monochronic cultures, such as the United States, the United Kingdom, and Germany, view time as a valuable commodity and punctuality as very important. People with a monochronic view of time will usually arrive at an appointment a few minutes early as a symbol of respect for the person they are meeting. In the United States, after first establishing a pleasant atmosphere with a few brief courtesies,

monochronic culture: a culture that views time as a valuable commodity and punctuality as very important (contrast with *polychronic culture*)

This man seems very concerned about time. Would his perception of time be considered monochronic or polychronic?

polychronic culture: a culture that sees time not as linear and simple but as complex and made up of many strands, none of which is more important than any other—hence such culture's relaxed attitude toward time (contrast with *monochronic culture*)

conflict: real or perceived incompatibilities of processes, understandings, and viewpoints between people

conflict-as-opportunity culture: a culture based on four assumptions: that conflict is a normal, useful process; that all issues are subject to change through negotiation; that direct confrontation and conciliation are valued; and that conflict is a necessary renegotiation of an implied contract—a redistribution of opportunity, a release of tensions, and a renewal of relationships (contrast with *conflict-as-destructive culture*)

people will likely bring up the matter of business fairly early in the conversation.

Polychronic Culture

If you think of time as the ever-rolling cycle of the seasons or something more open-ended, you are thinking in terms of *polychronic time,* where independent and unconnected tasks can be done simultaneously and also where people may carry out multiple conversations with different people at the same time.

Polychronic cultures have a relaxed attitude toward time. Indeed, as Calero (2005) noted, the predominant U.S. notion of time translates as "childishly impatient" to polychronic cultures. This notion of time is true even in relation to food, specifically in, say, Italy or France where two-course meals can take three hours. In polychronic societies, "promptness" is not particularly important, and as long as the person shows up sometime during the right day, that will count as doing what was required. Some Mediterranean and Arab countries do not regard as impolite being late to an appointment or taking a very long time to get down to business. Indeed, placing so much emphasis on time that people's relationships are ignored is regarded as rude and pushy; instead, time should be taken to build the relationships. In the same way, it is important in some countries not to get to the point too quickly, and a lot of time is spent talking about relational issues or other matters before it is polite to bring up a business question.

Future and Past Orientations

Cultures also differ in the way they pay attention to the past, the present, and the future. Different cultures tend to assume that the present is influenced either by one's goals and the future or by past events. In the latter case, fatalism and preordained destiny are seen as the controlling force over what happens in the present. Some Asian societies pay more attention to the distant future and, like South American and Mediterranean cultures, tend to assume a greater influence of the past on the present. Destiny or karma affects what happens to us in the present moment (Martin & Nakayama, 2007).

Conflict

Cultures can also be compared according to their understanding of and approach to **conflict**, which involves real or perceived incompatibilities of processes, understandings, and viewpoints between people. Communication scholars Judith Martin and Thomas Nakayama (2007, pp. 404–413)—drawing from the work of Augsburger (1992)—differentiate two cultural approaches to conflict: conflict as opportunity and conflict as destructive.

Conflict-as-Opportunity Cultures

Conflict-as-opportunity cultures tend to be individualist, such as the United States. This approach to conflict is based on the four assumptions listed in Table 12.2 (Martin & Nakayama, 2007, p. 404).

Table 12.2 The Four Assumptions of Conflict-as-Opportunity Cultures

1. Conflict is a normal, useful process.
2. All issues are subject to change through negotiation.
3. Direct confrontation and conciliation are valued.
4. Conflict is a necessary renegotiation of an implied contract—a redistribution of opportunity, a release of tensions, and a renewal of relationships.

SOURCE: Martin & Nakayama, (2007, p. 404).

On this view conflict is a normal and useful process, an inherent part of everyday life. Naturally experienced when interacting with people, conflict will lead, if handled constructively, to the enhancement of personal and relational life. This cultural view of conflict also understands all issues as subject to change, meaning that all personal or relational processes, goals, or outcomes can be altered. When a person wants to make changes in his or her relationships or personal life, he or she is expected to fully express and work with others to achieve these desires. Finally, members of these cultures view conflict not only as normal and useful but also as a necessary requirement for renewing relationships and for achieving overall well-being.

Conflict-as-Destructive Cultures

Stressing group and relational harmony above individual needs and desires, **conflict-as-destructive cultures** tend to be collectivist or community-oriented such as many Asian cultures. Religious groups, such as the Amish and Quakers, also view conflict as destructive. David's dad attended Quaker meetings as a child and adhered to pacifist ideals even on the playground. He has told stories of other children hitting him, knowing he would not fight back. As instructed in the Bible, he would literally turn the other cheek, and the other children would promptly hit that cheek as well. Nevertheless, David's dad remained steadfast in his culturally based belief in the destructive nature of conflict. As with conflict-as-opportunity cultures, four assumptions guide this approach to conflict, as listed in Table 12.3 (Martin & Nakayama, 2007, p. 406).

Contrary to conflict-as-opportunity cultures, this cultural approach views conflict not as a natural part of everyday experience but rather as unnecessary, detrimental, and to be avoided. Also contrary to conflict-as-opportunity cultures and reflective of collectivist cultures in general, members of conflict-as-destructive cultures do not view individual desires as more important than group needs and

Make your case

Do Cell Phones Alter Cultural Perceptions of Time?

The United States is typically regarded as monochronic, focused on time, dedicated to the steadfast accomplishment of the task at hand, and generally industrious and focused. However, the increased use of cell phones has tended to alter our perception of time. For instance, schedules are frequently loosened as a result of being able to contact someone immediately and alter plans. People often use cell phones to multitask (for example, sending texts while participating in a class).

QUESTIONS TO CONSIDER

1. Do you believe that it makes sense for communication scholars to treat the United States as essentially monochronic, or has technology overtaken that perception?
2. How have cell phones impacted your own views of time?

Table 12.3 The Four Assumptions of Conflict-as-Destructive Cultures

1. Conflict is a destructive disturbance of the peace.
2. The social system should not be adjusted to meet the needs of members; rather, members should adapt to established values.
3. Confrontations are destructive and ineffective.
4. Disputants should be disciplined.

SOURCE: Martin & Nakayama (2007, p. 406).

conflict-as-destructive culture: a culture based on four assumptions: that conflict is a destructive disturbance of the peace; that the social system should not be adjusted to meet the needs of members, but members should adapt to established values; that confrontations are destructive and ineffective; and that disputants should be disciplined (contrast with *conflict-as-opportunity culture*)

established norms. Furthermore, rather than valuing direct confrontation, members consider confrontations futile and harmful to relationships and the group as a whole. Accordingly, those who engage in confrontation should be disciplined to discourage such destructive behaviors.

However, even within particular cultures there are gender differences in the treatment of conflict, which raises once again the possibility that genders are themselves a particular kind of culture. On top of the broad nationalistic cultural analysis we can easily find differences in discourses of conflict. In broad terms, women see conflict as an opportunity and prefer to discuss issues and resolve them, whereas, equally broadly speaking, men see conflict as a battle for power, where one of them wins and the other is humiliated (Nelson & Brown, 2012).

Managing Conflict

Of course, conflict occurs in all relationships and among all groups, even those viewing conflict as destructive. However, the management of conflict will also differ among cultural groups. When conflict occurs, people generally engage in one of five styles of conflict management: (1) dominating, (2) integrating, (3) compromising, (4) obliging, and (5) avoiding (Rahim, 1983; Ting-Toomey, 2004).

Dominating. Dominating styles involve forcing one's will on another to satisfy individual desires regardless of negative relational consequences. For example, you and a friend decide to order a pizza, and as you call in the order, your friend mentions a desire for pepperoni. You would rather have sausage and reply, "Too bad. I'm making the call, and we are having sausage."

The person on the left did not want to engage in conflict, so he did not say anything when his friend wanted to order a pizza topping he did not like. What cultural orientation to conflict do his actions represent, and what style did he use to manage the conflict?

Integrating. Integrating styles necessitate a great deal of open discussion about the conflict at hand to reach a solution that completely satisfies everyone involved. You and your friend differ on what pizza topping you would like, so you openly discuss your positions and the options available until you reach a solution that fulfills both of your desires—perhaps getting both toppings or half sausage and half pepperoni.

Compromising. Compromising styles are often confused with integrating styles because a solution is reached following discussion of the conflict. However, making a compromise demands that everyone must give something up to reach the solution, and as a result, people never feel fully satisfied. Returning to the pizza quagmire, you and your friend discuss the conflict and decide to get mushrooms instead of sausage or pepperoni.

Obliging. Obliging styles of conflict management involve giving up one's position to satisfy another's. This style generally emphasizes areas of agreement and deemphasizes areas of disagreement. Using this style of conflict management, as you and your friend discuss what topping to include on your pizza, you probably mention that the important thing is you both want pizza and then agree to order pepperoni instead of sausage.

Avoiding. Finally, avoiding styles of conflict are just that: People avoid the conflict entirely either by failing to acknowledge its existence or by withdrawing from a situation when it arises. So, your friend expresses a desire for pepperoni on that pizza, and even though you really want sausage, you indicate that pepperoni is fine and place the order.

Skills You Can Use: Using Culture to Persuade

When attempting to persuade someone or to develop a positive relationship with someone, communicating in a manner consistent with his or her culture will increase your chances of success.

Transacting Culture

You may have noticed that although we said culture was not equivalent to nation or geography, many of the features we have focused on so far do actually make exactly that equation of culture and geography. This is because that is what the research is focused on, instead of what we think is most important. If you think geography defines cultures, then you can look for geographic differences in such things as attitudes to time or conflict. If on the other hand you treat culture as based in language and meaning practices rather than geography, then you will look for a different sort of difference! You will ask, for example, what are the differences between the meanings found in discourses of heterosexual and homosexual people, men and women, bikers and naturalists, Baptists and Mormons, Republicans and Democrats. What markers in their speech identify them as members of a particular community?

The preceding section emphasized a set of broad and general differences resulting from seeing culture in structural or geographical terms. Structural discussions of cultural characteristics treat culture very broadly and categorically: If you are a Westerner, you will behave and communicate in the Western way. Although such broad-brush ideas are sometimes helpful, especially when traveling to other countries, dealing with international relationships, or discussing the clash of cultures and/or diversity, it is important to go beyond the broad ideas and add some finer detail. And of course just because we have made this into a separate chapter it does not mean you should forget everything you have learned about nonverbal communication and the way in which different cultures treat haptics, chronemics, and kinesics (Chapter 5).

Indeed, a lot of *who you are* depends on *where you are,* or at least on *where you come from,* as well as on the groups you belong to and how they expect people to behave. You are not alone: You *belong* and do not always have a choice. You belong to many groups, some small (groups of friends or neighbors), some large (your citizenship or your ethnic group), some central to your life (family, friends), and some probably peripheral (your tax group, your shoe size). Somewhere in there, somewhere in your sense of yourself, however, is the culture(s) that you see as yours.

Studying culture as a transaction focuses on how culture is created symbolically through communication and is reinforced through your relationships with others

ETHICAL ISSUE

We just offered you a skill you can use, but can this suggestion sometimes be unethical? Specifically, is it unethical to mirror someone else's communication in order to achieve a goal if doing so violates or runs counter to how you would normally communicate? Are there boundaries making some matching of communication styles ethical and other matching of communication styles unethical?

By the way...

How Culture Re-creates Itself

In a sense, people create culture symbolically and then are bound by that which they create. For example, during a personal conversation, standing a certain distance from a particular person might be considered the norm among members of a cultural group (say 1 or 2 feet apart in the United States), because proper distances have been socially constructed over time. Personal spaces are used in personal interactions, but social distances, 3 to 6 feet, are used in formal interactions or interactions with superiors (see Chapter 5). These distances differ between cultures, yet members of each cultural group are constrained and must adhere to what their culture has created, because there may be repercussions if cultural norms involving distance are violated.

QUESTIONS TO CONSIDER

1. Cultural norms may change, but this change does not come easily or quickly. How might norms be changed within a culture?
2. What norms within your own culture have changed, and are there some cultural norms that will never change?

and your everyday experiences. Cultural codes are embedded within your communication, and you "speak" culture each time you communicate. Accordingly, it is through communication that cultural groups are established and cultural membership is achieved.

Culture Is Embedded Within Your Communication

Your culture is coded in your communication not only in the language you speak but also in the thoughts you express and the assumptions you make. Obviously, talk accomplishes this in the straightforward sense: French men and women speak French. But they also speak "*being* French." Accordingly, every time a person communicates, other people know something about his or her culture. When someone is seen wearing "cultural clothes," difference is assumed, but that person actually *wears* his or her culture in talk and behavior, too.

Your two authors, Steve and David, are different. Steve is English; David is American. When we travel in the United States, people say to Steve, "I love your accent," but when we travel in the United Kingdom, they say it to David. So which of us has an accent? No one in either place ever says with marvel to us, "You speak good English," though when we go to France, people might say, "You speak good French" (if we did). In the United Kingdom, people can tell that Steve is from "the West country," and in the United States, they know David is *not* from "the South." All of them can tell, even on the phone, that we are not ethnic Dutch or Indonesian. They also know we are not women or 5 years old. This is not only a result of vocalic differences but also a result of what we say and how we say it.

When Steve first met a new colleague (an Eastern European), the conversation lasted only briefly before the colleague said, "You're not American." Steve said, "Oh, the old accent gives me away yet again!" but the colleague said, "No, actually. I'm not a native English speaker, and I can't tell the difference between English and American accents. It was something in your *style* that announced you as 'other.'"

David grew up on a farm in rural Indiana, and like everyone, his communication styles and assumptions about the world were influenced and informed by people around him. He views the world differently and communicates differently than someone who was raised in the city, someone who grew up wealthy, or someone who has never worked the land. His rural Indiana cultural beliefs and values are displayed by what he says and how he says it. Rural Indiana communication styles and patterns are embedded in his talk.

Culture Goes Beyond Physical Location

Notwithstanding the importance of a person's place of origin, Steve is not just "West country," and David is not just "rural Indiana." Steve is a coxswain. David is a radio announcer. Steve is a father. David is a bartender/bouncer. Steve is a genealogist. David is a singer. Both of us are academics. These cultural activities and roles—past and present—have influenced our views of the world and our communication styles.

Furthermore, each is cultural in its own right. Steve communicates coxswain culture, father culture, genealogy culture, and academic culture. David communicates radio announcer culture, bartender/bouncer culture, singer culture, and academic culture. At times one may be more pronounced than others. Also at times it may be more important to enact membership into one culture than another. For instance, at academic conferences, we tend to communicate academic culture rather than coxswain or bartender/bouncer culture—although doing the latter may be a way to liven up future conferences!

Would someone studying biker culture within the Untied States be more likely to take a structural approach to culture or a transacted approach to culture?

What ultimately becomes clear—other than we have just spent too much time talking about ourselves—is that people belong to multiple cultures and that cultural membership is enacted through communication.

Cultural Groups Are Created Through Communication

As we have discussed in great detail, a structural understanding of culture as being encompassed by a nation-state, a region, an ethnicity, or a religion is restrictive. It does not give an entirely accurate depiction of culture in everyday life. For instance, several cultures may exist within one country (Houston & Wood, 1996). These cultural groups are recognized and differentiated through their unique communication and meaning systems.

Co-Cultures

Co-cultures are smaller groups of culture within a larger cultural mass. For instance, most countries have regions regarded as different and distinctive (the South, the Midwest, Yorkshire, the Valley). The belief systems in these small and diverse groups are often recognized as distinct from those within the larger society or nation. A large group like "Americans" can be broken down into smaller groups ("Northern Americans" and "Southern Americans") containing smaller sets of both nations and societies, such as Irish Americans, Southerners, Sioux, African Americans, Iowans, or Republicans.

Sociologically and demographically, discussions of co-cultures are significant because they underscore the vast number of cultures that can be explored and that encompass a person's life. However, there is still the tendency to take on a structural approach to their study. Accordingly, someone might say, "Republicans communicate this way, while Democrats communicate that way."

Speech Communities

A more communication-based view labels these cultures as speech communities (Hymes, 1972; Philipsen, 1975, 1997). **Speech communities** are cultures defining membership in terms of speaking patterns and styles that reinforce beliefs and values of the group. Essentially, cultural groups are set apart based on their unique communication styles. In this way, various **speech (communication) codes**, or a culture's verbalizations of meaning and symbols, tend to have built into them certain ways of understanding the world that guide the particular talk patterns people use in conversation with one another.

co-cultures: smaller groups of culture within a larger cultural mass

speech communities: sets of people whose speech codes and practices identify them as a cultural unit, sharing characteristic values through their equally characteristic speech

speech (communication) codes: sets of communication patterns that are the norm for a culture, and only that culture, hence defining it as different from others around it

How might break time at a factory be an opportunity to learn about and enact cultural membership within this culture?

One characteristic of any culture is what it takes for granted. For example, in a particular culture, certain topics can be talked about and certain ideas are taken for granted, even during persuasion. Kristine Muñoz (Fitch, 2003) has written about these taken-for-granted assumptions as **cultural persuadables**, certain topics that people in a society never bother to persuade anyone else about because their arguments are always raised against a background of common understanding and shared beliefs. For instance, some speech communities adhere to very traditional notions of gender roles. Accordingly, it is unnecessary to say anything directly about these gender roles because they are implicit in everything that is communicated. Also, in the United States, people may just say "because it is the right thing to do" without elaborating on why something is the right thing for the principle on which the judgment is based (life, liberty, pursuit of happiness).

Teamsterville and Nacirema

So, multiple cultures exist based on the unique ways in which they communicate and what is taken for granted in communication. As mentioned earlier, we can therefore pinpoint and study an essentially limitless number of cultures throughout the world. Two classic studies examining the cultures of "Teamsterville" and "Nacirema" exemplify this approach and laid the groundwork for subsequent research.

Communication scholar Gerry Philipsen (1975) explored the talk in Teamsterville, a pseudonym for a working-class community in Chicago showing a "man's communication style." For members of this community, the style of speech occasionally prefers action to words and is based on talking only when power is equal or symmetrical. In this community, a man demonstrates power by punching someone rather than talking about a problem. Speech is regarded as an inappropriate and ineffective way of communicating in situations when demonstrating power. For example, if a man were insulted by a stranger, the culturally appropriate way to deal with the insult would be to inflict physical damage rather than discuss the issue. In Teamsterville, speech in such a situation would be characterized as weak. On the other hand, when a man in Teamsterville is among friends, his speech is permitted to establish his manliness. If a man's friend made a derogatory remark about the man's girlfriend, the man would either take the remark as a tease or simply tell the friend not to say such things, and violence would not result as it would in the case of strangers saying the same thing.

In addition to his identification of the cultural Code of Honor carried out by the men of Teamsterville as they "do manliness," Philipsen (1997) identified a cultural Code of Dignity, which he identified as characteristic of the "Nacirema" (*American* spelled backward). This communication code emphasizes relationships, work, communication, and individual/self and is quite easily discovered on TV talk shows and in the broader context of speech in large parts of the United States.

cultural persuadables: the cultural premises and norms that delineate a range of what may and what must be persuaded (as opposed to certain topics in a society that require no persuasive appeal because the matters are taken for granted)

Cultural Membership Is Enacted Through Communication

Enacting membership in a cultural group means communicating and assigning meaning in ways similar to other members of that group. For instance, musicians enact membership into a musician culture by communicating like members of that culture. It can be broken down further, and we can distinguish musician cultures related to jazz, blues, death metal, hip-hop, rhythm and blues, country, bluegrass, rockabilly, and barbershop just to name a few. Once again, each cultural group communicates in unique ways, and enacting membership requires communicating as such.

ETHICAL ISSUE

Is it unethical to attempt to enact membership into a cultural group if you are not a legitimate member?

However, enacting membership into a cultural group is more complicated and restrictive than it may initially appear. If you want to be a rapper, you cannot just talk like a rapper and suddenly become one. It is not just the act of communicating that establishes membership into a cultural group; it is also, and more important, knowing the meaning of that communication that does so. A cultural understanding is required. If you do not know how to perform membership in a particular community, you are excluded from it. Membership in a culture can be represented in and restricted by one's knowledge of speech (communication) codes.

The unique ways of communication and the underlying meaning of that communication create a sense of otherness or separateness. Some cultural groups may rejoice in their exclusivity. For instance, certain clubs or organizations may have secret ways of communicating concealed from everyone but their members like their secret handshake. When "outsiders" attempt to enact membership into certain cultural groups, they may be referred to as "fakes" or "wannabes." Members of rural communities often view people who move into the area with suspicion. These new people may be living in the same area, but they do not automatically become members of the culture.

Cultural speech (communication) codes must be learned and understood before a person can fully enact membership into a group. Doing so requires interacting and forming relationships with members of that cultural group. It is through relating that cultural understanding is transferred and maintained. Cultural understanding is fundamental to enacting cultural membership, and it is through relationships that this understanding is learned.

Focus Questions Revisited

What does it mean to view culture as structured?

Viewing culture from a structural standpoint has a long history in the communication discipline. This way of seeing culture focuses on large-scale differences in values, beliefs, goals, and preferred ways of acting among nations, regions, ethnicities, and religions. Research using this perspective is often referred to as either cross-cultural communication or intercultural communication.

What does it mean to view culture as transacted?

When viewing culture from a transactional standpoint, culture is seen as a coded system of meaning. Culture is a set of beliefs, a heritage, and a way of being that is transacted in communication. When viewing culture as a system of norms, rituals, and beliefs, any group with a system of shared meaning can be considered a culture.

How is communication organized to reflect cultural beliefs about context, collectivism/individualism, time, and conflict?

Cultures can be categorized as either high context or low context. High-context cultures place a great deal of emphasis on the total environment or context where speech and interaction take place. In a low-context culture, people try to separate their relationships from the messages and to focus on the details and the logic.

Cultures can be categorized as either individualist or collectivist. Collectivist cultures place greater importance on the whole group, stressing common concerns and the value of acting not merely for oneself but for the common good. Individualist cultures focus on the individual person and his or her personal dreams, goals and achievements, and right to make choices.

Cultures can be categorized as either monochronic or polychronic. Monochronic cultures view time as valuable and adhere to schedules. Polychronic cultures view time more holistically and have a much more relaxed attitude toward schedules. Cultures also differ in their orientation to past, present, and future events.

Cultures can be categorized as viewing conflict as either opportunity or destructive. Cultures viewing conflict as opportunity perceive conflict as a normal and useful process, an inherent part of everyday life. Cultures viewing conflict as destructive perceive conflict as unnecessary, detrimental, and something to be avoided.

What does it mean to say culture is coded into communication?

Culture is coded in communication not only in the language spoken but also in thoughts expressed and assumptions made. Every time a person communicates, other people know something about his or her culture. Cultural beliefs and values are displayed by a person's communication.

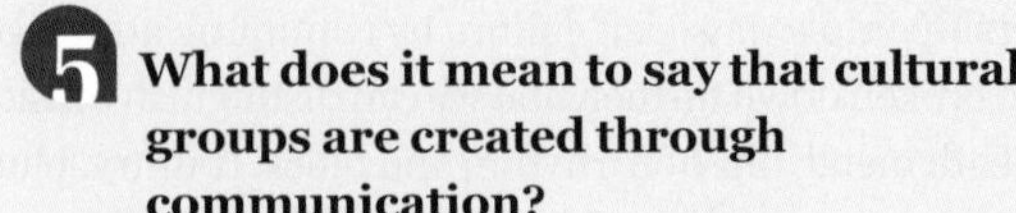

What does it mean to say that cultural groups are created through communication?

Multiple cultural groups are recognized and differentiated through their unique communication and meaning systems. Speech communities are cultures defining membership in terms of speaking patterns and styles that reinforce beliefs and values of the group. Essentially, cultural groups are set apart based on their unique communication styles.

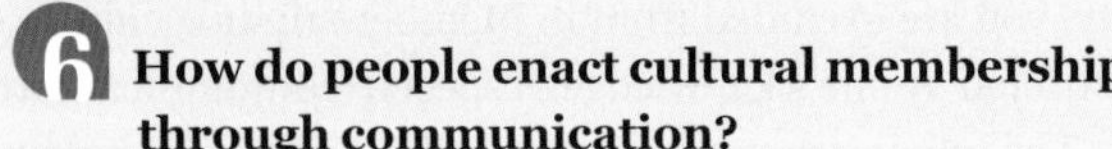

How do people enact cultural membership through communication?

Enacting membership in a cultural group means communicating and assigning meaning in ways similar to other members of that group. However, it is not just the act of communicating that establishes membership into a cultural group; it is also, and more important, knowing the meaning of that communication that does so. Membership in a culture can be represented in and restricted by one's knowledge of speech (communication) codes.

Key Concepts

co-cultures 257
coded system of meaning 247
collectivist 249
conflict 252
conflict-as-destructive culture 254
conflict-as-opportunity culture 252
cross-cultural communication 245
cultural persuadables 258
ethnocentric bias 243
high-context culture 248
individualist 250
intercultural communication 246
low-context culture 249
monochronic culture 251
polychronic culture 252
speech (communication) codes 257
speech communities 257

Questions to Ask Your Friends

1. As you did in the Analyzing Everyday Communication box, have your friends tell you about their favorite children's stories, and then discuss the themes demonstrated by those stories and connect them to the cultural ideals.
2. Ask your friends in how many cultures they view themselves as having established membership. In what ways do they establish these memberships?
3. Ask your friends to describe a recent intercultural experience. What did they find most challenging? What did they find most rewarding?

Media Connections

1. Select and analyze a movie with intercultural themes (e.g., *The Namesake*) to show how individuals from different cultures build relationships and develop understanding. Describe how culturally relevant concepts and ideas from this chapter are shown in the movie's characters, plot, setting, script, and acting styles.
2. How are different cultures represented on television and in movies? Compare current with 30- or 40-year-old shows and movies. What differences do you see?
3. How are other cultures represented by newspapers, television news, or online news sources? Can you identify any ethnocentric bias in these reports?

Student Study Site

Sharpen your skills with SAGE edge at edge.sagepub.com/duckciel2e

SAGE edge for students provides a personalized approach to help you accomplish your coursework goals in an easy-to-use learning environment.

Chapter Outline

Perceptions of Technology and Media

- Cave Drawings and Other Concerns
- Every Technology Is Relational
- Impact of Technology

The Relational Uses of Technology and Media

- The Use of Technology and Media Is a Shared Relational Activity
- Technology and Media Inform People About Relationships
- Technology and Media Function as Alternatives to Personal Relationships
- Technology and Media Are Used in Everyday Talk

Cell Phones: Constructing Identities and Relationships

- Constructing Identities Using Cell Phones
- Relating Through Cell Phones

Constructing Identities and Maintaining Relationships Online

- Social Networking Sites and the Construction of Identities
- Online Communication and Relationships

Focus Questions Revisited

Key Concepts

Questions to Ask Your Friends

Media Connections

13 Technology and Media in Everyday Life

How much time each day do you think the average person spends watching television, listening to music, reading, playing video games, and using the Internet? If you base your answer on how much time you spend engaging in these activities, doubling that number will provide a more accurate answer.

The Middletown Media Studies discovered that people actually spend twice the amount of time using media than they believe. These studies also established that people do not use media in isolation but often use two or more media systems simultaneously, an activity referred to as **concurrent media use**. For example, you may be reading this book while listening to the radio or watching television. Including concurrent media use, the most media-active person observed in these studies spent more than 17 hours using media each day, and the least media-active person observed spent a bit more than 5 hours using media each day. The average amount of time spent using media daily was nearly 11 hours (Papper, Holmes, & Popovich, 2004).

Now consider how often people send text messages in a given day. Focusing only on teenagers, the median (half send more, and half send fewer) number of texts sent each day is 60, with 18% of teenagers sending over 200 text messages daily (Lenhart, 2012). Adults send fewer texts on average than teenagers (A. Smith, 2011). However, the frequency of adult texting is rising, and current teenagers will soon become adults and bring many of their texting habits with them.

While the sheer amount of time spent using technology and media is reason enough for their importance as an area of study, perhaps more significant is the impact of technology and media on relationships and the impact of relationships on the use of technology and media. Technology and media use at home frequently occurs in the presence of family members, close friends, and romantic partners, while technology and media use outside the home often occurs with those with whom you share more social relationships, such as classmates, coworkers, acquaintances, and even strangers.

The use of technology and media takes place in the context of relationships, and our knowledge of technology and media can be best developed through a relational perspective and by examining their use in everyday life. In what follows, we discuss how people tend to view technology and media. We then explore the relational uses of technology and media. Finally, we specifically examine the ways in which people construct identities and relate through two prominent technologies: cell phones and the Internet.

FOCUS QUESTIONS

1. How do people generally perceive technology and media?
2. What are the relational uses of technology and media?
3. How are cell phones used in the construction of identities?
4. How do cell phones influence relationships?
5. How are identities constructed online?
6. How does online communication influence relationships?

concurrent media use: use of two or more media systems simultaneously

By the way...

Early Technological Fear

Perhaps the earliest recorded instance of technological fear is attributed to Socrates. He was concerned that writing would ruin people's memories. Ironically, his concerns are remembered because they were written down by Plato.

QUESTIONS TO CONSIDER

1. Why do you suppose people tend to view emerging technologies with such fear?
2. On the other hand, why do you suppose some people view emerging technologies as lifesavers?

Perceptions of Technology and Media

A person's perspective will influence how something is understood and how it is studied. Accordingly, your view of technology and media will influence how you comprehend and evaluate the information provided in this chapter. Within this initial section, we discuss how emerging technologies are traditionally viewed by people in general along with how relationships play a fundamental position in the ways in which technologies are used and understood. We will also address whether technology and media impact people, or whether it is the other way around.

Cave Drawings and Other Concerns

When a new technology is introduced in a society, it is generally framed both as something that will save the world and as something that is intrusive and threatening. It also tends to be evaluated according to standards and criteria associated with previously existing technology rather than being studied and evaluated according to its own unique standards and norms. More often than not, technological fears are more common than technological praises.

The emergence of any new communication technology has historically elicited choruses of concern and anxiety, surprisingly similar in nature. People tend to worry about the effects of emerging technologies on family, community, and, of course, children. While no evidence exists, we imagine focus groups were developed by well-meaning cave people to examine the potentially negative impact of cave drawings on innocent and susceptible cave children.

Documented criticism of more recent technologies shows people expressed similar fears when radio began appearing in homes in the 1920s, and these fears were nearly identical to those expressed about television when it began appearing in homes during the 1950s. Comic books were going to turn children into criminals, and video games were going to rot their brains. The Internet was going to destroy society by isolating people. Many of these criticisms are still being expressed, even though most have been proven wrong. In some cases, such as with concerns that the Internet would lead to isolation, the exact opposite has actually taken place.

Every Technology Is Relational

Technologies do influence the world in which you live. Regardless of whether its influences are positive or negative, each technology changes how people communicate and interact. The one constant among all technologies, from cave drawings to the Internet to whatever technologies arise next, is that they are inherently relational in their understanding and use.

At the center of all criticism and even praise of technologies rest their influence and effect on social interaction and connections among people. This influence is probably why criticism and praise surrounding each emerging technology have sounded so similar; relationships among people have been the one constant throughout all human technological development. Adapted to accomplish and meet relational needs, all technologies have influenced how you interact and relate with others.

Impact of Technology

So, technologies do influence your world, and this influence is especially evident when it comes to relationships. However, a question arises as to whether technologies are impacting humans or humans are impacting technologies. If you ask us—and we are certainly glad that you did—the answer is both. There are three primary views associated with the impact of technology.

What social influence may be impacting the use of technology in this picture?

Technological Determinism

Technological determinism is the belief that technologies determine social structure, cultural values, and even how we think. People are essentially viewed as powerless against the force of technology. As you might gather, people viewing technologies as deterministic are the same people most likely to evaluate emerging technologies with fear and suspicion.

Somewhat related to technological determinism is the belief that people are powerless against media content. Taken to the extreme, whatever is shown on television, for instance, will have the intended impact of producers and impact everyone in the audience in the exact same manner. Of course, people are not passive consumers of media. Rather, they actively interpret and evaluate media in a variety of ways for a variety of reasons.

Social Construction of Technology

Social construction of technology is the belief that people determine the development of technology and ultimately determine social structure and cultural value. The social constructionist view of technology reminds us that there are many factors in the development and emergence of technologies beyond the technology itself (Bijker, Hughes, & Pinch, 1987). These factors include human innovation and creativity, economics, government regulation, and actual users of technology.

We can use radio as an extended example when looking at the ways in which these human factors influence the emergence of technologies in society. Radio was created through the innovation and creativity of Guglielmo Marconi. His work was based on the earlier electromagnetic work of Nikola Tesla. From an economic standpoint, although there are claims made from both WWJ in Detroit and KDKA in Pittsburgh as the first licensed station, it is important to note the owner of the latter. The owner was Westinghouse—a radio set manufacturer interested in selling more sets! From a governmental standpoint, the Radio Act of 1927 established more control over licensing. The Federal Communications Commission (FCC) was created in 1934 to ensure decency on the airwaves. Ultimately, actual users exert tremendous influence on the development of any technology, determining its use, development, and place within society. In the case of radio, users influenced such factors as where it would be used and thus be made available (home, automobile, and outdoors), along with what content would be offered by broadcasters in pursuit of larger audiences.

technological determinism: belief that technologies determine social structure, cultural values, and even how people think (compare with *social shaping of technology* and *social construction of technology*)

social construction of technology: belief that people determine the development of technology and ultimately determine social structure and cultural value (compare with *social shaping of technology* and *technological determinism*)

Do you think using the Internet as a family will become a shared media experience like watching television as a family?

Social Shaping of Technology

Social shaping of technology is the belief that both people and technologies exert influence on social structure and cultural values. Many factors determine the development and emergence of technologies, including characteristics of the technology itself (MacKenzie & Wajcman, 1985). We can use a hammer as an example. People may ultimately determine what to do with a hammer. However, that hammer is better at accomplishing some things rather than others. Accordingly, the characteristics of a hammer will influence what people end up doing with it.

So, social shaping of technology views both humans and technology as responsible for what happens in the world. This perspective influenced research conducted by David (McMahan & Chesebro, 2003) concerning political structure and primary technologies of all of the world's nation-states. It was discovered that a nation-state's primary technology likely influences its political system and any political transformation that may take place.

Technologies do influence society and humans. At the same time, humans exert influence on technologies and society through such factors as innovation and creativity, economics, regulation, and the actual use of technology.

The Relational Uses of Technology and Media

Individuals do not use technology and media. Rather, *relators* use technology and media. It might sound like we are getting too technical or abstract. However, we make that distinction for a very specific reason. Your use of technology and media is always done in the context of relationships. Accordingly, that is the most accurate way to understand technology and media in everyday life. In this section, we talk about their various relational uses.

The Use of Technology and Media Is a Shared Relational Activity

People often use technology and media with others and for specific relational reasons. Most technologies—especially digital and electronic technologies—enable interaction to take place and quite frequently are the actual basis for interaction.

Even when people are not at the same location, a sense of connection also exists through shared experience with technology and media. In the case of television, sometimes millions of people are watching the same material as you, frequently at the exact same time. This sense of connection is being enhanced through the growing number of people making comments and chatting with others online while watching a television program (Proulx & Shepatin, 2012).

The use of technology and media as a shared relational activity enables people to accomplish certain relational needs. Table 13.1 presents four relational needs satisfied through the shared use of technology and media.

social shaping of technology: belief that both people and technologies exert influence on social structure and cultural values (compare with *social construction of technology* and *technological determinism*)

Table 13.1 Relational Needs and the Shared Use of Technology and Media

Promoting Interaction
Technology and media enable interactions to take place. Even in technology- and media-rich households with multiple television sets, computers, and other technology and media systems, families often use technology and consume media together, which provides an opportunity for interactions to occur. Gantz (2013), for example, found that television sports are often viewed with others, and watching sports is an activity that can maintain and enhance existing relationships.

Withdrawing From Interactions
Technology and media also allow people to withdraw from social interaction. Texting and accessing materials using cell phones and digital tablets allow people to disengage from others when desired. People sometimes even pretend to use their cell phones in order to avoid interactions (Baron & Campbell, 2012).

Differentiating Relationships
The shared use of technology and media has even been shown to distinguish particular relationships from others. Over 30 years ago, it was discovered that watching television was the most frequent activity shared by spouses (Argyle & Furnham, 1982). More recently, Padilla-Walker, Coyne, and Fraser (2012) found cell phones and watching television and movies to be among the most common media shared by families.

Enacting and Evaluating Roles
The shared use of technology and media also enables people to establish and enact specific relational roles, expectations, and boundaries (Lull, 1980). For instance, relational boundaries must be evaluated when parents and children "friend" one another on Facebook (Kanter, Afifi, & Robbins, 2012).

Technology and Media Inform People About Relationships

People base their understanding of relationships and their actions within relationships in part on media representations. Books, magazines, newspapers, the Internet, movies, songs, and television programs feature both fictional and real social and personal relationships. Of course, a variety of sources inform your understanding of relationships, and you can compare the information you gain from one source with the information you gain from other sources as you develop your own unique understanding of relationships.

Media Representations Inform About How Relationships Should Look

Media representations of relationships provide information about relational roles and demographic characteristics. Essentially, people can learn about what relationships look like and what to expect from them based on media depictions.

Relationships depicted on television and through other technologies are not always realistic, however. People have the ability to compare media depictions of relationships with relationships observed or enacted in their physical lives, but media representations of relationships may nevertheless create unrealistic expectations and beliefs about how relationships should look (e.g., Osborn, 2012).

Further, relationships depicted in media do not always look like those that audiences personally experience. Multiple races, religions, sexual orientations, socioeconomic categories, and relationship configurations are underrepresented in television and in all media (e.g., Dubrofsky, 2006). Even though media

Make your case

Positive and Negative Influences

There are positive and negative aspects to all three positions regarding the impact of technology. Make your case for and against each of them.

QUESTIONS TO CONSIDER

1. After making your arguments, which position do you support the most, and why?
2. Which position do you support the least, and why?

ETHICAL ISSUE

Do you believe that producers of such media products as television programs have an ethical obligation to combat the underrepresentation of certain groups in media content?

portrayals of relationships are often less than realistic, people may tend to believe that those relationships are normal and that their relationships should be compared to those in media.

Media Representations Inform About How to Behave in Relationships

Media representations also inform people about behaviors and interactions within relationships. These depictions provide models of behavior that inform people about how to engage in relationships. This use of media encompasses the **socialization impact of media.**

Like relational roles and demographic characterizations, however, media portrayals of relationship interactions and behaviors may not always mirror those in people's lives. Family life on television, for instance, has historically and consistently been portrayed as quite positive (e.g., Bryant, Aust, Bryant, & Venugopalan, 2001). Actual family life is not always positive, and unrealistic media depictions may create unrealistic expectations about relationship behavior (e.g., Taylor, 2005).

ANALYZING EVERYDAY COMMUNICATION

Media Depictions of College

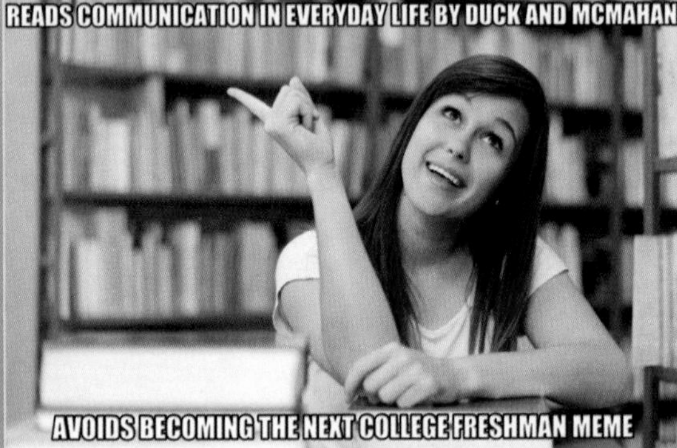

Before coming to college, most of what you knew about the experience probably came from media depictions. Naturally, some depictions of college life are more accurate than others.

QUESTIONS TO CONSIDER

1. What are the differences between what you now know about college and what you thought you knew based on media portrayals?
2. Have you had any difficulty managing expectations and realities?

Technology and Media Function as Alternatives to Personal Relationships

Technology and media provide many of the same uses and provide many of the same benefits as personal relationships. Needs and desires gained from personal relationships, such as companionship, information, support, control, intimacy, and entertainment, can be gained from media with the same level of satisfaction and fulfillment.

Notice that the header for this section of the chapter labels technology and media as *alternatives* to rather than *substitutions* or *compensations* for personal relationships. People do not necessarily turn to technology and media to compensate for a lack of companionship. Rather, technology and media use has actually been found to enrich already satisfied social and personal lives (Perse & Butler, 2005). Furthermore, words like *substitution* imply an inferior entity is filling in or taking the place of a superior reality. As we will discuss, technology, media, and personal relationships are equally functional and interchangeable alternatives.

Companionship and Relational Satisfaction From the Actual Use of Technology and Media

The relational and social satisfaction derived from technology and media comes in part from their actual use and position within the home. Some people may actually prefer the companionship provided by technology to that provided by those in their social network. Certainly, on some occasions people would rather search the Internet, listen to music, or watch a movie than be with other people.

The use of technology and media can actually provide the same amount of relational satisfaction, if not more, than engaging in a personal relationship. Cohen and Metzger (1998) previously observed that many motives for using technology and media

socialization impact of media: depictions of relationships in media provide models of behavior that inform people about how to engage in relationships

correspond with motives for engaging in personal relationships. These authors specifically compared social and relational needs surrounding feelings of security, such as intimacy, accessibility, control, and relaxation. In all instances but intimacy, media seem to have the advantage.

Byron Reeves and Clifford Nass (2002) have discovered that people actually interact with technology using the same basic patterns of interaction used with other humans. The **media equation** maintains that interactions with technology are the same as interactions with other people, and people use the same social rules and expectations when interacting with both. You interact with your computer and other technologies as if they are an actual person.

When they first hear about the media equation, many people deny that they treat technology similarly to people. Yet, why, just as some people seem more trustworthy than others, are some smart car technologies perceived to be more trustworthy than other smart car technologies (see Verberne, Ham, & Midden, 2012)? Perhaps the digital "voice" of some automobiles sounds more confident than that of other automobiles. Or have you ever pleaded with your computer to go faster when experiencing a slow connection or yelled at your computer when it crashed? It may not be so inconceivable that your interactions with technology mirror your interactions with other people, especially given the interactive nature of more recent technological innovations.

A number of studies have been conducted in support of the media equation. Table 13.2 provides three of Reeves and Nass's (2002) initial findings.

By the way...

Love and Sex With Robots

People's relationships with technology may become especially close in the relatively near future. David Levy (2007) convincingly argues in the book *Love and Sex With Robots* that by the year 2050 "robots will be hugely attractive to humans as companions because of their many talents, senses, and capabilities. They will have the capacity to fall in love with humans and to make themselves romantically attractive and sexually desirable to humans" (p. 22).

QUESTIONS TO CONSIDER

1. Do you believe that this will be the case in the year 2050?
2. Can you ever see yourself with a robot as a romantic partner?

Table 13.2 Media Equation Research Findings

Personality
When it comes to being dominant or submissive, people generally prefer to be around and interact with people who are similar to them rather than people who are different. It turns out people can not only perceive computers as having dominant or submissive personalities, through prompts and other means, but also prefer computers whose personality is similar to their own.

Flattery
People like other people who compliment them, and the same evaluative response holds true for computers. People, it was discovered, like computers who offer them praise more than computers that offer no evaluation.

Politeness
When someone asks for your feedback on a project he or she has completed or asks about his or her performance on a task, you generally provide him or her with a positive response. If someone else asked you about that person's performance, your response would be more negative than if that person asked you directly. Not necessarily deceitful, you are just not being as negative as you could be because you do not want to hurt his or her feelings. The same patterns of interaction were found to take place with computers. When asked to evaluate a computer while using the same computer to type their responses, people responded much more positively than when typing their responses on a different computer.

Companionship and Relational Satisfaction From Parasocial Relationships

While technologies themselves can satisfy relational needs, many of these needs are met through relationships established with media characters and personalities, known as **parasocial relationships** (Horton & Wohl, 1956). Relationships people form with media characters and personalities have proved just as real and

media equation: people use the same social rules and expectations when interacting with technology as they do with other people

parasocial relationships: "relationships" established with media characters and personalities

meaningful as those within their physical social networks. People consider and treat media characters and personalities just like they do family and friends.

As with the media equation, when first learning about parasocial relationships, students often consider the concept a bit outrageous and often claim they do not form such relationships. They often associate these relationships with stalkers or those who are obsessed with particular characters or media personalities. However, these relationships are actually quite normal and extremely common. In fact, we are fairly confident that you have formed parasocial relationships with media characters and, at a minimum, thought of and talked about fictional characters as if they were actual people.

Parasocial relationships have consistently been found to parallel relationships in physical social networks. Table 13.3 lists some research findings throughout the years.

Table 13.3 Parasocial Relationships Research Findings

- Similar to other relationships, people are often attracted to media characters and personalities with whom they perceive a certain degree of similarity (Turner, 1993).
- People use similar cognitive processes when developing parasocial relationships and other relationships (Perse & Rubin, 1989).
- People follow the same attachment styles used in physical relationships in their other relationships (Cole & Leets, 1999).
- Tweeting increasingly enables public figures to establish both parasocial and social relationships with followers (Frederick, Lim, Clavio, Pedersen, & Burch, 2012).
- Parasocial and other relationships provide similar levels of satisfaction (Kanazawa, 2002).
- As with face-to-face contact, parasocial contact has been shown to lower levels of prejudice (Schiappa, Gregg, & Hewes, 2005).
- Parasocial relationships are measured using similar criteria to those used to evaluate other relationships (Koenig & Lessan, 1985).
- Parasocial relationships impact the body images of both men and women (Young, Gabriel, & Hollar, 2013; Young, Gabriel, & Sechrist, 2012).
- Parasocial relationships and relationships with people in physical social networks have been found to follow similar patterns of development, maintenance, and dissolution. When parasocial relationships end (e.g., when a television character "dies"), people experience this loss in much the same manner as they do losing a close friend (Cohen, 2003).

Technology and Media Are Used in Everyday Talk

Technology and media frequently provide the basis for conversation in social and personal relationships. Reports have indicated that anywhere from 10.5% to half of all conversations involve media content to some extent (Alberts, Yoshimura, Rabby, & Loschiavo, 2005; Allen, 1975, 1982; Greenberg, 1975). Even using a conservative estimate, these numbers position technology and media as among the most frequent topics—if not the most frequent topic—of conversation among people.

Technology and Media Provide a General Topic of Conversation

Technology and media have long been recognized as providing people with a general topic of conversation (Berelson, 1949; Boskoff, 1970; Compesi, 1983; E. Katz, Hass, & Gurevitch, 1973; Lazarsfeld, 1940; Mendelsohn, 1964; Scannell, 1989; D. Smith, 1975). Much like discussing the weather, they enable people to establish a shared topic of discussion that in many cases will not lead to a heated disagreement.

As a general topic of conversation, technology and media play a vital social and relational role. Yet, even when media simply appear to provide a topic of conversation, important social and relational work takes place, and other functions of technology and media talk discussed here are ultimately accomplished.

Talk About Technology and Media Impacts Their Value and Understanding

Talking about technology and media significantly affects such things as the meanings derived from them as well as emotional responses and attitudes. You may have previously discussed with others the value of certain types of technology and media. For instance, you and a friend may have discussed the release of a new cell phone or a great website that one of you had discovered. Although not always immediately recognized as doing so, such discussions have likely influenced your use and understanding of technology and media (see Parry, Kawakami, & Kishiya, 2012).

Talk about such media content as a song, a movie, or an online video often results in new understandings of those products. An example is discussing what you watched on television the previous evening with friends at work or school the next day. Such discussions of media products can clarify the meanings attached, alter convictions about their significance, and adjust levels of appreciation. Increasingly, such discussions are taking place through online discussions (Proulx & Shepatin, 2012).

Talk About Technology and Media Impacts Their Dissemination and Influence

Discussions of technology and media aid in the dissemination (spread) of their use and messages. The use of technology spreads through word of mouth among friends more than through any other means. When you learned of the most recent digital tablet, cell phone, gaming system, or other technological product, chances are that information came from someone you know and was more influential than an advertisement by the manufacturer (see Kawakami, Kishiya, & Parry, 2013).

Media content also spreads through interactions with others. Even when someone has not watched a program on television or visited a particular website, discussing it with others can still spread the information contained within the program or site. You may not have caught a recent video online, but when friends who have watched the video tell you about it, the content of that video has nevertheless been spread to you. Especially with online content and podcasts, these conversations may lead to personal viewing or coviewing (Haridakis & Hanson, 2009). Media information is being spread, and relational connections are being enhanced at the same time.

The influence of media content may also be enhanced through their discussion with others (see Kam & Lee, 2012). Because of the issues of trust and concern inherent in close relationships, information gained from media but conveyed through a friend, a family member, or another close relationship may quite possibly be considered more significant and valid than information received directly from a media source. A magazine article about the dangers of texting while driving, for instance, may not convince you to stop this dangerous and completely stupid behavior. However, a friend may read this article and pass along the information to you. Since this information comes from someone with whom you share a close personal relationship, you may view it as more meaningful than if reading it in the magazine.

Talk About Technology and Media Promotes the Development of Media Literacy

Media literacy entails the learned ability to access, interpret, and evaluate media products. Discussion of media content impacts people's understanding and evaluation of this material, as well as their comprehension of its production and influence.

media literacy: the learned ability to access, interpret, and evaluate media products

Talking about media with those with whom you share close relationships significantly influences your actual use of media and your development of media literacy.

Communication regarding the use and interpretation of media often occurs among family members (see Davies & Gentile, 2012). Parents, for instance, influence children's television literacy both indirectly and directly (Austin, 1993). *Indirect influences* include children's modeling of viewing behaviors exhibited by their parents. *Direct influences* include rule making and actively mediating children's interpretations of television content through communication about observations on television.

Of course, the promotion of media literacy through discussions of media is not limited to those occurring among family members (Geiger, Bruning, & Harwood, 2001). Much of what people know about media literacy and their ability to critically evaluate media products has developed from interactions with friends, classmates, coworkers, romantic partners, and others with whom they share a relationship.

Talk About Technology and Media Influences Identification and Relationship Development

Talking about technology and media enables people to recognize and promote shared interests, understanding, and beliefs, while also serving to highlight differences among people. Perceptions of similarity and difference derived from conversations about technology and media can be fundamental in the evaluation of others and can play a strong role in the development of relationships.

A discussion with someone about movies you both have seen may promote feelings of similarity. These discussions are influential not only because they allow people to recognize shared media experiences but also because they allow people to recognize shared understanding of those experiences. At the same time, feelings of division or separation with someone can develop if there exists little or no overlap of technology and media experience. Likewise if there is not shared understanding of these experiences.

Of course, discussions of media content can uncover areas of similarity and difference beyond actual media use and evaluation. For example, discussing a blog entry can lead to the realization that you share certain political views with someone else. Talking with a romantic partner about a romantic relationship portrayed in a movie can provide a sense of how that person views relationships and whether or not you share such views. The topics included in media are essentially limitless, and so too are the areas of similarity and difference that can be explored through their discussion.

Talk About Technology and Media Enables Identity Construction

Technology and media that you use and enjoy are a significant part of who you are as an individual and play a major role in informing people of your identity. Discussions of technology and media allow people to enact identities related to technology use and media preferences, which are just as meaningful as other identities (McMahan, 2004). These discussions can provide a sense of voice and empowerment (Brown, 1994; Jewkes, 2002), while serving a vital role in the enactment of multiple types of identities, such as age and gender (Aasebo, 2005). Such discussions have also been found to enact professional and workplace identities (Stein, Galliers, & Markus, 2013).

technology and media profile: a compilation of your technology and media preferences and general use of technology and media; informs others about who you are as a person or at least the persona you are trying to project

Your **technology and media profile**, a compilation of your technology and media preferences and general use of technology and media, informs others about who you are as a person or at least the persona you are trying to project. David, for instance, loves watching television. He has numerous favorite shows, with *The Andy Griffith Show* at the top of the list. He enjoys most music and especially likes blues, classic soul, alternative music from the 1980s and 1990s, and anything by Eric Clapton and Prince. Thanks to Steve's introduction, David also enjoys listening to the music of Ralph Vaughan Williams but does not care much for Symphony No. 7. His favorite movie of all time, *The Blues Brothers,* is probably responsible for his initial interest in and enjoyment of blues and soul music. He rarely plays video games but tends to do well when he does play them. He never reads fiction (except for the Jack Reacher series by Lee Child, introduced to him by his friend, Julia) but is a voracious reader of history, newspapers, and academic literature. His Internet use is primarily dedicated to news sites along with watching television programs and listening to music. He prides himself on having had a Facebook account and a Twitter account before most people had even heard of the sites. Paradoxically, he rarely uses them.

What does David's technology media profile inform you about him? What does it tell you about who he is as a person, where and when he grew up, his past experiences, and his additional interests and preferences, along with the beliefs, attitudes, and values he might hold?

COMMUNICATION + **YOU**

Your Own Profile

Create your own technology and media profile, using the questions listed in Table 13.4 as a guide.

QUESTIONS TO CONSIDER

1. What do you think your technology and media profile would tell people about you?
2. Do you discuss aspects of your technology and media use and preferences with some people and not others? If so, why do you think this is the case?

Table 13.4 Creating Your Technology and Media Profile

1. Do you like watching television? If so, what are some of your favorite programs?
2. Do you like listening to music? If so, what are some of your favorite artists and songs?
3. Do you like watching movies? If so, what are some of your favorite movies?
4. Do you like to read? If so, what are some of your favorite books, newspapers, and magazines?
5. Do you like playing video games? If so, what are some of your favorite games?
6. Do you like using the Internet? If so, what are some of the sites you visit most often?
7. What television programs, music, movies, print material, video games, and Internet sites do you dislike?
8. Do you access television programs, music, movies, and books/newspapers/magazines through the Internet or your cell phone?
9. How often do you use e-mail? To whom are you most likely to send an e-mail message?
10. How often do you use your cell phone to call or text someone? To whom are you most likely to contact through voice or text?
11. Do you use a social networking site? If so, what are your primary reasons for using it, and how often do you use it?

Cell Phones: Constructing Identities and Relationships

Having discussed technology and media in general up to this point, we want to focus on two technologies that are extremely prevalent in society. We first examine cell phones and then turn our attention to the Internet, especially social networking sites. Specifically, we will explore the use of cell phones and the Internet in the construction of identities and their use in the development and maintenance of relationships.

Constructing Identities Using Cell Phones

Cell phones do not merely connect you with other people or provide you with information, music, and video. Personal and relational identities are created and maintained through your use of them. We view cell phones, along with iPods, digital tablets, and other such devices, as **relational technologies** to emphasize the relational functions and implications of their use in society and within specific groups.

The Meaning of Relational Technology

Identities constructed through relational technologies are based in part on what it means for specific groups to use them. For instance, some groups view the cell phone less as a device to contact others and more as a means of displaying social status and membership (J. Katz, 2006; Suki, 2013). Perceiving and using technology in a manner consistent with these groups assists in establishing membership into these groups and developing particular identities.

Relational Technology and Generations

A major influence on people's perceptions and use of technology is the generation in which they were born. Looking specifically at such technologies as print and television, communication scholars Gary Gumpert and Robert Cathcart (1985) were the first to suggest that the traditional notion of separating generations according to time can be replaced by separating generations according to technology and media experience.

What separates generations is not just the chronological era in which they were born but also the technology that encompasses their world. **Technology and media generations** are differentiated by unique technology grammar and consciousness based on the technological and media environment in which they were born. Accordingly, members of different technology and media generations view the use of certain technology and media differently. For example, if you were born into a generation that does not know a time when cell phones were not used, you perceive their use differently than someone born prior to the introduction of cell phones, and vice versa.

Relational Technology and Social Networks

Your social network is an equally powerful force in guiding perceptions and use of technology. While generational influence is largely determined by the *availability* of technology, the influence of social networks on your use and perceptions of technology is determined by the actual *use and incorporation* of technology and the social meanings that subsequently develop.

Friends, family, classmates, coworkers, and others with whom you share a particular relationship direct and shape your assumptions about the value of technology and what its use represents both relationally and personally. Cell phone adoption is often shared among members of a social network. Likewise, your use of relational technologies and your attitude toward them are likely to mirror those of your friends and other members of your social network (see Archambault, 2013).

relational technologies: such technologies as cell phones, iPods, and PDAs whose use has relational functions and implications in society and within specific groups

technology and media generations: those differentiated by unique technology grammar and consciousness based on the technological and media environment in which they are born

Skills You Can Use: Medium and Appropriateness

The medium through which you contact someone can make a difference in his or her perception of your message. The purpose of your message and the technological preferences of the person you are contacting will determine the appropriateness of face-to-face, telephone, or online communication.

Technological Products and Service Providers

In addition to adoption and incorporation of relational technologies, identities are created through the use of specific products and services. Specific meanings are associated with the use of particular products and service providers within a social system.

Cell phones and other relational technologies are symbolically connected to certain lifestyles, activities, or media personalities. The use of these devices allows people to associate themselves with accompanying perspectives and attitudes. In fact, one study (Lobet-Maris, 2003) found that, when purchasing a cell phone, young people are influenced less by quality or available features and more by the images or personas associated with that particular phone. Through both consumer adoption and manufacturer advertising, phones and other relational technologies may be associated with hipsters, youth, elderly, or other groups.

The actual service provider may even be associated with particular groups or issues. Individuals in the study just mentioned linked cell phone networks with humanitarianism, professionalism, and family. Thus, the use of specific networks may enable people to feel associated with groups sharing certain values or orientations.

Ringtones

Ringtones and other notifications do not simply inform someone of an incoming call or message; they can be viewed as a method of identity construction (see Pfleging, Alt, & Schmidt, 2012). People frequently select favorite music or dialogue from television programs or movies. Using these media products as ringtones announces your media preferences to others and underscores their importance in your life. Other ringtones are humorous or simply unique in some way. Whichever the case, the selection of ringtones is meaningful and is based largely on how a person wants to be perceived by others.

Of course, some people tend to keep their cell phone set on silent or vibrate rather than an audible ringtone. This decision could be an indication that the person does not desire to draw attention to his or her use of the technology. It could also indicate that the person does not wish to be socially compelled to answer, which provides greater choice in social contexts. Once again, this selection is not just personal but also relational and is influenced by how a person wishes to be perceived by others.

Performance of Relational Technology

Finally, the use of relational technologies can be considered a performance through which identities are constructed. The proper use or performance of technology has been established socially and will likely change over time. However, behaviors are judged according to present norms and prevailing expectations. Violating social standards associated with the use of technology often leads to negative responses and evaluations by others (Forma & Kaplowitz, 2012; Miller-Ott, Kelly, & Duran, 2012).

The appropriate use of technology is often determined by location and occasion. For instance, there are numerous locations and occasions where the use of technology may be deemed socially unacceptable. For instance, the use of relational technology is usually discouraged in the classroom. Your instructors may ban the use of cell phones in the classroom, but they are not the only ones who disapprove. Other students consider cell phones ringing or vibrating during class to be just as distracting and annoying as faculty do (Campbell, 2006).

Relating Through Cell Phones

Relationships and changes in technology can be seen as both relatively simple and more complex. In a very basic way, changes in technology simply allow people to achieve relatively stable relational goals in new ways. For instance, people exchange birthday greetings through sending e-cards rather than sending a traditional card through the postal service. From a more advanced view, technological transformations also change what can be accomplished, creating new relational goals and norms.

Cell phones are changing how people communicate and form relationships with others, as well as altering established relational goals and norms. In what follows, we examine the impact of cell phones on interactions among people.

Constant Connection and Availability

Cell phones position people as being constantly connected and constantly available to others. If you have your cell phone with you, you have your social network with you as well. The ability to make instant contact with another person regardless of geographic location creates a symbolic connection unlike that created by any previous communication technology.

This constant connection has led people to make contact with others more often than ever before. There are times when the content of these messages is less important than the actual contact itself. Such instances are similar to how seemingly mundane everyday talk keeps relationships going without necessarily adding much in terms of substance. Connecting with another person reestablishes the existence and importance of the relationship, confirming for both parties its existence and value in their lives.

New relational expectations have also developed as a result of this constant availability. For instance, when texting someone or calling a cell phone, there is an expectation of an immediate response. No response, or that a response does not occur in a timely manner, can constitute a violation in the relationship (Ling, 2004). Constant availability has also impacted how relationships develop, are maintained, and dissolve, especially among teenagers and younger adults (Bergdall et al., 2012).

Boundaries and Closeness

Cell phones have come to represent constant connection to those who possess your cell phone number, and how freely people give out that number varies. Giving or denying someone access to your cell phone number establishes both the *boundaries* and the *degree of closeness* desired and expected within the relationship. Limiting the availability of contact with a person establishes specific relational boundaries. How that person views and evaluates such limits depends on your relationship. Refusing to provide a cell phone number to a friend may be viewed negatively; physicians not providing clients with their numbers may be viewed as legitimate (see Wong, Tan, & Drossman, 2010).

Providing another person with your cell phone number suggests a desire for connection with that individual and perhaps an indication of the type of relationship you wish to establish. For instance, making your number available to an acquaintance could imply a desire to develop a closer type of relationship. As above, the evaluation and the meaning of this action generally depend on your relationship with the other person.

In what ways could the use of a cell phone create shared experiences?

Shared Experience

We can discuss shared experience derived from the use of cell phones in two ways. First, the actual use of cell phones constitutes shared technological experience, as was discussed earlier. More than simply transmitting information, the act of sending and receiving text messages both announces and establishes shared membership and acceptance into a group.

Cell phones also enable people to engage in shared experience even when physically separated. The immediate transmission of voice, picture, sound, and video provides people with the sense of experiencing an event or occasion together.

Social Coordination

One of the greatest relational consequences of the cell phone encompasses its use in coordinating physical encounters with others. Face-to-face interactions are frequently created and synchronized through the use of cell phones. Coordination of physical encounters can be accomplished through phone calls and text messages as well as through location-sharing applications (Patil, Norcie, Kapadia, & Lee, 2012).

Cell phones enable people to synchronize their activities to the point of microcoordination. Making plans to meet someone previously involved establishing a fixed time and physical location for the interaction to occur, but the massive adoption of cell phones has resulted in time and physical location for contact becoming increasingly fluid. **Microcoordination** refers to the unique management of social interaction made possible through cell phones. Rich Ling (2004) has observed three varieties of microcoordination: (1) midcourse adjustment, (2) iterative coordination, and (3) softening of schedules (see Table 13.5).

ETHICAL ISSUE

Do you believe physicians have an ethical obligation to provide their cell phone number to their patients?

Constructing Identities and Maintaining Relationships Online

Having discussed the influence of cell phones on the construction of identities and on relationships, we now turn our attention to online communication. Internet use is transforming knowledge, realities, commerce, politics, education, and essentially all aspects of everyday life (see Chesebro, McMahan, & Russett, in press).

While there are a number of areas to investigate, we specifically examine the online construction of identities and maintenance of relationships. These are not only intriguing topics but also fundamental to many of the other changes taking place.

microcoordination: the unique management of social interaction made possible through cell phones

Table 13.5 Ling's (2004) Three Varieties of Microcoordination

Midcourse Adjustment	Involves changing plans once a person has already set out for the encounter—for example, contacting the other person to change locations or to request that he or she pick up someone else on the way.
Iterative Coordination	Involves the progressive refining of an encounter. Cell phones have made actually establishing location and time unnecessary. Instead, people increasingly plan to meet without specifying an exact time or location. For instance, friends may agree to meet sometime tomorrow. As a result of progressive calls or messages, they eventually "zoom in on each other" (p. 72).
Softening of Schedules	Involves adjusting a previously scheduled time. If you planned to meet a friend for coffee at 3:30 p.m. but a meeting with your advisor took longer than expected and you are running late, cell phones make it much easier to reach your friend and inform him or her of the delay.

SOURCE: Ling (2004).

Social Networking Sites and the Construction of Identities

Social networking sites such as Facebook and Twitter are generally promoted for their social or relational benefits. However, they also happen to be locations where many of the transformations listed above are taking place.

We examine the use of social networking sites in terms of relationships later in the chapter. Now, we want to explore an aspect of social networking sites that people may tend to overlook. They have become important tools in the construction of identities.

Friends

The list of connections on a person's social networking site profile is an important tool in the construction of identities. For instance, the number of friends listed on a social networking site can be used by others when making social judgments about the user (Tong, Van Der Heide, Langwell, & Walther, 2008). People with a large number of friends are often perceived to be outgoing and socially connected. However, there is a point at which an excessive number of friends actually diminishes a person's appearance as socially connected (Zweir, Araujo, Boukes, & Willemsen, 2011). When someone lists 10,000 friends, others begin to wonder just how legitimate that list and those friendships actually are!

What activities are related to identity construction on social networking sites like Facebook?

Appearance is another way in which friends impact the identity construction of users. It has been discovered that the physical attractiveness of friends influences perceptions of the user's physical and social attractiveness (Jaschinski & Kommers, 2012; Walther, Van Der Heide, Kim, Westerman, & Tong, 2008). Essentially, people with good-looking friends are more likely to be perceived as good looking. People with not very attractive friends are more likely to be perceived as less attractive. Quick! Stop reading immediately and remove all the ugly people from your friends list! Make sure you come back when you are done, though. As always, we will be here waiting on you.

This next item does not require you to give immediate attention to your social networking site profile. However, you may want to examine the posts left by your friends, regardless of their level of physical attractiveness. In the same study mentioned above (Walther et al., 2008), it was discovered that socially complimentary or positive posts left by friends can improve perceptions of a user's social attractiveness and credibility.

There appears to be a gender difference when it comes to posts left by others, however. Female users were judged positively when friends left socially positive comments and were judged negatively when friends left socially negative comments. Male users, on the other hand, were actually judged positively when friends left comments about drinking, promiscuous behavior, and similar morally questionable behavior.

Photographs

The display of photographs on the pages of social networking site users is another tool in the construction of identities. One study (Pempek, Yermolayeva, & Calvert, 2009) discovered that the majority of users indicate that these photographs help them express who they are to other users. Furthermore, users tend to be very selective about the photographs that are posted online.

The selection of photographs is frequently based on which ones are the most physically flattering. Likewise, dissatisfaction with their personal appearance is the primary reason users give for "untagging" themselves in photographs of other users.

Another reason for untagging themselves in photographs is when they are shown engaging in morally questionable activities. Ironically, given the above discussion about friends' posts, male users are more likely than female users to cite being engaged in such activities as a reason for untagging themselves.

By the way...

The Future of Social Networking Sites

The number of adults in the United States using social networking sites reached 50% in 2011. When data were first gathered 6 years earlier, only 5% of adults in the United States reported using social networking sites. By the time adults finally reached 50%, teenagers in the United States were already at 76%. When the Internet-using population is specifically examined, the percentages of social networking site users increase to 65% of adults and 80% of teenagers (Lenhart et al., 2011; Madden & Zickuhr, 2011).

QUESTIONS TO CONSIDER

1. What percentages of the population do you believe will be using social networking sites in 10 years?
2. What percentages of the population do you believe will be using social networking sites in 20 years?

Media Preferences

As mentioned earlier in the chapter, technology and media preferences are frequently a basis for identity construction. In addition to their development through talk, technology and media identities are constructed through social networking sites.

Many social networking sites encourage users to list favorite media. Technology and media are also topics included in posts, and users have the opportunity to "like" certain technology or media products on Facebook. Of course, the corporations owning social media usually also sell other kinds of media that they encourage people to use in defining themselves on their profiles—such as music, movies, and books.

Media preferences, in particular, have been found to be an even more important aspect of identity for social networking site users than such "classic identity markers" as gender, political view, hometown, relationship status, and other categories frequently listed on a user's profile (Pempek et al., 2009).

Strategic

Identity construction on social networking sites tends to be quite strategic. Research indicates that users put thought into their comments and profiles (Ellison, Heino, & Gibbs, 2006). This is possible since, compared to face-to-face communication, online communication in general provides more time for people to develop their thoughts and actions.

As discussed above, people tend to carefully consider the photographs posted on their sites and consider whether or not to remain tagged in the photographs of others. Beyond photographs, all comments and activities on social networking sites can be used in the construction of identities and may be given a great deal of attention. It is not surprising to find that people believe they are better able to convey their identities online than off-line (Bargh, McKenna, & Fitzsimons, 2002).

ETHICAL ISSUE

- Students have been suspended from some schools for content on social networking sites. Should schools be allowed to suspend students for this content? Would your assessment change depending on whether the content did or did not pertain to school-related issues, activities, or people?
- Employers have based hiring decisions on social networking site content. Do you believe these actions are justified? In what ways do employers using social networking sites for the evaluation of job candidates compare and contrast with school officials using these sites for student discipline?

Public Disclosure

The *good news* about social networking sites is that they provide an opportunity for a great deal of self-disclosure. The *bad news* about social networking sites is that they provide an opportunity for a great deal of self-disclosure. We do not care how much you restrict access to your profile or how many privacy measures you enact on these sites. Consider everything that you post online to be within the public domain. Your relatives, elementary school teachers, and future employers, along with such scandal and tabloid programs and sites as TMZ, will be able to see it all.

With that said, we are here to provide an education along with such helpful advice. So, we want to take a look at what this massive public disclosure actually means when it comes to identity construction.

For the study of communication, this public disclosure of information calls into question traditional beliefs about self-disclosure and relationship development (Altman & Taylor, 1973). These views maintained that self-disclosure takes place gradually, with information shared becoming more personal as relationships gain intimacy or closeness. When it comes to disclosure on social networking sites, the disclosure of personal information takes place immediately. Further, this information is provided to everyone, regardless of relational closeness.

For users of social networking sites, this public disclosure of information provides opportunities for public confirmation and comparison. Activities and thoughts publically shared through updates are confirmed by others and given social legitimacy (Manago, Graham, Greenfield, & Salimkahn, 2008). This confirmation occurs off-line as well, but not publically and not by as many people.

core ties: people with whom you have a very close relationship and are in frequent contact; a person often discusses important matters in life with these people and often seeks their assistance in times of need (compare with *significant ties*)

Furthermore, the public disclosure of others enables comparison among users when evaluating themselves. Once again, of course, this behavior takes place off-line. There are a couple of important distinctions, though. First, public disclosure is being offered by many people, which provides more opportunities for comparison. Second, the information being shared tends to be strategic (as discussed above) and therefore more likely to be favorable and positive. Comparisons are being made to idealized images of others, which may lead to more negative evaluations of the self and to increasing pressure to enhance the image being portrayed on one's own profile.

By the way...

Early and Developing Social Networking Sites

It can be argued that social networking sites began in the form of online communities. If this is the case, Well.com, launched in 1985, would be among the first. In their current form—in which people create a profile, compile a list of connections, and visit the profiles of other members—Classmates.com, launched in 1995, and SixDegrees.org, launched in 1997, were among the first social networking sites. There are now over 200 sites based throughout the world and dedicated to a variety of groups and interests.

QUESTIONS TO CONSIDER

1. If you were to create a social networking site, on what group or interest would you focus?
2. What is the strangest social networking site you have ever come across or heard about?

Online Communication and Relationships

Having discussed the construction of identities online, we now turn our attention to online communication and relationships. Online communication enables people to maintain and enhance existing relationships, reinvigorate previous relationships, and create new relationships. In fact, increased use of the Internet actually leads to increased interaction with friends and family, not only online but also face-to-face and over the telephone (Jacobsen & Forste, 2011).

Fears that the Internet will decrease social interaction and diminish the quality of relationships appear unfounded. There are still people who champion face-to-face communication as the superior form of interaction (e.g., Turkle, 2012). However, these arguments tend to be based on opinion rather than based on unbiased evidence or actual studies.

Maintaining Relationships and Social Networks

Although online communication can lead to the creation of new relationships, it tends to be used more for the maintenance or continuation of existing relationships. This is especially true when it comes to social networking sites (Baym & Ledbetter, 2009; Ellison, Steinfeld, & Lampe, 2007; Kujath, 2011). The average Facebook user, for instance, has met 93% of his or her *friends* at least once. High school friends represent the largest category of Facebook friends, followed by extended family, coworkers, college friends, immediate family, people from volunteer groups, and neighbors (Hampton, Goulet, Rainie, & Purcell, 2011). As mentioned above, relational maintenance does not just occur online. Rather, online communication is associated with increased interactions using other forms of communication.

Online communication is also positively influencing social networks. Studying the impact of the Internet on social networks, Boase, Horrigan, Wellman, and Rainie (2006, p. 5) distinguished two types of connections in social networks: core ties and significant ties (see Table 13.6).

significant ties: people who are more than mere acquaintances but with whom a strong connection does not exist; a person is not overly likely to talk with these people or seek help from these people, but they are still there when needed (compare with *core ties*)

Internet users tend to have a greater number of significant ties than nonusers. Internet activity does not appear to increase the number of core ties. However, Internet use has been shown to increase the diversity of core ties. For instance, Internet users are more likely to have nonrelatives as members of their core network (Hampton, Sessions, Her, & Rainie, 2009).

Another consequence of online communication is the geographic diversity of social networks. Physical proximity still plays a large role in the development of social networks. However, online communication has resulted in more geographically dispersed networks (Boase et al., 2006). At the same time, Internet users are still just as likely as nonusers to visit with their neighbors (Hampton et al., 2009).

Table 13.6 Core Ties and Significant Ties

Core ties include people with whom you have a very close relationship and are in frequent contact. You often discuss important matters in life with core ties, and you often seek their assistance in times of need.

Significant ties, though more than mere acquaintances, represent a somewhat weaker connection. You make less contact with significant ties and are less likely to talk with them about important issues in your life or to seek help from them, but they are still there for you when needed.

DISCIPLINARY DEBATE

The Value of Social Networking Sites

The relational benefits of social networking sites are overwhelming. However, there are a few scholars in the discipline who view social networking sites negatively. For these scholars, relationships maintained online are not as valuable or genuine as those maintained through face-to-face communication.

QUESTIONS TO CONSIDER

1. What do you consider the strengths of this position?
2. What do you consider the weaknesses of this position?

Overall, social networking site users, in particular, also indicate feeling less isolated. They are also more likely to receive social support (Hampton, Goulet, Marlow, & Rainie, 2012; Hampton et al., 2011).

The increased likelihood of receiving support may not be based solely on Internet users being more helpful than nonusers. The greater number of significant ties and the overall diversity of an Internet user's social networks also increase the network resources. In other words, they increase the likelihood of finding someone who is willing to help. And, perhaps more importantly, they increase the likelihood of finding someone who possesses the ability to help.

Explaining the Benefits

From what we have just discussed, Internet use seems to greatly assist the maintenance of relationships and enhance social networks. However, we have not discussed why this may be true. Accordingly, we will examine the nature of both online communication and social networking sites as possible reasons why this is the case.

In what ways does a webcam affect the potentially asynchronous nature of online communication?

Characteristics of Online Communication. A characteristic of online communication is that it can be both synchronous and asynchronous. In **synchronous communication**—for example, an interaction through Skype—people interact essentially in real time and can send and receive messages at once. In **asynchronous communication**—for example, an interaction through e-mail—there is a delay between messages, and interactants must alternate between sending and receiving. Both types of communication have advantages and disadvantages.

When it comes to maintaining relationships, the asynchronous nature of online communication makes it easier for people to interact. People do not have to coordinate their schedules in order to interact. Rather, interaction can take place whenever it is most convenient for those involved. The ease with which contact can be made online may very well increase the likelihood that contact will take place at all.

Asynchronous communication also provides time for people to be more thoughtful and strategic. This additional time can make the interactions more meaningful and more likely to convey what a person wants to share and get across.

synchronous communication: communication in which people interact in real time and can at once both send and receive messages (contrast with *asynchronous communication*)

Characteristics of Social Networking Sites. The characteristics of social networking sites also explain why Internet users are better able to maintain larger and more diverse social networks, why they feel less isolated, and why they are more likely to receive assistance when needed (see Chesebro, McMahan, & Russett, in press).

One characteristic responsible is the *list of connections* users compile on these sites. These lists help people keep track of their social networks and can serve to make these connections more real and available. In terms of maintenance, we talked about Sigman's (1991) relational continuity constructional units in Chapter 7. These lists can serve as introspective units, reinforcing the existence of a relationship when people are physically apart.

Participation is easy on social networking sites. For one thing, you may have a power user in your list of connections. Power users are a group of users who tend to be active when it comes to posting, making comments on other users' walls, making friendship requests, and engaging in other activities (Hampton et al. 2012). It does not take a great deal of effort to participate, regardless.

Another characteristic of these sites, which helps explain the above findings, is that they *normalize the sharing of the mundane*. We have maintained that it is not the discussion of deep subjects or the sharing of private information that is most responsible for the development of relationships. Rather, it is the more common discussions of everyday, seemingly mundane information that drive the development and maintenance of personal relationships.

Social networking sites often encourage users to post what they are doing at a given moment. Most people are not saving the world; they are throwing out moldy bread or scraping something off of their shoes. Tong and Walther (2011) have observed that these sites normalized the discussion of these unremarkable events.

In spite of the existence of and potential for negative experiences, participation in social networking sites tends to be quite *positive*. The vast majority of both teen and adult users believe that people are mostly kind on these sites. Twice as many teen users, specifically, report positive outcomes when using these sites as report negative outcomes (Lenhart et al., 2011). These positive experiences are liable to increase the likelihood that people will continue using these sites and gain relational satisfaction and comfort from doing so.

By the way...

Emoticons

Although online communication is increasingly incorporating video and audio, it is still largely text based. Accordingly, another characteristic of online communication has been its lack of nonverbal cues to determine meaning. **Emoticons**, text-based symbols used to express emotions online, help alleviate this problem. The first "smiley face" emoticon :) was used at 11:44 a.m. on September 19, 1982, by Scott E. Fahlman while contributing to an online bulletin board.

QUESTIONS TO CONSIDER

1. Although helpful, can emoticons ever be overused?
2. As interacting online becomes increasingly video/audio based, how do you suppose that will impact the ways in which people assign meaning?

A final characteristic of social networking sites explaining their benefits is that *relating is the point*. These sites are constructed in ways that enable connection to take place. Intimacy, security, entertainment, knowledge, self-worth, and other needs generated from relationships are also provided through the use of these sites.

Further, people are able to learn more about relationships in general and their own relationships specifically through these sites. Relationships are played out through these sites, with some entirely documented through updates, photos, and other features. Relational knowledge can be developed through the use of these sites. Such knowledge may assist in the development and maintenance of relationships online as well as off-line.

asynchronous communication: communication in which there is a slight or prolonged delay between the message and the response; the interactants must alternate between sending and receiving messages (contrast with *synchronous communication*)

emoticons: text-based symbols used to express emotions online, often to alleviate problems associated with a lack of nonverbal cues

Focus Questions Revisited

How do people generally perceive technology and media?

People frequently view technology and media with suspicion, especially initially. Ultimately, all technology and media have influenced relationships in some manner, which has made responses to technology and media historically quite similar. Technology and media are viewed by some people as controlling societal development and by other people as being merely tools without great influence.

What are the relational uses of technology and media?

The use of technology and media is a shared relational activity that enables people to come together, withdraw from relationships, and enact specific relational roles. Media content informs people about how relationships should look and how people should behave in relationships. Technology and media function as coequal alternatives to personal relationships. Technology and media are also used in everyday talk. Beyond providing a general topic of conversation, talk about technology and media impacts their interpretation and understanding. Talk about technology and media also impacts their dissemination and influence, promotes the development of media literacy, influences identification and relationship development, and enables identity construction.

How are cell phones used in the construction of identities?

Identities constructed through relational technologies are based in part on what it means for groups to use them, such as generations and social networks. Identities are also created through the use of specific products and services, as well as through ringtones and the actual performance of cell phones.

How do cell phones influence relationships?

Cell phones have come to represent constant connection to those who possess your number. Giving someone your cell phone number or denying someone access to your number establishes both the boundaries and the degree of closeness desired and expected within your relationship with that person. A new relational expectation of constant availability has subsequently developed. Also, shared experience develops from the actual use of cell phones and from the immediate transmission of voice, picture, sound, and video. Finally, the use of cell phones makes possible the microcoordination of physical social interaction.

How are identities constructed online?

Examining social networking sites specifically, identities are constructed through lists of connections, photographs, media preferences, strategic work, and massive public disclosure.

How does online communication influence relationships?

Although online communication can lead to the creation of new relationships, it tends to be used more for the maintenance or continuation of existing relationships. Examining social networking sites specifically, benefits to relationships can be explained by the nature of online communication and the general characteristics of such sites.

Key Concepts

asynchronous communication 283
concurrent media use 263
core ties 280
emoticons 283
media equation 269
media literacy 271
microcoordination 277
parasocial relationships 269
relational technologies 274
significant ties 281
social construction of technology 265
social shaping of technology 266
socialization impact of media 268
synchronous communication 282
technological determinism 265
technology and media generations 274
technology and media profile 272

Questions to Ask Your Friends

1. Ask your friends to estimate the amount of time they spend using media every day. How do their responses compare with the average daily media use revealed by the Middletown Media Studies? If there is a significant difference between your friends' estimations and the numbers discovered in the Middletown Media Studies, why do you think this discrepancy exists?
2. Ask a few of your friends separately to describe their technology and media profile, and then compare their responses. Do you notice any similarity among their responses? If so, why do you think this similarity exists? What impact would this similarity of technology and media uses and preferences have on the relationships among your friends?
3. If you have your own page on a social networking site, ask your friends to compare how you present yourself on this page to how you present yourself off-line. In what ways are they different and similar?

Media Connections

1. Examine how characters on television programs use and perform relational technology. Do their use and performance of technology parallel those of your friends, family, coworkers, or classmates?
2. Describe how relationships are featured in the television, print, and Internet advertisements of cell phone companies.
3. Compare recent media depictions of relationships with media depictions of relationships from previous decades. What changes do you recognize?

Student Study Site

SAGE edge™

Sharpen your skills with SAGE edge at edge.sagepub.com/duckciel2e

SAGE edge for students provides a personalized approach to help you accomplish your coursework goals in an easy-to-use learning environment.

Chapter Outline

Public Address and Relating to Audiences

Analyzing Audiences

Speeches to Convince and Speeches to Actuate

Speeches to Convince

Speeches to Actuate

Sequential Persuasion

Foot in the Door

Door in the Face

Pregiving

Emotional Appeals

Fear: Buy This Book and No One Gets Hurt!

Guilt: Have You Ever Seen Two Grown Professors Cry?

Lost Emotions

Compliance Gaining

Relational Influence Goals

Secondary Goals of Compliance Gaining

Compliance Gaining Strategies

Focus Questions Revisited

Key Concepts

Questions to Ask Your Friends

Media Connections

14 Public and Personal Influence

From "Hey, *buddy,* can you spare a dime?" to "*Dad,* I need a ride to Mason's at six o'clock tonight," relational claims and reminders are the basis of much persuasion and influence. Many forms of persuasion are based on relational themes and implied obligations of connections among people, and they are so common that people do not even realize it is happening. You do favors for your friends, for example, because that is what friends do. Beyond personal relationships, politicians, organizations, and businesses strive to develop personal connections with voters, supporters, and customers in order to influence them.

This chapter looks at social and personal influence, partly as it has been conceived in previous research on persuasion techniques and partly in terms of the underlying relational assumptions that persuasion basically relies upon. You will gain a better understanding of persuasion taking place within personal relationships in your role as the persuader and your role as the target of persuasive attempts. You will also gain a better understanding of persuasion taking place through sales attempts and through acts of civic engagement.

In what follows, we examine four major areas of public and personal influence: (1) public address, (2) sequential persuasion, (3) emotional appeals, and (4) compliance gaining. We begin by discussing public address from a relational perspective and examining types of persuasive presentations. Sequential persuasion will assist you not only when developing a campaign to secure donations or volunteers but also in your everyday life when attempting to influence or being influenced by others. The study of emotions is a growing area of the discipline of communication—and for good reason. Emotions are powerful tools of persuasion. Finally, compliance gaining specifically focuses on personal attempts at influence that occur each day, and we explore various strategies used when attempting to persuade others.

As you read this chapter, one particular question might arise: What is with all the tables? There are more tables included within this chapter than the other chapters, but there is a reason for including so many. There is a great deal of information to consider within this area of study, and it is very easy to get overwhelmed by the various categories and components included within these sections. Accordingly, the tables are used to help synthesize this information and present it in as clear a manner as possible. So, there are a lot of tables, but they hopefully will assist your exploration of the material.

FOCUS QUESTIONS

1. What are areas to consider when analyzing audiences?
2. What are the types of persuasive presentations?
3. What are the techniques of sequential persuasion?
4. Are emotions physical or symbolic and relational, and why should they be included in a chapter on public and personal influence?
5. What are the relational influence goals of compliance gaining?
6. What are the original five strategies (categories) of compliance gaining?
7. What contextual influences impact the selection of compliance gaining strategies?

Can public and personal influence be studied without considering relationships?

Public Address and Relating to Audiences

At first glance, public speaking—in which both the speaker and the audience play active roles based on and guided through socially established norms and expectations—may appear as merely the enactment of social roles. If public speaking were simply the enactment of social roles, a speaker and an audience would be interchangeable—much like a given customer at a fast-food restaurant and a given cashier. However, public speaking more closely resembles the unique personal relationships that you share with your friends, family, and romantic partners in which the people are irreplaceable; that is, if a speaker or an audience were replaced, the interaction would be totally different.

Recognition of the relationship between speakers and an audience begins with acknowledging the similarities between public speaking and personal relationships. In personal relationships, people seek to inform, understand, persuade, respect, trust, support, connect, satisfy, and evoke particular responses from one another, and such objectives exist in public speaking situations. In personal relationships, people must adjust to one another just as speakers must adjust to each unique audience to satisfy the goals of a public presentation. People transact their personal relationships through communication and create meaning and understanding that go beyond the simple exchange of symbols, and the same transactions occur during public presentations.

Relational connections with audiences are often established by noting identification with the audience or how the speaker and the audience are alike in some manner or form, through discussing shared experiences, shared connections with the topic, or shared hopes, fears, joys, and concerns (Burke, 1969). People tend to trust and like others whom they perceive as similar to them. Additionally, through identification, the meaning framework of a speaker becomes apparent. People feel as if they understand the way a speaker thinks and views the world because of the similarities between them. Consequently, a speaker's words become more understandable and more believable because the audience members are able to match the speaker's ways of thinking to their own.

Analyzing Audiences

Analyzing audiences and adapting a presentation and its delivery accordingly are fundamental to effective public speaking. As a speaker, you must determine the best way to develop and maintain a positive relationship between yourself and audiences and between audiences and the material. In what follows, we discuss various factors that will impact approaches to the audience and provide suggestions and guidelines for developing effective presentations.

Does public speaking simply involve the enactment of social roles?

Relationship With the Speaker

As mentioned above, you must establish and maintain an appropriate relationship with an audience and base all decisions about a speech in part on that relationship. A relationship with an audience may already exist outside the public speaking context. An audience, for example, may consist of colleagues, supervisors, employees, classmates, group members, or community members, and their preexisting relationships with you will impact how they view you personally and what they expect from your presentation.

How an audience views you personally has a profound impact on presentations. A speaker's credibility is crucial to the success of a presentation. The most successful individuals tend to be those who are (a) considered knowledgeable about the topic, (b) trusted, and (c) concerned about the audience.

These characteristics touch on the three primary dimensions of credibility: knowledge, trustworthiness, and goodwill (Gass & Seiter, 2011). Notice that these components are often attributed to those with whom you share a personal relationship. In fact, perceptions of credibility are often based largely on the actual relationship shared with someone (i.e., you trust a person because he or she is your *friend*, or you distrust someone because he or she is your *enemy*).

Relationship With the Issue and Position

You must also determine an audience's relationship with the issue being addressed or the position being advanced. An audience may have a positive, a negative, or an impartial view of an issue before a speaker even begins to speak. You must take this existing evaluation into consideration when preparing a speech because it will likely impact how the audience receives the presentation and the audience's relationship with you.

Previous knowledge of the issue by an audience will also impact a presentation. The audience may be very knowledgeable or have little knowledge about the issue. The level of audience knowledge and understanding of an issue will dictate the depth and intricacy of a speech and what evidence and support material are used, the language used and whether terminology must be defined or explained, and how much time must be spent orienting the audience to the topic.

Skills You Can Use: Attitudes, Beliefs, and Values in Everyday Communication

Most of what is included within this chapter can be used to improve your skills as a communicator. However, you can use this opportunity to expand your skills beyond what is being offered here. When discussing attitudes, beliefs, and values, we are focused on their use when analyzing audiences for public presentations. However, the same ideas discussed here can be used when attempting to influence a single person.

By the way...

Given Beliefs

Depending on an audience's beliefs, some statements or claims of belief may need more or less support. If claiming that "the Earth is round," you might feel fairly confident that an audience will not look for proof, and unless that statement is critical to your argument, you will not need to include a great deal of support and development. Statements such as this are considered **given beliefs**—that is, the majority of people in the audience hold the same perspective of either true or false.

QUESTIONS TO CONSIDER

1. What might you consider to be given beliefs? (Be careful when compiling your list. People do not always view the world in the same way—and some do not want to go near the edge.)
2. Has anyone ever spoken to you using what he or she considered to be a given belief but you did not? If so, how did that impact his or her argument?

Attitudes, Beliefs, and Values

Determining audience attitudes, beliefs, and values also provides a speaker with insight into how an audience may evaluate and respond to an issue and how audience members may view their relationship with him or her.

Attitudes. Attitudes are learned predispositions to evaluate something in a positive or negative way that guide thinking and behavior (Fishbein & Ajzen, 1975). For example, you may dislike the taste of a particular type of food, which will guide your response to decline eating it should a plateful be passed your way at dinner. Attitudes usually do not change readily but instead remain relatively constant. Generally, the longer you hold an attitude and the more support you discover in its favor, the less likely you will be to change it. Audiences' attitudes will impact their view of you as a speaker, the topic, the occasion, and even the evidence provided to develop and support an argument.

Beliefs. Beliefs, or what people hold to be true or false, are formed like attitudes through your direct experience, as well as through media, public and personal relationships, and cultural views of the world. Whereas attitudes are evaluations of something as favorable or unfavorable, beliefs are evaluations of something as true or false. Like attitudes, your beliefs can change, but they are generally even more stable than attitudes.

Knowing the beliefs of audience members will help determine their attitudes, but the value of this knowledge does not stop there. Knowing the beliefs of an audience can also assist in determining whether certain statements or views will be accepted without the need for support or whether the audience will need to be convinced of their accuracy. Such social issues as those involving abortion, climate change, gun control, health care, illegal immigration, and sexual preference, for example, encompass many opposing and strongly held beliefs.

Values. Values are deeply held and enduring judgments of significance or importance that often provide the basis for both beliefs and attitudes. The values you hold are what you consider most important in this world. When listing values, people often include such things as life, family, truth, knowledge, education, personal growth, health, freedom, and wealth. Although all the items on this list might sound good to you, people do not agree on their importance. For instance, a person may not view wealth as all that important in life, and not all people believe in the importance of family.

attitudes: learned predispositions to evaluate something in a positive or negative way that guide people's thinking and behavior

beliefs: what a person holds to be true or false

values: deeply held and enduring judgments of significance or importance that often provide the basis for both beliefs and attitudes

Speeches to Convince and Speeches to Actuate

Now that we have discussed connecting to audiences and analyzing audiences, we can turn our attention to the two basic types of persuasive presentations: speeches to convince and speeches to actuate. These types of persuasive speeches are distinguished by their specific purpose. In both cases, though, establishing a positive relationship with the audience is vital to the success of a presentation.

Speeches to Convince

Speeches to convince are delivered in an attempt to impact audience thinking. They encompass a primary claim—essentially, what you are trying to convince your audience to believe. The four primary types of persuasive claims that can be developed through a speech to convince include (a) policy, (b) value, (c) fact, and (d) conjecture.

Claims of Policy

A **claim of policy** maintains that a course of action should or should not be taken. For example, you may wish to convince the audience that same-sex marriage should be legalized in your state. When supporting a particular policy, a speaker must demonstrate the need for such a policy, how the policy will satisfy that need, and that the policy can be successfully enacted. A speaker may also be required to prove that the policy advocated is superior to an existing policy or another policy being proposed.

A claim of policy does not have to support a policy. You could also oppose the legalization of same-sex marriage. When opposing a policy, a speaker could argue that the need for such a policy does not exist. If a need for such a policy does exist, a speaker might demonstrate that a proposed policy does not satisfy the need, that the policy could not be successfully enacted, or that other policies are superior to the one being presented for consideration.

Claims of Value

A **claim of value** maintains that something is good or bad, beneficial or detrimental, or another evaluative criterion. Claims of value deal largely with attitudes, which were discussed earlier. For instance, you may want to convince your audience that playing video games is beneficial to child development.

When developing a claim of value, you must let the audience know what criteria you used to determine and judge the value you support. Then, you need to exhibit how the object, person, or idea meets those criteria. You would need to explain to your audience what you mean by "beneficial to child development" and why playing video games meets those criteria. Claims of value go beyond simply offering your opinion about something. You must establish criteria and provide evidence to support your claim.

Claims of Fact and Claims of Conjecture

Claims of fact and claims of conjecture are related but have one key distinction. A **claim of fact** maintains that something is true or false at the *present time* or was true or false in the *past*. A **claim of conjecture**, though similar to a claim of fact in that something is determined to be true or false, contends what will be true or false in the *future* (Gouran, Wiethoff, & Doelger, 1994). An example of a claim of fact would be convincing your audience that laws banning the use of cell phones while driving decrease traffic fatalities. An example of a claim of conjecture might be that laws banning gun possession would result in an increase in crime.

Both claims of fact and claims of conjecture require solid evidence and support. Claims of conjecture are somewhat unique, however, since a speaker is arguing that something will be the case or will exist in the future. Accordingly, you are speculating about what might happen and do not have established facts or statistics to support

given belief: a belief that the majority of people in an audience will view as either true or false

speech to convince: a speech delivered in an attempt to impact audience thinking; encompasses a primary claim, or essentially what the speaker is trying to convince the audience to believe

claim of policy: a claim maintaining that a course of action should or should not be taken

claim of value: a claim maintaining that something is good or bad, beneficial or detrimental, or another evaluative criterion

claim of fact: a claim maintaining that something is true or false

claim of conjecture: a claim maintaining that something will be true or false in the future

your claim. However, existing facts and statistics can be used to support the presentation. Such evidence is used all the time when economic and other such predictions are made.

Audience Approaches to Speeches to Convince

Regardless of the type of claim being advanced, an audience's existing beliefs and attitudes will influence what you attempt to achieve with your presentation and the methods you employ. They will also influence how the audience members perceive you and your relationship with them. You can impact the thinking of your audience in the three different ways discussed in Table 14.1.

Table 14.1 Impacting Audience Thinking

Reinforcing an Existing Way of Thinking	In this case, you desire to strengthen your audience members' convictions and ensure them of their accuracy and legitimacy. Speeches that reinforce an existing way of thinking usually offer additional reasons in support of a particular way of thinking along with new or recent evidence. In these situations, audiences generally view their relationship with the speaker in a very positive manner.
Altering an Existing Way of Thinking	Here, you essentially tell the audience members that their current way of thinking is wrong or should be modified. This approach does not automatically mean that the audience will be hostile toward you or your position. However, when attempting to bring about this change, it is especially important to develop a very positive relationship with the audience. It is also especially important to enhance audience perceptions of your credibility, particularly of your goodwill.
Creating a New Way of Thinking	In this situation, members of your audience will probably be more willing to accept your claim than they would if you attempted to change their position. However, you may need to spend additional time developing the audience members' relationship with the material and stressing the importance of the issue in their lives. As always, establishing a positive relational connection with your audience will increase your likelihood of success.

Speeches to Actuate

Speeches to actuate are delivered in an attempt to impact audience behavior. You may want members of your audience to join your cause, volunteer with a charitable organization, limit their consumption of natural resources, or vote Glenn Quagmire for mayor of Quahog. You may end up influencing audience thinking as a consequence of a speech to actuate, but that is not the ultimate goal of such a speech. The ultimate goal of a speech to actuate is to impact the behavior of your audience. You can impact your audience in the five different ways discussed in Table 14.2.

Sequential Persuasion

Persuasion as a gradual process is the primary idea behind methods of sequential persuasion. These methods are most commonly used when attempting to secure donations for a community organization or charity but are also evident in everyday interactions with friends, family, and crafty salespeople (see Chan & Au, 2011; Dolinski, 2012; Feeley, Anker, & Aloe, 2012). Whether you are developing a donation campaign for a local organization, attempting to borrow money from a friend, or trying to increase your monthly sales, sequential methods of persuasion can help. In what follows, we will examine (a) foot in the door, (b) door in the face, and (c) pregiving.

speech to actuate: a speech that is delivered in an attempt to impact audience behavior

Table 14.2 Impacting Audience Behavior

Reinforcing an Existing Behavior	In this case, you desire to strengthen audience members' conviction about performing a behavior and ensure that they continue performing it. Reinforcing existing behavior often entails providing new reasons or evidence for enacting this behavior, along with increasing audience confidence and excitement about performing the behavior.
Altering an Existing Behavior	Here, you are asking the audience not to stop performing a certain behavior or to enact a totally new behavior but to modify an existing behavior. It is important that you stress the value of continuing to perform this action and its positive influence in audience members' lives, but you must urge them to perform this action in the more effective or beneficial manner you suggest.
Ceasing an Existing Behavior	An audience will probably be less supportive of this type of presentation, since you are essentially telling audience members that they are doing something wrong. Be careful not to offend them but be resolute in your support of ceasing that behavior. It is especially important to develop a positive relationship with the audience. Stress that you are doing this for members' well-being.
Enacting a New Behavior	The key to successfully persuading your audience members to enact a new behavior is determining why they are not behaving this way in the first place. Are they opposed to the behavior? Do they not know the behavior can be done? Do they not recognize the value of the behavior? Do they believe that performing the behavior is more trouble than it is worth? Do they view the behavior as unaccomplishable? Answering these questions will enable you to develop the presentation in a relational manner that best fits your audience and that will most likely persuade audience members to enact the desired behavior.
Avoiding a Future Behavior	When attempting to impact an audience in this manner, you are not necessarily reinforcing an existing behavior but encouraging your audience to avoid a specific new behavior. Such behaviors may be a concern now or in the future. These speeches often require that you provide the audience members with reasons and strategies for avoiding this behavior.

Foot in the Door

The **foot-in-the-door technique** involves making a small request and then following up with a second, larger request. The thinking is that once a person complies with a simple and small request, he or she will be more likely to comply with another, larger request—even one that is much larger than the initial request—even though it is one that would have been rejected outright if it had been asked for at first.

So, imagine that we stop by your house collecting donations for the Retired Professors Fund. We ask you to donate $20 to this worthy cause, and you comply by giving us a crisp $20 bill. You are greeted by smiling faces, profound thanks, and assurances of your kindness. Someone else then returns a few days later to further thank you and to let you know that you can do even more to support this worthy group. For only $100 a month, you can "adopt" a needy professor. You will even be sent a picture of your professor and receive periodic updates about your professor. Having previously contributed, you see yourself as the type of person who supports this sort of organization and pledge the $100 a month. According to the foot-in-the-door technique, complying with the initial request greatly increases the chances of compliance with the second, larger request and so saves some deserving professor from destitution.

Table 14.3 presents two theories explaining why the foot-in-the-door technique works. Notice, although these theories are traditionally aimed at understanding

foot-in-the-door technique: sequential method of persuasion that involves making a small request and then following up with a second, larger request

Table 14.3 Why Does Foot in the Door Work?

Self-Perception Theory (Bem, 1972)	People come to understand their attitudes, beliefs, and values through their actions. The foot-in-the-door technique works because upon contributing (an initially small amount) to a cause, a person begins seeing him- or herself as the type of person who supports a particular organization or worthy causes in general.
Cognitive Dissonance Theory (Festinger, 1957)	People prefer their actions to be consistent with their attitudes, beliefs, and values because inconsistency elicits negative feelings. The foot-in-the-door technique works because complying with the second request (even though it is larger) would be consistent with previous decisions and would likely prevent the possibility of negative feelings resulting from inconsistency.

By the way...

Internal Perceptions

Internal perceptions of social responsibility (Tusing & Dillard, 2000) and concerns of guilt (O'Keefe & Figge, 1999) have also been offered as possible explanations of the foot-in-the-door technique. Once again, though, these internal factors are based on external social and relational influences. Relationships come with certain responsibilities, and not accepting these responsibilities would be socially irresponsible and may very well lead to feelings of guilt.

QUESTIONS TO CONSIDER

1. Have you ever felt guilty when not performing actions associated with being in a particular relationship?
2. If so, did that influence your behavior?

internal matters, both the self-perception theory and the cognitive dissonance theory can be more fully understood by taking into account *relationships with others*. In the case of the self-perception theory, people may come to understand attitudes, beliefs, and values through their actions, but the continuation and evaluation of those actions and all behavior for that matter are based in large part on the reactions of others. In the case of the cognitive dissonance theory, if someone behaves in a way that is inconsistent with past behaviors, people tend to notice and may seek to uncover that inconsistency and compel the other person to behave according to expectations.

We can also examine when the foot-in-the-door technique is most successful. Factors leading to the successful use of foot in the door are presented in Table 14.4.

Door in the Face

Unlike the foot-in-the-door technique, the door-in-the-face technique does not aim for compliance with the initial request. In fact, the desire is to be turned down flat and have the "door" slammed in your face. Essentially, the **door-in-the-face technique** involves making a request so large that it will be turned down and then following up with a second, smaller request. The thinking is that people will

Table 14.4 When Is Foot in the Door Most Successful?

Prosocial Reasons (Dillard, Hunter, & Burgoon, 1984)	The foot-in-the-door technique is most effective when seeking donations for a charity, providing volunteer activities for an organization, or supporting another worthy cause. It is less effective when selling items or for other self-serving reasons.
Different People (Chartrand, Pinckert, & Burger, 1999)	The foot-in-the-door technique works best when different people make the requests. Complying with a second request made by a different person than the one who made the initial request reinforces attitudes, beliefs, and values. Essentially, a person would be saying that he or she would comply with this sort of request regardless of who was asking.
Significant Request (Fern, Monroe, & Avila, 1986)	The foot-in-the-door technique works best if the initial request is large enough that it will be meaningful to the person being asked. A small request may soon be forgotten and have little impact on a person's evaluation of attitudes, beliefs, and values.
No Material Incentives (Burger, 1999)	The foot-in-the-door technique works best when people are not given material incentives to comply. The reason is that a person would not necessarily see him- or herself as the type of person who supports such a cause but instead sees him- or herself as a person who supports such causes when there is something in it for him or her.

generally comply with the second, smaller request for a variety of reasons we discuss below.

So, here we come again collecting for the Retired Professors Fund. We ask if you would be willing to donate $200 each month for the adoption of a needy professor. Even though it is a worthy cause, you turn us down since that would be quite a bit of money each month. We then ask if you would be willing to donate $100 each month instead. According to the door-in-the-face technique, you will probably comply with this request.

The woman in this photo turned down the volunteer's initial request to become a volunteer herself but did agree to a relatively smaller request to sign a petition. What method of sequential persuasion may have been used here? If she agreed to the second request because she did not want to be viewed in a negative way, what would this be called?

As with foot in the door, we can examine why this technique works and when it is most successful. Table 14.5 provides the three primary reasons why the door-in-the-face technique works. Notice, again as with the previously discussed technique, that the second two reasons for why door in the face works involve the relationship with the person making the request. Table 14.6 provides factors leading to successful use of this technique.

Pregiving

How would you like an *I Love Professors* T-shirt for your very own? We would be happy to send you one. By the way, we just happen to be collecting for the Retired Professors Fund; would you care to donate? If you are thinking, "Wow, Steve and David are nice enough to send me a shirt; the least I can do is donate to this worthy cause," then you succumbed to the pregiving technique. The **pregiving technique** maintains that when a person is given something or offered favors by someone else, that person is more likely to comply with a subsequent request. After all, organizations do not send out return address labels along with a request for donation just because they want to make addressing envelopes easier for people.

As was done with the first two techniques of sequential persuasion, we can examine why this technique works (Table 14.7) and when it is most effective (Table 14.8). Once again, relational connections help explain why this technique is effective.

door-in-the-face technique: sequential method of persuasion that involves making a request so large that it will be turned down and then following up with a second, smaller request

pregiving technique: sequential method of persuasion maintaining that when a person is given something or offered favors by someone else, that person is more likely to comply with a subsequent request

Emotional Appeals

When it comes to persuasion and argumentation, the discipline of communication studies has traditionally focused primarily on logic and reasoning. This focus

Table 14.5 Why Does Door in the Face Work?

Perceptual Contrast Effect (Miller, Seligman, Clark, & Bush, 1976)	People generally comply with the second request because compared to the initial request it appears much smaller.
Reciprocal Concessions (Cialdini et al., 1975)	People generally comply with the second request because they feel that since the person making the request is willing to concede something, they should match the concession and also be willing to concede something.
Self-Presentation (Pendleton & Bateson, 1979)	People are concerned that other people (most notably the person making the request) may view them in a negative light and that complying with the second request might prevent or decrease those negative perceptions.

remains an important element within communication. At the same time, there is an increasing awareness of the importance of emotion when studying human behavior in general and when studying human motivation specifically (see Broda-Bahm, 2012; Yan, Dillard, & Shen, 2012).

Table 14.6 When Is Door in the Face Most Successful?

Prosocial Reasons (Dillard, Hunter, & Burgoon, 1984)	The door-in-the-face technique is most effective when seeking donations for a charity or volunteer activities. However, many salespeople tend to show the high-priced items first and then show more reasonably priced items, perhaps in an attempt to take advantage of the perceptual contrast effect.
Same Person (O'Keefe & Hale, 1998)	The door-in-the-face technique works best when the same person makes the second request. When the same person makes the request, it is more likely that reciprocal concessions will come into play.
Brief Delay (Fern, Monroe, & Avila, 1986)	The door-in-the-face technique also works best when there is a relatively brief delay between requests. Delaying the second request decreases the perceptual contrast effect. Further, concerns about self-presentation may have diminished if the delay between requests is too long.

By the way...

And Watch Television

The Nielsen television rating company sends two very crisp dollar bills when asking selected households to complete surveys about their television viewing habits. Beyond the possibility of saving their favorite show from cancelation, people in these households often complete these surveys because of receiving the two dollars.

QUESTIONS TO CONSIDER

1. Does pregiving work on you? Why, or why not?
2. Have you used pregiving on others? If so, was it successful or unsuccessful, and why?

Table 14.7 Why Does Pregiving Work?

Norm of Reciprocity (Cialdini & Goldstein, 2004)	People comply with requests following receipt of gifts or favors because they want to pay back the person who provided such gifts.
Increased Liking	When someone does something for a person or gives something to a person, the giver may be viewed more positively.

Table 14.8 When Is Pregiving Most Successful?

Same Person or Organization	The pregiving technique works best when the same person or organization makes the request. The same person or organization making the request takes advantage of the norm of reciprocity and increased liking that is derived from receiving the gift or favor.
Brief Delay	The pregiving technique also works best when there is a relatively brief delay between receiving the gift or favor and the request. If the delay is too long, feelings of obligation and increased liking may diminish.
No Bribe or Ulterior Motive (Groves, Cialdini, & Couper, 1992)	The pregiving technique works best when the gift or favor is seen not as a bribe or as having an ulterior motive but rather as an act of kindness.

Still, discussing emotion in a communication textbook may initially strike some people as peculiar. Emotions are often considered things that people *feel internally,* which seems far removed from the discussion of symbolic activity. It is true that emotions involve internal activities and feelings. Neuroscientists can even pinpoint changes in the brain when people experience specific emotions. Changes in heart rate, blood pressure, and temperature and a host of other physical changes occur when you experience any emotion.

Yet, emotion is also very much a *symbolic activity* and a *relational activity.* Symbolically, emotions and the feelings that accompany them are given meaning within a culture or society. Emotions bring about physical change, but this physical change is understood and evaluated according to established meaning. People use socially developed labels to determine what they are experiencing.

These symbolic characteristics of emotions are learned relationally. Relationships are about knowledge, connecting symbolically to others, and understanding the world. Accordingly, it is through everyday communication and interactions with friends, family, classmates, neighbors, romantic partners, and acquaintances that people come to understand emotion.

So, having discussed what emotions are and their connection with everyday life, we can now examine their use when influencing others. First, we discuss the use of fear, which is the most researched emotion when it comes to social influence. Next, we look at the use of guilt. Finally, we examine some of the "lost" emotions of persuasion.

Fear: Buy This Book and No One Gets Hurt!

Consider the many uses of fear you encounter on a daily basis. Television commercials for high-end home alarm systems warn you that an intruder may be scoping out your residence this very moment. Insurance companies claim they will have you covered if the home alarm system does not work. Politicians exclaim that if a certain package is not passed in Congress, then the country will be on the brink of collapse. Billboards caution you that drinking and driving kills, as does reading too many billboards instead of watching the road. Fear appeals are pervasive persuasive techniques, because they work very well—as long as they are properly implemented.

In all actuality, while often effective, fear appeals do not always work. It is not a matter of fear not being an effective tool of persuasion; rather persuaders do not always recognize all the elements connected with fear. Fear is a lot more complicated than expected.

Extended Parallel Process Model

Fortunately, Witte (1992, 1998) introduced the **extended parallel process model**, which explains the process of fear appeals and has been speculated to explain additional emotional processes (Lewis, Watson, & White, 2013). In order for a fear appeal to be effective, the target must perceive the threat as substantial and probable. The target must also perceive the solution as viable and possible. If the threat and solution are not perceived as such, the fear appeal will likely fail.

Two key elements of this model are *perceived threat* and *perceived efficacy*. The perceived threat entails (a) the extent to which a person believes that he or she is susceptible to the threat and (b) the severity of the threat. A person essentially asks, "How likely is it that this will happen to me, and how bad will it be?"

extended parallel process model: explains the process of fear appeals using the key elements of perceived threat and perceived efficacy

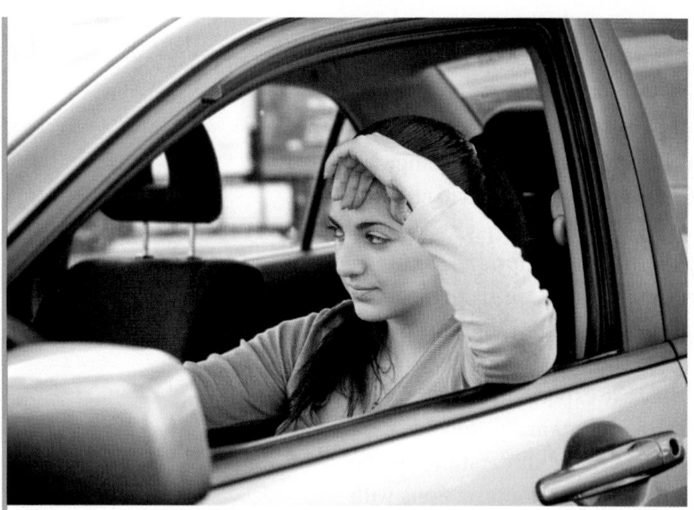

Is the use of emotion something that involves only internal feelings?

What some persuaders fail to do when using a fear appeal is offer people a way out of trouble or make this way out explicit. When a way out is offered, people then determine *perceived efficacy*. Perceived efficacy entails (a) the extent to which a person believes a recommended course of action will work and (b) whether or not he or she is capable of performing the recommended action. Here, a person essentially asks, "Will this action work, and am I capable of implementing it?"

If a person does experience fear as a result of a perceived threat, he or she will likely do something about it. A person will engage in either (a) fear control or (b) danger control, and this choice will be determined by reactions to perceived efficacy. When engaging in *fear control,* people focus on fear itself by denying its existence, not thinking about it, or simply taking deep breaths and hoping it goes away. When engaging in *danger control,* people do something about the threat, likely adopting the measure suggested by the persuasive appeal.

ETHICAL ISSUE

Is it ethical to manipulate someone's emotions in order to persuade him or her? Based on how you answered that question, are there any situations or circumstances that would justify the opposite view?

Guilt: Have You Ever Seen Two Grown Professors Cry?

Although the role of guilt in persuasive attempts has not been studied to the extent of fear, it remains a powerful persuasive tool in personal relationships and persuasive campaigns such as those representing charity organizations.

Guilt appeals are frequently used in advertisements (Turner & Underhill, 2012), and they are usually made up of two components: (1) evocation of guilt and (2) path to atonement (O'Keefe, 2002). So, a Retired Professors Fund television commercial might show needy professors with sorrowful eyes staring at the camera while an announcer discusses their horrendous plight. Then, the announcer will discuss how you can help this needy group for less than the price of a latte each day, which in essence will enable you to eliminate feelings of guilt brought on by pictures of professors in need. Naturally, you did not cause this particular tragedy, but since your life appears much better in comparison and you do not like to see people in need (guilt), you want to do something about it, so you think that donating to this worthy organization is the way to minimize these feelings (atonement).

The use of guilt is often used in everyday interactions. A series of studies by Vangelisti, Daly, and Rudnick (1991) uncovered that persuasion was the primary reason for inducing guilt in conversations and that guilt is more likely to be used among those sharing a close personal relationship. Further, stating relationship obligations ("A true friend would do this for me") and referring to sacrifices ("I went through 72 hours of labor to bring you into this world, so the least you could do is pick up a pair of socks off the floor") were the most common techniques for creating guilt in others.

Lost Emotions

Fear and guilt are certainly not the only emotions used in persuasion, but they tend to receive most of the attention from communication scholars. Nevertheless,

Table 14.9 Lost Emotions of Persuasion

Anger	Anger, like fear, appears positively related to changes in attitude. In other words, the angrier someone gets about an issue, the more likely that person will be persuaded. Of course, it is important that the anger is intentional and is positioned in the appropriate direction.
Disgust	Disgust has been found to be negatively correlated with attitude change when it comes to be associated with a position.
Happiness	Happiness has often been associated with humor in terms of its persuasive power—people tend to be happy when they find something humorous. Although findings are mixed when trying to determine whether happiness and humor lead to persuasion, they do not hurt matters in many cases.
Hope	In spite of its prevalent use by lottery officials, the use of hope in persuasion has received little attention. Like fear appeals, it seems likely that hope would be effective only if audiences found a suggested action to be a viable path to achieving whatever is being hoped for.

Robin Nabi (2002) has provided an examination of some of these "lost" emotions, some of which are included, along with what is known about their role in persuasion, in Table 14.9. Emotions are prevalent and influential features in persuasion, and we *hope* more research into their roles in persuasion is soon conducted.

This man is attempting to get this woman to comply by reminding her that they are best friends. Which compliance gaining strategy is he using?

Compliance Gaining

While the previous areas of influence are evident in both public and personal persuasive attempts, we will not focus on influence occurring specifically in actual dyadic (involving two people) relationships.

Compliance gaining involves interpersonal attempts at influence, especially attempts to influence someone's behavior. Compliance gaining has become one of the most researched areas of persuasion and possesses qualities that make it unique from other areas of research.

First, rather than focusing on campaigns or other attempts at mass influence, compliance gaining is focused on relational or dyadic influence. The focus is on what happens among friends, romantic partners, family members, acquaintances, neighbors, and people in other sorts of relationships in everyday life and everyday communication.

Second, rather than focusing on the person being persuaded, compliance gaining is more focused on the person doing the persuading.

Third—and certainly connected—rather than focusing on which persuasive techniques are most successful, compliance gaining is more concerned with which strategies are most likely to be selected. Moreover, compliance gaining research is concerned with discovering *why* certain strategies are selected in certain situations and when certain interactants (relationships) are involved.

Finally, rather than focusing only on the primary goal of compliance, compliance gaining recognizes the existence and importance of secondary goals, which we will discuss below.

compliance gaining: involves interpersonal attempts at influence, especially attempts to influence someone's behavior

Table 14.10 Goals of Relational Influence

Gaining Assistance	A relational influence goal dedicated to obtaining resources or services
Giving Advice	A relational influence goal dedicated to providing guidance
Sharing Activities	A relational influence goal dedicated to engaging in joint endeavors
Changing Orientations	A relational influence goal dedicated to changing a person's position on an issue
Changing Relationships	A relational influence goal dedicated to altering the relationship of the interactants
Obtaining Permission	A relational influence goal dedicated to receiving authorization for an action
Enforcing Rights and Obligations	A relational influence goal dedicated to making someone fulfill a commitment or role

Make your case

What Is Missing?

Changing orientations made the list as a relational influence goal, but what about *reinforcing orientations?* In this situation someone already agrees with a position you support, and you want to keep it that way.

QUESTIONS TO CONSIDER

1. Should reinforcing orientations be included?
2. Are any other goals missing from this list that you believe should be included?

Relational Influence Goals

The question that arises pertains to what people are generally trying to achieve by influencing others. Dillard, Anderson, and Knobloch (2002) have observed that while it may seem as if there are numerous reasons why people may attempt to influence others, there are seven primary goals of influence that tend to emerge.

As we discuss these goals, notice that all but one deal directly with *behavior*. When it comes to compliance gaining, changing someone's beliefs, attitudes, and values is rarely the goal and often may not even be a consideration. If you want someone to give you a ride, for example, it probably does not matter to you if that person's beliefs, attitudes, and values related to driving people around are changed. What matters is whether or not you are sitting in a vehicle heading toward your desired destination. With this distinction in mind, the seven primary goals of relational influence are provided in Table 14.10.

Secondary Goals of Compliance Gaining

The primary goal of compliance gaining is to influence someone, especially that person's behavior. Yet, there exist four secondary relational goals that impact how people go about seeking compliance: identity goals, interaction goals, resource goals, and arousal goals (Dillard, 1989; Dillard, Segrin, & Harden, 1989). These secondary goals are explained in Table 14.11. You might notice how secondary goals not only impact the primary goal of compliance gaining but also impact one another.

ETHICAL ISSUE

People frequently comply with requests from others because of their relationship. What are requests you would consider unethical to pose to a friend, even though a friend might comply? How about a romantic partner?

Compliance Gaining Strategies

Now that we have introduced compliance gaining and discussed the secondary goals of compliance gaining, we can begin to examine strategies people use to impact the behaviors of others in everyday life. Researchers have offered a number of compliance gaining technique classification systems. In what follows, we examine typologies

Table 14.11 Secondary Goals of Compliance Gaining

Identity Goals	These recognize that people desire to act in accordance with the personal and relational identities they attempt to transact and/or the personal and relational identities most appropriate in a given situation.
Interaction Goals	These recognize the desire to act appropriately when attempting to gain compliance. There exist appropriate ways of behaving and communicating in certain contexts and especially in certain relational contexts. When attempting to gain compliance, people will generally desire to conform to existing standards of interaction.
Resource Goals	These recognize the desire to maintain relational resources. When attempting to get someone to comply, people want to avoid doing something that will prevent him or her from being a potential resource in the future.
Arousal Goals	These recognize the desire to keep arousal at an acceptable level. People generally do not wish to appear upset, angry, or nervous or to display other such emotions. At the same time, people may not wish to appear too upbeat, happy, or excited.

and categories of compliance gaining strategies that have been developed. We then examine contextual factors influencing the strategy selection.

Original Typology

The earliest classification system was provided by Gerald Marwell and David Schmitt in 1967 and set the stage for many subsequent studies. These authors presented a total of 16 compliance gaining strategies but grouped these strategies into five categories: rewarding activities, punishing activities, expertise activities, activation of impersonal commitments, and activation of personal commitments. These five categories are presented in Table 14.12. As you consider these categories, note the many ways in which relationships serve as their foundation.

Contextual Influences

Compliance gaining may seem fairly straightforward at first (Person A wants to impact the behavior of Person B and selects a strategy to accomplish this goal). However, compliance gaining becomes a bit more complicated when taking into account the many contextual influences that affect a person's selection of the most appropriate and, hopefully, successful category. These contextual elements influence which tactics are used when attempting to gain compliance as well as which tactics are avoided when attempting to gain compliance. In what follows, we will examine seven contextual factors discussed in compliance gaining research (Cody & McLaughlin, 1980; Cody, Woelfel, & Jordan, 1983).

ETHICAL ISSUE

Dominance exists in relationships, but is it ethical to use dominance to get someone to comply?

Dominance. Dominance is a contextual influence of compliance gaining based on power dimensions within a relationship. French and Raven (1960) noted five bases of power that people use when attempting to influence each other: reward power, coercive power, expert power, legitimate power, and referent power. These power bases, presented in Table 14.13, continue to be relevant over a half-century after they were first offered.

dominance: contextual influence of compliance gaining based on power dimensions within a relationship

DISCIPLINARY **DEBATE**

Methodological Consequences

There is some disagreement in compliance gaining research as to how strategies should be compiled and tested. Such disagreement may lead to recall methodological problems with the social scientific approach discussed in Chapter 2. Some researchers provide study participants with a ready-made list of strategies and ask them to select which ones they would likely use in given situations. Other researchers ask study participants to provide their own strategies rather than selecting them from a ready-made list. These researchers argue that participants may select strategies from ready-made lists that they have never even considered before but mark them because they seem like good ideas. In both cases participants may offer more positive strategies than negative strategies because they want the researcher to see them in a positive manner.

QUESTIONS TO CONSIDER

1. Which research methodology do you believe is most appropriate when studying compliance gaining?
2. What other strategies could be used in future compliance gaining research?

Intimacy. **Intimacy** is a contextual influence of compliance gaining based on the relational connection among interactants. You would most likely select different compliance gaining strategies when attempting to influence someone with whom you share a close personal relationship such as a friend, a family member, or a romantic partner than you would when attempting to influence a stranger, an acquaintance, or a new neighbor. People generally are more concerned about not upsetting someone with whom they share a close relationship than they are about not upsetting someone with whom they are not close. Further, people who are close to you know intimate details of your life and could potentially use them against you.

intimacy: contextual influence of compliance gaining based on the relational connection among interactants

Resistance. **Resistance** is a contextual influence of compliance gaining based on anticipated opposition. Your selection of a compliance gaining strategy will be influenced by whether or not you think the other person will go along with your request or will oppose your request. People are generally fairly adept at determining potential resistance, but these assessments are not always accurate. For example, there has probably been an occasion when you were convinced that someone was going to resist your request,

Table 14.12 Compliance Gaining Strategies

Rewarding Activities	These seek compliance through positivity. Someone seeking compliance may make promises or act nicely.
Punishing Activities	These seek compliance through negativity. Someone seeking compliance may make threats or punish another person.
Expertise Activities	These seek compliance through perceptions of credibility or wisdom. Someone seeking compliance may advise another person to do something based on knowledge of the situation or the ways of the world.
Activation of Impersonal Commitments	This seeks compliance through the manipulation of internal feelings of obligation and appropriate behavior. Someone seeking compliance may describe positive or negative self-feelings that could result.
Activation of Personal Commitments	This seeks compliance through appealing to obligations to others. The basis of activation of personal commitments is the obligation that comes with being in a relationship. *

* We would actually prefer calling activation of impersonal commitments *personal commitments* and activation of personal commitments *relational commitments*, but Marwell and Schmitt did not ask us. Still, that might help you distinguish these two categories as long as you remember their actual names should they come up while taking an examination.

Table 14.13 Bases of Power

Reward Power	This is used when someone has something that another person wants or possesses the ability to provide it.
Coercive Power	This is used when someone is capable of imposing punishment on another person.
Expert Power	This is used when someone possesses needed knowledge or information.
Legitimate Power	This is used when someone holds a formal position or role.
Referent Power	This is used when someone wants to influence another person who wishes to emulate or happens to admire him or her.

spent quite a bit of time determining your strategy, and had already become a bit irritated that the person would even consider denying your wishes only to discover that the person was perfectly agreeable. Of course, the opposite situation has probably happened as well when you were met with unexpected resistance to your request.

Relational Consequences. Relational consequences is a contextual influence of compliance gaining based on the perceived effects a compliance gaining strategy might have on a relationship. Relational consequences can be examined in three different ways.

First, attempting to gain compliance comes with the potential of harming a relationship. A negative compliance gaining strategy may cause strife within a relationship, perhaps leading to relational disengagement or disintegration of the relationship in its present form.

Second and certainly connected, attempting to gain compliance could result in losing a source of future support and other resources. A negative compliance gaining strategy could be successful at obtaining a desired response from a person at the present time but could result in not being able to come back to that person in the future.

Third and finally, attempting to gain compliance could actually lead to the enhancement of a relationship and the reinforcement of a potential source. The negative consequences tend to be addressed more often than the positive consequences, but the positive relational consequences are just as likely. For instance, someone with the potential to use negative compliance gaining strategies but who chooses to use positive compliance gaining strategies may be looked upon more favorably. These actions may thus result in increased liking and dependability.

ANALYZING EVERYDAY COMMUNICATION

Case of the Cool Professor

You may have taken a class with a professor whom you really liked or related to. Consider how instructors use the five forms of power (Table 14.13) in the classroom—especially referent power! (The coolness factor of professors remains unparalleled!)

QUESTIONS TO CONSIDER

1. Which of these forms of power do you believe are most effective?
2. What contextual factors might influence your choices?

Personal Benefit. Personal benefit is a contextual influence of compliance gaining based on potential personal gain. It is also possible to consider the personal gain of the person being influenced. For instance, if someone is doing something dangerous or placing others in harmful situations, a negative strategy may be

resistance: contextual influence of compliance gaining based on anticipated opposition

relational consequences: contextual influence of compliance gaining based on the perceived effects a compliance gaining strategy might have on a relationship

personal benefit: contextual influence of compliance gaining based on potential personal gain

COMMUNICATION + YOU

Multiple Contextual Consequences

People often must take multiple contextual consequences into account. For instance, a friend may be dating someone who is not very good for him or her. You know your friend would benefit from leaving this person, but mentioning this may threaten your friendship.

QUESTIONS TO CONSIDER

1. Can you recall a time when you were faced with a situation impacting both relational consequences and personal benefits of a friend? What did you do?
2. What situations justify risking a friendship out of concern for a friend?

selected because compliance is so important that successful influence will outweigh the potential negative consequences. If compliance is simply important for whatever reason, strategies will be selected with decreased regard for relational drawbacks. Any negative consequences would be considered worth it in order to achieve the desired compliance.

Rights. Rights is a contextual influence of compliance gaining based on the degree to which the desired outcome seems justified. If a neighbor is playing loud music in the middle of the night, you might feel justified to ask him or her to turn down the music if it is disturbing you. If you think the neighbor's clothes are ugly and wish he or she would change fashions, you might feel less justified in making such a request. Sometimes the right to seek compliance is obvious, but it can get tricky. Relationships frequently inform people of whether or not attempts at compliance are justified, but even then, each unique relationship will vary as to what is considered justified. Asking a neighbor, a coworker, a stranger, or an acquaintance to improve his or her clothing choices may seem less justified than, say, asking the same of a friend, a romantic partner, or a family member, but justification in these relationships may still be tenuous. Other issues complicate things even more. Consider attempting to get a parent to discipline his or her child, for instance. Certain relationships might increase a person's right to make such a request, but there may nevertheless be disagreement as to whether a person is actually justified. Whatever the case, the extent to which a person does or does not feel justified will influence the selection of compliance gaining strategy.

Apprehension. Apprehension is a contextual influence of compliance gaining based on anxiety resulting from the circumstances. Certain compliance gaining situations are more stressful than others—for instance, asking a supervisor for a raise, seeking a higher grade on an assignment from an instructor, or asking someone out on a date. Other compliance gaining situations such as asking someone to pass the salt or asking someone to close a window may be less stressful. Of course, things are never quite as straightforward as they appear, and these examples may or may not lead to apprehension. Contextual factors encompassing the compliance gaining situation offer more accurate predictions of apprehension than the situation itself. Simply glance at the above items for a few prime examples. Each can influence whether or not a situation will lead to apprehension. This is an important point, because it underscores that these contextual influences do not exist in isolation; they exist together and impact one another.

rights: contextual influence of compliance gaining based on the degree to which the desired outcome seems justified

apprehension: contextual influence of compliance gaining based on anxiety resulting from the circumstances

Focus Questions Revisited

What are areas to consider when analyzing audiences?

When analyzing audiences, it is important to consider an audience's relationship with the speaker and the audience's relationship with the issue and position. It is also important to consider the attitudes, beliefs, and values of an audience.

What are the types of persuasive presentations?

The two primary types of persuasive speeches are speeches to convince and speeches to actuate. Speeches to convince are delivered in an attempt to impact audience thinking, and they encompass a primary claim—essentially, what you are trying to convince your audience to believe. The following are the four primary types of persuasive claims that can be developed through a speech to convince: (1) policy, (2) value, (3) fact, and (4) conjecture. Speeches to actuate are delivered in an attempt to impact audience behavior.

What are the techniques of sequential persuasion?

Techniques of sequential persuasion include (a) foot in the door, (b) door in the face, and (c) pregiving. The foot-in-the-door technique involves making a small request and then following up with a second, larger request. The door-in-the-face technique involves making a request so large that it will be turned down and then following up with a second, smaller request. The pregiving technique maintains that when a person is given something or offered favors by someone else, that person is more likely to comply with a subsequent request.

Are emotions physical or symbolic and relational, and why should they be included in a chapter on public and personal influence?

Emotions are both physical and symbolic and relational. Often considered something that people feel internally, emotion is also very much a symbolic and relational activity. Symbolically, emotions and the feelings that accompany them are given meaning within a culture or society. Further, these symbolic characteristics of emotions are learned relationally. When it comes to persuasion, the discipline of communication studies has traditionally focused primarily on logic and reasoning. This focus remains an important element, but there is an increasing awareness of the importance of emotion when studying human behavior in general and when studying human motivation specifically.

What are the relational influence goals of compliance gaining?

There are seven relational influence goals of compliance gaining. *Gaining assistance* is a relational influence goal dedicated to obtaining resources. *Giving advice* is a relational influence goal dedicated to providing guidance. *Sharing activities* is a relational influence goal dedicated to engaging in joint endeavors. *Changing orientations* is a relational influence goal dedicated to changing a person's position on an issue. *Changing relationships* is a relational influence goal dedicated to altering the relationship of the interactants. *Obtaining permission* is a relational influence goal dedicated to receiving authorization for an action. Finally, *enforcing rights and obligations* is a relational influence goal dedicated to making someone fulfill a commitment or role.

What are the original five strategies (categories) of compliance gaining?

Gerald Marwell and David Schmitt's (1967) 16 compliance gaining strategies were grouped into five categories: (1) rewarding activities, (2) punishing activities, (3) expertise activities, (4) activation of impersonal commitments, and (5) activation of personal commitments. Rewarding activities seek compliance through positivity. Punishing activities seek compliance through negativity. Expertise activities seek compliance through perceptions of credibility or wisdom. Activation of impersonal commitments seeks compliance through the manipulation of internal feelings of obligation and appropriate behavior. Activation of personal commitments seeks compliance through appealing to obligations to others.

What contextual influences impact the selection of compliance gaining strategies?

There are seven contextual factors that impact the selection of compliance gaining strategies. *Dominance* is a contextual influence of compliance gaining based on power dimensions within a relationship. *Intimacy* is based on the relational connection among interactants. *Resistance* is based on anticipated opposition. *Relational consequences* are based on the perceived effects a compliance gaining strategy might have on a relationship. *Personal benefit* is based on potential personal gain. *Rights* are based on the degree to which the desired outcome seems justified. *Apprehension* is based on anxiety resulting from the circumstances.

Key Concepts

activation of impersonal commitments 302
activation of personal commitments 302
apprehension (contextual influence) 304
arousal goals 301
attitudes 290
beliefs 290
claim of conjecture 291
claim of fact 291
claim of policy 291
claim of value 291
cognitive dissonance theory 294
compliance gaining 299
dominance (contextual influence) 301
door-in-the-face technique 295
expertise activities 302
extended parallel process model 297
foot-in-the-door technique 293
given belief 291
identity goals 301
interaction goals 301
intimacy (contextual influence) 302
perceptual contrast effect 295
personal benefit (contextual influence) 303
pregiving technique 295
punishing activities 302
reciprocal concessions 295
relational consequences (contextual influence) 303
resistance (contextual influence) 303
resource goals 301
rewarding activities 302
rights (contextual influence) 304
self-perception theory 294
self-presentation 295
speech to actuate 292
speech to convince 291
values 290

Questions to Ask Your Friends

1. Ask your friends to describe their most recent attempt to influence someone's behavior. What techniques did they use? Were they successful? If so, why do you think they were successful? If not, what do you think would have led to success?

2. Ask your friends to describe the most recent attempt by someone to influence their behavior. What techniques did that person use? Was the person successful? If so, why do you think that person was successful? If not, what do you think would have led to success?

3. Produce a compliance gaining scenario for your friends such as, asking someone to give them a ride. Then ask them to describe how they would go about gaining compliance with a friend, a romantic partner, a colleague/classmate, a neighbor, and an acquaintance. How do their strategies change depending on the relationship?

Media Connections

1. Watch a series of commercials on television and determine what emotions were used. What emotions are most predominant? Are certain emotions used when selling particular products?

2. Look closely at the next mailer you receive from an organization seeking a donation. Is the organization using a technique of sequential persuasion? Do you think it will be successful? If so, what has the organization done correctly? If not, what could it have done differently?

3. Try to convince a friend to do something for you while interacting face-to-face. Now try to convince another friend to do the exact same thing; only this time do it through e-mail or text message. What differences did you notice in the two attempts? What similarities did you notice in the two attempts?

Student Study Site

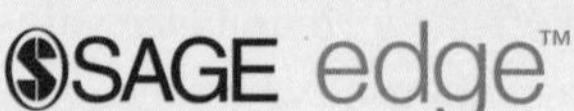

Sharpen your skills with SAGE edge at edge.sagepub.com/duckciel2e

SAGE edge for students provides a personalized approach to help you accomplish your coursework goals in an easy-to-use learning environment.

Chapter Outline

Preparing for an Interview
- Cover Letters and Résumés
- Résumés

Interviews
- Characteristics of an Interview
- Types of Interviews

Pre-interview Responsibilities
- Interviewer Responsibilities
- Interviewee Responsibilities

Beginning an Employment Interview
- Greeting and Establishing Appropriate Proxemics
- Negotiating Relational Connection and Tone
- Establishing Purpose and Agenda

Asking the Questions During an Employment Interview
- Primary and Secondary Questions
- Open and Closed Questions
- Neutral and Leading Questions
- Directive and Nondirective Questioning
- Avoiding Illegal Questions

Answering the Questions During an Employment Interview
- Adjusting the Interview Frame
- Learning From Successful and Unsuccessful Interviewees
- Answering Common Questions
- Dealing With Illegal Questions

Concluding an Employment Interview
- Interviewer Responsibilities
- Interviewee Responsibilities

Post-interview Responsibilities
- Interviewer Responsibilities
- Interviewee Responsibilities

Focus Questions Revisited

Key Concepts

Questions to Ask Your Friends

Media Connections

15 Interviewing

This chapter is dedicated to something that will be of great importance through your professional life—interviews. An **interview** is a goal-driven transaction characterized by questions and answers, clear structure, control, and imbalance. An interview is usually a dyadic transaction, meaning that it takes place between two people. A talk show host asking questions of a celebrity is one example of a dyadic interview. Sometimes, however, a person may be interviewed by two or more people or by a panel. Consider, for instance, when someone testifies before Congress and is asked a series of questions by a panel of senators.

We introduce various types of interviews in this chapter, but we primarily focus on employment interviews, since those are the types of interviews the majority of people reading this book are most concerned about at this point in their lives. Of course, interviews share many characteristics with other types of communication. Certainly, all of the properties of communication discussed throughout the book remain intact. Communication within an interview is transactional and symbolic (both verbal and nonverbal), requires meaning, is both presentational and representational, and requires the use of frames for understanding. An interview also requires effective listening (engaged, relational, and critical) on the part of everyone involved in order to be successful. Furthermore, identity work, relational work, and cultural work are all being conducted during an interview. We look at both similarities and differences between interviews and other sorts of communication as we go along.

This chapter focuses on how to conduct and participate in employment interviews. First, since most people will not be invited to interview with an organization without an effective cover letter and résumé, we discuss the construction of these vital application tools. Then we discuss the preparation for an interview. We then examine what must take place during the beginning of an interview. Next, we explore what happens during the question-and-answer portion of an interview. *From an interviewer standpoint,* we discuss ways to develop different types of questions, sequencing the questions, directive and nondirective questioning, and avoiding illegal questions. *From an interviewee standpoint,* we discuss adjusting the interview frame for greater success, learning from successful and unsuccessful interviews, answering common interview questions, and handling illegal questions. We then examine what must take place during the conclusion of an interview. We next discuss the responsibilities of interviewers and interviewees following an interview.

FOCUS QUESTIONS

1. What are a cover letter and résumé?
2. What are the characteristics of an interview?
3. What are the types of interviews?
4. What are the pre-interview responsibilities of interviewers and interviewees?
5. How should a person begin an employment interview?
6. What types of questions and questioning styles may an interviewer use?
7. How should interviewees respond to questions during an interview?
8. How should a person conclude an employment interview?
9. What are the post-interview responsibilities of interviewers and interviewees?

Preparing for an Interview

You will not be invited to an employment interview without a quality cover letter and résumé. Accordingly, we first address some key elements in the construction of these essential items. We begin by discussing the cover letter, which is the tool used to get a potential employer to actually review your résumé. It is quite surprising how little common sense average applicants show at this stage. (1) You guarantee your application going into the shredder if you do not appreciate that the person reading these applications is likely very busy, so do not waste the person's time by making your letter or application hard to read or understand. (2) Do not use exotic fonts or layouts, and make sure the font size is big enough for a (possibly older) person to read. (3) You are going to be one of perhaps a hundred applicants for the job, and the reader gets tired of reading the same old stuff—your responsibility is to stand out, but in a good way (one of our departments once had an application on special notepaper with the applicant dressed up as a devil. *Shred!*). (4) Everything you do to make the reader's job easier will help you. Busy people do not want to read poorly structured or "off point" applications that start with a funny story about your grandmother. Keep it all relevant; make it easy for the reader to take in; and never forget the first point: Readers are busy.

interview: a goal-driven transaction characterized by questions and answers, clear structure, control, and imbalance

cover letter: a letter sent when seeking employment, which has four purposes: (1) declare interest in the position, (2) provide a summary of qualifications, (3) compel the person to read your résumé, and (4) request an interview

Cover Letters and Résumés

A **cover letter** has four purposes: (1) declare interest in the position, (2) provide a summary of qualifications, (3) compel the person to read your résumé, and (4) request an interview. Employers often receive numerous applications for a single position, and quite often application materials are given only slight attention. Therefore, hopeful employees should do everything possible to ensure that their materials stand out from the rest and receive adequate attention. In what follows, we present the key elements of effective cover letters.

ANALYZING EVERYDAY COMMUNICATION

Look at Your Résumé

Evaluate your most recent cover letter and résumé using the guidelines and suggestions offered in this chapter. If you have never written a cover letter and résumé, prepare them for a fictional position in your career field or for an actual position you wish to obtain. Even if you are not currently seeking employment, it is never too early to develop or update these important career tools.

QUESTIONS TO CONSIDER

1. In what ways could your cover letter be improved?
2. In what ways could your résumé be improved?

Address Letter to Specific Person

Many applicants do not take the time to confirm who will be reading their materials and consequently do not address their cover letter to a specific person. Simply addressing the letter "To Whom It May Concern" will not make your cover letter stand out from the rest and will elicit *little* concern from the receiver. A quick phone call to the organization will likely provide you with the name of the person to whom the letter should be addressed, if it is unavailable in the job announcement/advertisement. Be certain to use the person's last name only and to address the person using his or her proper title.

Identify the Position

Identify the position for which you are applying in the first paragraph of the letter. An organization may have multiple positions available, and you want to ensure that you are being considered for the one you intend. You should also indicate how you discovered the position's availability. Finally, you should display knowledge about and positive regard for the organization. Including this information shows that you have taken the time to learn about the organization and that you view it favorably. Some applicants—especially those applying for hundreds of positions—use form cover letters and change nothing but the name and address of the company. Such form letters will generate less interest than letters in which the applicant is clearly knowledgeable about the organization and actively interested in working there.

Summarize Qualifications and Promote Résumé

Summarize the qualifications that make you an ideal fit for the position in the second paragraph. You may discuss such items as your education and training, experiences, special skills, and activities that have prepared you for the position and that will enable you to successfully fulfill the duties of the position. Be sure to emphasize what you can provide for the organization, not what it can do for you. At the end of this paragraph, you should encourage the reader to refer to your résumé. You can do this by mentioning specific information that can be discovered there or by simply mentioning the additional information that can be discovered through its examination.

Reaffirm Interest and Request an Interview

Reaffirm your interest in the position and request an interview in the final paragraph of the cover letter. You may want to indicate your intention to contact this person in the future ("I will contact you in two weeks to see if you require additional information about my credentials or desire any additional materials"). Another option in the final paragraph is to request a date to meet with the employer. This might be especially appropriate if you are presently located in an area other than the organization and will happen to be visiting that area ("I will be in the Misery City area June 30–July 5 and would appreciate the opportunity to meet with you during that time to discuss my qualifications in more detail").

Sign Off With Respect and Professionalism

When ending the letter, you should use the term *Sincerely* or *Respectfully* or *Cordially* rather than *Yours Truly* or *Yours Faithfully,* which is too personal when corresponding with someone you likely do not know, and rather than *Best Wishes* or *Cheers,* which is too informal for a professional letter. Use your full name and do not use a nickname. Sign the letter using dark ink in a legible and professional manner, avoiding unnecessary flourish (i.e., no swirly lines at the end or smiley face emoticons). You should end the letter properly to ensure the quality of the letter established thus far is maintained.

Résumés

The purpose of a **résumé** is to present your experiences and credentials for a position in a clear and concise manner. Employers may spend less than a minute looking at your résumé, so the information included should be not only clear and concise but also positive and obviously appropriate to the position for which you are applying. Many readers do a "first pass" review, merely glancing at the materials and sorting them into a "shred" pile and "follow up" file, which they then read more closely. Your job is to make sure they approve your materials for a closer read. In what follows, we discuss the key elements of effective résumés.

résumé: document used when seeking employment that presents credentials for a position in a clear and concise manner

Skills You Can Use: Following the Rules and What It Tells People When You Do Not

Cover letters and résumés should be easy for the employer to read. They should be sent flat rather than folded and printed on light-colored paper rather than dark-colored paper. Of course, some employers prefer to receive application material digitally (Schullery, Ickes, & Schullery, 2009). Furthermore, many career networking sites enable applicants to post video résumés. *Be sure to read position announcements carefully* to determine an employer's preferred method of delivery. You may have lots of clever ideas about the convincing way to present yourself, but if you do not follow the format required by the employer, you are wasting your cleverness to no avail. It is routine for employers to ignore applications that are not submitted in the correct format as requested. They will get enough good applicants that they can afford to throw out wrongly formatted applications without risk of having no good applicants left. They also know from the format—and whether or not you follow instructions about it—whether you are a person who is attentive to details, careful to follow instructions, or difficult to manage, a person who will take up a lot of their time later having to have tasks explained once again and whose work will always need to be done a second time in order to have it done correctly. This wastes precious managerial time.

Name and Contact Information

As with your cover letter, you should use your full name when constructing a résumé and avoid using nicknames. Include the following contact information: (1) address, (2) telephone number, and (3) e-mail address. Include a personal website address only if it is solely professional or academic. If you are a student, you may have both a campus address and telephone number and a permanent address and telephone number. If this is the case, include both your campus contact information and your permanent contact information. Make sure that your e-mail address adheres to professional standards. Someone whose e-mail address begins *Lazydrunk93* will not receive many interview offers!

Career Objective

Next, you must include your career objective. This objective should be one sentence and never over two sentences. It should also be explicitly tailored to meet the needs of the organization and the position for which you are applying. The employer will be asking what you can do for the organization, not what the organization can do for you. A vague statement of interests and a lack of commitment to the organization will not work.

Education and Training

Education and training should follow your career objective. List your degrees or training in reverse chronological order so that your most recent (and likely most relevant) information appears first. Listing your high school degree is not necessary if you are presently enrolled in or have completed college. This section should include the following information: (1) degree completion (or expected completion) date along with all majors or minors, (2) college name and location, and (3) awards, honors, or certificates. Use your own best judgment as to whether you should include your grade point average. Some fields may place more importance on this number than others.

Experiences

The experiences section of your résumé will include your employment history and other endeavors such as volunteer work if they happen to be directly relevant to the position for which you are applying, or else should show your commitment to the various values and concerns of the employer (community service, general engagement in the world as a thinking citizen with leadership potential). As with your education history, list your experiences in reverse chronological order. This section should include the following information: (1) position, (2) name of the organization along with location (city and state), (3) dates of employment or service (month and year), and (4) responsibilities and accomplishments. Your responsibilities and accomplishments are especially important in this section, and you should emphasize those that are most applicable to the position you are hoping to receive. These responsibilities and accomplishments are usually not written in complete sentences. Instead, begin each phrase with a verb that implies action (e.g., *spearheaded, updated, developed, increased*).

Skills

Next, include the skills that are most relevant to the position for which you are applying. These skills could include abilities in such areas as computer programs, languages, laboratory protocol, machinery, tools, or whatever areas most fit the position. If you possess multiple skills within a particular category, you may wish to use that category as a heading. For instance, you may possess skills in multiple computer programs and include these under a header titled *Computer Skills.*

Activities

When listing activities on your résumé, you should include those most relevant to the position first. However, in this case, feel free to also list activities that are not necessarily related to the position. Of course, you should only include those activities that reflect favorably on you, but listing activities can indicate a well-rounded person with many life experiences from which to draw when dealing with people and participating in organizational life.

Interviews

Assuming that the employer follows up and invites you to an interview, there are some important points you need to consider about the best way to present yourself. Interviews are both similar to and different from normal conversations, and you need to consider these points carefully.

Characteristics of an Interview

Interviews encompass unique characteristics that distinguish them from other types of communication. In what follows, we examine five characteristics of interviews: (1) goal-driven, (2) question–answer, (3) structured, (4) controlled, and (5) unbalanced.

Interviews are generally more *goal-driven* than other types of communication, especially those taking place between two people. All communication achieves something beyond the simple exchange of symbols, but these achievements and creations are not always purposeful and intended. Interviews have a clear purpose, a goal to be achieved. Information may be desired, a problem may need to be resolved, persuasion may be desired, someone may need assistance with a personal problem, or an employer may be seeking the best person for a job opening and a potential employee may be looking for a good employer.

Another characteristic of interviews is the *question–answer* nature of the transaction. The majority of an interview consists of one person (sometimes more than one) asking questions and another person answering those questions. Everyday communication includes occasional questions and answers—especially if people are getting to know one another—but not to the extent of an interview. Furthermore, in most everyday communication, it is not usually the case that one person is in charge of asking the questions while the other person is in charge of answering them.

Interviews also tend to be more *structured* than other types of communication. Whereas a casual interaction between two people may happen spontaneously and have no clear focus, interviews involve planning and preparation and tend to have a clear sequence. Certain actions are expected during an interview in order to reach a clearly defined goal.

Interviews are generally *controlled* by an interviewer, who is responsible for moving the interview toward its intended goal. The amount of control exerted during an interview depends on this goal, which is achieved in part by the questions asked and the communication environment established. Once again, this—specifically whether an interview is characterized as *directive* or *nondirective*—is a topic that deserves fuller attention later in the chapter.

A final characteristic of interviews is that the time spent talking by an interviewee and an interviewer is usually *unbalanced*. Typically, an interviewer will speak for 30% of the time, and an interviewee will speak for 70% of the time. Of course, the type of interview will dictate exactly how much time each party spends talking, but more often than not, an interviewee will talk more and an interviewer will talk less.

Types of Interviews

Now that we have discussed the characteristics of an interview, we can examine various types of interviews. You may have already experienced some of these interviews in the past and will likely encounter them many times throughout your personal and professional life. We will begin with the employment interview, since this type of interview will receive the most attention in the remainder of the chapter. Note that the first three types of interviews discussed encompass the workplace. Initial employment is not the only place you will come across interviews in your professional life.

Employment Interviews

When people think of interviews, an employment interview is probably what comes immediately to mind. **Employment interviews** are those in which a potential employer interviews a potential employee. Both parties have a great deal riding on the success of an interview. The potential employee is not only seeking employment but also determining whether the job is one that would be accepted if offered. The potential employer is searching not only for a qualified applicant but also for someone who would actually benefit the organization. Potential employers also want to convince potential employees that the position is one they would accept if offered.

employment interviews: interviews in which a potential employer interviews a potential employee

Performance Interviews

Also known as *performance reviews*, **performance interviews** are those in which an individual's activities and work are discussed. These interviews are most often conducted between employees and supervisors, but you may also experience them in educational and other settings. For instance, students frequently discuss their progress toward a degree with an advisor or perhaps even a committee of professors. In both situations, a person's strengths and weaknesses are discussed with the ultimate goal being to improve his or her performance. Naturally such interviews can be stressful, but they can also provide people with valuable information that can be used to strengthen their performance and to help them achieve personal and professional goals. These interviews are also an opportunity for the goals and culture of an organization to be reinforced.

Exit Interviews

Exit interviews are those that occur when a person chooses to leave a place of employment. The conventional wisdom is that someone who is leaving may be more likely to provide honest answers about organizational cultures, policies, supervisors, compensation, and other aspects of the workplace. If used correctly, these interviews can provide employers with valuable insight that can be incorporated to improve employee satisfaction and thus the productivity and success of an organization. These interviews are also increasingly common in education and among multiple types of groups, such as volunteer organizations.

Make your case

Are Exit Interviews Useful?

An exit interview is often conducted by a company or an institution when an employee voluntarily leaves to take employment elsewhere. The company/institution has an interest in knowing why people leave and whether there is anything it could have done to retain the employee. Obviously this is not done purely from altruism; it costs quite a lot to train new employees up to the standard of reliability that can be obtained from an established employee, and everyone everywhere is trying to find ways to reduce the costs of operation. Also, if the employee leaves because of a sense that opportunities for advancement are not available within the present organization or that employees are not adequately recognized, then the organization might be able to do something to improve the atmosphere in the future. Thus exit interviews are essentially information-gathering exercises and may even include questions asking the employee to give frank assessments of superiors, management styles, organizational culture, and other elements of life in the workplace that the employee may have found to be hindrances to good work.

QUESTIONS TO CONSIDER

1. Do exit interviews provide accurate and useful information to employers? Or will employees leaving an organization still hesitate to provide full disclosure of the positive and negative aspects of the organization?
2. What factors may determine whether an exit interview will be worthwhile?

Information-Gaining Interviews

You may have previously experienced an information-gaining interview and not even realized it as such. **Information-gaining interviews** are those in which a person solicits information from another person. You have likely responded to surveys, which is one form of information-gaining interview. A doctor asking you about your symptoms during an office visit is another example of this form of interview. You may conduct information-gaining interviews when preparing speeches and papers for school or work. These sorts of interviews are also frequently seen on webcasts and included in newspapers, magazines, and blogs.

Persuasive Interviews

Persuasive interviews are those that have influence as the ultimate goal. The interviewer may appear to be gaining information but is actually attempting to influence the thoughts or actions of the interviewee. This form of interview may sound a bit manipulative and underhanded, but it is quite common. When salespeople ask your opinion about a product or service, they often do so in a way that attempts to sway you toward what they want you to purchase. At other times, what appears to be a survey is in reality an attempt to persuade. Political workers have frequently been accused of dirty tricks under the guise of conducting straightforward surveys. They

performance interviews: interviews in which an individual's activities and work are discussed

exit interviews: interviews that occur when a person chooses to leave a place of employment

information-gaining interviews: interviews in which a person solicits information from another person

persuasive interviews: interviews that have influence as the ultimate goal

What is the difference between information-gathering interviews like the one pictured here and persuasive interviews? Is the difference always obvious to the person being interviewed?

attempt to plant a seed of doubt or concern in the mind of the interviewee. For instance, imagine being asked, "If the incumbent were convicted of running a cockfighting ring, would this influence your vote in the upcoming election?" Depending on your opinion of roosters or animal cruelty in general, such questions often influence voter perceptions of candidates and result in rumors being circulated.

Problem-Solving Interviews

When experiencing difficulties or facing an unknown challenge, people may engage in **problem-solving interviews**, those in which a problem is isolated and solutions are generated. These types of interviews may be conducted by someone with greater experience or insight than the person being interviewed. Students, for example, may be questioned by their professors in order to determine why they may be experiencing difficulties in a class. Sometimes problem-solving interviews are conducted by someone with general knowledge of a situation but whose fresh approach can be beneficial. For instance, a colleague may be asked to engage in a problem-solving interview when difficulties are encountered with a project at work. Someone not involved with a situation will often provide alternative approaches to solving a problem.

Helping Interviews

Unlike problem-solving interviews, **helping interviews** are always conducted by someone with expertise in a given area and whose services are engaged by someone in need of advice. The most obvious example of a helping interview is a psychologist asking questions of a client. However, other helping interviews include those conducted by credit card counselors with people facing a heavy debt load or by attorneys advising clients on legal matters.

Pre-interview Responsibilities

Having examined the characteristics of interviews and different types of interviews, we now focus our attention fully on employment interviews. Although other types of interviews are important, as mentioned previously employment interviews are likely the most important for people reading this book. The entire employment interview process is discussed, from pre-interview responsibilities of both an interviewer and an interviewee to post-interview responsibilities of both an interviewer and an interviewee. Along the way, we explore the beginning of an interview, how interviewers should ask questions, how interviewees should answer questions, and how an interview should come to a close. So, we start by discussing what should be done in preparation for an interview.

As just mentioned, our focus on employment interviews is due to their importance in the lives of those most likely to be reading this book—you and other students! As you prepare for your future career, you may also be more concerned with

problem-solving interviews: interviews in which a problem is isolated and solutions are generated

helping interviews: interviews conducted by someone with expertise in a given area and whose services are engaged by someone in need of advice

the responsibilities of an interviewee rather than an interviewer. We discuss the responsibilities of both because you will likely be called to interview someone at some point in your career, perhaps sooner than you anticipate. Plus, knowing the responsibilities of everyone involved in the interview process will assist you when interviewing for positions.

ETHICAL ISSUE

If an interviewee is not interested in a position and simply desires interview experience, is it ethical for him or her to take part in an interview? If an interviewer already has a job candidate selected for the position, is it ethical for him or her to interview other candidates for the position in order to simply fulfill legal or other requirements?

Interviewer Responsibilities

We begin our discussion of pre-interview responsibilities by focusing on the duties of an interviewer. There are four primary responsibilities of the interviewer before the interview: (1) reviewing application materials, (2) preparing questions and an interview outline, (3) gathering materials, and (4) beginning on time.

Review Application Material

The interviewer should review a job candidate's application material before the interview. Accordingly, you should not use the interview itself to review the application material. Doing so conveys a lack of preparation and respect, and it wastes valuable time that should be used to conduct the interview. Furthermore, as we next discuss, reviewing a job candidate's application material should be done beforehand in order to develop specific questions to ask each individual interviewee.

Prepare Questions and an Interview Outline

The interviewer should prepare a list of questions in advance of the interview. (Various types of interview questions are discussed later in the chapter.) Preparing questions in advance helps ensure that the appropriate information will be elicited from the job candidate. It also helps ensure that the interview will be conducted within the proper time constraints. If multiple job candidates are being interviewed, using common questions will make it easier to compare and contrast candidates. However, each interview will demand the inclusion of unique questions adapted to each individual interviewee.

These questions should be included in an interview outline, which reminds the interviewer of his or her duties during the various parts of an interview. For instance, as we discuss later, an interviewer should provide the interviewee with a purpose and an agenda at the beginning of an interview and summarize the interview, ask for questions, and preview future action and the schedule among other tasks in the conclusion. Including these tasks in an interview outline will help make sure they are included during the interview. We urge you to be diligent in your creation of interview questions and interview outlines. This task can be the difference between conducting a successful interview and conducting a poor interview.

The person in this picture is reviewing application material prior to interviewing a job candidate. What are the other responsibilities of an interviewer prior to the interview?

Gather Materials

The interviewer should gather materials for the interview before the interviewee arrives rather than afterward. Searching for the application material, interview

By the way...

Other People's Knowledge About the Workplace

Many schools have career centers, or similarly named offices, that provide assistance for students when seeking employment. Among their many services, some even conduct mock interviews for practice. These resources should be easy for you to find on the college website, and there are people in these offices with lots of skills you can use. They are employed there because they understand how recruitment officers for corporations and other colleges work, when they might be visiting campus, what kinds of interview preparation you may need to do, and how you go about assessing your own skills and suitability for jobs you may not even have considered. We strongly encourage you to seek out such opportunities on your campus.

QUESTIONS TO CONSIDER

1. In addition to school career centers, do you know anyone who could assist you with your interviewing and job search skills?
2. What sources to assist you with your interviewing and job search skills can you find on the Internet?

outline, and writing materials for notes—even if these things are close by—indicates a lack of preparation and, consequently, a lack of respect for the interviewee. It also takes up valuable time that should be dedicated to conducting the interview.

Begin on Time

The interviewer should strive to begin the interview on schedule rather than causing a delay. As with failing to gather materials beforehand, making the interviewee wait past the scheduled time is unprofessional and conveys a lack of respect for the interviewee. Avoid scheduling a meeting or another activity that may run long immediately before an interview. If multiple interviews are being conducted during a single day or period, make sure some time is scheduled between them and maintain adherence to the schedules of the interviews themselves. Ideally, there will be enough time before an interview to gather materials and review the application material and enough time following an interview to review your performance and evaluate the interviewee.

Interviewee Responsibilities

An interviewee also has responsibilities before the interview. There are a total of seven duties that must be conducted by the interviewee: (1) gathering information, (2) preparing questions, (3) practicing, (4) ensuring a professional personal appearance, (5) arriving on time, (6) bringing materials, and (7) turning off the cell phone.

Gather Information

Before an employment interview, an interviewee must gather information about the organization, about the profession, and about himself or herself. Communication professionals have traditionally focused on the need to gather information about the organization, but the latter two areas are just as significant.

Exhibiting knowledge about the organization during the interview will indicate proper preparation, enthusiasm for the position, and a desire to become part of the organization. Exhibiting knowledge about the organization is a distinguishing characteristic of successful interviewees. Such information may include the organization's history, future plans, challenges, accomplishments, and other characteristics. Exhibiting knowledge about the profession during the interview will also be beneficial. A job candidate will most likely possess knowledge about the profession before gathering information. However, it is especially important that interviewees appear knowledgeable of the latest developments within the profession. Furthermore, addressing such developments in relation to the organization's needs and goals will be especially impressive.

An interviewee should also gather information about himself or herself. Perhaps *gather* is not as appropriate as the term *formulate*. People already possess knowledge and information about themselves, but this information is not necessarily composed in a way that can be clearly articulated. It may not even be clear to them. When it comes to the interview, though, this information needs to be conveyed in a clear and supportive manner. Accordingly, gathering *or* formulating information about oneself must be done in preparation for an interview. Table 15.1 offers some questions to help guide this formulation.

Table 15.1 Formulating Information About Oneself

- What are my long-term professional goals? How will they be achieved?
- What are my short-term professional goals? How will they be achieved?
- What are my greatest achievements? What did I learn from them?
- What are my greatest failures? What did I learn from them?
- What are my greatest strengths? How am I using them and developing them?
- What are my greatest weaknesses? How am I overcoming them?
- Why did I choose this profession?
- Why do I want this position? How does this position fit with my professional goals?
- Why do I want to work for this organization? How does this organization fit with my professional goals?
- What professional experiences have made me an ideal candidate for this position?
- What education and training have made me an ideal candidate for this position?
- What skills make me an ideal candidate for this position?

Prepare Questions

An interviewee should also prepare a list of questions to ask the interviewer concerning the organization and the position. Questions about the organization could surround future goals, organizational structure, perceived challenges and strengths of the organization, organizational culture, and management style. Questions concerning the position could include such topics as experiences of previous employees, history of the position, evaluation of performance, percentage of time devoted to various responsibilities of the position, perceived challenges and opportunities of the position, amount of supervision, and why the position is now available.

There are a few lines of questioning that should be avoided by an interviewee. Questions deemed illegal when asked by an interviewer should not be asked by an interviewee. Asking these questions would not result in legal consequences, but they are just as discriminatory and inappropriate when asked by an interviewee as when asked by an interviewer. (We discuss illegal questions later in this chapter.) Also, an interviewee should not ask questions with answers available on an organization's website or in material already provided by the organization. Asking such questions would suggest, appropriately, a lack of preparation on the part of an interviewee. An interviewee should also avoid asking about salary or benefits. If you are like us, answers to questions about salary and benefits would seem helpful in determining whether or not the position would be accepted if offered. However, most professional cultures deem such questions inappropriate, so it is advisable to not ask them until you get the offer.

Practice

An interviewee should also practice the interview as part of his or her preparation. Compile a list of questions that you might be asked during an interview. (Some of the most common interview questions are discussed later in this chapter.) Once these questions have been compiled, practice answering them aloud. Having an idea about what you might say is not sufficient. Actually articulating your thoughts and hearing the words come out of your mouth will better prepare you for the actual interview. If possible, have someone else play the role of the interviewer and ask you questions (some of which may come from your list and some of which may not). Make the interview situation as complete and as realistic as possible, including arrival at the interview setting, initiating the interview, answering the questions, concluding the interview, and leaving the interview setting. You may even want to dress as you will at the actual interview. Practicing will also enable you to diminish some of those unknown elements of interviewing that often lead to nervousness and anxiety.

Professional Personal Appearance

Personal appearance—including clothing, hairstyles, tattoos, jewelry, makeup, and hygiene—is a reflection of how you perceive yourself, how you wish to be perceived by others, and your relationship with others. People make judgments, accurately or not, based on the appearance of others. Accordingly, interviewees should strive to convey credibility and professionalism through their personal appearance, and should appear in a manner consistent with expectations of the interviewer in order to establish relational connections with him or her. Rather than developing a one-size-fits-all model of interview appearance, it is best to dress according to the position for which you are interviewing. The general rule of thumb is dressing one step above how you would generally dress for the position if hired. And when in doubt, it is always better to be overdressed rather than underdressed.

If an interviewee arrives early for an interview, is it a good idea for him or her to catch up on rest while waiting?

Arrive on Time

Few other behaviors make a worse impression than arriving late to an interview. Arriving late not only is unprofessional and disrespectful but also may result in decreasing the amount of time available for the interview. Of course, arriving too early might make an interviewee seem overeager. So, we are not suggesting you arrive 2 hours before the interview is scheduled. Planning to arrive 15 minutes early will enable you to be punctual without appearing overly enthusiastic or nervous. If you do happen to arrive early, use that time to freshen up and review your materials.

Bring Materials

Speaking of materials, an interviewee should bring some to the interview. You should plan on bringing (1) additional copies of your résumé, (2) paper and writing utensils, and (3) a list of questions to ask the interviewer. In most situations, these items should be housed within a briefcase or professional-looking folder. Copies of your résumé will allow you to provide the interviewer with an additional copy if necessary and to review specific items with the interviewer if he or she so desires. The paper and writing utensils will allow you to take notes during the interview. The list of questions exhibits preparation and will enable you to remember specific questions you want to ask.

For some people, asking them to bring paper and writing utensils might be like asking them to bring a stone tablet, chisel, and hammer. In other words, it may seem outdated since these people (perhaps you) primarily record items using a laptop computer or digital notebook. At this point, in the majority of workplaces, technological expectations would not include the use of a laptop computer or digital notebook during an interview. Accordingly, the interviewer may find its use strange and perhaps even unprofessional. However, perceptions of technology are continuously changing (Chapter 13), and the use of a laptop or notebook may be more acceptable in the near future. Furthermore, there may be some organizations and industries in which it is acceptable now. The use of such items may also make you appear technologically savvy and progressive, which could be seen as a bonus by some interviewers. Use your best judgment as to whether a laptop computer or digital notebook would be appropriate, given the expectations of the interviewer and the identity you wish to convey during the interview.

By the way...

Using Technology in the Interview Process

Much of what is discussed in this chapter involves face-to-face interviews, but you may also be asked to interview by telephone or webcam. Here are some tips for these types of interviews.

Telephone Interviews

1. Select a quiet place that is free of potential distractions.
2. Do not eat, drink, or chew gum.
3. Even though the interviewer will not see you smile, doing so will come through in your voice.
4. Stand or sit up straight in order to strengthen your voice.
5. Avoid nonfluencies such as *um* and *uh,* since these are even more obvious over the telephone.
6. Have your résumé, notes, and other materials available should you need them.

Skype and Webcam Interviews

1. Select a quiet place that is free of potential distractions.
2. Test the camera and speaker before the interview.
3. Be aware of what appears in the background and remove anything that could be distracting.
4. Your personal appearance should mirror your appearance for a face-to-face interview.
5. Look directly at the camera, but avoid staring at it, much like you would avoid staring at someone with whom you are talking face-to-face.
6. Remember that the interviewer may be able to see and hear you before and immediately following the interview.

QUESTIONS TO CONSIDER

1. Have you ever had a phone or Skype interview? If so, did you prepare for it in the same way you would for a face-to-face interview?
2. If not, how might you prepare for such interviews?

COMMUNICATION + **YOU**

Discuss Your Interview Experiences

You can learn a lot about interviewing by talking with other people and sharing experiences. Do not forget what we said above—that preparation for interviews begins before the interview is even set up—and include in your discussion a description of your cover letter and résumé as well as the impression that you feel these items create. Consider cases where you have *not* been called for an interview and try to identify the differences in your successes and failures. Each of you can describe interviews you have participated in and can report on what went right and what went wrong, what difficulties there were, and so forth, and you should recall employment interviews in which you were either the interviewee or the interviewer. As you read this chapter, consider how your entire performance could be improved. If you have never participated in an employment interview, ask someone who has done so to describe his or her interview experiences to you.

QUESTIONS TO CONSIDER

1. Thinking about your previous interview experiences, which aspects of the interviews went well, and which aspects needed improvement?
2. What would you do differently next time?

Turn Off the Cell Phone

Perceptions of technology are continuously changing, but it will be a long time before the ringing of a cell phone is deemed an appropriate occurrence during an employment interview. You should turn off your cell phone completely and keep it out of sight during an interview. Your sole focus should be on the interviewer and the discussion at hand. We sincerely hope it never happens to you, but if you do forget to turn off your cell phone during an interview and it happens to ring, quickly apologize to the interviewer and turn it off at that time. Do not answer the call—even to tell the person you will call him or her back. Certainly do not carry on a conversation with the person who called. Your professionalism and respect for the interviewer (along with yourself) will be called into question by a ringing cell phone.

Beginning an Employment Interview

Now that the pre-interview responsibilities have been accomplished, it is time to begin the interview. When beginning an interview, the participants must (1) greet one another and establish proxemics, (2) negotiate the relational connection and tone of the interview, and (3) establish the purpose and agenda of the interview.

Greeting and Establishing Appropriate Proxemics

Initial impressions have a tremendous impact on perceptions of another person and whether additional contact is desired. Accordingly, the opening moments are crucial to the success of an interview, especially for an interviewee (Barrick et al., 2012).

As an interviewee, you must convey respect for an interviewer's space. If the interview takes place in an office, always knock and wait for permission to enter before entering, even if the door is open. Unless directed to do otherwise, address the interviewer using his or her last name and a formal or professional title (Dr., Mr., Ms., Your Holiness). Exchange greetings and introduce yourself, if necessary, while initiating a professional handshake with the interviewer to establish a positive relational connection and to suggest confidence. Shaking hands with a firm grip while looking the other person in the eye has been shown to increase ratings of employment suitability by interviewers (G. L. Stewart, Dustin, Barrick, & Darnold, 2008). Fist bumps or high fives are never appropriate, unless the interviewer is a Wonder Twin or has just completed an incredible athletic feat! Wait for the interviewer to direct you to where you will be positioned during the interview, rather than moving to an area or being seated beforehand.

As an interviewer, strive to make the interviewee feel welcomed and appreciated through your greeting. Initiate a handshake, if the interviewee has not already done so. Prepare in advance where the interviewee will be positioned for the interview and direct him or her to that space accordingly. As we discuss, where you and the interviewee are positioned will impact the relational connection and tone of the interview.

Negotiating Relational Connection and Tone

During most employment interviews, the interviewer possesses more power than the interviewee. The extent of that power distance and the tone of the interview (formal, relaxed, humorous, serious) will be negotiated by the interviewer and interviewee. This negotiation will take place throughout the course of an interview but is often established during its opening moments. Although interviewees are free to attempt to develop whatever relational connection and tone they desire, it is generally best for them to follow the verbal and nonverbal cues of the interviewer, especially if they want the job.

Verbal cues from an interviewer will inform an observant interviewee of the desired tone and relationship. If an interviewer asks to be called by his or her first name, that could be an indication of a relatively relaxed interview context and a sense of equality with the interviewee. If an interviewer makes a joke at the beginning of an interview, that might also be an indication of a generally relaxed interview context. Self-disclosure, or perhaps even self-deprecation, may be an indication of a desire for equality. An interviewer may very well verbally announce a desire for a relaxed interview context. If an interviewer does none of these things or does not verbally indicate informality or equality in other ways, he or she probably expects a formal, traditional interview context.

Accompanying nonverbal cues from an interviewer will also inform an interviewee of the desired tone and relationship. Smiling along with other positive nonverbal behaviors will certainly indicate a different tone than would frowning and other negative nonverbal behaviors. Beyond these cues, however, the placement of an interviewee in relation to the interviewer may indicate the degree of formality of the interview and the relational connection the interviewer wishes to develop. For instance, an interviewer seated on one side of a desk and an interviewee seated on the other side would indicate a more formal interview and a less equal relationship. On the other hand, an interviewer seated next to an interviewee, perhaps on chairs positioned at right angles with one another, would indicate a more relaxed interview and a more equal relationship.

By the way...

Do Not Forget the Nonverbal Communication in Interviews!

Don't forget to genuinely smile during your next employment interview. Interviewees with genuine dynamic smiles are evaluated more favorably by interviewers than those with fake smiles or neutral facial expressions (Krumhuber, Manstead, Cosker, Marshall, & Rosin, 2009). If you can fake sincerity, though, you have got it made!

QUESTIONS TO CONSIDER

1. Do you think you would have a better impression after interviewing someone who was highly qualified for the job, but was very serious and did not smile very much during the interview, or someone who had adequate qualifications but who was very genuine and friendly?
2. Is it possible to fake sincerity?

Establishing Purpose and Agenda

Establishing the purpose and agenda is the responsibility of the interviewer. The purpose of an employment interview is fairly obvious, but establishing the agenda is especially important. As an interviewer, you should inform the interviewee how long the interview will take place. You may also want to preview the areas of questioning or other features to make an interviewee more comfortable through the partial removal of unknown variables. Doing so also establishes your expectations as an interviewer of how the interview will be conducted.

Asking the Questions During an Employment Interview

Now that the interview has begun, it is time to address the matter of questions and answers. We first examine the types of questions that an interviewer can ask during the interview and then examine different styles of questioning. You may be at the point in your professional life where you are more concerned about being an interviewee than an interviewer. However, even if this is the case, you may very well be conducting interviews in the future. Further, knowing what the interviewer is doing will help you immensely as an interviewee.

There are three pairs of question types that may be asked during an interview: (1) primary and secondary, (2) open and closed, and (3) neutral and leading. There also exist different styles of questioning involving the amount of control exerted by the interviewer. As an interviewer, you must also be aware of illegal lines of questioning that must be avoided. We begin our exploration of asking the questions by examining the different types of questions that can be asked.

Primary and Secondary Questions

Before an interview, an interviewer should have compiled a list of questions covering the primary topics to discuss with an interviewee. Questions that introduce new topics during an interview are known as **primary questions**. Examples of primary questions include the following:

- What led to your interest in digital storytelling?
- What responsibilities did you have at your last job?
- What experience do you have working with flux capacitors?
- In what ways has your major prepared you for a position like this one?

Interviewee responses to questions will likely lead an interviewer to ask follow-up questions to seek elaboration or further information. These types of questions are known as **secondary questions**, of which there are two main types: probing questions and mirror questions. **Probing questions** are brief statements or words such as "Go on," "Uh-huh," and "What else?" that urge an interviewee to continue or to elaborate on a response. **Mirror questions** paraphrase an interviewee's previous response to ensure clarification and to elicit elaboration. For instance, an interviewer may ask, "From what you said, it seems you have previous experience with this product line, but have you had direct experience working in this market?" Additional examples of secondary questions include the following:

- What other aspects did you find most rewarding?
- In what ways?
- Which of those did you most dislike?
- Is that correct?

The best way to distinguish primary and secondary questions is that secondary questions only make sense when preceded by a primary question and subsequent response. Beginning a series of questions with any of the preceding examples would not make any sense.

primary questions: questions that introduce new topics during an interview (contrast with *secondary questions*)

secondary questions: follow-up questions asked when seeking elaboration or further information (see *probing questions* and *mirror questions*; contrast with *primary questions*)

probing questions (secondary questions): brief statements or words that urge an interviewee to continue or to elaborate on a response

mirror questions (secondary questions): questions that paraphrase an interviewee's previous response to ensure clarification and to elicit elaboration

Open and Closed Questions

The questions asked during an interview will be either open or closed. **Open questions** enable and prompt interviewees to answer in a wide range of ways. Examples of open questions include the following:

- Tell me about your decision to become a Foley artist.
- What led you to volunteer with the Retired Professors Fund?
- Describe a time when you had to work with a group.
- How would you describe your work ethic?

Open questions serve three important functions. First, and most obvious, open questions enable interviewers to gather information about an interviewee. Second, these questions enable an interviewer to assess the communication skills of an interviewee in the interviewee's own words and style. Third, open questions provide valuable insight into the worldview of an interviewee. Recalling both the presentational nature of communication discussed in Chapter 1 and Kenneth Burke's pentad discussed in Chapter 4, words and stories have meaning beyond that which appears on the surface and provide a glimpse into how people perceive situations, themselves, and others.

Contrary to open questions, **closed questions** are those that limit the range of an interviewee's response. Examples of closed questions include the following:

- Where did you attend college?
- What positions did you hold at your previous company?
- Are you willing to work weekends?
- What was the most difficult aspect of your past job?

Closed questions serve important functions during an interview. Closed questions do not take up as much time as open questions, so they can be especially valuable when time is limited. These questions can also be used to gather specific information about an interviewee. Finally, the answers to closed questions make it relatively easy to compare and contrast candidates for a position. Such evaluations are especially easy to make when dealing with **bipolar questions**, a type of closed question that forces an interviewee to select one of two responses. The answers to bipolar questions are frequently either yes or no. The third example in the preceding list is considered a bipolar question that would be answered with either an affirmative or a negative. Some bipolar questions ask interviewees to select between two presented choices. For instance, an interviewer might ask, "Which do you believe is most important to success at work—hard work or talent?"

Neutral and Leading Questions

When developing questions for an interview, it is best to include neutral questions and to avoid leading questions. **Neutral questions** provide an interviewee with no indication of a preferred way to respond. Examples of neutral questions include the following:

- Why did you select communication studies as a major?
- What do you think of our new product line?

open questions: questions that enable and prompt interviewees to answer in a wide range of ways

closed questions: questions that limit the range of an interviewee's response

bipolar question: a type of closed question that forces an interviewee to select one of two responses

neutral questions: questions that provide an interviewee with no indication of a preferred way to respond (contrast with *leading questions*)

- What are your thoughts on labor unions?
- Describe the qualities of your previous supervisor.

Notice that these examples do not direct an interviewee toward a specific response or one that is obviously preferred by the interviewer. Some people might believe that the second example involving a "new product line" would direct an interviewee toward a favorable response. However, an interviewer may want to determine whether the interviewee is someone who would not be afraid to express opinions and who would be able to improve and enhance the company's products.

Leading questions suggest to an interviewee a preferred way to respond. Examples of these types of questions include the following and are based on those in the preceding list:

- What influenced your incredibly wise decision to major in communication studies?
- You do approve of our new product line, don't you?
- What are some of the problems you see with labor unions?
- What did you like most about your previous supervisor?

In these examples, an interviewer would be guiding an interviewee toward a specific type of answer. (We know that the decision to major in communication studies is obviously incredibly wise, but the first one still counts!) Generally, it is best to avoid leading questions during interviews and not to give interviewees an indication about how they should answer. Still, leading questions are sometimes used to determine whether an interviewee is someone who would hold his or her ground. Once again, the production line example could be a test to determine an interviewee's confidence and ability to voice concerns.

Directive and Nondirective Questioning

The fact that interviews are controlled is one of their characteristics mentioned earlier in this chapter. However, the amount of control exerted during an interview will vary, based especially on the specific goal of an interview. Some types of interviews require great control by the interviewer, while other types of interviews require little control and more flexibility by the interviewer.

leading questions: questions that suggest to an interviewee a preferred way to respond (contrast with *neutral questions*)

directive interviews: interviews that are greatly controlled by an interviewer

Directive interviews are greatly controlled by an interviewer. Questions tend to be closed and perhaps leading (C. J. Stewart & Cash, 2000). A directive interviewer tends to follow a clear line of questioning, deviating only to guide an interviewee back

Figure 15.1 A Continuum of Interviewer Control

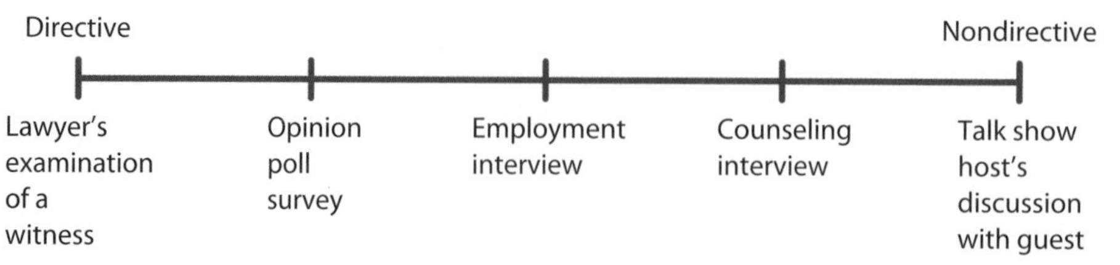

on topic or when wanting an interviewee to elaborate. Watch an attorney cross-examining a witness on *Law & Order* for a good example of a directive interview. The questions are certainly leading, and many tend to be closed. Further, the person being questioned on the stand is not allowed to deviate from the line of questioning, with the attorney being fully in control.

Nondirective interviews, on the other hand, are those in which the direction of the interview is primarily given to the interviewee. A nondirective interviewer generally introduces fairly broad topic areas and then allows an interviewee to "take off" in whatever direction desired. Accordingly, the questions asked tend to be open and neutral (C. J. Stewart & Cash, 2000). For an example of a nondirective interview, watch a talk show host interviewing a celebrity. A pre-interview of sorts has occurred before the program in which members of the staff have asked what the celebrity would like to talk about and have discussed possible questions the host might ask. During the actual program, the host will ask a general question ("How's the weather?"), knowing the celebrity will take it from there. The examples featured in Figure 15.1 are those offered by Gouran, Wiethoff, and Doelger (1994) and exhibit the range of directive and nondirective interviews.

DISCIPLINARY DEBATE

Where to Draw the Line on Appropriateness?

We—along with the federal government—encourage you to avoid asking illegal questions as part of the interview process. You can learn more about illegal questions and workers' rights by visiting the Equal Employment Opportunity Commission website at www.eeoc.gov. However, some people may find value in asking these questions.

QUESTIONS TO CONSIDER

1. Aside from instances of bona fide occupational qualifications, are there instances during which asking such questions would be beneficial?
2. Should illegal interview questions be made legal?

Avoiding Illegal Questions

When seeking the best candidate for a job, it may seem like a good idea to ask as many questions as possible and to learn as much as possible about someone, including many intricate details of his or her life. However, there are some questions that cannot be asked and for good reason—they are potentially discriminatory. Equal employment opportunity (EEO) laws have been established, in part, to prevent possible discrimination during the hiring process, whether it is done intentionally or unintentionally. Even the most well-intentioned comment or question can be discriminatory; therefore, you should be aware of questions that must be avoided.

Common areas that cannot be discussed with potential employees include age, marital/family status, ethnicity/national origin, religion, affiliations, and disabilities. In some cases, however, otherwise illegal areas of questioning are allowed. Some jobs demand certain abilities or requirements, known as *bona fide occupational qualifications*. For instance, it is illegal to inquire about the age of an applicant unless there is a minimum age requirement for a job or unless the job is one where a retirement age is enforced, such as a commercial airline pilot. Working for a religious organization may require affiliation with that religion. Furthermore, some occupations require certain physical abilities. However, bona fide occupational qualifications that counter discriminatory questions are not as common as you might think, and it is best to avoid areas of potential discrimination. Table 15.2 presents areas to avoid along with examples of illegal and legal questions.

ETHICAL ISSUE

Is it ethical for an interviewee to embellish his or her accomplishments during an interview? Where is the line drawn between describing accomplishments in a positive manner and fabricating these accomplishments?

nondirective interviews: interviews in which the direction of the interview is primarily given to the interviewee

Table 15.2 Avoiding Illegal Questions

CATEGORY	ILLEGAL QUESTIONS	LEGAL QUESTIONS
Age	How old are you? What year were you born?	Are you 21 years old or older, and therefore legally allowed to accept this position if offered? Are you under the age of 60 years old, and therefore legally allowed to accept this position if offered?
Marital/ Family Status	Are you married or living with a partner? Are you pregnant? Do you have any children or plan on having children?	There is a great deal of travel involved with this position. Do you foresee any problems with this requirement? Will the long hours required of this job pose any problems for you? Would you be willing to relocate if necessary? Do you have any responsibilities that may prevent you from meeting the requirements of this position?
Ethnicity/ National Origin	What is your ethnicity? Where is your family from? Were you born in the United States? What is your native language?	Do you have any language abilities that would be helpful in this position? Are you authorized to work in the United States?
Religion	Are you religious? What religion are you? Do you worship regularly at a church/mosque/ temple? Do you believe in God? Are there any months when you won't be needing lunch, Ramadan for example?	Are you able to work on Saturday evenings/Sunday mornings, if needed?
Affiliations	What clubs or social organizations do you belong to? Are you a Republican or a Democrat? Are you now or have you ever been a member of the Communist Party?	Do you belong to any professional organizations that would benefit your ability to perform this job?
Disabilities	What is your medical history? Do you have any disabilities? How would you describe your family's health? What resulted in your disability?	This job requires that a person be able to lift 100 pounds. Would you have any problems fulfilling that requirement?

Answering the Questions During an Employment Interview

Having examined the asking of questions during an interview, we can now explore the answering of questions. We first discuss how adjusting the interview frame can greatly benefit interviewees. Next, we investigate some of the lessons learned from both successful and unsuccessful interviewees. Then, methods for answering some of the most common interview questions are offered. Finally, we discuss how to answer illegal questions should they be asked during an interview.

Adjusting the Interview Frame

Before you began reading this chapter, you probably had a good idea about what happens during an interview. It is possible that you have been through at least one before. Yet even if you have not personally experienced an interview, you have likely seen them depicted in movies or television programs, and you have likely talked about interviews with people who have experienced them. Therefore, you are well aware of the *frames* surrounding interviews. Frames were introduced in Chapter 1, and we even included interviews as an example. They are basic forms of knowledge that enable people to define a scenario, which in turn helps them determine meaning and understand the roles and expectations of the participants. In the interview frame, one person generally asks a lot of questions and the other one answers them, but you are hopefully recognizing that it is more complex than this description.

By the way...

Are You Reading This Critically?

You are hopefully engaged in critical analysis and evaluation as discussed in Chapter 6. If so, you might find the use of a study (Einhorn, 1981; see Table 15.3) that is over 30 years old a bit suspect. We would be the first to tell you to be cautious when coming across apparently dated sources. In this case, however, the age of the source has not diminished the value of its findings. Still, maintain a critical stance when reading this or any book.

QUESTIONS TO CONSIDER

1. Do you think the information from this source is still valid, given the passing of time?
2. Will this information still be valid 30 years from now?

How a person frames a situation often dictates what will happen. If a person frames a situation as one in which he or she will play the role of bumbling fool, then the person will likely act like a bumbling fool. Coined by Robert Merton (1957), a **self-fulfilling prophecy** maintains that if someone believes a particular outcome will take place, his or her actions will often lead to its fruition. Accordingly, if you think you will succeed (or fail) at a task, you are more likely to do so, because your actions will likely be those that lead to success (or failure). Therefore, you should always expect to perform well during an interview. Naturally, just because you expect to perform well and end up doing so does not mean that you will get the position you seek. However, it will certainly improve your chances.

We can go a bit deeper with this notion of framing an interview, though. Many interviewees frame an interview as a situation in which they are on trial to determine whether they are capable or worthy of a position and must defend themselves. Anderson and Killenberg (2009, p. 229) have suggested that an interviewee instead frame the interview less threateningly as (1) *an opportunity rather than a test,* (2) *a learning experience rather than a demonstration,* and (3) *a dialogue rather than a monologue.*

You should strive to avoid viewing the interview as a test through which your worthiness as a potential employee, your skills, and your knowledge, along with your value as a human being, are all being called into question. Instead, view the interview as an opportunity to discuss the many ways you could contribute to an organization, to display the skills and knowledge that make you qualified for the position, and, of course, to confirm your value as a human being. In most instances, you would not be asked to interview unless an employer already viewed you as capable of performing the duties of a position and doing so successfully.

Furthermore, do not view the interview merely as a performance in which the above attributes are displayed. Rather, view the interview as an opportunity to learn about yourself. Preparation for and participation in an interview require determining your strengths, weaknesses, and goals, as well as reviewing how your past

self-fulfilling prophecy: principle maintaining if someone believes a particular outcome will take place, his or her actions will often lead to its fruition

Table 15.3 Learning From Successful and Unsuccessful Interviewees

CATEGORY	SUCCESSFUL INTERVIEWEES	UNSUCCESSFUL INTERVIEWEES
Clear Career Goals	Able to clearly articulate their career goals and explain how those goals relate with the position for which they are interviewing	Provide no clear indication of career goals or how those goals might relate to the position for which they are interviewing
Identification with Employers	Mention the organization by name often and exhibit knowledge of the organization	Rarely mention the organization by name and demonstrate little to no previous knowledge of the organization
Support for Arguments	Provide illustrations, comparisons and contrasts, statistics, and even testimony from colleagues, supervisors, and instructors	Provide little evidence or support material when answering questions
Participation	Actively involved in the development of the interview throughout the entire process and spend a great deal of the interview talking	Play a passive role in the development of the interview and talk very little during the interview
Language	Use active, concrete, and positive words along with technical jargon associated with the position	Use passive, ambiguous, and negative words while using little or no technical jargon
Nonverbal Delivery	Speak loudly and confidently while using vocal variety and avoiding nonfluencies. They incorporate meaningful gestures and support interviewer comments with positive nonverbal feedback such as nodding and smiling.	Speak softly and provide little vocal variety while including longer-than-appropriate pauses. They use few gestures and engage in distracting mannerisms such as rubbing their hands or shaking their legs. They also engage in little or no eye contact with the interviewer.

experiences have brought you to your current place in this world. It is an opportunity to establish personal and professional goals.

Finally, do not view the interview as something that is dominated by one person, while the other person is relegated to a subordinate or immaterial position. Instead, an interview should be viewed as something that is created (transacted) by all participants, who are equally responsible and necessary for its development and who can all potentially gain from the experience. Both an interviewee and an interviewer gain personally and professionally from the interview. They are able to learn about themselves and others; an interviewee has an opportunity to acquire a potentially fulfilling work position, and an interviewer has an opportunity to acquire the services of someone who could potentially improve an organization.

Learning From Successful and Unsuccessful Interviewees

Reframing the interview means that an interview can be successful even if you are not offered a position. After all, each interview can be a learning experience that allows you to grow personally and professionally. However, we recognize that such growth does not matter to someone whose primary goals are simply being offered a job and not living out of his or her vehicle. So, for the moment, let's focus on success as being offered a position following an interview.

A great deal can be learned about such success from the people doing the hiring, and this is exactly what was done in a study conducted by Lois Einhorn (1981). As part of this study, the communicative choices of successful and unsuccessful interviewees were examined and categorized. Table 15.3 outlines six key differences between successful and unsuccessful interviewee communication.

Would keeping his hands clasped throughout the interview improve or diminish this interviewee's chances of being offered the position?

Answering Common Questions

There are many questions you might be asked during an interview, so it is impossible to cover them all. At the same time, there are a few questions (in various forms and phrases) that come up more than others. In what follows, we address 10 of the most common questions and discuss some of the best ways to answer them during your interview.

Tell Me a Little About Yourself

When asking you to describe yourself during an interview, the interviewer could not care less about such items as your astrological s ign, favorite restaurants, achievements in youth sports, or high school prom theme. An interviewer wants to know how you could benefit the organization, and you should answer accordingly. You should discuss your education, previous work experience, career highlights, and achievements, being sure to emphasize how this information fits the position and would benefit the organization.

What Are Your Greatest Strengths?

This sort of question will almost always arise during an interview in some form or another. Going into the interview, you should have a ready-made list of three or four strengths that you can discuss. Be sure to have concrete examples to support each one and show how these strengths will enable you to succeed at the position.

What Are Your Greatest Weaknesses?

If you say, when asked the preceding question, "Well, I'm pretty lazy, and things would probably start disappearing from around the office if you hired me," you probably will not get the job. It is a responsibility of the interviewee to answer all questions honestly. Doing so is ethically appropriate—and employers may be able to uncover dishonesty (Reinhard, Scharmach, & Müller, 2013). That being said, you can certainly phrase your responses in a way that minimizes any weaknesses you might mention. Communication professionals often suggest the time-honored tactic of offering a weakness that sounds more like a strength. ("I am such a hard worker that I often get drained by the end of the day. And I tend to work too many weekends.") However, such responses sound misleading, have become a bit cliché, and do not indicate a genuine ability or interest in recognizing and addressing areas in need of improvement. You may instead want to offer a genuine weakness along with what you are doing to overcome it.

("My Excel skills are in need of development, so I have been taking a night class devoted to the program.") This tactic is especially helpful if there is an obvious skill or ability that you are lacking but that is required for the position or would benefit the position.

What Do You Know About This Organization?

When asked this question, you should exhibit an awareness of such items as the organization's mission, history, growth, and future plans, and perhaps its key personnel. It is a prime opportunity to underscore your enthusiasm for the position and demonstrate how you could benefit the organization based on its present and future endeavors.

Why Do You Want to Work Here?

This question provides another opportunity to reinforce your knowledge of the organization. Likewise, it is another chance for you to discuss your enthusiasm for the position and the organization. Finally, it is a chance to show how your abilities suit the organization and how hiring you would be mutually beneficial. In doing so, you must provide clear, explicit explanations and support for your assertions. For instance, it is not enough to say you could help the organization expand; rather, you must fully explain how you could do so. Remember, the extent of support for arguments is one of the distinguishing characteristics of successful and unsuccessful interviewees.

What Is Your Ideal Job?

This is a tricky question, because you should not necessarily say, "This one"—unless that is true, in which case you should discuss why. At the same time, if you mention a job other than the position for which you are applying, it may appear as if you are uninterested or you plan to move on as soon as something better comes along. Accordingly, you should play it safe and simply *describe* attributes of an ideal position (i.e., meaningful, challenging, fulfilling) while also discussing how the present position meets that description.

Why Do You Want to Leave Your Current Job?

Your current employer may be an idiotic, unprofessional, and unethical ogre who treats you like dirt and may very well eat small children, but you should probably not be that descriptive during an interview. If there are major problems, you may want to address but not dwell on them, taking partial responsibility while discussing what you have learned from the situation. Doing so may be especially wise if the interviewer is possibly aware of these problems. More often than not, however, it is best to focus on the positive attributes of your current (or previous) job, discussing how you have developed professionally and offering legitimate reasons for wanting to leave (e.g., moving to a new location, desire for professional growth). One of the reasons interviewers ask this question is to determine whether you will be happy and likely to stay if offered the position in their organization. Therefore, it is wise to discuss how this position better fits your professional goals and desires when compared to your current position.

What Are Your Expectations in Terms of Salary?

This is another very tricky question, because you do not want to put yourself out of reach and you do not want to sell yourself short. Some people suggest placing the question back on the interviewer ("What do people with my experience usually earn here?"), but the question asks for *your* expectations for salary, not his or her expectations. A good way to address this question is by conducting research beforehand to learn the average salaries for a particular position in a particular area. ("Based on the research I have conducted, I would expect the salary to be between $40,000 and $48,000 each year in addition to incentive bonuses.")

Where Do You See Yourself in 5 Years?

This question is usually asked to gauge a person's ambitions, sense of reality, and fit with the company. Your answer will depend, of course, on where you actually want to be in your professional life 5 years from that moment. If you anticipate holding the very position for which you are interviewing, you should say so while also talking about the professional growth that will have taken place and your plans to enhance the organization through that position. If you anticipate moving through the ranks of the organization, your rise to the top should be properly ambitious and realistic. Further, you should stress your plans for professional growth and anticipated contributions to the organization that would justify such advancement. If you anticipate not being with the organization in 5 years, indicating as much may be justifiable if the position is considered short-term. However, you should stress how your time at the organization would be mutually beneficial.

ETHICAL ISSUE

If an interviewer inadvertently asks an illegal question, should he or she be reported to the proper authorities? Is it possible to distinguish purposeful and inadvertent behavior in such situations? Should the consequences be different?

Why Should We Hire You?

When asked this question, you should have a very good answer. If you do not know why the organization should hire you, the interviewer will surely not know either. It may sound as if the interviewer is questioning your abilities, but he or she simply wants to know how you would benefit the organization. Accordingly, this is a perfect opportunity to reinforce your strengths and abilities by discussing how they will benefit the organization.

Dealing With Illegal Questions

We previously discussed illegal questions that should not be asked during an interview, but just because they *should not be* asked does not mean that they *will not be* asked. Sometimes this violation is intentional, while at other times it is unintentional. Whichever the case, you may very well be asked an illegal question while being interviewed for a position. How you deal with such a violation depends on such factors as your perception of its intentionality and, in all honesty, how badly you want the job. However, when it comes to the latter, if such violations occur in the interview

Table 15.4 Strategies for Answering Illegal Questions

CATEGORY	ILLEGAL QUESTIONS	STRATEGIES
Tactful refusal	Where are your parents from?	I don't believe my parents' places of origin matter for this position.
Direct but brief answer	How did you injure your leg?	It was injured while jogging.
Tactful inquiry	Where do you go to church?	How does that question pertain to the position?
Neutralize concern	Do you have children?	Yes, but that would not interfere with my work here.
Exploit the question	Is English your native language?	No. My native language is Ket, which would be beneficial for this company since it plans on opening offices in central Siberia next year.

process, you may need to seriously question whether the position and the employer are right for you. C. J. Stewart and Cash (2000, pp. 294–295) have offered strategies, outlined in Table 15.4, that can be utilized if you are asked an illegal question during an interview and choose to continue the meeting.

Concluding an Employment Interview

When concluding an employment interview, it is important that positive relational connections among the participants be maintained. Important information needs to be offered during the conclusion of an interview, and certain functions must take place. So, let's explore the responsibilities of both interviewers and interviewees during the conclusion of an employment interview.

Interviewer Responsibilities

We will begin with the responsibilities of an interviewer. There are six things an interviewer must do during the conclusion of an interview: (1) provide a wrap-up signal, (2) summarize the interview, (3) ask for questions, (4) preview future actions and schedule, (5) offer thanks, and (6) engage in farewells.

Wrap-Up Signal

Responsibility for controlling an interview rests with the interviewer. Therefore, the interviewer should initiate the conclusion of the interview through a **wrap-up signal**, a phrase indicating the beginning of the conclusion (e.g., "As we near the end of the interview," "As we begin to conclude our discussion"). An interviewer should always allow enough time for both parties to adequately perform their responsibilities of the conclusion, rather than trying to cram everything into the final moments of the interview.

Summarize the Interview

The interviewer should provide a straightforward, relatively brief summary of the information provided by the interviewee during the interview. Doing so will make the interviewee feel understood and will allow him or her to make any necessary clarifications. Interviewers should be careful not to sound either overly enthusiastic or overly dismissive when summarizing this information. This approach will prevent giving the interviewee either false hope or the feeling of failure.

Ask for Questions

The interviewer should always ask the interviewee for questions about the position and about the organization. The answers to these questions should be truthful and provide an accurate reflection of the position and organization. Hiring someone who has been given false impressions may lead to negative feelings and the need to conduct another search should that person decide that the position and organization are not the good fit he or she was led to believe. The questions asked by an interviewee will also provide additional information about that person, including knowledge and motivations.

Preview Future Actions and Schedule

The interviewer should also provide the interviewee with information pertaining to what will happen next and the schedule for decisions about the position. Interviewers are not required to provide any guarantees or odds of employment, nor do they have to disclose how many other job candidates are being interviewed for the position.

wrap-up signal: a phrase, usually uttered by the interviewer, that signals the beginning of an interview's conclusion

Offer Thanks

It is common to erroneously perceive an employment interview as something an interviewer is doing as a favor or because of some grand benevolence. However, the interview is being conducted, in part, because an interviewer (representing an organization) is in need of someone's professional services. Furthermore, the interviewee has invested time, energy, and emotion into the interview process. Accordingly, sincere thanks for participation in the interview should be offered.

Is it the responsibility of the interviewer or the interviewee to bring a formal end to the interview?

Farewells

Finally, it is the responsibility of an interviewer to formally end the interview by offering a handshake and expressing a professional farewell remark to the interviewee. There is certainly no reason to prolong the formal ending of the interview, but you should avoid making it seem as if you are rushing an interviewee out of the office. Otherwise, positive relational connections that may have been established will be diminished, and an otherwise constructive interview may be viewed negatively.

Interviewee Responsibilities

Along with the interviewer, the interviewee also has responsibilities during the conclusion of an interview. There are five things an interviewee must do during this part of an interview: (1) ask questions, (2) reinforce qualifications and enthusiasm, (3) inquire about the future schedule, (4) offer thanks, and (5) engage in farewells.

Ask Questions

Interviewees should have questions prepared and written out during their preinterview preparations. As part of most interviews, an interviewer will ask whether an interviewee has any questions he or she would like to ask. Not asking any questions would indicate a lack of preparation and enthusiasm, so it is a good idea to have some developed. An interviewer may occasionally fail to provide an interviewer an opportunity to ask questions. If it is clear that the interview is ready to end and that the interviewer does not plan on asking for questions, it is acceptable to politely ask if you may pose a few questions. Remember, an interview is not just about whether an interviewee will be offered a position but also about whether an interviewee will accept the position, if offered.

Reinforce Qualifications and Enthusiasm

An interviewee should also briefly summarize the qualifications that make him or her an ideal candidate, along with underscoring his or her enthusiasm for the position. Doing so will help reinforce strengths and abilities while ensuring that key experiences, education, training, and other information have been conveyed. It may also assist the interviewer in remembering and documenting these items.

Inquire About Schedule (If Not Provided)

The interviewer is responsible for providing an interviewee with a schedule of future contact and decision making. However, it is perfectly acceptable to inquire about this information should an interviewer fail to provide it.

By the way...

Constant Evaluation

Remember that both an interviewer and an interviewee are being evaluated at all times, not just when questions are being asked and answered. An interviewee's behaviors before and following a meeting can be used when forming judgments about his or her overall character and professionalism. When interviewing, you should avoid any odd behaviors while waiting for the interview to take place or when leaving the interview location, while also remembering to be respectful of the office staff—they generally deserve such respect regardless of whether you are attempting to make a good impression. Also, interview sessions occasionally include tours of buildings, introductions to members of the organization, meals, and transportation to or from the interview location. An interviewee will be evaluated throughout all of these situations, so make sure you remain aware that assessments are being made. Such occasions and activities are also a good opportunity to evaluate the interviewer and determine whether the position or organization is right for you.

QUESTIONS TO CONSIDER

1. Is it fair to evaluate an interviewee aside from the formal interview setting?
2. Do you think information discovered by both interviewers and interviewees is more genuine in these settings?

Offer Thanks

As mentioned earlier, an interviewer should be grateful for the time, energy, and emotion that an interviewee has put into the interview process. Likewise, an interviewee should be grateful for the work of an interviewer. As this chapter indicates, there is a lot more work involved when interviewing people for a position, and items such as searching for job candidates (constructing the job announcement, gaining approval through human resources, advertising, reviewing applications) and completing the hiring process (deciding who gets the offer, negotiating compensation, dealing with human resources) are not even addressed. Accordingly, sincere thanks should be offered to the interviewer.

Farewells

The interviewer should initiate the formal end of the interview. An interviewee should follow the lead of the interviewer and not unnecessarily prolong the departure. A smile and professional handshake will help maintain a positive relational connection with the interviewer. As an interviewee, you should keep the "By the Way" box in mind when making an exit, and remember that your evaluation as a job candidate will continue until you completely leave the interview location.

Post-Interview Responsibilities

Just because the interview has been concluded does not mean that the work is done. Both interviewers and interviewees have post-interview responsibilities that are vital to their professional development and that will improve interviewees' chances of being offered the position and help interviewers determine the best candidate for the organization. We begin our discussion with the responsibilities of an interviewer.

Interviewer Responsibilities

Following the interview, an interviewer must complete the following three tasks: (1) review the job candidate, (2) assess his or her personal performance, and (3) contact the interviewee with a final decision about the position.

Assess the Job Candidate

An interviewer should record his or her evaluation of the interviewee along with any additional thoughts or information as soon as possible following the interview. Recording impressions and other relevant information is especially important if many interviews are being conducted, and doing so as soon as possible will reduce the amount of information that is lost with time. Contact with references, documented experience, training, and other background information will be used when making final employment decisions, but information gleaned from the interview is also very important when making such decisions and should be properly documented. Table 15.5 provides areas that can be addressed when evaluating a job candidate following the interview.

Table 15.5 Assessing a Job Candidate

- What are the candidate's strengths?
- What are the candidate's weaknesses?
- How does this candidate compare with other candidates?
- How suitable does the candidate seem for the specific requirement of the position?
- How would the candidate fit with the organization's climate?
- How knowledgeable about the position and the organization does the candidate seem?
- Are there any concerns about whether the candidate would be successful in this position?
- What additional questions or information about the candidate need to be addressed?

Assess Personal Performance

The interviewer should also assess his or her performance in order to improve both personally and professionally. Focus equally on the positive and negative aspects of the interview performance. Regardless of how much interviewing experience you may possess, there is always room for improvement. Table 15.6 provides a few questions you may pose when evaluating your performance as an interviewer.

Table 15.6 Assessing Performance as Interviewer

- Did I make the interviewee comfortable and establish the desired tone of the interview? How can I improve these aspects of the interview?
- Did my questions elicit the information needed to fully evaluate the job candidate? How can I improve these questions to enhance the quality of the information gained?
- Did I avoid illegal questions?
- What nonverbal communication most benefited my performance? How can I improve my nonverbal communication?
- How well did I listen during the interview? How can I improve my listening?
- Were my responses to the questions posed by the interviewee complete and accurate? In what ways can I improve my responses?
- Did I provide the interviewee with information about future contact and a realistic timetable for decisions about the position?
- Was the interview conducted within the time constraints? Did all portions of the interview receive the appropriate amount of attention? How can I improve my use of time?

Contact Interviewee

The interviewer should ensure that *all* interviewees are contacted about the final decision. This contact should come either personally or through whatever method is used by the organization. Contacting interviewees is a professional courtesy that, unfortunately, is increasingly absent during many job searches. There exists no legitimate excuse for not contacting and acknowledging a job candidate who did not receive an offer. Not contacting job candidates is not only unprofessional but also cruel! Additionally, a person may not have been suited for this position, but he or she may be ideal for a future position. A lack of contact may prevent a well-suited candidate from applying for a future position—for good reason. A person who is mistreated during the interview process may eventually be in a position that could negatively influence the organization. Ultimately, interviewers should simply contact all interviewees because it is the humane thing to do.

Interviewee Responsibilities

An interviewee has three responsibilities following an interview: (1) assess the interview, (2) send a follow-up letter, and (3) avoid irritating the interviewer.

Assess the Interview

Following the interview, an interviewee should develop a candid assessment of his or her performance. The sooner this assessment can be conducted, the fresher the

Table 15.7 Assessing Performance as Interviewee

- Which questions were answered well? What made these good answers?
- What questions were not answered well? How can I improve these answers?
- Were my questions appropriate? How can I improve these questions?
- What nonverbal communication most benefited my performance? How can I improve my nonverbal communication?
- How well did I listen during the interview? How can I improve my listening?

Table 15.8 Assessing Position and Organization

- What are the pros and cons of the position?
- What are the pros and cons of the organization?
- How does this position compare with other available positions?
- How does this organization compare with other organizations?
- How has my understanding and evaluation of this career/profession changed?

information and the more accurate the recollection. Strive to give equal attention to the aspects of the interview that went well and those that need improvement. Regardless of how you might feel about the interview, even the best interview can be improved, and an awful interview is never as bad as it seems. The best way to improve as an interviewee is through an honest assessment of your performance.

An interviewee should also develop an honest assessment of the position and organization. Developing this assessment will help determine whether the position is something you will accept if offered. It will also increase your understanding about careers and industries for which you are interviewing. Tables 15.7 and 15.8 provide questions to assess your performance, the position, and the organization.

Send Follow-Up Letter

An interviewee should also send a letter of thanks following the interview. In addition to thanking the interviewer for his or her time, it is an opportunity to reinforce interest in the position and remind the interviewer of qualifications and experience. If something was not mentioned during the interview, this letter is a good opportunity to add that information. Interviewers occasionally ask for additional information or materials. These items can be included with the letter as well. Do not appear overly confident about the interview, nor should you apologize for a less-than-stellar interview. The letter should also be viewed as a professional correspondence. Accordingly, it should be respectful, well written, and free of grammatical errors. The letter can be handwritten, typed, or e-mailed, although some people disagree about which of these is most appropriate. People and organizations view technology in different ways (Chapter 13), so use your best judgment as to whether it will be deemed an appropriate method of correspondence.

Avoid Irritating the Interviewer

This post-interview requirement may seem obvious, but you should avoid irritating the interviewer by inquiring about the progress of a job search. Do not send the interviewer numerous letters, leave phone messages every hour on the hour, or send the interviewer a Facebook friendship request. We understand that waiting for an employment decision can be excruciatingly painful, but waiting is something that must be done. Irritating the interviewer will in no way increase your chances of being offered the position and will likely hinder those chances. If you have not heard from the interviewer by the time he or she indicated you would be contacted, however, it is acceptable to politely inquire about the status of the position. A number of variables can lead to a delay in the search process, so it is not uncommon, nor is it necessarily a personal affront against you. The organization may very well be busy renting a truck to dump a load of money on your doorstep.

Focus Questions Revisited

What are a cover letter and résumé?

A cover letter declares interest in a position, summarizes qualification, focuses attention on the résumé, and requests an interview. The key features of a cover letter include (1) a focus on a specific person, (2) identification of the position, (3) a summary of qualifications and the promotion of the résumé, (4) a reaffirmation of interest and a request for an interview, and (5) a professional and respectful sign-off. The purpose of a résumé is to present your credentials for a position in a clear and concise manner. The key elements of a résumé include (1) name and contact information, (2) career objective, (3) education and training, (4) experiences, (5) skills, and (6) activities.

What are the characteristics of an interview?

Interviews are goal-driven, structured, controlled, and unbalanced and feature questions and answers.

What are the types of interviews?

The following are the most common types of interviews: (1) employment interviews, (2) performance interviews, (3) exit interviews, (4) information-gaining interviews, (5) persuasive interviews, (6) problem-solving interviews, and (7) helping interviews.

What are the pre-interview responsibilities of interviewers and interviewees?

Before an interview, an interviewer must review application material, prepare questions and an interview outline, gather material, and ensure the interview begins on time. An interviewee must gather information, prepare questions, practice, bring materials, form a professional personal appearance, and arrive on time.

How should a person begin an employment interview?

During the beginning of an interview, participants must greet one another and establish proxemics, begin to negotiate the desired relational connection and tone of the interview, and establish the purpose and agenda of the interview.

What types of questions and questioning styles may an interviewer use?

The different types of questions that an interviewer may ask include (1) primary and secondary, (2) open and closed, and (3) neutral and leading. The interviewer may not ask questions that are potentially discriminatory. The type of control exerted by the interview can be either directive or nondirective.

How should interviewees respond to questions during an interview?

When answering the questions, interviewees should attempt to adjust the interview frame in order to view the interview as an opportunity, a learning experience, and a dialogue rather than a test, a demonstration, or a monologue. They should also learn from successful interviewees, who articulate clear goals; identify with employers; provide support for arguments; participate in the development of the interview; use active, concrete words; and display dynamic nonverbal communication. Interviewees should be prepared to answer common questions asked during employment interviews and also be prepared should they be asked an illegal question.

How should a person conclude an employment interview?

When concluding an employment interview as an interviewer, you should provide a wrap-up signal, summarize the interview, ask for questions, preview future actions and schedule, extend thanks, and offer farewells. When concluding an employment interview as an interviewee, you should ask questions, reinforce qualifications and enthusiasm, inquire about the schedule if it has not been offered, extend thanks, and offer farewells.

What are the post-interview responsibilities of interviewers and interviewees?

Following an interview, an interviewer must review the job candidate, assess his or her performance, and contact the interviewee with a final decision about the position. An interviewee must assess the interview, develop a follow-up letter, and avoid irritating the interviewer.

Key Concepts

bipolar questions 325
closed questions 325
cover letter 310
directive interviews 326
employment interviews 314
exit interviews 315
helping interviews 316
information-gaining interviews 315
interview 310
leading questions 326
mirror questions 324
neutral questions 325
nondirective interviews 327
open questions 325
performance interviews 315
persuasive interviews 315
primary questions 324
probing questions 324
problem-solving interviews 316
résumé 310
secondary questions 324
self-fulfilling prophecy 329
wrap-up signal 334

Questions to Ask Your Friends

1. Ask a friend to describe his or her most recent employment interview. What aspects of the interview went well? What aspects of the interview needed improvement? Having read this chapter, provide your friend with advice about how to improve his or her performance during interviews.
2. Ask a friend to participate in mock interviews with you. You should alternate between being an interviewer and being an interviewee. Evaluate your performances and pinpoint areas for improvement and development.
3. Ask a friend to review your cover letter and résumé. What suggestions for improvement does he or she make?

Media Connections

1. Watch an interview conducted on television or available online. What open and closed questions are included? Are the questions mostly neutral or mostly leading? Are secondary questions included? Is this a directive or a nondirective interview?
2. Watch an interview conducted on television or available online with the sound muted. What does the nonverbal communication of the interviewer and interviewee suggest in terms of their relational connection and the tone of the interview? Next, watch the interview with the sound turned on. Does the verbal communication of the interviewer and interviewee match your perceptions of their relational connection and the tone of the interview conveyed nonverbally?
3. Find a clip from *Law & Order* or another fictional program featuring a lawyer questioning a witness. Next, find a clip from a television news program in which someone is being interviewed. Finally, find a clip from a late-night talk show in which a celebrity is being interviewed about his or her latest project. How would you rank these examples in terms of being directive or nondirective? What features caused you to rank them in that order?

Student Study Site

SAGE edge™

Sharpen your skills with SAGE edge at edge.sagepub.com/duckciel2e

SAGE edge for students provides a personalized approach to help you accomplish your coursework goals in an easy-to-use learning environment.

Glossary

accommodation: when people change their accent, their rate of speech, and even the words they use to indicate a relational connection with the person to whom they are talking

accounts: forms of communication that go beyond the facts and offer justifications, excuses, exonerations, explanations, or accusations

act: element of the pentad involving what happened (see *agency, agent, scene, purpose*)

action-facilitating support: providing information or performing tasks for others

activation of impersonal commitments: seeking compliance through the manipulation of internal feelings of obligation and appropriate behavior

activation of personal commitments: seeking compliance through appealing to obligations to others

adjourning (Tuckman's group development): when a group reflects on its achievements, underlines its performative accomplishments, and closes itself down (see *forming, norming, performing, storming*)

advisory group: that which is task specific, usually with the intention of producing an outcome that is a focused "best solution" to a specific problem or arrangement of an event

agency: element of the pentad involving how an act was accomplished (see *act, agent, scene, purpose*)

agent: element of the pentad involving who performed an act (see *act, agency, scene, purpose*)

altercasting: how language can impose a certain identity on people, and how language can support or reject the identity of another person

appeal to authority (fallacious argument): when a person's authority or credibility in one area is used to support another area

appeal to people (fallacious argument): claims that something is good or beneficial because everyone else agrees with this evaluation (also called *bandwagon appeal*)

appeal to relationships (fallacious argument): when relationships are used to justify certain behaviors and to convince others of their appropriateness

apprehension: contextual influence of compliance gaining based on anxiety resulting from the circumstances

argument against the source (fallacious argument): when the source of a message, rather than the message itself, is attacked (also called *ad hominem* argument)

arousal goals: secondary goals of compliance gaining recognizing the desire to keep arousal at an acceptable level

asynchronous communication: communication in which there is a slight or prolonged delay between the message and the response; the interactants must alternate between sending and receiving messages (contrast with *synchronous communication*)

attending: the second step in the listening process when stimuli are perceived and focused on

attitude of reflection (symbolic interactionism): thinking about how you look in other people's eyes, or reflecting on the fact that other people can see you as a social object from their point of view

attitudes: learned predispositions to evaluate something in a positive or negative way that guide people's thinking and behavior

authority structure: in some families the authority structure stresses the role of one parent as head of the family; others stress equality of all the mature members

avoidance (politeness strategy): when a person avoids a face-threatening act altogether (see *bald on record, negative politeness, off record, positive politeness*)

backchannel communication: vocalizations by a listener that give feedback to the speaker to show interest, attention, and/or a willingness to keep listening

back region: a frame where a social interaction is regarded as not under public scrutiny, so people do not have to present their public face (contrast with *front region*)

bald on record (politeness strategy): when a person acts directly without concern for face needs (see *avoidance, negative politeness, off record, positive politeness*)

beliefs: what a person holds to be true or false

bidirectionality hypothesis: the idea that power can work in two directions; that is, at some points and times it works one way when parents control or influence their young kids, but power also goes the other way and sometimes kids can control or influence parents, for example, by throwing temper tantrums

binuclear family: two families based on the nuclear form (e.g., the children's father, their stepmother, and her children, if any, as well as the children's mother and their stepfather and his children, if any)

bipolar question: a type of closed question that forces an interviewee to select one of two responses

blended family: when parents adopt nongenetic offspring, divorce, or remarry other partners, then so-called blended families are the result

body buffer zone: a kind of imaginary aura around you that you regard as part of yourself and your personal space

boundary management: focuses on the way marital couples manage talking about private matters with each other and how they coordinate communication boundaries in balancing a need for disclosure with the need for privacy

certainty-uncertainty dialectic: the need for predictability and routine in a relationship and the need for novelty and change in a relationship (also called *novelty-predictability dialectic*)

change (relational dialectics): movement in relationships that occurs in part through dealing with relational contradictions; in relationships, change is the constant element; relationships are perpetually in motion, unfinished business, and constantly evolving

children and parents (patient-provider relationship): the provider clearly portrays a dominant role of expert while the patient assumes a submissive and dependent role; this view of provider and patient relationships is the most traditional and still most common

chronemics: the study of use and evaluation of time in interactions

claim of conjecture: a claim maintaining that something will be true or false in the future

claim of fact: a claim maintaining that something is true or false

claim of policy: a claim maintaining that a course of action should or should not be taken

claim of value: a claim maintaining that something is good or bad, beneficial or detrimental, or another evaluative criterion

closed questions: questions that limit the range of an interviewee's response (contrast with *open questions*)

co-cultures: smaller groups of culture within a larger cultural mass

coded system of meaning: a set of beliefs, a heritage, and a way of being that is transacted in communication

coercive power: that which is derived from the ability to punish

cognitive dissonance theory: people prefer their actions to be consistent with their attitudes, beliefs, and values, because inconsistency elicits negative feelings; explains foot-in-the-door technique

cohesiveness: working together and feeling connected

collectivist: subscribing to a belief system that stresses group benefit and the overriding value of working harmoniously rather than individual personal advancement (contrast with *individualist*)

collectivist talk: that which is characterized as stressing group benefit and harmony rather than personal needs and advancement (contrast with *individualist talk*)

communication as action: the act of sending messages—whether or not they are received

communication as interaction: an exchange of information between two (or more) individuals

communication as transaction: the construction of shared meanings or understandings between two (or more) individuals

communication frame: a boundary around a conversation that pulls one's attention toward certain things and away from others

communication privacy management theory: explains how people create and manage privacy boundaries in their relationships

compliance gaining: involves interpersonal attempts at influence, especially attempts to influence someone's behavior

composition fallacy (fallacious argument): argues that the parts are the same as the whole

concurrent media use: use of two or more media systems simultaneously

conflict: real or perceived incompatibilities of processes, understandings, and viewpoints between people

conflict (Fisher's group progression): occurs when a group argues about possible ways of approaching the problem and begins to seek solutions (see *emergence, orientation, reinforcement*)

conflict-as-destructive culture: a culture based on four assumptions: that conflict is a destructive disturbance of the peace; that the social system should not be adjusted to meet the needs of members, but members should adapt to established values; that confrontations are destructive and ineffective; and that disputants should be disciplined (contrast with *conflict-as-opportunity culture*)

conflict-as-opportunity culture: a culture based on four assumptions: that conflict is a normal, useful process; that all issues are subject to change through negotiation; that direct confrontation and conciliation are valued; and that conflict is a necessary renegotiation of an implied contract—a redistribution of opportunity, a release of tensions, and a renewal of relationships (contrast with *conflict-as-destructive culture*)

connectedness-separateness dialectic: the need to be with a relational partner and the need to be away from a relational partner (also called *connection-autonomy dialectic*)

connotative meaning: the overtones, implications, or additional meanings associated with a word or an object

consistency: a message is free of internal contradiction and is in harmony with information known to be true

constitutive approach to communication: communication can create or bring into existence something that has not been there before, such as an agreement, a contract, or an identity

consumers (patient-provider relationship): patients viewing themselves as paying providers for specific information and expecting them to carry out their wishes

content (representational) listening: obstacle to listening when people focus on the content level of meaning, or literal meaning, rather than the social or relational level of meaning

continuation of identity: parts of your identity carry over from your normal practices of everyday talk into the workplace, but some parts of your identity are transformed by the workplace

contradiction (relational dialectics): interplay between two things that are connected at the same time they are in opposition

conventionality-uniqueness dialectic: the need of people to feel as if their relationship is like the relationships of others and the need to feel as if their relationship is special

convergence: a person moves toward the style of talk used by the other speaker (contrast with *divergence*)

conversational hypertext: coded messages within conversation that an informed listener will effortlessly understand

core ties: people with whom you have a very close relationship and are in frequent contact; a person often discusses important matters in life with these people and often seeks their assistance in times of need (compare with *significant ties*)

cover letter: a letter sent when seeking employment, which has four purposes: (1) declare interest in the position, (2) provide a summary of qualifications, (3) compel the person to read your résumé, and (4) request an interview

creative group: that which is focused on the evaluation of concepts or on the creation of new products or approaches to complex problems

critical approach: seeks to identify the hidden but formidable symbolic structures and practices that create or uphold disadvantage, inequity, or oppression of some groups in favor of others

critical listening: the process of analyzing and evaluating the accuracy, legitimacy, and value of messages

cross-cultural communication: compares the communication styles and patterns of people from very different cultural/social structures, such as nation-states

cultural persuadables: the cultural premises and norms that delineate a range of what may and what must be persuaded (as opposed to certain topics in a society that require no persuasive appeal because the matters are taken for granted)

***cum hoc ergo propter hoc* (fallacious argument):** argues that if one thing happens at the same time as another, it was caused by the thing with which it coincides; Latin for "with this; therefore, because of this"

decoding: drawing meaning from something you observe

denotative meaning: the identification of something by pointing it out ("that is a cat")

Devil terms: powerfully evocative terms viewed negatively in a society (contrast with *God terms*)

dialectic tension: occurs whenever one is in two minds about something because one feels a simultaneous pull in two directions

directive interviews: interviews that are greatly controlled by an interviewer

disruptive roles: those functioning in opposition to group productivity and cohesion

divergence: a person moves away from another's style of speech to make a relational point, such as establishing dislike or superiority

division fallacy (fallacious argument): argues the whole is the same as its parts

dominance: contextual influence of compliance gaining based on power dimensions within a relationship

door-in-the-face technique: sequential method of persuasion that involves making a request so large that it will be turned down and then following up with a second, smaller request

dyadic process: part of the process of breakdown of relationships that involves a confrontation with a partner and the open discussion of a problem with a relationship

dynamic: elements of nonverbal communication that are changeable during interaction (e.g., facial expression, posture, gesturing; contrast with *static*)

egocentric listening: obstacle to listening when people focus more on their message and self-presentation than on the message of the other person involved in an interaction

elaborated code: speech that emphasizes the reasoning behind a command; uses speech and language more as a way for people to differentiate the uniqueness of their own personalities and ideas and to express their own individuality, purposes, attitudes, and beliefs than as a way to reinforce collectivity or commonality of outlook (contrast with *restricted code*)

emblems: gestures that represent feelings or ideas not necessarily being expressed verbally

emergence (Fisher's group progression): occurs when consensus begins to dawn, and a group sees the emergence of possible agreement (see *orientation, conflict, reinforcement*)

emoticons: text-based symbols used to express emotions online, often to alleviate problems associated with a lack of nonverbal cues

emotional support: type of nurturing support enabling people to express their feelings and to have those feelings validated by others

employment interviews: interviews in which a potential employer interviews a potential employee

encoding: putting feelings into behavior through nonverbal communication

engaged listening: making a personal relational connection with the source of a message that results from the source and the receiver actively working together to create shared meaning and understanding

environmental distraction: obstacle to listening that results from the physical location where listening takes place and competing sources

equivocation (fallacious argument): relies on the ambiguousness of language to make an argument

essential function of talk: a function of talk that makes the relationship real and talks it into being, often by using coupling references or making assumptions that the relationship exists

esteem support: type of nurturing support making someone feel competent and valued

ethnocentric bias: believing that the way one's own culture does things is the right and natural way to do them

exit interviews: interviews that occur when a person chooses to leave a place of employment

experiential superiority: obstacle to listening when people fail to fully listen to someone else because they believe that they possess more or superior knowledge and experience than the other person

expertise activities: seeking compliance through perceptions of credibility or wisdom

expert power: that which is derived from possessing special knowledge

extended family: a family that has at its center a nuclear family but also includes grandparents, aunts, cousins, and all other living forms of blood relatives

extended parallel process model: explains the process of fear appeals using the key elements of perceived threat and perceived efficacy

external dialectics: those involving a relational unit and other relational units or people within their social networks

eye contact: extent to which someone looks directly into the eyes of another person

facework: the management of people's dignity or self-respect, known as "face"

factual diversion: obstacle to listening that occurs when so much emphasis is placed on attending to every detail of a message that the main point becomes lost

fallacious argument: an argument that appears legitimate but is actually based on faulty reasoning or insufficient evidence

false alternatives (fallacious argument): occurs when only two options are provided, one of which is generally presented as the poor choice or one that should be avoided

family identity: a sense of the special or unique features of the family; often revolves around intergenerational storytelling, where the elders talk about dead relatives or relate stories about particular family characters who defined the essence of being a member of their family

family narratives: in the process of storytelling families create a shared sense of meaning about the family experience, whether it is something positive like a birth or an adoption or something negative such as a death or divorce

family of choice: a family created through adoption, or simply the group of people you decide is your "true" family even though there is no genetic connection

family of descent: the whole historical family tree from which you are descended, both living and dead

family of generativity: the family where you are one of the parents of at least one child

family of origin: the family where you are the child of two parents, and in the majority of cases you will have spent some of your life with one or both of them

family storytelling: families have stories about remarkable figures or events in their history that help define the nature of that particular family; telling such stories is a way of bonding and uniting the family as well as identifying some of its key characteristics

feminine talk: that which is characterized as nurturing, harmonious, and compromising (contrast with *masculine talk*)

foot-in-the-door technique: sequential method of persuasion that involves making a small request and then following up with a second, larger request

formal group: that which is task oriented and outcome focused, generally with a formal structure, a restricted membership, and an established chair or leader

formality/hierarchy: creates distance between workers and management and can represent a strain or restraint on relationships as an individual is forced to adopt a professional face rather than a personal identity when dealing with people at work

formal power: that which is formally allocated by a system or group to particular people (compare with *informal power*)

formal roles: specific functions to which group members are assigned and that they are expected to perform within the group

forming (Tuckman's group development): when a group comes into existence and seeks direction from a leader about the nature of its tasks and procedures (see *adjourning, norming, performing, storming*)

frames: basic forms of knowledge that provide a definition of a scenario, either because both people agree on the nature of the situation or because the cultural assumptions built into the interaction and the previous relational context of talk give them a clue

front region: a frame where a social interaction is regarded as under public scrutiny, so people have to be on their best behavior or acting out their professional roles or intended "face" (contrast with *back region*)

gaze: involves one person looking at another person

given belief: a belief that the majority of people in an audience will view as either true or false

God terms: powerfully evocative terms that are viewed positively in a society (contrast with *Devil terms*)

grave dressing process: part of the breakdown of relationships that consists of creating the story of why a relationship died and erecting a metaphorical tombstone that summarizes its main events and features from its birth to its death

group culture: the set of expectations and practices that a group develops to make itself distinctive from other groups and to give its members a sense of exclusive membership (e.g., dress code, specialized language, particular rituals)

group norms: rules and procedures that occur in a group but not necessarily outside it and that are enforced by the use of power or rules for behavior

group roles: positions or functions within a group (see *disruptive roles, formal roles, informal roles, social roles, task roles*)

group sanctions: punishments for violating norms

groupthink: a negative kind of consensus seeking through which members place a higher priority on keeping the process running smoothly and agreeably than they do on voicing opinions that contradict the majority opinion (or the opinion of the leader)

haptics: the study of the specific nonverbal behaviors involving touch

hasty generalization (fallacious argument): when a conclusion is based on a single occurrence or insufficient data or sample size

hearing: the passive physiological act of receiving sound that takes place when sound waves hit a person's eardrums

helping interviews: interviews conducted by someone with expertise in a given area and whose services are engaged by someone in need of advice

high code: a formal, grammatical, and very correct—often "official"—way of talking

high-context culture: a culture that places a great deal of emphasis on the total environment (context) where speech and interaction take place, especially on the relationships between the speakers rather than just on what they say (contrast with *low-context culture*)

high-context talk: that which is characterized as relying on the context in which it takes place, with words used sparingly and the relationship shared by interactants being extremely important (contrast with *low-context talk*)

historiography: the study of the persuasive effect of writing history in particular ways and the reasons why particular reports and analyses are offered by specific authors

identity: a person's uniqueness, represented by descriptions, a self-concept, inner thoughts, and performances, that is symbolized in interactions with other people and presented for their assessment and moral evaluation

identity goals: secondary goals of compliance gaining recognizing that people desire to act in accordance with the personal and relational identities they attempt to transact and/or the personal and relational identities most appropriate in a given situation

illustrators: gestures that visualize or emphasize verbal communication

inclusion-seclusion dialectic: the need for people in a relationship to be around others in a social network and the need for people in a relationship to be by themselves

indexical function of talk: demonstrates or indicates the nature of the relationship between speakers

individualist: one who subscribes to a belief system that focuses on the individual person and his or her personal dreams, goals and achievements, and right to make choices (contrast with *collectivist*)

individualist talk: that which is characterized as stressing individual needs and achievement (contrast with *collectivist talk*)

industrial time: the attention to punctuality and dedication to a task that is connected with the nature of industry (clocking in, clocking out, lunch breaks, etc.)

informal power: operates through relationships and individual reputations without formal status (e.g., someone may not actually be the boss but might exert more influence on other workers by being highly respected; compare with *formal power*)

informal roles: those to which someone is not officially assigned but that serve a function with a group

informational support: type of action-facilitating support providing someone with information in order to increase his or her knowledge and understanding of health issues

information-gaining interviews: interviews in which a person solicits information from another person

instrumental function of talk: when what is said brings about a goal that you have in mind for the relationship, and talk is the means or instrument by which it is accomplished (e.g., asking someone on a date or to come with you to a party)

instrumental goals: are predominant at work and are directed at completion of duties; can also involve a direct assessment of performance

instrumental support: type of action-facilitating support performing tasks for someone

interaction goals: secondary goals of compliance gaining recognizing the desire to act appropriately when attempting to gain compliance

intercultural communication: examines how people from different cultural/social structures speak to one another and what difficulties or conflicts they encounter, over and above the different languages they speak

interdependence: the reliance of each member of a team or group on the other members, making their outcomes dependent on the collaboration and interrelated performance of all members (e.g., a football team dividing up the jobs of throwing, catching, and blocking)

internal dialectics: those occurring within a relationship itself

interpreting: the third step in the listening process when meaning is assigned to sounds and symbolic activity

interpretivist approach: views communication as creative, uncertain, and unpredictable, and thus rejects the idea that a single reality exists or can be discovered; researchers using this approach primarily seek to understand and describe communication experience

interview: a goal-driven transaction characterized by questions and answers, clear structure, control, and imbalance

intimacy: compliance gaining based on the relational connection among interactants

intrapsychic process: part of the process of breakdown of a relationship where an individual reflects on the strengths and weaknesses of a relationship and begins to consider the possibility of ending it

introspective units: one of three types of relational continuity constructional units that keep the memory of the relationship alive during the physical separation of the members involved; introspective units are reminders of the relationships during an absence, examples being photographs of a couple, wedding bands, or fluffy toys that one partner gave to another

kinesics: the study of movements that take place during the course of an interaction

kin keeping: the act of serving as a reservoir for information about members of the family, which is passed along to the other members of the network

kin networks: the extended relational network of cousins, second cousins, children of cousins, uncles, aunts, and even long-term friends who are considered family, too

langue: the formal grammatical structure of language (contrast with *parole*)

leading questions: questions that suggest to an interviewee a preferred way to respond (contrast with *neutral questions*)

leakage: unintentional betrayal of internal feelings through nonverbal communication

legitimate power: that which is derived from a person's status or rank

listening: the active process of receiving, attending to, interpreting, and responding to symbolic activity

long-distance relationships (LDRs): relationships characterized by the distance between partners that prevents them from meeting face-to-face frequently (e.g., commuter marriages, relationships where one person lives on the East Coast and one on the West Coast)

low code: an informal and often ungrammatical way of talking

low-context culture: assumes that the message itself means everything, and it is much more important to have a well-structured argument or a well-delivered presentation than it is to be a member of the royal family or a cousin of the person listening (contrast with *high-context culture*)

low-context talk: that which is characterized as straightforward, with the message speaking for itself and relationship separated from the message as much as possible (contrast with *high-context talk*)

machines and mechanics (patient-provider relationship): providers are viewed as competent experts analytically diagnosing a physical problem and then fixing it; patients are passive and allow the expert mechanic to give them a proper tune-up with little or no input or objection

masculine talk: that which is characterized as tough, aggressive, and competitive (contrast with *feminine talk*)

meaning: what a symbol represents

media equation: people use the same social rules and expectations when interacting with technology as they do with other people

media literacy: the learned ability to access, interpret, and evaluate media products

medium: means through which a message is conveyed

medium distraction: obstacle to listening that results from limitations or problems inherent in certain media and technology, such as mobile phones or Internet connections

message complexity: obstacle to listening when a person finds a message so complex or confusing that he or she stops listening

microcoordination: the unique management of social interaction made possible through cell phones

mirror questions (secondary questions): questions that paraphrase an interviewee's previous response to ensure clarification and to elicit elaboration

monochronic culture: a culture that views time as a valuable commodity and punctuality as very important (contrast with *polychronic culture*)

narrative: any organized story, report, or talk that has a plot, an argument, or a theme and in which speakers both relate facts and arrange the story in a way that provides an account, an explanation, or a conclusion

negative face wants: the desire not to be imposed upon or treated as inferior (contrast with *positive face wants*)

negative politeness (politeness strategy): when a person acknowledges the possibility of negative face, offering regrets or being pessimistic (see *avoidance, bald on record, off record, positive politeness*)

networking group: that which is focused on obtaining, building, or sustaining relationships, usually online

neutral questions: questions that provide an interviewee with no indication of a preferred way to respond (contrast with *leading questions*)

nondirective interviews: interviews in which the direction of the interview is primarily given to the interviewee

nonverbal communication: any symbolic activity other than the use of language

norming (Tuckman's group development): when a group establishes its procedures to move more formally toward a solution (see *adjourning, forming, performing, storming*)

norms: the habitual rules for conducting any family activity

nuclear family: the parents plus their genetically related children

nurturing support: helping people feel better about themselves and the issues they are experiencing

off record (politeness strategy): when a person hints or presents a face-threatening act in a vague manner (see *avoidance, bald on record, negative politeness, positive politeness*)

openness-closedness dialectic: the need to talk to a relational partner and the need to not talk to a relational partner; also, the need to disclose some information to a *relational* partner and to not disclose other information to a relational partner

open questions: questions that enable and prompt interviewees to answer in a wide range of ways (contrast with *closed questions*)

orientation (Fisher's group progression): occurs when group members get to know one another and come to grips with the problems they have convened to deal with (see *emergence, conflict, reinforcement*)

out-groups: cells of disgruntled members who feel undervalued, mistreated, disrespected, not included, or overlooked; these members can be either disruptive or constructive

parasocial relationships: "relationships" established with media characters and personalities

parole: how people actually use language: where they often speak using informal and ungrammatical language structure that carries meaning to us all the same (contrast with *langue*)

partners (patient-provider relationship): patients and providers work together to solve a problem and are viewed as equals, each bringing special knowledge to the interaction

past experience with the source: obstacle to listening when previous encounters with a person lead people to dismiss or fail to critically examine a message because the person has generally been right (or wrong) in the past

peer culture: the set of attitudes and beliefs that create influence from children or adults of the same age/generation as the target person

pentad: five components of narratives that explain the motivation of symbolic action

perception: process of actively selecting, organizing, and evaluating information, activities, situations, people, and essentially all the things that make up your world

perceptual contrast effect: explains door-in-the-face technique; people generally comply with the second request because compared to the initial request it appears much smaller

performance interviews: interviews in which an individual's activities and work are discussed

performative self: a self that is a creative performance based on the social demands and norms of a given situation

performing (Tuckman's group development): when a group performs its task, having previously established how this performance will be carried out (see *adjourning, forming, norming, storming*)

personal benefit: contextual influence of compliance gaining based on potential personal gain

personal constructs: bipolar dimensions used to measure and evaluate things

personal relationships: relationships that only specified and irreplaceable individuals (such as your mother, father, brother, sister, or very best friend) can have with you (compare with *social relationships*)

personal space: space legitimately claimed or occupied by a person for the time being; the area around a person that is regarded as part of the person and in which only informal and close relationships are conducted

persuasive interviews: interviews that have influence as the ultimate goal

pitch: highness or lowness of a person's voice

plausibility: the extent to which a message seems legitimate

polychronic culture: a culture that sees time not as linear and simple but as complex and made up of many strands, none of which is more important than any other—hence such culture's relaxed attitude toward time (contrast with *monochronic culture*)

polysemy: the fact that multiple meanings can be associated with a given word or symbol rather than just one unambiguous meaning

positive face wants: the need to be seen and accepted as a worthwhile and reasonable person (contrast with *negative face wants*)

positive politeness (politeness strategy): when a person focuses on positive face, often through flattery or by offering something in return (see *avoidance, bald on record, negative politeness, off record*)

***post hoc ergo propter hoc* (fallacious argument):** argues that something is caused by whatever happens before it; Latin for "after this; therefore, because of this"

praxis (relational dialectics): the notion that activities of the partners in a relationship are a vital component of the relationship itself; people are both actors and the objects of action in relationships

pregiving technique: sequential method of persuasion maintaining that when a person is given something or offered favors by someone else, that person is more likely to comply with a subsequent request

presentation: one person's particular version of, or "take" on, the facts or events (contrast with *representation*)

primary questions: questions that introduce new topics during an interview (contrast with *secondary questions*)

privacy management: see *boundary management*

probing questions (secondary questions): brief statements or words that urge an interviewee to continue or to elaborate on a response

problem-solving interviews: interviews in which a problem is isolated and solutions are generated

professional face: the behaviors, courtesy, and comportment that are appropriate for people to present to others in a workplace

prospective units: one of three types of relational continuity constructional units that keep the memory of the relationship alive during the physical separation of the members involved; prospective units are recognitions that a separation is about to occur

provisions of relationships: the deep and important psychological and supportive benefits that relationships provide

proxemics: the study of space and distance in communication

punishing activities: seeking compliance through negativity

purpose: element of the pentad involving an act that took place (see *act, agency, agent, scene*)

rate (of speech): how fast or slowly a person speaks, generally determined by how many words are spoken per minute

receiving: the initial step in the listening process where hearing and listening connect

reciprocal concessions: explains door-in-the-face technique; people generally comply with the second request because they feel that since the person making the request is willing to concede something, they should match the concession and also be willing to concede something

red herring (fallacious argument): the use of another issue to divert attention away from the real issue

referent power: that which is derived from the allegiance of one group of people to another person or group

reflecting (paraphrasing): summarizing what another person has said to convey understanding of the message

regulators: nonverbal actions that indicate to others how you want them to behave or what you want them to do

reinforcement (Fisher's group progression): occurs when a group explicitly consolidates consensus to complete the task, or the leader does it for the group by thanking the members (see *emergence, conflict, orientation*)

relational consequences: contextual influence of compliance gaining based on the perceived effects a compliance-gaining strategy might have on a relationship

relational continuity constructional units (RCCUs): small-talk ways of demonstrating that the relationship persists during absence of face-to-face contact

relational dialectics: the study of contradictions in relationships, how they are played out and how they are managed

relational goals: typically involve intimacy and support and usually serve recreational or supportive purposes

relational listening: recognizing, understanding, and addressing the interconnection of relationships and communication during the listening process

relational technologies: such technologies as cell phones, iPods, and PDAs whose use has relational functions and implications in society and within specific groups

Relationship Filtering Model: demonstrates how sequences of cues are used to determine which people are selected to develop close relationships

representation: describes facts or conveys information (contrast with *presentation*)

resistance: contextual influence of compliance gaining based on anticipated opposition

resource goals: secondary goals of compliance gaining recognizing the desire to maintain relational resources

responding: final step in the listening process that entails reacting to the message of another person

restricted code: a way of speaking that emphasizes authority and adopts certain community/cultural orientations as indisputable facts (contrast with *elaborated code*)

résumé: document used when seeking employment that presents credentials for a position in a clear and concise manner

resurrection process: part of the breakdown of relationships that deals with how people prepare themselves for new relationships after ending an old one

revelation-concealment dialectic: the need to let others know about the existence of a relationship and the need to prevent others from knowing about the existence of a relationship; also, the need to disclose some information about the relationship to outsiders and the need to hide other information about the relationship from outsiders

rewarding activities: seeking compliance through positivity

reward power: that which is derived from the ability to provide, manage, or withhold benefits

rights: contextual influence of compliance gaining based on the degree to which the desired outcome seems justified

rituals: particularly formalized ways for handling, say, the routines of mealtimes or birthday gift giving in a family

rules: norms for "family" that monitor the way in which family life should be carried out

Sapir-Whorf hypothesis: the idea that it is the names of objects and ideas that make verbal distinctions and help you make conceptual distinctions rather than the other way around

scene: element of the pentad involving the situation or location of an act (see *act, agency, agent, purpose*)

schemata: mental structures that are used to organize information in part by clustering or linking associated material

secondary questions: follow-up questions asked when seeking elaboration or further information (see *probing questions* and *mirror questions;* contrast with *primary questions*)

sedimentation: the process by which repeated everyday practices create a "structure" for performance in the future, as a river deposits sediment that alters or maintains its course over time

selective exposure: the idea that you are more likely to expose yourself to that which supports your values and attitudes, that you will be more likely to pick up on activities that support your views of the world, and that you will pay less attention to those that do not

selective listening: obstacle to listening when people focus on the points of a message that correspond with their views and interests and pay less attention to those that do not

self-description: description that involves information about self that is obvious to others through appearance and behavior

self-disclosure: the revelation of personal information that others could not know unless the person *made* it known

self-fulfilling prophecy: principle maintaining if someone believes a particular outcome will take place, his or her actions will often lead to its fruition

self-perception theory: explains foot-in-the-door technique; people come to understand their attitudes, beliefs, and values through their actions

self-presentation: explains door-in-the-face technique; people are concerned that other people (most notably the person making the request) may view them in a negative light and that complying with the second request might prevent or decrease those negative perceptions

semantic diversion: obstacle to listening that occurs when people are distracted by words or phrases used in a message through negative response or unfamiliarity

sexual harassment: "any unwelcome sexual advance or conduct on the job that creates an intimidating, hostile, or offensive working environment; any conduct of a sexual nature that makes an employee uncomfortable" (England, 2012, p. 3)

sign: a consequence or an indicator of something specific, which cannot be changed by arbitrary actions or labels (e.g., "wet streets are a sign of rain")

significant ties: people who are more than mere acquaintances but with whom a strong connection does not exist; a person is not overly likely to talk with these people or seek help from these people, but they are still there when needed (compare with *core ties*)

silence: meaningful lack of sound

single-parent family: family where there are children but only one parent caregiver; singleness may be a choice, a preference, or an unwanted outcome (e.g., as a result of an undesired divorce or unexpected death)

social construction: the way in which symbols take on meaning in a social context or society as they are used over time

social construction of technology: belief that people determine the development of technology and ultimately determine social structure and cultural value (compare with *social shaping of technology* and *technological determinism*)

social process: telling other people in one's social network about dissatisfaction and about possible disengagement or dissolution of a relationship

social relationships: relationships in which the specific people in a given role can be changed and the relationship would still occur (e.g., customer–client relationships are the same irrespective of who is the customer and who is the client on a particular occasion; compare with *personal relationships*)

social roles: those functioning to encourage group members and to develop and maintain positive communication and relationships among group members

social scientific approach: views the world as objective, causal, and predictable; researchers using this approach primarily seek to describe communication activity and to discover connections between phenomena or causal patterns

social shaping of technology: belief that both people and technologies exert influence on social structure and cultural values (compare with *social construction of technology* and *technological determinism*)

socialization: the process by which a child comes to understand the way the surrounding culture "does things"—that is, holds certain values to be self-evident and celebrates particular events or festivals

socialization impact of media: depictions of relationships in media provide models of behavior that inform people about how to engage in relationships

socioemotional leaders: those focusing on making group members feel comfortable, satisfied, valued, and understood (compare with *task leaders*)

source distraction: obstacle to listening that results from auditory and visual characteristics of the message source

speech (communication) codes: sets of communication patterns that are the norm for a culture, and only that culture, hence defining it as different from others around it

speech communities: sets of people whose speech codes and practices identify them as a cultural unit, sharing characteristic values through their equally characteristic speech

speech to actuate: a speech that is delivered in an attempt to impact audience behavior

speech to convince: a speech delivered in an attempt to impact audience thinking; encompasses a primary claim, or essentially what the speaker is trying to convince the audience to believe

static: elements of nonverbal communication that are fixed during interaction (e.g., shape of the room where an interaction takes place, color of eyes, clothes worn during an interview; contrast with *dynamic*)

status of the source: obstacle to listening when a person's rank, reputation, or social position leads people to dismiss or fail to critically examine a message

storming (Tuckman's group development): when a group determines leadership and roles of its members (see *adjourning, forming, norming, performing*)

structurational approach: to look at how people enact and enable or contain future interactions through their talk

structuration theory: points to the regularities of human relationships that act as rules and resources drawn on to enable or constrain social interaction

support group: that which is focused on advising, comforting, sharing knowledge, spreading information, and raising consciousness about specific issues

symbolic interactionism: how broad social forces affect or even transact an individual person's view of who he or she is

symbolic self: the self that is transacted in interaction with other people; that arises out of social interaction, not vice versa; and hence that does not just "belong to you"

symbols: arbitrary representations of ideas, objects, people, relationships, cultures, genders, races, and so forth

synchronous communication: communication in which people interact in real time and can at once both send and receive messages (contrast with *asynchronous communication*)

systems theory: deals with (among other phenomena) family and social events as systems made up of parts but operating as a whole system that can achieve functions that individuals alone cannot and that also creates an environment in which those individuals must exist; the behavior of one part (person) affects the atmosphere and behavior of other parts (persons) of the family

task leaders: those focusing on the performance of tasks to ensure the achievement of group goals (compare with *socioemotional leaders*)

task roles: those functioning to ensure a group achieves its goals and is productive

technological determinism: belief that technologies determine social structure, cultural values, and even how people think (compare with *social shaping of technology* and *social construction of technology*)

technology and media generations: those differentiated by unique technology grammar and consciousness based on the technological and media environment in which they are born

technology and media profile: a compilation of your technology and media preferences and general use of technology and media; informs others about who you are as a person or at least the persona you are trying to project

territoriality: the establishment and maintenance of space that people claim for their personal use

totality (relational dialectics): the notion that relational contradictions do not occur in isolation from one another and that the whole complexity of relationships must be taken into account as each element or part of the relationship influences other parts

turn taking: when one speaker hands over speaking to another person

values: deeply held and enduring judgments of significance or importance that often provide the basis for both beliefs and attitudes

verbal communication: the use of language

verifiability: an indication that the material being provided can be confirmed by other sources or means

vocalics (paralanguage): vocal characteristics that provide information about how verbal communication should be interpreted and how the speaker is feeling

vocational anticipatory socialization: the preparation for becoming a worker; takes place from early moments of childhood onward, including through exposure to the media and depiction of the workplace in comedy and other shows

volume: loudness or softness of a person's voice

wandering thoughts: obstacle to listening involving daydreams or thoughts about things other than the message being presented

wrap-up signal: a phrase, usually uttered by the interviewer, that signals the beginning of an interview's conclusion

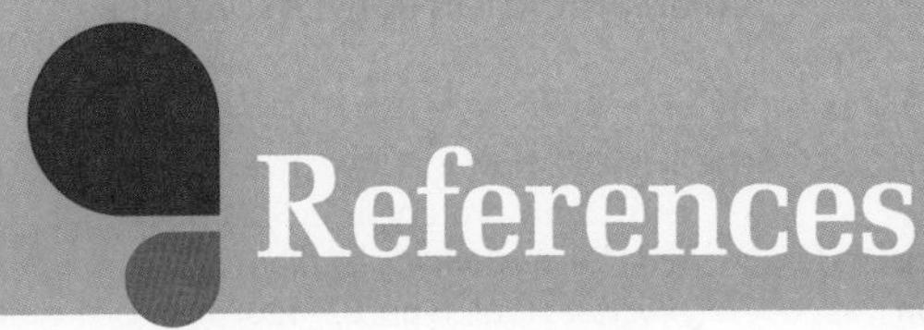

References

Chapter 1

Dance, F. E. X., & Larson, C. E. (1976). *The functions of human communication: A theoretical approach.* New York: Holt, Rinehart & Winston.

Griffin, E. (2012). *Communication theory: A first look* (8th ed.). New York: McGraw-Hill.

Watzlawick, P., Beavin, J., & Jackson, D. (1967). *Pragmatics of human communication: A study of interactional patterns, pathologies and paradoxes.* New York: Norton.

Wood, J. T., & Duck, S. W. (Eds.). (2006). *Composing relationships: Communication in everyday life.* Belmont, CA: Thomson Wadsworth.

Chapter 2

Borisoff, D., Hoel, P. C., & McMahan, D. T. (2010). Interpersonal communication: Trajectories and challenges. In J. W. Chesebro (Ed.), *A century of transformation: Studies in honor of the 100th anniversary of the Eastern Communication Association* (pp. 205–235). New York: Oxford University Press.

Brock, B. L., Scott, R. L., & Chesebro, J. W. (1990). *Methods of rhetorical criticism* (3rd ed.). Detroit, MI: Wayne State University Press.

Carey, J. W. (1979). Graduate education in mass communication. *Communication Education, 28,* 282–293.

Chang, Y. (2012). Is that fair? A cultural analysis of Chinese criminal courtroom communication. *China Media Research, 8,* 95–105.

Chesebro, J. W. (2010). *A century of transformation: Studies in honor of the 100th anniversary of the Eastern Communication Association.* New York: Oxford University Press.

Cohen, H. (1994). *The history of speech communication: The emergence of a discipline, 1914–1945.* Annandale, VA: Speech Communication Association.

Delia, J. G. (1987). Communication research: A history. In C. R. Berger & S. H. Chaffee (Eds.), *Handbook of communication science* (pp. 20–98). Newbury Park, CA: Sage.

Dhaenens, F. (2012). Gay male domesticity in the small screen: Queer representation of gay homemaking in *Six Feet Under* and *Brothers & Sisters. Popular Communication, 10,* 217–230.

Donovan-Kicken, E., McGlynn, J., & Damron, J. C. H. (2012). When friends deflect questions about sensitive information: Questioners' cognitive complexity and explanations for friends' avoidance. *Western Journal of Communication, 76,* 127–147.

Duck, S. W., & McMahan, D. T. (2012). *The basics of communication: A relational perspective* (2nd ed.). Thousand Oaks, CA: Sage.

Gass, R. H., & Seiter, J. S. (2011). *Persuasion, social influence, and compliance gaining* (4th ed.). Boston: Allyn & Bacon.

Glaser, B. G., & Strauss, A. (1967). *Discovery of grounded theory: Strategies for qualitative research.* Mill Valley, CA: Sociology Press.

Gouran, D. S. (2010). Emergent and evolving perspectives on communication in small groups. In J. W. Chesebro (Ed.), *A century of transformation: Studies in honor of the 100th anniversary of the Eastern Communication Association* (pp. 161–184). New York: Oxford University Press.

Harris, K. L., Palazzolo, K. E., & Savage, M. W. (2012). "I'm not sexist, but . . .": How ideological dilemmas reinforce sexism in talk about intimate partner violence. *Discourse & Society, 23,* 643–656.

Holt, L. (2012). Using laugh responses to defuse complaints. *Research on Language and Social Interaction, 45,* 430–448.

Hovland, C., Janis, I., & Kelley, H. H. (1953). *Communication and persuasion.* New Haven, CT: Yale University Press.

Jackson, R. L., II. (2010). Mapping cultural communication research: 1960s to the present. In J. W. Chesebro (Ed.), *A century of transformation: Studies in honor of the 100th anniversary of the Eastern Communication Association* (pp. 272–292). New York: Oxford University Press.

Lederman, L. C. (2010). Health communication: The first twenty-five years. In J. W. Chesebro (Ed.), *A century of transformation: Studies in honor of the 100th anniversary of the Eastern Communication Association* (pp. 236–254). New York: Oxford University Press.

McCroskey, J. C. (1968). *An introduction to rhetorical communication.* Englewood Cliffs, NJ: Prentice Hall.

McCroskey. J. C. (1970). Measures of communication-bound anxiety. *Speech Monographs, 37,* 269–277.

McCroskey, J. C. (2010). Communication apprehension and related communication traits. In J. W. Chesebro (Ed.), *A century of transformation: Studies in honor of the 100th anniversary of the Eastern Communication Association* (pp. 329–337). New York: Oxford University Press.

McMahan, D. T. (2004). What we have here is a failure to communicate: Linking interpersonal communication and mass communication. *Review of Communication, 4,* 33–56.

McMahan, D. T. (2011). Heartland: Symbolic displays of aggression and male masculinity in rural America. *Qualitative Research Reports in Communication, 12,* 51–59.

Metts, S., Sprecher, S., & Cupach, W. R. (1991). Retrospective self-reports. In B. M. Montgomery & S. W. Duck (Eds.), *Studying interpersonal interaction* (pp. 162–178). New York: Guilford Press.

Morreale, S., Hugenberg, L., & Worley, D. (2006). The basic communication course at U.S. colleges and universities in the 21st century: Study VII. *Communication Education, 55,* 415–437.

Norwood, K. (2013a). Grieving gender: Trans-identities, transition, and ambiguous loss. *Communication Monographs, 80,* 24–45.

Norwood, K. (2013b). Meaning matters: Framing trans identity in the context of family relationships. *Journal of GLBT Family Studies, 9,* 152–178.

Olson, L. C. (2010). Rhetorical criticism and theory: Rhetorical questions, theoretical fundamentalism, and the dissolution of judgment. In J. W. Chesebro (Ed.), *A century of transformation: Studies in honor of the 100th anniversary of the Eastern Communication Association* (pp. 37–72). New York: Oxford University Press.

Olson, L. C., Finnegan, C. A., & Hope, D. S. (2008). *Visual rhetoric: A reader in communication and American culture.* Thousand Oaks, CA: Sage.

Papper, R. A., Holmes, M. E., & Popovich, M. N. (2004). Middletown Media Studies: Media multitasking . . . and how much people really use the media. *International Digital Media & Arts Association Journal, 1,* 4–56.

Richmond, V. P., & Frymier, A. B. (2010). Communication education and instructional development. In J. W. Chesebro (Ed.), *A century of transformation: Studies in honor of the 100th anniversary of the Eastern Communication Association* (pp. 310–328). New York: Oxford University Press.

Turner, L. H., & West, R. (Eds). (2015) *The SAGE handbook of family communication.* Thousand Oaks, CA: Sage.

Trent, J. S., & Friedenberg, R. V. (2010). Political communication: A flourishing field of study and scholarship. In J. W. Chesebro (Ed.), *A century of transformation: Studies in honor of the 100th anniversary of the Eastern Communication Association* (pp. 143–160). New York: Oxford University Press.

Wiemann, J. M., Hawkins, R. P., & Pingree, S. (1988). Fragmentation in the field—and the movement toward integration in communication science. *Human Communication Research, 15,* 304–310.

Wilcox, W. (1959). Historical trends in journalism education. *Journalism Educator, 14,* 2–7, 32.

Williams, K. D. (2013). The effects of video game controls on hostility, identification, and presence. *Mass Communication & Society, 16,* 26–48.

Wright, C. N. (2012). Education orientation and upward influence: An examination of student-to-student connectedness as power in the classroom. *Communication Education, 61,* 271–289.

Chapter 3

Altman, I., & Taylor, D. (1973). *Social penetration: The development of interpersonal relationships.* New York: Holt, Rinehart & Winston.

Altman, I., Vinsel, A., & Brown, B. B. (1981). Dialectic conceptions in social psychology: An application to social penetration and privacy regulation. In L. Berkowitz (Ed.), *Advances in experimental social psychology* (Vol. 14, pp. 107–160). New York: Academic Press.

Baxter, L. A. (2004). Distinguished scholar article: Relationships as dialogues. *Personal Relationships, 11*(1), 1–22.

Baxter, L. A. (2011). *Voicing relationships: A dialogic perspective.* Thousand Oaks, CA: Sage.

Baxter, L. A., & Braithwaite, D. O. (2008). Relational dialectics theory: Crafting meaning from competing discourses. In L. A. Baxter & D. O. Braithwaite (Eds.), *Engaging theories in interpersonal communication* (pp. 349–361). Thousand Oaks, CA: Sage.

Baxter, L. A., & Montgomery, B. M. (1996). *Relating: Dialogs and dialectics.* New York: Guilford Press.

Berscheid, E., & Reis, H. T. (1998). Attraction and close relationships. In D. T. Gilbert, S. F. Fiske, & G. Lindzey (Eds.), *The handbook of social psychology* (4th ed., pp. 139–281). Boston: McGraw-Hill.

Burke, K. (1969). *A grammar of motives.* Berkeley: University of California Press.

Burleson, B. R., Holmstrom, A. J., & Gilstrap, C. M. (2005). "Guys can't say that to guys": Four experiments assessing the normative motivation account for deficiencies in the emotional support provided by men. *Communication Monographs, 72*(4), 468–501.

Caughlin, J. P., & Afifi, T. D. (2004). When is topic avoidance unsatisfying? Examining the moderators of the association between avoidance and dissatisfaction. *Human Communication Research, 30*(4), 479–513.

Cupach, W. R., & Metts, S. (1994). *Facework.* Thousand Oaks, CA: Sage.

Derlega, V. J., Metts, S., Petronio, S., & Margulis, S. T. (1993). *Self-disclosure.* Newbury Park, CA: Sage.

Dindia, K. (2000). Self-disclosure, identity, and relationship development: A dialectical perspective. In K. Dindia & S. W. Duck (Eds.), *Communication and personal relationships* (pp. 147–162). Chichester, UK: Wiley.

Duck, S. W. (2011). *Rethinking relationships: A new approach to relationship research.* Thousand Oaks, CA: Sage.

Fehr, B. (1993). How do I love thee: Let me consult my prototype. In S. W. Duck (Ed.), *Understanding relationship processes* (Vol. 1, pp. 87–120). Newbury Park, CA: Sage.

Goffman, E. (1959). *Behaviour in public places.* Harmondsworth, UK: Penguin Books.

Hess, J. A. (2000). Maintaining a nonvoluntary relationship with disliked partners: An investigation into the use of distancing behaviors. *Human Communication Research, 26,* 458–488.

Huisman, D. (2008). *Intergenerational family storytelling.* Iowa City: University of Iowa Department of Communication Studies.

Jourard, S. M. (1964). *The transparent self.* New York: Van Nostrand Reinhold.

Jourard, S. M. (1971). *Self-disclosure.* New York: Wiley.

Kellas, J. K. (2008). Narrative theories: Making sense of interpersonal communication. In L. A. Baxter & D. O. Braithwaite (Eds.), *Engaging theories in interpersonal communication* (pp. 241–254). Thousand Oaks, CA: Sage.

Kelly, G. A. (1955). *The psychology of personal constructs.* New York: Norton.

Marwell, G., & Schmitt, D. R. (1967). Dimensions of compliance-gaining behavior: An empirical analysis. *Sociometry, 30,* 350–364.

Mead, G. H. (1934). *Mind, self, and society.* Chicago: University of Chicago Press.

Metts, S. (2000). Face and facework: Implications for the study of personal relationships. In K. Dindia & S. W. Duck (Eds.), *Communication and personal relationships* (pp. 74–92). Chichester, UK: Wiley.

Norwood, K. M. (2010, April 26). *Here and gone: Competing discourses in the communication of families with a transgender member.* Unpublished PhD thesis, Department of Communication Studies, University of Iowa.

Payne, A. (Director). (2004). *Sideways* [Motion picture]. United States: Fox Searchlight Pictures.

Petronio, S. (2002). *Boundaries of privacy.* Albany: State University of New York Press.

Petronio, S., & Durham, W. T. (2008). Communication privacy management theory: Significance for interpersonal communication. In L. A. Baxter & D. O. Braithwaite (Eds.),

Engaging theories in interpersonal communication (pp. 309–322). Thousand Oaks, CA: Sage.

Shotter, J. (1984). *Social accountability and selfhood.* Oxford, UK: Basil Blackwell.

Tracy, K. (2002). *Everyday talk: Building and reflecting identities.* New York: Guilford Press.

Wood, J. T., & Duck, S. W. (Eds.). (2006). *Composing relationships: Communication in everyday life.* Belmont, CA: Thomson Wadsworth.

Chapter 4

Arrindell, W. A., van Well, S., Kolk, A. M., Barelds, D. P. H., Oei, T. P. S., & Lau, P. Y. (2013). Higher levels of masculine gender role stress in masculine than in feminine nations: A thirteen-nations study. *Cross-cultural Research, 47,* 51–67.

Bernstein, B. (1971). *Class, codes, and control.* London: Routledge.

Brown, P., & Levinson, S. C. (1978). Universals in language usage: Politeness phenomena. In E. E. Goody (Ed.), *Questions and politeness* (pp. 56–289). Cambridge, UK: Cambridge University Press.

Burke, K. (1966). *Language as symbolic action: Essays on life, literature and method.* Berkeley: University of California Press.

Burke, K. (1969). *A grammar of motives.* Berkeley: University of California Press.

Charee, M. T., Romo, L. K., & Dailey, R. M. (2013). The effectiveness of weight management influence messages in romantic relationships. *Communication Research Reports, 30,* 34–45.

Cupach, W. R., & Metts, S. (1994). *Facework.* Thousand Oaks, CA: Sage.

Du, H., & King, R. B. (2013). Placing hope in self and others: Exploring the relationships among self-construals, locus of hope, and adjustment. *Personality & Individual Differences, 54,* 332–337.

Duck, S. W. (2002). Hypertext in the key of G: Three types of "history" as influences on conversational structure and flow. *Communication Theory, 12*(1), 41–62.

Duck, S. W. (2007). *Human relationships* (4th ed.). London: Sage.

Duck, S. W., & Pond, K. (1989). Friends, Romans, Countrymen; lend me your retrospective data: Rhetoric and reality in personal relationships. In C. Hendrick (Ed.), *Review of social psychology and personality: Close relationships* (Vol. 10, pp. 17–38). Newbury Park, CA: Sage.

Engels, J. (2011). Demophilia: A discursive counter to demophobia in the early republic. *Quarterly Journal of Speech, 97,* 131–154.

Fisher, W. R. (1985). The narrative paradigm: An elaboration. *Communication Monographs, 52,* 347–367.

Giles, H., Linz, D., Bonilla, D., & Gomez, M. L. (2012). Police stops of and interactions with Latino and White (non-Latino) drivers: Extensive policing and communication accommodation. *Communication Monographs, 79,* 407–427.

Giles, H., Taylor, D. M., & Bourhis, R. Y. (1973). Towards a theory of interpersonal accommodation through language use. *Language in Society, 2,* 177–192.

Goffman, E. (1971). *Relations in public: Microstudies of the public order.* New York: Harper & Row.

Gudykunst, W. (2000). *Asian American ethnicity and communication.* Thousand Oaks, CA: Sage.

Jiqun, L. (2012). The comparison of the cultural connotations of animal terms in Chinese and French. *Canadian Social Science, 8,* 225–230.

Kelly, G. A. (1969). Ontological acceleration. In B. Mather (Ed.), *Clinical psychology and personality: The collected papers of George Kelly* (pp. 7–45). New York: Wiley.

Kirkpatrick, C. D., Duck, S. W., & Foley, M. K. (Eds.). (2006). *Relating difficulty: The processes of constructing and managing difficult interaction.* Mahwah, NJ: Lawrence Erlbaum.

Komatsu, E. (Ed.). (1993). *Saussure's third course of lectures on general linguistics (1910–1911)* (R. Harris, Trans.). London: Pergamon.

McMahan, D. T. (2004). What we have here is a failure to communicate: Linking interpersonal and mass communication. *Review of Communication, 4,* 33–56.

Metts, S. (2000). Face and facework: Implications for the study of personal relationships. In K. Dindia & S. W. Duck (Eds.), *Communication and personal relationships* (pp. 72–94). Chichester, UK: Wiley.

Morsbach, H. (2004). *Customs and etiquette of Japan.* London: Global Books.

Ogden, C. K., & Richards, I. A. (1946). *The meaning of meaning* (8th ed.). New York: Harcourt Brace Jovanovich.

Samovar, L. A., Porter, R. E., & McDaniel, E. R. (2010). *Communication between cultures* (7th ed.). Belmont, CA: Wadsworth.

Sapir, E. (1949). *Selected writings in language, culture and personality* (D. Mandelbaum, Ed.). Berkeley: University of California Press.

Scott, M. B., & Lyman, S. M. (1968). Accounts. *American Sociological Review, 33,* 46–62.

Whorf, B. (1956). *Language, thought, and reality: Selected writings of Benjamin Lee Whorf* (J. Carroll, Ed.). Boston: MIT Press.

Chapter 5

Bradshaw, S. (2006). Shyness and difficult relationships: Formation is just the beginning. In C. D. Kirkpatrick, S. W. Duck, & M. K. Foley (Eds.), *Relating difficulty: The processes of constructing and managing difficult interaction* (pp. 15–41). Mahwah, NJ: Lawrence Erlbaum.

Burgoon, J. K., Coker, D. A., & Coker, R. A. (1986). Communicative effects of gaze behavior: A test of two contrasting explanations. *Human Communication Research, 12,* 495–524.

Dolcos, S., Sung, K., Argo, J. J., Flor-Henry, S., & Dolcos, F. (2012). The power of a handshake: Neural correlates of evaluative judgments in observed social interactions. *Journal of Cognitive Neuroscience, 24,* 2292–2305.

Duck, S. W. (2007). *Human relationships* (4th ed.). London: Sage.

Elfenbein, H. A. (2013). Nonverbal dialects and accents in facial expressions of emotion. *Emotion Review, 5,* 90–96.

Ellsworth, P. C., Carlsmith, J. M., & Henson, A. (1972). The stare as a stimulus to flight in human subjects: A series of field experiments. *Journal of Personality and Social Psychology, 21,* 302–311.

Erlandson, K. (2012). Stay out of my space! Territoriality and nonverbal immediacy as predictors of roommate satisfaction. *Journal of College and University Student Housing, 38,* 46–61.

Farley, S. D., Hughes, S. M., & LaFayette, J. N. (2013). People will know we are in love: Evidence of differences between vocal samples directed toward lovers and friends. *Journal of Nonverbal Behavior, 37,* 23–138.

Giles, H. (2008). Communication accommodation theory. In L. A. Baxter & D. O. Braithwaite (Eds.), *Engaging theories in interpersonal communication* (pp. 161–173). Thousand Oaks, CA: Sage.

Goodboy, A. K., & Brann, M. (2010). Flirtation rejection strategies: Toward an understanding of communicative disinterest in flirting. *The Qualitative Report, 2,* 268–278.

Guerrero, L. K., & Floyd, K. (2006). *Nonverbal communication in relationships.* Mahwah, NJ: Lawrence Erlbaum.

Hall, E. T. (1966). *The hidden dimension.* New York: Doubleday/Anchor.

Heslin, R. (1974). *Steps toward a taxonomy of touching.* Paper presented at the meeting of the Midwestern Psychological Association, Chicago.

Jourard, S. M. (1971). *Self-disclosure.* New York: Wiley.

Kalman, Y. M., Scissors, L. E., Gill, A. J., & Gergle, D. (2013). Online chronemics convey social information. *Computers in Human Behavior, 29,* 1260–1269.

Kendon, A., & Ferber, A. (1973). A description of some human greetings. In R. P. Michael & J. H. Crook (Eds.), *Comparative ecology and behavior of primates* (pp. 591–668). New York: Academic Press.

Knapp, M. L., & Hall, J. A. (2002). *Nonverbal communication in human interaction* (5th ed.). New York: Holt, Rinehart & Winston.

Koppensteiner, M., & Grammer, K. (2010). Motion patterns in political speech and their influence on personality ratings. *Journal of Research in Personality, 44,* 374–379.

Manusov, V., & Patterson, M. L. (2006). *Handbook of nonverbal communication.* Thousand Oaks, CA: Sage.

Matsumoto, D., & Hwang, H. S. (2012). Culture and emotion: The integration of biological and cultural contributions. *Journal of Cross-Cultural Psychology, 43,* 91–118.

Peace, K. A., Porter, S., & Almon, D. F. (2012). Sidetracked by emotion: Observers' ability to discriminate genuine and fabricated sexual assault allegations. *Legal and Criminological Psychology, 17,* 322–335.

Pretsch, J., Flunger, B., Heckmann, N., & Schmitt, M. (2013). Done in 60 s? Inferring teachers' subjective well-being from thin slices of nonverbal behavior. *Social Psychology of Education, 16,* 421–434.

Puccinelli, N. M., Andrzejewski, S. A., Markos, E., Noga, T., & Motyka, S. (2013). The value of knowing what customers really want: The impact of salesperson ability to read non-verbal cues of affect on service quality. *Journal of Marketing Management, 29,* 356–373.

Remland, M. S. (2004). *Nonverbal communication in everyday life* (2nd ed.). New York: Houghton Mifflin.

Roberts, S. C., Saxton, T. K., Murray, A. K., Burriss, R. P., Rowland, H. M., & Little, A. C. (2009). Static and dynamic facial images cue similar attractiveness judgements. *Ethology, 115,* 588–595.

Sanford, K. (2012). The communication of emotion during conflict in married couples. *Journal of Family Psychology, 26,* 297–307.

Seiter, J. S., & Sandry, A. (2003). Pierced for success? The effects of ear and nose piercing on perceptions of job candidates' credibility, attractiveness, and hirability. *Communication Research Reports, 20*(4), 287–298.

Sheeler, R. (2013). Nonverbal communication in medical practice. In D. Matsumoto, M. G. Frank, & H. S. Hwang (Eds.), *Nonverbal communication: Science and applications* (pp. 237–246). Thousand Oaks, CA: Sage.

Chapter 6

Barker, L., Edwards, R., Gaines, C., Gladney, K., & Holley, F. (1980). An investigation of proportional time spent in various communication activities by college students. *Journal of Applied Communication Research, 8,* 101–109.

Beall, M. L., Gill-Rosier, J., Tate, J., & Matten, A. (2008). State of the context: Listening in education. *International Journal of Listening, 22,* 123–132.

Cialdini, R. B. (1993). *Influence: The psychology of persuasion.* New York: Morrow.

Flynn, J., Valikoski, T.-R., & Grau, J. (2008). Listening in the business context: Reviewing the state of research. *International Journal of Listening, 22,* 141–151.

Gouran, D. S., Wiethoff, W. E., & Doelger, J. A. (1994). *Mastering communication* (2nd ed.). Boston: Allyn & Bacon.

Halone, K. K., & Pechioni, L. L. (2001). Relational listening: A grounded theoretical model. *Communication Reports, 14,* 59–71.

Janusik, L. A., & Wolvin, A. D. (2009). 24 hours in a day: A listening update to the time studies. *International Journal of Listening, 23,* 104–120.

Osgood, C. E., Suci, G. J., & Tannenbaum, P. H. (1957). *The measurement of meaning.* Urbana: University of Illinois Press.

Pearson, J. C., & Nelson, P. E. (2000). *An introduction to human communication* (8th ed.). New York: McGraw-Hill.

Preiss, R. W., & Gayle, B. M. (2006). Exploring the relationship between listening comprehension and rate of speech. In B. M. Gayle, R. W. Preiss, N. Burell, & M. Allen (Eds.), *Classroom communication and instructional processes* (pp. 315–327). Mahwah, NJ: Lawrence Erlbaum.

Rankin, P. T. (1928). The importance of listening ability. *English Journal, 17,* 623–630.

Sahlstein, E. M. (2000). *Relational rhetorics and RRTs (relational rhetorical terms).* Unpublished manuscript, Iowa City, IA.

Schnapp, D. C. (2008). Listening in context: Religion and spirituality. *International Journal of Listening, 22,* 133–140.

Steil, L. K. (1997). Listening training: The key to success in today's organizations. In M. Purdy & D. Borisoff (Eds.), *Listening in everyday life: A personal and professional approach* (pp. 213–237). Lanham, MD: University Press of America.

Urdang, L., Hunsinger, W. W., & LaRouche, N. (1991). *A fine kettle of fish and other figurative phrases.* Detroit, MI: Invisible Ink.

Weinrauch, J. D., & Swanda, R., Jr. (1975). Examining the significance of listening: An exploratory study of contemporary management. *Journal of Business Communication, 13,* 25–32.

Wood, J. T. (2009). *Communication in our lives* (5th ed.). Boston: Wadsworth Cengage Learning.

Chapter 7

Acitelli, L. K. (1988). When spouses talk to each other about their relationship. *Journal of Social and Personal Relationships, 5,* 185–199.

Baxter, L. A. (2004). A tale of two voices: Relational dialectics theory. *Journal of Family Communication, 4,* 181–192.

Baxter, L. A., & Montgomery, B. M. (1996). *Relating: Dialogs and dialectics.* New York: Guilford Press.

Bergmann, J. R. (1993). *Discreet indiscretions: The social organization of gossip.* New York: Aldine de Gruyter.

Byrne, D. (1997). An overview (and underview) of research and theory within the attraction paradigm. *Journal of Social and Personal Relationships, 14,* 417–431.

Carl, W. J. (2006). What's all the buzz about? Everyday communication and the relational basis of word-of-mouth and buzz marketing practices. *Management Communication Quarterly, 19,* 601–634.

Duck, S. W. (1982). A topography of relationship disengagement and dissolution. In S. W. Duck (Ed.), *Personal relationships 4: Dissolving personal relationships* (pp. 1–30). London: Academic Press.

Duck, S. W. (1998). *Human relationships* (3rd ed.). London: Sage.

Duck, S. W. (1999). *Relating to others* (2nd ed.). Milton Keynes, UK: Open University Press.

Duck, S. W. (2007). *Human relationships* (4th ed.). London: Sage.

Duck, S. W. (2011). *Rethinking relationships.* Thousand Oaks, CA: Sage.

Hess, J. A. (2000). Maintaining a nonvoluntary relationship with disliked partners: An investigation into the use of distancing behaviors. *Human Communication Research, 26,* 458–488.

Kahn, J. R., McGill, B. S., & Bianchi, S. M. (2011). Help to family and friends: Are there gender differences at older ages? *Journal of Marriage and Family, 73,* 77–92.

Kerckhoff, A. C. (1974). The social context of interpersonal attraction. In T. L. Huston (Ed.), *Foundations of interpersonal attraction* (pp. 61–77). New York: Academic Press.

Leatham, G. B., & Duck, S. W. (1990). Conversations with friends and the dynamics of social support. In S. W. Duck, with R. C. Silver (Eds.), *Personal relationships and social support* (pp. 1–29). London: Sage.

O'Connell, R. L. (2011). *The ghosts of Cannae: Hannibal and the darkest hour of the Roman Republic.* New York: Random House.

Petronio, S. (2013). Brief status report on communication privacy management theory. *Journal of Family Communication, 13,* 6–14.

Quinn, S., & Oldmeadow, J. A. (2013). Is the *i*generation a "we" generation? Social networking use among 9- to 13-year-olds and belonging. *British Journal of Developmental Psychology, 31,* 136–142.

Rollie, S. S., & Duck, S. W. (2006). Stage theories of marital breakdown. In J. H. Harvey & M. A. Fine (Eds.), *Handbook of divorce and dissolution of romantic relationships* (pp. 176–193). Mahwah, NJ: Lawrence Erlbaum.

Sahlstein, E. M. (2004). Relating at a distance: Negotiating being together and being apart in long-distance relationships. *Journal of Social and Personal Relationships, 21*(5), 689–710.

Sahlstein, E. M. (2006). The trouble with distance. In C. D. Kirkpatrick, S. W. Duck, & M. K. Foley (Eds.), *Relating difficulty: Processes of constructing and managing difficult interaction* (pp. 119–140). Mahwah, NJ: Lawrence Erlbaum.

Sanchez-Nunez, M. T., Fenandez-Berrocal, P., & Latorre, J. M. (2013). Assessment of emotional intelligence in the family: Influences between parents and children on their own perceptions and that of others. *Family Journal, 21,* 65–73.

Sigman, S. J. (1991). Handling the discontinuous aspects of continuous social relationships: Toward research on the persistence of social forms. *Communication Theory, 1,* 106–127.

Straus, S., Johnson, M., Marquez, C., & Feldman, M. D. (2013). Characteristics of successful and failed mentoring relationships: A qualitative study across two academic health centers. *Academic Medicine, 88,* 82–89.

Sunnafrank, M. (1983). Attitude similarity and interpersonal attraction in communication processes: In pursuit of an ephemeral influence. *Communication Monographs, 50,* 273–284.

Sunnafrank, M., & Ramirez, A. (2004). At first sight: Persistent relational effects of get-acquainted conversations. *Journal of Social and Personal Relationships, 21*(3), 361–379.

Theiss, J. A., & Nagy, M. E. (2013). A relationship turbulence model of partner responsiveness and relationship talk across cultures. *Western Journal of Communication, 77,* 186–209.

Thibaut, J. W., & Kelley, H. H. (1959). *The social psychology of groups.* New York: Wiley.

Vangelisti, A., & Banski, M. (1993). Couples' debriefing conversations: The impact of gender, occupation and demographic characteristics. *Family Relations, 42,* 149–157.

Weiss, R. S. (1974). The provisions of social relationships. In Z. Rubin (Ed.), *Doing unto others* (pp. 17–26). Englewood Cliffs, NJ: Prentice Hall.

Weiss, R. S. (1998). A taxonomy of relationships. *Journal of Social and Personal Relationships, 15,* 671–683.

Wood, J. T. (2000). *Relational communication: Continuity and change in personal relationships* (2nd ed.). Belmont, CA: Wadsworth.

Wood, J. T. (2006). Chopping carrots: Creating intimacy moment by moment. In J. T. Wood & S. W. Duck (Eds.), *Composing relationships: Communication in everyday life* (pp. 24–35). Belmont, CA: Wadsworth.

Chapter 8

Afifi, T. D. (2003). "Feeling caught" in stepfamilies: Managing boundary turbulence through appropriate communication privacy rules. *Journal of Social and Personal Relationships, 20*(6), 729–755.

Afifi, T. D., & Hamrick, K. (2006). Communication processes that promote risk and resiliency in postdivorce families. In M. A. Fine & J. H. Harvey (Eds.), *Handbook of divorce and relationship dissolution* (pp. 435–456). Mahwah, NJ: Lawrence Erlbaum.

Bateson, G. (1972). *Steps to an ecology of mind.* New York: Ballantine Books.

Baxter, L. A., Braithwaite, D. O., Bryant, L., & Wagner, A. (2004). Stepchildren's perceptions of the contradictions in communication with stepparents. *Journal of Social and Personal Relationships, 21*(4), 447–467.

BBC News. (2006, October 15). *Woman gives birth to grandchild.* Retrieved from http://news.bbc.co.uk/2/hi/asia-pacific/6052584.stm

BBC News. (2008, April 5). *Families in meltdown, judge says.* Retrieved from http://news.bbc.co.uk/1/hi/uk/7331882.stm

Blieszner, R. (2006). A lifetime of caring: Dimensions and dynamics in late-life close relationships. *Personal Relationships, 13*(1), 1–18.

Bosticco, C., & Thompson, T. (2005). The role of communication and story telling in the family grieving system. *Journal of Family Communication, 5*(4), 255–278.

Bruess, C. J. S., & Hoefs, A. (2006). The cat puzzle recovered: Composing relationships through family rituals. In J. T. Wood & S. W. Duck (Eds.), *Composing relationships: Communication in everyday life* (pp. 65–75). Belmont, CA: Wadsworth.

Buzzanell, P. M., & Turner, L. H. (2003). Emotion work revealed by job loss discourse. Backgrounding—foregrounding of feelings, construction of normalcy, and (re)instituting of traditional masculinities. *Journal of Applied Communication Research, 31,* 27–57.

Cohen, D. (2013). *Family secrets: Shame and privacy in modern Britain.* Oxford: Oxford University Press.

Colby, M., Hecht, M. L., Miller-Day, M., Krieger, J. R., Syvertsen, A. K., Graham, J. W., & Pettigrew, J. (2013). Adapting school-based substance use prevention curriculum through cultural grounding: A review and exemplar of adaptation processes for rural schools. *American Journal of Community Psychology, 51*(1–2), 190–205.

Coleman, S., & May-Chahal, C. (2003). *Safeguarding children and young people.* London: Routledge.

Duck, S. W. (2007). *Human relationships* (4th ed.). London: Sage.

Duck, S. W. (2011). *Rethinking relationships.* Thousand Oaks, CA: Sage.

Galvin, K. M. (2007). Diversity's impact on defining the family: Discourse-dependence and identity. In L. H. Turner & R. West (Eds.), *The family communication sourcebook* (pp. 1–27). Thousand Oaks, CA: Sage.

Galvin, K. M., & Bylund, C. L. (2009). Family communication. In H. T. Reis & S. Sprecher (Eds.), *Encyclopedia of human relationships.* Thousand Oaks, CA: Sage.

Golliher, R. (2006). *Relationships with the dead in Japan.* Unpublished manuscript, University of Iowa, Iowa City.

Griffin, E. (2012). *Communication: A first look at communication theory* (8th ed.). New York: McGraw-Hill.

Huisman, D. (2008). *Intergenerational family storytelling.* Unpublished PhD thesis, Communication Studies, University of Iowa, Iowa City.

Kayser, K., & Rao, S. S. (2006). Process of disaffection in relationship breakdown. In M. A. Fine & J. H. Harvey (Eds.), *Handbook of divorce and relationship dissolution* (pp. 201–221). Mahwah, NJ: Lawrence Erlbaum.

Kellas, J. K., & Trees, A. R. (2006). Finding meaning in difficult family experiences: Sense making and interaction processes during joint family storytelling. *Journal of Family Communication, 6*(1), 49–76.

Koerner, A. F. (2006). Models of relating—not relationship models: Cognitive representations of relating across interpersonal relationship domains. *Journal of Social and Personal Relationships, 23*(5), 629–653.

Koerner, A. F., & Fitzpatrick, M. A. (2002). Toward a theory of family communication. *Communication Theory, 12*(1), 70–91.

Le Poire, B. A. (2006). *Family communication: Nurturing and control in a changing world.* Thousand Oaks, CA: Sage.

Le Poire, B. A., Hallett, J., & Erlandson, K. T. (2000). An initial test of inconsistent nurturing as control theory: How partners of drug abusers assist their partners' sobriety. *Human Communication Research, 26,* 432–4547.

Lloyd, J., & Anthony, J. (2003). Hanging out with the wrong crowd: How much difference can parents make in an urban environment? *Journal of Urban Health—Bulletin of the New York Academy of Medicine, 80*(3), 383–399.

May-Chahal, C., & Antrobus, R. (2012). Engaging community support in safeguarding adults from self-neglect. *British Journal of Social Work, 42*(8), 1478–1494.

May-Chahal, C., Mason, C., Rashid, A., Greenwood, P., Walkerdine, J., & Rayson, P. (2012). Safeguarding cyborg childhoods: Incorporating the on/offline behaviour of children into everyday social work practices. *British Journal of Social Work.* Retrieved from http://bjsw.oxfordjournals.org/content/early/2012/08/10/bjsw.bcs121

Miller-Day, M., Hecht, M., & Marks, S. (2000). *Adolescent relationships and drug resistance.* Mahwah, NJ: Lawrence Erlbaum.

Nicholson, J. H. (2006). "Them's fightin' words": Naming in everyday talk between siblings. In J. T. Wood & S. W. Duck (Eds.), *Composing relationships: Communication in everyday life* (pp. 55–64). Belmont, CA: Wadsworth.

Pearson, J. C. (1996). Forty-forever years? In N. Vanzetti & S. W. Duck (Eds.), *A lifetime of relationships* (pp. 383–405). Pacific Grove, CA: Brooks/Cole.

Petronio, S. (2002). *Boundaries of privacy.* Albany: State University of New York Press.

Petronio, S., & Durham, W. T. (2008). Communication privacy management theory: Significance for interpersonal communication. In L. A. Baxter & D. O. Braithwaite (Eds.), *Engaging theories in interpersonal communication* (pp. 309–322). Thousand Oaks, CA: Sage.

Petronio, S., Sargent, J. D., Andea, L., Reganis, P., & Cichocki, D. (2004). Family and friends as health-care advocates: Dilemmas of confidentiality and privacy. *Journal of Social and Personal Relationships, 21*(1), 33–52.

Pettit, G., & Lollis, S. (1997). Reciprocity and bidirectionality in parent-child relationships: New approaches to the study of enduring issues. *Journal of Social and Personal Relationships, 14,* 435–440.

Pickhart, C. (2013). *Surviving your child's adolescence.* San Francisco: Jossey-Bass/Wiley.

Powell, K. A., & Afifi, T. D. (2005). Uncertainty management and adoptees' ambiguous loss of their birth parents. *Journal of Social and Personal Relationships, 22*(1), 129–151.

Regnerus, M. (2012). How different are the adult children of parents who have same-sex relationships? Findings from the New Family Structures Study. *Social Science Research, 41,* 752–770.

Rholes, W. S., Simpson, J. A., & Friedman, M. (2006). Avoidant attachment and the experience of parenting. *Personality and Social Psychology Bulletin, 32*(3), 275–285.

Rollie, S. S. (2006). Nonresidential parent-child relationships: Overcoming the challenges of absence. In C. D. Kirkpatrick, S. W. Duck, & M. K. Foley (Eds.), *Relating difficulty: Processes of constructing and managing difficult interaction* (pp. 181–202). Mahwah, NJ: Lawrence Erlbaum.

Rowe, A. C., & Carnelley, K. B. (2005). Preliminary support for the use of a hierarchical mapping technique to examine attachment networks. *Personal Relationships, 12*(4), 499–519.

Rowe, A. C., Carnelley, K. B., Harwood, J., Micklewright, D., Russouw, L., Rennie, C. L., & Liossi, C. (2012). The effect of attachment orientation priming on pain sensitivity in pain-free individuals. *Journal of Social and Personal Relationships, 29*(4), 488–507.

Sahlstein, E. M. (2006). Relational life in the 21st century: Managing people, time and distance. In J. T. Wood & S. W. Duck (Eds.), *Composing relationships: Communication in everyday life* (pp. 110–118). Belmont, CA: Wadsworth.

Sahlstein, E. M. (2010). Communication and distance: The present and future interpreted through the past. *Journal of Applied Communication Research, 38,* 106–114.

Sahlstein, E. M., Maguire, K. C., & Timmerman, L. (2009). Contradictions and praxis contextualized by wartime deployment: Wives' perspectives revealed through relational dialectics. *Communication Monographs, 76,* 421–442.

Segrin, C., & Flora, J. (2005). *Family communication.* Mahwah, NJ: Lawrence Erlbaum.

Socha, T. J. (2012). *Lifespan communication: Children, families, and aging.* New York: Peter Lang.

Socha, T. J., & Yingling, J. A. (2010). *Families communicating with children: Building positive developmental foundations.* Cambridge, UK: Polity.

Steuber, K. R., & Solomon, D. H. (2012). Relational uncertainty, partner interference, and privacy boundary turbulence: Explaining discrepancies in spouses' infertility disclosures. *Journal of Social and Personal Relationships, 29,* 3–27.

Stone, L. (1979). *The family, sex, and marriage in England 1500–1800.* New York: Harper Colophon.

Straus, M. A., Gelles, R. J., & Steinmetz, S. K. (1980). *Behind closed doors: Violence in the American family.* New York: Anchor.

Suter, E. A. (2006). He has two mommies: Constructing lesbian families in social conversation. In J. T. Wood & S. W. Duck (Eds.), *Composing relationships: Communication in everyday life* (pp. 119–127). Belmont, CA: Wadsworth.

Vangelisti, A. L., & Caughlin, J. P. (1997). Revealing family secrets: The influence of topic, function and relationships. *Journal of Social and Personal Relationships, 11,* 679–705.

Von Bertalanffy, L. (1950). An outline of general systems theory. *British Journal for the Philosophy of Science, 1*(2), 63–79.

Watzlawick, P., Beavin, J., & Jackson, D. (1967). *Pragmatics of human communication: A study of interactional patterns, pathologies and paradoxes.* New York: Norton.

Weston, K. (1997). *Families we choose: Lesbians, gays, kinship* (Revised and updated paperback ed.). New York: Columbia University Press.

Wright, P. H., & Wright, K. D. (1995). Co-dependency: Personality syndrome or relational process? In S. W. Duck & J. T. Wood (Eds.), *Confronting relationship challenges: Understanding relationship processes 5* (pp. 109–128). Thousand Oaks, CA: Sage.

Zwick, J. (Director). (2002). *My big fat Greek wedding* [Motion picture]. United States: Gold Circle Films.

Chapter 9

Bales, R. F. (1950). *Interaction process analysis.* Cambridge, MA: Addison-Wesley.

Carli, L. L., & Eagly, A. H. (2011). Gender and leadership. In A. Bryman, D. Collinson, K. Grint, B. Jackson, & M. Uhl-Bien (Eds.), *The SAGE handbook of leadership* (pp. 103–117). Thousand Oaks, CA: Sage.

Chhokar, J. S., Brodbeck, F. C., & House, R. J. (Eds.). (2012). *Culture and leadership across the world: The GLOBE book of in-depth studies of 25 societies.* New York: Routledge.

Clampitt, P. G. (2005). *Communicating for managerial effectiveness.* Thousand Oaks, CA: Sage.

Dando-Collins, S. (2004). *Caesar's legion: The epic saga of Julius Caesar's elite tenth legion and the armies of Rome.* Chichester, UK: Wiley.

Emery, C. (2012). Uncovering the role of emotional abilities in leadership emergence: A longitudinal analysis of leadership networks. *Social Networks, 34,* 429–437.

Evans, C. R., & Dion, K. L. (2012). Group cohesion and performance: A meta-analysis. *Small Group Research, 43,* 690–701.

Fisher, B. A. (1970). Decision emergence: Phases in group decision making. *Speech Monographs, 37,* 53–66.

French, J. R. P., Jr., & Raven, B. (1960). The bases of social power. In D. Cartwright & A. Zander (Eds.), *Group dynamics* (pp. 607–623). New York: Harper & Row.

Frey, L. R. (2003). *Group communication in context: Studies in bona fide groups.* Mahwah, NJ: Lawrence Erlbaum.

Frings, D., Hurst, J., Cleveland, C., Blascovich, J., & Abrams, D. (2012). Challenge, threat, and subjective group dynamics: Reactions to normative and deviant group members. *Group Dynamics: Theory, Research, and Practice, 16,* 105–121.

Gully, S. M., Devine, D. J., & Whitney, D. J. (2012). A meta-analysis of cohesion and performance effects of level of analysis and task interdependence. *Small Group Research, 43,* 702–725.

Harden Fritz, J. M., & Omdahl, B. L. (2006). Reduced job satisfaction, diminished commitment, and workplace cynicism as outcomes of negative work relationships. In J. M. Harden Fritz & B. L. Omdahl (Eds.), *Problematic relationships in the workplace* (pp. 131–151). New York: Peter Lang.

Hepburn, J. R., & Crepin, A. E. (1984). Relationship strategies in a coercive institution: A study of dependence among prison guards. *Journal of Social and Personal Relationships, 1,* 139–158.

Janis, I. (1972). *Victims of groupthink.* Boston: Houghton Mifflin.

Jordan, J., Brown, M. E., Treviño, L. K., & Finkelstein, S. (2013). Someone to look up to: Executive–follower ethical reasoning and perceptions of ethical leadership. *Journal of Management, 39,* 660–683.

Kantabutra, S., & Rungruang, P. (2013). Perceived vision-based leadership effects on staff satisfaction and commitment at a Thai energy provider. *Asia-Pacific Journal of Business Administration, 5*(2), 157–178.

Meeussen, L., Delvaux, E., & Phalet, K. (2013). Becoming a group: Value convergence and emergent work group identities. *British Journal of Social Psychology.* doi: 10.1111/bjso.12021

Moser, K. S., & Axtell, C. M. (2013). The role of norms in virtual work. *Journal of Personnel Psychology, 12,* 1–6.

Mumby, D. K. (2006). Constructing working-class masculinity in the workplace. In J. T. Wood & S. W. Duck (Eds.), *Composing relationships: Communication in everyday life* (pp. 166–174). Belmont, CA: Wadsworth.

Nezlek, J. B., Wesselmann, E. D., Wheeler, L., & Williams, K. D. (2012). Ostracism in everyday life. *Group Dynamics: Theory, Research, and Practice, 16,* 91–104.

Northouse, P. G. (2012). *Leadership: Theory and practice* (6th ed.). Thousand Oaks, CA: Sage.

O'Connell, R. L. (2011). *The ghosts of Cannae: Hannibal and the darkest hour of the Roman Republic.* New York: Random House.

Purvanova, R. K. (2013). The role of feeling known for team member outcomes in project teams. *Small Group Research, 44,* 298–331.

Putnam, L. L., & Stohl, C. (1990). Bona fide groups: A reconceptualization of groups in context. *Communication Studies, 41,* 248–265.

Smith, G. (2001). Group development: A review of the literature and a commentary on future research directions. *Group Facilitation, 3,* 14–45.

Tuckman, B. W. (1965). Developmental sequence in small groups. *Psychological Bulletin, 63,* 384–399.

Chapter 10

Allen, B. J. (2006). Communicating race at WeighCo. In J. T. Wood & S. W. Duck (Eds.), *Composing relationships: Communication in everyday life* (pp. 146–154). Belmont, CA: Wadsworth.

Bastien, D., McPhee, R., & Bolton, K. (1995). A study and extended theory of the structuration of climate. *Communication Monographs, 62,* 87–109.

Berry, L. L. (1983). Relationship marketing. In L. L. Berry, G. L. Shostack, & G. D. Upah (Eds.), *Emerging perspectives on service marketing* (pp. 25–28.). Chicago: American Marketing Association.

Carl, W. J. (2006). What's all the buzz about? Everyday communication and the relational basis of word-of-mouth and buzz marketing practices. *Management Communication Quarterly, 19*(4), 601–634.

Cockburn-Wootten, C., & Zorn, T. (2006). Cabbages and headache cures: Work stories within the family. In J. T. Wood & S. W. Duck (Eds.), *Composing relationships: Communication in everyday life* (pp. 137–144). Belmont, CA: Wadsworth.

Dillard, J. P., & Miller, K. I. (1988). Intimate relationships in task environments. In S. W. Duck (Ed.), *Handbook of personal relationships* (pp. 449–465). New York: Wiley.

Duck, S. W. (2011). *Rethinking relationships.* Thousand Oaks, CA: Sage.

England, D. C. (2012). *The essential guide to handling workplace harassment & discrimination* (2nd ed.). Berkeley, CA: NOLO.

Fairhurst, G. T. (2007). *Discursive leadership.* Thousand Oaks, CA: Sage.

Fairhurst, G. T., & Sarr, R. (1996). *The art of framing: Managing the language of leadership.* San Francisco: Jossey-Bass.

Fournier, S. (1998). Consumers and their brands: Developing relationship theory in consumer research. *Journal of Consumer Research, 24,* 343–373.

Fournier, S., & Alvarez, C. (2012). Brands as relationship partners: Warmth, competence and in-between. *Journal of Consumer Psychology, 22,* 77–185.

Giddens, A. (1991). *Modernity and self-identity: Self and society in the late modern age.* Cambridge, UK: Polity Press.

Goodman, W. B., & Crouter, A. C. (2009). Longitudinal associations between maternal work stress, negative work-family spillover, and depressive symptoms. *Family Relations, 58*(3), 245–258.

Ice, R. (1991). Corporate publics and rhetorical strategies: The case of Union Carbide's Bhopal crisis. *Management Communication Quarterly, 4*(3), 341–362.

Kram, K. E., & Isabella, L. A. (1985). Mentoring alternatives: The role of peer relationships in career development. *Academy of Management Journal, 28*(1), 110–132.

Lutgen-Sandvik, P., & McDermott, V. (2008). The constitution of employee-abusive organizations: A communication flows theory. *Communication Theory, 18*(2), 304–333.

Mokros, H. B. (2006). Composing relationships at work: Three minutes at a wholesale produce market. In J. T. Wood & S. W. Duck (Eds.), *Composing relationships: Communication in everyday life* (pp. 175–185). Belmont, CA: Wadsworth.

Morgan, G. (2006). *Images of organizations.* Thousand Oaks, CA: Sage.

Mumby, D. K. (2006). Constructing working-class masculinity in the workplace. In J. T. Wood & S. W. Duck (Eds.), *Composing relationships: Communication in everyday life* (pp. 166–174). Belmont, CA: Wadsworth.

National Transportation Safety Board. (1993, November 15). *Tall strike during go-around, Boeing 727–227* [Report No. CHI94FA039]. Retrieved from http://www.fss.aero/accident-reports/look.php?report_key=817

Northouse, P. G. (2012). *Leadership: Theory and practice* (6th ed.). Thousand Oaks, CA: Sage.

Petronio, S. (2002). *Boundaries of privacy.* Albany: State University of New York Press.

Sias, P. M. (2009). *Organizing relationships: Traditional and emerging perspectives on workplace relationships.* Thousand Oaks, CA: Sage.

Totten, L. D. (2006). Who am I right now? Negotiating familial and professional roles. In J. T. Wood & S. W. Duck (Eds.), *Composing relationships: Communication in everyday life* (pp. 186–193). Belmont, CA: Wadsworth.

Univision. (2008, April 21). [Advertisement]. *The New York Times,* p. C10.

Waldron, V. R. (2000). Relational experiences and emotions at work.

In S. Fineman (Ed.), *Emotion in organizations* (pp. 64–82). Thousand Oaks, CA: Sage.

Weick, K. (1995). *Sense-making in organizations.* Thousand Oaks, CA: Sage.

Weiss, R. S. (1974). The provisions of social relationships. In Z. Rubin (Ed.), *Doing unto others* (pp. 17–26). Englewood Cliffs, NJ: Prentice Hall.

Zorn, T. (1995). Bosses and buddies: Constructing and performing simultaneously hierarchical and close friendship relationships. In J. T. Wood & S. W. Duck (Eds.), *Under-studied relationships: Off the beaten track* (pp. 122–147). Thousand Oaks, CA: Sage.

Zweig, D. (2005). Beyond privacy and fairness concerns: Examining psychological boundary violations as a consequence of electronic performance monitoring. In J. Weckert (Ed.), *Electronic monitoring in the workplace: Controversies and solutions* (pp. 37–52). Hershey, PA: Idea Group.

Zweig, D., & Webster, J. (2002). Where is the line between benign and invasive? An examination of psychological barriers to the acceptance of awareness monitoring systems. *Journal of Organizational Behavior, 23,* 605–622.

Chapter 11

Aldeis, D., & Afifi, T. D. (2013). College students' willingness to reveal risky behaviors: The influence of relationship and message type. *Journal of Family Communication, 13,* 92–113.

Bankoff, S. M., McCullough, M. B., & Pantalone, D. W. (2013). Patient-provider relationship predicts mental and physical health indicators for HIV-positive men who have sex with men. *Journal of Health Psychology, 18*(6), 762–772.

Barnes, M. K., & Duck, S. W. (1994). Everyday communicative contexts for social support. In B. R. Burleson, T. L. Albrecht, & I. G. Sarason (Eds.), *Communication of social support: Messages, interactions, relationships, and community* (pp. 175–194). Thousand Oaks, CA: Sage.

Beaudoin, C. E., & Tao, C. C. (2007). Benefiting from social capital in online support groups: An empirical study of cancer patients. *CyberPsychology & Behavior, 10,* 587–590.

Berge, J. M., Arikian, A., Doherty, W. J., & Neumark-Sztainer, D. (2012). Healthful eating and physical activity in the home environment: Results from multifamily focus groups. *Journal of Nutrition Education and Behavior, 44,* 123–131.

Buettner, C. K., & Debies-Carl, J. S. (2012). The ties that bind: bonding versus bridging social capital and college student party attendance. *Journal of Studies on Alcohol and Drugs, 73,* 604.

Bute, J. J. (2013). The discursive dynamics of disclosure and avoidance: Evidence from a study of infertility. *Western Journal of Communication, 77*(2), 164–185.

Carl, W. J., & Duck S. W. (2004). How to do things with relationships. In P. Kalbfleisch (Ed.), *Communication yearbook* (Vol. 28, pp. 1–35). Thousand Oaks, CA: Sage.

DeSantis, A. D. (2002). Smoke screen: An ethnographic study of a cigar shop's collective rationalization. *Health Communication, 14,* 167–198.

Diem, S. J., Lantos, J. D., & Tulsky, J. A. (1996). Cardiopulmonary resuscitation on television—Miracles and misinformation. *New England Journal of Medicine, 334,* 1578–1582.

Dorflinger, L., Kerns, R. D., & Auerbach, S. M. (2013). Providers' roles in enhancing patients' adherence to pain self-management. *Translational Behavioral Medicine, 3,* 39–46.

du Pre, A. (2005). *Communicating about health: Current issues and perspectives* (2nd ed.). New York: McGraw-Hill.

Duck, S. W. (2007). *Human relationships* (4th ed.). London: Sage.

Duclos, C. W., Eichler, M., Taylor, L., Quintela, J., Main, D. S., Pace, W., & Staton, E. W. (2005). Patient perspectives of patient–provider communication after adverse events. *International Journal for Quality in Health Care, 17*(6), 479–486.

Eisenman, A., Rutetski, V., Zohar, Z., & Stolero, J. (2012). Subconscious passive learning of CPR techniques through television medical drama. *Journal of Emergency Primary Health Care, 3,* 3.

Fitzgerald, A., Fitzgerald, N., & Aherne, C. (2012). Do peers matter? A review of peer and/or friends' influence on physical activity among American adolescents. *Journal of Adolescence, 35,* 941–958.

Flatt, J. D., Agimi, Y., & Albert, S. M. (2012). Homophily and health behavior in social networks of older adults. *Family & Community Health, 35*(4), 312–321.

Fournier, A. K., Hall, E., Ricke, P., & Storey, B. (2013). Alcohol and the social network: Online social networking sites and college students' perceived drinking norms. *Psychology of Popular Media Culture, 2,* 86–95.

Fox, S. (2006, October 29). *Online health search 2006.* Washington, DC: Pew Internet & American Life Project.

Fox, S., & Duggan, M. (2013, January 15). *Health online 2013.* Washington, DC: Pew Research Center.

Frosch, D. L., Grande, D., Tarn, D. M., & Kravitz, R. L. (2010). A decade of controversy: Balancing policy with evidence in the regulation of prescription drug advertising. *Journal Information, 100,* 24–32.

Gross, A. F., Stern, T. W., Silverman, B. C., & Stern, T. A. (2012). Portrayals of professionalism by the media: Trends in etiquette and bedside manners as seen on television. *Psychosomatics, 53,* 452–455.

Hargittai, E., Fullerton, L., Menchen-Trevino, E., & Thomas, K. Y. (2010). Trust online: Young adults' evaluation of web content. *International Journal of Communication, 4,* 468–494.

Harris, D., & Willoughby, H. (2009). Resuscitation on television: Realistic or ridiculous? A quantitative observational analysis of the portrayal of cardiopulmonary resuscitation in television medical drama. *Resuscitation, 80,* 1275–1279.

Hether, H. J., & Murphy, S. T. (2010). Sex roles in health storylines on prime time television: A content analysis. *Sex Roles, 62,* 810–821.

Hetsroni, A. (2009). If you must be hospitalized, television is not the place: Diagnoses, survival rates and demographic characteristics of patients in TV hospital dramas. *Communication Research Reports, 26*(4), 311–322.

Holman, A., & Sillars, A. (2012). Talk about "hooking up": The influence of college student social networks on nonrelationship sex. *Health Communication, 27,* 205–216.

Jain, P., & Slater, M. D. (2013). Provider portrayals and patient–provider communication in drama and reality medical entertainment television shows. *Journal of Health Communication, 18*(6), 703–722.

Jayne, M., Valentine, G., & Gould, M. (2012). Family life and alcohol consumption: The transmission of "public" and "private" drinking cultures. *Drugs: Education, Prevention and Policy, 19,* 192–200.

Jensen, J. D., Moriarty, C. M., Hurley, R. J., & Stryker, J. E. (2010). Making sense of cancer news coverage trends: A comparison of three comprehensive content analyses. *Journal of Health Communication, 15,* 136–151.

Kinsella, J. (1989). *Covering the plague: AIDS and the American media.* New Brunswick, NJ: Rutgers University Press.

Lakon, C. M., & Valente, T. W. (2012). Social integration in friendship networks: The synergy of network structure and peer influence in relation to cigarette smoking among high risk adolescents. *Social Science & Medicine, 74*(9), 1407–1417.

Lindsay, S., Smith, S., Bellaby, P., & Baker, R. (2009). The health impact of an online heart disease support group: A comparison of moderated versus unmoderated support. *Health Education Research, 24,* 646–654.

Loane, S. S., & D'Alessandro, S. (2013). Communication that changes lives: Social support within an online health community for ALS. *Communication Quarterly, 61,* 236–251.

MacKenzie, R., Chapman, S., Barratt, A., & Holding, S. (2007). "The news is [not] all good": Misrepresentations and inaccuracies in Australian news media reports on prostate cancer screening. *Medical Journal of Australia, 187,* 507.

Martin, K. D., Roter, D. L., Beach, M. C., Carson, K. A., & Cooper, L. A. (2013). Physician communication behaviors and trust among black and white patients with hypertension. *Medical Care, 51,* 151–157.

Mathews, A. W. (2012, December 20). Doctors move to webcams. *Wall Street Journal.* Retrieved from http://online.wsj.com/article/SB10001424127887324731304578189461164849962.html

Mathews, A. W. (2013, February 4). Should doctors and patients be Facebook friends? *Wall Street Journal.* Retrieved from http://online.wsj.com/article/SB10001424127887324900204578283900262408308.html

Moeller, A. D., Moeller, J. J., Rahey, S. R., & Sadler, R. M. (2011). Depiction of seizure first aid management in medical television dramas. *Canadian Journal of Neurological Sciences, 38,* 723–727.

Mohler, J. L., & Mishel, M. (2012). Patient satisfaction influenced by interpersonal treatment and communication for African American men. The North Carolina–Louisiana Prostate Cancer Project (PCaP). *American Journal of Men's Health, 6,* 409–419.

Myneni, S., Iyengar, S., Cobb, N. K., & Cohen, T. (2013). Identifying persuasive qualities of decentralized peer-to-peer online social networks in public health. In *Persuasive Technology* (pp. 155–160). Springer Berlin Heidelberg.

Nguyen, S. N., Von Kohorn, I., Schulman-Green, D., & Colson, E. R. (2012). The importance of social networks on smoking: Perspectives of women who quit smoking during pregnancy. *Maternal and Child Health Journal, 16,* 1312–1318.

Nichols, W. L. (2012). Deception versus privacy management in discussions of sexual history. *Atlantic Journal of Communication, 20,* 101–115.

Petronio, S. (2002). *Boundaries of privacy: Dialectics of disclosure.* Albany: State University of New York Press.

Petronio, S. (2010). Communication privacy management theory: What do we know about family privacy regulation? *Journal of Family Theory & Review, 2,* 175–196.

Petronio, S. (2013). Brief status report on communication privacy management theory. *Journal of Family Communication, 13,* 6–14.

Pingree, S., Boberg, E., Patten, C., Offord, K., Gaie, M., Schenskey, A., . . . Ahluwalia, J. (2004). Helping adolescents quit smoking: A needs assessment of current and former teen smokers. *Health Communication, 16,* 183–194.

Primack, B. A., Roberts, T., Fine, M. J., Dillman Carpentier, F. R., Rice, K. R., & Barnato, A. E. (2012). *ER* vs. ED: A comparison of televised and real-life emergency medicine. *Journal of Emergency Medicine, 43*(6), 1160–1166.

Rasmussen, E., & Ewoldsen, D. R. (2013). Dr. Phil and psychology today as self-help treatments of mental illness: A content analysis of popular psychology programming. *Journal of Health Communication, 18*(5), 610–623.

Roter, D. L., & Hall, J. A. (2006). *Doctors talking with patients/Patients talking with doctors* (2nd ed.). Westport, CT: Praeger.

Saguy, A. C., & Gruys, K. (2010). Morality and health: News media constructions of overweight and eating disorders. *Social Problems, 57,* 231–250.

Salvy, S. J., De La Haye, K., Bowker, J. C., & Hermans, R. C. (2012). Influence of peers and friends on children's and adolescents' eating and activity behaviors. *Physiology & Behavior, 106*(3), 369–378.

Schoenthaler, A., Allegrante, J. P., Chaplin, W., & Gbenga Ogedegbe, M. D. (2012). The effect of patient–provider communication on medication adherence in hypertensive black patients: Does race concordance matter? *Annals of Behavioral Medicine, 43,* 372–382.

Secklin, P. L. (2001). Multiple fractures in time: Reflections on a car crash. *Journal of Loss and Trauma, 6,* 323–333.

Shaw, B. R., Hawkins, R., McTavish, F., Pingree, S., & Gustafson, D. H. (2006). Effects of insightful disclosure within computer mediated support groups on women with breast cancer. *Health Communication, 19,* 133–142.

Tenzek, K. E., Herrman, A. R., May, A. R., Feiner, B., & Allen, M. (2013). Examining the impact of parental disclosure of HIV on children: A meta-analysis. *Western Journal of Communication, 77,* 323–339.

Turow, J. (2012). Nurses and doctors in prime time series: The dynamics of depicting professional power. *Nursing Outlook, 60,* S4–S11.

Uchino, B. N. (2009). Understanding the links between social support and physical health: A life-span perspective with emphasis on the separability of perceived and received support. *Perspectives on Psychological Science, 4,* 236–255.

VanLear, C. A., Sheehan, M., Withers, L. A., & Walker, R. A. (2005). AA online: The enactment of supportive computer mediated communication. *Western Journal of Communication, 69,* 5–26.

Venetis, M. K., Robinson, J. D., & Kearney, T. (2013). Consulting with a surgeon before breast cancer surgery: Patient question asking and satisfaction. *Journal of Health Communication, 18*(8), 943–959.

Wright, K. B., Sparks, L., & O'Hair, H. D. (2012). *Health communication in the 21st century* (2nd ed.). Malden, MA: Blackwell.

Yang, C., Davey-Rothwell, M., & Latkin, C. (2012). "Drinking buddies" and alcohol dependence symptoms among African American men and women in Baltimore, MD. *Drug and Alcohol Dependence, 128*(1–2), 123–129.

Ye, J., Rust, G., Fry-Johnson, Y., & Strothers, H. (2010). E-mail in patient–provider communication: A systematic review. *Patient Education and Counseling, 80,* 266–273.

Young, J. H. (1992). *The medical messiahs: A social history of health quackery in twentieth-century America.* Princeton, NJ: Princeton University Press.

Chapter 12

Augsburger, D. W. (1992). *Conflict mediation across cultures: Pathways and patterns.* Louisville, KY: Westminster/John Knox.

Burleson, B. R., Holmstrom, A. J., & Gilstrap, C. (2005). "Guys can't say that to guys": Four experiments assessing the normative motivation account for deficiencies in the emotional support provided by men. *Communication Monographs, 72,* 468–501.

Calero, H. (2005). *The power of nonverbal communication: What you do is more important than what you say.* Aberdeen, WA: Silver Lake.

Chiang, S.-U. (2009). Dealing with communication problems in the instructional interactions between international teaching assistants and American college students. *Language and Education, 23,* 461–478.

Fitch, K. L. (1998). *Speaking relationally: Culture, communication, and interpersonal connection.* New York: Guilford Press.

Fitch, K. L. (2003). Cultural persuadables. *Communication Theory, 13*(1), 100–123.

Fox, K. (2005). *Watching the English.* London: Hodder & Stoughton.

Gudykunst, W. (2000). *Asian American ethnicity and communication.* Thousand Oaks, CA: Sage.

Gudykunst, W. B., & Kim, Y. Y. (1984). *Communicating with strangers: An approach to intercultural communication.* New York: Random House.

Houston, M., & Wood, J. T. (1996). *Gendered relationships.* Mountain View, CA: Mayfield.

Hymes, D. (1972). Models of the interaction of language and social life. In J. Gumperz & D. Hymes (Eds.), *Directions in sociolinguistics: The ethnography of communication* (pp. 35–71). New York: Holt, Rinehart & Winston.

Jin, B., & Oh, S. (2010). Cultural differences of social network influence on romantic relationships: A comparison of the United States and South Korea. *Communication Studies, 61,* 156–171.

Le, Q., & Chiu, C. (2009). Culturally-informed health metaphors on health service delivery. *International Journal of Social Health Information Management, 2,* 48–59.

Martin, J. N., & Nakayama, T. K. (2007). *Intercultural communication in context* (4th ed.). New York: McGraw-Hill.

McClelland, D. C. (1961). *The achieving society.* New York: Free Press.

Morsbach, H. (2004). *Customs and etiquette of Japan.* London: Global Books.

Nakayama, T. K., Martin, J. N., & Flores, L. A. (Eds.). (2002). *Readings in intercultural communication* (2nd ed.). New York: McGraw-Hill.

Nelson, A., & Brown, C. D. (2012). *The gender communication handbook: Conquering conversational collisions between men and women.* San Francisco: Pfeiffer.

Paxman, J. (1999). *The English: A portrait of a people.* Harmondsworth, UK: Penguin.

Philipsen, G. (1975). Speaking "like a man" in Teamsterville: Culture patterns of role enactment in an urban neighborhood. *Quarterly Journal of Speech, 61*(1), 13–22.

Philipsen, G. (1997). A theory of speech codes. In G. Philipsen & T. Albrecht (Eds.), *Developing theories in communication* (pp. 119–156). Albany: State University of New York Press.

Rahim, M. A. (1983). A measure of styles of handling interpersonal conflict. *Academy of Management Journal, 26,* 368–376.

Samovar, L. A., Porter, R. E., & McDaniel, E. R. (2010). *Communication between cultures* (7th ed.). Belmont, CA: Wadsworth.

Sandemose, A. (1936). *En flyktning krysser sitt spor* 1933, translated as *A fugitive crosses his tracks.* New York: Alfred Knopf.

Seki, K., Matsumoto, D., & Imahori, T. T. (2002). The conceptualization and expression of intimacy in Japan and the United States. *Journal of Cross-Cultural Psychology, 33*(3), 303–319.

Ting-Toomey, S. (2004). The matrix of face: An updated face-negotiation theory. In W. Gudykunst (Ed.), *Theorizing about intercultural communication* (pp. 71–92). Thousand Oaks, CA: Sage.

Wood, J. T. (2004). Monsters and victims: Male felons' accounts of intimate partner violence. *Journal of Social and Personal Relationships, 21*(5), 555–576.

Chapter 13

Aasebo, T. S. (2005). Television as a marker of boys' construction of growing up. *Young: Nordic Journal of Youth Research, 13,* 185–203.

Alberts, J. K., Yoshimura, C. G., Rabby, M., & Loschiavo, R. (2005). Mapping the topography of couples' daily conversation. *Journal of Social and Personal Relationships, 22,* 299–322.

Allen, I. L. (1975). Research report—Everyday conversations about media content. *Journal of Applied Communications Research, 3,* 27–32.

Allen, I. L. (1982). Talking about media experiences: Everyday life as popular culture. *Journal of Popular Culture, 16,* 106–115.

Altman, I., & Taylor, D. (1973). *Social penetration: The development of interpersonal relationships.* New York: Holt, Rinehart & Winston.

Archambault, J. S. (2013). Cruising through uncertainty: Cell phones and the politics of display and disguise in Inhamane, Mozamique. *American Ethnologist, 40,* 88–101.

Argyle, M., & Furnham, A. (1982). The ecology of relationships. *British Journal of Social Psychology, 21,* 259–262.

Austin, E. W. (1993). Exploring effects of active parental mediation of television content. *Journal of Broadcasting & Electronic Media, 37,* 147–158.

Bargh, J. A., McKenna, K. Y. A., & Fitzsimons, G. M. (2002). Can you see the real me? Activation and expression of the "true self" on the Internet. *Journal of Social Issues, 58,* 33–48.

Baron, N. S., & Campbell, E. M. (2012). Gender and mobile phones in cross-national context. *Language Sciences, 34,* 13–27.

Baym, N. K., & Ledbetter, A. (2009). Tunes that bind? Predicting friendship strength in a music-based social network. *Information, Communication & Society, 12,* 408–427.

Berelson, B. (1949). What "missing the newspaper" means. In P. F. Lazarsfeld & F. N. Stanton (Eds.), *Communications research 1948–1949* (pp. 111–129). New York: Harper & Brothers.

Bergdall, A. R., Kraft, J. M., Andes, K., Carterm, M., Hatfield-Timajchy, K., Hock-Long, L. (2012). Love and hooking up in the new millennium: Communication technology and relationships among urban African American and Puerto Rican young adults. *Journal of Sex Research, 49,* 570–582.

Bijker, W. E., Hughes, T. P., & Pinch, T. J. (1987). *The social construction of technological systems: New directions in the sociology and history of technology.* Cambridge, MA: MIT Press.

Boase, J., Horrigan, J. B., Wellman, B., & Rainie, L. (2006). *The strength of Internet ties: The Internet and e-mail aid users in maintaining their social networks and provide pathways to help when people face big decisions.* Washington, DC: Pew Research Center.

Boskoff, A. (1970). *The sociology of urban regions* (2nd ed.). Englewood Cliffs, NJ: Prentice Hall.

Brown, M. E. (1994). *Soap opera and women's talk.* Thousand Oaks, CA: Sage.

Bryant, J., Aust, C. F., Bryant, J. A., & Venugopalan, G. (2001). How psychologically healthy are America's prime-time television families? In J. Bryant & J. A. Bryant (Eds.), *Television and the American family* (2nd ed., pp. 247–270). Mahwah, NJ: Lawrence Erlbaum.

Campbell, S. W. (2006). Perceptions of mobile phones in college classrooms: Ringing, cheating, and classroom policies. *Communication Education, 55,* 280–294.

Chesebro, J. W., McMahan, D. T., & Russett, P. C. (in press). *Internet communication.* New York: Peter Lang.

Cohen, J. (2003). Parasocial breakups: Measuring individual differences in responses to the dissolution of parasocial relationships. *Mass Communication & Society, 6,* 191–202.

Cohen, J., & Metzger, M. (1998). Social affiliation and the achievement of ontological security through interpersonal and mass communication. *Critical Studies in Mass Communication, 15,* 41–60.

Cole, T., & Leets, L. (1999). Attachment styles and intimate television viewing: Insecurely forming relationships in a parasocial way. *Journal of Social and Personal Relationships, 16,* 495–511.

Compesi, R. J. (1983). Gratifications of daytime TV serial viewers. *Journalism Quarterly, 57,* 155–158.

Davies, J. J., & Gentile, D. A. (2012). Responses to children's media use in families with and without siblings: A family development perspective. *Family Relations, 61,* 410–425.

Dubrofsky, R. E. (2006). *The Bachelor:* Whiteness in the harem. *Critical Studies in Media Communication, 23,* 39–56.

Ellison, N., Heino, R., & Gibbs, J. (2006). Managing impressions online: Self-presentation processes in the online dating environment. Journal of Computer-Mediated Communication, 11(2), 415–441.

Ellison, N., Steinfield, C., & Lampe, C. (2007). The benefits of Facebook "friends": Exploring the relationship between college students' use of online social networks and social capital. *Journal of Computer-Mediated Communication, 12,* 1143–1168.

Forma, J., & Kaplowitz, S. A. (2012). The perceived rudeness of public cell phone behavior. *Behaviour & Information Technology, 31,* 947–952.

Frederick, E., Lim, C. H., Clavio, G., Pedersen, P. M., & Burch, L. M. (2012). Choosing between the one-way or two-way street: An exploration of relationship promotion by professional athletes on Twitter. *Communication & Sport.* Retrieved from http://com.sagepub.com/content/early/2012/11/29/2167479512466387

Gantz, W. (2013). Reflections on communication and sport: On fanship and social relationships. *Communication & Sport, 1,* 176–187.

Geiger, W., Bruning, J., & Harwood, J. (2001). Talk about TV: Television viewers' interpersonal communication about programming. *Communication Reports, 14,* 49–57.

Greenberg, S. R. (1975). Conversations as units of analysis in the study of personal influence. *Journalism Quarterly, 52,* 128–130.

Gumpert, G., & Cathcart, R. (1985). Media grammars, generations, and media gaps. *Critical Studies in Mass Communication, 2,* 23–35.

Hampton, K. N., Goulet, L. S., Marlow, C., & Rainie, L. (2012). *Why most Facebook users get more than they give: The effect of Facebook "power users" on everybody else.* Washington, DC: Pew Research Center.

Hampton, K. N., Goulet, L. S., Rainie, L., & Purcell, K. (2011). *Social networking sites and our lives.* Washington, DC: Pew Research Center.

Hampton, K. N., Sessions, L. F., Her, E. J., & Rainie, L. (2009). *Social isolation and new technology.* Washington, DC: Pew Research Center.

Haridakis, P., & Hanson, G. (2009). Social interaction and co-viewing with YouTube: Blending mass communication reception and social connection. *Journal of Broadcasting & Electronic Media, 53,* 317–335.

Horton, D., & Wohl, R. R. (1956). Mass communication and para-social interaction: Observations on intimacy at a distance. *Psychiatry, 19,* 215–229.

Jacobsen, W. C., & Forste, R. (2011). The wired generation: Academic and social outcomes of electronic media use among university students. *Cyberpsychology, Behavior, and Social Networking, 14,* 275–280.

Jaschinski, C., & Kommers, P. (2012). Does beauty matter? The role of friend's attractiveness and gender on social attractiveness ratings of individuals on Facebook. *International Journal of Web Based Communities, 8,* 389–401.

Jewkes, Y. (2002). The use of media in constructing identities in the masculine environment of men's prisons. *European Journal of Communication, 17,* 205–225.

Kam, J. A., & Lee, C.-J. (2012). Examining the effects of mass media campaign exposure and interpersonal discussions on youth's drug use: The mediating role of visiting pro-drug websites. *Health Communication, 28*(5), 473–485.

Kanazawa, S. (2002). Bowling with our imaginary friends. *Evolution and Human Behavior, 23,* 167–171.

Kanter, M., Afifi, T., & Robbins, S. (2012). The impact of parents "friending" their young adult child on Facebook on perceptions of parental privacy invasions and parent-child relationship quality. *Journal of Communication, 62,* 900–917.

Katz, E., Hass, H., & Gurevitch, M. (1973). On the use of the mass media for important things. *American Sociological Review, 38,* 164–181.

Katz, J. E. (2006). *Magic in the air: Cell communication and the transformation of social life.* New Brunswick, NJ: Transaction.

Kawakami, T., Kishiya, K., Parry, M. E. (2013). Personal word of mouth, virtual word of mouth, and innovation use. *Journal of Product Innovation Management, 30,* 17–30.

Kennedy, T. L. M., Smith, A., Wells, A. T., & Wellman, B. (2008). *Networked families.* Washington, DC: Pew Internet & American Life Project.

Koenig, F., & Lessan, G. (1985). Viewers' relations to television personalities. *Psychological Reports, 57,* 263–266.

Kujath, C. (2011). Facebook and MySpace: Complement or substitute for face-to-face interaction? *Cyberpsychology, Behavior, and Social Networking, 14,* 75–78.

Lazarsfeld, P. F. (1940). *Radio and the printed page: An introduction to the study of radio and its role in the communication of ideas.* New York: Duell, Sloan, and Pearce.

Lenhart, A. (2012, March 19). *Teens, smartphones, and texting.* Washington, DC: Pew Internet & American Life Project.

Lenhart, A., Madden, M., Smith, A., Purcell, K., Zickuhr, K., & Rainie, L. (2011). *Teens, kindness and cruelty on social networking sites: How American teens navigate the new world of digital citizenship.* Washington, DC: Pew Research Center.

Levy, D. (2007). *Love and sex with robots: The evolution of human-robot relationships.* New York: HarperCollins.

Ling, R. (2004). *The cell connection: The cell phone's impact on society.* San Francisco: Morgan Kaufmann.

Lobet-Maris, C. (2003). Cell phone tribes: Youth and social identity. In L. Fortunati, J. E. Katz, & R. Riccini (Eds.), *Mediating the human body: Technology, communication, and fashion* (pp. 87–92). Mahwah, NJ: Lawrence Erlbaum.

Lull, J. (1980). The social uses of television. *Human Communication Research, 6,* 197–209.

MacKenzie, D., & Wajcman, J. (1985). *The social shaping of technology.* Milton Keynes, UK: Open University Press.

Madden, M., & Zickuhr, K. (2011). *65% of online adults use social networking sites.* Washington, DC: Pew Internet & American Life Project.

Manago, A. M., Graham, M. B., Greenfield, P. M., & Salimkhan, G. (2008). Self-presentation and gender on MySpace. *Journal of Applied Developmental Psychology, 29,* 446–458.

McMahan, D. T. (2004). What we have here is a failure to communicate: Linking interpersonal and mass communication. *Review of Communication, 4,* 33–56.

McMahan, D. T., & Chesebro, J. W. (2003). Media and political transformations: Revolutionary changes of the world's cultures. *Communication Quarterly, 51,* 126–153.

Mendelsohn, H. (1964). Listening to the radio. In L. A. Dexter & D. M. White (Eds.), *People, society, and mass communications* (pp. 239–249). New York: Free Press.

Millier-Ott, A. E., Kelly, L., & Duran, R. L. (2012). The effects of cell phone usage rules on satisfaction in romantic relationships. *Communication Quarterly, 60,* 17–34.

Osborn, J. L. (2012). When TV and marriage meet: A social exchange analysis of the impact of television viewing on marital satisfaction and commitment. *Mass Communication and Society, 15,* 739–757.

Padilla-Walker, L. M., Coyne, S. M., & Fraser, A. M. (2012). Getting a high-speed family connection: Associations between family media use and family connection. *Family Relations, 61*(3), 426–440.

Papper, R. A., Holmes, M. E., & Popovich, M. N. (2004). Middletown Media Studies: Media multitasking . . . and how much people really use the media. *International Digital Media & Arts Association Journal, 1,* 4–56.

Parry, M. E., Kawakami, T., & Kishiya, K. (2012). The effect of personal and virtual word-of-mouth on technology acceptance. *Journal of Product Innovation Management, 29,* 952–966.

Patil, S., Norice, G., Kapadia, A., & Lee, A. J. (2012). Reasons, rewards, regrets: Privacy consideration in location sharing as an interactive practice [Article no. 5]. *Proceedings of the Eighth Symposium on Usable Privacy and Security.* New York: Association for Computing Machinery.

Pempek, T. A., Yermolayeva, Y. A., & Calvert, S. L. (2009). College students' social networking experiences on Facebook. *Journal of Applied Developmental Psychology, 30,* 227–238.

Perse, E. M., & Butler, J. S. (2005). Call-in talk radio: Compensation or enrichment? *Journal of Radio Studies, 12,* 204–222.

Perse, E. M., & Rubin, R. B. (1989). Attribution in social and parasocial relationships. *Communication Research, 16,* 59–77.

Pfleging, B., Alt, F., & Schmidt, A. (2012). Meaningful melodies: Personal sonification of text messages for mobile devices. *Proceedings of the International Conference on Human-Computer Interaction With Mobile Devices and Services Companion, 14,* 189–192.

Proulx, M., & Shepatin, S. (2012). *Social TV: How marketer can reach and engage audiences by connecting television to the web, social media and mobile.* Hoboken, NJ: Wiley.

Reeves, B., & Nass, C. (2002). *The media equation: How people treat computers, television, and new media like real people and places.* Stanford, CA: Center for the Study of Language and Information.

Scannell, P. (1989). Public service broadcasting and modern public life. *Media, Culture, and Society, 11,* 135–166.

Schiappa, E., Gregg, P. B., & Hewes, D. E. (2005). The parasocial contact hypothesis. *Communication Monographs, 72,* 92–115.

Sigman, S. J. (1991). Handling the discontinuous aspects of continuous social relationships: Toward research on the persistence of social forms. *Communication Theory, 1,* 106–127.

Smith, A. (2011, September 19). *Americans and text messaging.* Washington, DC: Pew Internet & American Life Project.

Smith, D. M. (1975). Mass media as a basis for interaction: An empirical study. *Journalism Quarterly, 52,* 44–49, 105.

Stein, M.-K., Galliers, R. D., & Markus, M. L. (2013). Towards an understanding of identity and technology in the workplace. *Journal of Information Technology, 28*(3), 167–182.

Suki, N. M. (2013). Students' dependence on smart phones: The influence of social needs, social influences and conveniences. *Campus-wide Information Systems, 30*(2), 124–134.

Taylor, L. D. (2005). All for him: Articles about sex in American lad magazines. *Sex Roles, 52,* 153–163.

Tong, S. T., Van Der Heide, B., Langwell, L., & Walther, J. B. (2008). Too much of a good thing? The relationship between number of friends and interpersonal impressions on Facebook. *Journal of Computer-Mediated Communication, 13,* 531–549.

Tong, S. T., & Walther, J. B. (2011). Relational maintenance and CMC. In K. B. Wright & L. M. Webb (Eds.), *Computer-mediated communication in personal relationships* (pp. 79–118). New York: Peter Lang.

Turkle, S. (2012, April 21). The flight from conversation. *The New York Times.* Retrieved from http://www.nytimes.com/2012/04/22/opinion/sunday/the-flight-from-conversation.html?pagewanted=all

Turner, J. R. (1993). Interpersonal and psychological predictors of parasocial interaction with different television performers. *Communication Quarterly, 41,* 443–453.

Verberne, M. F., Ham, J., & Midden, C. J. (2012). Trust in smart systems: Sharing driving goals information to increase trustworthiness and acceptability of smart systems in cars. *Journal of the Human Factors and Ergonomics Society, 54,* 681–686.

Walther, J. B., Van Der Heide, B., Kim, S.-Y., Westerman, D., & Tong, S. T. (2008). The role of friends' appearance and behavior on evaluations of individuals on Facebook: Are we known by the company we keep? *Human Communication Research, 34,* 28–49.

Wong, R. K. M., Tan, J. S. M., & Drossman, D. A. (2010). Here's my phone number, don't call me: Physician accessibility in the cell phone and e-mal era. *Digestive Diseases and Sciences, 55,* 662–667.

Young, A. F., Gabriel, S., & Hollar, J. L. (2013). Batman to the rescue! The protective effects of parasocial relationships with muscular superheroes on men's body images. *Journal of Experimental Social Psychology, 49,* 173–177.

Young, A. F., Gabriel, S., & Sechrist, G. B. (2012). The skinny on celebrities: Parasocial relationships moderate the effects of thin media figures on women's body image. *Social Psychological and Personality Science, 3,* 659–666.

Zweir, S. Araujo, T., Boukes, M., & Willemsen, L. (2011). Boundaries to the articulation of possible selves through social networking sites: The case of Facebook profilers' social connectedness. *Cyberpsychology, Behavior, and Social Networking, 14,* 571–576.

Chapter 14

Bem, D. J. (1972). Self-perception theory. In L. Berkowitz (Ed.), *Advances in experimental social psychology* (pp. 2–62). New York: Academic Press.

Broda-Bahm, K. (2012). Reasoning with emotion. *The Jury Expert, 24,* 20–22.

Burger, J. M. (1999). The foot-in-the-door compliance procedure: A multiple process analysis and review. *Personality and Social Psychology Review, 3,* 303–325.

Burke, K. (1969). *A rhetoric of motives.* Berkeley: University of California Press.

Chan, A. C., & Au, T. K. (2011). Getting children to do more academic work: Foot-in-the-door versus door-in-the-face. *Teaching & Teacher Education, 27,* 982–985.

Chartrand, T., Pinckert, S., & Burger, J. M. (1999). When manipulation backfires: The effects of time delay and requester on the foot-in-the-door technique. *Journal of Applied Social Psychology, 29,* 211–221.

Cialdini, R. B., & Goldstein, N. J. (2004). Social influence: Compliance and conformity. *Annual Review of Psychology, 55,* 591–621.

Cialdini, R. B., Vincent, J. E., Lewis, S. K., Catalan, J., Wheeler, D., & Darby, B. L. (1975). Reciprocal concessions procedure for inducing compliance: The door-in-the-face technique. *Journal of Personality and Social Psychology, 37,* 2221–2239.

Cody, M. J., & McLaughlin, M. L. (1980). Perceptions of compliance gaining situations: A dimensional analysis. *Communication Monographs, 47,* 132–148.

Cody, M. J., Woelfel, M. L., & Jordan, W. J. (1983). Dimension of compliance-gaining situations. *Human Communication Research, 9,* 99–113.

Dillard, J. P. (1989). Types of influence goals in personal relationships. *Journal of Social and Personal Relationships, 6,* 293–308.

Dillard, J. P., Anderson, J. W., & Knobloch, L. K. (2002). Interpersonal influence. In M. Knapp & J. A. Daly (Eds.), *Handbook of interpersonal communication* (3rd ed., pp. 425–474). Thousand Oaks, CA: Sage.

Dillard, J. P., Hunter, J. E., & Burgoon, M. (1984). Sequential-request persuasive strategies: Meta-analysis of foot-in-the-door and door-in-the-face. *Human Communication Research, 10,* 461–488.

Dillard, J. P., Segrin, C., & Harden, J. M. (1989). Primary and secondary goals in the production of interpersonal influence messages. *Communication Monographs, 56,* 19–38.

Dolinski, D. (2012). The nature of the first small request as a decisive factor in the effectiveness of the foot-in-the-door technique. *Applied Psychology: An International Review, 61,* 437–453.

Feeley, T. H., Anker, A. E., & Aloe, A. M. (2012). The door-in-the-face persuasive message strategy: A meta-analysis of the first 35 years. *Communication Monographs, 79,* 316–343.

Fern, E. F., Monroe, K. B., & Avila, R. A. (1986). Effectiveness of multiple request strategies: A synthesis of research results. *Journal of Marketing Research, 23,* 144–152.

Festinger, L. (1957). *A theory of cognitive dissonance.* Stanford, CA: Stanford University Press.

Fishbein, M., & Ajzen, I. (1975). *Belief, attitude, intention, and behavior: An introduction to theory and research.* Reading, MA: Addison-Wesley.

French, J. R. P., Jr., & Raven, B. (1960). The bases of social power. In D. Cartwright & A. Zander (Eds.), *Group dynamics* (pp. 607–623). New York: Harper & Row.

Gabel, S. (2011). Power in the face of the medical director: What it is and how to get more. *Administration & Policy in Mental Health & Mental Health Services Research, 38,* 211–214.

Gass, R. H., & Seiter, J. S. (2011). *Persuasion, social influence, and compliance gaining* (4th ed.). Boston: Allyn & Bacon.

Gouran, D. S., Wiethoff, W. E., & Doelger, J. A. (1994). *Mastering communication* (2nd ed.). Boston: Allyn & Bacon.

Groves, R. M., Cialdini, R. B., & Couper, M. P. (1992). Understanding the decision to participate in a survey. *Public Opinion Quarterly, 56,* 475–495.

Lewis, I., Watson, B., & White, K. M. (2013). Extending the explanatory utility of the EPPM beyond fear-based persuasion. *Health Communication, 28,* 84–98.

Marwell, G., & Schmitt, D. R. (1967). Dimensions of compliance gaining behavior: An empirical analysis. *Sociometry, 30,* 350–364.

Miller, G. R., Seligman, C., Clark, N. T., & Bush, M. (1976). Perceptual contrast versus reciprocal concession as mediators of induced compliance. *Canadian Journal of Behavioral Sciences, 8,* 401–409.

Nabi, R. L. (2002). Discrete emotions and persuasion. In J. P. Dillard & M. Pfau (Eds.), *The persuasion handbook: Developments in theory and practice* (pp. 289–308). Thousand Oaks, CA: Sage.

O'Keefe, D. J. (2000). Guilt and social influence. In M. E. Roloff (Ed.), *Communication yearbook* (Vol. 23, pp. 67–101). Thousand Oaks, CA: Sage.

O'Keefe, D. J. (2002). Guilt as a mechanism of persuasion. In J. P. Dillard & M. Pfau (Eds.), *The persuasion handbook: Developments in theory and practice* (pp. 329–344). Thousand Oaks, CA: Sage.

O'Keefe, D. J., & Figge, M. (1999). Guilt and expected guilt reduction on door in face. *Communication Monographs, 66,* 312–324.

O'Keefe, D. J., & Hale, S. L. (1998). The door-in-the-face influence strategy: A random effects meta-analytic review. In M. E. Roloff (Ed.), *Communication yearbook* (Vol. 21, pp. 1–33). Thousand Oaks, CA: Sage.

Pendleton, M. G., & Bateson, C. D. (1979). Self-presentation and the door-in-the-face technique for inducing compliance. *Personality and Social Psychology Bulletin, 5,* 77–81.

Turner, M. M., & Underhill, J. C. (2012). Motivating emergency preparedness behaviors: The differential effects of guilt appeals and actually anticipating guilty feelings. *Communication Quarterly, 60,* 545–559.

Tusing, K. J., & Dillard, J. P. (2000). The psychological reality of the door-in-the-face: It's helping not bargaining. *Journal of Language and Social Psychology, 19,* 5–25.

Vangelisti, A. L., Daly, J. A., & Rudnick, J. R. (1991). Making people feel guilty in conversations: Techniques and correlates. *Human Communication Research, 18,* 3–39.

Witte, K. (1992). Putting the fear back into fear appeals: The extended parallel process model. *Communication Monographs, 59,* 330–349.

Witte, K. (1998). Fear as motivator, fear as inhibitor: Using the extended parallel process model to explain fear appeal successes and failures. In P. A. Anderson & L. K. Guerrero (Eds.), *The handbook of communication and emotion: Research, theory, applications, and contexts* (pp. 423–450). San Diego, CA: Academic Press.

Yan, C., Dillard, J. P., & Shen, F. (2012). Emotion, motivation, and the persuasive effects of message framing. *Journal of Communication, 62,* 682–700.

Chapter 15

Anderson, R., & Killenberg, G. M. (2009). *Interviewing: Speaking, listening, and learning for professional life.* New York: Oxford University Press.

Barrick, M. R., Dustin, S. L., Giluk, T. L., Stewart, G. L., Shaffer, J. A., & Swider, B. W. (2012). Candidate characteristics driving initial impressions during rapport building: Implications for employment interview validity. *Journal of Occupational and Organizational Psychology, 85*(2), 330–352.

Einhorn, L. J. (1981). An inner view of the job interview: An investigation of successful communicative behaviors. *Communication Education, 30,* 217–228.

Gouran, D. S., Wiethoff, W. E., & Doelger, J. A. (1994). *Mastering communication* (2nd ed.). Boston: Allyn & Bacon.

Krumhuber, E., Manstead, A. S. R., Cosker, D., Marshall, D., & Rosin, P. L. (2009). Effects of dynamic attributes of smiles in human and synthetic faces: A simulated job interview setting. *Journal of Nonverbal Behavior, 33,* 1–16.

Merton, R. K. (1957). *Social theory and social structure.* Glencoe, IL: Free Press.

Reinhard, M. A., Scharmach, M., & Müller, P. (2013). It's not what you are, it's what you know: Experience, beliefs, and the detection of deception in employment interviews. *Journal of Applied Social Psychology, 43*(3), 467–479.

Schullery, N. M., Ickes, L., & Schullery, S. E. (2009). Employer preferences for résumés and cover letters. *Business Communication Quarterly, 72,* 153–176.

Stewart, C. J., & Cash, W. B., Jr. (2000). *Interviewing: Principles and practices* (9th ed.). New York: McGraw-Hill.

Stewart, G. L., Dustin, S. L., Barrick, M. R., & Darnold, T. C. (2008). Exploring the handshake in employment interviews. *Journal of Applied Psychology, 93,* 1139–1146.

Photo credits

4: © iStockphoto.com /Robert Churchill; **5:** ©Thinkstock **6:** ©Creatas /Thinkstock; **7:** ©iStockphoto.com/pbsubhash; **8:** © iStockphoto.com/Kolbz; **9:** ©Fuse / Thinkstock; **11:** ©Fuse /Thinkstock; **13:** ©Christopher Robbins/Photodisc/ Thinkstock; **14:** ©JupiterImages/Brand X Pictures/Thinkstock; **16:** ©Ryan McVay/ Lifesize/Thinkstock; **20:** © iStockphoto. com/ Pgiam; **24:** © iStockphoto.com/ PowerChild; **26:** © Getty Images / Thinkstock; **27:** ©Creatas /Thinkstock **;** **28:** ©Purestock /Thinkstock **;** **31:** ©Thinkstock; **33:** © Jack Hollingsworth / Photodisc /Thinkstock; **34:** © iStockphoto. com/wdstock; **36:** ©Christopher Robbins/ Photodisc/Thinkstock; **37:** © Digital Vision /Photodisc /Thinkstock; **40:** © Jupiterimages/Comstock/Thinkstock; **48:** © iStockphoto.com/mammamaart; **50:** © Jupiterimages /Brand X Pictures/ Thinkstock; **51:** © iStockphoto.com/ redhumv; **53:** © GMP/ Associated Press; **56:** ©Digital Vision/Thinkstock; **57:** © iStockphoto.com/somamix1; **58:** © iStockphoto.com/ranplett; **61:** © iStockphoto.com/mammamaart; **62:** © iStockphoto.com/ Hocus Focus Studio; **63:** © Erik Isakson/Tetra Images/Corbis; **65:** © iStockphoto.com/ Yuri; **68:** © Digital Vision/ThinkStock; **70:** ©iStockPhoto. com/llhoward ; **71:** © Ingram Publishing /Thinkstock; **72:** ©CBS Photo Archive/ CBS/Getty Images; **74:** ©Digital Vision/ Thinkstock; **77:** ©BananaStock/ThinkStock; **78:** © Jason Moore/ZUMA Press/Corbis; **79:** ©Jupiterimages/Brand X Pictures/ Thinkstock; **80:** ©Nancy R. Schiff/Hulton Archive/Getty; **83:** ©Stockbyte/Thinkstock; **84:** ©Fuse/Thinkstock; **88:** ©iStockPhoto. com/Mlenny; **90:** ©Walter B. McKenzie/ Stone/Getty; **92:** ©Jupiterimages/ Goodshoot/Thinkstock; **93:** ©CLOVER/ Associated Press; **95:** ©Erik Snyder/ Thinkstock; **97:** © Radius Images/Corbis; **98:** ©Digital Vision/Thinkstock; **99:** ©Sam Panthaky/AFP/Getty; **101:** ©Keystone/ ©Keith Brofsky/Stockbyte/Thinkstock; **106:** © Hemera/Thinkstock; Hulton Archive/ Getty; **110:** © E. Dygas/Thinkstock; **112:** © Digital Vision/Thinkstock; **113:** ©Jupiter Images/Brand X Pictures/Thinkstock; **116:** © Juniperimages/Comstock/ThinkStock; **117:** © Stockbyte/Thinkstock; **120:** © Maria Teijeiro/Thinkstock; **121:** © Digital Vision/ Photodisc/Thinkstock; **124:** © MICHAEL REYNOLDS/epa/Corbis; **125:** © iStockphoto.com/igorr1; **126:** © iStockphoto.com/Yuri; **132:** © iStockphoto.com/franckreporter; **134:** © iStockphoto.com/Shane Hansen; **135:** © iStockphoto.com/Yuri; **137:** © iStockphoto.com/diane39; **138:** ©Wavebreak Media/Thinkstock; **142:** © iStockphoto.com/wakila; **143:** © iStockphoto/Claudiad; **147:** © iStockphoto.com/monkeybusiness images; **148:** ©Goodshoot/Thinkstock; **150:** © iStockphoto.com/drxy; **158**: © iStockphoto.com/Mark Bowden; **159:** © Donna Elkow-nash/iStockphoto; **162:** ©Elena Korenbaum/iStockphoto; **163:** © Ocean/Corbis; **164:** ©Ryan ©McVay/ Photodisc/Thinkstock; **166:** ©sturti/ Thinkstock; **170:** © Peter Beck/ CORBIS; **172:** © Goodshoot /Thinkstock; **173:** ©Digital Vision /Photodisc/Thinkstock; **178:** © Comstock/Thinkstock; **180:** ©Grant Faint/The Image Bank/Getty; **183:** © iStockphoto.com/GlobalStock; **184:** © Björn Andrén/Matton Collection/ Corbis; **187:** © B.S.P.I./Corbis; **188:** © iStockphoto.com/wynnter; **188:** ©David De Lossy/Photodisc/Thinkstock; **189:** ©Purestock/Thinkstock; **192**: © Bernd Vogel/Corbis; **199:** © iStockphoto.com/ gehringj; **200:** © Bettmann/CORBIS; **202:** © iStockphoto.com/4774344sean; **204:** © US Marines Photo / Alamy; **208:** ©Digital Vision/Photodisc/Thinkstock; **212:** © Brad Killer/iStockphoto; **213:** ©Digital Vision/Getty Images/Thinkstock; **217:** © Bruce Ayres/Stone/Getty; **219:** © iStockphoto.com/Robert Churchill; **222**: © iStockphoto.com/vgajic; **224:** © iStockphoto.com/ClarkandCompany; **226:** ©Getty Images/Comstock / Thinkstock; **227:** ©iStockphoto / Thinkstock; **228:** ©Ryan McVay /Digital Vision/Thinkstock; **229:** © iStockphoto. com/monkeybusinessimages; **231:** ©Fuse/Thinkstock; **234:** ©iStockphoto / Thinkstock; **236:** © iStockphoto.com/ garymilner; **238**: © Justin Paget/Corbis; **242:** ©Robert Ginn/Getty; **244:** © iStockphoto.com/rhyman007; **246:** © iStockphoto.com/morganl; **247:** © Jacob Ehnmark; **249:** ©Monkey Business/Thinkstock; **251:** © iStockphoto. com/mediaphotos;**252**: © StockByte/Think Stock; **253:** ©iStockphoto/Thinkstock; **254:** © Fuse/Getty Images; **256:** ©iStockphoto/Thinkstock; **257:** ©Can Stock Photo Inc./monkeybusiness; **258:** © Jetta Productions/Blend Images/Corbis; **264:** ©iStockphoto/Thinkstock; **265:** © Fancy/ JuniperImages; 266: ©Marili Forastieri/Photodisc/Thinkstock; **268:** ©iStockphoto/Thinkstock; **275:** ©Monkey Business/Thinkstock; **277:** © iStockphoto. com/fotostorm; **278:** ©Chris Jackson/Getty; **279:** © iStockphoto.com/Mark Bowden; **282:** © iStockphoto.com/scanrail; © iStockphoto.com/video1; **283:** ©browndogstudios/iStock Vectors/ Getty; **286:** ©Comstock/Thinkstock; **288:** ©Monkey Business/Thinkstock; **289:** © Getty Images/Thinkstock; **290:** ©Stockbyte/Thinkstock; **295:** © Sean Locke/iStockphoto; **296:** © iStockphoto. com/rayheinsius; **298:** © iStockphoto. com/anneleven; **299:** © iStockphoto. com/twohumans; **303:** ©Creatas/ Thinkstock; **308:** © iStockphoto/ AlexRaths; **310:** ©Creatas/Thinkstock; **312:** ©Creatas/Thinkstock; **316:** ©iStockphoto/wdstock; **317:** © Getty Images/Thinkstock; **318**: © iStockphoto. com/elfinima; **320:** © iStockphoto. com/sturti; **321:** © iStockphoto.com/ arekmalang; **323:** © iStockphoto.com/ AlexRaths; **331:** ©Polka Dot Images/ Thinkstock; **335:** ©Creatas/Thinkstock; **336:** ©Brand X Pictures/Thinkstock.

Index

Accommodation, language, 78, 342
Action-facilitating support, 230, 342
Active listening. *See* Listening
Afifi, T. D., 61
Altercasting, 64
Alvarez, C., 211
Andea, L., 172
Anderson, J. W., 299
Appeal to authority, 123, 342
Appeal to people (bandwagon appeal), 123, 342
Appeal to relationships, 123–124, 342
Apprehension, 304, 342
Aristotle, 26
Associations, communication, 25
Asynchronous communication, 282, 342
Attitude of reflection, 58, 342
Attitudes, audience, 290, 342
Audience analysis. *See* Public speaking
Authority structure in families, 166–167, 342

Backchannel communication, 104, 342
Bandwagon appeal, 123, 342
Bastien, D., 206
Baxter, L. A., 144, 168
Beavin, J., 11
Beliefs, audience, 290, 342
Bernstein, Basil, 75
Berry, L. L., 211
Bidirectionality hypothesis, 167, 342
Boase, J., 281
Body buffer zone, 99
Bolton, K., 206
Bonilla, D., 78
Boundaries, relational, 61–62, 168–169, 276–277
Boundary management, 169, 234, 342
Bourhis, R. Y., 78
Braithwaite, D. O., 168
Breakdown Process Model
- dyadic process, 150, 344
- grave dressing process, 150, 345
- intrapsychic process, 148, 150, 346
- overview, 148, 149 (figure)
- resurrection process, 150–151, 348
- social process, 150, 349
- *See also* Relationships, personal

Brown, Penelope, 82
Bruess, Carol, 167
Bryant, L., 168
Burgoon, J. K., 103
Burke, Kenneth, 79, 80
Buzzanell, P. M., 171

Carlsmith, J. M., 102
Cash, W. B., Jr., 334
Cathcart, Robert, 274
Caughlin, J. P., 61
Central States Communication Association, 25
Chang, Y., 34
Change in relationships, 145, 171–173, 342
- *See also* Relational dialectics; Relationships, personal

Chiang, S. -U., 246
Chronemics, 105–106, 342
Cichocki, D., 172
Cockburn-Wootten, C., 201
Co-cultures, 257, 343
Code, elaborated, 75, 344
Code, restricted, 75, 348
Coded system of meaning, 247, 343
Cohen, J., 268
Cohesiveness, group, 181–182, 343
Coker, D. A., 103
Coker, R. A., 103
Collectivist culture, 249–250, 343
Communication education, 38
Communication frames
- conversational, 76–77
- in families, 158
- and perspective, 13
- relational, 78
- types of, 12–13, 17, 343
- workplace environment, 202–206

Communication privacy management theory, 233–234, 343
Communication studies
- associations, 25
- communication journals, 25 (table)
- communication theory, 38, 39 (table)
- constitutive approach, 16
- critical approach, 36–37
- disciplines of, 37–43
- historiography, 23–24
- interpersonal communication, 26–27, 28
- interpretivist approach, 30 (table), 33–35
- mass communication, early history of, 27–28
- relational perspective in, 29
- rhetoric and rhetorical criticism, 26, 28, 42–43, 43 (table)
- social scientific approach to, 30–33, 30 (table)
- *See also* Relational perspective

Communication theory, 38, 39 (table)
Compliance gaining
- definition of, 299, 343
- goals of, 299–300, 301 (table)
- strategies in, 301–305, 302 (table)
- *See also* Influence

Composition fallacy, 126
Conflict
- definition of, 252, 343
- as destructive, 253–254, 253 (table), 343
- management of, 254–255
- as opportunity, 252–253, 253 (table), 343

Connotative meaning, 70–72, 343
Constitutive approach to communication, 16, 343
Content listening, 119, 343
Continuation of identity, 203, 343
Convergence, 78, 343
Conversation. *See* Talk; Verbal communication
Conversational hypertext, 74–75, 343
Crepin, A. E., 190
Critical approach, 30 (table), 36–37, 343
Critical cultural communication, study of, 38
Critical listening
- consistency, evaluation of, 122, 343
- definition of, 120–121, 343
- and fallacious arguments, 122–126, 344
- plausibility, evaluation of, 121, 347
- status of the source, 121–122, 123, 349
- verifiability, evaluation of, 122, 350
- *See also* Listening

Cultural communication, study of, 38
Cultural norms, 246
Cultural persuadables, 258, 343
Culture
- co-cultures, 257
- collectivism/individualism, 249–251
- and conflict, 252–255
- context of, 248–249
- and conflict management, 254–255
- cross-cultural communication, study of, 38
- definition of, 245–246, 343
- ethnocentric bias, 243
- and group membership, 258–259
- identities, effect on, 56
- influences on communication, 10–11, 17, 243–244, 256–257
- intercultural communication, 38, 246, 346

and minorities, 245
and nonverbal communication, 92
and relationship development, 141
as structure, 245–246
and time, perception of, 251–252
as transaction, 246 -247, 255–257
and verbal communication, 75–76, 76 (table)
Cum hoc ergo proptor hoc, 124, 343
Cupach, W. R., 82
Cybernetics, 162–164

Daly, J. A., 298
Damron, J. C. H., 32
Dance, Frank, 5
Decision making, group, 11
Decoding, 90–91, 91 (table), 344
Denotative meaning, 70–72, 344
DeSantis, A. D., 229
Devil terms, 72–73, 73 (table), 344
Dhaenens, F., 36
Dialectics, relational. *See* Relational dialectics
Dialectic tension, types of, 60–61, 344
Dillard, J. P., 299
Dindia, K., 60
Direct observation, 34
Divergence, 78, 344
Diversity, benefits of, 244, 245
Division fallacy, 126, 344
Doelger, J. A., 327
Dominance, 301, 344
Donovan-Kicken, E., 32
Duck, John, 58
Duck, Steve, 58–59, 73, 83, 138, 148
du Pre, Athena, 225
Durham, W. T., 60, 61, 62
Dynamic nonverbal communication, 91, 344

Eastern Communication Association, 25
Egocentric listening, 119, 344
Einhorn, Lois, 330
Ellsworth, P. C., 102
Emblems, 102, 344
Emoticons, 283, 344
Emotional support, 231, 344
Encoding, 90–91, 91 (table), 344
Environmental distractions, 118–119, 344
Equivocation (as fallacious argument), 126, 344
Erlandson, K. T., 156
Esteem support, 231, 344
Ethnocentric bias, 243, 344
Experiential superiority, 120
Experimental research methods, 31
Extended parallel process model, 297–298, 344
Eye contact, 102–103, 344

Facework, 65, 81–83, 344
Facial expressions, 102
Factual diversion, 118, 344
Fahlman, Scott E., 283
Fairhurst, G. T., 208
Fallacious arguments, types of, 122–126, 344
False alternatives, 125, 344
Family, types of
binuclear, 159, 342
blended, 159, 168, 342
of choice, 159, 344
of descent, 158, 159, 344
extended family, 158, 344
of generativity, 158, 159, 344
kin networks, 158, 346
nuclear family, 158, 347
of origin, 158, 159, 344
same-sex parents, 159
single-parent, 159
Family narratives, 169–170, 344
See also Narratives
Family relationships
and boundaries, 168–169
and change, 171–173
children, 164–165
communication styles in, 165–167, 174
as communication systems, 160–162
family identity, creation of, 169–170, 344
genograms, 160, 161 (figure)
negative aspects, 157, 163–164
norms and rituals, 165, 167–168, 347, 348
and peer culture, 164
positive aspects of, 155–156
privacy and secrets, 169–170
storytelling, 169–170, 345
as structures, 158–159
study of, 39–40
as systems, 162–164
See also Family, types of
Farley, S. D., 104
Ferber, A., 96
Fisher, Aubrey, 186
Fisher, W. R., 78
Fitzpatrick, M. A., 161
Flora, J., 158
Flores, L. A., 245
Foley, M., 73
Formality/hierarchy, 205, 209–210, 345
Fournier, Susan, 212
Fox, Kate, 251
Frames. *See* Communication frames
French, J. R. P., Jr., 191, 193
Friedenberg, R. V., 42
Frymier, A. B., 38

Galvin, Kathleen, 156, 164, 168, 174
Gaze, 102–103, 345
Genogram, 160, 161 (figure)
Gestures, 92, 101–102
Giddens, A., 207
Giles, H., 78, 104
Goals, types of, 205
God terms, 72–73, 73 (table), 202, 345
Goffman, Erving, 65, 82
Gomez, M. L., 78
Gouran, D. S., 40, 327
Greeting ritual, 96 (table)
Grounded theory, 33–34
Group culture, 185, 345
Group norms, 183, 345
Group roles
disruptive, 185
formal, 184, 198–199, 345
informal, 184, 199, 345
social, 184
task, 184
Groups
characteristics of, 180–185, 181 (table)
culture, creation of, 185
and decision making, 11, 185–188
development stages of, 186–187, 186 (table), 187 (table)
leadership of, 188–193
relational aspects of, 187–188, 193
research on, 40, 179, 186
roles of members, 184–185
types of, 179–180, 181 (table)
See also Leadership; Organizational communication
Group sanctions, 184, 345
Groupthink, 182, 345
Gumpert, Gary, 274

Hall, E. T., 99
Hall, J. A., 226
Hallett, J., 156
Haptics, 106–107, 106 (table), 345
Harris, K. L., 36
Hasty generalization (fallacious argument), 125, 345
Health communication
and Internet technology, 237–238, 237 (table)
and media, 235–237
patient-provider relationships, 224–228, 227 (table)
research in, 41
and social networks, 228–232
Hearing, 114, 345
See also Critical listening; Listening skills
Henson, A., 102
Hepburn, J. R., 190
Heslin, R., 96, 106
Hess, J. A., 61, 141
High-context cultures, 248–249, 345
Historiography, 23–24, 345
Hoefs, Anna, 167
Holt, L., 35
Horrigan, J. B., 281
Hughes, S. M., 104

Identity
boundary management and, 61–62
definitions of, 49–50, 345
influences on, 53–54
as narratives, 62–63
and the Onion Model, 49, 52–53, 52 (figure)
and perception, 51, 54–55
as performance, 64–65
relational aspects of, 55–56, 64
self-disclosure and, 58–61
and social networking, 62, 278–281
in social roles, 51, 65
symbolic transactions of, 56–58
in the workplace, 203–205
Illustrators, 102, 345
Imahori, T. T., 245
Individualist culture, 250–251, 345
Industrial time, 210–211, 345
Influence
and power, 303 (table)
through emotional connections, 296–299
through persuasive techniques, 294–296
through public speaking, 290–292
See also Compliance gaining; Persuasion; Sequential persuasion
Informational support, 230, 346
Instructional communication, 38
Instrumental goals, 205, 346
Instrumental support, 231, 346
Interdependence, group, 182, 346
International Association for Relationship Research, 25
International Communication Association, 25
Interpersonal communication
in organizational culture, 212–213, 212 (table)
study of, 26–28, 39, 40
Interpretivist approach, 30 (table), 33–35, 346
Interviewing
as communication frame, 328–330
communication strategies during employment interview, 322–324
cover letter, 310–311
directive, 326–327, 344
employment interview preparation, 314, 316–322
exit interviews, 315
helping interviews, 316, 345
information-gaining interviews, 315, 345
interview characteristics, 313–314
nondirective, 327, 347
nonverbal communication in, 323
performance interviews, 315
persuasive interviews, 315, 347
post-interview responsibilities, 336–338
problem-solving interviews, 316, 347
questions, types of, 324–329, 328 (table), 331–333
as research method, 35
résumé, 311–313
tips for conclusion, 334–336
wrap-up signal, 334, 350
See also Questions, types of
Intimacy
and compliance, 302, 346
cultural differences in, 246–247
and self-disclosure, 59–60
Intracultural communication, 38
Introspective units, 143, 173, 346
Iowa Communication Association, 25
Isabella, L. A., 217

Jackson, D., 11
Jackson, R. L., II, 38
Janis, Irving, 182
Jin, B., 246
Jourard, Sidney, 59, 96, 106

Kellas, J. K., 62, 169
Kelly, George, 55
Kendon, A., 96
Kenneth Burke Society, 25
Kinesics, 101–102, 346
Kin keeping, 170, 346
Kinsella, J., 236
Kirkpatrick, C. D., 73
Knobloch, L. K., 299
Koerner, A. F., 161
Kram, K. E., 217

LaFayette, J. N., 104
Language
and accommodation, 78
and perception, 71
and speaking, 77
as symbolic, 69–70
See also Verbal communication
Langue, 78, 346
Larson, Carl, 5
Law of Jante, 249, 250 (table)
Leadership
and ethics, 192
as formal position in group, 188–189, 199, 209–210
and power, 190–191, 191 (table), 198–199
styles of, 189–190
and vision, 191–192
See also Organizational communication
Leakage (of feelings), 94, 346
Lederman, L. C., 41
Le Poire, B. A., 156, 158
Levinson, Steven, 82
Levy, David, 269
Ling, Rich, 277, 278
Linz, D., 78
Listening
active process of, 114–115
critical listening, 120–126, 343
definition of, 114, 346
engaged, 115–116, 344
importance of, 112–113
objectives of, 113–114, 114 (table)
obstacles to, 117–120
relational, 116–117, 348
See also Critical listening; Listening process
Listening process
attending, 114, 342
interpreting, 114–115, 346
receiving, 114, 117 (table), 348
reflecting, 115, 348
responding, 115, 348
See also Listening
Long-distance relationships, 170, 346
Low-context cultures, 250, 346

Martin, J. N., 245
Marwell, Gerald, 301, 305
Mass communication, 27–28, 40–41
See also Media
Matsumoto, D., 245
McClelland, D. C., 246
McCroskey, J. C., 38
McGlynn, J., 32
McMahan, David, 34
McPhee, R., 206
Mead, George Herbert, 58
Meaning
in nonverbal communication, 92–93, 93 (table)
in organizational culture, 200–201
relational aspect of, 74–75
symbols and, 8–10, 12–13, 70, 346
and words, 70–72
Media
concurrent media use, 263
and everyday talk, 270–273
and health communication, 235–237
media studies, 40–41
as relational activity, 266–270
See also Mass communication; Technology
Media equation, 269, 269 (table), 346
Media literacy, 271–272, 346
Merton, Robert, 329
Message complexity, 120, 346
Metts, S., 82
Metzger, M., 268
Microcoordination, 277, 278 (table), 346
Monochronic culture, 251–252, 346
Montgomery, B. M., 144
Morgan, Gareth, 200
Mumby, D. K., 185, 210
Muñoz, Kristine, 258

Nabi, Robin, 298
Nakayama, T. K., 245
Narratives
 elements of, 79–81, 80 (table), 346
 family identity and, 169–170
 and identity, 62–63
 presentational aspect of, 78–79
Nass, Clifford, 269
National Association of Academic Teachers, 25
National Communication Association, 22, 22 (table), 25
Networking group. *See* Social networking
Nonverbal communication
 assigning meaning, 92–93, 93 (table)
 cultural aspects of, 92, 99, 105
 decoding, 90–91, 91 (table), 344
 definition of, 89–90, 347
 encoding, 90–91, 91 (table), 344
 functions of, 94–97
 gestures, 92, 101–102
 in interviews, 323
 and kinesics, 101–102
 as regulator, 95–96, 348
 relational aspect of, 97
 and space/territory, use of, 98–101, 106
 and symbols, 89–91
 and touch, 105, 106–107, 106 (table)
 types of, 7
 use of time, 105–106, 210–211
 with verbal communication, 94–95, 103–105
 in workplace, 203
 See also Symbols
Norwood, K., 34
Nurturing support, 230–231, 347

O'Connell, R. L., 151
Oh, S., 246
Onion Model, 49, 52–53, 52 (figure)
Online communication, 281–283
 See also Social networking
Online relationships. *See* Social networking; Technology
Organizational communication
 abusive communication, 217, 219
 and boundaries, 215–218
 and company surveillance, 215–216
 as context of interpersonal relationships, 212–213, 212 (table), 217–218
 in customer-client relationships, 211–212
 and hierarchy, 209–210
 and identity, 203–205
 and meaning making, 199, 208–209
 peer relationships, 217–219, 218 (table)
 relational perspective of, 197–199, 212–214
 rules and norms, 209–211
 socialization, effect of, 200
 and structuration theory, 207–208
 study of, 41
 types of, 203–205
Organizational culture, 206–207
Out-groups, 183, 347

Palazzolo, K. E., 36
Parasocial relationships, 269–270, 270 (table), 347
Parole, 78, 347
Participant observation, 34
Paxman, Jeremy, 251
Peer culture, 164, 347
Pentad in narratives, 79–81, 80 (table), 347
Perceived efficacy, 297–298
Perceived threat, 297–298
Perception and identity, 51, 53–54, 347
Performative self, 64–65, 347
Personal benefit, 303, 347
Personal constructs, 55, 347
Personality. *See* Identity
Personal relationships. *See* Relationships, personal
Personal space, 99–100, 100 (figure), 347
Persuasion, 23, 41–42, 258
 See also Persuasive speeches; Sequential persuasion techniques
Persuasive speeches
 to actuate, 292
 claim of conjecture, 291–292, 343
 claim of fact, 291–292, 343
 claim of policy, 291, 343
 claim of value, 291, 343
 See also Sequential persuasion techniques
Petronio, Sandra, 60, 61, 62, 168, 172
Pew Research Center's Internet and American Life Project, 237
Philipsen, Gerry, 258
Politeness theory, 82–83, 83 (table)
Political communication, study of, 42
Polychronic culture, 252, 347
Pond, K., 83
Post hoc ergo propter hoc, 124, 347
Power
 assessment of, 37
 formal role of, 190, 209–210, 345
 and influence, 303 (table)
 informal role of, 190, 209–210, 345
 types of, 191 (table)
 See also Leadership
Precepts (Ptahhotep), 24
Presentational communication, 13–14
Privacy management, 169, 347
Professional face, 203, 205, 347
Prospective units, 143, 173, 348
Provisions of relationships, 136–137, 348
Proxemics, 98–101, 348
Public disclosure, 280
Public relations, study of, 42
Public speaking
 as area of study, 25, 26
 and audiences, effect on, 289–290, 292 (table), 293 (table)
 and emotion, importance of, 295–299, 299 (table)
 and fear, use of, 297–298
 and guilt, use of, 298
 relational connections in, 288–290
 sequential persuasion techniques, 292–295
 speaker credibility, 289
 speeches to convince, 290–292, 349
 See also Compliance gaining; Persuasive speeches; Sequential persuasion techniques

Questionnaires/surveys, 31–32
Questions, types of
 closed, 325, 343
 illegal interview, 327, 328 (table), 333, 333 (table)
 leading, 326, 346
 neutral, 325–326, 347
 open, 325, 347
 primary and secondary, 324, 347, 348

Rainie, L., 281
Raven, B., 191, 193
Red herring fallacy, 125, 348
Reeves, Byron, 269
Reganis, P., 172
Regnerus, M., 159
Regulators, 95–96, 97, 348
Relational consequence, 303, 348
Relational continuity constructional units, 143–144, 173, 283, 348
Relational dialectics
 change in relationship, 145, 342
 contradiction, 144, 343
 definition of, 144, 348
 external, 145, 146 (table), 344
 internal, 145, 146 (table), 346
 praxis, 145, 347
 totality, 145, 350
Relational goals, 205, 348
Relational perspective
 definition of, 4
 dialectic tensions, 61–62
 of groups, 187–188
 of identity, 55–56
 of influence, 299–300, 300 (table), 303
 in leadership, 192–193
 of listening, 116–117
 in organizations, 197–199
 in political communication, 42
 in public relations, 42
 and symbols, 9
 in technology use, 266–270
 and verbal communication, 73–75

Relational technologies, 274–277, 348
Relationship Filtering Model, 138–141, 139 (figure), 348
Relationships, personal
  benefits of, 134–137
  and Breakdown Process Model, 148–151
  conflict management, 254–255
  maintenance of, 143–146
  and relational technology, 276–277
  Relationship Filtering Model, 138–141, 139 (figure)
  symptoms of decline in, 147–148
  types of, 133–134, 347
  verbal communication in, 141–143
  workplace interference in, 214–215
  See also Family relationships; Relational dialectics
Representational communication, 13–14, 348
Resistance, 302, 348
Rhetoric, study of, 26, 41
Rhetorical criticism, approaches to, 26, 42–43, 43 (table)
Richmond, V. P., 38
Robert, Henry Martyn, 182
Robert's Rules of Order (Robert), 182
Rollie, Stephanie, 173
Roter, D. L., 226
Rudnick, J. R., 298

Sahlstein, Erin, 123, 170
Sandemose, Aksel, 248, 249
Sapir, Edward, 71
Sapir-Whorf hypothesis, 71, 348
Sargent, J. D., 172
Saussure, Ferdinand de, 78
Savage, M., 36
Schemata, 55, 348
Schmitt, David, 301, 305
Segrin, C., 158
Seki, K., 245
Selective exposure, 55, 348
Selective listening, 119, 348
Self
  core of, 49–50, 57
  performative, 64–65
  reflection on, 58
  symbolic identity of, 56–58
  See also Identity; Self-disclosure
Self-disclosure
  benefits of, 59–60
  and boundaries, 61–62
  components of, 58–59, 348
  during interview process, 323
  and relational dialectics, 60–61
  and social networking, 280
Self-fulfilling prophecy, 329, 348
Semantic diversion, 118–119, 349
Sequential persuasion techniques
  door in the face, 294–295, 295 (table), 296 (table)
  foot in the door, 293–294, 294 (table), 345
  pregiving, 295, 296 (table), 347
Sexual harassment, 217, 219, 349
Sias, P. M., 212
Sideways (movie), 67
Sigman, S. J., 143, 283
Signs, definition of, 7, 349
Small-group research, 40
  See also Groups
Social class and shared meanings, 75
Socialization
  effect on the workplace, 200–202
  family roles in, 156
  impact of media, 268, 349
Social networking sites
  benefits of, 282–283
  characteristics of sites, 282–283
  identity construction, 62, 278–281
  to maintain relationships, 281–282
  and relational technology, 274
  types of connections, 281
  See also Technology
Social networks and health communication, 41, 228–232
Social performance, 65
Social relationships, 134, 349
Social rules, 156
Social scientific approach
  assumptions, 31
  methodology, 31–33
  overview, 30–31, 30 (table), 349
Social support, types of, 230–232, 233 (table)
Socioemotional leaders, 189
Socrates, 26
Southern States Communication Association, 25
Speaking. *See* Public speaking; Talk; Verbal communication
Speech codes, 257, 259, 349
Speech communities, 257–258, 349
Speeches. *See* Persuasive speeches; Public speaking
Static nonverbal communication, 91–92, 349
Stewart, C. J., 334
Storytelling. *See* Narratives
Structuration theory, 207–208, 349
Support. *See* Social support, types of
Surveys/questionnaires, 31–32
Suter, E. A., 164
Symbolic interactionism, 58, 349
Symbolic self, 57–58, 349
  See also Self
Symbols
  cultural significance of, 6, 7–8, 247
  definition of, 7, 17, 349
  and identity, 56–58
  as language, 69–72
  and meaning, 8–10, 12–13, 17, 70
  in nonverbal communication, 89–91
  norms and rituals, 167–168
  social construction of, 8–9
Synchronous communication, 282, 349
Systems theory, 162–164, 349

Talk
  cultural styles of, 76 (table)
  functions of, 83–84, 141–143
  speech codes, 257, 259
  technology and media, 270–273
  vocal characteristics of, 103–105
  in workplace, 205–206
  See also Public speaking; Verbal communication
Task leaders, 189, 349
Taylor, D. M., 78
Teamwork. *See* Groups
Technological determinism, 265, 349
Technology
  concurrent media use, 263
  as distraction, 118
  and everyday talk, 270–273
  and health communication, 41, 237–238, 237 (table)
  impact on communication, 10, 40, 265–266
  and media generations, 274, 350
  and media profile, 272–273, 350
  parasocial relationships, 269–270, 270 (table), 347
  and perception of time, 253
  relational uses of, 41, 264, 266–270, 274–277
  social construction of, 265
  social networking sites, 278–283
  social shaping of, 266, 349
  See also Media; Social networking sites
Territoriality, 98–99, 350
Textual analysis, 35, 36
Time, use of, 105–106, 210–211, 251–252
Tong, S. T., 283
Totten, L. D., 215
Touch. *See* Nonverbal communication
Tracy, K., 57
Transaction
Transactional communication, 16–17, 192–193, 246–247
  See also Symbols
Transparency, 60
Trees, April, 129
Trent, J. S., 42
Tuckman, Bruce, 186
Turner, L. H., 171
Turn taking (conversational), 104–105, 350

Values, audience, 290
Vangelisti, A. L., 298

Verbal communication
and conversational frames, 76–77
cultural aspect of, 75–76, 76 (table)
and facework, 81–83
in families, 161–162, 165–168, 170
and meaning, 70–72, 74
as narratives, 78–80, 169–170
with nonverbal communication, 94–95
and politeness theory, 82–83, 83 (table)
presentational aspect of, 78–81
relational aspect of, 73–75, 83, 141–143
speaking codes, 77
as symbolic, 69–70
talk, functions of, 83–84
types of, 7
values of words, 72–73, 72 (table)
vocalics of, 103–105
in workplace, 203–204, 205 (table)
See also Talk
Vocal characteristics. *See* Vocalics
Vocalics
definition of, 103, 350
as distraction, 118
pitch, 103, 347
rate, 104, 348
as regulator, 104–105
in relationships, 104
and silence, 104, 349
volume, 104, 350
Vocational anticipatory socialization, 201–202, 350
Von Bertalanffy, L., 162

Wagner, A., 168
Walther, J. B., 283
Wandering thoughts, 119–120, 350
Watzlawick, P., 11
Weick, K., 208
Weiss, Robert, 136–137, 198
Wellman, B., 281
Western States Communication Association, 25
Whorf, Benjamin, 71
Wiethoff, W. E., 327
Williams, K. D., 31
Witte, K., 297
Wood, J. T., 147
Words. *See* Verbal communication
Workplace communication. *See* Organizational communication
World Communication Association, 25
Wright, C. N., 31

Zorn, T., 201
Zweig, D., 215, 216